INTERNATIONAL BUSINESS PLANNING: POLICY & PROCEDURE

By

Antonio Mendoza
Professor of Law
Pepperdine University
School of Law

AMERICAN CASEBOOK SERIES®

WEST GROUP

A THOMSON COMPANY

ST. PAUL, MINN., 2001

West Group has created this publication to provide you with accurate and authoritative information concerning the subject matter covered. However, this publication was not necessarily prepared by persons licensed to practice law in a particular jurisdiction. West Group is not engaged in rendering legal or other professional advice, and this publication is not a substitute for the advice of an attorney. If you require legal or other expert advice, you should seek the services of a competent attorney or other professional.

American Casebook Series, and the West Group symbol
are registered trademarks used herein under license.

ISBN 0–314–21131–4

 TEXT IS PRINTED ON 10% POST
CONSUMER RECYCLED PAPER

"I will praise you O Lord, with all my heart;
I will tell of all your wonders."
Psalm 9:1

Dedication

To my Wife, Maria

And Daughters, Marisela & Anna

*

Preface

This casebook is a study of international business transactions using a transaction-based approach. It covers the inbound and outbound international sale of goods and services, transfer of technology, and foreign direct investment in the Western Hemisphere. The materials also include a basic analysis of the U.S. federal income taxation of international business transactions. Although the casebook focuses on international business planning between Mexico and the United States, the strategies used are applicable to international business transactions occurring anywhere in the world since it concentrates on U.S. domestic law and on international agreements applicable to many parts of the world.

The casebook is timely. We are experiencing a sea change of attitude towards international business in Latin America and the developing world as a whole. Old protectionist attitudes are giving way to a spirit of free trade and open borders. Trade and economic integration agreements are being negotiated at an unprecedented pace. Domestic legal systems are changing to allow market access to foreign goods and services, and increasing the protection of intellectual property rights and capital owned by foreigners. Privatization of state owned companies also continues to attract foreign investment. My hope is to acquaint the U.S. law student with the challenges and opportunities of international business transactions in Mexico. The study of the experiences in Mexico can provide guidance for business transactions in other developing regions of the world— Eastern Europe, Vietnam, China, and other countries.

The casebook is divided into seven chapters. Chapter 1 provides an introduction to the various types of international business transactions and the trade and economic relationships that may exist between countries. It also analyzes the different types of international agreements and how they are converted into rights enforceable in domestic legal systems. There is also a discussion on the history of economic integration agreements in the Americas. The effect that differences in culture, political and legal systems, and economic development levels have on economic integration among countries is also addressed. A brief overview of the civil law legal system in general and the Mexican legal system in particular is also included.

Chapter 2 looks at the inbound foreign direct investment using a hypothetical Mexican company as the foreign investor purchasing an U.S. business enterprise. The federal statutory laws that can either restrict or require a reporting of the transaction are examined. There is also a review of U.S. statutory law and NAFTA on business immigration Visas for executives of the Mexican company to enter and work in the United States. Strategies to use in the actual making and structuring of the investment including financial statement review, due diligence, and the methods used in determining the value of a business are also discussed. The problems associated with the movement of cash across national borders in the Americas including the anti-money laundering and asset forfeiture laws are presented in the context of a foreign direct investment.

Since this casebook adopts a transactions based approach, Chapter 2 introduces three important factors that investors consider in the making of a foreign direct investment—control, limiting the risk, and profit maximization and distribution. These three factors are addressed throughout the materials on foreign direct investment both inbound and outbound. The effect the choice of entity decision has on the three important factors and a basic introduction to the U.S. federal income tax implications of international business transactions are also covered. The tax materials discuss the relevant Internal Revenue Code provisions and the role that bilateral tax treaties play in determining the tax implications of an international business transaction.

Chapter 3 examines the outbound foreign direct investment using a hypothetical U.S. company making a wholly owned foreign direct investment in Mexico. The focus is on the protections and dispute resolution procedures afforded foreign investors generally under international agreements—specifically NAFTA and U.S. bilateral investment treaties —and Mexican domestic law. The various sources of laws are analyzed using the three important factors of control, limiting the risk, and profit maximization and distribution. The World Bank Guidelines on foreign direct investment are also discussed in creating a type of "Hospitality Index" through which a developing country's attitude toward foreign direct investment can be assessed.

The chapter also examines the choice of entity decision facing the U.S. Company under the Mexican domestic legal system. It addresses the choice of entity decision in light of the three important factors of control, limiting the risk, and profit maximization and distribution. There is also a discussion of the unique role played by the civil law notary and the great differences between a civil law and common law notary. The section also explores the issues surrounding the "proving up" of the authority to sign on behalf of a foreign corporation in the Mexican legal system. Finally, the chapter considers the problems faced by U.S. companies in the illegal payments to corrupt foreign officials.

Chapter 4 examines the outbound foreign direct investment using a hypothetical U.S. company making a foreign direct investment in Mexico through an international equity joint venture (IEJV) with a Mexican Company. In the hypothetical, the U.S. Company is taking a minority position in the joint venture. The materials explain the pros and cons of IEJVs and the role of the lawyer in negotiating and drafting the IEJV and the collateral agreements. The key factors in negotiating and structuring the IEJV in light of the three important factors of control, limiting the risk, and profit maximization and distribution are also examined. There is also particular attention given to the capitalization, valuation, and termination issues arising out of an IEJV.

The chapter also studies the international transfer of technology through an international licensing agreement entered into by an U.S. and Mexican Company. The materials address the relationship between licensor and licensee, and the international and domestic laws protecting the ownership of intellectual property. The applicable rules are from the TRIPS, NAFTA, U.S. domestic law, and Mexico's Industrial Property Law. There is also a discussion on the protection of the value of the technology.

The international sale of goods and services are also discussed in this chapter. The materials include contract formation issues for the international sale of goods, market access for the international sale of services and government procurement rules. The chapter concludes with an analysis of the U.S. federal income tax implications of capitalizing and operating the International Equity Joint Venture. It also discusses the tax implications of the transfer pricing decision with respect to the international transfer of technology and the international sale of goods and services.

Chapters 5, 6 & 7 deal with the issues surrounding the international sale of goods. Chapter 5 analyzes the use of letters of credit in financing the international sale of goods. The materials consider the documentary transaction and the legal issues arising from the presentation of conforming documents. There is also a discussion on the effect that fraud in the transaction has on the payment of a documentary letter of credit.

Chapter 6 analyzes the role the Carriage of Goods by Sea Act plays on the international carriage and delivery of goods. The materials review the Bill of Lading and its role as a contract of carriage between Shipper and Carrier, and the risks each party faces in the case where goods are lost or damaged. The chapter ends with an examination of the Federal Bill of Lading Act and the Bill of Lading in its role as a document of receipt and a document of title.

Chapter 7 uses a transaction-based approach on the issue of trade regulation. It discusses the country categorization and product classification rules that are used in determining the trade barriers that may be present to the free movement of goods. The chapter also analyzes the product rules of origin under the GATT and NAFTA and other regional agreements and their effect on the movement of goods across national borders. The chapter also examines the rules governing dutiable value. The materials end with a discussion of free trade zones and *maquiladoras*.

*

Acknowledgements

I wish to acknowledge the help and moral support in writing this book to the many colleagues, friends and students that have helped me along the way. I give very special thanks to Ron Phillips our former dean who suggested the casebook in the first place, to Professors Bryan Liang and Jack Coe whose initial readings, ideas and moral support were invaluable to me.

It is difficult to name all of the people who have helped but special thanks are here given to Dean Richard Lynn, Professors Baxter Dunaway, Charles Nelson, Harry Caldwell, Mark Scarberry, Greg Ogden, Robert Cochran, and Wayne Estes. There is also special recognition given to students Jeremy Dolnick, Heidi Kettler, Izabella Kasprzyk, and David Adams. Special thanks are also given to Candace Warren and the other faculty secretaries who did yeoman work on finalizing the various drafts.

*

Summary of Contents

Table of Contents

*

Table of Cases

The principal cases are in bold type. Cases cited or discussed in the text are roman type. References are to pages. Cases cited in principal cases and within other quoted materials are not included.

INTERNATIONAL BUSINESS PLANNING: POLICY & PROCEDURE

*

Chapter 1

INTERNATIONAL BUSINESS PLANNING

SECTION 1.1 INTRODUCTION

A. THE TYPES OF INTERNATIONAL BUSINESS TRANSACTIONS

Businesses are formed to benefit their owners. Management strives to maximize the profit and value of the company, giving the highest return to the owners at the least possible risk. The traditional business plan calls for establishing a market for the products of the company. It then will sell its products at a profit sufficient to satisfy its owners and to preserve or increase its market share and invest in research and development, advertising, and other expenditures aimed at increasing value in the long run. A company that is growing with domestic sales at a rate that satisfies its owners does not need to consider entering the international arena. Therefore, engaging in international business transactions is not necessarily a part of normal corporate growth but a response to external factors.

The factors that compel a company to engage in international business largely result from forces outside the company. Growing domestic competition both from domestic and foreign sources may shrink the domestic market share. This is particularly the case with the phenomenon of market globalization where foreign products can easily enter domestic markets. This often requires a company to look to foreign markets to maintain their sales volume. In addition, vast changes in the world—Eastern Europe, Asia, and Latin America are making formerly inaccessible markets open to U.S. products. Finally, the undeniable fact that developing countries have labor rates much lower than developed countries creates a substantial economic incentive to 'think internationally'. Thus, U.S. companies usually engage in international business transactions either to access a new market or to lower their operating costs or both. They do this in order compete effectively.

1

In spite of these factors favoring international business transactions there is a resistance to engage in international transactions. This stems from the natural reluctance to deal with the unknown or unfamiliar since this requires a change, usually unwelcome, in the way one does business and interacts with people. Take for example the following case: The marketing manager of a large and highly successful U.S. oil industry service company once told me that his company originally would only do business with people that had a 'Texas accent.'

Despite creating such a limited market, the company grew to a very substantial size. However, growing global competition apparently caused a change of corporate direction because the statement took place in a conference room in Mexico City as negotiations were taking place between it and a Mexican corporation to jointly pursue business in Mexico. The company was doing business with someone that did not even speak English.

Another factor that can have a chilling effect on international transactions is the increased risk and complexity of international transactions vis-a-vis purely domestic ones. The differences in language, currency, culture, and political and legal systems contribute to that inherent complexity. The distrust in the rule of law in a foreign country or the lack of faith in the domestic legal institutions that protect the rights of the foreign investor is also a major obstacle. In addition, the different development levels of the countries add complications that may increase the trepidation of business decision-makers considering international business transactions.

Some of the apprehensions are justified. For example, private companies from developed countries engaging in business activities in a developing country usually are surprised and dismayed at the level of host government involvement in what is essentially a purely commercial transaction. The private company's goal of profit maximization and market share is frequently at odds with the goals of the developing country's government to maintain control of their economy, keep currency and capital in their country or other specialized desires of the relevant public decision-makers in the developing country.

Engaging in international business almost always involves a balancing of benefits and risks. Describing strategies for maximizing benefits while minimizing risk is a goal of this casebook. The planning issues that surface in an international business transaction are directly related to the type of international transaction contemplated. The degree of complexity is a function of the type of international transaction involved. International business transaction can be divided into three categories— the sale of goods and services, transfer of technology, and foreign investment.

Each category has its unique set of issues and relative complexity. Generally, the easiest entry and lowest risk in international business is the sale of goods and services. The transfer of technology and foreign investment are more complex and usually create more risk to the business enterprise. A Company chooses the type of international transaction that most fits its needs. The lawyer should always keep in mind to use the simpler and less risky international business transaction when possible. It is also useful to keep in mind that the international business transaction can also be segmented by its direction. For our purposes an outbound transaction is where the U.S. Company is selling goods, transferring technology or capital to a foreign country. An inbound transaction is one where a foreign person is doing business or investing in the United States. The following hypothetical involves an outbound transaction.

The Hypothetical Case of Delta, Inc.

Delta Inc. is a Texas Corporation engaged in the sale of goods and services used in the petroleum industry. It is structured into three divisions.

Its oldest division [Division I] manufactures and sells "Blow Out Preventers" [BOP]. The BOP is a safety device essential in offshore drilling activities. The BOP is a high-tech device covered by an U.S. patent. It has a very good reputation for reliability and ease of operation. In spite of its high cost it is the most popular brand worldwide. Delta is currently operating below capacity in Division I because of decreased domestic demand.

Division II contains Delta's geology and engineering group. This division provides technical expertise on the locating of oil reserves and in the drilling of exploratory wells. It also develops plans and strategies to use in the development of oil wells in zones where there are proven reserves. Delta believes there may be a substantial market for these services in light of market globalization and privatization efforts currently taking place worldwide. The Division has expertise in on —shore as well as off-shore activities.

Delta's Division III owns several valuable patents for the manufacturing of concrete additives used in oil well drilling. The additive, known as "Quick Dry" makes concrete harden rapidly. The making of "Quick Dry" is a labor-intensive process. Delta has been losing U.S. market share on account of lower cost European additives of comparable quality. Division III is Delta's core business accounting for seventy-five percent of its annual sales. Delta is convinced that it must reduce its labor cost in manufacturing the additive or risk losing a substantial portion of its market.

1. The International Sale of Goods and Services

The international sale of goods and services is generally more complex than a purely domestic sale. One complicating factor is governmental involvement where there is a physical transfer of goods across national borders. In the case above, the sale of the BOP will require an U.S. export license. This can be a cumbersome process depending on the product involved and its ultimate destination. Likewise, the foreign government could impose trade barriers on products entering the country. These can be either tariff barriers or non-tariff barriers.

The community of nations has been very active in eliminating trade barriers that can impede the sale of goods across international borders. Multilateral trade agreements like the General Agreement on Tariff and Trade and regional agreements like the North American Free Trade Agreement have targeted the elimination of tariff and non-tariff barriers. The success has been quite remarkable. Indeed, the phenomenon of market globalization has provoked great interest in formerly non-market economies to join in agreements reducing trade barriers. The effect of these agreements on trade regulation is discussed in Chapter 7, infra.

Notwithstanding the political willingness of countries to promote the free flow of goods across national borders the business risk continues to be a complicating factor. Delta is concerned with getting paid on the sale while the buyer simply wants to receive the product under the conditions and at the bargained price. Delta could minimize its risk by consummating the sales transaction in the U.S. Depending on its bargaining power, the foreign buyer may be compelled to come to Delta's place of business and assume the responsibility to take the product home. This could eliminate some of the costs of shipping and returning the goods and the payment of export and import fees. To Delta, from a business standpoint, this would be like a domestic transaction. However, the structure would not eliminate Delta's obligation of obeying any applicable U.S. export laws.

Delta, however, may not be able to compel the Buyer to come to it. The Buyer may have several sources for the goods and could refuse the terms offered by the seller. Competition and the realities of the marketplace may oblige Delta to consummate the sales transaction in the Buyer's home country. The Buyer may require that Delta consummate the transaction in their country. The business community has devised a system known as a Documentary Transaction that is useful in bridging the risk gap faced by the buyer and seller. The Documentary Transaction financed with a letter of credit is discussed in Chapter 5.

The international sale of goods has been the focus of trade agreements for a long time with keen interest shown in removing trade barriers. The efforts in removing trade barriers from the international sale of services are of more recent vintage. Developed countries are substantial exporters of services while developing countries are importers of services. This is due to the types of goods that countries sell. Exports from developing countries are usually commodities like oil and agricultural products. Developed countries export manufactured goods with a high degree of technology. A service component is usually a necessary part of selling high technology products.

Historically, developing countries have not felt a need to negotiate the removal of barriers to services. This hurt service providers like Delta since their primary interest is to gain market access. However, recent changes in multilateral trade agreements like the General Agreement on

Tariff and Trade (GATT) and the North American Free Trade Agreement (NAFTA) have included the international sale of services. These agreements permit access to domestic markets by service providers like Delta. Delta's Division II is a good candidate for the international sale of services.

Complications still exist, even after gaining access to the domestic foreign market. Many developing countries are or have been statist economies. Delta will likely have to do business with a governmental unit since it will be the purchaser of the services. There will be governmental procurement rules with which to contend. Another possibility is that Delta may have to enter into a contractual joint venture with a private company that has a contract with the host government. In addition, since Delta will be sending personnel to the host country their immigration status abroad and their health and safety concerns will be important issues. Section 4.3, infra addresses the issues arising from contractual joint ventures and government procurement.

2. *The International Transfer of Technology*

Technology, also known as an intellectual property right (IPR) or intangible property, is a product of the mind. IRC § 936 (h)(3)(B)(1986) is helpful in provides a broad useful definition: "Y The term 'intangible property' means any . . . patent, invention, formula, process, design, pattern, or knowhow . . . copyright, literary, musical, or artistic competition, . . . trademark, tradename, or brand name, . . . franchise, license, or contract . . . method, program, system, procedure, campaign, survey, study, forecast, estimate, customer list, or technical data . . . or . . . any similar item . . . which has substantial value independent of the services of any individual." Delta's Division III patent qualifies as technology.

IPR's are an important asset to the U.S. economy. Over the years, the protectionist politicians have railed against the trade deficit in basic U.S. made goods. No such claim can be made on IPR's. The United States is an exporter of technology. It has a substantial surplus in the international transfer of technology[1] while Latin America, as a region of developing countries, is a net importer of technology. Intellectual property in the aggregate is a very important asset to the U.S. economy. Because of the high economic importance to the U.S. economy, technology protection is a major pillar of U.S. trade policy.

Technology is also important to developing countries, albeit for different reasons. Developing countries take the position that technology coming within its borders is an asset, the benefit of which should flow down to its citizens, particularly where the IPR involves pharmaceuticals or some other health and safety IPR. The divergent interests, known as the North–South debate, have caused policy differences[2] among devel-

---

1. In 1990 U.S. receipts on international patent and licensing transactions total 15.3 billion dollars while expenditures were 2.7 billion dollars. There was a 12.6 billion surplus in that year. *See* Daniel F. Perez, *Exploitation and Enforcement of Intellectual Property Rights*, 10 COMPUTER L., No. 8 at 10, 17 (1993).

2. For a discussion of the so-called North–South Debate see Gloria L. Sandri-

oped and developing countries. Some developing countries view the protection of the IPR rights of foreign persons as a low priority. In those cases, the intellectual property of the foreign owners will not be protected in the domestic legal system.

Developing countries have begun to provide more effective protection to foreign IPR owners. Multilateral international agreements like the Trade Related Aspects of International Property Rights [TRIPS] negotiated under the auspices of the GATT and the intellectual property chapter under the NAFTA provide rules for the protection of intellectual property as well as an enforcement mechanism. In addition to the rules provided in the international agreements countries that have been criticized for lax IPR protection (like Mexico) have enacted domestic legislation that greatly enhances the protection of foreign IPR owners. See Section 4.2, infra for a discussion of these laws. The change is the result of a drastic need of foreign capital and technology by developing countries. This policy change is contributing to a great increase in the international transfer of technology. This bodes well for companies like Delta.

Delta's Division III is a candidate for a transfer of technology arrangement for a variety of reasons. The first is cost—the "Quick Dry" made in the U.S. is too expensive on account of the high U.S. labor and other operating costs. Delta could sell the additive at a competitive price if it could tap the large pool of low cost labor in Latin America. The lowering of costs is a primary motivation for the transfer of technology. Another reason is that a technology transfer is a good way to test a market without the need for the more expensive alternative of establishing an actual physical presence in the country. Lastly, the host government may be unwilling to allow Delta access to its domestic market unless it establishes some type of presence in that country.

The factors that impel a transfer of technology arrangement are mainly external to the company. Delta management would likely resist the idea of a technology transfer for fear that it could lose the IPR through counterfeiting or piracy. In spite of the recent proliferation of international agreements protecting intellectual property, the most effective protection rules arise principally from domestic law. Therefore, if the particular domestic system does not provide adequate protection or if it lacks an effective enforcement regime, the protection of the IPRs could be in serious doubt.

The transfer of technology can be structured in several ways. Delta could sell the patent to an unrelated party. This may not be an acceptable alternative to Delta especially if the patent represents its core technology. It could transfer the technology to a wholly owned foreign subsidiary. This transaction is more in the nature of a foreign direct investment discussed below. Delta could also license the use of the

no, *The NAFTA Investment Chapter and Foreign Direct Investment in Mexico: A*   *Third–World Perspective*, 27 VAND J. TRANS-NAT'L L. 259 (1994).

patent and other intellectual property to an unrelated party. The typical transfer of technology arrangement uses the latter method.

In a Licensing Agreement, Delta as the patent owner will allow the Licensee to use the patent for the production of the additive. The Licensee then sells the additive and receives the profits from the sale. Delta's ''profits'' result from the royalties it charges the Licensee. The value of the patent, therefore, is a function of the royalty Delta can negotiate. This highlights the second risk facing Delta—the loss of the value of the IPR. Since the value of the IPR is determined by the royalty rate, the higher the royalty rate, the higher the value of the IPR. Conversely, a low royalty amount diminishes the value.

The royalty rate is a matter of negotiation between Delta and the Licensee. In a domestic context licensing agreements are contracts of adhesion where the Licensor is in a stronger bargaining position. The Licensee is often faced with a take it or leave it attitude by the Licensor. In an international context the Licensee may also be a large and sophisticated company, thus making the royalty rate a matter of negotiation. However, the host developing country may also limit the royalty amount. These are known as performance requirements and can substantially reduce Delta's royalty amount. For example, assume that a twelve-percent royalty reflects the fair market value of the patent. A performance requirement limiting the royalty to four percent reduces the value of the patent by two-thirds.

The host country could also impose currency controls that limit the ability of the Licensor to repatriate its royalties in a hard currency. This can also have a substantial negative effect on the value of the IPR. International agreements have been very helpful in eliminating performance requirements. The elimination of currency controls and caps on royalties helps maintain the value of the transferred technology. The protection of the value coupled with the rules protecting the ownership of the IPR has created a hospitable environment to the foreign IPR transferor. The countries that adopted these rules are seeing an influx of technology within their borders.

Delta faces the following questions on the transfer—Can the patent be protected under the laws of the host country? Can the Licensee be trusted? Can an appropriate royalty be charged? How will Delta be paid? These and other facets of the International Licensing Agreement are discussed in Section 4.2, infra.

If Delta cannot find a trustworthy Licensee it could organize a foreign subsidiary and transfer the patent in return for stock of the newly formed foreign corporation. It could also form the foreign corporation and either sell or license the patent to the subsidiary. In either of these cases Delta would have to establish a physical presence—a foreign direct investment in the host country. This may be the only alternative given the great importance of the patent to Delta. The foreign direct investment [FDI] is the most complex and riskiest form of international business transaction.

3. *The Foreign Direct Investment*

Like the sale of goods and transfer of technology the foreign direct investment (FDI) is not necessarily a part of normal growth, rather it arises from external factors. The FDI, sometimes referred to as a bricks and mortar investment, involves the transfer of capital and establishing a physical presence in a foreign country. In this context, the country that is receiving the capital is known as the host country. The country from where the capital is coming is the exporting country. For our purposes, an inbound FDI is where the U.S. is the host country *i.e.* a foreign person is investing in the United States. An outbound FDI is where an U.S. person is investing abroad.

The U.S., as the largest industrial country in the world, is the leading exporter of capital. It is also a very strong magnet for the inbound FDI. Some of the reasons for the U.S. attracting so much foreign capital are the size of the U.S. consumer market, the political stability, and the availability of managerial know-how. The U.S. is also blessed with an efficient and highly skilled labor force, and a large and a well-developed capital market. There is also easy access to intellectual property with a high degree of the most advanced technology.

Because of its free trade tradition, the U.S. enjoys an absence of economic controls, and minimal governmental intervention in purely commercial transactions. It is also the place where profits are earned in dollars. Even though the U.S. attracts much foreign capital there are many laws with which to contend. Foreign direct investment is subject to great scrutiny. Indeed, the popular notion in some circles is that international trade generally is bad for the United States. This may be because of the dramatic rise in foreign direct investment or the belief that the U.S. is losing jobs to low wage countries. There have been protests against free trade on the belief that it will tend to hurt the environment. The lawyer helping the foreign investor will find an array of ever-increasing U.S. rules that regulate inbound FDI.

As the U.S. contends with protectionist tendencies, Latin America and other regions of the world like Eastern Europe and the far east continue with programs of free trade and open borders. These countries are moving away from a highly statist economies where the governments owned much of the industry. Presently, there is a great privatization movement occurring in these areas. Governments are divesting themselves of ownership in industries such as telecommunications and power generation. As a result, massive amounts of capital are expected to flow into these areas as they privatize and build up their infrastructure.

This pent-up demand for capital, along with the changed attitude towards FDI has created opportunities for foreign investors. However, the opportunity carries risk. The FDI transaction is the most complex and riskiest of international business transaction. It involves the transfer of capital but is usually accompanied by a sale of goods, services, and technology component. The foreign investor should embark on an FDI only when one of the simpler forms of international transactions will not work. This is where the lawyer's help can be invaluable—look for simpler ways to achieve the desired result.

In some cases the host country will mandate the physical presence of the investor as a condition to accessing the domestic market. In the typical case however, the investor decides on the FDI for reduction of costs, maximizing control, and limiting its risk. Take for example Delta's Division III. The Division represents seventy-five percent of total Delta revenue. The company is being driven to a low labor rate country. It is unlikely that such an important revenue producer would be licensed to an unrelated party. Delta would want to maintain direct control over this core technology. The FDI alternative is the one that makes the most economic sense. The outbound foreign direct investment is discussed in chapters three and four infra.

The outbound foreign direct investment promises to continue to grow creating opportunities to tap these new investment markets. One of the principal reasons that there has been a growth spurt in the FDI is the willingness on the part of formerly closed countries to allow foreign investment. They have this willingness because of the need for capital and technology. The eagerness to receive the FDI manifests itself in the negotiation of international agreements. These accords create obligations at the international level. The following materials describe the rules through which international agreements form part of domestic legal systems.

B. THE SOURCES AND APPLICATION OF INTERNATIONAL LAW

1. *Governmental Trade Policy and International Business*

The business goals of the private company must take into account the regulatory environment in which it will operate. Just as private parties develop a plan to maximize profits and minimize risks, governments develop international trade policy to further their national interests. Oftentimes this means creating barriers to the free flow of international business transactions. For example, if the host government is protectionist, trade barriers will impose a higher cost for doing business in the country or prevent the entry of the foreign business altogether. This type of governmental regulation can affect all three categories of international business transactions.

Governments have come to recognize that in order to enhance the free and unfettered flow of international business transactions, a favorable regulatory climate must be achieved. The attitude in Latin America and the world generally is to move towards free trade and open borders, enhancing the international sale of goods, transfer of technology, and foreign investment. There are a variety of international trade and economic agreements that countries can enter into to further their trade policy.

International trade and economic relationships can be generally grouped into five categories—agreements that reduce trade barriers to the movement of goods and services, free trade agreements, customs union, common markets, and economic unions. As a general rule, trade relationships flourish between countries when there are fewer trade barriers. The simplest agreement is where two or more countries agree to reduce trade barriers by bestowing on the respective country some favored treatment. This status is known as "most favored nation" and is generally gained through admission into the General Agreement on Tariff and Trade/ World Trade Organization. The impact of these efforts to reduce trade barriers is discussed in chapter 7, infra.

The Free Trade Agreement eliminates, in some cases after a phase-in period, all trade barriers among the countries that make up the free trade group. The North American Free Trade Agreement (NAFTA) falls in this category. Canada, Mexico, and the U.S. as members of NAFTA, in effect receive better than 'most favored nation' status in transactions among them. The Customs Union incorporates the principles of a free trade agreement and adds a common external tariff. The Common Market incorporates the principles of a Customs Union and adds the free movement of the factors of production—capital and personnel in the common market area.

The deepest integration agreement among countries is the Economic Union. The Economic Union embraces common market principles and adds to it a common currency and common company's laws. Generally, the deeper trade relationships between countries arise when there is a similar economic development level among the signatory countries. Conversely, countries with a great disparity in economic development cannot sustain full economic integration. See Section 1.2, infra for a discussion of an analysis of the impediments to economic integration agreements in the Americas.

Economic and trade relationships between countries begin as obligations of the countries at the international level. It is initially a political decision. The political decision comes from the willingness, at least among the negotiating governments, for the success of going forward on a trade deal. The momentum can lead to other substantial changes. For example, the process of negotiating NAFTA led Mexico to enact sweeping new domestic legislation liberalizing foreign direct investment and strengthening the intellectual property rights of foreigners. The new political emphasis has helped invigorate the governments in Latin America to negotiate other trade and economic agreements. International agreements are being negotiated at a record pace in the Western Hemisphere because of the potential benefits that can be derived.

2. The International Agreement

a. Introduction

The international agreement is a principal source of international law and the most useful for international business planning. It replaces the domestic legal system to a certain extent. They are essentially contractual undertakings between countries wherein the countries agree to be legally bound to the terms of the agreement pursuant to the principles of international public law. The negotiating process allows a country to provide for its interests. Thus, by using an international agreement there is an approval of the trade process by the government at least as of the time the agreement is negotiated.

Oftentimes, even areas that are not specifically covered are affected by the goodwill surrounding the negotiation of trade pacts. Apart from the utility of the actual terms in the signed document, agreements between countries signal a political willingness of the governments to enhance free trade and open borders. The Western Hemisphere countries have been actively negotiating agreements to achieve trade liberalization and economic integration. The activity is continuing with a fever pitch. It is a remarkable change in attitude particularly among Latin American countries. Since the legal planner must consider the regulatory environment of the countries impacted by the transaction one can get a sense of the regulatory environment by analyzing the type of agreements between the countries in question.

Another important benefit in using international agreements is legal harmonization. As contracts between countries they constitute the governing law at the international level. They harmonize the law with respect to the coverage area. In addition, through dispute resolution provisions they provide mechanisms to harmonize the interpretation of the law. International agreements also facilitate finding the law because the agreements will be included in existing international legal databases. Also the agreement's official text is often in two or more languages.

International agreements also have some important limitations. By definition, they only affect the issues that have been negotiated. They are, therefore, much narrower in scope than any domestic body of law. Furthermore, they are static memorializing the circumstances that existed at the time the agreement was executed. In addition, enforcement of an international agreement, absent supra-national authority, must be done through the domestic legal system. Finally, international agreements constitute an obligation of the contracting state at the international level. They do not automatically create a private right enforceable at the domestic level.

For a private person to assert a right under an international agreement it must be recognized or received in the particular domestic legal system. This process of transforming an international right into a private right enforceable in the domestic legal system varies from country to country. The following materials describe these rules.

b. The Reception of International Agreements in the Domestic Legal System: The General Rules

STATUS OF TREATIES IN DOMESTIC LEGAL SYSTEMS: A POLICY ANALYSIS

John H. Jackson

86 Am. J. Int'l L. 310 (1992).

* * *

In connection with treaties, the basic concepts of "monism" and "dualism" have long been used to explain some of the relationships of treaty law to domestic law.

* * *

In traditional explanations of the effect of treaties (going back a century or more), a distinction is made between "monist" and "dualist" states. This terminology has been criticized, and clearly it is too "dichotomous" in flavor, since there are various degrees of direct application of treaties, to say nothing of the considerable confusion about it. Nevertheless, even though not precise, these terms are used and may help to demonstrate the major alternative approaches.

Let us assume that state M is considered "monist" and state D is considered "dualist," and in each state a citizen of the other has been refused rights to own property by the national government even though that state's citizens possess those rights. What is the national legal situation?

Traditionally, the "monist" state's legal system is considered to include international treaties to which M is obligated. Thus, a citizen of D can sue as an individual in the courts of M to require that he be treated in accordance with the treaty standard.

On the other hand, the term "dualist" has been used to describe the contrary result in state D. In a dualist state, international treaties are part of a separate legal system from that of the domestic law (hence a "dual" system). Therefore, a treaty is not part of the domestic law, at least not directly. Without further facts, a citizen of M who is refused the property ownership privilege in D that D's citizen has there, has no way to sue in the courts of D because those courts apply the law of D, which does not include the rule expressed in the treaty (at least not yet). The citizen of M's only recourse is to persuade his own government to use diplomatic means to encourage D to honor its obligation and assure him equal property ownership rights.

It is generally said that for the treaty rule to operate in the domestic legal system of a dualist state, there must be an "act of transformation," that is, a government action by that state incorporating the treaty norm into its domestic law. This may be a statute duly enacted by the parliament that uses all or part of the treaty language and incorporates it as a statutory matter into domestic law. Sometimes such a statute may paraphrase the treaty language, or "clarify" or elaborate on the treaty language. In all these cases, the domestic law is that of the act of transformation, but the treaty language usually has "relevance" in interpreting the statutory language, under various theories of domestic jurisprudence. Other legal instruments can also serve as an act of transformation, including a regulation of an administrative body (if its authority so permits), and possibly even an action or decision of a court or tribunal (again, depending on the authority of the tribunal). Like other concepts discussed here, "act of transformation" is not uniformly defined, and there are several other terms that compete with, or may (in the view of some) be subsumed within this phrase, such as "incorporation," "adoption," "reception," and similar terms. Likewise, the term "implementation" of treaties must be contrasted with, and in some cases embraces, the "act of transformation," as well as "direct applicability."

* * *

The United Kingdom is generally considered the prime example of a dualist system. Treaties never have direct "statutelike" application in the United Kingdom, but of course may have other internal effects. Many national systems derived from that of the United Kingdom, such as the Canadian and Australian systems, follow similar approaches. The legislature may enact laws that incorporate ("transform") treaties or treaty norms into domestic law, but, interestingly, the UK Parliament does not have a formal role in treaty making. Treaties are entered into by the "Crown" (today, obviously with the counsel of ministers). Sometimes (such as with the UK European Communities Act of 1972) a parliament can make provision for the "transformation" in advance. Variations on this approach are found in many other countries, for example, Germany and Italy.

At the other extreme, perhaps, is the Constitution of the Netherlands, which could generally be called "monist" since it expressly provides that certain treaties are directly applied and that in such cases these treaties are deemed superior to all laws, including constitutional norms!

* * *

———————

The article describes the two broad categories that are used by states to receive international agreements into the domestic legal system. In the Monist State, the creation of an international obligation at the international level also creates a right enforceable at the domestic level at the same time. No other action is necessary—the agreement is the domestic law. In the Dualist State, the creation of an obligation at the international level has no effect at the domestic level. The effect at the local level can come only from enabling legislation enacted pursuant to the terms of the international agreement. In the Dualist State, the domestic legislation is the law, not the international agreement. The U.S. legal system combines the Monist and Dualist system. In the U.S., the type of international agreement determines whether the monist or dualist system will be followed.

c. International Agreements in the U.S. Legal System

(1) Introduction

International agreements can be broadly grouped in three categories—Treaties, Congressional Agreements, and Executive agreements. The type of international agreement to be used in any given situation is initially a political decision subject to Constitutional limitations and ultimate judicial review. The following describes the guidelines the Executive uses in determining what type of agreement should be used.

U.S. DEPT. OF STATE, FOREIGN AFFAIRS MANUAL
Circular No. 175 (2d ed. 1985).

§ 720.2 General Objectives

The objectives [of these procedures] are:

a. That the making of treaties and other international agreements for the United States is carried out within constitutional and other appropriate limits;

* * *

c. That timely and appropriate consultation is had with congressional leaders and committees on treaties and other international agreements;

* * *

§ 721.3 Considerations for Selecting Among Constitutionally Authorized Procedures

In determining a question as to the procedure which should be followed for any particular international agreement, due consideration is given to the following factors along with [constitutional requirements]:

a. The extent to which the agreement involves commitments or risks affecting the nation as a whole;

b. Whether the agreement is intended to affect State laws;

c. Whether the agreement can be given effect without the enactment of subsequent legislation by the Congress;

d. Past U.S. practice with respect to similar agreements;

e. The preference of the Congress with respect to a particular type of agreement;

f. The degree of formality desired for an agreement;

g. The proposed duration of the agreement, the need for prompt conclusion of an agreement, and the desirability of concluding a routine or short-term agreement; and

h. The general international practice with respect to similar agreements.

In determining whether any international agreement should be brought into force as a treaty or as an international agreement other than a treaty, the utmost care is to be exercised to avoid any invasion or compromise of the constitutional powers of the Senate, the Congress as a whole, or the President.

§ 721.4 *Questions as to Type of Agreement to Be Used; Consultation With Congress.*

* * *

c. Consultations on such questions will be held with congressional leaders and committees as may be appropriate.

The Executive Branch is responsible for negotiating any of the three categories of international agreements—executive agreements, treaties, and congressional agreements. The guidelines describe the criteria to be used in the selection of a particular agreement. The terms in an executive agreement can come into force by the action of the President acting alone. The treaty requires the advice and consent of the Senate. The Congressional Agreement requires the approval of both the Senate and the House of Representatives. The decision of the President in the choice of agreement is subject to judicial review.

(2) The Executive Agreement

UNITED STATES v. BELMONT

United States Supreme Court, 1937.
301 U.S. 324, 57 S.Ct. 758, 81 L.Ed. 1134.

Mr. Justice SUTHERLAND delivered the opinion of the Court.

This is an action at law brought by petitioner against respondents in a federal District Court to recover a sum of money deposited by a Russian corporation (Petrograd Metal Works) with August Belmont, a private banker doing business in New York City under the name of August Belmont & Co. August Belmont died in 1924; and respondents are the duly appointed executors of his will. A motion to dismiss the complaint for failure to state facts sufficient to constitute a cause of action was sustained by the District Court, and its judgment was affirmed by the court below. (C.C.A.) 85 F.(2d) 542. The facts alleged, so far as necessary to be stated, follow.

The corporation had deposited with Belmont, prior to 1918, the sum of money which petitioner seeks to recover. In 1918, the Soviet government duly enacted a decree by which it dissolved, terminated, and liquidated the corporation (together with others), and nationalized and appropriated all of its property and assets of every kind and wherever situated, including the deposit account with Belmont. As a result, the deposit became the property of the Soviet government, and so remained until November 16, 1933, at which time the Soviet government released and assigned to petitioner all amounts due to that government from American nationals, including the deposit account of the corporation with Belmont. Respondents failed and refused to pay the amount upon demand duly made by petitioner.

The assignment was effected by an exchange of diplomatic correspondence between the Soviet government and the United States. The purpose was to bring about a final settlement of the claims and counterclaims between the Soviet government and the United States; and it was agreed that the Soviet government would take no steps to enforce claims against American nationals; but all such claims were released and assigned to the United States, with the understanding that the Soviet government was to by duly notified of all amounts realized by the United States from such release and assignment. The assignment and requirements for notice are parts of the larger plan to bring about a settlement of the rival claims of the high contracting parties. The continuing and definite interest of the Soviet government in the collection of assigned claims is evident; and the case, therefore, presents a question of public concern, the determination of which well might involve the good faith of the United States in the eyes of a foreign government. The court below held that the assignment thus effected embraced the claim here in question; and with that we agree.

That court, however, took the view that the situs of the bank deposit was within the state of New York; that in no sense could it be regarded as an intangible property right within Soviet territory; and that the nationalization decree, if enforced, would put into effect an act of confiscation. And it held that a judgment for the United States could not be had, because, in view of that result, it would be contrary to the controlling public policy of the state of New York. The further contention is made by respondents that the public policy of the United States would likewise be infringed by such a judgment. The two questions thus presented are the only ones necessary to be considered.

We take judicial notice of the fact that coincident with the assignment set forth in the complaint, the President recognized the Soviet government, and normal diplomatic relations were established between that government and the government of the United States, followed by an exchange of ambassadors. The effect of this was to validate, so far as this country is concerned, all acts of the Soviet government here involved from the commencement of its existence. The recognition, establishment of diplomatic relations, the assignment, and agreements with respect thereto, were all parts of one transaction, resulting in an international compact between the two governments. That the negotiations, acceptance of the assignment and agreements and understandings in respect thereof were within the competence of the President may not be doubted. Governmental power over internal affairs is distributed between the national government and the several states. Governmental power over external affairs is not distributed, but is vested exclusively in the national government. And in respect of what was done here, the Executive had authority to speak as the sole organ of that government. The assignment and the agreements in connection therewith did not, as in the case of treaties, as that term is used in the treaty-making clause of the Constitution (article 2, s 2), require the advice and consent of the Senate.

A treaty signifies 'a compact made between two or more independent nations, with a view to the public welfare.' B. Altman & Co. v. United States, 224 U.S. 583, 600, 32 S. Ct. 593, 596, 56 L.Ed. 894. But an international compact, as this was, is not always a treaty, which requires the participation of the Senate. There are many such compacts, of which a protocol, a modus vivendi, a postal convention, and agreements like that now under consideration are illustrations. See 5 Moore, Int. Law Digest, 210–221. The distinction was pointed out by this court in the Altman Case, supra, which arose under section 3 of the tariff Act of 1897 (30 Stat. 151, 203), authorizing the President to conclude commercial agreements with foreign countries in certain specified matters. We held that although this might not be a treaty requiring ratification by the Senate, it was a compact negotiated and proclaimed under the authority of the President, and as such was a 'treaty' within the meaning of the Circuit Court of Appeals Act (26 Stat. 826), the construction of which might be reviewed upon direct appeal to this court.

Plainly, the external powers of the United States are to be exercised without regard to state laws or policies. The supremacy of a treaty in this respect has been recognized from the beginning. Mr. Madison, in the Virginia Convention, said that if a treaty does not supersede existing state laws, as far as they contravene its operation, the treaty would be ineffective. 'To counteract it by the supremacy of the state laws, would bring on the Union the just charge of national perfidy, and involve us in war.' 3 Elliot's Debates 515. And see Ware v. Hylton, 3 Dall. 199, 236, 237, 1 L.Ed. 568. And while this rule in respect of treaties is established by the express language of clause 2, article 6, of the constitution, the same rule would result in the case of all international compacts and agreements from the very fact that complete power over international affairs is in the national government and is not and cannot be subject to any curtailment or interference on the part of the several states. Compare United States v. Curtiss–Wright Export Corporation, 299 U.S. 304, 316 et seq., 57 S.Ct. 216, 219, 81 L.Ed. 255. In respect of all international negotiations and compacts, and in respect of our foreign relations generally, state lines disappear. As to such purposes the state of New York does not exist. Within the field of its powers, what ever the United States right-fully undertakes, it necessarily has warrant to consummate. And when judicial authority is invoked in aid of such consummation, State Constitutions, state laws, and state policies are irrelevant to the inquiry and decision. It is inconceivable that any of them can be interposed as an obstacle to the effective operation of a federal constitutional power. * * * And nothing we have said is to be construed as foreclosing the assertion of any such claim to the fund involved, by intervention or other appropriate proceeding. We decide only that the complaint alleges facts sufficient to constitute a cause of action against the respondents.

Judgment reversed.

The Executive Agreement is used in those cases where the President is given sole Constitutional authority to act. They generally relate to foreign relations and rarely impact private interests. For example, an Executive Agreement can be used in cases involving the establishment of foreign relations to include any agreements negotiated and executed in the furtherance of those goals. Another example would be the signing of any agreements incidental to the establishment of an U.S. Embassy in a foreign country.

The Executive Agreement can have different names—compact, protocol, or some other like term. Regardless of the name, the Agreement is monist in nature. It will become an international obligation and a right enforceable in U.S. domestic courts upon signing by the President, so long as it comports with Constitutional limitations. Executive Agreements are also supreme over State law. They can, however, be superseded by later international agreements or federal law enacted by Congress acting within its Constitutional authority.

(3) The Treaty

A treaty requires ratification by a two-thirds vote of the Senate. It becomes an obligation under international law only after Senate action. Treaties can be of two types—self-executing and non self-executing. Under the Constitution treaties, (both self-executing and non self-executing) as well as federal statutory law are both the supreme law of the land. The difference between the types of treaties is in their transformation into a right enforceable in the domestic legal system. Self-executing treaties become enforceable at the domestic level when they become legal obligations at the international level. Therefore, a self-executing treaty is monist in nature since there is no need for enabling domestic legislation.

A non self-executing treaty is dualist in nature. It has no domestic effect unless there is enabling legislation. The practical difference is that a self-executing treaty involves the President and Senate whereas non self-executing treaties involve the President, the Senate and the House of Representatives. One can readily see the political implications in choosing the particular type of agreement to deal with the international issue. When President Carter decided to turn over the Panama Canal to Panama he chose a self-executing treaty. He felt the Senate would agree politically to go along with the transaction. However, he did not want to involve the House of Representatives because the idea was very politically unpopular there. The decision by Carter led to a lawsuit by sixty members of Congress.

EDWARDS v. CARTER

United States District Court, District of Columbia, 1978.
445 F.Supp. 1279.

* * *

[S]ixty members of the House of Representatives, sought a declaratory judgment that the exclusive means provided in the Constitution for disposal of United States property requires approval of both Houses of Congress, See Art. IV, s 3, cl. 2, and that therefore the Panama Canal Zone may not be returned to Panama through the Treaty process, which invests the treaty-making power in the President by and with the advice and consent of two-thirds of the Senators present, See Art. II, s 2, cl. 2. Appellee contends that the Constitution permits United States territory to be disposed of either through congressional legislation or through the treaty process, and that therefore the President's decision to proceed under the treaty power is constitutionally permissible. * * *

II

Article IV, s 3, cl. 2 of the Constitution states in its entirety: The Congress shall have Power to dispose of and make all needful Rules and Regulations respecting the Territory or other Property belonging to the United States; and nothing in this Constitution shall be so construed as to Prejudice any Claims of the United States, or of any particular State. Appellants contend that this clause gives Congress exclusive power to convey to foreign nations any property, such as the Panama Canal, owned by the United States. We find such a construction to be at odds with the wording of this and similar grants of power to the Congress, and, most significantly, with the history of the constitutional debates. * * *

The grant of authority to Congress under the property clause states that "The Congress shall have Power ... ," not that only the Congress shall have power, or that the Congress shall have exclusive power. In this respect the property clause is parallel to Article I, s 8, which also states that "The Congress

shall have Power...." Many of the powers thereafter enumerated in s 8 involve matters that were at the time the Constitution was adopted, and that are at the present time, also commonly the subject of treaties. The most prominent example of
this is the regulation of commerce with foreign nations, Art. 1, s
8, cl. 3, and appellants do not go so far as to contend that the
treaty process is not a constitutionally allowable means for
regulating foreign commerce. It thus seems to us that, on its
face, the property clause is intended not to restrict the scope of
the treaty clause, but, rather, is intended to permit Congress to
accomplish through legislation what may concurrently be accomplished through other means provided in the Constitution.

The American Law Institute's Restatement of Foreign Relations, directly addressing this issue, comes to the same conclusion we reach: The mere fact, however, that a congressional
power exists does not mean that the power is exclusive so as to
preclude the making of a self-executing treaty within the area of
that power. ALI Restatement of Foreign Relations Law (2d), s
141, at 435 (1965). The section of the Restatement relied on by
the dissent merely states that the treaty power, like all powers
granted to the United States, is limited by other restraints
found in the Constitution on the exercise of governmental
power. (Rest.For.Rel. s 117). Of course the correctness of this
proposition as a matter of constitutional law is clear. See Reid v.
Covert, 354 U.S. 1, 77 S.Ct. 1222, 1 L.Ed.2d 1148 (1957); De
Geofroy v. Riggs, 133 U.S. 258, 10 S.Ct. 295, 33 L.Ed. 642
(1890); Asakura v. Seattle, 265 U.S. 332, 44 S.Ct. 515, 68 L.Ed.
1041 (1924), also relied on by the dissent. To urge, as does the
dissent, that the transfer of the Canal Zone property by treaty
offends this well-settled principle that the treaty power can only
be exercised in a manner which conforms to the Constitution
begs the very question to be decided, namely, whether Art. IV, s
3, cl. 2 places in the Congress the Exclusive authority to dispose
of United States property. * * *

There are certain grants of authority to Congress, which
are, by their very terms, exclusive. In these areas, the treaty-
making power and the power of Congress are not concurrent;
rather, the only department of the federal government authorized to take action is the Congress. For instance, the Constitution expressly provides only one method [of] congressional enactment for the appropriation of money: No Money shall be
drawn from the Treasury, but in Consequence of Appropriations
made by Law. Art. I, s 9, cl. 7. Thus, the expenditure of funds by
the United States cannot be accomplished by self-executing
treaty; implementing legislation appropriating such funds is
indispensable. Similarly, the constitutional mandate that "all
Bills for raising Revenue shall originate in the House of Representatives," Art. 1, s 7, cl. 1, appears, by reason of the restric-

tive language used, to prohibit the use of the treaty power to impose taxes. * * *

These particular grants of power to Congress operate to limit the treaty power because the language of these provisions clearly precludes any method of appropriating money or raising taxes other than through the enactment of laws by the full Congress. This is to be contrasted with the power-granting language in Art. 1, s 8, and in Art. IV, s 3, cl. 2. Rather than stating the particular matter of concern and providing that the enactment of a law is the only way for the federal government to take action regarding that matter, these provisions state simply that Congress shall have power to take action on the matters enumerated.

Thus it appears from the very language used in the property clause that this provision was not intended to preclude the availability of self-executing treaties as a means for disposing of United States property. The history of the drafting and ratification of that clause confirms this conclusion. * * *

V

While certain earlier judicial interpretations of the interplay between the property clause and the treaty clause may be somewhat confused and less than dispositive of the precise issue before us, past treaty practice is thoroughly consistent with the revealed intention of the Framers of these clauses. In addition to the treaties with Indian tribes upheld in the cases discussed above, there are many other instances of self-executing treaties with foreign nations, including Panama, which cede land or other property assertedly owned by the United States. That some transfers have been effected through a congressional enactment instead of, or in addition to, a treaty signed by the President and ratified by two-thirds of the Senate present lends no support to appellants' position in this case, because, as stated previously, self-executing treaties and congressional enactments are alternative, concurrent means provided in the Constitution for disposal of United States property. * * *

The transfer of property contemplated in the current instance is part of a broader effort in the conduct of our foreign affairs to strengthen relations with another country, and indeed with the whole of Latin America. The Framers in their wisdom have made the treaty power available to the President, the chief executant of foreign relations under our constitutional scheme, by and with the advice and consent of two-thirds of the members of the Senate present, as a means of accomplishing these public purposes. * * *

For the foregoing reasons, the judgment of the District Court dismissing the complaint is Affirmed.

The President makes the initial decision on the type of international agreement to be used. The guidelines developed by the Department of State provide various criteria that should be followed. One is appropriate consultation. This may fall to the wayside in some cases given the political nature of presidential decisions. However, the decision is subject to judicial review especially where enabling legislation may be required. A self-executing would not be appropriate in those cases where Congress has the exclusive Constitutional authority to act through legislation. The court named two instances—appropriations and the raising of revenue. In those cases non self-executing treaties must be used.

Another case where a non self-executing treaty must be used is when commitments or risks facing the nation as a whole are being made. An example is the General Agreement on Tariff and Trade / World Trade Organization (GATT/WTO). The GATT/WTO is a broad trade agreement affecting the entire nation. It is a non self-executing treaty. The provisions of the GATT/ WTO became rights enforceable in U.S. domestic courts through the enactment of the Uruguay Round Agreements Act [URAA].[3] In this case, the GATT/WTO—the non self-executing treaty—is not the applicable domestic law, the federal legislation—the URAA is the controlling law. The URAA should mirror the terms of the GATT/WTO international agreement. What happens when there is a difference between the two?

Examples of self-executing treaties are the network of bilateral tax treaties[4] and the United Nations Convention on Contracts for the International Sale of Goods (UNCISG)[5]. These types of treaties create a right enforceable under the domestic legal system without enabling legislation. They are monist in nature. Constitutional authority for the raising of revenue rests with the House of Representatives. Tax legislation must begin there. Why does the bilateral tax treaty not need action by the House of Representatives? Tax treaties and the UNCISG are discussed in Sections 2.3 and 5.1, infra.

(4) The Congressional Agreement

The Congressional Agreement is in many respects like a non self-executing treaty. The North American Free Trade Agreement (NAFTA)[6] is a Congressional Agreement. The agreement is dualist in nature. The entry into force both at the domestic level is determined by the Agreement itself. The NAFTA is different from a treaty, however, because congressional approval was required even before it became an interna-

---

3. 5 Pub. Law 103–465, 108 Stat. 4809.

4. As of April 1, 2000, there were sixty-four bilateral income tax treaties to which the United States was a party. For an analysis of these treaties see RHOADES & LANGER, U.S. INTERNATIONAL TAXATION AND TAX TREA-

TIES (Mathew Bender & Co., Lexis Publishing)(2000).

5. 19 I.L.M. 671 (1980)

6. See 19 U.S.C.A. § 3301. North American Free Trade Agreement Implementation Act, Pub. L. 103–82 (1993)

tional obligation. The language in the enabling federal legislation is illustrative of the type of pressure that Congress can bring to bear.

NORTH AMERICAN FREE TRADE AGREEMENT IMPLEMENTATION ACT
19 U.S.C. § 3311.

Sec. 101 (c)(2) Conditions for entry into force of the agreement—The president is authorized to exchange notes with the Government of Canada and Mexico providing for the entry into force, on or after January 1, 1994, of the Agreement for the United States with respect to such country as * * * The President * * * determines that such country has implemented statutory changes necessary to bring that country into compliance with its obligations under the Agreement and has made provision to implement the Uniform Regulations provided for under article 511 of the Agreement regarding the interpretation, application, and administration of the rules of origin, and * * * transmits a report to the House of Representatives and the Senate setting forth the determination under subparagraph (A) and including, in the case of Mexico, a description of the specific measures taken by that country to * * * bring its laws into conformity with the requirements of the Schedule of Mexico in Annex 1904.15 of the Agreement , and * * * otherwise ensure the effective implementation of the binational panel review process under chapter 19 of the Agreement regarding final antidumping and countervailing duty determinations; and * * * the government of such country exchanges notes with the United States providing for the entry into force of the North American Agreement on Environmental Cooperation and the North american Agreement on Labor Cooperation for that country and the United States. * * *

The NAFTA implementation Act gave the President authorization to exchange notes with the respective governments only after determining that the countries had enacted specific statutory changes in their domestic system. The legislation also required the President to report the foreign domestic enactment to the Senate and the House. In addition, with respect to Mexico the President had to include in his report the specific measures taken by Mexico to bring its laws into conformity with Annex 1904.15 which detailed certain amendments to Mexican law that dealt in large part with antidumping and countervailing duties laws. The legislation also called upon the President to ensure the effective implementation of the binational panel review process on antidumping and countervailing duties. Finally, the act allowed the exchange of notes only after the entry into force of the North American Agreement on Environmental Cooperation and the North American Agreement on Labor Cooperation.

Politics also entered into the choice of a Congressional Agreement. The NAFTA, heavily endorsed by then President Bush, is a prime example of political exigencies. Recognizing the political implications, President Bush opted to get the House involved from the beginning. The political debate on the benefits of NAFTA raged in the House but ultimately passed under President Clinton's Administration. The Senate passed the NAFTA quickly thereafter. In Mexico, the NAFTA is referred to as the *Tratado de Libre Comercio*. In Spanish, *Tratado* means treaty. Politically, in Mexico, it was important to use the phraseology "treaty," even though it was not a treaty for U.S. purposes.

3. *The Relationship Between Treaties and Federal Statutory Law*

Under the U.S. Constitution, treaties and federal statutory law are both the supreme law of the land. They must, of course, meet the requirements of the Constitution. The hierarchical status of treaties and federal legislation is important to the lawyer in an international business-planning context. A lawyer advising a foreign person doing business in the U.S. and claiming a right under a treaty provision must make sure that the treaty provision is valid law. The issue does not arise in the case of a non self-executing treaty since the enabling legislation and not the treaty provides the rules. However, there can be conflict in the case of a non self-executing treaty.

Assume Congress enacted federal legislation that conflicts with the treaty provision. If the treaty and federal legislation are both the supreme law of the land which controls? The Supreme Court has dealt with this issue in two ways. The first involves the method of interpreting the conflicting provisions. In an early case *The Charming Betsy,* 6 U.S. (2 Cranch) 64, 2 L.Ed. 208 (1804)) Chief Justice Marshall wrote that an act of Congress ought never to be construed to violate the law of nations if any other construction is possible. Thus the starting point is to construe the conflict away.

SUMITOMO SHOJI AMERICA, INC. v. AVAGLIANO
United States Supreme Court, 1982.
457 U.S. 176, 102 S.Ct. 2374, 72 L.Ed.2d 765.

* * *

Chief Justice BURGER delivered the opinion of the Court.

We granted certiorari to decide whether Article VIII (1) of the friendship, Commerce and Navigation treaty between the United States and Japan provides a defense to a Title VII employment discrimination suit against an American subsidiary of a Japanese company.

I.

Petitioner, Sumitomo Shoji America, Inc., is a New York corporation and a wholly owned subsidiary of Sumitomo Shoji Kabushiki Kaisha, a Japanese general trading company or sogo shosha. Respondents are past and present female secretarial employees of Sumitomo. All but one of the respondents are United States citizens; that one exception is a Japanese citizen living in the United States. Respondents brought this suit as a class action claiming that Sumitomo's alleged practice of hiring only male Japanese citizens to fill executive, managerial, and sales positions violated both 42 U.S.C. § 1981 and Title VII of the Civil Rights Act of 1964, 78 Stat. 253, as amended, 42 U.S.C § 2000e et seq. (1976 ed. And Supp. IV). Respondents sought both injunctive relief and damages.

Without admitting the alleged discriminatory practice, Sumitomo moved under Rule 12(b)(6) of the Federal Rules of Civil Procedure to dismiss the complaint. Sumitomo's motion was based on two grounds: (1) discrimination on the basis of Japanese citizenship does not violate Title VII or § 1981; and (2) Sumitomo's practices are protected under Article VIII(1) of the Friendship, Commerce and Navigation treaty between the United States and Japan, Apr. 2, 1953, [1953] 4 U.S.T. 2063, T.I.A.S. No. 2863. The District Court dismissed the § 1981 claim, holding that neither sex discrimination nor national origin discrimination are cognizable under that section. 473 F. Supp. 506 (S.D.N.Y.1979). The court refused to dismiss the Title VII claims, however; it held that because Sumitomo is incorporated in the United States it is not covered by Article VIII(1) of the Treaty. The District Court then certified for interlocutory appeal to the Court of Appeals under 28 U.S.C. § 1292(b) the question of whether the terms of the treaty exempted Sumitomo from the provisions of Title VII.

* * *

We granted certiorari, 454 U.S. 962, 102 S. Ct. 501, 70 L.Ed. 2d 377 (1981), and we vacate and remand.

II

Interpretation of the Friendship, Commerce and Navigation treaty between Japan and the United States must, of course, begin with the language of the Treaty itself. The clear import of treaty language controls unless "application of the words of the treaty according to their obvious meaning effects a result inconsistent with the intent or expectations of its signatories." Maximov v. United States, 373 U.S. 49, 54, 83 S. Ct. 1054, 1057, 10 L. Ed. 2d 184 (1963). See also The Amiable Isabella, 6 Wheat. (19 U.S.) 1, 72, 5 L.Ed. 191 (1821).

Article VIII(1) of the Treaty provides in pertinent part:

"[C]ompanies of either Party shall be permitted to engage, within the territories of the other Party, accountants and other technical experts, executive personnel, attorneys, agents and other specialists of their choice." (Emphasis added.)

* * *

Clearly Article VIII(1) only applies to companies of one of the Treaty countries operating in the other country. Sumitomo contends that it is a company of Japan, and that Article VIII(1) of the Treaty grants it very broad discretion to fill its executive, managerial, and sales positions exclusively with male Japanese citizens.

* * *

Article VIII(1) does not define any of its terms; the definitional section of the treaty is contained in article XXII. Article XXII(3) provides: "As used in the present Treaty, the term 'companies' means corporations, partnerships, companies and other associations, whether or not with limited liability and whether or not for pecuniary profit. Companies constituted under the applicable laws and regulations within the territories of either Party shall be deemed companies thereof and shall have their juridical status recognized within the territories of the other Party." (Emphasis added.)

Sumitomo is "constituted under the applicable laws and regulations: of New York; based on Article XXII(3), it is a company of the United States, not a company of Japan. As a company of the United States operating in the United States, under the literal language of Article XXII(3) of the treaty, Sumitomo cannot invoke the rights provided in Article VIII(1), which are available only to companies of Japan operating in the United States and to companies of the United States operating in Japan.

The Governments of Japan and the United States support this interpretation of the Treaty. Both the Ministry of Foreign Affairs of Japan and the United States Department of State agree that a United States corporation, even when wholly owned by a Japanese company, is not a company of Japan under the Treaty and is therefore not covered by Article VIII(1). The Ministry of Foreign Affairs stated its position to the American Embassy in Tokyo with reference to this case: "The Ministry of Foreign Affairs, as the Office of [the Government of Japan] responsible for the interpretation of the [Friendship, Commerce and Navigation] Treaty, reiterates its view concerning the application of Article 8, Paragraph 1 of the Treaty: For the purpose of the Treaty, companies constituted under the applicable laws . . . of either Party shall be deemed companies thereof and, therefore, a subsidiary of a Japanese company which is incorporated under the laws of New York is not covered by Article 8 Paragraph 1 when it operates in the United States."

* * *

The United States Department of State also maintains that Article VIII(1) rights do not apply to locally incorporated subsidiaries. Although not conclusive, the meaning attributed to treaty provisions by the Government agencies charged with their negotiation and enforcement is entitled to great weight. Kolovrat v. Oregon, 366 U.S. 187, 194, 81 S.Ct. 922, 926, 6 L.Ed.2d 218 (1961).

* * *

Our role is limited to giving effect to the intent of the Treaty parties. When the parties to a treaty both agree as to the meaning of a treaty provision, and that interpretation follows from the clear treaty language, we must, absent extraordinarily strong contrary evidence, defer to that interpretation.

* * *

We are persuaded, as both signatories agree, that under the literal language of Article XXII(3) of the Treaty, Sumitomo is a company of the United States; we discern no reason to depart from the plain meaning of the Treaty language. Accordingly, we hold that Sumitomo is not a company of Japan and is thus not covered by Article VIII(1) of the Treaty. The judgment of the Court of Appeals is vacated, and the case is remanded for further proceedings consistent with this opinion.

Vacated and remanded.

In many cases the rule of construction does not help because there is a clear conflict. This happened when the Tax Reform Act of 1986 enacted anti-treaty shopping provisions that conflicted with several self-executing bilateral tax treaties. In cases where there is an irreconcilable conflict the courts have adopted the later-in-time-rule. The later-in-time rule provides that the later enactment trumps the earlier provision. Thus, subsequent federal law can rescind even a provision in a monistic international agreement, such as a self-executing treaty. The converse is also true—a treaty can trump previously enacted federal legislation. Note that the action by Congress could be a breach of the treaty at the international level. However, this does not affect the private person attempting to assert a right in federal district court.

SECTION 1.2   IMPEDIMENTS TO ECONOMIC INTEGRATION IN THE AMERICAS

A.   INTRODUCTION

U.S. Trade policy has traditionally favored 'fair' trade as distinguished from free trade. Providing an environment that enhances the exportation of goods and services and the protection of U.S. capital and technology has been a linchpin of U.S. trade policy. The 'fairness' of trade is, of course, in the eye of the beholder. U.S. trade policy has been attacked as a capitulation to corporate and 'one world government' interests. The meeting in Seattle of the GATT/WTO provoked riots in the streets of Seattle. Organized labor, environmentalists, and human rights activists complained that free trade policy was in fact an attempt by corporations to increase profits at the expense of people and the environment. Protectionist politicians see in the WTO/GATT the NAF-TA and other trade agreements the ceding of U.S. sovereignty to foreign interests.

Attempts at linking trade policy with other political interests are not new. During the Nixon administration, bilateral attempts to promote a freer trade environment between the U.S. and Russia failed in part due to U.S. Congressional efforts to link Russian Jewish emigration policy to the trade accord. More recently, the NAFTA gained House of Representatives approval only after two side agreements on labor and the environment were negotiated. Latin American trade policy seems to be focused on fear, either real or imagined, of U.S. economic hegemony. In spite of this there has been some growth in the concept of free trade and open borders. This section discusses some of the strides that have been made and an analysis of the impediments that exist for deeper economic relationships.

1.   *Agreements Reducing Trade Barriers*

The most basic level of trade relationships between countries is the agreement to reduce trade barriers between countries. The largest agreement of this type is the General Agreement on Tariff & Trade / World Trade Organization[7] [GATT/WTO]. The GATT/WTO had its beginnings in 1947. Shortly after the hostilities of World War II ended, the victorious parties minus Russia met to set out trade, economic, and monetary policy. In what came to be known as the Bretton Woods Conference the countries agreed to unite and form three institutions— the World Bank, the International Monetary Fund, and the World Trade Organization.

The World Bank was formed to provide loans to developing countries for infrastructure development projects. The International Monetary Fund was designed to help countries with exchange rate fluctuations. The third leg—the GATT was to focus on trade. Due in large part to U.S. resistance the trade institution was not finalized. Installed in its place was installed a framework agreement known as the General Agreement on Tariff and Trade [GATT]. The intention of the GATT is to reduce trade barriers—both tariff and non-tariff—among its member countries. The trade barrier is discussed in chapter 7, infra.

Since its inception in 1947, the GATT has had great success in removing tariff barriers. Worldwide tariff rates after the depression were extremely high—around ninety percent. Under the auspices of the GATT and through the various negotiating rounds, the overall world tariff rate among GATT signatory countries now ranges from three to five percent—a substantial reduction. The removal of non-tariff barriers has presented a more intractable problem. These types of barriers can take the form of quotas or health and safety regulations. The problem is that some member countries disguise protectionist policies through safety concerns of dubious application.

The 1947 GATT framework agreement covered only goods. Its main thrust was and is still on market access. The methodology is to require non-discrimination, national treatment, and most favored nation [MFN] treatment for the goods and nationals of the member countries. The

---

7. The GATT / WTO is a non self-executing treaty. The terms of the GATT / WTO became a right enforceable in the U.S. domestic legal system through Pub. L. 103–465, 108 Stat. 4809.

GATT Article I establishes the Most Favored Nation Principle. The wording of the clause is illustrative: "____ With respect to any ... advantage, favour, privilege or immunity granted by any contracting party to any product originating in or destined for any other country shall be accorded immediately and unconditionally to the like product originating in or destined for the territories of all other contracting states ..." This immediate and unconditional promise of non-discrimination is a key concept in MFN treatment.

Throughout the various negotiating rounds, pressures were brought to bear by the developed countries to increase the coverage of the GATT to include services as well as goods as well as to provide rules for the protection of technology and foreign capital. The developed countries prevailed. The latest GATT round—known as the Uruguay Round, resulted in many changes to the 1947 GATT framework agreement that the developed countries had been pressing for a long time. The Uruguay Round resulted in three treaties—the General Agreement on Tariff and Trade (GATT), the General Agreement on Trade in Services (GATS), and the Agreement on Trade–Related Aspects of Intellectual Property Rights (TRIPS). Foreign Direct Investment was also briefly addressed through the Trade Related Investment Measures (TRIM) agreement. The WTO administers the international rules found in these agreements. The impact of these agreements is discussed in different sections of this book.

2.   *The Free Trade Agreement*

The next step in the economic integration between countries is the free trade agreement. Free trade agreements are reciprocal arrangements where the signatory countries agree, in some cases after a phase-in period, to mutually remove tariff and non-tariff barriers on the movement of goods and services within the free trade area. Unlike agreements reducing trade barriers, this type of agreement removes rather than reduces trade barriers. The member countries constitute the free trade area within which the goods and services move freely. The service component, however, does not provide for the free mobility of people.

There are several free trade agreements in the Americas. The Group of Three, which includes Colombia, Venezuela, and Mexico, was signed on June 13, 1994. Chile enacted bilateral free trade agreements with Mexico (September 22, 1991), Venezuela (April 2, 1993), Colombia (December 6, 1993), and Ecuador (January 1, 1995). Mexico, in 1999, also entered into a free trade agreement with the European Union (EU). The largest free trade agreement in the Americas and the world is the North American Free Trade Agreement (NAFTA).[8] The NAFTA was signed on January 1, 1994 and includes Canada, Mexico and the United States.

---

8. The NAFTA is a Congressional Agreement. The enabling legislation can be found in 19 U.S.C.A. § 3301 et seq., the North American Free Trade Agreement Implementation Act, Pub. L. 103–82 (1994)

The NAFTA is the first free trade agreement entered into between a developed and developing country. While the NAFTA's aim is the phased removal of tariff and non-tariff barriers, it also contains chapters dealing with foreign investment, intellectual property, and dispute resolution. The NAFTA also includes side agreements that deal with labor and environment issues. The NAFTA is also significant in that pursuant to its negotiation, Mexico enacted laws protecting intellectual property rights and capital of foreigners in Mexico. This is one of the collateral benefits of entering into trade and economic relationships; it spawns a governmental willingness to further protect the interests of the foreign person.

U.S. trade policy has always focused on enhancing the exportation of U.S. goods and services. The NAFTA provided a mechanism whereby a previously protectionist state opened its large domestic market for U.S. produced goods and services. It was essentially a one-way street since the U.S. had for a number of years allowed the entry of many Mexican goods free from tariffs under the General System of Preferences.[9] In addition, the added bonus of technology and capital protection, and dispute settlement procedures under the NAFTA was very attractive to U.S. interests. The added feature of substantial changes in Mexican domestic law involving intellectual property and foreign investment protection made the entry irresistible.

There are few negatives to the U.S. in entering the NAFTA on account of its status as a free trade agreement. The negatives arise from the collateral effect a NAFTA type agreement can have on U.S. jobs. The 'giant sucking sound' of jobs leaving the United States as colorfully stated by an alarmist politician gave the NAFTA a status it did not deserve. To be sure, the so-called rust belt has lost many jobs. However, the loss of U.S. jobs has more to do with the enormous difference in labor rates between the U.S. and Mexico than with the NAFTA. In fact, Mexico had been welcoming foreign direct investment within its borders since the late 1980s even without the NAFTA.

The NAFTA is not geographic specific. The parties contemplated the potential accession of other Latin American countries or groups of countries. Chile and the South American Customs Union *Mercosur*, whose members include Argentina, Brazil, Paraguay, and Uruguay were often cited as potential candidates. The current NAFTA countries plus Chile and *Mercosur* constitute ninety five percent of the Western Hemisphere gross domestic product. Chile was often mentioned as the first candidate.

In fact negotiations had begun with Chile but were suspended when President Clinton lost fast track authority in negotiating trade agreements. Under 'fast track', the U.S. Congress can only vote yes or no on trade legislation. The trade package as a whole must be approved or disapproved. This is an important feature because without it special interest groups will be able to exert pressure on Congress to remove

9. 12 110 Stat. 1755 (1996).

certain products or industries from the agreement. The type of line item exclusions that can result from the absence of an up or down vote chills the enthusiasm of potential trading partners.

The denial by Congress of Presidential fast track authority is an interesting phenomenon. Historically, the United States has been the champion of fair trade and open borders. Latin America had always been highly protectionist. Currently, it appears that Latin America wants to engage the U.S. in continuing trade and open borders with the U.S. holding back. The following materials describe prior Latin American efforts and contrast it with the current change in attitude.

a. An Historical Perspective

Mexico engaged in the unilateral opening of its borders to foreign goods and foreign investment in the late 1980s and entered into the NAFTA for two basic reasons—it needed technology and foreign capital. The result was due to economic efforts among Latin American countries that did not work. Why were Mexico and all of Latin America in such dire need of technology and capital? The following materials discuss this issue.

The idea of political and economic integration or trade cooperation in the Americas is not new. In his Jamaica letter of 1815, Simon Bolívar called for South American political integration. Similarly, Jeffrey Blaine, Secretary of State during the Garfield administration in 1890 called for the establishment of a Customs Union in the Americas countries. Despite such far-sighted efforts, early economic and political integration efforts in the Western Hemisphere ended in failure. Indeed the record of trade cooperation between the U.S. and other Western Hemisphere countries is dismal. The only exception is the relationship between the U.S. and Canada.

The U.S. and Canada have enjoyed a long and successful history of trade agreements dating back to 1854. They are also very much alike in culture, language and economic development. Conversely, until recently trade agreements between the U.S. and Latin America have been nonexistent. By 1988, the only important successful bilateral trade negotiations between the U.S. and Latin America were the Mexican *Bracero* (guest farm-worker) program, the Mexican *Maquiladora* (product assembly) program, and the U.S.-Mexico Understanding on Subsidies and Countervailing Duties.

There are many factors in the lack of trade cooperation between the U.S. and Latin America. One is the Latin American fear of economic domination by the "colossus of the north". The economic disparity coupled with the legal, political, and cultural differences has created fear, distrust, and mutual suspicion between Latin America and the U.S. Furthermore, the anti-foreign and protectionist cycles that the U.S. itself occasionally goes through have heightened the distrust and fed the mutual lack of cooperation. Even Canada, with its similarities to the United States and record of trade cooperation, has been apprehensive of the United States. Former Canadian Prime Minister Elliot Trudeau once likened U.S. Canada relations to sleeping with an elephant; even an unintended turn could kill you. Canada has especially been concerned with maintaining its cultural distinctiveness from the U.S.

Latin American fear of U.S. economic domination reached a high in the 1930s. Reeling from the devastating effect of the worldwide depression, Latin American countries felt that only by uniting could they protect themselves against real or perceived U.S. economic hegemony. Latin American economists argued for intra-Latin American economic integration using import substitution and protectionism as the development strategy of the region. Under import substitution domestically produced goods replace imports. The theory is that by erecting protectionist barriers imports will either be denied admission into the region or the cost, because of the government import duties, will make the domestic sales price of the imported goods prohibitive. In that way, it was believed, those domestically produced goods would be substituted for imports.

The following two articles describe the macroeconomic policies of import substitution and protectionism adopted in Latin America, the debt crisis they generated, and the devastating effect these macroeconomic policies have had on Latin American economies.

LAW, HIERARCHY, AND VULNERABLE GROUPS IN LATIN AMERICA: TOWARDS A COMMUNAL MODEL OF DEVELOPMENT IN A NEOLIBERAL WORLD

Enrique R. Carrasco
30 Stan. J. Int'l L. 221 (1994).

A.　The Import–Substitution Model of Development

The origins of the import-substitution model of development can be traced to development economists who in the 1930s and 1940s began to focus on the causes of poverty in developing countries and attempted to develop long-term formulas for economic progress. Although trained in the neo-classical tradition of free trade and capitalism, these economists faced empirical data that cast doubt upon the applicability of these theories to developing countries. Prior to the 1930s, Latin American countries pursued outward-oriented free trade policies. They exported primarily agricultural and mineral raw materials in which they had a comparative advantage, and they imported primarily manufactured goods from Europe. The severe drop in export earnings during the worldwide depression of the 1930s, however, emphasized to these countries the vulnerability of their exports (and hence their economic development) to global trade cycles induced by the industrialized countries.

They consequently turned their economies inward via import-substitution policies and sought to replace imported manufactures with domestically produced goods. The state used its financial regulatory regime to perform the temporary protective function needed to transform Latin American countries into industrialized states. High tariffs and non-tariff barriers such as import quotas and licensing requirements provided protection from the external sphere.

* * *

In the 1950s, Raul Prebisch, Hans Singer, and others provided theoretical support for these policies. Their arguments became associated with the "structuralist school" of international trade and development advanced by the United Nations Economic Commission for Latin America (ECLA), now Economic Commission for Latin America and the Caribbean (ECLAC)), of which Prebisch was Executive President.

The structuralists argued that there was a structural bias in the global trading system against developing countries that exported primary commodities.

* * *

Because of this structural bias, the import-substitution model rejected the assumption that international division of labor based on comparative advantage would yield an equitable distribution of benefits between developing and developed countries. The structuralist school, like the neoclassical school, did emphasize the importance of trade to economic development; however, they argued, instead of exporting primary goods, the state should supervise a process of industrialization through backwards linkages, starting with light industry and concluding with capital goods production. Regional trading among developing countries would then help infant industries achieve economies of scale, enabling developing countries to launch an export drive to the rest of the world.

* * *

Given the underdeveloped domestic capital markets in Latin America, only the state could provide the significant investments required for the establishment of intermediate and capital goods industries. Moreover, Latin American countries viewed such strategic investments as vital to their sovereignty.

* * *

The state's tasks of guiding strategic investments and encouraging foreign investment created friction between Latin American governments and multinationals, and led to the enactment of laws in the 1960s and early 1970s that sought to control foreign investment.

* * *

In sum, under the import-substitution model of development, the state generated the economic laws and regulations described above and created state-owned enterprises that would protect, transform, and propel Latin American countries into global capitalism from an autonomous platform. The unfettered free market simply could not perform this function.

* * *

B.   The Development Debate and the Makings of the Debt Crisis

* * *

As the development debate continued, the OPEC countries deposited in U.S. and European banks billions of dollars in profits they received after the 1974 price hike in oil. The banks lent these so-called petrodollars at a profit to developing countries, particularly to Latin American countries that were willing to borrow in order to finance their export drives and, for oil importers such as Brazil, to meet higher energy bills. Latin American governments recognized that this relatively cheap money could supplement historically low domestic savings, which then could be invested to sustain economic growth. Moreover, loans from foreign commercial banks did not require borrowers to abide by specified macroeconomic policies. The heavy borrowing, especially by the public sector, enabled Latin America to sustain relatively impressive growth rates between 1975–80.

* * *

Over time, however, the borrowing strategy resulted in excessive public expenditures and high fiscal deficits. External borrowing financed the widening trade deficits and postponed the day of reckoning. As domestic demand increased during the economic boom, so did inflation.

When the debt crisis officially commenced in August of 1982, Latin American debtor countries faced a number of serious economic problems that stemmed from both internal and external factors: (i) a staggering level of external debt, a large proportion of which was contracted from foreign commercial banks at floating interest rates; (ii) high international interest rates, which made debt service costly and difficult; (iii) a marked deterioration of terms of trade due to the worldwide recession and protectionist barriers in industrialized countries; (iv) a dramatic reversal from net inward transfers of resources to net outward transfers, resulting from the steep drop in lending to the region and the flight of private capital out of debtor countries; (v) high fiscal deficits; (vi) high inflation rates; and (vii) overvalued currencies.

* * *

PERSPECTIVES ON THE NORTH AMERICAN FREE TRADE AGREEMENT REGIONAL TRADE ARRANGEMENTS IN THE WESTERN HEMISPHERE

Dr. Richard Bernal

8 Am. U. J. Int'l L. & Pol'y 683 (1993).

* * *

The extent of the economic stagnation in Latin America and the Caribbean which has prevailed throughout the 1980s and into the 1990s, is evident in the fact that GDP in real terms and GDP per capita are actually lower in 1990 than they were in 1977 for the region as a whole. Furthermore, the region has suffered a persistent de-capitalization through capital flight and heavy debt servicing. In 1991, debt service absorbed over 40% of export earnings and the debt-to-exports ratio was significant at 287%. Latin America and the Caribbean have also suffered a negative net transfer of resources between 1980 and 1990, reaching a high of $31 billion in 1983. Compounding these problems is rampant inflation, which in 1990 reached 7,000% in Peru and over 13,000% in Nicaragua.

Against this background, the severe economic crisis of Latin America and the Caribbean during the 1980s compelled a re-examination of economic policy. The region responded to the economic stagnation with a reorientation of economic policies to focus on economic reform, stabilization, and structural adjustment in an attempt to initiate a private-sector, market-driven, outward-looking growth strategy. Import-substitution and state-led development strategies have been renounced and dismantled in favor of outward-oriented approaches. Most Latin American countries, as well as many Central American and Caribbean countries have reduced tariffs, removed quantitative trade restrictions and vigorously implemented programs of privatization. A change in Latin American integration strategy from an inward-oriented approach aimed at strengthening stalled import-substitution industrialization, to an outward-oriented approach complementing internal market liberalization has also taken place. Regional trade liberalization was a logical outgrowth of market-oriented policies because it sought to enlarge the market.

* * *

Latin American countries originally formulated grand regional and sub-regional economic integration systems, planned and nurtured by the ECLAC to unite against the United States. During its formative years the ECLAC was greatly influenced by its Executive Secretary, Dr. Raul

Prebisch, an Argentine economist who believed that economic integration was the key to Latin American well being. He became a leading force in formulating policies directed at integrating the Latin American economies.

Under the ECLAC, the Latin American Free Trade Association (LAFTA), a framework agreement for Latin American economic integration was enacted. The members included Argentina, Brazil, Bolivia, Chile, Mexico, Paraguay, Peru, and Uruguay. The LAFTA framework inspired the formation of The Central American Common Market, the Andean Pact, and the Caribbean Community. These sub-regional economic integration systems endorsed the protectionist, inward-looking views espoused by the ECLAC and LAFTA. The central idea in the early integration efforts was creating a common external barrier while creating border-less regions within the member countries. The U.S., as a strong advocate of free trade, did not agree with much of the Latin American integration efforts of the 1930s.

The import substitution development strategy was a failure. The protectionist rules prevented low cost foreign equity investments from entering the country. The huge levels of debt at high interest rates precipitated the Latin American debt crisis of the 1980s. Adding to the misery, the debt funding of infrastructure development was impeded by inefficiencies and corruption by the governments of the developing countries. Additionally, the domestic products produced, because of the lack of technology, were inferior to products available in the world market.

The protectionist system restricted the entry of much needed manufacturing technology. In the 1970s, this writer represented a group of Mexican bus companies seeking to purchase buses for use in their domestic routes. They were willing to purchase U.S. buses that were over ten years old and pay the near 100% import tax rather than buy new but inferior Mexican buses. However, from the debacle of import substitution and protectionism, there emerged a new attitude towards free trade in the 1990s.

b. A Change in Attitude

By the end of the 1980s, the reality of the failed policies was settling in. In the world at large communism was a failure, the Union of Soviet Socialist Republics had dissolved, the cold war ended, and democratically elected governments came forth everywhere in the world, including Latin America. The military rule in Chile, Argentina, and Paraguay ended. A rapprochement towards free trade and open markets started taking place in Latin America.

By 1980, the by then moribund LAFTA was replaced by the more progressive Latin American Integration Association (LAIA) (Spanish acronym ALADI). The members of LAIA; Argentina, Bolivia, Brazil, Chile, Colombia, Ecuador, Mexico, Paraguay, Uruguay, and Venezuela shared the common aim of the formation of a Latin American Common

Market. Even though the LAIA framework adhered to protectionist barriers and import substitution policies, it encouraged regional and sub-regional efforts, inspiring changes to the Central American Common Market, The Andean Pact, and the Caribbean Community. It also inspired the formation of the *Mercado Comun Del Cono* Sur (*Mercosur*)[The Common Market of the Southern Cone (countries of South America)] that focuses on removing barriers to trade, removing restrictions on foreign investment, and to some extent, protecting intellectual property rights.

In 1990, the U.S. weighed in on the side of economic integration in the Americas by announcing the Enterprise for the Americas Initiative (EAI). Through the EAI, the U.S. encouraged integration efforts in the Americas by reducing trade barriers, increasing investments into Latin America, and providing for debt relief. The EAI was well received in Latin America. Under its auspices, the U.S. negotiated framework agreements to expand trade and liberalize foreign investment laws with the *Mercosur*, Caribbean Community, and over ten individual countries. The framework agreements provided for Trade and Investment Councils (TICs) to act as forums to discuss the removal of barriers to trade and investment. The TICs are designed as precursors to negotiating free-trade agreements.

The late 1980s and early 1990s showed unprecedented activity in negotiating trade agreements. The U.S.-Canada Free Trade Agreement of 1987 and the North American Free Trade Agreement of 1993 were the largest. Latin American countries were also active in creating or modifying regional, sub-regional, and bilateral trade relationships. The motivation for Latin America's free trade initiatives was and is survival. The Latin American debt crisis of the 1980s and the lost decade of the 1970s, as Ambassador Bernal so appropriately describes it, caused a profound rethinking of macroeconomic policy in Latin America.

This change in attitude has led to an ambitious project named the Free Trade Agreement of the Americas (FTAA). The FTAA would create a free trade area from the Yukon to *Tierra del Fuego* with a combined population of eight hundred and fifty million people and a combined gross domestic product of thirteen trillion dollars, making it the largest free trade area in the world. In a remarkable meeting in Miami in December 1994, thirty-four democratically elected presidents of Western Hemispheric countries met agreeing in principle to create the FTAA by the year 2005. The FTAA is expected to build on the GATT/WTO and other regional and bilateral agreements already in place.

The FTAA while seeking to establish a free trade area has as an ultimate purpose the elimination of barriers to investment and technology transfers. The ultimate goal would include the integration of Western Hemisphere capital markets. The FTAA negotiators recognize that the efficient movement of goods, services, information, technology, and capital are the foundations of prosperity. The lofty goals adopted in the 1994 summit meeting[10] includes the preserving and strengthening of democracies, promoting prosperity, eradicating poverty and discrimination, guaranteeing sustainable development while conserving the natural environment. The goals are quite ambitious given the stark differences in the development level of the countries.

A variety of reasons can be given for U.S. involvement in trade liberalization in the Americas. The growing regionalization of global trade and the recognition that helping the developing countries in the Western Hemisphere achieve economic security is the only sure way to stanch the flow of illegal immigration and dependence on the illicit drug trade. U.S. recognition of the importance of existing trade in the Americas is another factor. However, misgivings about the potential loss of American jobs have stifled some of the enthusiasm for trade liberalization.

There has been a growing level of negative feelings towards free trade and open borders in the United States. In addition to the potential loss of jobs, the negative feelings may be due to dramatic increases of inbound foreign investment and foreigners "buying up America." These fears create a sense that the U.S. is losing its position as the preeminent world economic power because of the rise of Japanese industrial power, Arab money centers, and the European Community.

Whatever the reason, some members of Congress and other political leaders have been obsessed with the notion that U.S. nationals are not competing at a level playing field and that unfair foreign competition is hurting U.S. business interests. The result is an air of protectionism that directly contradicts the long held U.S. views of free fair trade and open borders. However, the biggest impediment to deeper economic relationships in the Americas is not a lack of willingness among the countries but rather the economic, political, cultural, differences that exist in the region.

B. THE CHALLENGES TO ESTABLISHING ECONOMIC INTEGRATION AGREEMENTS IN THE AMERICAS

1. Introduction

The three types of agreements that represent a deeper economic integration among the member countries are the Customs Union, the Common Market, and the Economic Union. The Customs Union incorporates the principles of a free trade agreement providing for the free movement of goods and services within the borders of the signatory countries while adding a common external tariff to all other countries. This relationship establishes an "us versus them" position. For example, assume that Germany, an EU country wishes to access the U.S. market with one of its products. It could import the product free of tariff into

---

10. See Summit of the Americas: Declaration of Principles and Plan of Action, 34   I.L.M. 808.

Mexico, and so long as the NAFTA rules of origin are followed, could import the product into the U.S. market free of tariff under the NAFTA.

If, however, the NAFTA were a Customs Union, the German Company would encounter the same tariff whether it imported its product into Mexico, the U.S., or Canada. This type of relationship prevents Mexico from being a platform for the German goods. Essentially, the countries in a Customs Union are aligning their economic future very closely. Therefore, in order to keep any one-member country from being adversely affected, their economic development level should be very similar. A review of the Customs Unions in the Western Hemisphere[11] reveals this macroeconomic reality.

There are several Customs Unions in the Western Hemisphere among the Latin American countries. The latest in time and most important is the *Mercado Comun del Cono Sur (MERCOSUR)*. The MERCOSUR is the Spanish Language acronym for the Common market of the Southern Cone Countries of South America—Argentina, Brazil, Paraguay, and Uruguay. The MECOSUR was formed in 1991 and as the name *Mercado Comun* suggests was initially conceived as a common market. It has never achieved that status.

Although conceived as a common market, the Central American Common Market since its inception in 1958 has variously included the Central American countries of Guatemala, Honduras, El Salvador, Costa Rica, and Panama. The region has been ravaged by civil war. Its progress in economic integration has obviously not progressed as envisioned. The Andean Pact is another that since its inception in 1969 has included the countries in the Andes Mountains—Bolivia, Colombia, Chile, Ecuador, Peru and Venezuela. Political and economic differences among the countries have kept them from achieving their original plans. Finally, a group of thirteen Caribbean countries formed the Caribbean Community, which although intended to be a common market is a Customs Union. The Customs Union is the deepest level of involvement by any group of countries in the Americas. The United States is not a member of any Customs Union.

A Common Market incorporates the principles of a free trade agreement and Customs Union adding to it the free movement of the factors of production—people and capital. Thus, in a common market goods, services, people, and capital are allowed free movement within the member states while those countries outside the group face a common external tariff. An Economic Union represents a full economic integration between countries. In an economic union common currency and company laws are added to the principles of a common market.

11. The Western Hemisphere countries have been very active in formulating trade and economic agreements. There are eight major agreements—the GATT/World Trade Organization, the NAFTA, the Southern Cone Common Market, the Andean Pact, the Caribbean Community, the Central American Common Market, Group of Three, and a set of free trade agreements known as the Chilean Bilaterals. For a detailed discussion of the agreements, see *An Analytical Compendium of Western Hemisphere Trade Agreements,* Organization of American States Trade Unit, June 30, 1995.

An Americas common market or economic union is very far in the future. Even an America's customs union would be difficult to achieve. The stark differences in economic development between the U.S., Canada and Latin America are a major impediment. In addition, the major differences in cultural, legal and political systems pose formidable barriers to the notion of free trade and open borders.

Between the U.S. and Latin America, there is much diversity in culture, language, economics, political systems, and legal systems. In addition, relations between the countries have not always been friendly and at times have led to war. Fear of loss of sovereignty in Latin America, cultural identity of Canada, and jobs in the U.S. are the driving influences that create challenges to free trade and open borders. However, despite the mutual suspicion and distrust, the governments continue to move towards free trade and economic integration.

Governments in the Americas' countries realize that trade cooperation and some degree of economic integration is vital to the national interests of each individual country. Thus, the Americas are becoming a region of interdependent countries. There is also a growing awareness in the U.S. and Canada that a prosperous Latin America is the only true solution to illegal immigration and environmental concerns.

2. *The Cultural Differences*

The cultural diversity existing between the U.S., Canada, and the other countries in the Western Hemisphere, referred to in this work collectively as Latin America, is well known. Oftentimes, however, Latin America is viewed as a monolith, with little diversity within it. However, this is not true. In fact, there is probably more diversity between Peru and Chile than between Belgium and France. To many, the U.S. Mexico border cities—hot, dusty, poor and dirty—are representative of the rest of Latin America. Some are surprised to see Caucasian Latin Americans and the influence Western European countries have had in the people and culture there. The topography in Latin America is as varied as the people are, with deserts, tropical climates, icebergs, and fjords in the austral reaches of South America.

Recognizing and dealing with cultural diversity is important in international business planning. One goal of this casebook is to present America's diversity in an objective manner, remembering that cultural differences do not imply the inferiority or superiority of any given culture. The successful international lawyer approaches cultural distinctions in an unbiased manner. The international lawyer who can confront cultural diversity in an impartial manner will be a more effective counsel to a client and will become a better person in the process.

The following article compares and contrasts the cultural distinctions between the U.S. and Mexico. It is important to remember, however, that simply understanding the culture of Mexico may not necessarily explain fully the cultural nuances in other Latin American countries.

THE AMERICANIZATION OF MEXICAN LAW: NON-TRADE ISSUES IN THE NORTH AMERICAN FREE TRADE AGREEMENT

Stephen Zamora

24 LAW & POL'Y INT'L BUS. 391 (1993).

* * *

Cultural attitudes would not be so crucial if the United States and Mexico shared similar cultural backgrounds. However, the Anglo–Saxon/Protestant culture that has molded the U.S. legal system differs markedly from the hispanic-Catholic and indigenous heritage that has shaped Mexican law and society. One must be aware of the misunderstandings that can result from such differences, including mistaken assumptions about the presumed benefits of one culture's approach to problem-solving as a model for other societies.

* * *

Carlos Fuentes, the ubiquitous Mexican writer and astute observer of U.S.-Mexican relations, emphasizes these cultural differences:

The three-thousand-mile border [sic] between Mexico and the United States is more than a border between Mexico and the United States: it is the border between the United States and all of Latin America, for Latin America begins at the Mexican border.

It is the only frontier between the industrialized and the developing worlds.

It is the frontier between two memories: a memory of triumph and a memory of loss. . . .

It is the frontier between two cultures: the Protestant, capitalist, Nordic culture, and the southern, Indo–Mediterranean, Catholic culture of syncretism and the baroque. . . .

Every Latin American has a personal frontier with the United States.

And every North American, before this century is over, will find that he or she has a personal frontier with Latin America. . . .

* * *

In The Labyrinth of Solitude, Octavio Paz similarly contrasts the Mexican world view with that of the United States:

The history of Mexico is the history of a man seeking his parentage, his origins. He has been influenced at one time or another by France, Spain, the United States and the militant indigenists of his own country. . . . Our solitude has the same roots as religious feelings. It is a form of orphanhood, an obscure awareness that we have been torn from the All, and an ardent search: a flight and a return, an effort to re-establish the bonds that unite us with the universe.

* * *

Some people claim that the only differences between the North American and ourselves are economic. . . . I refuse to believe that as soon as we have heavy industry and are free of all economic imperialism, the differences will vanish.

* * *

A.   The Communitarian Culture

[T]he most important cultural difference between U.S. and Mexican society can be summed up thus: Mexican society stresses cooperation and subordination of the individual to the larger social group, while U.S. society stresses competition and glorifies individual freedom.

* * *

In the United States, individualism and competition are the legacies of a society in which a person's ties and obligations to the larger group have become weakened. The average U.S. citizen of the 1990s expects less protection and support from his or her extended family, church, municipality, company or labor union than his or her grandparents asked. This is in part a result of the high degree of mobility, geographical as well as socioeconomic, that characterizes U.S. society; the unbreakable support of one's larger social group is not expected if one so easily moves to a new job or a new city. Conversely, the individual expects that by working hard and competing successfully, he or she can gain wealth, social status, etc., without regard to the needs or requirements of a larger social group.

* * *

By comparison with his or her U.S. counterpart, the individual in Mexico depends on permanent ties to larger social groups for greater moral and physical support. The most basic group is the family—"Mexico's social security system," as Mexicans refer to it. In addition to the immediate family, Mexicans form bonds of support and cooperation with extended family members, and through the compadrazgo (godfather) system they create kinship-type bonds with those outside the family. The private sector economy in Mexico has traditionally been controlled through this system of family and personal alliances. Even the largest Mexican companies are primarily owned, and effectively controlled, by extended family groups. Venture capital is scarce and expensive, so that many new business enterprises are financed by returning to the network of personal relationships that one has established with family members or friends. In comparison with the United States, these relationships are more constant, and are dependant both on one's performance and on one's ability to fit into and cooperate with the group.

* * *

[T]he over-arching theme is the subordination of the individual person or enterprise to the group or system of which it is a part.

* * *

The average Mexican citizen—less mobile, individualistic and competitive than his or her U.S. counterpart—is linked to his or her society in positive and negative ways that have more to do with cooperation than with competition. It is important to recognize that the adherence to a hierarchically structured community and an emphasis on cooperation within that community are deeply embedded in Mexican society.

* * *

———————

Although cultural similarities exist among Latin American countries, the countries are not identical. The Spanish and indigenous population's influence is most pronounced between Mexico and countries at and to the north of the equator. The southern cone countries of South America have a small indigenous population. The Spanish influence in the South American cone competes with Italian, Portuguese, and to a lesser degree, German culture. In the Caribbean countries, the African culture is very prevalent.

The similarities among Latin America countries includes: catholicism, the family as an important social and financial support group, a communitarian culture adhering to a hierarchical ordering of society and a less mobile populace. Why is it important to recognize cultural differences important in international business planning? Dean Zamora discusses the family as an important element in Mexican society. What are some of the advantages of a family oriented society in a business setting? What are its disadvantages?

3.   *Economic Differences and International Trade Policy*

As different as the countries are in political, legal and cultural structure, these pale in comparison to the disparate economic development of countries in the Western Hemisphere. The difference in development level of countries is the single most important factor preventing substantial trade relationships and economic integration. The world's countries are often categorized as developed or developing countries with a variety of gradations within the broad classification. The Americas is comprised of countries in every stage of development ranging from the U.S. and Canada with a per capita gross domestic product (GDP) in excess of $20,000 to Haiti with a per capita GDP of less than $400. Mexico while being the most prosperous of Latin American countries has a GDP of almost $7,000, far below that of the U.S. and Canada.

The economic dividing line in the Americas is stark. The average worker in the U.S. and Canada enjoy a standard of living that is much higher than their Latin American counterparts. The wage differential is enormous and the ability to break out of the poverty cycle in the U.S. and Canada is much greater than in Latin America. A debate has raged for many years between the developed and developing countries focusing on determining the fair and just trade relationship that should exist among these countries. Developed countries have long espoused the position that fair treatment means equal treatment among countries. Developing countries believe that equal treatment between unequal parties is inherently unfair. The following article describes the general posture taken by developing countries.

INTERIM REPORT OF THE OAS SPECIAL COMMITTEE ON TRADE TO THE TRADE MINISTERS WESTERN HEMISPHERE TRADE MINISTERIAL

Denver, Colorado, June 30, 1995.

* * *

A few descriptive statistics underline the great discrepancies of countries in the region:

- The United States represents nearly 80% of the combined hemispheric GDP;

- While exports to the United States make up 52 percent of Latin America's total exports, they represent only 13% of total U.S. imports (half of which come from Mexico). On the other hand, only 14 percent of U.S. exports go to Latin America;

- This asymmetry is much greater in the case of the small Caribbean and Central American economies, which send over half the exports to the United States but account for only 1.5 percent of total US imports; and

- In spite of the unilateral liberalization efforts undertaken by Latin American countries, tariffs are much higher in Latin America and the Caribbean than in the United States, as a result of which the burden of adjustment posed by trade liberalization will fall more on the former than the latter.

These disparities greatly complicate the acknowledged need to accomplish a closer integration of developing countries in the global trade regime. While the global benefits of trade liberalization are generally recognized, the realization of these benefits by small and less developed countries will depend greatly on their capacity to adjust to shifts in market opportunities and to increased competition. When these countries cannot adjust appropriately and quickly enough, more often than not due to underlying structural weaknesses, their trade and economic prospects may worsen.

* * *

The development level of a country has a significant impact on the governmental attitude towards international trade. Latin America exports basic commodities such as agriculture and oil. There is overall very little trust in the quality of products manufactured in Latin America even among nationals of the countries themselves. Thus, the export markets for goods manufactured in Latin America are very small. In addition, Latin America is a net importer of technology and capital. The OAS report emphasizes the fact that many developing countries cannot readily move towards free trade on account of the structural weaknesses present in their economies.

The U.S. exports manufactured products containing a high degree of technology. It is a net exporter of technology and capital. In the case of technology, the flow is almost exclusively one-way. There is a large U.S. trade surplus on the transfer of technology. The amount of capital exported is also heavily skewed in favor of developed countries. U.S. trade policy reflects this reality. There is a heavy emphasis on promoting exports. The U.S. also promotes the foreign market access for the products and services its citizens are selling. It pushes for free competition and the elimination of trade barriers.

The rallying cry is to provide a level playing field for its nationals. This includes eliminating unfair trade practices, insisting on reciprocal trade preferences, protecting intellectual property rights, and safeguarding the capital investment made by its citizens. The following article describes the U.S. position.

WESTERN HEMISPHERE—ENTERPRISE FOR THE AMERICAS, 1995 NATIONAL TRADE DATA BANK MARKET REPORTS DEPARTMENT OF COMMERCE

March 21, 1995.

* * *

MOVING TOWARD FREE TRADE
INDICATORS OF READINESS

Which countries are to be future free trade agreement (FTA) partners is largely a self-selecting exercise. United States standards for entering FTA negotiations, however, will be high. The United States will consider whether an FTA would be in the economic interest of the United States, and consistent with overall hemispheric policy objectives. The United States does not intend to apply the GATT concept of special and differential treatment to FTA negotiations. Any decision to proceed would be taken after consultations with the U.S. Congress.

To be a realistic candidate, a country or group of countries must have the economic and institutional capacity to fulfill the long-term, serious commitments involved. A prospective FTA partner must be committed to a stable macroeconomic environment and market-oriented policies before negotiations are underway. Market-oriented policies include participation in good standing in the General Agreement on Tariffs and Trade, a willingness to open the economy to foreign investment and trade in services, and a commitment to enforce "world class intellectual property right protection." The international financial institutions, in particular the Inter–American Development Bank and the World Bank, are ready to help the region's nations adopt structural and investment policy reform programs with this goal in mind.

Another aspect of readiness is a country's commitment to the multilateral trading system. The EAI is compatible with, and supportive of, the multilateral trading system. Indeed, the U.S. uses the meetings of the Trade and Investment Councils, created by framework agreements, to coordinate positions in the GATT. The U.S. will only negotiate agreements fully consistent with the provisions of GATT Article XXIV * * *

———————

Latin American trade policy is in a state of flux. The massive reorientation from a statist economy to an economy embracing free trade has yet to run its course. Generally, Latin American trade policy is aimed at creating jobs for its underemployed population, increasing the amount and quality of technology within its borders, and increasing foreign investment as a means of infrastructure development. Latin America has essentially capitulated to the U.S. view of international trade embracing free and unfettered competition giving open and receptive treatment of foreign technology and investment. The result will be great opportunities for U.S. nationals. There will be new markets for U.S. products, reductions in labor costs when manufacturing jobs are sent to Latin America, and new capital investment opportunities.

The impact on Latin America could be very negative. Latin American industries will be hard pressed to compete with the onslaught of U.S. and Canadian products. Free trade has the potential of severely hurting nascent Latin American industries. In addition, U.S. and Canadian foreign investment could "buy up" Latin America due to the enormous economic disparity of the countries. Embracing the concept of free trade and open borders with the unequal bargaining position of the countries is a great challenge for the growth of free trade in the Americas.

A concern for the continuing of trade liberalization is the political reality of whether Latin American countries can continue the current trend. Questions regarding the political will of Latin American governments to stay the course of free trade will doubtless create much speculation. The current interest in free trade and open markets is perhaps different from other eras. Several distinguishing factors are present: (1) The emergence of democratically elected leaders, (2) a recognition by Latin America of past failed policies, and (3) the United States having initiated a major effort in trade liberalization through the Enterprise for the Americas Initiative.

The great challenge to free trade and open borders is the grinding poverty that exists in Latin America and the concomitant problem of illegal immigration. A healthy economy and the presence of a substantial middle class in Latin America are the only way to prevent illegal immigration in the United States. If Mexico ever achieves the status of the Canadian economy it would have the illegal immigration problem not the United States. Illegal immigration results from economic necessity. But for the lure of jobs, an illegal alien would quickly move back home.

As a developed country, goals of the U.S. are to require its trading partners to allow access to their domestic markets, eliminate unfair trade practices, protect intellectual property rights, and capital being exported. How realistic is U.S. policy as outlined in the Market Reports excerpt given the large economic difference between the countries? Developing countries view free trade and open borders as a means of creating jobs for its unemployed or under-employed citizens, increase the amount of modern technology within their borders, and attract capital to enhance the development of the country's infrastructure. What can a developing country lose by free trade and open borders?

4. The Political Differences

In addition to cultural diversity, there is much political diversity in the Western Hemisphere. The Americas' political heritage has been diverse—monarchies, socialism, communism, military dictatorships, and democracies. Governments have gained power through democratic elections, revolutions, wars, and countless military coups. Democracy has grown from this heritage, spreading rapidly in the Western Hemisphere, especially since the end of the cold war. A graphic example of democratic expansion was the economic summit of the Americas held in Miami, Florida in 1994 with thirty-four democratic republics attended. Cuba was the only country not in attendance.

The trend towards democracy tends to favor international business because of the historical willingness of democratic countries to embrace free trade and to open their borders to foreign investment. Of course, entering into international agreements liberalizing free trade and opening borders is much easier when there has been a history of friendly relations and when there are cultural, economic, and political similarities among the contracting states. Generally, the greater the diversity, the more difficult it is to establish deep international trade relationships.

The political difference between the United States and Latin America is most pronounced in the exercise of the inter-relationship between the three branches of government. Like the United States, Mexico and other Latin American countries have three branches of government—the Executive, Legislative, and Judiciary. Under the U.S. and Mexican Constitution there is a built-in system of checks and balances. The U.S. system of checks and balances works quite well as can be seen by the recent impeachment of President Clinton. In Mexico and much of Latin America, the system has not worked as well. In Latin America, the cultural predisposition of cooperation and the accepting of a hierarchically structured society has fostered the concept of *Presidencialismo*—the imperial presidency.

In spite of a shift away from military junta rule democratically elected chief executives in Latin America yield greater power than their U.S. or Canadian counterparts.

This difference in power was graphically illustrated during the NAFTA ratification process. In the U.S., much was written about the uncertainty of whether the House of Representatives would pass NAFTA. In Mexico, there was no discussion of that possibility. It was a foregone conclusion that the Mexican legislature would affirm what then President Salinas negotiated. In addition, there was no thought of the Judiciary challenging the NAFTA as being un-constitutional.

Presidencialismo has had a chilling effect on international business. The rules for domestic regulation of international trade emanate, either from a statute enacted by the legislature, or an international agreement. In either case the statute or treaty is subject to review by the judiciary to ensure that it comports with the Constitution. Once the legislation is passed, regulations explaining the law are promulgated under the authority of the chief executive. Regulations should merely explain the statute. The judiciary, as a counterbalance to improper exercise of presidential rule making, can nullify any regulation that broadens or limits the scope of the statute. This safeguard disappears in the absence of an independent judiciary.

Mexican history has shown that regulations can vary substantially from the statute—either making it more or less restrictive. Indeed, one commentator suggested that Mexican President Salinas issued regulations liberalizing foreign investment that not only varied the statute, but violated the Mexican Constitution as well. The effect of *Presidencialismo* is obvious. A president that can act like a monarch destroys the independence of the judiciary and legislature. In such a system uncertainty abounds in international business planning. A change in President can reverse a liberalization program and render useless a plan based on existing law. *Presidencialismo* also worsens the pervasive problem of corruption in Latin America strengthening the widely held view that Latin America is a region governed by relationships instead of law. The current attitude towards trade liberalization may weaken the concept of *Presidencialismo*, but only time will tell if it will ever be eliminated.

5.   *The Differences in Legal Systems*

To a great extent, the American views the Mexican legal system as corrupt and inefficient. The fact that there is a different language and culture only exacerbates the problem. The Mexican sees the U.S. system as illogical, expensive, slow, and biased in favor of the American. Neither view is totally correct but the chilling effect of this lack of trust stifles the growth of international trade. The hiring of local counsel may help to assuage some fears of dealing in a foreign jurisdiction but will not eliminate it. Another way of coping with these differences, although not to the exclusion of local counsel, is to understand the essential differences between the legal systems that exist in the Americas.

In the Americas there exists two legal systems—the civil and common law. The U.S. and Canada are common law countries while the rest of the Western Hemisphere, including Mexico, follows the civil law. Each system has its own tradition, style of legal texts, terminology, and approach to law. Understanding this diversity is the first step in the international business planning process. The differences in contract formation principles, the function of a civil law notary, and the corporate code principles are just a few of the many areas the differences of which can create traps for the unwary.

RELATIONSHIPS AMONG ROMAN LAW, COMMON LAW, AND MODERN CIVIL LAW

Peter G. Stein

66 TUL. L. REV. 1591 (1992).

* * *

The most obvious feature of modern civil law in the eyes of a common-law lawyer is that is it codified. * * * The civil-law conception of the written law as the sole source of private law and the highly systematic nature of modern codes of civil law lie behind the form of reasoning that characterizes the civil law.

* * *

Civil-law reasoning may loosely be described as deductive reasoning, by which one proceeds from a broad principle, expressed in general terms, then considers the facts of the particular case and finally, as in a syllogism, applies the principle to the facts so as to reach a conclusion. This form of reasoning leads the civil-law lawyer to present a legal argument as if there can be only one right answer to any legal problem, and disagreement on the application of the law to the facts of a case must, in this way of thinking, be the result of faulty logic by somebody.

Thus, civil-law judges in general do not give dissenting opinions and every judgment, even in appellate cases, is that of the court as a whole.

In the common law no formulation of a rule, whether by judge or academic, is final. A later judge can broaden or narrow the terms in which it is expressed. What is authoritative is not what is said but what is decided, and the difficulties of discovering what rule a particular decision has laid down are well known. The common law is thus open-ended in that new extensions to existing rules can be revealed at any time by the courts, but it has no existence as a body of material distinct from what the courts have decided. The common-law judge is the oracle of the law and takes personal responsibility for his decisions. If he dissents from his colleagues, it may be because he is ahead of them; today's dissenting opinion may be tomorrow's majority view. As a result of this prominence of the judges, academic lawyers in common-law countries have not enjoyed the same prestige as their colleagues in civil-law countries.

Traditionally the civil-law judge is * * * to apply the written law, and the meaning of that law is to be discovered from the writings of its academic exponents. The explanation of the authority accorded to academic writers in the civil law is partly historical. When the texts of Justinian's Corpus Iuris were rediscovered around the year 1100 after lying dormant for five hundred years, they were so complicated that no one could begin to understand them without the help of the medieval Gloss, so that the Gloss came to have as much authority as the texts themselves. The late medieval commentators offered the key to understanding the texts and the judges traditionally deferred to them. Thus, in the civil law, by contrast with the common law, the academic commentator seems to be the senior and the judge the junior partner in the legal process.

* * *

III.   Civil-Law Procedure and Common-Law Procedure

* * *

To the common-law lawyer the civil-law type of deductive logic seems to reverse the natural form of legal reasoning. The common-law lawyer begins his argument with an examination of the facts, with a view to identifying the precise legal issue raised by the case. When the relevant rules are derived from earlier cases cited as precedents, each party cites those precedents that favor his own position and emphasizes the facts of his case relevant to those precedents. They are then analyzed with a view to establishing which are the most significant precedents. At this point in the debate, there is usually much scope for argument; the common law is therefore never presented, like the civil law, as a set of certain rules that can be applied with inexorable logic.

* * *

When a common-law lawyer asks what the case is about, he is thinking of the facts, with a view to identifying the material circumstances of the case and to showing that they fall within the scope of one rule rather than another. When a civil-law lawyer asks what the case is about, he generally refers to the legal issue defined in a general way. Often the adversarial procedure of the common law has the advantage of identifying the issue with greater precision. In the civil-law procedure the real points at issue may only emerge gradually as the case proceeds.

* * *

The civil law emerges from legislative enactment. The legislature, not the judiciary, is the key element. One commentator noted that the heroes of the civil law are lawgivers—Justinian and Napoleon whereas in the common law the heroes are judges—Cardozo, Brandeis, etc. The reason for this can be attributed to the codified nature of the civil law. It is important for the common law lawyer to recognize, however, that a civil law code is not the same as a codification in the common law system. For example, the Internal Revenue Code is merely a compilation of laws that have been grouped together. The civil law code is not a mere collection of laws. The code is a comprehensive treatment giving the general principles of a specific subject area. The civil law code has been referred to as mini constitutions as opposed to a compilation of laws.

ON SOME PRACTICAL IMPLICATIONS OF THE DIVERSITY OF LEGAL CULTURES FOR LAWYERING IN THE AMERICAS

Alejandro M. Garro
64 Rev. Jur. U.P.R. 461 (1995).

* * *

There is a close affinity among Latin American legal systems to the extent they share a similar socioeconomic structure, political culture and a common legal heritage. However, the movement towards unification has been circumscribed, with varying degrees of success, in the areas of public law and private international law. In the area of private substantive law, the civil and commercial codes of the Latin American countries share a general framework from which general principles on commercial contracts may be derived. Despite such favorable conditions, the Latin American experience in the unification of private substantive law to date has not been very significant. This is especially disappointing, considering that countries lacking similar historical and cultural unity are progressively coming to terms with the international unification of law. Helped by the dynamics of economic integration, the movement for legal unification and harmonization has gained momentum in Western Europe with the internationalization of trade, investment and financing. In Latin America, efforts to deal with unification have been traditionally frustrated by chauvinistic perspectives of sovereignty. This trend appears to be changing.

One is tempted to draw the conclusion that an awareness of the advantages of uniformity has been lacking in Latin America. This is certainly not the case. Substantial efforts have been made in this regard, and it is not uncommon to hear Latin Americans advocate the advantages of harmonization and unification. * * * However, before speculating about the prospects of Latin America's future participation in regional and international unification efforts in the field of international commercial contracts and other areas of substantive law, one may need to consider the impact on unification of some political, economic, and cultural characteristics peculiar to the Latin American region. Those features and prevailing trends in areas such as legal education, access to basic tools of research, legal scholarship and judicial decisions play a significant role as contributing or retarding factors of legal harmonization and unification of substantive law.

* * *

Why, despite a common legal heritage that traces back almost five centuries, that is perpetuated by the reception of the European codification and its scholarly doctrine, and strengthened by similar socioeconomic and political structures, is the formal diversity of substantive private law the norm in Latin America and uniformity and harmonization still the exception? This question may be approached by discussing first the structural variables of an economic, political and legal nature that hinder Latin American progress toward a more harmonized or unified framework of private law at a regional level. Then one may discuss and even speculate about contemporary Latin American attitudes towards unification efforts of a more global or universal nature.

* * *

From a strict normative standpoint, Latin American nations are far less integrated than a federal union such as the United States or a supranational arrangement such as the European Community.

It may be surprising to foreign observers to realize how little informed Latin American lawyers are about the legal systems of their sister republics. This lack of information is a result of many factors among which include the difficulty posed by developing economies against the background of long distances and poor means of communication and transportation, the historical significance of international trade with Western Europe and the United States as opposed to the more modest trade relationships among the Latin American countries, and a traditional, and up to a certain extent, unavoidable Eurocentric approach that has prevailed in Latin American legal scholarship on private law.

Latin American law revision commissions, judges, law professors and lawyers communicate with each other very little, but most often in conferences that take place in Europe or the United States. The most sophisticated legal comparativists in Latin America are likely to be more acquainted with some aspect of the law of commercial transactions in France, Spain, Italy, or even Germany or New York than with the legal system of another Latin American country.

The foregoing structural and cultural features that inhibit the unification of Latin American law are also reflected in the difficulties posed to harmonization by non-legislative means through the training of lawyers by law schools, and the lack of access to research tools that may throw light on the judicial or doctrinal path followed by other Latin American countries. There are no Latin American law schools with exchange or summer programs for teaching or studying in other Latin American countries, such as those conducted by some U.S.-based law schools. The legal literature and judicial decisions in Latin America do not seem to have a potential impact as a vehicle for harmonization. This is in large measure due to the drastic limitations imposed by economic underdevelopment on the availability and quality of legal research. Basic research tools such as updated and comprehensive legislative and case-law reports of other Latin American countries are out of reach of most Latin American law libraries. Even if adequate sources were available, a notoriously underpaid academic community and an understaffed and overworked judiciary is unlikely to be able to process, digest and think over the many intricate issues posed by legal unification.

With the exception of a handful of countries, the legal literature indigenous to Latin America is comparatively scarce and of relative usefulness. Doctrinal materials include extensive references to broad scientific principles and citations to "classical" European legal commentators, but very little insight or personal observation as to what is the law in action in other Latin American countries.

* * *

Judicial decisions are not likely to prove an efficient means of Latin American legal unification. First, because in many Latin American countries it is uncertain in both theory and practice the extent to which precedents contribute to a unified interpretive approach of the domestic law. The prevailing style of legal scholarship rarely turns to the operative facts of prior cases in support of a legal proposition. Although most Latin American supreme courts, including the supreme court of a federal country such as Mexico, is meant to unify the interpretation of law within the country through the appellate jurisdiction, and despite the compromises in practice and in some instances in theory made to the traditional non-recognition of the binding forces of precedents, the lack of easy access to published precedents severely conspires against the use of judicial decisions as a vehicle of unification of law in the same jurisdiction.

Few Latin American countries have adequate systems of reporting court decisions. Those accustomed to computerized research tools and skillfully indexed and cross-referenced legal digests may not fully appreciate the critical nature of the indexing function to obtain a full and clear picture of the weight of authority in a Latin American country on a particular point or question. Even if foreign judicial decisions were widely available to the Latin American judge, it is doubtful the extent to which one may rely on the convenience of harmonization or the need to promote the uniform application of a uniform text as against other elements to be balanced in the complexities of the judicial process. To the extent that foreign court decisions are not binding, the paramount concern of most courts will be to reach a "fair" decision, even though not in harmony with decisions in similar cases reached by foreign courts.

* * *

_____

The Garro article points out that even coming from a common family of legal systems there is much diversity among Latin American countries. This legal diversity within Latin America can have a significant impact on international business planning. Even a company that has had experience in one Latin American country would be mistaken to believe that the same procedures and plan could be used in a different Latin American country.

Physically finding the law in Latin American countries can also be a problem. In the United States, we are blessed with vast electronic research resources. Additionally, the codification of statutes and the compiling of cases are great aids to find the appropriate law. It is important to remember, however, that rules do exist in Latin America and that difficulty in finding them does not reflect a qualitative inferiority of the system.

International agreements are useful in harmonizing legal rules. There have also been efforts to harmonize domestic rules like the Uniform Commercial Code in the United States. Some international organizations have made efforts in domestic legal harmonization. The Organization of American States (OAS) through one of its institutions called the Inter–American Juridical Committee (IAJC), has been very active in promoting the harmonization of national laws as well as promoting the development and codification of international law.

The IAJC efforts at harmonizing private law have been progressing under a specialized committee named the Inter–American Specialized Conferences on the Development of Private International Law. The committee conferences, widely known by the Spanish acronym CIDIP, have instituted five hemispheric—wide conferences on a range of subjects.

Note: An Overview of the Mexican Legal System

The Mexican legal system is illustrative of the Latin American civil law system. Mexico, like the United States is a federal republic. The following is a brief and broad explanation of the Mexican legal System:

An Introduction To The Mexican Legal System[12]

In order to study the Mexican legal system, it is useful to begin with an explanation of the world's contemporary legal environment and to specifically analyze, though briefly, the *Civil Law Tradition*, of which Mexico forms a part.

Subsequently, we will enter into an introductory and brief explanation of some of the most relevant areas of the Mexican legal system: the history of Mexican law, the concept of law and the classification of the law. Then we will examine the State and its institutions, wherein the Constitution and the federal system and its three branches (executive, legislative and judicial) are most notable. Next, special mention is made of the *Amparo* Trial. And, finally, we include observations regarding the notary public (as part of the Latin notary family) and the commercial public broker whose roles in the Mexican legal system are of utmost importance as they are required by applicable law.

THE CIVIL LAW TRADITION

The civil law tradition is both the oldest and the most widely distributed of the three legal traditions (civil law, common law, and socialist law) See

---

12. This note was prepared by Professor Roberto Rosas. Professor Rosas is a Mexican lawyer and Visiting Professor at St. Mary's University School of Law in San Antonio, Texas.

The Civil Law Tradition, John Henry Merryman, Stanford University Press, Second Edition, 1994. Its origins are traced back to 450 BC, the supposed date of publication of the XII Tables in Rome. Today, it is the dominant tradition in most of Western Europe, all of Latin America, many parts of Asia and Africa, and even of a few enclaves in the common law world (Louisiana, Quebec, and Puerto Rico).

The five sub-traditions within the civil law tradition: Roman civil law, canon law, commercial law, legal science and the western revolution are the principal historical sources of the concepts, institutions, and procedures of most of the civil law tradition. In modern form, as affected by revolutionary law and legal science, these sub-traditions are embodied in five basic codes typically found in a civil law jurisdiction: 1) civil code; 2) commercial code; 3) code of civil procedure; 4) penal code; and, 5) code of criminal procedure.

California has a number of codified statutes called codes, as do some other states in the United States. For example, the Uniform Commercial Code (UCC) has been adopted in most American jurisdictions. However, although these codes look like the codes in civil law countries, the underlying ideology, the conception of what a code is and of the functions it should perform in the legal process is not the same.

For purposes of understanding the civil law tradition, we should consider codification as an expression of ideology rather than a form. To begin the study of the civil law tradition, particularly the Mexican legal system, we should understand this ideology and why it achieves expression in code form.

THE SOURCES OF LAW

Legislation (*Legislación*)

The major driving forces behind the civil law tradition in Mexico are the legislation as manifested in the various codes and the rules and regulations promulgated thereunder. However, codes, statutes, rules, and regulations are not the only sources of law used in Mexico and other civil law countries. Article 14 of the Mexican Constitution has designated three sources of civil (in this context, as opposed to criminal) law—the law, jurisprudence, and should those fail general principles of law. The law can be interpreted to mean the letter of the law. Jurisprudence (*Jurisprudencia*) is derived from the judicial interpretation of the law. The general principles of law result are gleaned from the work of civil law legal thinkers of great renown throughout history. The *Legislación, Jurisprudencia,* and general principles of law are considered formal sources of the law under the Constitution. Doctrine (*Doctrina*) is derived from treatises and other legal writings of scholars. *Doctrina* is considered as a secondary and indirect source of law.

Jurisprudence (*Jurisprudencia*)

Mexican *Jurisprudencia* is based on case law decided at the Supreme Court Level or its equivalent. *Jurisprudencia* is established when at least five decisions issued by the Supreme Court of Justice with respect to a particular issue are substantiated in five consecutive like holdings uninterrupted by another holding to the contrary. The resolutions of the Circuit Collegiate Tribunals also establish *Jurisprudencia* in the same manner.

Decisions that elucidate contradictions of holdings of the Chamber and the Circuit Collegiate Tribunals (also known in the common law system as splits in the Circuits) also constitute jurisprudence. When less than five cases are decided in the same manner the decision is called a *Tesis de Jurisprudencia* (Jurisprudence Thesis) while not mandatory may be used as authority. These decisions are published in the Federal Judicial Weekly Report (*Semanario Judicial de la Federación*).

Doctrine (*Doctrina*)

Mexican *Doctrina* consists of legal writings or treatises published by legal scholars. Judges who are heavily influenced by legal scholarship utilize the ideas suggested to them by scholars without citing them and usually refer in a very general way to the doctrine. Professor Merryman in his book states that the doctrine can carry immense authority since "Y the teacher-scholar is the real protagonist of the civil law tradition. The civil law is a law of the professors ..." As a result "Y it is reasonably accurate to say that the law in a civil law jurisdiction is what the legal scholars say it is ..." *The Civil Law Tradition, John Henry Merryman, Stanford University Press, Second Edition, 1994*, pps 55–60.

BRIEF DESCRIPTION OF THE HISTORY OF MEXICAN LAW

History has distinguished five periods for the study of Mexican law: 1) the Pre-colonial period, predominantly under indigenous legislation and customs; 2) Colonial period, predominantly under the control of Spain during the *Nueva España* (New Spain); 3) Independent period, under Mexican legislation as an independent country; 4) Revolutionary period, during and after the Mexican Revolution; and, 5) Institutional period, under a regime that seeks to institutionalize the legal system.

THE MEXICAN LEGAL SYSTEM

In the Mexican legal system law has been defined as a set of legal rules created by the State to regulate the external conduct of individuals with judicial sanctions provided for in the event of non-compliance.

CLASSIFICATION OF THE LAW

Although many scholars have argued that there cannot be a separation or classification of the law, a classification of the law has been recognized for didactic purposes. The Mexican law system recognizes, for didactic purposes, a classification of the law into three main branches: Public Law, Private Law, and Social Law. Constitutional law, criminal law, administrative law, procedural law, and public international law fall within the scope of the public law classification. Civil law, commercial law, and international private law are under the umbrella of the private law classification. Finally, labor law and agrarian law rest on the social classification of the law.

THE STATE AND ITS INSTITUTIONS

Mexican Constitutions

Since the Mexican war of independence from Spain, three constitutions have been implemented in Mexico: The Constitution of 1824, the first

Constitution of independent Mexico; the Constitution of 1857, the second; and, as a result of the Mexican Revolution in 1910, the Constitution of 1917 that despite many amendments and reforms remains in force.

The Constitution of 1824 is the first federal constitution in Mexico. The distribution of the subject matter in this Constitution follows the classical constitutional model in its 171 articles. The two main parts of a constitution are clearly delineated therein: dogmatic and organic. The dogmatic part is focused on the rights of individuals and citizens along with other community principles. The organic part is focused on the separation of powers and provides precise regulations for their operation, powers, and functions. Interestingly, that constitution's preamble invokes God as the supreme legislator of society and states that Congress comes to enact this constitution in compliance with the duties that have been imposed upon it.

The dogmatic part lacks the classic declaration of individual and citizens' rights. However, these rights are addressed in subsequent parts of the Constitution where it delegates the power to legislate these issues to the state legislatures. Freedoms of speech and of the press are mentioned therein solely for the purpose of ensuring that the federal authorities police and guarantee said freedoms.

The organic part is covered in titles III, IV, and V, the organization of the three branches of government (Executive, Legislative, and Judicial, respectively). Title VI covers the function and organization of the states' branches of government.

The Constitution of 1857 is one of the most significant constitutional texts in Mexican constitutional law. Its content marked Mexico's separation from the past in its most important manifestations: the economical and political power of the church and the disappearance of military and religious immunity. Notably, it includes a separate title covering individual and citizens' rights. It is also significant that this constitution amply recognizes individual freedoms and rights and provides a legal mechanism to enforce those rights through the *Amparo* remedy.

The Constitution of 1917 was enacted on February 5, 1917. This Constitution, as do the Constitutions of 1824 and 1857, contains two parts: the dogmatic part and the organic part. The dogmatic part deals with fundamental human rights and individual guarantees. The organic part organizes the public power.

Individual Guarantees

The individual guarantees contained in the dogmatic part of the Constitution of 1917 include rights and liberties that protect individuals from governmental action. These guarantees are broadly classified in four groups: 1) Equality, contained in the Constitution's Articles 1, 2, 4, 12, and 13; 2) Liberty, contained in Articles 3–11 and 16, 24, and 28; 3) Property, contained in Article 27); and, 4) Legality, contained in Articles 14–23 and 27.

Interestingly, Article 29 of the Constitution regulates the suspension of individual guarantees in specific cases.

FEDERAL SYSTEM

The Mexican Republic consists of free and sovereign states that with respect to their internal regime are united in a Federation and are subject to the dispositions and principles contained in the political Constitution, which is the supreme law of the land.

The Mexican political system recognizes three levels of government: federal, state, and municipal. The country is made up of 32 political and administrative units, 31 of which are states and one is a Federal District or *Distrito Federal* (Mexico City), the home of the federal powers and the capital of Mexico.

As to the states, each one has its own constitution (within the framework of the Federal Constitution), a state Congress, and a Superior Justice Tribunal. Their system of administrative organization is the responsibility of the state governor elected by popular vote for a period of six years. The three branches of state government are based at the state capital.

The state entities are subdivided into administrative units called municipalities (*Municipios*), considered as the basis upon which the entire structure of the nation's government rests. Their management is under the responsibility of a City Council, also elected by popular vote, that is formed by a Mayor (*Presidente Municipal o Alcalde*), Councilmen (*Regidores*), and trustees who remain in office for three years.

For purposes of internal policy administration, the Federal District is divided into 16 delegations, each under the responsibility of a delegate who is elected by popular vote. The Federal District governor is elected by popular vote as well.

In order to exercise its supreme power, the federation is divided into legislative, administrative, and judicial branches. The legislative branch encompasses two chambers: the Chamber of Deputies and the Chamber of Senators. The executive branch is headed by the President of the United Mexican States. And, the judicial branch encompasses the Supreme Court of Justice of the Nation (*Suprema Corte de Justicia de la Nación*), Electoral Tribunal (*Tribunal Electoral*), Circuit Collegiate Tribunals (*Tribunales Colegiados de Circuito)*, Circuit Unitary Tribunals (*Tribunales Unitarios de Circuito*), District Courts (*Juzgados de Distrito*), and the Federal Judicial Council (*Consejo de la Judicatura Federal*).

Executive Branch

Federal Public Administration

The Federal Public Administration is divided into three branches: 1) the Centralized Public Administration that encompasses the President of the United Mexican States and Secretariats of State; 2) Quasi Governmental Public Administration which encompasses *Petróleos Mexicanos* (PEMEX), *Comisión Federal de Electricidad* (CFE), *Instituto Mexicano del Seguro Social* (IMSS), and *Universidad Nacional Autónoma de México* (UNAM), among others; and, 3) Attorney General of the Republic (PGR).

Judicial Branch

The judicial branch encompasses 1) the Supreme Court of Justice of the Nation, which sits 11 Justices *en banc* and functions in two chambers: a) civil and criminal and b) administrative and labor; 2) the Electoral Tribunal, which operates through a superior chamber (integrated by seven electoral magistrates) and regional chambers; 3) the Circuit Collegiate Tribunals which sit three magistrates (*Magistrados*) and can be of specialized subject matter jurisdiction or of general jurisdiction; 4) Circuit Unitary Tribunals which sit one magistrate (*Magistrados*); and, 5) District Judges which sit one judge and can be of specialized subject matter jurisdiction or general jurisdiction; 6) the Federal Judicial Council which sits seven members (*Consejeros*) *en banc* and administrative and disciplinary commissions;

Legislative Branch

The legislative branch encompasses two chambers, the Chamber of Deputies and the Chamber of Senators. The Chamber of Deputies is composed of national representatives elected every three years. There are 300 deputies of direct representation and 200 elected for proportional representation in each electoral district. The Chamber of Senators is composed of four senators for each state of the Union, three elected through direct representation and one through minority representation.

THE AMPARO TRIAL

The *Amparo* trial constitutes the means of defense for the governed against the arbitrary unlawful actions (unconstitutional acts) of the government committed by governmental entities or individuals.

The creation of the *Amparo* trial is owed to the illustrious jurists Mariano Otero (Guadalajara, Jalisco, 1817), Manuel Crescencio Rejón (Boloncheticul, Yucatán, 1799), and Ignacio Vallarta (Guadalajara, Jalisco, 1830). They are the forerunners of this great Juridical Institution that initially covered only criminal matters and subsequently came to cover all legal subject matters.

The *Amparo* is an original Mexican institution that has been referred to as a Mexican legal invention by some international scholars and which has had great influence on other Latin American countries.

Areas of Application

The *Amparo* Trial is a highly complex Legal Institution that protects practically all of the Mexican legal system, from the most elevated precepts of the Constitution to the modest disposition of a humble municipal rule.

In accordance with this broad spectrum of protected rights and the procedural function that it achieves, it is possible to delineate five areas or sections of application: 1) *Amparo* as a defense of individual rights or guarantees such as life, liberty, or personal dignity; 2) *Amparo* against laws—protects the individual from unconstitutional laws (*Amparo contra leyes); 3) Amparo in judicial matters—examines the legality of judicial proceedings (Amparo* Judicial); 4) Administrative *Amparo*—provides jurisdiction against official administrative acts and decisions affecting the individual

(*Amparo Administrativo*); and 5) *Amparo in agrarian matters—protects the communal*-ejidal rights of the peasants (*Amparo Social Agrario*).

Division Of The *Amparo* Trial

Direct *Amparo* and Indirect *Amparo*

When dealing with a definite civil, criminal or administrative decision or an award of the labor tribunals, direct *Amparo* applies. In other words, direct *Amparo* is the remedy that individuals whose constitutional rights have been violated can assert against any final decision rendered by tribunals or administrative judges with respect to a dispute following a trial proceeding.

When dealing with acts that are not of the same nature as the aforementioned legal resolutions but constitute violations of individual guarantees, the indirect *Amparo* (or *second instance Amparo*) is appropriate.

Jurisdiction

The Supreme Court of Justice or the Circuit Collegiate Tribunals have original jurisdiction over direct Amparo proceedings.

The District Courts have original jurisdiction over indirect *Amparo* proceedings.

Parties

The injured party, the responsible authority or party, the Attorney General Counsel's Office (*Ministerio Público Federal*), and, sometimes, a third interested party are parties to the Amparo trial.

Suspension of the Act Complained Of

In order to avoid enforcement of the resolution or act that is the basis of the complaint and to prevent incurring damages that are irreparable in nature or which are difficult to repair as a result of said enforcement upon the party seeking relief the *Amparo* Trial provides a precautionary measure known as a suspension of the act complained of (*Suspensión del acto reclamado*). This results in suspension of the authorities' actions and the enforcement of the resolution.

In an *Amparo* Trial, a party can obtain three different resolutions called sentences. A party can obtain a resolution that grants the *Amparo*, one that denies it or one that dismisses it.

The *Amparo* law also provides remedies within the *Amparo* proceeding: review, complaint, and claim. The sentences dictated by the District Judges in an *Amparo* proceeding can be challenged by the remedy of review. The sentences issued by a collegiate Tribunal or the Supreme Court are enforceable and constitute *res judicata* for all purposes. There is no remedy available to challenge a decision issued by the Supreme Court or Collegiate Tribunal. Thus, the law concerning the matter in question designates the Supreme Court's holding as *ejecutoria* (a judgment that cannot be challenged).

THE MEXICAN NOTARY

One of the biggest differences between the legal practice in the United States and Mexico is evidenced by the role of the notary public. While the notary public in the United States is typically a person who performs a largely ministerial function, the notary public in Mexico acts as a quasi public official.

A notary public in Mexico is a lawyer appointed by a state or the Federal District as a public official of considerable importance. Theoretically, notaries may practice law but are practically constrained by the time that is consumed in the performance of their notarial duties. Notaries are authorized to authenticate facts, thus, making them true irrebutable statements without the necessity of other witnesses. Authentication of certain witness statements, however, does not irrebuttably establish the underlying facts.

Notaries are also exclusively authorized to review wills, powers of attorney or contracts as to proper form, to perform real estate title searches and to act as public recorder. Accordingly, transactions that require the recording of documents invariably require the services of a notary.

Notaries are governed by the notarial law for the particular state or by the notary law of the Federal District, depending on what jurisdiction they operate under.

COMMERCIAL PUBLIC BROKER

In addition to the notary public, the commercial public broker plays an important role in Mexican law. Commercial public brokers, like notaries, are lawyers vested with public faith and can perform many of the same functions.

The principal difference between these two figures is that commercial public brokers can act only with respect to matters of a commercial nature. Commercial public brokers are governed by the Federal law of Commercial Brokers of the Ministry of Commerce and Industrial Development. (*SECO-FI*).

Despite the difference in nature between the notary public and the commercial public broker, there are some identical requirements to be met in becoming either a public notary or a commercial public broker. These requirements are—Mexican citizenship by birth with legal capacity; a law degree and, for notaries in the Federal District, Notary Public Law requires three years of professional practice. There is no practice time requirement for commercial public brokers. Other identical requirements include a passing grade on an examination and no convictions for an intentional crime.

These are the only identical requirements for becoming either a Notary Public or Commercial Public Broker in the Federal District. However, these and other requirements may differ within different jurisdictions. For a full description of requirements necessary for notaries public and commercial public brokers see *Ley del Notariado para el Distrito Federal and Ley Federal de Correduría Publica*. See also *Ley del Notariado* of different jurisdictions.

The Mexican legal system is similar to other civil law countries. As can be seen from the above excerpt it is derived from a rich and longstanding tradition. It is, however, quite different from the U.S. law, both as to substantive rules and procedures. In addition, as the Garro article points out, there is a lack of harmonization among Latin American countries. The unifying role that international agreements have should not be underestimated. To the extent that international law applies, resort to domestic legal systems would not be necessary.

There are many weaknesses in resorting to domestic legal systems. The greatest is in determining the appropriate law in a foreign domestic legal system and the enforcement of rights thereunder. The problem is most pronounced when there are differences in language, political systems, and legal culture. These differences tend to create distrust among the parties. Another weakness in using domestic legal systems is in their lack of harmonization. Chapters 2 and 3 review the U.S. domestic laws, international law, and Mexican law on the foreign direct investment.

Chapter 2

THE INBOUND FOREIGN DIRECT INVESTMENT

SECTION 2.1 ASSESSING THE REGULATORY ENVIRONMENT

The transfer of capital across national borders, also known as the foreign direct investment (FDI), can be segmented by its direction. For our purposes, an inbound foreign direct investment is where a foreign person is investing in the United States. The outbound FDI, discussed in chapters 3 and 4 infra, involves an U.S. person investing abroad. We have reviewed the impact that international trade and integration agreements can have on the FDI. For example, in a common market, private capital flows freely among the common market countries. The United States is not a party to a common market. In fact, there is no common market arrangement existing in the Western Hemisphere.

However, the U.S. is a party to various bilateral and multilateral agreements that do affect the movement of capital across national borders even though they do not create a common market. Examples of these types of agreements include the investment chapter of the NAFTA and the Bilateral Investment Treaty Program, commonly known as BITS. These agreements are discussed in chapter 3, infra in the materials dealing with the outbound FDI. The inbound foreign district investment essentially involves only U.S. law. International agreements do not substantially impact the U.S. regulation of the inbound foreign direct investment.

The hypothetical case below involves a Mexican corporation contemplating an investment in the United States. Since the emphasis is on U.S. law, the Mexican Corporation investor can be replaced by a national of practically any foreign country whether European, Asian, or from any part of the world. The rules they would confront are the same, although the application may be different.

The Hypothetical Case of
Industrial Del Sureste

Industrial del Sureste is a Mexican corporation based in Guadalajara, Jalisco, Mexico. It is organized into divisions each engaged in several business areas. One division is engaged in the offshore oil industry operating in Mexican waters of the Gulf of Mexico. The company has been very successful in its business operations and has captured a substantial portion of the market. It continues to have success in securing government contracts for the drilling of exploratory and developmental wells.

Industrial is now focusing on some contracts that will be opening in on-shore oil and gas areas. Although it has substantial contacts and business expertise, its technical knowledge in the industry is limited. The needed expertise has been obtained through independent contractors. It would like to bid on these new contracts but with 'in house' expertise. The Gomez family owns *Industrial* with Juan Gomez, the father as majority shareholder. Juan, through an U.S. business friend, became aware of a business enterprise having substantial expertise in the desired area. The friend is a Director and minority shareholder of Ace, Inc., a Texas corporation. Ace has been involved in the oil and gas drilling industry for over thirty years. The President and a majority of the board of directors have been with the company for a long time. They are very conservative and do not appear to be too interested in growing the company. They are, however, very well compensated. The shareholder discontent is growing with Ace's apparent lack of direction. Ace owns valuable intellectual property and has a team of employees that have a very good reputation for their technical expertise. It also has several other types of assets. Ace's Balance Sheet and income statement are as follows:

Ace, Inc.
Balance Sheet
December 31, 1999

Assets

	Cost	Fair Market Value
Cash	$ 500,000	$ 500,000
Equipment	500,000	750,000
Intellectual Property	5,000,000	8,000,000
Texas Ranch Land	3,000,000	2,750,000
Total Assets	$9,000,000	$12,000,000

Liabilities & Stockholders Equity

Liabilities	$1,000,000	$ 1,000,000

Stockholders Equity		
Capital Stock	$5,000,000	
Retained Earnings	3,000,000	
Total Stockholder's Equity	$8,000,000	$11,000,000
Total Liabilities and Stockholder's Equity	$9,000,000	$12,000,000

Ace, Inc.
Income Statement
For the year ended December 31, 1999

Revenue

Sales of Goods and Services	$3,500,000
Agricultural Income	10,000
Total Revenue	$3,510,000

Expenses

Operating Expenses	$1,500,000	
Federal income Tax	500,000	
Total Expenses		$2,000,000
Net Income After Taxes		$1,510,000

Juan is interested in the business opportunity for a variety of reasons. It provides a way for *Industrial* to purchase needed expertise and intellectual property that he hopes can be used in the Mexican operations. Ace is a viable business that is generating U.S. dollars, which can also be helpful. Also, Juan is interested in having his oldest son, Andres, immigrate and work in the United States. Andres holds a masters degree from the Harvard Business School with extensive high level managerial experience in *Industrial*. Juan would be the chief executive officer of the U.S. business operations. Either *Industrial*, Juan, or Andres could acquire the U.S. business. Each has substantial assets in the United States on investments that were previously made.

Juan has some concerns: Will the foreign investment be allowed? What are the reporting requirements, if any? How should the deal be structured—should he buy the company in his own name? Should *Industrial*? Should Andres? If *Industrial* buys the company, should it be as a branch or wholly owned subsidiary? What sort of due diligence procedures should be done on Ace, Inc? Should the purchase be structured as a purchase of Ace shares or its assets? Juan has heard that the U.S. is highly litigious—how can the purchaser limit the risk especially on the non-business U.S. assets? Will Andres be allowed to immigrate and work in the U.S.? What are the likely U.S. federal income tax implications to Juan, Andres, and *Industrial* on the business activities? These and other related questions are addressed in this chapter.

A. INITIAL CONSIDERATIONS: ASSESSING THE INVEST-MENT REGULATORY ENVIRONMENT

The first question to address is whether U.S. law permits the investment. The U.S. has historically encouraged the free flow of inbound and outbound foreign direct investment. In the early 1800's, when the U.S. was a developing country, inbound foreign direct investment helped build the nation's system of roads, canals, and railroads. As the economy grew and the U.S. transformed itself into a developed country, it became a substantial exporter of foreign direct investment. It also continues to be the destination of a substantial amount of inbound foreign direct investment. In a world of great uncertainty and political instability, the United States shines as a beacon, a safe haven for foreign direct investment.

Even though the U.S. has a policy of welcoming FDI, it does restrict foreign investment in certain sensitive industries. These federal statutory formulations have been in the books for many years and include shipping,[1] mining,[2] communications,[3] and aviation.[4] A trend towards restricting and regulating inbound foreign direct investment emerged in the early 1970's. The oil crisis in 1973, the rise of middle-eastern money centers and the growing economic prowess of Japan spurred a legislative activism that on occasion bordered on xenophobia. The great concern was that foreigners were 'buying up' America.

As a result, Congress enacted legislation that restricts certain foreign investments not based on a specific industry, but rather on the more nebulous concept of national security. There are also federal statutory rules that impose reporting requirements on the acquisition of a FDI. The maze of federal statutes is discussed below.

---

1. The Shipping Act of 1916, 39 Stat. 729 (1916) (codified as amended at 46 U.S.C. app. §§ 801–942 (1988)).

2. The Mining Act of 1872, ch. 152, 17 Stat. 91 (1872) (codified as amended at 30 U.S.C. § 22 (1988)); and The Mineral Leasing Act of 1920, ch. 85, 41 Stat. 437 (1920) (codified as amended at 30 U.S.C. §§ 181–287 (1988)).

3. The Communications Act of 1934, ch. 652, 48 Stat. 1064, 1086 (1934) (codified as amended at 47 U.S.C. 7310(a),(b)(1)–(2) (1988)).

4. The Federal Aviation Act of 1958, Pub. L. No. 85–726, 72 Stat. 731 (1958) (codified as amended at 49 U.S.C. app. §§ 1301–1567 (1988) and Federal Aviation Act of 1958, Pub. L. No. 95–163, § 14, 91 Stat. 1278, 1283 (1977) (codified as amended at 49 U.S.C. app. § 1401 (B) (1988)).

1. *A survey of the Statutes That Affect the Inbound FDI*

a. *Exon–Florio*

UNITED STATES: EXECUTIVE AUTHORITY TO DIVEST ACQUISITIONS UNDER THE EXON–FLORIO AMENDMENT—THE MAMCO DIVESTITURE

Jim Mendenhall

32 Harv. Int'l L.J. 286 (1991).

* * *

In the interests of national security, President Bush ordered the Chinese National Aero–Technology Corporation to divest itself of control over MAMCO, a U.S. corporation. His decision marked the first time a president exercised his power under the Exon–Florio Amendment to interfere with foreign acquisitions that potentially threaten U.S. national security. Furthermore, the MAMCO case expands executive authority beyond the conventionally defined parameters of the statute's language and intent; the executive now has discretion to impose economic sanctions on a foreign country for purposes largely unrelated to national security.

Concerned about the accelerating rate of foreign investment during the late 1980s, the sponsors of the amendment delegated to the executive extremely broad power to shape long-term economic planning and to shield vital domestic industries from foreign takeovers. The original House bill accordingly empowered the Secretary of Commerce to examine foreign acquisitions if they affected "national security" and "essential commerce." However, in order to quell executive fears that the proposed bill would undermine the traditional open policy of the United States toward international investment and trade, Congress excluded all references to "essential commerce" and "economic welfare." Consequently, the final version passed by Congress authorized the president to block or divest acquisitions of United States juridical persons by foreign corporations if such acquisitions would threaten to impair national security. Certain domestic and foreign commentators began, however, to read Congress's original intent back into the revised statute, arguing that the amendment's "national security" language could be used to protect both military and economic concerns. The amendment itself was written in broad terms and therefore neither explicitly included nor excluded economic welfare as a proper basis for presidential action. The statute's ambiguities have remained unresolved. * * *

The passage of the amendment in 1988 gave the executive the authority to implement and regulate the provisions of the statute. President Reagan consequently created a general institutional framework for conducting investigations into suspect acquisitions. In the months immediately following the amendment's adoption, Reagan issued a pair of executive orders authorizing the CFIUS to investigate completed and pending acquisitions potentially subject to executive suspension, prohibition, or divestment. At the outset of the review process, either a CFIUS member agency or one of the parties to the transaction notifies the CFIUS of a potentially problematic acquisition. After full investigation, the CFIUS recommends appropriate action to the president, who, on his own discretion, decides whether or not to block the acquisition or require divestment. While a court may review the remedy prescribed by the president, executive findings of fact are not reviewable. * * *

The MAMCO case reflected many of the problems inherent in the Exon–Florio amendment, most of which arose from the ambiguity of the statutory language. Under the umbrella justification of protecting national security, on February 1, 1990, President Bush ordered the China National Aero–Technology Import and Export Corporation CATIC), a Chinese government agency, to divest its holdings in MAMCO, a U.S. manufacturer of aircraft components.

CATIC acquired MAMCO on November 30, 1989 for $5 million. Described as little more than a "machine shop," MAMCO was a "metal basher" that produced metal airplane and helicopter components to client specifications for use in civilian aircraft. MAMCO did not design its products and did not employ full-time designers or engineers. The components, while made only for commercial use, could theoretically be converted for use in military aircraft as well. Although the federal government had not listed any of these components as items prohibited for sale to China, certain of MAMCO's products were subject to export control. However, MAMCO did not hold any classified contracts with the federal government at the time of the acquisition.

CATIC, a purchasing agent for the Chinese Ministry of Aerospace Industry, purchased, manufactured, and developed both civilian and military aircraft. CATIC had a reputation for disregarding foreign-export-control laws in order to obtain sensitive Western technology. In order to eliminate such problems, the United States imposed controls on its aerospace exports to China. However, the effort proved futile since CATIC proceeded to purchase and disassemble two General Electric airplane engines. * * *

The CFIUS began investigating the MAMCO transaction on December 5, 1989. The investigation followed a preliminary thirty-day "notice phase" review which apparently proved insufficient to quell official suspicions. According to a White House statement, CFIUS undertook the investigation "in order to assess MAMCO's present and potential production and technological capabilities and the national security implications of CATIC's purchase of MAMCO." After termination of its forty-five-day phase-two investigation, the commission unanimously recommended that President Bush order CATIC to divest its control of MAMCO. The official White House statement explained that "based on credible confidential information, the president determined that CATIC's continued control of MAMCO might threaten to impair the national security." On February 5, 1990, representatives from CATIC, the Chinese embassy, and the administration convened to discuss the issue, and thereafter CATIC was given three months to divest itself of control over MAMCO.

Even at that point, however, the fate of CATIC's ownership of MAMCO remained unsettled. Due to the difficulties in interpreting the language and legislative history of the statute, confusion arose over the exact meaning of the word, "divestiture." MAMCO did not possess and was unlikely to obtain sensitive or confidential technology. If Congress had designed the Exon–Florio Amendment specifically to block the flow of vital technology into foreign hands, CATIC could probably have found some way to retain actual ownership of MAMCO while still divesting itself of control. It was still possible to interpret the ambiguous divestiture order to mean that CATIC needed only to divest itself of direct control over MAMCO or to limit its direct access to whatever technology MAMCO possessed. CATIC fueled such speculation by refusing to admit that it would fully divest itself of the United States corporation, stating only that the agency would try to find a solution "acceptable to both sides."

Anxiety intensified when, on May 1, 1990, President Bush decided to grant a three-month extension for CATIC's divestiture. Again, CATIC refused to specify what action it would take, claiming only that "it would explore all possibilities for complying with the order." Finally, on August 2, CATIC resolved the problem with the announcement that it would sell MAMCO to a United States company, DeCrane Aircraft Holdings Inc. Consequently, the CFIUS advised CATIC that the sale fulfilled the requirements of the divestiture order.

President Bush's decision in the MAMCO case highlighted the confusion resulting from the still unresolved definition of "national security." The exact threat to national security posed by the MAMCO acquisition remained unclear throughout the months of official investigation. The president's laconic statement, while directly following the structure and rhetoric of the Exon–Florio provision, served only to complicate matters further with a cryptic reference to "confidential information." What appeared clear, however, was that the divestiture decision potentially expanded the realm of the president's Exon–Florio power. It seemed that the executive could now justify interference with a current or potential acquisition by claiming that it both protected the nation's military and economic security and furthered the administration's general foreign-policy goals.

The ambiguities in the Exon–Florio Amendment and the proposed regulations have proven a source of confusion for investors, politicians, and neutral observers. During its short life span, the amendment incited heated controversy regarding its proper role in relation to three vaguely defined and overlapping branches of national policy; military-industrial security, economic planning, and as a consequence of the MAMCO decision, foreign relations.

While some observers applauded President Bush's order as protecting an industry vital to military security, it was difficult to justify the divestiture on the grounds that MAMCO's production facilities provided technology and goods necessary to maintaining the integrity of the domestic defense industry. MAMCO produced metal brackets and other relatively simple components for civilian aircraft. * * *

If military sensitivity does not fully explain the divestiture, neither do economic concerns. The sale involved a few-million-dollars in a transaction involving non-vital technology. The Exon–Florio statute, if intended at all for economic protection, was designed to blunt the onslaught of foreign investment from major economic powers like England or Japan, and not China. Moreover, in light of the restraint that the administration has exhibited in the past, Bush appeared loathe to use Exon–Florio as a tool of economic protectionism. In fact, the administration's vigorous open-investment policy has enabled it to overcome any deterrent effect CFIUS notification may have had on potential foreign investors.

While the dynamics of the Exon–Florio order are difficult to explain in terms of economic or military policy, the order can be understood in the context of Bush's foreign policy. The administration may have viewed the transaction less as one between two private parties than as a deal between a domestic manufacturer and the Chinese government. If President Bush used Exon–Florio as a means for sanctioning the Chinese government, he may have implicitly converted Exon–Florio into a powerful foreign-policy weapon, one largely divorced from its original "national security" context. On the positive side, if Bush's decision was motivated not by commercial protectionism but by foreign-policy considerations, the order would not reflect a movement away from a commitment to open investment. * * *

––––––––

The Exon–Florio amendment[5] to the Omnibus Trade and Competitiveness Act of 1988 gives the president broad authority to investigate any merger, acquisition, or takeover of a U.S. person engaged in interstate commerce when a foreign person will be in control of the FDI. The president is empowered (mandated when the purchaser is a foreign government) to block any such transaction where the U.S. national security could be adversely affected.

Exon–Florio has been criticized as protectionist, unnecessary and vague. The vagueness assertion derives from the congressional decision not to define national security, the very reason why the president could block the transaction. Rather than specifically defining the term, the statute lists factors that the president or his designee can use. The listed factors[6] include the potential effect the transaction could have on sales of military application products to countries that engage in terrorism or are otherwise enemies of the U.S. In addition, the effect of control by a

5. 50 USC App. § 2170 et seq. (1988);   **6.** 50 USC App. § 2170(f) (1988).
31 C.F.R. Part 800 (1994).

foreign person may have on the capability and capacity of domestic industries to meet U.S. national defense requirements. Another factor that must be considered is the effect that the transaction could have on U.S. technology leadership in areas that affect national security.

Although the failure to define national security has been ameliorated somewhat by the various factors, there is room for abuse. For example, in the hypothetical, assume that *Industrial* is planning an unfriendly takeover of Ace, Inc. Assume further that Ace's management is against the takeover because they are fearful of losing their jobs. Management could assert Exon–Florio, arguing that the investment could impair national security. *Industrial* may be unwilling to go through with the deal and simply find another target, to the detriment of Ace's shareholders.

Exon–Florio is administered by the Committee on Foreign Investment In The United States known by its acronym of CFIUS. The CFIUS is composed of government personnel from the Departments of Treasury, State, Defense, Commerce, and Justice. It also has representatives from the U.S. Trade Representative, the Council of Economic Advisors, and the Office of

Management and Budget. Under the regulations a party may submit a voluntary notice on the transaction or a member of the CFIUS can submit a notice. The investigation must begin within 30 days of written notification and the President must take action within 15 days after that. The President could either permit the transaction or block it. Failure to comply with the statute allows the President, through the Attorney General, to seek appropriate relief including divestment of the FDI by the acquirer. Any action taken by the President is not subject to judicial review.

The *Hart-Scott-Rodino Antitrust Improvements Act of 1976 (HSR)*[7] can also block an acquisition either as a monopoly or restraint of trade. Under *HSR*, the acquisition of certain businesses defined in the act must file a *Notification and Report Form for Certain Mergers and Acquisitions*. The report must be filed with the Federal Trade Commission and the Assistant Attorney General in charge of the Antitrust Division of the Department of Justice of the proposed acquisition. The failure to file a report can subject the affected persons to civil penalties of $10,000 per day for failure to file. One of the reasons *Exon-Florio* was criticized as unnecessary is because of the existence of this statute. In addition, there are also federal restrictions on the renting of public lands by foreigners. These include homestead lands,[8] grazing lands,[9] mineral deposits,[10] offshore oil tracts,[11] and geothermal steam.[12] Additionally, some state stat-

---

7. 15 USC § 18a (1976); 16 C.F.R. Parts 800–803 (1976).

8. 43 C.F.R. § 2511.1(b)(3) (1993).

9. 43 U.S.C. § 315 (1998); 43 C.F.R. § 4110.1(a)(1998).

10. 30 U.S.C. §§ 22, 181 (1998); 43 C.F.R. 3102.1–.2(1993).

11. 43 U.S.C. § 1331(1998).

12. 30 U.S.C. § 1015(1998); 43 C.F.R. § 3203.1(1993).

utes[13] attempt to restrict the ownership of agricultural to non-foreign persons.

    b.   A summary of Investment Reporting Statutes

    (1) The International Investment and Trade Survey Act

AMERICAN JEWISH CONGRESS v. DEPARTMENT OF THE TREASURY

United States District Court, District of Columbia, 1982.
549 F.Supp. 1270.

* * *

BARRINGTON D. PARKER, District Judge:

In this proceeding under the Freedom of Information Act (FOIA or Act), 5 U.S.C. s 552 (1976), the American Jewish Congress (AJC) seeks to obtain from the Department of the Treasury (Department or Treasury) a copy of a document containing the most recent aggregate figures showing the amount of monies in United States banks deposited by, and the amount of Treasury bills owned or held by, foreign persons from three Arab countries—Saudi Arabia, Kuwait, and the United Arab Emirates. The Department denied the request and relied on two FOIA exemptions: Exemption (b)(3), 5 U.S.C. s 552(b)(3), and Exemption (b)(1), 5 U.S.C. s 552(b)(1). * * *

For the reasons set forth below the Court determines that although Exemption (b)(3) is inapplicable here, Treasury has properly invoked Exemption (b)(1) of the FOIA. The American Jewish Congress' request for the documents, therefore, is denied and the complaint dismissed. * * *

As to Exemption (b)(3), two statutes are cited by the government: the Bretton Woods Agreements Act (Bretton Woods Act), 59 Stat. 515, 22 U.S.C. § 286f, and the International Investment Survey Act of 1976 (Survey Act), 22 U.S.C. §§ 3101 et seq. Both Acts provide for the gathering of information on foreign investment in the United States. * * * Section 4(c)(1) of the Survey Act requires the President to conduct a "comprehensive benchmark survey of foreign portfolio investment in the United States at least once every five years...." 22 U.S.C. s 3103(c)(1). In order to collect that information, the Act authorizes the Secretary of the Treasury to promulgate regulations which "may require any person subject to the jurisdiction of the United States ... to furnish, under oath, any report containing information which is determined to be necessary to carry out the international investment surveys and studies conducted under [the] Act." Section 5(b)(2), 22 U.S.C. s 3104(b)(2).

---

13.   See Indiana Code § 32–1–8–2, Ken-   Neb. Rev Stat. § 76–401.
tucky   Rev.   Stat.Ann.   § 381.300(1),   and

Pursuant to those statutes, the Department of the Treasury's Office of International Financial Reports prepares statistical reports and analyses of the portfolio investments in the United States by foreign residents. The portfolio investment data collected on Treasury's report forms include bank deposits and Treasury bills, the two types of portfolio investment which are the subject of the plaintiff's FOIA request. * * *

The Department provided two reasons for its decision to withhold the information. First, it stated that the two statutes trigger Exemption (b)(3) and preclude Treasury from disclosing the information sought by the plaintiff. In each of the three Arab countries, the government or governmental financial institutions hold most of the country's portfolio investments. Thus, by revealing the aggregate figure for a particular country's investments, Treasury would, it asserted, indirectly reveal the investment of a particular government or governmental authority. Both statutes prohibit disclosure of the investments of an individual investor, and, therefore, Treasury concluded that the requested document was exempt from disclosure under FOIA. Second, the Department relied upon Exemption (b)(1) and refused the requested document, asserting that it was protected because of national defense or foreign policy concerns. * * *

Section 552(b)(3) exempts from disclosure matters that are ... specifically exempted from disclosure by statute ... provided that such statute (A) requires that the matters be withheld from the public in such a manner as to leave no discretion on the issue, or (B) establishes particular criteria for withholding or refers to particular types of matters to be withheld.

In asserting this exemption, Treasury relies on confidentiality provisions contained within both the Bretton Woods and the Survey Acts. * * * The confidentiality provision of the Survey Act prohibits the publication of "any information collected pursuant to subsection (b)(2) of this section in a manner that the person who furnished the information can be specifically identifiable except as provided in this section." The subsection continues: No person can compel the submission or disclosure of any report or constituent part thereof collected pursuant to this chapter, or any copy of such report or constituent part thereof, without the prior written consent of the person who maintained or furnished such report under subsection (b) of this section and without prior written consent of the customer, where the person who maintained or furnished such report included information identifiable as being derived from the records of such customer. * * *

The government's statutory argument is that the information sought by the American Jewish Congress qualifies as "detail" which discloses "the affairs of any person," in the language of the Bretton Woods Act, and as "information identifiable as being derived from the records of [a] customer," in the language of the Survey Act. The premise for the argument is that, beginning in 1974, official governmental authorities in the OPEC countries began to overwhelmingly dominate the portfolio investing within those countries. Because such a large percentage of the portfolio investments from those countries is held by the government, release of the information sought by the American Jewish Congress would be "tantamount to disclosure of the holdings in the United States of particular official monetary or financial authorities in each of these countries."

The contention is flawed. First, the premise for the argument is highly questionable. The link between the raw data sought by the plaintiff and the investments held by a particular investor are approximate. Neither Act restricts the release of data, which through approximation or interpolation, might provide a rough idea of the holdings of an individual investor.

Moreover, Treasury's argument is particularly unappealing in this case since it is the Department itself, which has furnished the data for those students of the world economy who might seek to determine the approximate governmental holdings of these Arab countries. Apparently, it is generally known among international economists that the bulk of the investment from the OPEC countries is made by the governmental authority. However, the most exact statement of the percentage of official investment provided the Court is contained within a document which Treasury submitted to a congressional subcommittee in 1978. * * *

Second, the legislative history of the Survey Act further undermines the statutory argument. The purpose of the Act was to provide "clear and unambiguous authority for the President to collect information on international investment and to provide analyses of such information to the Congress, the executive agencies, and the general public." Section 2(b), 22 U.S.C. s 3101(b). The overall purpose of the Act was to encourage as much disclosure of information on foreign investment as possible. Furthermore, the legislative history of the Act makes clear that Treasury may release "aggregate statistical data," such as that sought by the American Jewish Congress. * * *

The *International Investment and Trade In Services Survey Act (IITSA)*[14] is one of the earlier Congressional efforts which focused on gathering data[15] on foreign investment. In the early seventies, Congressional preoccupation with foreigners 'buying up America' resulted in a finding that there was no systematic process in place to gauge the extent and source of foreign investment in the United States. The IITSA fills that gap by providing statutory authority to develop a database that can be used to discover the extent and source of the FDI. It also gives the

---

14. 22 USC §§ 3101–3108 (1998); 15 C.F.R. Part 806 and 31 C.F.R. Part 129 (1998).

15. The reporting of an investment is also required under the Internal Revenue Code, see I.R.C. §§ 6038C and 6039C (1986).

President clear authority to establish a system and report the results of the data to Congress. It is intended to be a statute to collect and categorize data.

A related act, the *Foreign Direct Investment and International Financial Data*,[16] also grants the Department of Commerce the authority to compile data. The law permits the Department of Commerce to use data acquired under the *IITSA* as well as from other U.S. governmental agencies—the Departments of Labor, Treasury, and Energy as well as the U.S. Census Bureau in making its annual report on foreign investment in the United States.

The *IITSA* affects any U.S. business enterprise (known under the statute as an U.S. affiliate) whether or not incorporated when a foreign person owns a ten percent or more voting interest or an equivalent interest in an unincorporated FDI. The statute does not define the term 'equivalent interest' but the focus is a direct interest. Also, the term 'foreign person' is a geographic designation; therefore, an U.S. person living abroad can be a foreign person under the statute. The statute is broad affecting any FDI with the requisite foreign interest unless specific statutory exemptions apply.

One exception is for a real estate investment held exclusively for personal use and not for profit. Another is where the FDI is below one million dollars and involves less than 200 acres of real estate is exempt. However, in the latter case an exemption form must be filed in order to comply with the statute. An investment that is not exempt must report the investment transaction within forty-five days after consummation to the Department of Commerce, Bureau of Economic Analysis, International Investment Division.

The report must contain the financial information requested on the pre-printed form, an industry classification form, and it must reveal the Ultimate Beneficial Owner (UBO) of the FDI. In addition to the initial report, periodic reports, either annual or quarterly, must be filed. The criteria for reporting, involves the sales volume and asset value of the FDI. All of the reports must be supplied in pre-printed BEA forms. Penalties for failure to comply include civil and criminal penalties. The BEA has been lenient on imposing penalties. It seems the government would rather have the data than prosecute offenders.

(2) The Agricultural Foreign Investment Disclosure Act (AFIDA)

The *Agricultural Foreign Investment Disclosure Act (AFIDA)*[17] was enacted in 1978 and has the basic purpose of the *IITSA*—seeking to collect information. However, the *AFIDA* has a more limited focus, that of agricultural property. Under the Act, a foreign person must report an acquisition of agricultural property, or previously owned property that is converted to agricultural use. Under the statute, agricultural land is U.S.

---

16. 22 USC §§ 3141–3146(1998).   **17.** 7 USC §§ 3501–3508 (1978) and 7 C.F.R. Part 781 (1978).

land either currently used or used within the last five years for farming, ranching, forestry, or timber production.

There is a limited exception where the land in question is less than ten acres and has less than one thousand dollars of gross annual agriculture revenues. A foreign person is an individual who is neither a resident or citizen of the U.S., a foreign corporation, or a domestic corporation which is owned ten percent or more by a single foreign person or fifty percent or more by several foreign persons whether or not related.

The report must be made to the Agriculture Department within ninety days of the purchase transaction or the change of use to agricultural property. Unlike the *IITSA*, the information required on the report is of the type that most purchasers would prefer not to be made public. This information includes the name and address of the foreign person, purchase price, and the current estimated value of the land. In addition to providing the information, the data is posted in the county courthouse where the land is situated. The penalty for failing to submit a form or knowingly submitting a form that does not contain all of the required information can be as high as 25% of the fair market value of the property.

2. *The Application of the Law to the Hypothetical*

The balance sheet and income statement of Ace, Inc. is the place to look for the possible impact of these federal statutes. For example, one of Ace's assets is a patent. There needs to be a review of exactly what this patent covers. If the patent has some military application, the purchase could trigger national security concerns under *Exon-Florio*. The balance sheet and income statement also reveal that agricultural property and income from that property. The agricultural assets will require a report under the *AFIDA*.

The purchase transaction will also require a report under the *IITSA* and the various applicable Internal Revenue Code sections. Absent any application of Exon–Florio or Hart–Scott–Rodino, there are no restrictions for making the investment. The reporting statutes do apply, and the corresponding forms to report the acquisition should be made to avoid any penalties from being assessed.

B. IMMIGRATION ISSUES

1. *Introduction*

The movement of people across national borders is a hot political and economic issue in the Western Hemisphere, particularly illegal immigration of Mexicans into the United States. The increase in trade and business relations among the NAFTA countries will signal an increase of the movement of people. This movement will tend to exacerbate the lingering problems of illegal immigration. In the United States the issue of international labor mobility is addressed principally under domestic law. NAFTA Chapter 16—*Temporary Entry For Business Per-*

sons provides rules for the movement of business people, however, it uses as a base existing U.S. immigration law.

In our hypothetical, an integral part of the decision to make the FDI is to determine if Andres can immigrate and work in the United States. There are three basic purposes that U.S. immigration law[18] addresses. As it relates to business, it is intended to protect the U.S. worker and help the business owner in obtaining foreign workers. The system works by providing a regulatory scheme of either temporary or permanent Visas. A foreign worker in the U.S. must have a Visa. The penalty for violating the law is a sanction against the worker and the employer. The worker faces deportation and the business owner may face civil and/or criminal penalties for any violations.

Another basic purpose is to unite families. In this context, a family refers to husband, wife, and minor children. Another purpose is to protect the safety of U.S. citizens by excluding certain types of people— terrorists, anarchists, etc. Personnel of the Immigration and Naturalization Service (INS) administer the immigration laws. The materials in this section deal primarily with the business aspects of U.S. immigration law.

2. *Types of Visas Under U.S. Immigration Law*

IMMIGRATION FUNDAMENTALS FOR INTERNATIONAL LAWYERS

Michael Maggio, Larry S. Rifkin, Sheila T. Starkey, American
13 Am. U. Int'l L. Rev. 857.

* * *

III. Basic History of United States Immigration Law

America was basically an open border country with no immigration laws until 1882 when Congress placed a "head tax" on immigrants and barred "idiots, lunatics, convicts, and persons likely to become a public charge"—restrictions that still exist today. Most immigrants came freely, unlike other immigrants that were forcibly brought here as slaves. The first immigration laws were geared toward keeping out people because of criminal conduct and the possibility that they might become a public charge. This marked the beginning of the system that we still have today, where people must first show that they should be allowed in, that they are admissible.

In immigration law there is this concept of being admissible, being allowed in, and also the concept of being deportable for bad conduct that results in them being expelled from the United States. The first immigration laws in 1875 dealt with admissibility, and they were geared toward keeping out certain convicts and people who were likely to become public charges. These provisions still exist in immigration law today. * * * [T]here are basically two types of visas. Non-immigrant

---

18. 8 USC 1101 et. seq. (1998).

visas and immigrant visas; in other words, temporary visas and permanent visas. A non-immigrant visa is a permission to come into the United States on a temporary basis. * * * The H–1B1 visa is available to people who are going to be employed here in a specialty occupation, usually a professional occupation. * * * In addition to the H–1B1 visa, another visa * * * is the L-visa—the international manager or executive visa. This is the category that all the big multinational companies use, but you don't need to be a big multinational company to use it. You can be a small company with only a few employees to use this visa to bring yourself over here and open up a subsidiary office to carry on business.

Let me give you an example. A client comes to us from Venezuela. This person has a small manufacturing company in Venezuela with twenty-five employees, and they are looking for a market so they decide that it would be a good idea to open up an office here in Florida. What are the requirements for an L–1 visa? The owner of this company in Venezuela comes to me. What do I tell him? What can he do?

Well, in order to qualify as a manager or an executive to obtain an L–1 visa, one must have been employed by the company abroad for at least one year in any one of the last three years. It does not have to be immediate past employment; it is employment for at least one year in any one of the last three years. We had a situation where someone had terminated his employment with the company, yet the company maybe a year or two later, wanted to bring this person to the U.S. company as an L–1 in a reconciliation. But in our hypothetical situation, we have a simple case. We have the owner of this foreign company that has twenty-five employees who wants to open up a U.S. branch operation to distribute his goods. This individual has to have been employed with the foreign company for at least one year, and he has to be receiving a salary for his efforts. If this person has been employed with the foreign company for at least one year, and he is the president of the foreign company, you automatically assume you have to employ him as an executive or manager.

What is the definition of executive or manager for immigration purposes? That has changed throughout the years. Sometimes it has been interpreted very narrowly. Sometimes it has been interpreted broadly. Right now it is in the middle. * * * One is the traditional line definition that we are all familiar with, the factory. You've got the president of the factory, you've got the vice presidents, you've got the managers below them, and you've got the supervisors and skilled workers below them. This is the traditional line definition, but most companies do not operate this way.

In service-type organizations and smaller companies you typically have what is called the central function manager or executive system. This is the other definition. Is the person essential to the operation of business? Are they involved in essential activities of the company? Now, either under the line definition or the essential function manager or executive, remember they've got to function as a manager or executive.

They can't be sharpening pencils and typing letters and getting coffee. There normally must be other employees to qualify for an L-visa. You also have to look at the type of business they are engaged in. My example is a manufacturing company, but you could have an import-export company in Venezuela, for example, with one to three employees. Sometimes it comes down to an interpretation of what is traditional in the industry, and a lot of this is good old common sense. * * *

Getting back to our hypothetical, we've got the company in Venezuela with twenty-five employees, the individual has been working there for more than a year, and he satisfies the line definition of manager. If he wants to open up a company here, what do you need to do? Well, you file a petition with the Immigration Service. In your filing with the Immigration Service you have to prove corporate relationships. People often come to my office after they have been to another law firm, and they bring in a list of documents, and they present this list of documents. I tell these clients that there is no such thing as a standard list of documents that can prove relationships. The list is going to be different from one client to another. For a multinational company, we may only need an annual report. There is no standard list of documents because what you are trying to do is to prove a corporate relationship.

What creates a qualifying multinational organization? Well, you can have a parent subsidiary situation where the company in Venezuela owns the company here in the United States as the majority shareholder. Or the company in the United States could be the majority shareholder of the company in Venezuela, although that is less likely to occur because the foreign company is usually going to be the majority shareholder. So the foreign company owns at least fifty-one percent of the company here. * * *

My fictional client that owns the company in Venezuela can create a qualifying affiliate situation because he owns one hundred percent of the company in Venezuela and at least fifty-one percent of the company here. Changing my facts slightly, you could have a situation where the owners of the company in Venezuela–say there are three owners of the company in Venezuela who each own a third of the company in Venezuela—want to create an affiliate situation here in the United States because of the tax implications and other issues. Those three owners, Mr. A, Ms. B, and Ms. C have to be the same owners of the company in the United States in "approximately the same percentages." * * *

So, we've got our qualifying situation because we have either a subsidiary or affiliate situation. What do you need now to prove the relationships? As I mentioned earlier, there is no laundry list of documents. What do you need? If you are trying to prove an affiliate situation, you have to show that there is an affiliation between the two companies. You have to incorporate the company in the United States. You have to rent office space because the Immigration Service will look into this at the visa petition stage. Renting space is very key. And when my clients ask me if they can use my apartment, I tell them, "No, you can't use my apartment." Remember the common sense rule. It has to be a legitimate business situation. * * *

The E-visa comes into play only in certain countries where we have treaties of reciprocity whereby United States citizens can go over and do similar activities. Therefore, E-visas are not available for every country. * * * There are treaties with certain countries that allow two types of visas: E–1s and E–2s. The E–1 is based on trade in goods or services. * * * The E–2 visa involves something called "substantial investment." For the E–2 visa, the INS regulations and the State Department guidelines are chock full of discretion * * * "substantial investment" means * * * is not defined. * * *

There are generally two types of employment-based immigration cases. One type requires a test of the United States labor market for qualified United States workers through the running of an advertisement. This is called the labor certification process. The other type does not require one to undergo the labor certification process. * * *

There are three categories of first preference or priority cases. The first category is persons of extraordinary ability. This category is for persons with extraordinary ability in the sciences, arts, education, business, or athletics. This extraordinary ability has to be demonstrated by sustained national or international acclaim and the achievements must be evidenced through extensive documentation. This permanent residence category has many of the same requirements as the O nonimmigrant category.

The greatest benefit for persons of extraordinary ability is that the applicant does not need to undergo the labor certification or advertising process, nor does he or she need a petition from an employer, or an offer of employment. A person can petition for himself or herself. The petition goes directly to the Immigration and Naturalization Service. Although the applicant does not need a job offer, he or she does need to document plans to enter the United States to continue work in the field. This can be done through contracts to perform work here in the United States or through a personal statement detailing plans to work in the field in the United States.

The extraordinary ability category is intended for the small percentage of people who have risen to the very top of their field. * * *

There are other possibilities that also enable the beneficiary to avoid undergoing the labor certification and advertising process. Another is the Outstanding Professor and Researcher Category. * * *

To qualify in this category, the applicant must be recognized internationally as outstanding in a specific academic area, and the applicant must have three years of experience teaching or conducting research in that area. Again, the applicant does not have to undergo the labor certification process, but unlike persons of extraordinary ability, the applicant in this category does need a permanent full-time job offer, and the employer must petition for this person. Professors must have a tenured or tenure-tract position. For researchers, it must be a comparable position, one of indefinite or unlimited duration. The position does not have to be with a university; it can also be with a private employer if the employer has at least three full-time researchers and has achieved documented accomplishments in an academic field. * * *

There is a third category of priority workers who do not need to undergo the labor certification and advertisement process. This category is reserved for multinational executives and managers. The criteria are very similar to the criteria for obtaining an L–1 non-immigrant visa. In fact, many L–1s later obtain permanent residency in this category.

The employer must be conducting business in two or more countries, one of which is the United States, either directly or through an affiliate or subsidiary. To qualify in this category the applicant must have worked one of the preceding three years as an executive or manager with the overseas affiliate. The individual must be coming to work in the United States in a managerial or executive capacity. The U.S. employer must have been doing business in the United States for at least one year. "Doing business" means the regular, systematic, and continuous provision of goods and/or services. It does not mean the mere presence of an office.

Although there is a requirement that the U.S. employer has been doing business for one year, there is not a requirement that the qualifying relationship between the U.S. and foreign entity has existed for one year.

The definition of "managerial capacity" requires (1) management of an organization, department, component, or function; (2) supervision and control of other supervisory, managerial, or professional personnel or management of an essential function; (3) authority to make personnel decisions or functioning at a senior level if a function is managed; and (4) exercise of discretion over operations or a function. The definition of "executive capacity" requires (1) management of an organization or major component or function; (2) authority to establish goals and policies; (3) wide latitude in discretionary decision-making; and (4) only general supervision from higher executives, the board of directors, or stockholders. * * *

---

a.   The Non–Immigrant Visa

Under U.S. immigration law there are two categories of Visas people can obtain–immigrant and non-immigrant. The status of the person is reflected in the type of Visa issued. The immigrant category, also known as a "green card", permits the holder to live and work in the United States permanently. The non-immigrant is permitted to stay for the period allowed under the Visa. Some non-immigrant Visas allows the person to enter and work in the United States. At the end of the time the Visa stipulates the person must return to their country of origin. The key criterion is in having the applicant prove that she has the ability to support herself while in the U.S. If the burden of proof is not met to the satisfaction of the INS or Consular personnel, no Visa will be issued.

Recall that one basic policy of immigration law is the protection of U.S. jobs. This is the practical application of this policy. The INS and consular authorities are always vigilant against sham transactions. Therefore, good practice dictates that the non-immigrant category chosen must carefully fit the economic reality of a given transaction. There are several types of non-immigrant Visas that can be used by persons engaged in international business transactions.

(1) The Business Visitor Visa

The simplest business Visa that can be obtained is the Business Visitor, B–1 Visa. A person entering the U.S. as a business visitor can engage in light business activity. Some examples include attending corporate directors meeting, attending a conference, and signing business documents. In this Visa category the person cannot earn a salary. This Visa is not appropriate for the activities contemplated for Andres.

(2) The Intra–Company Transferee

The L–1 Visa is a good fit for Andres. Foreign managerial and executive personnel who need to work in the U.S can use the Visa. The foreign executive can draw a salary and bring his family. The L–1 Visa imposes certain requirements on the executive and the businesses that are requesting it. The person seeking the visa must be a high-level manager or executive of the business enterprise. He must have been a paid employee of the company working outside of the U.S. in any one of the last three years. Additionally, the U.S. business in which the applicant will be working must have employees.

The L–1 Visa was intended for use by large multi-national companies transferring executive personnel across national borders. However, smaller businesses can use the L–1 so long as the legal criteria are met. One important requirement is that the U.S. business requiring the services of the foreign executive has employees other than the family of the applicant. The reason is that in order for the applicant to come to the United States to be a manager, there must be people who she will manage. The non-family rule is to prevent sham transactions.

The relationship between the foreign business where the applicant was an employee and the new U.S. business enterprise must also be established. The connection between the foreign and domestic business can take one of a number of forms. The foreign business could establish a branch or form a domestic corporation as a wholly owned subsidiary. It could also establish a joint venture with another company so long as it has over fifty-one percent control over the U.S. Corporation. Another variation is where the shareholders of the foreign corporation own or control the U.S. Corporation. In addition to the organizational requirements, certain operational requirements must also be met.

The structure must demonstrate a valid business investment. There should be a business plan, a business location (whether purchased or rented), and a sufficient amount of money to show that the business plan as contemplated can be realized. In addition, the foreign business must prove that it is a valid business. Financial statements and tax returns filed in the home country can show this valid business requirement. The foreign business must also prove up its foreign employees and where the applicant is a manager or executive in their organizational structure.

The L–1 Visa seems to be a good fit for Andres. However, at the end of the Visa term Andres would have to return to Mexico unless he can successfully change his status to permanent resident. The benefit of an L–1 Visa is that this change of status is possible. See the materials on immigrant Visas, infra.

(3) The Treaty Trader or Treaty Investor

The E series Visa is another type of non-immigrant Visa available to certain foreign nationals where a treaty between their country of origin provides a type of immigration reciprocity with the United States. The North American Free Trade Agreement is one such agreement. The immigration

rules are supplemented in the international agreement but are referenced to U.S. domestic law covering the E series visa. The E Visa can be of two types—treaty trader (E–1) or treaty investor (E–2).

The treaty trader Visa (E–1) is available to a qualified person engaged in the trade of goods and services. The treaty trader must be an executive level person engaged in substantial business activity. The E–1 would not be a good fit for Andres. A person who makes a substantial investment with at risk capital can use the treaty investor Visa (E–2). There is great discretion bestowed on the U.S. consul granting the visa as to what constitutes 'substantial.' Like other subjective tests, the amount can vary. One million dollars is substantial while ten thousand dollars is probably not. The applicant needs to be careful with this test, especially when there will be a purchase of a going business.

For example, assume an applicant enters into an earnest money contract to purchase a business. The applicant intends to manage the business under an E–2 visa. If the investment is not deemed substantial, the Visa will not be granted but the applicant will still be contractually liable to go forward on the contract. In addition to a substantial investment, the investor must be at risk and the invested amount sufficient to make the business operational and viable. These are all fact sensitive questions. The rules are in place to prevent a person from using the E–2 visa as a vehicle to come to the United States and use the investment as a ploy to further their immigration desires.

The E–2 does not appear to be a good for Andres. The first problem is that Andres must make an at-risk investment to qualify. This may not fit the overall corporate strategy of *Industrial* or Juan Gomez. In addition, the E–2 does not provide for a change of status to immigrant status like the L–1.

(4) The TN Visa

NAFTA AND THE TRANSFER OF BUSINESS PERSONNEL

Austin T. Fragomen, Jr.,
Ethan E. Bensinger
515 PLI/Lit 65 (1994).

* * *

[T]he immigration-related provisions of NAFTA * * * relate to the same four nonimmigrant classifications which were impacted by the FTA: Business Visitor (B–1), Treaty Trader/Investor (E–1/2), Intracompany Transferee (L–1), and Professional (previously designated TC for Canadian citizens under FTA and redesignated TN for Canadian and Mexican citizens under NAFTA).

All of the substance regarding admissible classes of business persons is located in Annex 1603 of the agreement. Following are the principal elements of the immigration-related provisions:

• B–1 business visitor status for Canadian and Mexican business persons engaging in acceptable business activities listed on Schedule 1 included in NAFTA. The NAFTA B–1 provisions are parallel in most respects to the INS and State Department lists of acceptable B–1 activities for any foreign national. The NAFTA B–1 schedule, however, appears to include selected activities that non-immigrants other than those from Mexico or Canada would not normally be allowed to undertake. Most of those activities are usual incidents of cross-border commerce that had been restricted in a series of pre-FTA cases involving Mexican and Canadian nationals.

• E–1 and E–2 treaty trader and investor status for Canadian and Mexican nationals engaged in supervisory, executive, or "essential skills" capacity with an investment or trading enterprise. This provision of NAFTA essentially extends treaty benefits to Mexican nationals.

• L–1 intracompany transferee status for Canadian and Mexican nationals employed for one out of the prior three years with a qualifying organization. The U.S. provisions for intracompany transfers have traditionally been more liberal than those of other countries, and are not affected by the agreement. Rather, this provision should have the effect of liberalizing Mexican law with regard to such transfers, just as the FTA liberalized Canadian law in 1989.

• TN professional classification designed to replace the existing TC professional classification existing under the FTA, and extend that classification to Mexican nationals. Note, however, that significant restrictions that do not apply to Canadian nationals are placed by NAFTA on Mexican professionals. Those restrictions are discussed below.

All Mexican nationals must present a visa for U.S. entry. This requirement is rooted in the agreement itself, which provides, at Annex 1603, that: a Party may require a business person seeking temporary entry under this Part to obtain a visa or its equivalent prior to entry. Before imposing a visa requirement, such Party shall consult with a Party whose business persons would be affected with a view to avoiding the imposition of the requirement. Additionally, and of direct significance to Mexican nationals, is the provision that With respect to an existing visa requirement, a Party shall, at the request of a Party whose business persons are subject to the requirement, consult with that Party with a view to its removal.

The immigration segment of NAFTA, Annex 1603, states that each of the three countries will grant temporary entry to four categories of business persons. The term "business person" is defined at Article 1608 of NAFTA as "a citizen of a [the United States, Mexico, or Canada] who is engaged in the trade in goods, the provision of services or the conduct of investment activities." And, for purposes of NAFTA, the term "temporary entry" refers to an "entry into the territory of [the United States, Mexico, or Canada] by a business person of another Party without the intent to establish permanent residence." Further, the four categories relevant to business persons are very closely modeled on the existing categories of the U.S.-Canada Free Trade Agreement ("FTA"), which in turn closely reflect the relevant provisions of U.S. immigration law under the Immigration and Nationality Act ("INA"). * * *

B. TN PROFESSIONALS

For purposes of U.S. immigration law, a Professional is defined as an alien who "will perform services in a specialty occupation which requires theoretical and practical application of a body of highly specialized knowledge and attainment of a baccalaureate or higher degree or its equivalent as a minimum requirement for entry into the occupation in the United States, and who is qualified to perform services in the specialty occupation because he or she has attained a baccalaureate or higher degree or its equivalent in the specialty occupation."

One of the fundamental aspects of the TN Professional category under NAFTA is the disparate treatment of Canadian and Mexican nationals. Just as under the FTA, Canadian professionals under NAFTA need only present proof at the port-of-entry, that they are Canadian citizens, that they are seeking U.S. admission to engage in one of the professions listed in Appendix 1603.D.1, and that they possess the requisite educational documents.

To the contrary, Mexican nationals seeking TN status must comply with a procedure that is identical to that for H–1B classification for world-wide nationals. In other words, they must first apply for a "TN" visa, which will be adjudicated only on the basis of a previously approved I–129 petition. For purposes of the TN category, all I–129 petitions for Mexican nationals will be submitted to the Northern Regional Adjudications Center in Nebraska. And, similar to the H–1B petition, the I–129 petition seeking TN classification must be accompanied by an approved Labor Condition Application (Form 9035).

Further, NAFTA limits the number of Mexican national TN professionals to 5,500 per year, unless Mexico and the U.S. jointly agree to expand or eliminate this provision. Whereas the annual admission of Mexican nationals in H–1B status has hovered at approximately 3,000, government officials surmise that the annual limitation on TN applicants will not hamper the inflow of Mexican professionals. * * *

In order to acquire the status of a U.S. permanent resident ("Green Card" holder), the applicant must qualify under the Immigration Selection System. No one can become a resident alien of the United States unless he or she meets the restrictive criteria set forth in one of the available categories. * * *

The fifth preference is reserved for Employment–Creation Aliens. Eligible candidates are foreign investors who make an investment of $1 million ($500,000 in a high unemployment area) in a new commercial enterprise in the United States, resulting in the creation of ten employment positions for U.S. citizens or U.S. permanent residents. This category is allocated 10,000 visas annually, with 3,000 of the 10,000 reserved for those aliens making investments in "targeted," high unemployment areas. * * *

––––––––––

The NAFTA as a free trade agreement does not address the mobility of people across national borders. Recall that a common market and economic union are the only forms of country integration that provides immigration free borders. The NAFTA generally does not provide immigration rules but rather allows Mexicans to use the NAFTA as a means to access the E Visa Series regime. The rules focus on non-immigrant categories of Business Visitors (B–1), Treaty Trader/Investor (E–1 & E–2), Intra–Company Transferee (L–1) incorporating the general principles found in U.S. immigration law. A new addition to the immigration landscape provided by NAFTA is the Professional Category (TN).

The fact that NAFTA is not intended to promote the free movement of Mexicans is shown through the requirements imposed on professionals qualifying for the TN Visa. Canadian applicants can obtain the Visa by presenting proof of citizenship at an U.S. port of entry and that they are to engage in professional activity within the U.S. The Mexican professionals, however, must apply for a Visa and qualify as a temporary worker under Visa H–1B. The temporary worker has the onerous burden of obtaining a labor certification. A 'Labor Certification' is a lengthy process where through application and advertising, the Department of Labor and state employment offices certify that the job in question cannot be filled by a U.S. citizen. In addition to the application requirements, there is a numerical cap that limits the number of qualified TN

Visa applicants that can enter from Mexico. These same rules do not apply to Canadian applicants.

b. The Immigrant Visa

The immigrant visa allows a person to reside permanently in the United States. It is one step below obtaining citizenship. The immigrant visa also known as a 'green card' can be obtained through either a family or work relationship. The family relationship relates to one of the fundamental principles of immigration law–uniting families. As such, the highest preference is given to spouses and minor children of citizens or green card holders. Non-minor children and other members of the extended family like parents and siblings are given a lower priority.

The employment relationship, like the family relationship, also faces a preference category. The first preference category includes persons of extraordinary ability in the sciences, arts, education, business, or athletics—the Einsteins and other Nobel Laureates of this world. In this category of people, there is no need for labor certifications or petitions from an employer or offer of employment. The person must prove that they will continue to work in their field. Other people in this category include Professors and Researchers who have international renown in some specific academic area. The last group in this category is the executive or manager.

Second Preference Category includes applicants with advanced degrees and exceptional ability. Generally, a labor certification is required unless it can be proved that the applicant's job is in the national interest of the U.S. In those cases a national interest waiver can be obtained that would preclude the need to obtain a labor certification. There is a third category of workers that do not need to go through the cumbersome labor certification process. These are the multinational executives and managers. This is a type of L–1 Visa but for immigrant status. This is a good option for Andres.

Another avenue for obtaining a 'green card' is through employment creation. Under 8 USC § 1153(b)(5) immigrant visas are available to those immigrants that have invested or are in the process of investing at least one million dollars in capital in a U.S. business. The business must benefit the United States and create full time employment for no less than ten persons not counting the immigrant's family. The statute also provides for the granting of the immigrant visa with an investment of five hundred thousand dollars in certain target employment areas. Andres may be able to use this law if he will be the person investing in the U.S. business enterprise.

C. MAKING THE INVESTMENT

1. The Decision to Purchase

a. Reviewing the Financial Statements

At this point, *Industrial* and the Gomez family have determined that the investment can be made, although there will be a need to report the investment to several federal government agencies. It has also been discovered that Andres can come and run the new company as long as he meets the criteria set out under U.S. immigration law. The parties must now decide if the investment makes good business sense. This basic business decision is not usually the province of the lawyer. She can, however, assist the client in determining if this specific business opportunity is a good one. In reality, the 'international business lawyer' is one that advises foreign clients on U. S. law. Therefore, how can one become a good international lawyer? Become a good domestic lawyer!

The investment decision must be made with the needs of the client in mind. Recall that in the hypothetical, the primary motivation was to purchase expertise and intellectual property that could be used in the Mexican operations. Ace appears to fit that profile with its patent and team of employees. Evaluating the investment requires a due diligence review of the assets, liabilities, and operations of Ace. The next step is to determine a fair price. The third step looks to the structure of the actual transaction. The financial statements of a company are a good beginning point for review as they provide a wealth of information on the company.

Since financial statements are important, their reliability must first be established. It is advisable to obtain financial statements for several years so that any trends whether favorable or unfavorable can be detected. It is also usually a good idea to review financial statements given to banks and financial statements provided in federal income tax returns. The comparison of the two sometimes reveals some interesting discrepancies. It is also advisable to assess the competence of the accountants who prepared the financial statements.

Financial statement quality is an important matter. The problem of overstating assets and understating liabilities, the proper matching of income with expenses, along with many other questions related to the financial statements goes to the issue of reliability. Financial statements that are prepared by in-house accountants or outside non Certified Public Accountants (CPAs) should be examined very closely. Even financial statements prepared by outside CPA's should be scrutinized to see if management did not limit the CPA's scope of examination in preparing the statements.

There are three qualitative categories of statements that CPAs can issue—the compilation statement, the review, and the audit. The compilation statement offers virtually no critical review of the amounts by the CPA. It is the least costly, but it is also the least reliable. The second level—the review—is more comprehensive than the compilation but still does not match the reliability of an audit. Audited financial statements are the most costly and usually the most reliable. In audited financial statements, the CPA must render an opinion on the quality of the financial statements. Therefore, there is potential liability in tort against the CPA for misleading or erroneous financial statements.

Another complicating factor in international business transactions is determining the uniformity in the financial statements. Each country has its set of accounting rules, known as Generally Accepted Accounting Principles (GAAP). There can be substantial differences between the GAAP of countries. The lack of accounting harmonization is a major problem in financial statement analysis. The parties must be sure that the statements are in the same form as they are used to seeing. The crucial financial statements that should be reviewed are the balance sheet and income statement.

(1) The Balance Sheet

The balance sheet of a company takes a picture of the financial condition of the business enterprise as of a certain point in time. It reflects the assets, liabilities and stockholder's equity of a corporation as of a certain date, typically the end of the fiscal year. The assets of a corporation is everything the corporation owns whether tangible or intangible, real or personal. The amounts recorded under U.S. GAAP are reflected at their initial cost. The liabilities reflect those amounts that the corporation owes others. Monies owed to third parties are often referred to as outside debt whereas amounts owed to stockholders, as creditors, are known as inside debt. Liabilities are also reflected at their initial cost.

The third component of a corporate balance sheet is stockholder's equity. Stockholder's equity, also known as net worth or book value is composed of two parts—contributed capital and retained earnings. Contributed capital represents the money received from the sale of the corporation's capital stock. This is also referred to as legal capital. Retained earnings represent the cumulative excess of earnings over expenses of the business enterprise. If the operations have resulted, on a cumulative basis, in expenses over revenues the amount is referred to as a deficit. The typical balance sheet format lists the assets first reflecting the amount of total assets. It then adds the total liabilities and stockholder's equity amount to obtain a total that equals the total assets.

(2) The Income Statement

The income statement is another important financial statement. It reflects the results of the business operations over a period of time, usually a twelve-month period. It shows the revenue by type and amount. It also reflects the expenses incurred by the business in generating the reported revenue. The excess of revenue over expenses will yield net income (also known as net profit). If expenses are greater than revenue the result is known as a loss. The cumulative effect of the income statement is reflected in the balance sheet through the retained earnings amount. The income statement reflects the profitability of a company during a twelve-month period of time.

b. Due Diligence on the Assets, Liabilities, and Business Operations

Due diligence efforts should focus on any unrecorded or understated liabilities. Reviewing public lien records or lawsuit filings against the company could discover unrecorded liabilities or potential liabilities. A related problem is the possibility of loan acceleration. The balance sheet discloses a million-dollar loan. The terms of the loan agreement should be reviewed to make sure that it is not in default or if the documents contain an acceleration clause that is triggered by a change in company ownership. On the asset side, the investigation should address the problem of asset overstatement.

Recall that one main purpose for the purchase is the intellectual property owned by Ace. Does Ace really own the patent? Does Ace own the equipment and farmland? The target could also have valuable lease or contract rights. Are they about to expire? Will they survive the change in ownership? Are the values assigned to the assets accurate? These are the types of questions that should be investigated as part of the due diligence procedure.

Due diligence should also extend to a review of the operations of the business. The important question is whether the income stream reflected on the income statement is likely to continue. A review should be made of any labor disputes that could impair business operations. This is important to the foreign investor since there is a particular interest in the technical employee team. Related questions include—Are the contracts with key employees? Would they stay on with a change in ownership?

On the revenue side, one should look into Ace's customer base. For example, how many clients does Ace have? Is the revenue base clustered around a few clients? Are there contracts in place for the larger clients? Will they stay as clients through a change in ownership? The thrust of the questions related to operations should be in determining if the income stream reported on the income statement has a high probability of continuing at the same or higher level.

c.   *Valuation Methods*

The due diligence effort should result in confirming the reliability of the financial statements provided by the seller. Once this is established, determining a fair price for the investment can be addressed. Determining fair market value of a business enterprise is an imprecise art. Internal Revenue Code Regulations[19] provides a helpful description of fair market value: "... The fair market value is the price at which the property would change hands between a willing buyer and a willing seller, neither being under any compulsion to buy or to sell and both having a reasonable knowledge of relevant facts ..." The process of valuation is a fact intensive effort. The quest to determine the fair market value of a business enterprise begins by assembling a team of professionals that can help in the process.

The lawyer working with the client should determine what other people should become involved in the valuation effort. The typical parties involved are accountants, engineers, marketing personnel and specialized

---

19.   Treas. Reg. 20.2031(1)(b) (1965).

appraisers of personal and real property. The personal property may include tangible personal property like equipment or intangible property such as patents, trademarks and other types of intellectual property. In order for the lawyer to more clearly understand the valuation issue, she should have a passing familiarity with the financial statements of a business enterprise. This is not to replace the other professionals, but rather, to be able to help the client in determining who is needed.

Generally, determining the fair market value of a publicly held corporation is fairly simple. The value of the stock is determined by the purchase and sale transactions taking place in any given day. You simply look at the newspaper and determine the per share price of the corporation. The valuation of a closely held business enterprise is much more complicated. Recall that the standard is fair market value—that price paid by a willing buyer to a willing seller. The price a willing buyer will pay and the price a willing seller will accept is a function of the value determined through an analysis of the financial statements of the business enterprise. There are essentially three commonly used valuation techniques used—the book value method, the adjusted book value, and the earnings multiplier method which is also known as the discounted cash flow method.

The book value method establishes the price as the amount of stockholder's equity in the cost column of the balance sheet. In the hypothetical, the amount is eight million dollars. The book value method does not address any increase or decrease in the cost of the assets. Neither does it capture the synergistic value of the assets as a going concern. For these reasons, the book value method results in a conservative price amount. In the case where the assets have appreciated in value, the book value would be a bargain for the buyer and a bad price for the seller. It is, in many cases, not at all reflective of true fair market value.

The adjusted book value takes into account the fair market value of the assets. In a typical balance sheet, the numbers reflect the initial cost of the asset. The value of the business changes by the increase or decrease of the underlying assets. The property appraisers are very important in the adjusted book value method. Their determinations of value of the underlying assets will be very important. Although typically more reflective of 'just value' than the book value method, the adjusted book value method has the deficiency of not taking into account the going concern value of a business enterprise. In our hypothetical, the adjusted book value method results in a price of twelve million dollars.

The earnings multiplier method takes into account the synergism created by the grouping of the particular assets, management team, and market niche of the company. This method focuses on net earnings and establishes a value based on a multiple of the earnings amount. The problem in this case is twofold—determining the quality of the income stream and establishing the correct earnings multiplier. The quality of the income stream can be determined by the due diligence procedures described above.

The earnings multiplier rate is inversely proportional to risk. A higher risk results in a lower earnings multiplier, which yields a lower value. Conversely a lower risk will support a higher rate and corresponding higher value. The risk focuses on the income stream. The basic question—What is the probability that the historical income stream will continue or increase? If the probability were high, then the risk is said to be low. However, if the business is an industry where profits are very volatile, the risk would be high and the rate would be lower. Returning to our hypothetical, assuming an earnings multiplier of ten, Ace's value would be fifteen million one hundred thousand dollars. What value would you suggest to Gomez?

2. *Structuring the Transaction*

Assume that the agreed price for Ace is twelve million dollars. The next step in the process is in structuring the actual purchase transaction. There are a variety of ways in which a transaction can be structured. The potential investors are *Industrial* (the foreign corporation), Juan Gomez, its principal shareholder, or Andres, the chief executive officer. Determining the most appropriate investor is a fact question that is answered by looking at the needs of the client. We will assume that *Industrial* will be the investor. How should *Industrial* or an entity designated by it make the actual purchase? See Section 2.2, infra for the discussion on the choice of entity.

Industrial could make a cash purchase offer to the existing Ace shareholders. The tender offer would need to comply with any state and federal securities laws. In addition, it should provide for a threshold number of shares to consummate the transaction—either eighty or one hundred percent. A variation of this method would be where *Industrial* purchases newly issued Ace shares in such an amount that it could reach the ownership threshold desired. Any minority shareholders could be bought out through a stock redemption agreement, perhaps even by receiving *Industrial* stock.

In the first method—the purchase of shares from existing Ace shareholders—may not even require corporate action by Ace. Its virtue is in its simplicity. The second alternative is more complicated because it requires action at the corporate level, perhaps even amendment of the corporate charter. It could, however, potentially have additional benefits because the corporation would receive the funds instead of the shareholders. In either one of these two alternatives, Ace, Inc. remains intact. The change occurs at the corporate level.

This can have positive and negative implications. The disadvantage is that any Ace liabilities, whether recorded or unrecorded, remain in place regardless of the change in ownership. In addition, the premium paid for the shares does not increase the cost basis of the individual assets. This is disadvantageous for tax purposes. However, keeping Ace intact could also be beneficial. In many cases there could be favorable contractual arrangements or tax attributes that could be lost if Ace does not continue. Additionally, keeping Ace intact would retain any goodwill associated with its name.

Another alternative for *Industrial* is to purchase Ace's assets. In this alternative, *Industrial* could pick and choose the assets it wants to buy. This way, through certain state bulk sales laws unrecorded liabilities do not follow the assets. In addition, the purchase of the individual assets allows for a step-up in the tax basis of the assets a valuable tax attribute. In many cases it is more advisable to purchase the assets of a business, unless of course, Ace, Inc. has valuable attributes inherent to it as mentioned above.

These alternatives have to be assessed in light of the needs of the client and the particular circumstances.

D. THE MOVEMENT OF CASH ACROSS NATIONAL BORDERS

The foreign direct investment requires the movement of capital across national borders. Capital can take the form of cash, negotiable monetary instruments, stocks, bonds, tangible property, and intangible property. The movement of cash and monetary instruments, especially when there is a Latin American connection, provokes, in many cases unjustifiably, suspicions of money laundering activities. Assume for a moment that *Industrial* is to purchase Ace's assets. The transfer of the cash to Ace can create some serious problems for *Industrial*.

Illegal drug sales and its harmful effect on the U.S. population are obvious. The high crime rate can be in great part attributed to illegal drug consumption. The efforts of U.S. governmental entities such as the Drug Enforcement Agency (DEA), the Federal Bureau of Investigation (FBI), and the Criminal Investigation Division of the Internal Revenue Service (CID) have been given great power in fighting the tidal wave of drugs coming into the country from Latin America.

The fight is on two fronts—the first front is to impede the physical flow of the illegal drugs, a formidable task given the many ways to enter the United States, which albeit successful in part, have not stopped the flow of the drugs. The second method is by removing the profit from the drug dealers. Congress has enacted money laundering[20] and asset forfeiture laws that are very broad in scope in an effort to remove the profit from illegal drug dealing. These money-laundering laws can snag honest and dishonest entrepreneurs alike. Even the mere opening of a bank account can cause problems.

KEEPING DRUG MONEY FROM REACHING THE WASH CYCLE: A GUIDE TO THE BANK SECRECY ACT

Peter E. Meltzer
108 Banking L.J. 230 (1991).

* * *

---

20. See 18 U.S.C. §§ 1956, 1957 (1994).

The laundering of illegal drug profits is a $300 billion annual business, including $110 billion generated in the United States alone. An essential prerequisite to the success of any drug operation is a successful money-laundering system in which profits generated from illegal activities are converted into financial assets that appear to have legitimate origin. Because money laundering is principally accomplished through the use of legitimate financial institutions, money laundering is the potential Achilles' heel of the illegal drug business.

The Bank Secrecy Act was enacted into law in 1970 as an effort to prevent laundering of profits resulting from drug sales. Congress reasoned that if it were possible to create a paper trail of all transactions in which customers deposit, withdraw, mail, or in any way attempt to transfer cash sums in excess of $10,000 at one time, the money-laundering process, which is so essential to any drug operation, would be made far more difficult. * * *

Laundering typically consists of three distinct stages, known as placement, layering, and integration. Placement is the physical disposal of bulk cash proceeds into a financial institution. Layering is the process of transferring these funds among various accounts through a series of complex financial transactions that are intended, to the greatest extent possible, to separate these funds from their original sources. Finally, integration is the process of shifting the laundered funds to legitimate organizations that have no apparent link to organized crime. In other words, an apparently legitimate explanation is provided for the illicit proceeds.

The theory behind the Bank Secrecy Act and its reporting requirements is that the money laundering process is most vulnerable at the placement stage. In an address before the American Bankers Association, Attorney General Richard Thornburgh described the "greatest dilemma" of drug dealers as follows:

The annual gross income from drug sales in this country is estimated at over $100 billion. On the street, a crack sale is done for five or ten dollars, so that the largest denomination of currency in street circulation is usually a twenty-dollar bill. Together [the bundles of cash] would weigh about 26 million pounds.

Here is the problem: how do you push 26 million pounds of these twenties through a bank window? An even tougher problem: how do you shove $100 billion in twenties through a bank window without attracting attention?

If a paper trail can be created at the moment that the cash proceeds enter the banking system, a fundamental pre-requisite to the success of the money-laundering system—the absence of a documentary connection between the placement, layering and integration stages—is hampered. * * *

A cornerstone of the Bank Secrecy Act is its requirement that financial institutions file a currency transaction report (CTR) for all deposits, withdrawals, exchanges, or transfers of currency in excess of $10,000 during any one business day. The CTR system represents Congress's attempt to begin creation of the paper trail at the placement stage of the money-laundering process.

Early enforcement of the Bank Secrecy Act was sporadic, and compliance levels were low. As late as 1983, banks were filing a total of 500,000 CTR forms a year. In the mid–1980s, however, several large regional banks were levied large fines for failing to properly file CTRs, and shortly thereafter, compliance with the Act sharply increased. This year, it is projected that banks will file in excess of 8 million CTR forms. * * *

There have been a number of cases decided and administrative rulings issued that have helped define the parameters of the reporting obligations of a financial institution under the Bank Secrecy Act. For example, what happens if a customer is "smurfing" or intentionally structuring transactions to keep them below the $10,000 threshold? In a structuring situation, the same person deposits between $9,000 and $9,900 on a daily basis, often going to different tellers each day. In short, the customer has "structured" the deposits so as not to trigger the bank's obligation to file a CTR, which appears to be precisely the customer's goal.

The cases that were interpreting the un-amended version of the Bank Secrecy Act (i.e., prior to the Money Laundering Control Act of 1986) were divided as to whether individuals could be held criminally liable for structuring currency transactions to avoid the CTR reporting requirement. Some courts rejected attempts to impose liability either because they concluded that the Bank Secrecy Act did not provide customers with fair warning that structuring was unlawful or because they believed there could be no accessory liability since the financial institution was not obligated to aggregate separate currency transactions into one reportable transaction. Other courts, on the other hand, affirmed structuring convictions, at least where the defendant engaged in multiple currency transactions totaling more than $10,000 at a single bank in a single day.

In 1986, Congress created the anti-structuring provision of the Bank Secrecy Act, which was intended to address this situation and resolve the conflict then existing in the courts. This provision reads as follows:

No person shall for the purpose of evading the reporting requirements of section 5313(a) with respect to such transaction–1. cause or attempt to cause domestic financial institution to fail to file a report required under section 5313(a); 2. cause or attempt to cause a domestic financial institution to file a report required under section 5313(a) that contains a material omission or misstatement of fact; or 3. structure or assist in structuring, or attempt to structure or assist in structuring, any transaction with one or more domestic financial institution.

Under the foregoing anti-structuring provision, tellers will have "assisted in structuring" if they provide any advice to a customer as to how to avoid triggering the bank's obligation to file a CTR. For example, if the customer wants to deposit $15,000 in cash and the teller suggests that the deposits be made in two equal installments on separate days, this advice would be considered as assisting in structuring.

In addition to the liability imposed on a customer for structuring and on a bank for assisting in structuring, there have also been administrative rulings issued regarding a bank's general obligations when a customer appears to be structuring. Even if the bank is not technically required to file a CTR as a result of the customer's deposits, the bank should nevertheless contact the criminal investigation division of the Internal Revenue Service (IRS) if it appears that intent to avoid the CTR process is present. * * *

The regulations relating to exemptions from CTR reporting requirements impose certain duties on banks who have a degree of personal knowledge of each of their customers who deposit or withdraw currency in excess of $10,000. It is partly for this reason that the "know your customer" standard has developed in recent years as a significant step not only in preventing money laundering generally but in being able to comply with the requirements imposed on banks relating to exemptions by the federal regulations.

The know-your-customer policy serves several purposes. First, it may deter potential customers who would use the bank for illicit purposes because of their reluctance to reveal information about themselves. Second, the investigation of the potential customer may reveal matters calling into question the legitimacy of the potential customer. Third, the investigation will give the institution a database against which the customer's transactions can be evaluated to determine if they are consistent with the customer's legitimate activities. Fourth, it will assist the bank in evaluating whether the transactions are in amounts that are "commensurate with the customary conduct of the lawful domestic business of the customer," as required by the federal regulations.

It is true that the techniques and methodologies of the money launderers have become far more sophisticated in the past several years. Gone are the days when a money launderer entered a bank in southern Florida and simply deposited a suitcase of cash. Nevertheless, there are ways to distinguish between a legitimate business and business created for the sole purpose of laundering cash. As one Drug Enforcement Administration official has stated:

No matter what the trafficker says when it comes to the bank and no matter what business he claims to represent, generally speaking most of these traffickers do not request or require the broad spectrum of banking services. They are looking to deposit cash. They are not depositing checks. They are not requesting lines of credit. They are not doing the sort of routine business that bankers would expect on the scale that the people are handling money.

There are a number of activities of which a bank should beware that could indicate that a customer is laundering money. For example, a bank should be particularly careful when a customer does the following: 1. Opens a number of accounts under one or more names and subsequently makes many deposits of less than $10,000; 2. Opens an account without references, a local address, or identification; 3. Is reluctant to proceed with the transaction after being informed that a CTR would have to be filed. 4. Is reluctant to provide the information needed to file the CTR;

5. Buys a number of cashier's checks, money orders, or travelers's checks for large amounts under the $10,000 reporting limit or consistently buys such items without apparent legitimate reasons; or Converts large amounts of money from small to large-bill denominations, which are easier to transport.

There is also conduct of non-customers that should make a bank particularly careful. For example, a bank should beware when the following occurs:

A non-customer receives incoming or makes outgoing wire transfers involving currency near the reporting threshold or that involves many traveler's checks; A non-customer receives wire transfers under instructions to the bank to "pay upon proper identification" or to convert the funds to cashier checks and mail them to the non-customer; 1. There is a significant change in currency shipment patterns between correspondent banks or unusually large transactions between a small out-of-the-way bank and a larger bank; 2. Any individual discusses CTR filing requirements with bank personnel with the apparent intent of determining how to avoid these requirements; or 3. Any bank employee avoids taking a vacation.

It is hoped that if a bank is thorough and diligent in practicing the know-your-customer standard, then not only may the launderers own goal be frustrated, but also the bank may be assisting itself in avoiding both civil and criminal liability for possible carelessness. * * *

Each person who physically transports, mails, or ships currency or other monetary instruments in a aggregate amount exceeding $10,000 at one time into or out of the United States is required under 31 C.F.R. s 103.23(a) to file a Form 4790 Currency Monetary Instrument Report (CMIR) with the U.S. Customs Service. The person who receives in the U.S. currency or other monetary instruments in the aggregate amount exceeding $10,000 as to which a report has not been filed under 31 C.F.R. s 103.23(a) must, under 31 C.F.R. s 103.23(b), file a CMIR within fifteen days of receipt of the currency or monetary instrument.

The CMIR must be filed with the U.S. Customs officer in charge at any port of entry or departure. If the currency or monetary instrument is not physically accompanying a person entering or departing from the United States, the CMIR may be filed by mail on or before the date of entry, departure, mailing, or shipping. Thus, a CMIR must be filed in the following instances: 1. A person is about to board an international flight with an amount in excess of $10,000 of U.S. currency in his possession— a CMIR must be filed before boarding the flight; 2. A $100,000 bearer bond is to be mailed to a relative overseas—a CMIR must be filed on or before the date the bond is mailed and; 3. A package is received from overseas containing $12,000 in U.S. currency–a CMIR must be filed within fifteen days after receipt of the currency. * * *

The failure of a financial institution to act with due care with respect to its Bank Secrecy Act obligations can result in both criminal and civil liabilities for the institution as well as its officers and directors. * * *

UNITED STATES v. THOMPSON

United States Court of Appeals, Fifth Circuit, 1979.
603 F.2d 1200.

* * *

CHARLES CLARK, Circuit Judge:

On March 12, 1979, George Thompson, III was found guilty of unlawfully causing the Ridglea Bank of Fort Worth, Texas, to fail to file a currency transaction report (CTR), 31 U.S.C. ss 1059, 1081, with the knowledge that this violation was committed in the furtherance of violations of other federal laws, in that Thompson, in violation of 18 U.S.C. s 2(b), aided and abetted Michael E. Welch in knowingly and intentionally possessing with the intent to distribute, and in distributing, cocaine in violation of 21 U.S.C. s 841(a)(1). Thompson was sentenced to three years imprisonment and fined $20,000.00. He appeals his conviction arguing first that the statute and regulations under which he was prosecuted are unconstitutionally vague as applied to him, second that he is entitled to structure a single transaction in currency as multiple loans so as to avoid reporting requirements, and third that the evidence is insufficient to establish that he caused the bank to fail to file the CTR. We reject appellant's arguments and affirm his conviction. * * *

George Thompson, III was Chairman of the Board of Ridglea Bank. The evidence presented at trial established that beginning in 1974, Thompson authorized a series of loans to Michael E. Welch. These loans were to enable Welch, an aspiring jazz musician, to purchase musical instruments. Welch experienced difficulty in repaying these loans and in April 1976 approached Thompson with a plan by which Thompson would arrange for additional loans to Welch. Welch proposed using the proceeds of these loans to purchase marijuana that he would in turn resell, utilizing the profits derived from the venture to repay the initial indebtedness. A series of loans followed, all approved by Thompson and disbursed in cash to Welch. Welch testified that Thompson knew at the time these loans were made that the proceeds would be used to purchase marijuana. Thompson denied such knowledge, claiming that he did not know nor did he want to know what the loans were to be used for. Some time prior to March 9, 1977, Welch approached Thompson and proposed a plan whereby the proceeds of additional loans would be used to purchase cocaine which, when sold, would generate a much greater profit than had the sales of marijuana. Again, Welch planned to use the profits to discharge his indebtedness at the Ridglea Bank. Previously having become aware of currency transaction reporting requirements, Thompson advised Welch that any future monies loaned by Ridglea Bank would be in amounts of less than $10,000 in order to avoid filing a currency transaction report. On March 9, 1977, Welch met with Thompson at Ridglea Bank in order to obtain $45,000.00. Welch again testified that Thompson knew at the time of the loan transaction that the proceeds would be used to purchase cocaine. Thompson again denied having such knowledge, claiming that he did not know nor did he want to know what the loans would be used for. Thompson had five notes prepared, each in the amount of $9,000.00 and each bearing a different maturity date. He admitted intentionally structuring the transaction in such a manner to avoid filing a currency transaction report. Thompson personally processed the notes by receiving five cash tickets from the bank's Loan and Discount Department and, upon presentation to a commercial teller, receiving $45,000.00 in cash in five separate $9,000.00 bundles. Thompson immediately transferred the entire $45,000.00 in cash to Welch at one time. Welch testified that after obtaining the $45,000.00 he purchased almost two pounds of cocaine. * * *

No CTR was filed by the Ridglea Bank for the March 9, 1977, transaction. The commercial teller who disbursed the $45,000.00 in cash to Thompson, and whose responsibility it was to file a CTR, testified that Thompson provided him no information from which a report could be filed. The teller further testified that Thompson was the only person who could have provided the information necessary to enable a CTR to be filed as there was no information on the loan application and Welch had no accounts with the bank. The teller explained his failure to file a CTR as based on a reliance on Thompson's authority as Chairman of the Board and on an assumption that Thompson would tell him to file a CTR were one needed. * * *

Appellant contends that the statute and regulations under which he was prosecuted are unconstitutionally vague as applied to him in that the terms "transaction" and "currency transaction" are nowhere defined. We reject this argument.

Congress enacted the Currency and Foreign Transactions Reporting Act "to require certain reports or records where such reports or records have a high degree of usefulness in criminal, tax, or regulatory investigations or proceedings." 31 U.S.C. s 1051. The Act provides that:

Transactions involving any domestic institution shall be reported to the Secretary (of the Treasury) at such time, in such manner, and in such detail as the Secretary may require if they involve the payment, receipt, or transfer of United States currency, or such other monetary instruments as the Secretary may specify, in such amounts, denominations, or both, or under such circumstances, as the Secretary shall by regulation prescribe.

31 U.S.C. s 1081. The pertinent regulation requires that: Each financial institution shall file a report of each deposit, withdrawal, exchange of currency or other payment or transfer, by, through, or to such financial institution which involves a Transaction in currency of more than $10,000. 31 C.F.R. s 103.21(a) (emphasis added). The regulations expressly define a "transaction in currency" as being "(a) transaction involving the physical transfer of currency from one person to another." 31 C.F.R. s 103.11. The regulation's definition of "transaction in currency" is reprinted in its entirety on the reverse side of Form 4789, which is utilized by financial institutions in filing CTRs. The terms "currency" and "person" also are defined in the regulations with similar specificity. * * *

The "void for vagueness" doctrine requires that a law give a person of ordinary intelligence a reasonable opportunity to know what is prohibited so that he may act accordingly. Grayned v. City of Rockford, 408 U.S. 104, 108, 92 S.Ct. 2294, 33 L.Ed.2d 222 (1972). A statute is fatally vague only when it exposes a potential actor to some risk or detriment without giving him fair warning of the proscribed conduct. Rowan v. United States Post Office Dep't, 397 U.S. 728, 740, 90 S.Ct. 1484, 25 L.Ed.2d 736 (1970). While criminal statutes must fairly apprise those who are subject to them as to the conduct that is proscribed, no more than a reasonable degree of certainty can be demanded. * * *

With reference to the above authorities, we cannot say that the applicable statute and regulations as defined failed to afford appellant fair notice of what constitutes a "transaction in currency of more than $10,000." Rather, the government's proof at trial clearly established a violation of the reporting requirements as defined, in that an unreported physical transfer of $45,000.00 in cash from the Ridglea Bank to Welch occurred on March 9, 1977. The mere fact that appellant intentionally structured the $45,000.00 transfer as five $9,000.00 loans with different maturity dates does not remove the transaction from the ambit of the reporting requirements, where these loans were executed by the same borrower, on the same day, in the same bank, and where the proceeds of the loans totalling in excess of $10,000.00 were physically transferred by the financial institution to the borrower at the same time and place. * * *

Appellant argues that he was entitled to structure a single transaction in currency as multiple loans, thus avoiding the obligation to report pursuant to s 1081 and the relevant regulations. Appellant analogizes this to a taxpayer structuring a financial transaction in a certain manner to avoid, rather than evade, the payment of taxes. The analogy is inapposite. Congress has lawfully required reporting of transactions in currency of more than $10,000.00 as an aid to criminal, tax, or regulatory investigations or proceedings. In the instant case, appellant intentionally sought to defeat the statutory requirements by engaging in an unreported transaction in currency of more than $10,000.00. Appellant cannot flout the requirements of s 1081 with impunity. The decision to structure a $45,000.00 transaction in currency as five $9,000.00 loans with the intent to annul the reporting requirements does not equate to a decision to structure a financial transaction in a lawful manner so as to minimize or avoid the applicability of a tax covering only specific activity.

* * *

————————

Money laundering is the process by which illicit funds are made to appear legitimate. Drug dealers will not be able to reap their profit except though this money laundering effort. The law enforcement effort against money laundering focuses in three areas—the placement, layering and integration of the illicit funds into clean businesses. The principal governmental agencies that are involved are the FBI and the Criminal Investigation Division of the Internal Revenue Service (CID). The IRS can also be involved through its civil audit branch. A revenue agent conducting a civil audit can refer a case to the CID when the company meets the profile of a money laundering enterprise.

The placement stage involves the depositing of the funds, usually in small denominations, in banks or in transporting the currency across the U.S. border. The *Bank Secrecy Act* (BSA) described above attempts to stop this activity by requiring banks or those who transport currency across national borders to file a report when the transaction, whether involving cash or negotiable instruments is in excess of ten thousand dollars. The BSA also makes it an offense to structure a transaction in such a way that the amount falls below the ten thousand dollar threshold—the so-called 'smurfing' of funds. The transport of the funds in and of itself is not a violation of the BSA but the failure to report is. In addition to the criminal penalties under the act, the government is allowed to seize the undeclared currency or monetary instruments.

The layering process also involves the use of banks. Layering is an attempt to disguise the true source of funds by using multiple bank accounts to deposit and transfer (layer) monies through different accounts in different banks. The BSA is used against layering activities by requiring the cash transaction report. In addition, federal regulations compel the banks to 'know your clients.' The know-your-client or KYC rules essentially turn banks into spies for the government. Under the KYC rules, banks are to monitor the deposit activities of their customers reporting any suspicious activity to the government. In some cases, they are required to not tell the customer of their action.

The integration phase of the money laundering cycle focuses on the capital investment of laundered funds into legitimate business enterprises. The integration is the end goal—the generation of legal profits. If the government can identify the receptacle entities, federal civil and criminal forfeiture laws[21] can be used to seize these businesses. The interaction of

21. 18 USC §§ 981,982,984, & 986 (1998).

these rules can be troublesome for *Industrial*. Latin America is considered to be a major center of money laundering activities. The flow of funds from Mexico and the purchase of Ace could stir suspicions.

There are two U.S. policy objectives potentially in conflict. One is drug interdiction, while the other is the opening of the border for the free flow of investment capital. The broad scope of the money laundering laws, coupled with the suspicious policeman mentality can stifle international investment. This is particularly true when the foreign capital is coming from Latin America. This is a type of racial profiling that ensnares the innocent along with the guilty. The singling out of Latin Americans is discriminatory and may breach international law.

The NAFTA promise of fair and equitable treatment, full protection and security as well as most favored nation treatment (See NAFTA Chapter 11 Article 1105 1. And Article 1103) could be jeopardized by this conflict. It is probably a safe bet to say that the purchase of Ace by *Industrial*, a Mexican corporation, would be subjected to closer scrutiny than if the purchaser were a Canadian company. In addition, it is arguable that the forfeiture laws could violate NAFTA Article 1110 on expropriation because there is no compensation paid to owners when their property is seized by the government.

SECTION 2.2   THE CHOICE OF ENTITY DECISION

A. INTRODUCTION

At this point it has been decided that *Industrial* will be the investor. Assume that the transaction has been structured as a purchase of Ace's assets for twelve million dollars. *Industrial* will be the investor but it may not be the actual buyer of the assets. Establishing the actual buyer can only be made after determining the appropriate form of doing business in the United States. The lawyer has an important role to advise the client on the appropriate form of business organization to use.

There is no one form of business organization inherently superior to another. The 'best' form is the one that fits best for the owners of the enterprise. The choice of entity decision should based on the existing facts and circumstances, the laws of the exporting and host country, and the needs of the client. The best 'fit' is determined by assessing the needs of the client and comparing them with the legal, tax and formation characteristics of the available entities. The choice of entity decision should be made with three important factors in mind —profit maximization and distribution, control, and limitation of risk on non-business assets. The entity that provides the legal and tax attributes most beneficial to the client should be used.

There are a variety of entities available for use in an inbound transaction. The task is to assess the needs of the client and to choose an entity that best fits those needs. Entities can be broadly divided into two categories–the corporation and the non-corporate form. The corporation itself can be of various types—the General Business Corporation, the Closely Held Corporation, the Professional Corporation, and the Professional Association. Each type of corporation varies in its formation and governance specifics but share common corporate attributes. The discussion in these materials will focus on the General Business Corporation. The corporation is an entity separate and apart from its owners—the shareholders. The corporation offers attractive attributes as well as great disadvantages.

The non-corporate forms vary in their attributes. Some, like the branch and general partnership, are considered to be an aggregation or conduit of their owners. Other non-corporate forms like the Limited Liability Company, the Limited Partnership, and the Limited Liability Partnership have corporate-like characteristics as well as aggregate or conduit attributes. The conduit form of business organization has some very attractive features as well as some great disadvantages. While all of the entities should be reviewed for their legal and tax attributes, the analysis below traces the impact of the 'three important factors' in the case where *Industrial* will choose a branch (conduit entity) or a wholly owned subsidiary (a corporate entity).

B. LIMITING THE RISK ON THE INVESTMENT

The branch is treated as a conduit of the corporate owner. The liabilities of the branch are the liabilities of the corporation. Therefore, if the branch has a judgment creditor, the creditor can attach the assets of the branch and of *Industrial*, whether in the United States or Mexico, if the branch assets are insufficient to satisfy the judgment. The same result occurs to the partners of a general partnership—the owners of the business are jointly and severally and personally liable for the debts of the entity. A judgment creditor can attach the business assets and proceed to the personal non-business assets of the owners. Unlimited liability is a very negative attribute of the conduit form of business organization.

The corporate form generally limits the shareholder loss to the amount of the investment. The Limited Liability Company, Limited Partnership, and the Limited Liability Partnership share in this beneficial corporate attribute. The so-called limited liability rule is subject to several important exceptions. Under traditional corporate law concepts creditors can 'pierce the corporate veil' in a variety of situations. The following cases discuss the exceptions to the limited liability general rule.

FLETCHER v. ATEX
United States Court of Appeals, Second Circuit, 1995.
68 F.3d 1451.

JOSE A. CABRANES, Circuit Judge.

This is a consolidated appeal from a final judgment of the United States District Court for the Southern District of New York * * * granting defendant-appellee Eastman Kodak Company's motion for summary judgment and dismissing all claims against it in two actions * * * The plaintiffs-appellants filed suit against Atex, Inc. ("Atex") and its parent, Eastman Kodak Company ("Kodak"), to recover for repetitive stress injuries that they claim were caused by their use of computer keyboards manufactured by Atex. * * *

The Fletcher and Hermanson plaintiffs filed their respective complaints on December 4, 1992, and February 25, 1994, seeking recovery from Atex and Kodak, among others, for repetitive stress injuries that they claim were caused by their use of Atex computer keyboards. From 1981 until December 1992, Atex was a wholly-owned subsidiary of Kodak. In 1987, Atex's name was changed to Electronic Pre–Press Systems, Inc., ("EPPS"), but its name was changed back to Atex in 1990. In December 1992, Atex sold substantially all of its assets to an independent third party and again changed its name to 805 Middlesex Corp., which holds the proceeds from the sale. Kodak continues to be the sole shareholder of 805 Middlesex Corp.

After extensive discovery, Kodak moved for summary judgment in Fletcher on April 21, 1994, and in Hermanson on April 28, 1994. The plaintiffs opposed Kodak's motion, arguing that genuine issues of material fact existed as to Kodak's liability under any number of theories, including (1) that Atex was merely Kodak's alter ego or instrumentality; (2) that Atex was Kodak's agent in the manufacture and marketing of the keyboards; (3) that Kodak was the "apparent manufacturer" of the Atex keyboards; and (4) that Kodak acted in tortious concert with Atex in manufacturing and marketing the allegedly defective keyboards.

In support of their first theory, the plaintiffs argued that Kodak "dominated and controlled" Atex by maintaining significant overlap between the boards of directors of the two companies, "siphoning" off funds from Atex through use of a cash management system, requiring Kodak's approval for major expenditures, stock sales, and real estate acquisitions, participating in negotiations involving the sale of Atex to a third party, and including references to Atex as a "division" of Kodak and to the "merger" between Atex and Kodak in Atex's promotional literature and Kodak's Annual Report. * * *

Plaintiffs argue that the district court should have denied Kodak's motion for summary judgment on the ground that genuine issues of material fact existed regarding each of the plaintiffs' four theories of liability. We consider the plaintiffs' arguments on each of these theories in turn. * * *

The plaintiffs claim that the district court erred in granting Kodak's motion for summary judgment on their alter ego theory of liability. The plaintiffs offer two arguments in this regard. First, they contend that the district court was estopped from granting Kodak's motion for summary judgment because the New York state court found in King v. Eastman that issues of material fact existed regarding Kodak's domination of Atex. Second, they argue that even if collateral estoppel does not apply in the instant case, genuine issues of material fact remain that preclude a grant of summary judgment in favor of Kodak.

The district court correctly noted that "[u]nder New York choice of law principles, '[t]he law of the state of incorporation determines when the corporate form will be disregarded and liability will be imposed on shareholders.' " * * * Because Atex was a Delaware corporation, Delaware law determines whether the corporate veil can be pierced in this instance.

Delaware law permits a court to pierce the corporate veil of a company "where there is fraud or where [it] is in fact a mere instrumentality or alter ego of its owner." * * * Although the Delaware Supreme Court has never explicitly adopted an alter ego theory of parent liability for its subsidiaries, lower Delaware courts have applied the doctrine on several occasions, as has the United States District Court for the District of Delaware. * * * Thus, under an alter ego theory, there is no requirement of a showing of fraud. * * * To prevail on an alter ego claim under Delaware law, a plaintiff must show (1) that the parent and the subsidiary "operated as a single economic entity" and (2) that an "overall element of injustice or unfairness . . . [is] present." * * *

In the New York state action of King v. Eastman, the court granted Kodak's motion for summary judgment, relying on an erroneous interpretation of Delaware's alter ego doctrine. The court noted that although the plaintiffs had raised "ample questions of fact regarding the first element of the piercing theory—domination," they made "no showing that Kodak used whatever dominance it had over Atex to perpetrate a fraud or other wrong that proximately cause[d] injury to them." This was an error; under Delaware law, the alter ego theory of liability does not require any showing of fraud. * * *

To prevail on an alter ego theory of liability, a plaintiff must show that the two corporations " 'operated as a single economic entity such that it would be inequitable . . . to uphold a legal distinction between them.' " * * * Among the factors to be considered in determining whether a subsidiary and parent operate as a "single economic entity" are: "[W]hether the corporation was adequately capitalized for the corporate undertaking; whether the corporation was solvent; whether dividends were paid, corporate records kept, officers and directors functioned properly, and other corporate formalities were observed; whether the dominant shareholder siphoned corporate funds; and whether, in general, the corporation simply functioned as a facade for the dominant shareholder." * * * As noted above, a showing of fraud or wrongdoing is not necessary under an alter ego theory, but the plaintiff must demonstrate an overall element of injustice or unfairness. * * *

A plaintiff seeking to persuade a Delaware court to disregard the corporate structure faces "a difficult task." * * * Courts have made it clear that "[t]he legal entity of a corporation will not be disturbed until sufficient reason appears." Id. Although the question of domination is generally one of fact, courts have granted motions to dismiss as well as motions for summary judgment in favor of defendant parent companies where there has been a lack of sufficient evidence to place the alter ego issue in dispute. * * *

Kodak has shown that Atex followed corporate formalities, and the plaintiffs have offered no evidence to the contrary. Significantly, the plaintiffs have not challenged Kodak's assertions that Atex's board of directors held regular meetings, that minutes from those meetings were routinely prepared and maintained in corporate minute books, that appropriate financial records and other files were maintained by Atex, that Atex filed its own tax returns and paid its own taxes, and that Atex had its own employees and management executives who were responsible for the corporation's day-to-day business. The plaintiffs' primary arguments regarding domination concern (1) the defendant's use of a cash management system; (2) Kodak's exertion of control over Atex's major expenditures, stock sales, and the sale of Atex's assets to a third party; (3) Kodak's "dominating presence" on Atex's board of directors; (4) descriptions of the relationship between Atex and Kodak in the corporations' advertising, promotional literature, and annual reports; and (5) Atex's assignment of one of its former officer's mortgage to Kodak in order to close Atex's asset-purchase agreement with a third party. The plaintiffs argue that each of these raises a genuine issue of material fact about Kodak's domination of Atex, and that the district court therefore erred in granting summary judgment to Kodak on the plaintiffs' alter ego theory. We find that the district court correctly held that, in light of the undisputed factors of independence cited by Kodak, "the elements identified by the plaintiffs ... [were] insufficient as a matter of law to establish the degree of domination necessary to disregard Atex's corporate identity." Fletcher, 861 F.Supp. at 245.

First, the district court correctly held that "Atex's participation in Kodak's cash management system is consistent with sound business practice and does not show undue domination or control." Id. at 244. The parties do not dispute the mechanics of Kodak's cash management system. Essentially, all of Kodak's domestic subsidiaries participate in the system and maintain zero-balance bank accounts. All funds transferred from the subsidiary accounts are recorded as credits to the subsidiary, and when a subsidiary is in need of funds, a transfer is made. At all times, a strict accounting is kept of each subsidiary's funds.

Courts have generally declined to find alter ego liability based on a parent corporation's use of a cash management system. * * * The plaintiffs offer no facts to support their speculation that Kodak's centralized cash management system was actually a "complete commingling" of funds or a means by which Kodak sought to "siphon[ ] all of Atex's revenues into its own account."

Second, the district court correctly concluded that it could find no domination based on the plaintiffs' evidence that Kodak's approval was required for Atex's real estate leases, major capital expenditures, negotiations for a sale of minority stock ownership to IBM, or the fact that

Kodak played a significant role in the ultimate sale of Atex's assets to a third party. Again, the parties do not dispute that Kodak required Atex to seek its approval and/or participation for the above transactions. However, this evidence, viewed in the light most favorable to the plaintiffs, does not raise an issue of material fact about whether the two corporations constituted "a single economic entity." Indeed, this type of conduct is typical of a majority shareholder or parent corporation. * * *

The plaintiffs' third argument, that Kodak dominated the Atex board of directors, also fails. Although a number of Kodak employees have sat on the Atex board, it is undisputed that between 1981 and 1988, only one director of Atex was also a director of Kodak. Between 1989 and 1992, Atex and Kodak had no directors in common. Parents and subsidiaries frequently have overlapping boards of directors while maintaining separate business operations. In Japan Petroleum, the Delaware district court held that the fact that a parent and a subsidiary have common officers and directors does not necessarily demonstrate that the parent corporation dominates the activities of the subsidiary. * * * Since the overlap is negligible here, we find this evidence to be entirely insufficient to raise a question of fact on the issue of domination.

Fourth, the district court properly rejected the plaintiffs' argument that the descriptions of the relationship between Atex and Kodak and the presence of the Kodak logo in Atex's promotional literature justify piercing the corporate veil. Fletcher, 861 F.Supp. at 245. The plaintiffs point to several statements in both Kodak's and Atex's literature to evidence Kodak's domination of its subsidiary. For example, plaintiffs refer to (1) a promotional pamphlet produced by EPPS (a/k/a Atex) describing Atex as a business unit of EPPS and noting that EPPS was an "agent" of Kodak; (2) a document produced by Atex entitled "An Introduction to Atex Systems," which describes a "merger" between Kodak and Atex; (3) a statement in Kodak's 1985 and 1986 annual reports describing Atex as a "recent acquisition[ ]" and a "subsidiar[y] . . . combined in a new division"; and (4) a statement in an Atex/EPPS document, "Setting Up TPE 6000 on the Sun 3 Workstation," describing Atex as "an unincorporated division of Electronic Pre–Press Systems, Inc., a Kodak company." They also refer generally to the fact that Atex's paperwork and packaging materials frequently displayed the Kodak logo.

It is clear from the record that Atex never merged with Kodak or operated as a Kodak division. The plaintiffs offer no evidence to the contrary, apart from these statements in Atex and Kodak documents that they claim are indicative of the true relationship between the two companies. Viewed in the light most favorable to the plaintiffs, these statements and the use of the Kodak logo are not evidence that the two companies operated as a "single economic entity." * * *

Fifth, the plaintiffs contend that Atex's assignment of its former CEO's mortgage to Kodak in order to close the sale of Atex's assets to a third party is evidence of Kodak's domination of Atex. We reject this argument as well. The evidence is undisputed that Kodak paid Atex the book value of the note and entered into a formal repayment agreement with the former CEO. Formal contracts were executed, and the two companies observed all corporate formalities.

Finally, even if the plaintiffs did raise a factual question about Kodak's domination of Atex, summary judgment would still be appropriate because the plaintiffs offer no evidence on the second prong of the alter ego analysis. The plaintiffs have failed to present evidence of an "overall element of injustice or unfairness" that would result from respecting the two companies' corporate separateness. * * *

In the instant case, the plaintiffs offer nothing more than the bare assertion that Kodak "exploited" Atex "to generate profits but not to safeguard safety." There is no indication that Kodak sought to defraud creditors and consumers or to siphon funds from its subsidiary. The plaintiffs' conclusory assertions, without more, are not evidence, * * * and are completely inadequate to support a finding that it would be unjust to respect Atex's corporate form.

For all of the foregoing reasons, the district court's order entering summary judgment on the plaintiffs' alter ego theory of liability is affirmed. * * *

We affirm the district court's order granting summary judgment for the defendant on each of the plaintiffs' four theories of liability. * * * We agree with the district court's conclusion that the defendant was entitled to summary judgment on the plaintiffs' alter ego theory of liability. * * * The elements

identified by the plaintiffs were insufficient to raise a material issue of fact regarding domination, and further, the plaintiffs failed to offer evidence of injustice that would justify disregarding Atex's corporate form. * * *

COOK v. ARROWSMITH SHELBURNE, INC.
United States Court of Appeals, Second Circuit, 1995.
69 F.3d 1235.

* * *

WINTER, Circuit Judge:

Mary Cook appeals from Judge Billings's grant of summary judgment and dismissal of her amended complaint. The amended complaint alleged that the various appellees fired her because of her gender in violation of the Vermont Fair Employment Practices Act, 21 V.S.A. s 495 et seq. ("VFEPA") and Title VII of the Civil Rights Act of 1964, 42 U.S.C. § 2000e et seq. It also alleged state common law claims of wrongful discharge and intentional infliction of emotional distress. Because Cook has established a prima facie case of gender discrimination, we reverse the grant of summary judgment as to the Title VII and VFEPA claims. We also reverse the grant of summary judgment for the parent corporation concerning its liability for the discriminatory acts of its wholly owned subsidiary. * * *

Cook worked for defense contractor Arrowsmith Shelburne, Inc. ("ASI"), a wholly owned subsidiary of KDT Industries, Inc. From 1987 to 1992, she was a Senior Buyer and Materials Manager responsible for, inter alia, negotiating procurement contracts to build technical military equipment. Cook was highly regarded by her supervisors, Ned Arcouette and Robert Martin, and the ASI controller, Michael Morgan, and received outstanding performance evaluations throughout her employment with ASI.

In 1991, appellee Clifton Lind assumed the title of General Manager of ASI. Lind was, however, on KDT's payroll. Lind did little to conceal his negative view of women. * * *

On December 17, 1992, Cook filed the present action against ASI, KDT, and Lind. * * *

In Spirt v. Teachers Ins. & Annuity Ass'n * * * we held with regard to Title VII that the term "employer" is "sufficiently broad to encompass any party who significantly affects access of any individual to employment opportunities, regardless of whether the party may technically be described as an 'employer' . . . at common law." * * * However, Spirt involved the relationship between an employer and a third-party insurer, not, as here, a relationship between a corporate parent and a corporate subsidiary. * * *

Courts of appeals that have addressed the question of parent-subsidiary liability have adopted a flexible four-part test aimed at determining the degree of interrelationship between the two entities. * * * Thus, the Fifth Circuit has held that [A] parent and subsidiary cannot be found to represent a single, integrated enterprise in the absence of evidence of (1) interrelation of operations, (2) centralized control of labor relations, (3) common management, and (4) common ownership or financial control. * * *

The National Labor Relations Board originally developed this test as a means for ascertaining whether two entities constituted a single employer in the context of labor disputes, and that test was subsequently approved by the Supreme Court in Radio & Television Broadcast Technicians Local Union 1264 v. Broadcast Service of Mobile, Inc., 380 U.S. 255, 85 S.Ct. 876, 13 L.Ed.2d 789 (1965) (per curiam). However, "[c]ourts applying this four-part standard in Title VII and related cases have focused on the second factor: centralized control of labor relations." * * * The Fifth Circuit has held that "this criterion has been further refined to the point that the critical question to be answered then is: What entity made the final decisions regarding employment matters related to the person claiming discrimination?" * * *

Therefore, as the Sixth Circuit has held, the four-factor test may be satisfied "by a showing that there is an amount of participation [that] is sufficient and necessary to the total employment process, even absent total control or ultimate authority over hiring decisions." * * *

We believe that the appropriate test under Title VII for determining when parent companies may be considered employers of a subsidiary's employees is the four-part test adopted by the Fifth, Sixth, and Eighth circuits. We focus our inquiry, as those circuits do, on the second factor, centralized control of labor relations. Applying this test, we conclude that KDT is not entitled to summary judgment because all four factors weigh powerfully in favor of allowing the action against KDT to continue. ASI is a wholly owned subsidiary of KDT. In addition, there is substantial evidence of an interrelation of operations between KDT and ASI. KDT ran ASI in a direct, hands-on fashion, establishing the operating practices and management practices of ASI. Moreover, KDT clearly maintained control of labor relations at ASI. For example, applications for employment with ASI went through KDT; all personnel status reports were approved by KDT; and ASI cleared all major employment decisions with KDT. Indeed, Mary Cook was herself hired as an ASI purchaser by Scott Zinnecker, the vice president of Human Resources at KDT, and was fired at the direction of Lind, who was paid directly by KDT. Finally, KDT and ASI maintained a common management structure. The President of ASI, Gordon Graves, operated out of the Texas office of KDT. There is thus sufficient evidence in the record to preclude summary judgment for KDT. * * *

Given the litigious nature of U.S. society what business form would be advisable for *Industrial*? What advice can you give Industrial to ensure that the general rule of corporate limited liability is maintained? It is important not to assume that these rules regarding risk limitation exists in other jurisdictions. See Section 3.4, infra for a contrast with the choice of entity under the Mexican legal system.

C. CONTROL OVER THE BUSINESS ENTITY

Control is another important factor in establishing an FDI, especially in the case where there is more than one owner. In a branch scenario, control is exerted directly from the corporation. The branch manager is an employee of the corporation. Therefore, the owner of the branch—the corporation—has direct control over it. In a similar fashion, the partner in a general partnership can have great control over the business. Since a partnership is a conduit entity the partner has a percentage ownership interest in the actual assets. The direct ownership of individual assets creates in the partner a right of partition. This right gives a partner with a small ownership interest a great amount of leverage over the partnership.

The owner of the corporation, however, has only indirect control over the subsidiary. The same can be generally said of the other corporate-like entities—the Limited Liability Company, Limited Partnership, and the Limited Liability Partnership. The owners of the corporation are the shareholders. Shareholder control over the corporation is indirect. This can place minority shareholders at a distinct disadvantage *vis a vis* the majority shareholders. There are three sources of corporate control—statutory, company level, and contractual or operational. Statutory control is found in the state corporate statute enacted by the legislatures of the particular state.

The management of the corporation is effected through the board of directors. Any effort to vest control on any other group of persons would not be allowed regardless of the agreement between the parties. The company level control can come from the Articles of Incorporation and from the corporate by-laws. The articles of incorporation must be in accordance with the state statute. The by-laws must be in accordance with the state statute and articles of incorporation.

McQUADE v. STONEHAM
New York Court of Appeals, 1934.
263 N.Y. 323, 189 N.E. 234.

* * * POUND, Chief Judge.

The action is brought to compel specific performance of an agreement between the parties, entered into to secure the control of National Exhibition Company, also called the Baseball Club (New York Nationals or 'Giants'). This was one of Stoneham's enterprises, which used the New York polo grounds for its home games. McGraw was manager of the Giants. McQuade was at the time the contract was entered into a city magistrate. He resigned December 8, 1930.

Defendant Stoneham became the owner of 1,306 shares, or a majority of the stock of National Exhibition Company. Plaintiff and defendant McGraw each purchased 70 shares of his stock. Plaintiff paid Stoneham $50,338.10 for the stock he purchased. As a part of the transaction, the agreement in question was entered into. It was dated May 21, 1919. Some of its pertinent provisions are 'VIII. The parties hereto will use their best endeavors for the purpose of continuing as directors of said Company and as officers thereof the following: 'Directors: 'Charles A. Stoneham, 'John J. McGraw, 'Francis X. McQuade '—with the right to the party of the first part [Stoneham] to name all additional directors as he sees fit: 'Officers: President $45,000 Vice President 7,500 Treasurer 7,400. 'Charles A. Stoneham, President, 'John J. McGraw, Vice–President, 'Francis X. McQuade, Treasurer. 'IX. No salaries are to be paid to any of the above officers or directors, except as follows: 'X. There shall be no change in said salaries, no change in the amount of capital, or the number of shares, no change or amendment of the by-laws of the corporation or any matters regarding the policy of the business of the corporation or any matters which may in anywise affect, endanger or interfere with the rights of minority stockholders, excepting upon the mutual and unanimous consent of all of the parties hereto. * * *

'XIV. This agreement shall continue and remain in force so long as the parties or any of them or the representative of any, own the stock referred to in this agreement, to wit, the party of the first part, 1,166 shares, the party of the second part 70 shares and the party of the third part 70 shares, except as may otherwise appear by this agreement. * * * '

In pursuance of this contract Stoneham became president and McGraw vice president of the corporation. McQuade became treasurer. In June, 1925, his salary was increased to $10,000 a year. He continued to act until May 2, 1928, when Leo J. Bondy was elected to succeed him. The board of directors consisted of seven men. The four outside of the parties hereto were selected by Stoneham and he had complete control over them. At the meeting of May 2, 1928, Stoneham and McGraw refrained from voting, McQuade voted for himself, and the other four voted for Bondy. Defendants did not keep their agreement with McQuade to use their best efforts to continue him as treasurer. On the contrary, he was dropped with their entire acquiescence. At the next stockholders' meeting he was dropped as a director although they might have elected him.

The courts below have refused to order the reinstatement of McQuade, but have given him damages for wrongful discharge, with a right to sue for future damages.

The cause for dropping McQuade was due to the falling out of friends. McQuade and Stoneham had disagreed. The trial court has found in substance that their numerous quarrels and disputes did not affect the orderly and efficient administration of the business of the corporation; that plaintiff was removed because he had antagonized the dominant Stoneham by persisting in challenging his power over the corporate treasury and for no misconduct on his part. The court also finds that plaintiff was removed by Stoneham for protecting the corporation and its minority stockholders. We will assume that Stoneham put him out when he might have retained him, merely in order to get rid of him.

Defendants say that the contract in suit was void because the directors held their office charged with the duty to act for the corporation according to their best judgment and that any contract, which compels a director to vote to keep any particular person in office and at a stated salary is illegal. Directors are the exclusive executive representatives of the corporation, charged with administration of its internal affairs and the management and use of its assets. They manage the business of the corporation. * * * 'An agreement to continue a man as president is dependent upon his continued loyalty to the interests of the corporation.' * * * So much is undisputed.

Plaintiff contends that the converse of this proposition is true and that an agreement among directors to continue a man as an officer of a corporation is not to be broken so long as such officer is loyal to the interests of the corporation and that, as plaintiff has been found loyal to the corporation, the agreement of defendants is enforceable.

Although it has been held that an agreement among stockholders whereby it is attempted to divest the directors of their power to discharge an unfaithful employee of the corporation is illegal as against public policy (Fells v. Katz, supra), it must be equally true that the stockholders may not, by agreement among themselves, control the directors in the exercise of the judgment vested in them by virtue of their office to elect officers and fix salaries. Their motives may not be questioned so long as their acts are legal. The bad faith or the improper motives of the parties does not change the rule. * * * Directors may not by agreements entered into as stockholders abrogate their independent judgment. * * *

Stockholders may, of course, combine to elect directors. That rule is well settled. As Holmes, C. J., pointedly said (Brightman v. Bates, 175 Mass. 105, 111, 55 N. E. 809, 811): 'If stockholders want to make their power felt, they must unite. There is no reason why a majority should not agree to keep together.' The power to unite is, however, limited to the election of directors and is not extended to contracts whereby limitations are placed on the power of directors to manage the business of the corporation by the selection of agents at defined salaries.

The minority shareholders whose interests McQuade says he has been punished for protecting, are not, aside from himself, complaining about his discharge. He is not acting for the corporation or for them in this action. It is impossible to see how the corporation has been injured by the substitution of Bondy as treasurer in place of McQuade. As McQuade represents himself in this action and seeks redress for his own wrongs, 'we prefer to listen to [the corporation and the minority stockholders] before any decision as to their wrongs.' * * *

It is urged that we should pay heed to the morals and manners of the market place to sustain this agreement and that we should hold that its violation gives rise to a cause of action for damages rather than base our decision on any outworn notions of public policy. Public policy is a dangerous guide in determining the validity of a contract and courts should not interfere lightly with the freedom of competent parties to make their own contracts. We do not close our eyes to the fact that such agreements, tacitly or openly arrived at, are not uncommon, especially in close corporations where the stockholders are doing business for convenience under a corporate organization. We know that majority stockholders, united in voting trusts, effectively manage the business of a corporation by choosing trustworthy directors to reflect their policies in the corporate management. Nor are we unmindful that McQuade has, so the court has found, been shabbily treated as a purchaser of stock from Stoneham. We have said: 'A trustee is held to something stricter than the morals of the market place' (Meinhard v. Salmon, 249 N. Y. 458, 464, 164 N. E. 545, 546, 62 A. L. R. 1), but Stoneham and McGraw were not trustees for McQuade as an individual. Their duty was to the corporation and its stockholders, to be exercised according to their unrestricted lawful judgment. They were under no legal obligation to deal righteously with McQuade if it was against public policy to do so.

The courts do not enforce mere moral obligations, nor legal ones either, unless some one seeks to establish rights, which may be waived by custom and for convenience. We are constrained by authority to hold that a contract is illegal and void so far as it precludes the board of directors, at the risk of incurring legal liability, from changing officers, salaries, or policies or retaining individuals in office, except by consent of the contracting parties. On the whole, such a holding is probably preferable to one, which would open the courts to pass on the motives of directors in the lawful exercise of their trust.

* * *

———

Is control an important issue in the case of a wholly owned subsidiary? The lawyer plays a very important role in assisting the client in understanding and using this information to realize the client's plan. Control over the FDI can also be affected through contractual undertakings. See negotiating the International Equity Joint Venture, Section 4.1, infra for a discussion of different control strategies that can be used.

D.   PROFIT MAXIMIZATION AND DISTRIBUTION

Maximizing profit can be achieved by either increasing revenue or lowering expenses. The increase in revenue is the result of market and operational factors. *Industrial* would like to maximize the profit in its U.S. investment. The choice of entity decision does not have a direct correlation with increased revenue. However, the decision could have a substantial effect on its income tax. The income tax effect of the choice of entity is discussed in Section 2.3, infra. Also for a complete discussion of profit maximization and distribution see also Sections 3.1 and 4.1, infra.

Profit distribution follows control. In the case of the branch the profit distribution is direct—the corporate owner makes the distribution. In the General Partnership, Limited Partnership and Limited Liability Partnership, profit distributions are made pursuant to the contract that formed the entity. In the case of a corporation and Limited Liability Company, the owners have indirect control over the profit distribution. In the case of a corporation, the board of directors makes the decision. In the Limited Liability Company, the Board of Managers decides.

DODGE v. FORD MOTOR CO.
Michigan Supreme Court, 1919.
204 Mich. 459, 170 N.W. 668.

* * *

When plaintiffs made their complaint and demand for further dividends, the Ford Motor Company had concluded its most prosperous year of business. The demand for its cars at the price of the preceding year continued. It could make and could market in the year beginning August 1, 1916, more than 500,000 cars. Sales of parts and repairs would necessarily increase. The cost of materials was likely to advance, and perhaps the price of labor; but it reasonably might have expected a profit for the year of upwards of $60,000,000. It had assets of more than $132,000,000, a surplus of almost $112,000,000, and its cash on hand and municipal bonds were nearly $54,000,000. Its total liabilities, including capital stock, were a little over $20,000,000. It had declared no special dividend during the business year except the October, 1915, dividend. It had been the practice, under similar circumstances, to declare larger dividends. Considering only these facts, a refusal to declare and pay further dividends appears to be not an exercise of discretion on the part of the directors, but an arbitrary refusal to do what the circumstances required to be done. These facts and others call upon the directors to justify their action, or failure or refusal to act. In justification, the defendants have offered testimony tending to prove, and which does prove, the following facts: It had been the policy of the corporation for a considerable time to annually reduce the selling price of cars, while keeping up, or improving, their quality. * * *

It is hoped, by Mr. Ford, that eventually 1,000,000 cars will be annually produced. The contemplated changes will permit the increased output. The plan, as affecting the profits of the business for the year beginning August 1, 1916, and thereafter, calls for a reduction in the selling price of the cars. It is true that this price might be at any time increased, but the plan called for the reduction in price of $80 a car. The capacity of the plant, without the additions thereto voted to be made (without a part of them at least), would produce more than 600,000 cars annually. This number, and more, could have been sold for $440 instead of $360, a difference in the return for capital, labor, and materials employed of at least $48,000,000. In short, the plan does not call for and is not intended to produce immediately a more profitable business, but a less profitable one; not only less profitable than formerly, but less profitable than it is admitted it might be made. The apparent immediate effect will be to diminish the value of shares and the returns to shareholders.

It is the contention of plaintiffs that the apparent effect of the plan is intended to be the continued and continuing effect of it, and that it is deliberately proposed, not of record and not by official corporate declaration, but nevertheless proposed, to continue the corporation henceforth as a semi-eleemosynary institution and not as a business institution. In support of this contention, they point to the attitude and to the expressions of Mr. Henry Ford.

Mr. Henry Ford is the dominant force in the business of the Ford Motor Company. No plan of operations could be adopted unless he consented, and no board of directors can be elected whom he does not favor. One of the directors of the company has no stock. One share was assigned to him to qualify him for the position, but it is not claimed that he owns it. A business, one of the largest in the world, and one of the most profitable, has been built up. It employs many men, at good pay.

'My ambition,' said Mr. Ford, 'is to employ still more men, to spread the benefits of this industrial system to the greatest possible number, to help them build up their lives and their homes. To do this we are putting the greatest share of our profits back in the business.'

'With regard to dividends, the company paid sixty per cent. on its capitalization of two million dollars, or $1,200,000, leaving $58,000,000 to reinvest for the growth of the company. This is Mr. Ford's policy at present, and it is understood that the other stockholders cheerfully accede to this plan.'

He had made up his mind in the summer of 1916 that no dividends other than the regular dividends should be paid, 'for the present.'

'Q. For how long? Had you fixed in your mind any time in the future, when you were going to pay—A. No.

'Q. That was indefinite in the future? A. That was indefinite; yes, sir.'

The record, and especially the testimony of Mr. Ford, convinces that he has to some extent the attitude towards shareholders of one who has dispensed and distributed to them large gains and that they should be content to take what he chooses to give. His testimony creates the impression, also, that he thinks the Ford Motor Company has made too much money, has had too large profits, and that, although large profits might be still earned, a sharing of them with the public, by reducing the price of the output of the company, ought to be undertaken. We have no doubt that certain sentiments, philanthropic and altruistic, creditable to Mr. Ford, had large influence in determining the policy to be pursued by the Ford *506 Motor Company—the policy which has been herein referred to. * * *

A business corporation is organized and carried on primarily for the profit of the stockholders. The powers of the directors are to be employed for that end. The discretion of directors is to be exercised in the choice of means to attain that end, and does not extend to a change in the end itself, to the reduction of profits, or to the non-distribution of profits among stockholders in order to devote them to other purposes.

There is committed to the discretion of directors, a discretion to be exercised in good faith, the infinite details of business, including the wages which shall be paid to employees, the number of hours they shall work, the conditions under which labor shall be carried on, and the price for which products shall be offered to the public.

It is said by appellants that the motives of the board members are not material and will not be inquired into by the court so long as their acts are within their lawful powers. As we have pointed out, and the proposition does not require argument to sustain it, it is not within the lawful powers of a board of directors to shape and conduct the affairs of a corporation for the merely incidental benefit of shareholders and for the primary purpose of benefiting others, and no one will contend that, if the avowed purpose of the defendant directors was to sacrifice the interests of shareholders, it would not be the duty of the courts to interfere.

We are not, however, persuaded that we should interfere with the proposed expansion of the business of the Ford Motor Company. In view of the fact that the selling price of products may be increased at any time, the ultimate results of the larger business cannot be certainly estimated. The judges are not business experts. It is recognized that plans must often be made for a long future, for expected competition, for a continuing as well as an immediately profitable venture. The experience of the Ford Motor Company is evidence of capable management of its affairs. It may be noticed, incidentally, that it took from the public the money required for the execution of its plan, and that the very considerable salaries paid to Mr. Ford and to certain executive officers and employees were not diminished. We are not satisfied that the alleged motives of the directors, in so far as they are reflected in the conduct of the business, menace the interests of shareholders. It is enough to say, perhaps, that the court of equity is at all times open to complaining shareholders having a just grievance.

Assuming the general plan and policy of expansion and the details of it to have been sufficiently, formally, approved at the October and November, 1917, meetings of directors, and assuming further that the plan and policy and the details agreed upon were for the best ultimate interest of the company and therefore of its shareholders, what does it amount to in justification of a refusal to declare and pay a special dividend or dividends? The Ford Motor Company was able to estimate with nicety its income and profit. It could sell more cars than it could make. Having ascertained what it would cost to produce a car and to sell it, the profit upon each car depended upon the selling price. That being fixed, the yearly income and profit was determinable, and, within slight variations, was certain. * * *

The plight of the Dodge brothers highlights the classic case of an attempted minority shareholder freeze out by the majority. In a corporation, control over the board means control over the benefits a corporation can provide. For example, the minority cannot easily compel the payment of dividends. There are many ways to avoid the result in *Ford* where the minority shareholders won. The board of directors also makes decisions on hiring and the letting of contracts. Avoiding minority freeze-outs is discussed in Section 4.1, infra.

E.   FORMATION OF THE ENTITY

1.   *Articles of Incorporation*

Articles of Incorporation

The Articles of Incorporation are signed by the Incorporator for the purpose of forming a Corporation Under The Texas General Business Corporation Act as follows:

Article 1

NAME

§ 1.1   Name: The name of the corporation is Industrial, Inc.

Article 2

PURPOSE

§ 2.1   Purpose: The purpose for which the Corporation is organized is to transact all lawful business for which Corporations may be organized under the Business Corporation Act of the State of Texas.

Article 3

SHARES

§ 3.1   Authorized Stock: The total authorized stock is twenty million common shares having no par value.

Article 4

DIRECTORS

§ 4.1   Initial Directors: The initial Board shall consist of two Directors and the names and addresses of the persons who shall serve as Directors until the first meeting of Stockholders or until their successors can be elected and qualified are:

Juan Gomez   1000 Plaza Industrial
Guadalajara, Jalisco,
Mexico

Andres Gomez   1000 Plaza Industrial
Guadalajara, Jalisco,
Mexico

Article 5

REGISTERED OFFICE

§ 5.1   Registered Office: The address of the initial registered office is: 1735 Avenue of The Americas, San Antonio, Texas. The name of the initial registered agent at such address is John Smith.

Article 6

INCORPORATORS

§ 6.1   Incorporators: The name and address of the Incorporator is as follows:

Andres Gomez   1000 Plaza Industrial
                    Guadalajara, Jalisco,
                    Mexico

Article 7

TERM

§ 7.1   Term: The term of existence of the Corporation shall be perpetual.

In witness whereof, the undersigned, the Incorporator of the above-named Corporation, has hereunto signed these Articles of Incorporation on this the 30th day of June, 2000.

_____   1000 Plaza Industrial
Andres Gomez   Guadalajara, Jalisco,
                          Mexico

_____

The corporation is a creature of statute. The legislation governing its formation is found in state law. The various state statutes vary in certain detail but are generally the same. The branch is formed in a particular jurisdiction by registering the foreign corporation pursuant to the particular state statute. The articles of incorporation excerpted above are sufficient to form a Texas corporation. The branch, like the corporation is also a creature of statute. However, in the case of a branch, it is the foreign corporation that must be registered. The Limited Liability Company formation procedures are similar to the corporation. The General Partnership is formed through contract. The Limited Partnership and Limited Liability Partnership are also formed by contract and through state registration.

2.   *Formation Procedures*

a.   *Preparing the Articles of Incorporation*

The procedure for forming a corporation is simple yet formal and rigid. The first step in the incorporation process is to prepare the articles of incorporation. The articles of incorporation included above are an example of a simple incorporation document. The articles include the bare statutory minimum. The needs of the client may require a more detailed document and the lawyer should act accordingly. A corporation is created by state law. Therefore, care should be taken that the particular state requirements are being met. If the statutory requirements are not met, the Secretary of State will reject the articles of incorporation.

(1) The Name of the Corporation

Each corporation must have a name. It is best to get several alternative names and check the availability with the secretary of state of the particular state before finalizing. The name can be checked through the telephone or the Internet. The availability of a name, and the use of it on the articles, does not create any protection of the name as an intellectual property right. In order to protect the name for those purposes there must be further federal and state registrations which is beyond the scope of this casebook. The MBCA requires the inclusion of the term incorporation, corporation, company or limited or an abbreviation of those terms. Articles without this designation will not be accepted for filing.

(2) Purpose and Duration

It is generally best to include a broad business purpose. The broad purpose allows a change of corporate business without having to possibly amend the articles of incorporation. The corporation is allowed to exist in perpetuity. This is usually the best alternative since dissolving and liquidating the company at some arbitrary point in time could have negative business and tax implications.

(3) Authorized Capital

Article 3.1 states "The total authorized stock is twenty million common shares without par value." These shares are logically referred to as the authorized shares. Once shares are sold they are said to be issued and outstanding. The holders of the issued and outstanding shares are the owners of the corporation. For example, assume the corporation sells ten million shares. The holders of the ten million shares own one hundred percent of the corporation. The ten million remaining authorized shares have no effect until they are issued.

Of course the entire twenty million shares could be sold at the inception. In that case the owners of the corporation would be the holders of the twenty million shares issued and outstanding shares. A better practice is to refrain from selling all of the authorized shares at the formation. Keeping authorized shares allows for the future issuance of stock without having to amend the articles of incorporation. Determining the amount of shares to sell is part of the broader issue of corporate capitalization. For a discussion of the myriad of issues that emerge in the corporate capitalization issue, see Section 4.1, infra.

(4) The Persons Involved in the Corporate Formation

MBCA Section 2.02. states that the name and address of the registered agent and incorporator must be included in the articles of incorporation. The initial board of directors and their addresses may also be included, although it is not required. The shareholders and officers of the corporation are not listed in the articles of incorporation. The Incorporator is responsible for signing the Articles of Incorporation, sending the articles of incorporation to the Secretary of State and performing any function called upon him pursuant to MBCA § 2.05.(a)(2). The initial board members are to serve in the capacity of directors until the organizational meeting.

b. The Organizational Meeting

The next step in the corporate formation process is the organizational meeting. Once the Secretary of State accepts the Articles of Incorporation, a corporate charter (or license) is granted. The organizational meeting is called by either a majority of the initial board of directors or Incorporators, whatever the case may be. The organizational meeting is the occasion when the initial sale of shares is done. The bylaws and fiscal year of the corporation are also adopted at the organizational meeting. Other important matters concluded in the organizational meeting include the appointment of officers and the execution of any employment contracts.

Other typical items on the agenda include establishing the principal office, naming the bank with which the corporation will do business, adopting the corporate seal, and conducting any other business that may be needed. That is the only public information that is found on the Articles of Incorporation. The action taken at the organizational meeting is not public information. The shareholders remain confidential. The by-laws of the corporation, which provide the important private rules on how the corporation will be governed, are also confidential. The following is a summary of the typical inclusions in the by-laws.

(1) General Information

The by-laws are private rules adopted at the corporate level. They must, however, be consistent with the state corporation statute and the articles of incorporation. Any by-law that conflicts with these two are void. The by-laws typically include the address of the principal offices and the rules on a variety of administrative issues. This includes information on naming the capital stock transfer agent and registrar, determining the stockholders entitled to vote, maintaining the stock transfer ledger, and any restrictions that have been placed on the transfer of stock.

Also included is who has the authority to sign contracts, checks, and proxies. Additionally, the buy-laws will describe the form of the corporate seal, adopt the fiscal year of the corporation and the procedures for amending the by-laws. The by-laws also provide the very important rules on corporate governance. The corporation may be a legal person but is must act through others. The by-laws provide the procedures for the people who can speak for the corporation—the shareholders, directors, and officers.

Generally, the board of directors appoints the officers of the corporation. The officers, headed by the president, manage the day-to-day operations. The board of directors manages the overall operations of the corporation making many of the critical decisions that need to be made. The board of directors serves at the pleasure of the shareholders that elect them. The shareholders are the owners of the corporation and as such have the final say on corporate matters.

(2) The Shareholders, Directors, and Officers

The shareholders of a corporation must meet at least once a year. The by-laws add details to this requirement by providing the time, place, and notice requirements for these annual meetings. Shareholders are also permitted to have special meetings. The by-laws identify the person or persons who can call the meeting, and gives the time, place, and notice requirements. They also provide information on quorum and voting requirements (e.g. simple majority or supermajority) or whether a written consent can serve in lieu of a meeting.

The by-laws also provide the rules for the number of directors the corporation will have and the board committees that will be established. The qualifications, term, and how the board members are elected and removed is also typically included. Other rules relating to filling board vacancies and the compensation of board members are also provided. Like shareholders, directors are obliged to meet at least once a year or more often if necessary. The by-laws provide the time, place, and notice requirements for the annual meetings. They also identify the person or persons who can call the meeting, and gives the time, place, notice requirements, quorum and voting requirements. The by-laws also include what officer positions the corporation will have—President, Vice–President(s), Secretary, and Treasurer. They will also include qualifications for the officers, how they will be selected, their term of office, removal procedures, their duties and their salaries.

SECTION 2.3   THE U.S. FEDERAL INCOME TAX ON INTERNATIONAL TRANSACTIONS

A. INTRODUCTION

Apart from the international and domestic rules regulating international trade, there is a distinct, complex, and pervasive body of law that affects international business transactions—the income tax law. The income tax rates, which in some countries reach as high as 50%, constitutes a substantial cost greatly impacting profitability. A complicating factor is the absence of the government's direct input in the deal planning process. For example, in negotiating a sales contract, there is active involvement by the Buyer and Seller in striking a deal.

Hopefully, issues that have negative cost implications are resolved prior to the consummation of the transaction. However, the government's view on a particular tax issue may not even arise until several years after the deal is consummated, when the taxpayer is audited. Acting like a silent partner, the government comes in after the transaction has been completed and extracts its due, not necessarily respecting the transaction as structured. Moreover, in an international transaction, there may be two or more countries assessing an income tax on the same income.

In the Western Hemisphere, domestic tax rules and enforcement mechanisms have been disparate. The U.S. system for reporting and paying income taxes is voluntary. The 'voluntary' nature of the system is helped along by the aggressive audit and collection attitude of the Internal Revenue Service. Many Latin American businesses are aware that, historically, tax compliance is enforced more efficiently in the U.S. than in their countries. In Latin America, the lack of computer capability as well as corruption by lower level government auditors has created an environment where compliance with tax laws is poor.

Many Latin Americans are careful to plan their affairs in the U.S. with scant planning for the tax implications in their own country. Presently, the trend is changing. For better or worse, Latin American tax authorities are looking to the U.S. model for examining returns. In Mexico, there are now cases being reported of high-level business owners being charged with tax evasion. Tax strategies in the Western Hemisphere will become more complex in the future since these countries are tightening up the substantive income tax laws and are increasing their enforcement.

To many lawyers, the income tax system is a black box—information is submitted to a tax lawyer or CPA and answers come out. My experience has been that superb business lawyers go to great lengths in avoiding tax issues, eschewing even a rudimentary analysis of the factors that play a part in a tax strategy. The problem with this attitude is that income tax rules are pervasive, inescapable, touching virtually all types of international business transactions. In my experience there was never a case where the client requested advice on an international business transaction while having no interest in the income tax effect. In many cases the income tax is the tail that wags the dog.

The international business lawyer that has a basic understanding of the tax implications in a transaction becomes more valuable to her clients, helping them steer clear of the income tax traps for the unwary. But keep heart, as we go through the materials, you will discover that the incomes tax rules are fairly logical albeit technical. In addition, the tax materials in this casebook are intended to provide a thumbnail sketch of the applicable tax rules for the non-tax international business-planning lawyer. It is assumed the reader has no prior knowledge of tax law or accounting concepts. The purpose is to analyze the basic tax rules that can prevent costly errors.

There are two legal systems that govern the tax implications of international business transactions—the internal revenue code and the bilateral tax treaty network. The Internal Revenue Code[22] governs domestic and international transactions entered into by U.S. and non-U.S. persons. It is lengthy, arcane, and in some cases almost indecipherable. The bilateral tax treaty network on the other hand simplifies many of the tax rules. Since only one system can apply to a given transaction, in order to determine the applicable system there must be an analysis of the relationship between the code and treaty provision, the transaction in question, and the taxpayer engaging in it. The analysis begins with the basic rules under the Internal Revenue Code.

B.   THE RULES UNDER THE INTERNAL REVENUE CODE

The rules affecting international business transactions are scattered in the over nine thousand sections of the much-maligned Internal Revenue Code found in *26 USC § 1 et seq*. While the basic law is contained in the Code, explanations are found in Treasury Regulations, Revenue Rulings, and other pronouncements from the Internal Revenue Service. There are also treatises that deal with international tax issues. The first step in the process is in determining if there is a taxable event.

1.   *The Taxable Event*

While a detailed analysis of this question requires a course in tax fundamentals, a brief explanation will suffice for our purposes. A taxable event generally occurs when a taxpayer has gross income. Under *I.R.C. § 61 (1986)* gross income is defined as "... all income from whatever source derived ..." While the Code uses a circular definition—gross income is income—courts have more precisely and broadly construed the term. The range of transactions that can yield gross income is broad. Virtually any transaction that yields an economic benefit to the taxpayer is gross income unless some Code provision specifically excludes the item as gross income.

For example, Uncle Harry leaves Taxpayer a million dollars in his will as an inheritance. The taxpayer upon receipt of the money has a clear economic benefit. However, *I.R.C. § 102(a)(1986)* provides that "... gross income does not include the value of property acquired by ... inheritance." Therefore, Taxpayer receives the money tax-free. On the other hand, assume taxpayer finds a one hundred-dollar bill in the street. The finder has an economic enrichment of one hundred dollars. Since there is no Code section that comes to the rescue, the taxpayer is subject to tax on her good fortune. She has gross income. Analyzing all the possible scenarios in order to determine gross income is beyond the scope of this book. For purposes of simplicity, in this chapter we assume that a taxable event exists.

2.   *Determining Status*

The Code divides people in two categories—U.S. Persons or non-U.S. persons. Status has a profound effect on the jurisdiction to impose the U.S. federal income tax. U.S. persons pay tax on worldwide income while

---

22.   26 USC § 1 et. seq. (1986).

non-U.S. persons generally pay tax only on U.S. source income. Under *IRC § 7701(a)(30)(A)-(C) (1986)* an U.S. person is a citizen or resident of the United States, a domestic corporation, or a domestic partnership. Conversely, a non-U.S. person is one who is not an U.S. person. Determining the status of corporations is fairly straightforward. The determining characteristic in the case of corporations is the place of incorporation. If a corporation is formed in a foreign country, it is a non-U.S. person. Conversely, if formed in one of the fifty states, it is an U.S. person regardless of the citizenship of the owners.

Determining the status of an individual is more complex. A citizen or resident of the U.S. is a U.S. person for tax purposes. Citizenship is determined by place of birth or where naturalized. Residency for tax purposes is defined by a technical set of rules found in *I.R.C. § 7701(b) (1986)*. A resident alien is an individual who either holds an U.S. Green Card or is deemed to be substantially present in the U.S. as determined under *I.R.C. § 7701(b)(3)(1986)*. It is important to note that immigration status is different from tax status. An individual may be a non-immigrant under the immigration and naturalization laws and a resident alien for tax purposes.

A nonresident alien (NRA) is considered as a non-U.S. person and taxed on U.S. source income unless the NRA was an U.S. citizen who renounced citizenship for tax avoidance purposes. In that case the NRA can be taxed as an U.S. person. Whether a person renounced citizenship for tax purposes is a fact question.

FURSTENBERG v. C.I.R.
United States Tax Court, 1984.
83 T.C. 755.

* * *

FEATHERSTON, Judge:

Respondent determined deficiencies in petitioner's Federal income taxes as set forth below:

Year	Deficiency
1975	$ 595,017
1976	1,476,718
1977	3,207,600

After concessions, the issues for decision are as follows:

1. Whether petitioner's loss of her United States citizenship on December 23, 1975, had as one of its principal purposes the avoidance of United States taxes within the meaning of section 877(a) * * *

At the time she filed her petition in this case, petitioner resided at 34 Boulevard D'Italie, Monte Carlo, Monaco. * * *

Petitioner was born on December 17, 1919, in Houston, Texas. She is the daughter of Sarah Campbell Blaffer and Robert Lee Blaffer; her father was one of the founders of Humble Oil & Refining Co., the predecessor of Exxon Corporation.

Petitioner's formal education began at Kincaid, a day school in Houston. She then went to the Ethel Walker School in Connecticut. During World War II, petitioner attended a French school for girls in New York where instruction was exclusively in French. She later studied languages and art at the University of Mexico.

Because of the financial success of her father, petitioner's family was able to travel a great deal. As a child, petitioner traveled extensively with her family, visiting Europe, in particular, France.

Petitioner had a close relationship as a child with her governess, a Frenchwoman named Suzanne Glemet, described by petitioner as a 'second mother.' She spent several summers in France at the family home of her governess in Charent, in the southwest part of France near Bordeaux.

Petitioner learned to speak French as her 'first language,' i.e., before she learned to speak English. She is so fluent in French, in fact, that she is taken for a French person when she speaks. In addition to English and French, petitioner also speaks Spanish and German.

PETITIONER'S MARRIAGES TO E. J. HUDSON AND RICHARD J. SHERIDAN

On August 7, 1945, petitioner married E. J. Hudson (Hudson), a petroleum engineer. * * * Petitioner was divorced from Hudson on March 14, 1963. * * *

On January 25, 1968, petitioner married Richard M. Sheridan (Sheridan), an international executive of Mobil Oil Corporation, in Tokyo, Japan. * * * Petitioner separated from Sheridan in the summer of 1970, and was divorced from him on November 29, 1971. * * *

PETITIONER'S MOVE TO PARIS

In August 1969, petitioner obtained an option for the purchase of an apartment in a building to be constructed at 33 Avenue Foch in Paris; she purchased the apartment in January 1970. When construction of the apartment was completed, petitioner moved in, taking her personal belongings from London. It is stipulated that petitioner was a resident of France from 1970 through 1977, the last year here in controversy. * * *

By this time in her life, petitioner had a great many friends in France and other European countries; indeed, the majority of her close friends were in Europe. While living in Paris, petitioner pursued her interest in the art world, visiting many museums and attending art exhibits, openings and auctions both in Paris and elsewhere in Europe. * * *

PETITIONER'S MARRIAGE TO PRINCE TASSILO VON FURSTENBERG

Petitioner first met Prince Tassilo von Furstenberg (Furstenberg) in Trieste, Italy, in 1961. When they met, petitioner was in the process of obtaining her divorce from Mr. Hudson. Furstenberg, who was living in Italy at the time, was married to Clara Agnelli (Agnelli), an Italian woman from whom he had been separated for years. At that time, however, divorces were prohibited under Italian law. * * *

Petitioner and Furstenberg were married in Paris on October 17, 1975, in a civil ceremony attended only by their children and a few close friends. A buffet luncheon reception was given after the wedding at the apartment of Baron and Baroness Hubert von Pantz, Austrian friends of the Furstenbergs, and was attended by approximately 150 persons including Baron Otto Eiselberg, the Austrian Ambassador to France. The ambassador, assuming that petitioner would adopt the Austrian citizenship of her new husband, assured petitioner that he could simplify naturalization procedures for her. * * *

PETITIONER'S ADOPTION OF AUSTRIAN CITIZENSHIP

Members of Furstenberg's family first became princes of the Holy Roman Empire in 1664. He was and is a citizen of Austria; his Austrian heritage and ties are very important to him. At the time they decided to marry in early 1975, Furstenberg explained to petitioner the importance of his Austrian heritage and expressed to her his desire that she adopt Austrian nationality.

Cognizant of the fact that 'it was more or less expected of that type of European aristocracy,' petitioner confirmed her decision with her commitment to Furstenberg that she would be 'very proud to marry him, bear his name, his title, and his nationality.' Although she had been living outside of the United States for some years, at no time did petitioner ever consider the possibility of adopting European citizenship until her engagement to Furstenberg.

Petitioner felt that part of bearing Furstenberg's name and title 'was to be Austrian the way he wished it.' Further, by 1975, petitioner had been living in Europe continuously for 7 years; she preferred living in Europe more than anywhere else. Finally, petitioner felt that by adopting Austrian citizenship, she 'was going back to (her own) * * * European heritage and roots.' At the time petitioner agreed to adopt Furstenberg's Austrian nationality, in early 1975, when they decided to marry, she did not know that by so doing, she would lose her United States citizenship. Further, she did not know what the tax consequences of such an action would be.

During their honeymoon, Furstenberg reminded petitioner of her agreement to become an Austrian citizen. Petitioner told her husband that she would attend to the matter as soon as she could. * * *

As he had promised at petitioner's wedding reception, the naturalization process was simplified for petitioner at the request of Baron

Eiselberg, Austrian Ambassador to France. Petitioner obtained Austrian citizenship by naturalization on her own application on December 23, 1975; she thereby lost her United States citizenship on the same day under the provisions of section 349(a)(1) of the Immigration and Nationality Act of 1952, 66 Stat. 267.

Petitioner's Discussions With Her Accountant

During the 1970's, petitioner's United States tax returns were prepared by Arthur Young & Company, an accounting firm. The individual at Arthur Young with whom petitioner discussed her tax returns was Gordon S. Moore (Moore), who is now deceased. Petitioner's practice was to meet with Moore once a year to discuss her current year's tax return, although some years she may have met with Moore twice.

In late April or early May 1975, after her decision to marry Furstenberg and adopt his citizenship, petitioner met with Moore when she came to Houston to attend to her mother who was terminally ill. At their meeting, petitioner informed Moore that she intended to marry Furstenberg, adopt Austrian citizenship, and live with her husband in Paris. She asked Moore to advise her concerning the income tax consequences of her plans.

Moore informed petitioner at this meeting that her plan to marry and adopt Austrian nationality would 'complicate' her taxes. He warned petitioner about French taxes, telling her that the French taxes could be very high, and that they were rising. Moore told petitioner that he would look into it for her. * * *

Petitioner's Tax Returns: 1974—1977

Petitioner filed income tax returns and reported income and tax liability for 1974 through 1977 as described below:

1974: As a United States citizen for the entire year, petitioner filed a Form 1040 for 1974. She reported total income of $766,297.08, consisting principally of dividend income from various sources in the amount of $688,766.55. Her total United States tax liability for the year, computed under the graduated rates applicable to United States citizens, was $155,990.54.

1975: For 1975, petitioner filed a Form 1040NR, U.S. Nonresident Alien Income Tax Return, attaching to it a Form 1040. Schedule 1 of the Form 1040NR is entitled 'General Information' and states in relevant part:

Taxpayer was a resident of France during the entire year of 1975. She was a U.S. Citizen until December 23, 1975 on which date she acquired the nationality of Austria by naturalization.

* * *

Opinion

* * *

Petitioner, a United States citizen by birth, adopted Austrian citizenship on December 23, 1975, thereby losing her United States citizenship. The controversy at hand centers on the income tax consequences flowing from petitioner's expatriation.

Until December 23, 1975, the date of her expatriation, petitioner reported her income and paid United States income taxes based on the graduated tax rates applicable to all United States citizens. Thereafter, as an Austrian citizen residing in Paris, petitioner became a nonresident alien for United States tax purposes. She reported her United States source income as a nonresident alien for the last week of 1975 (December 23–31) and for 1976 and 1977. In her nonresident alien returns (Forms 1040NR) for the periods at issue, petitioner reported that, as a nonresident alien resident in France, she was taxable under section 871 and the French Tax Treaty as follows:

1. She was subject to tax on her United States source dividends and interest at the respective rates of 15 percent and 10 percent under Articles 9 and 10 of the French Tax Treaty. Petitioner received substantial trust distributions in late 1975, which she reported on her 1975 nonresident alien return as dividends taxable at the 15 percent rate under the French Tax Treaty;

2. She was subject to tax on her other items of United States source income not covered by the treaty (royalties, rent, director's fees) at the flat rate of 30 percent under section 871; and

3. She was not subject to United States tax on her capital gains under Article 12 of the French Tax Treaty. Respondent contends that the loss of petitioner's citizenship had for one of its principal purposes the avoidance of United States taxes so as to subject petitioner's United States source income and capital gains to taxation under the graduated tax rates made applicable by section 877 to former United States citizens who expatriate for tax avoidance purposes. Petitioner, in the first instance, urges us to resolve this factual issue in her favor by finding that tax avoidance was not one of her principal purposes in expatriating, thus finding her to be taxable as a nonresident alien under the more favorable rates prescribed by section 871 and the French Tax Treaty. * * *

In general, section 877 provides that a nonresident alien individual who loses his United States citizenship shall be subject to tax on his United States source income, for the 10–year period following such loss, at the graduated tax rates applicable to United States citizens rather than more favorable rates applicable to nonresident aliens, unless the loss of citizenship did not have for one of its principal purposes the avoidance of United States taxes. * * * Section 877(e) specifically assigns the burden of proving the lack of a tax avoidance motive on the expatriate if respondent establishes that it is reasonable to believe that the individual's loss of United States citizenship would result in a substantial reduction in taxes. The parties have stipulated that respondent has met his initial burden of proof under section 877(e). Thus, the burden is on petitioner to demonstrate that tax avoidance was not one of her principal purposes in expatriating. The issue is purely factual.

Although we have never specifically interpreted the phrase 'one of its principal purposes' in the context of section 877, we find instructive the following definition set forth in Dittler Bros., Inc. v. Commissioner, 72 T.C. 896, 915 (1979), affd. without published opinion 642 F.2d 1211 (5th Cir.1981), in which the Court was called upon to determine, under section 367, whether or not a certain translation was in 'pursuance of a plan having as one of its principal purposes the avoidance of Federal income taxes:' (W)e believe that the term 'principal purpose' should be construed in accordance with its ordinary meaning. Such a rule of statutory construction has been endorsed by the Supreme Court. Malat v. Riddell, 383 U.S. 569, 571 (1966). Webster's New Collegiate Dictionary defines 'principal' as 'first in rank, authority, importance, or degree.' Thus, the proper inquiry hereunder is whether the exchange of manufacturing know-how was in pursuance of a plan having as one of its 'first-in-importance' purposes the avoidance of Federal income taxes.

After careful consideration of all the evidence, we conclude that petitioner has carried her burden under section 877(e); we are convinced that petitioner did not have tax avoidance as one of her principal or 'first in importance' purposes in expatriating.

With respect to her intent in expatriating, petitioner testified that: She and Furstenberg decided to marry in early 1975. At that time, Furstenberg, a titled Austrian aristocrat, requested that petitioner adopt his Austrian citizenship. Although she had been living abroad for over 7 years, petitioner had never before considered expatriation. Desiring, however, to do what she could to make her third marriage a success and cognizant of the fact that it was general European custom for a wife to adopt the nationality of her husband, petitioner committed herself at the time of her decision to marry Furstenberg in early 1975 to 'bear his name, his title, and his nationality.'

Petitioner's decision to expatriate at the time of her marriage was further motivated, as she testified, by her ever-increasing, life-long ties to Europe; her preference for living in Europe rather than anywhere else; her personal and professional interest in the arts; the fact that, as of 1975, her social life was centered in Europe, where she had been living for over 7 years; and the fact that both of her parents were dead and her children were grown. In sum, her expatriation was the result of both her commitment to marry Furstenberg and the ultimate culmination of her life-long ties to Europe. Petitioner specifically declared that tax avoidance was neither a principal purpose, nor any purpose whatsoever, in her decision to adopt Austrian citizenship. We found petitioner to be a straightforward and credible witness; we have no reason to disbelieve or doubt her testimony.

Respondent, citing cases dealing with determinations of fraud under section 6653(b), contends that intent, or the lack thereof, can seldom be established by direct proof and, therefore, urges us to examine petitioner's entire course of conduct to determine her intent in expatriating. It is true that in the context of a fraud determination, seldom will an individual be forthcoming with direct evidence of his fraudulent intent, and respondent, in order to carry his burden of proof, is often forced to present indirect evidence of the individual's conduct on which inferences as to fraudulent intent may be drawn. In this case, however, petitioner has the burden of proof, and she has squarely addressed the issue of her intent through her uncontroverted testimony. Moreover, an examination of petitioner's conduct with respect to her expatriation, in our view, only serves to corroborate her testimony concerning her lack of tax avoidance motives.

Petitioner met with her accountant, Gordon Moore, in late April or early May 1975, only after her decision to marry Furstenberg and her commitment to adopt Austrian citizenship had been made. She asked him to advise her concerning the income tax consequences of her planned marriage and expatriation. At that time, he warned petitioner that her plan to marry and expatriate would 'complicate' her taxes; that French taxes could be very bad and were getting worse. Petitioner had no further discussions with Moore until March 1976, after her expatriation, when he advised her of the risk of double taxation on her dividends by France and United States. * * *

The foregoing chronology of events makes clear that at the time of her expatriation, petitioner was aware not of any possible tax advantages, but only of possible negative tax consequences which could follow from giving up her United States citizenship. Petitioner's decision to sell her securities was made after her expatriation. Avoidance of taxes, therefore, could not have been a consideration either as of the date of her decision to expatriate or the date of expatriation itself.

Further, rather than concluding that the timing of petitioner's expatriation points to her tax avoidance motives, as urged by respondent, we think the timing of her expatriation is compelling evidence itself that petitioner's expatriation was inextricably linked only to her commitment to marry Furstenberg, rather than to any plan of tax avoidance. Petitioner expatriated on December 23, 1975, only 4 days following her return from her honeymoon and the day of her scheduled departure for a Christmas holiday in Italy. Had her expatriation not been tied to her marriage to Furstenberg, petitioner, who had been living in Europe for over 7 years and in France for at least 5 years, could have expatriated years earlier. She could have, thereby, claimed the benefits of the French Tax Treaty years earlier. * * *

Petitioner's actions here are clearly distinguishable from those of Max Kronenberg, the taxpayer in Kronenberg v. Commissioner, 64 T.C. 428 (1975), the only other case in which the Court has decided the issue of tax avoidance as a principal purpose in expatriation under sec. 877. Kronenberg was a naturalized United States citizen who had retained his Swiss citizenship. From 1955 through 1966, Kronenberg owned 95.30 percent of the outstanding stock and was the president and co-director, with his wife, of PIC, Inc., a mica importing business. In 1966, Kronenberg decided to sell the business and considered moving back to Switzerland. On Feb. 26, 1966, PIC's shareholders voted to effect a complete liquidation under sec. 337 to be completed by Feb. 25, 1967. In Dec. 1966, Kronenberg learned from his accountant that if he lost his United States citizenship prior to receiving the liquidating distribution from PIC, Inc., it would not be subject to tax by the United States. The Court described Kronenberg's subsequent activities as follows (64 T.C. at 434–435):

After learning of such tax advantage, he engaged in a flurry of activity: he engaged attorneys to prepare the papers and complete the liquidation of PIC; he sold the family house; he made all the necessary arrangements for the transportation of his family and possessions to Switzerland; on February 20, 1967, the shareholders and directors of PIC met and took the necessary actions to complete the liquidation of the corporation; he instructed his attorneys to distribute to him all the assets of PIC at the latest possible time; he and his family actually left the United States on February 21, 1967, and arrived in Zurich on the following day; on February 23, 1967, he and his wife renounced their U.S. citizenship; and in accordance with his instructions, the transfer of funds from PIC to his personal account was carried out by his attorneys on February 24, 1967.

Finding Kronenberg's activities of Jan. and Feb. 1967 'too perfect to be unplanned,' (supra at 435) the Court concluded that the evidence failed to show that Kronenberg gave any consideration to renouncing his United States citizenship before he learned of the tax advantages of doing so. The Court was 'compelled' to find that Kronenberg had expatriated for tax avoidance purposes.

In contrast, petitioner's activities were too imperfect from a tax standpoint to have been planned. As we have discussed, petitioner engaged in no 'flurry of activity' in connection with her expatriation. She decided to expatriate before she knew anything about the tax consequences thereof; she had lived in Europe for over 7 years; at the time of her expatriation she knew of only possible negative tax effects; and her activity, or lack of it, viz-a-viz the trust distributions indicates that she did no planning whatsoever to delay them until after her expatriation.

Respondent has offered no evidence to refute or impeach petitioner's testimony concerning her motives for expatriating. He urges us, however, to infer a tax avoidance motive because petitioner never resided in Austria after adopting Austrian citizenship; because of the 'fortunate' timing of her expatriation concomitant with the Testamentary Trust distribution of various securities, in 1976 and 1977, resulting in the realization of substantial capital gains which, but for her expatriation, enabled petitioner to reap significant tax benefits; and because petitioner is a wealthy, intelligent woman who in the past had relied on tax counsel. This we decline to do.

First, we do not find as troubling as does respondent the fact that petitioner never resided in Austria after adopting Austrian citizenship. It merely corroborates petitioner's testimony that she adopted the Austrian citizenship of her husband as part of her marriage commitment, and reflects her belief that she was conforming to the custom of the European aristocracy which she was entering by her marriage. Petitioner testified that she was not adverse to living in Austria; indeed, she spent over a month there in the summer of 1975, staying at Furstenberg's hunting lodge in Strobl. We think it quite reasonable, nonetheless, for petitioner and Furstenberg to have settled in Paris after their marriage. Furstenberg, who was 71 years old at the time of the marriage, had himself been living outside of Austria for many years, and he did not like living in Austria's harsh climate. Petitioner had lived in her Paris apartment for 5 years and was obviously settled into the social life there. That they chose to live in Paris rather than Austria, therefore, raises no suspicion of tax avoidance motives. * * *

Finally, although it is true that petitioner is a wealthy and intelligent woman, she has no more than a layman's knowledge of the tax law; indeed, she admitted that she did not read or understand her tax returns for the years at issue, she merely signed what was presented to her by her accountants. Thus, we cannot infer a tax avoidance motive merely by virtue of her wealth and intelligence.

Petitioner, in this case, has had the burden of proving a negative, i.e., a lack of intent. Admittedly, this is usually a difficult thing to do. She testified that tax avoidance was not a purpose in her expatriation; her actions and the surrounding circumstances support her testimony. There is no evidence other than the magnitude of the deficiencies here in dispute to suggest otherwise. Although those deficiencies are sufficient to place the burden of proof on petitioner under section 877(e), they are not enough to refute the direct credible testimony presented by petitioner and the corroborating facts and circumstances. We think petitioner has adequately met her burden of proving a lack of tax avoidance motives. Thus, we conclude that because tax avoidance was not one of petitioner's principal purposes in expatriating, she is not taxable under section 877. * * *

In the case of *Industrial*, if it decides to use a branch, the entity would be a non-U.S. person because the branch is a conduit of the foreign corporation *Industrial*. If, however, *Industrial* elects to use the Texas Corporation the entity would be an U.S. person even if wholly owned by a non-U.S. person. If Juan Gomez were to own the business entity it would be a non-U.S. person so long as Juan does not become a resident alien by applying for a green card or through the substantial presence test. Likewise, Andres would be a nonresident alien. However, since he is to live and work in the United States he will be a resident alien whether he uses an immigrant or non-immigrant Visa.

3. *The Income Tax effect of Status*

COOK v. TAIT

United States Supreme Court, 1924.
265 U.S. 47, 44 S.Ct. 444, 68 L.Ed. 895.

Plaintiff is a native citizen of the United States, and was such when he took up his residence and became domiciled in the city of Mexico. A demand was made upon him by defendant in error, designated defendant, to make a return of his income for the purpose of taxation under the revenue laws of the United States. Plaintiff complied with the demand, but under protest; the income having been derived from property situated in the city of Mexico. A tax was assessed against him in the sum of $1,193.38, the first installment of which he paid, and for it, as we have said this action was brought.

The question in the case, and which was presented by the demurrer to the declaration is, as expressed by plaintiff, whether Congress has power to impose a tax upon income received by a native citizen of the United States who, at the time the income was received, was permanently resident and domiciled in the city of Mexico, the income being from real and personal property located in Mexico.

Plaintiff assigns against the power, not only his rights under the Constitution of the United States, but under international law, and in support of the assignments cites many cases. It will be observed that the foundation of the assignments is the fact that the citizen receiving the income and the property of which it is the product are outside of the territorial limits of the United States. These two facts, the contention is, exclude the existence of the power to tax. Or to put the contention another way, to the existence of the power and its exercise, the person receiving the income and the property from which he receives it must both be within the territorial limits of the United States to be within the taxing power of the United States. The contention is not justified, and that it is not justified is the necessary deduction of recent cases. * * *

The contention was rejected that a citizen's property without the limits of the United States derives no benefit from the United States. The contention, it was said, came from the confusion of thought in 'mistaking the scope and extent of the sovereign power of the United States as a nation and its relations to its citizens and their relation to it.' And that power in its scope and extent, it was decided, is based on the presumption that government by its very nature benefits the citizen and his property wherever found, and that opposition to it holds on to citizenship while it 'belittles and destroys its advantages and blessings by denying the possession by government of an essential power required to make citizenship completely beneficial.' In other words, the principle was declared that the government, by its very nature, benefits the citizen and his property wherever found, and therefore has the power to make the benefit complete. Or, to express it another way, the basis of the power to tax was not and cannot be made dependent upon the situs of the property in all cases, it being in or out of the United States, nor was not and cannot be made dependent upon the domicile of the citizen, that being in or out of the United States, but upon his relation as citizen to the United States and the relation of the latter to him as citizen. The consequence of the relations is that the native citizen who is taxed may have domicile, and the property from which his income is derived may have situs, in a foreign country and the tax be legal—the government having power to impose the tax.

Judgment affirmed. * * *

In *Cook*, the Supreme Court has held the only necessary nexus for taxation is citizenship.[23] Note that the focus is on the taxpayer—the entity that is realizing the taxable event, not on the owners. The U.S. person pays tax on worldwide income computed on a net basis at the graduated rates provided in *IRC §§ 1 and 11*. The problem with the worldwide income tax effect is the possibility of double taxation. For example, assume that the U.S. person earns income in Argentina. The United States, under *Cook*, will tax the income. Argentina may also impose a tax on the same income. To ameliorate the harshness of this double tax, the Code[24] provides for a credit on creditable foreign income taxes actually paid. The foreign tax credit, although helpful, is laden with exceptions. In addition, the credit is only available if the U.S. person has non-U.S. source income.

A non-U.S. person pays tax only on U.S. source income, unless she has revoked citizenship or residency[25] for tax avoidance purposes or if she has an U.S. office[26] to which the income in question is attributable. The tax strategy for the foreigner, therefore, is to keep income 'offshore' and to not establish an U.S. office. Conversely, to the U.S. person, there is no 'off-shore' since the tax is imposed on worldwide income. Determining the source of the income in question is of paramount importance to the non-U.S. person. It is also important to the U.S. person because foreign tax credits are only available in those cases where there is non-U.S. source income.

4. *Determining the Source and Category of the Income*

a. *The Source Rules*

The source of income is determined through a technical set of rules found in *I.R.C. §§ 861–865 (1986)*. The Code source rules divide income by type—interest and dividend income is sourced by the residence of the seller. Personal services are sourced by where the services are performed. The source of the rental income generated on tangible property

---

23. Treas Reg.1.871–1(a)(1980) extends the worldwide income approach to resident aliens.

24. IRC § 901 et seq.

25. See Treas Reg. IRC § 877(e)(1986).

26. IRC § 865(e). See also the discussion on determining the source of income, infra.

is referenced by where the property is located. Royalty income from intangible property is sourced with reference to where the property is used. The residence of the seller sources the gain on sale of non-inventory personal property. The gain on sale of inventory property is determined by where the sale is consummated. The *Balanovski* case illustrates the tortuous route that must be navigated in determining the source of income[27] derived from the sale of inventory. Generally, great care must be taken in any transaction that has some nexus with the U.S., lest the long reach of the Code visits some hapless taxpayer like Balanovski.

UNITED STATES v. BALANOVSKI

United States Court of Appeals, Second Circuit, 1956.
236 F.2d 298.

* * *

CLARK, Chief Judge.

This is an appeal by defendants and a cross-appeal by the United States of America from a decision of Judge Palmieri, sitting without a jury, adjudging defendant-taxpayers liable for almost $1,000,000 in income taxes and interest for the year 1947, and directing two New York banks to pay over funds belonging to the defendant partnership in part payment of the judgment. * * * In our view the recovery granted was insufficient, and we are therefore reversing on the appeal of the United States only.

Defendants Balanovski and Horenstein were copartners in the Argentine partnership, Compania Argentina de Intercambio Comercial (CADIC), Balanovski having an 80 per cent interest and Horenstein, a 20 per cent interest. Balanovski, an Argentinean citizen, came to the United States on or about December 20, 1946, and remained in this country for approximately ten months, except for an absence of a few weeks in the spring of 1947 when he returned to Argentina. His purpose in coming here was the transaction of partnership business; and while here, he made extensive purchases and sales of trucks and other equipment resulting in a profit to the partnership of some $7,763,702.20.

His usual mode of operation in the United States was to contact American suppliers and obtain offers for the sale of equipment. He then communicated the offers to his father-in-law, Horenstein, in Argentina.

Horenstein, in turn, submitted them at a markup to an agency of the Argentine Government, Instituto Argentino de Promocion del Intercambio (IAPI), which was interested in purchasing such equipment. If

27. Treas. Reg. 1–861–7(c) (1957) states that if bare legal title is retained the place where the risk of economic loss transfers to the buyer is the place of consummation. The regulation further provides that when the IRS feels that the transaction has been arranged in such a manner for the primary purpose of tax avoidance a new test emerges. In those cases, all factors including place of negotiation and execution of sales agreement, location of property, and the place of payment will be considered in sourcing the income.

IAPI accepted an offer, Horenstein would notify Balanovski and the latter would accept the corresponding original offer of the American supplier. In the meantime IAPI would cause a letter of credit in favor of Balanovski to be opened with a New York bank. Acting under the terms of the letter of credit Balanovski would assign a portion of it, equal to CADIC's purchase price, to the United States supplier. The supplier could then draw on the New York bank against the letter of credit by sight draft for 100 per cent invoice value accompanied by (1) a commercial invoice billing Balanovski, (2) an inspection certificate, (3) a nonnegotiable warehouse or dock receipt issued in the name of the New York bank for the account of IAPI's Argentine agent, and (4) an insurance policy covering all risks to the merchandise up to delivery F.O.B. New York City.

* * *

After the supplier had received payment, Balanovski would draw on the New York bank for the unassigned portion of the letter of credit, less 1 per cent of the face amount, by submitting a sight draft accompanied by (1) a commercial invoice billing IAPI, (2) an undertaking to ship before a certain date, and (3) an insurance policy covering all risks to the merchandise up to delivery F.A.S. United States Sea Port. The bank would then deliver the nonnegotiable warehouse receipt that it had received from the supplier to Balanovski on trust receipt and his undertaking to deliver a full set of shipping documents, including a clean on board bill of lading issued to the order of IAPI's Argentine agent, with instructions to notify IAPI. It would also notify the warehouse that Balanovski was authorized to withdraw the merchandise. Upon delivery of these shipping documents to the New York bank Balanovski would receive the remaining 1 per cent due under the terms of the letter of credit. Although Balanovski arranged for shipping the goods to Argentina, IAPI paid shipping expenses and made its own arrangement there for marine insurance. The New York bank would forward the bill of lading, Balanovski's invoice billing IAPI, and the other documents required by the letter of credit (not including the supplier's invoice billing Balanovski) to IAPI's agent in Argentina.

Twenty-four transactions following substantially this pattern took place during 1947. Other transactions were also effected which conformed to a substantially similar pattern, except that CADIC engaged the services of others to facilitate the acquisition of goods and their shipment to Argentina. And other offers were sent to Argentina, for which no letters of credit were opened. Several letters of credit were opened which remained either in whole or in part unused. In every instance of a completed transaction Balanovski was paid American money in New York, and in every instance he deposited it in his own name with New York banks. Balanovski never ordered material from a supplier for which he did not have an order and letter of credit from IAPI.

Balanovski's activities on behalf of CADIC in the United States were numerous and varied and required the exercise of initiative, judgment, and executive responsibility. They far transcended the routine or merely clerical. Thus he conferred and bargained with American bankers. He inspected goods and made trips out of New York State in order to buy and inspect the equipment in which he was trading. He made sure the goods were placed in warehouses and aboard ship. He tried to insure that CADIC would not repeat the errors in supplying inferior equipment that had been made by some of its competitors. And while here he attempted 'to develop' 'other business' for CADIC.

Throughout his stay in the United States Balanovski employed a Miss Alice Devine as a secretary. She used, and he used, the Hotel New Weston in New York City as an office. His address on the documents involved in the transactions was given as the Hotel New Weston. His supplier contacted him there, and that was the place where his letters were typed and his business appointments arranged and kept. Later Miss Devine opened an office on Rector Street in New York City, which he also used. When he returned to Argentina for a brief time in 1947 he left a power of attorney with Miss Devine. This gave her wide latitude in arranging for shipment of goods and in signing his name to all sorts of documents, including checks. When he left for Argentina again at the end of his 10–month stay, he left with Miss Devine the same power of attorney, [FN1] which she used throughout the balance of 1947 to arrange for and complete the shipment of goods and bank the profits.

When Balanovski left the United States in October 1947 he filed a departing alien income tax return, on which he reported no income. In March 1948 the Commissioner of Internal Revenue assessed $2,122,393.91 as taxes due on income for the period during which Balanovski was in the United States. In May 1953 the Commissioner made a jeopardy assessment against Balanovski in the amount of $3,954,422.41 and gave him notice of it. At the same time a similar jeopardy assessment, followed by a timely notice of deficiency, was made against Horenstein in the amount of $1,672,209.90, representing his alleged share of CADIC's profits on the above described sales of United States goods.

The government brought the present action to foreclose a federal tax lien on $511,655.58 and $42,529.49–amounts of partnership funds held in two United States banks—and to obtain personal judgments against Balanovski and Horenstein in the sums of $6,722,625.54 (of which $5,050,415.64 is now sought on appeal) and $1,672,209.90 respectively. Balanovski and Horenstein were served with process by mail in Argentina pursuant to 28 U.S.C. s 1655; and Miss Devine, the purported agent of Balanovski, was personally served in New York. Defendants then appeared by their attorneys and proceeded to defend the action. * * *

CADIC was actively and extensively engaged in business in the United States in 1947. Its 80 per cent partner, Balanovski, under whose hat 80 per cent of the business may be thought to reside, was in this country soliciting orders, inspecting merchandise, making purchases, and (as will later appear) completing sales. While maintaining regular contact with his home office, he was obviously making important business decisions. He maintained a bank account here for partnership funds. He operated from a New York office through which a major portion of CADIC's business was transacted. * * *

We cannot accept the view of the trial judge that, since Balanovski was a mere purchasing agent, his presence in this country was insufficient to justify a finding that CADIC was doing business in the United States. We need not consider the question whether, if Balanovski (an 80 per cent partner) were merely engaged in purchasing goods here, the partnership could be deemed to be engaged in business, since he was doing more than purchasing. Acting for CADIC he engaged in numerous transactions wherein he both purchased and sold goods in this country, earned his profits here, and participated in other activities, pertaining to the transaction of business. Cases cited in support of the proposition that CADIC was not engaged in business here are quite distinguishable. * * *

[A] nonresident alien engaged in business here derives income from the sale of personal property in 'the country in which (the goods are) sold.' By the overwhelming weight of authority, goods are deemed 'sold' within the statutory meaning when the seller performs the last act demanded of him to transfer ownership, and title passes to the buyer. * * *

Here, by deliberate act of the parties, title, or at least beneficial ownership, passed to IAPI in the United States. Under the letters of credit, Balanovski was paid in the United States and CADIC's last act to complete performance was done here. When Balanovski presented evidence of shipment—the clean ocean bill of lading made out to the account of an Argentine bank with the directive 'Notify IAPI'—he had completed CADIC's work and he received the final 1 per cent of IAPI's contract price.

The time when title to goods passes depends, of course, upon the intention of the parties. * * * When documents of title, such as a bill of lading, are given up, the presumption is that the seller has given up title, together with the documents. * * * In F.O.B. and F.A.S. contracts there is a presumption that title passes from the seller just as soon as the goods are delivered to the carrier 'free on board' or 'free alongside' the ship, as the case may be. * * * Both of these presumptions, which would tend to establish that title passed from CADIC to IAPI in the United States, are not altered by the use of a letter of credit. * * * Nor need we here consider whether more than 'beneficial' title passed immediately to IAPI or whether a 'security' or 'legal' title rested with the intermediary bank. * * *

All the available evidence confirms, rather than rebuts, these presumptions of passage of title in the United States. All risk of loss passed before the ocean voyage. IAPI took out the marine insurance. CADIC performed all acts to complete the transaction, retained no control of the goods, and there was no possibility of withdrawal.

Judge Palmieri apparently did not contest that title to the goods passed in the United States. But he applied a test based upon the 'substance of the transaction' to hold that Argentina was the place where the income-producing contracts were negotiated and concluded, the place of the buyer's business, and the destination of the goods. This led him to conclude that Argentina, rather than the United States, was the place of sale. The judge further buttressed this result by observing that IAPI, rather than CADIC, had insisted upon the passing of title in the United States.

Although the 'passage of title' rule may be subject to criticism on the grounds that it may impose inequitable tax burdens upon taxpayers engaged in substantially similar transactions, such as upon exporters whose customers require that property in the goods pass in the United States—see Hearings before the House Committee on Ways and Means on Forty Topics Pertaining to the General Revision of the Internal Revenue Code, 83d Cong., 1st Sess., pt. 2, at 1458 (1953)—no suitable substitute test providing an adequate degree of certainty for taxpayers has been proposed. Vague 'contacts' or 'substance of the transaction' criteria would make it more difficult for corporations engaged in Western Hemisphere trade to plan their operations so as to receive the special deduction granted them if they derive at least 95 per cent of their income from sources outside the United States. Int.Rev.Code of ss 1954, 921, 922; see also s 941. See Note, supra, 69 Harv.L.Rev. 567.

Careful study was given this problem by the experts working on the Income Tax Project of the American Law Institute. They did give consideration to an alternative test of 'place of destination.' But this was open to criticism on the ground that it unduly favored exporters. * * * After much deliberation the American Law Institute has retained the 'title passage' rule in its 1954 draft of a model Internal Revenue Code. * * * Further, in substantially re-enacting s 119(e)(2) of the 1939 Code, Congress did not further define 'the place of sale,' thus apparently accepting the prevailing 'passage of title' test. See Int.Rev.Code of 1954, ss 861(a)(6), 862(a)(6).

Of course this test may present problems, as where passage of title is formally delayed to avoid taxes. Hence it is not necessary, nor is it desirable, to require rigid adherence to this test under all circumstances. But the rule does provide for a certainty and ease of application desirable in international trade. Where, as here, it appears to accord with the economic realities (since these profits flowed from transactions engineered in major part within the United States), we see no reason to depart from it. Hence we hold that the partners are liable for taxes on the entire profits of the partnership sales amounting to $7,763,702.20.

* * *

In *Balanovski*, the taxpayer was a non-U.S. person—an Argentine Partnership. It is a good example of how a seemingly innocuous decision can have devastating consequences. The taxpayer, by using the commer- cial term *FOB New York* title and risk of loss transferred in the United States thus creating U.S. source income. The substance of the transac- tion is only reviewed when title and risk of loss is transferred outside the United States. If Balanovski had negotiated for the title and risk of loss to transfer in Buenos Aires, the examination of the substance of the transaction would be in order. Assuming there had been non-U.S. source income, would the income generated by the partnership be taxable in the United States?

b. Categorizing the Income

Once income is determined to be U.S. source, it must be categorized to determine its tax effect. There are two basic categories—trade or business[28](also known as ECI[29]) or investment income.[30] Only non-U.S. persons face these income categorization rules. Recall that U.S. persons pay income tax on the net amount under the graduated rates provided by the Code. The non-U.S. person faces this tax consequence on trade or business income.[31] In this regard, non-U.S. persons with U.S. source trade or business income is taxed like an U.S. person. Likewise, non-U.S. source income attributable to an U.S. office is taxed as income from a trade or business.

Investment income is itself divided into two categories—fixed, deter- minable, annual or periodic income (known as FDAP[32]) and other in- come.[33] FDAP is taxed on the gross amount at a thirty-percent rate[34] or lower treaty amount. There are some benefits to non-U.S. persons in this area. For example, interest income paid by U.S. financial institutions or other interest qualifying as 'portfolio interest' is exempt from tax. The category—other income—which essentially includes capital gains from the sale of non-U.S. real property, is also exempt[35] from U.S. taxation. The gain on sale of an U.S. real property interest, however, is taxable as trade or business income.[36] Also, the profits from an U.S. branch of a foreign corporation are subject to U.S. taxation even though the income is not repatriated to the foreign corporation.

28. IRC §§ 871(b); 882(1986).

29. IRC § 864(c)(1986).

30. IRC §§ 871(a); 881(1986).

31. IRC §§ 871(b); 882(a)(1986).

32. FDAP income includes interest ... dividends, rents, ... and other fixed or determinable annual or periodical gains, profits, and income. IRC § 871(a)(1)(A)(1986).

33. IRC § 871(a)(2)(1986)

34. IRC §§ 871(a)(1); 881(a). However, certain types of interest income are exempt from tax—§§ 871(h); 881(c)(1986)

35. IRC § 871(a)(2)(1986)

36. IRC § 897(a)(1986)

C. THE RULES UNDER THE NETWORK OF BILATERAL TAX TREATIES

1. *Introduction*

THE U.S. AND MEXICO TAX TREATY: LONG OVERDUE BUT FALLING SHORT OF ITS POTENTIAL

ANTONIO MENDOZA

17 Hous. J. Int'l L. 27(1994).

* * *

The free movement of goods between nations is an important trade goal of the United States. Tax treaties help achieve this goal by reducing tax barriers to trade and investment. The Convention Between the Government of the United States of America and the Government of the United Mexican States for the Avoidance of Double Taxation and the Prevention of Fiscal Evasion with Respect to Taxes on Income (Convention) is one such treaty.

From the perspective of the United States government, the Convention advances several trade and fiscal policy goals, including: (1) strengthening the free movement of goods and capital between the United States and Mexico, thereby improving mutual economic relations; (2) providing a mechanism for the exchange of information; and (3) assisting in the fulfillment of the goals embraced by the North American Free Trade Agreement (NAFTA).

In addition to preserving tax benefits permitted under the Internal Revenue Code (Code), the Convention promotes business opportunities by promising tax simplification; reducing the Code income tax rate on certain types of income; promising U.S. nationals nondiscriminatory treatment; and providing relief from double taxation for those qualified to participate. * * *

B. *The Interaction Between the Code and Convention*

1. Treaties v. Federal Statutory Law: The Later–In–Time Rule

Both treaties and federal statutes have the force of federal law. They are equal, which creates the necessity for a rule to establish primacy in cases of conflict. In the United States, the later-in-time rule determines which is controlling when there is a conflict. Under the later-in-time rule, an inconsistent, subsequent federal statute will preempt a provision in the Convention. Even though the Convention continues to be a binding international obligation, the preempted provision will have no effect in the United States.

The Code provides for the equal status of treaties and statutes and a rule of construction to prevent unintentional preemptions of the treaty. Intentional preemptions continue to be a potential source of instability.

Congress may effectively negate the Convention if it so wishes. Because the intention to preempt an earlier treaty may not always be clear from the statute itself, the governing law may be difficult to ascertain. The tax planning implications from this uncertainty can be readily appreciated.

2. Code Provisions That Apply After the Convention: The Code as a Gap Filler

Under the later-in-time rule, a subsequently enacted treaty provision preempts a pre-existing Code provision. However, a treaty may only preempt those Code provisions that directly conflict with the treaty. Since the Code contains many more provisions than even the lengthiest tax treaty, many Code provisions continue to apply. In effect, the Code fills in gaps the Convention left unaddressed. As a result, the treaty will be supplemented by many complicated and arcane Code provisions, rendering tax simplification under the Convention illusory.

III.   The Convention and Code: A Combined System of Federal Income Taxation on Inbound Transactions

A.   *The Savings Clause*

The use of the Code as a gap filler, along with the later-in-time rule, creates a combined system of federal income taxation for transactions between residents of Mexico and the United States. Nonetheless, the savings clause reserves a right for contracting states to tax its citizens and resident aliens under the Code as if the Convention was not in effect. From the perspective of U.S. citizens and resident aliens, the Code is the only system of federal income taxation. For certain Mexican residents, both the Convention and the Code are applicable. * * *

The U.S. Mexico tax treaty, although unique in that it is the only bilateral tax treaty between a developed and developing country, has characteristics similar to other U.S. bilateral tax treaties. For example, all tax treaties have a goal to eliminate the double taxation of income, all contain a savings clause, all simplify the rules relating to business profits, and all reduce the tax rate assessed on certain types of investment income.

One main feature of a bilateral tax treaty is to prevent two countries from taxing the same income. It is in this area where simplification has been achieved. The treaty describes exactly when a contracting state can tax a national from the other contracting state. In addition, the treaty will identify and allow a credit against the tax of one contracting state when paid to the other contracting state. This eliminates the necessity of determining whether a foreign enactment is truly a creditable tax.

Tax treaties are also used in preventing tax evasion. Contracting states are required to exchange financial information involving its nationals with the other contracting state. The U.S. is quite insistent in imposing this requirement in all its tax treaties. Indeed, a treaty for the exchange of financial information was the precursor to the U.S./Mexico tax treaty.

There are several weaknesses in the treaty system. For example, at the federal level, tax treaties replace only prior inconsistent federal statutes. Treaties may contain thirty plus articles whereas the internal revenue code has over nine thousand sections. There are, therefore, many cases where the treaty does not cover a particular tax problem. There are also many countries with which there is no treaty. In the Western Hemisphere Canada, Mexico, and Venezuela have negotiated tax treaties with the United States. In the cases where there is no treaty, the domestic law provides the rules.

In order to assess the tax implications of any given international business transaction, the lawyer must first determine if the foreign party is a national of a state that is a treaty partner. She must then determine whether the treaty addresses the particular tax issue in question. If so, federal legislation enacted subsequent to the treaty adoption date must then be examined to determine if the particular treaty provision has not been superseded. If there is no such legislation, the treaty rules prevail. The income tax system is truly a combined treaty-Code system.

2. *An Analysis of the Major Issues*

   a. Selected Articles

CONVENTION BETWEEN THE GOVERNMENT OF THE UNITED STATES OF AMERICA AND THE GOVERNMENT OF THE UNITED MEXICAN STATES FOR THE AVOIDANCE OF DOUBLE TAXATION AND THE PREVENTION OF FISCAL EVASION WITH RESPECT TO TAXES ON INCOME

The Government of the United States of America and the Government of the United Mexican States, desiring to conclude a convention for the avoidance of double taxation and the prevention of fiscal evasion with respect to taxes on income, which shall hereafter be referred to as the "Convention", have agreed as follows:

ARTICLE 1

General Scope

1.   This Convention shall apply to persons who are residents of one or both of the Contracting States, except as otherwise provided in the Convention.

2.   The Convention shall not restrict in any manner any exclusion, exemption, deduction, credit, or other allowance now or hereafter accorded: a) by the laws of either Contracting State; or b) by any other agreement between the Contracting States.

3.   Notwithstanding any provision of the Convention except paragraph 4, a Contracting State may tax its residents (as determined under Article 4 (Residence)), and by reason of citizenship may tax its citizens, as if the Convention had not come into effect. For this purpose, the term

"citizen" shall include a former citizen whose loss of citizenship had as one of its principal purposes the avoidance of tax, but only for a period of 10 years following such loss.

* * *

ARTICLE 4

Residence

1. For the purposes of this Convention, the term "resident of a Contracting State" means any person who, under the laws of that State, is liable to tax therein by reason of his domicile, residence, place of management, place of incorporation, or any other criterion of a similar nature. However, this term does not include any person who is liable to tax in that State in respect only of income from sources in that State.

2. Where by reason of the provisions of paragraph 1, an individual is a resident of both Contracting States, then his residence shall be determined as follows: a) he shall be deemed to be a resident of the State in which he has a permanent home available to him; if he has a permanent home available to him in both Contracting States, he shall be deemed to be a resident of the State with which his personal and economic relations are closer (center of vital interests); b) if the State in which he has his center of vital interests cannot be determined, or if he does not have a permanent home available to him in either State, he shall be deemed to be a resident of the State in which he has an habitual abode; c) if he has an habitual abode in both States or in neither of them, he shall be deemed to be a resident of the State of which he is a national; d) in any other case, the competent authorities of the Contracting States shall settle the question by mutual agreement.

3. Where by reason of the provisions of paragraph 1 a person other than an individual is a resident of both Contracting States, such person shall not be treated as a resident of either Contracting State for purposes of this Convention.

ARTICLE 5

Permanent Establishment

1. For the purposes of this Convention, the term "permanent establishment" means a fixed place of business through which the business of an enterprise is wholly or partly carried on.

2. The term "permanent establishment" includes especially a) a place of management; b) a branch; c) an office; d) a factory; e) a workshop; and f) a mine, an oil or gas well, a quarry, or any other place of extraction of natural resources.

3. The term "permanent establishment" shall also include a building site or construction or installation project, or an installation or drilling rig or ship used for the exploration or exploitation of natural resources, or supervisory activity in connection therewith, but only if such building site, construction or activity lasts more than six months.

4.   Notwithstanding the preceding provisions of this Article, the term "permanent establishment" shall be deemed not to include: a) the use of facilities solely for the purpose of storage, display, or delivery of goods or merchandise belonging to the enterprise; b) the maintenance of a stock of goods or merchandise belonging to the enterprise solely for the purpose of storage, display, or delivery; c) the maintenance of a stock of goods or merchandise belonging to the enterprise solely for the purpose of processing by another enterprise; d) the maintenance of a fixed place of business solely for the purpose of purchasing goods or merchandise, or of collecting information, for the enterprise; e) the maintenance of a fixed place of business solely for the purpose of advertising, supplying information, scientific research, or for the preparations relating to the placement of loans, or for similar activities which have a preparatory or auxiliary character, for the enterprise; f) the maintenance of a fixed place of business solely for any combination of the activities mentioned in subparagraphs a) to e), provided that the total activity of the combination is of preparatory or auxiliary character.

5.   Notwithstanding the provisions of paragraphs 1 and 2, where a person—other than an agent of an independent status to whom paragraph 7 applies—is acting in a Contracting State on behalf of an enterprise of the other Contracting State, that enterprise shall be deemed to have a permanent establishment in the first-mentioned State in respect of any activities which that person undertakes for the enterprise, if such person: a) has and habitually exercises in that State an authority to conclude contracts in the name of the enterprise, unless the activities of such person are limited to those mentioned in paragraph 4 which, if exercised through a fixed place of business, would not make this fixed place of business a permanent establishment under the provisions of that paragraph; or b) has no such authority but habitually processes in the first-mentioned State on behalf of the enterprise goods or merchandise maintained in that State by that enterprise, provided that such processing is carried on using assets furnished, directly or indirectly, by that enterprise or any associated enterprise.

6.   Notwithstanding the foregoing provisions of this Article, an insurance enterprise of a Contracting State shall, except in regard to reinsurance, be deemed to have a permanent establishment in the other Contracting State if it collects premiums in the territory of that other State or insures risks situated therein through a representative other than an agent of an independent status to whom paragraph 7 applies.

7.   An enterprise shall not be deemed to have a permanent establishment in a Contracting State merely because it carries on business in that State through a broker, general commission agent, or any other agent of an independent status, provided that such persons are acting in the ordinary course of their business and that in their commercial or financial relations with the enterprise conditions are not made or imposed that differ from those generally agreed to by independent agents.

8. The fact that a company which is a resident of a Contracting State controls or is controlled by a company which is a resident of the other Contracting State, or which carries on business in that other State (whether through a permanent establishment or otherwise), shall not of itself constitute either company a permanent establishment of the other.

* * *

ARTICLE 7

Business Profits

1. The business profits of an enterprise of a Contracting State shall be taxable only in that State unless the enterprise carries on or has carried on business in the other Contracting State through a permanent establishment situated therein. If the enterprise carries on or has carried on business as aforesaid, the business profits of the enterprise may be taxed in the other State but only so much of them as is attributable to a) that permanent establishment; b) sales in that other State of goods or merchandise of the same or similar kind as the goods or merchandise sold through that permanent establishment. However, the profits derived from the sales described in subparagraph (b) shall not be taxable in the other State if the enterprise demonstrates that such sales have been carried out for reasons other than obtaining a benefit under this Convention.

2. Subject to the provisions of paragraph 3, where an enterprise of a Contracting State carries on or has carried on business in the other Contracting State through a permanent establishment situated therein, there shall in each Contracting State be attributed to that permanent establishment the business profits which it might be expected to make if it were a distinct and independent enterprise engaged in the same or similar activities under the same or similar conditions.

3. In determining the business profits of a permanent establishment, there shall be allowed as deductions expenses which are incurred for the purposes of the permanent establishment, including executive and general administrative expenses so incurred, whether in the State in which the permanent establishment is situated or elsewhere. However, no such deduction shall be allowed in respect of such amounts, if any, paid (otherwise than towards reimbursement of actual expenses) by the permanent establishment to the head office of the enterprise or any of its other offices by way of royalties, fees or other similar payments in return for the use of patents or other rights, by way of commission, for specific services performed or for management, or except in the case of a banking enterprise, by way of interest on moneys lent to the permanent establishment.

4. No business profits shall be attributed to a permanent establishment by reason of the mere purchase by that permanent establishment of goods or merchandise for the enterprise.

5.   For the purposes of this Convention, the business profits to be attributed to the permanent establishment shall include only the profits or losses derived from the assets or activities of the permanent establishment and shall be determined by the same method year by year unless there is good and sufficient reason to the contrary.

6.   Where business profits include items of income which are dealt with separately in other Articles of the Convention, then the provisions of those Articles shall not be affected by the provisions of this Article.

---

b.   Determining Residency

The tax treaty simplifies the process of determining status and the resultant tax effect. The status of the person turns on residency as defined in Article Four. Therefore, if a person is deemed to be a resident of Mexico under Article Four, the treaty will provide the rules unless the treaty is silent on an issue in which case the Code will provide the answer. If however, a person is deemed to be a resident of the United States pursuant to Article Four of the treaty or is a U.S. citizen, for U.S. tax purposes, the Code will apply. This is the operation of the so-called 'savings' clause that is present in all U.S. tax treaty. What benefit is a tax treaty to an U.S. resident or citizen? Will *Industrial* be able to use the tax treaty? Will its wholly owned subsidiary?

c.   The Source and Category of Income and the Resulting Tax Effect

(1) Investment Income

Under the Code, the source and category rules are very technical and detailed. The tax treaties offer somewhat of a breath of fresh air. Specific articles provide the answers for types of income. For example, Article 10 provides the source rules and tax effect on dividends, Article 11 focuses on interest income, and Article 12 addresses royalty income. The analysis is simple. In addition, the tax rate is reduced from the thirty percent FDAP rate imposed by the Code.

(2) Trade or Business Income

Even in the case of business profits there is relative simplicity. Article Seven provides for U.S. tax on Mexican residents only in the case where the Company has a permanent establishment in the United States. Therefore, the critical question is the existence of a 'permanent establishment.'

SIMENON v. C.I.R.
United States Tax Court, 1965.
44 T.C. 820.

* * *

HARRON, Judge:

The respondent determined a deficiency in income tax for the taxable year 1955 in the amount of $22,895.57. The main question is whether petitioner had a 'permanent establishment' in the United States until March 19, 1955, within the meaning of the income tax convention between the United States and France and respondent's regulations adopted thereunder, with the consequence that author's royalties from U.S. sources received while he was in France are not tax exempt.

FINDINGS OF FACT

The stipulated facts are so found and are incorporated herein by reference.

Beginning March 28, 1955, through November 29, 1955, concerns in the United States (U.S. sources) paid petitioner royalties, as consideration for the right to use copyrights and analogous rights with respect to literary works of the petitioner, in the total sum of $25,291.95, as follows, none of which was included in gross income in the return for 1955 filed by petitioner:

Date paid in 1955	Payor	Amount
Mar. 28	Doubleday & Co	$5,000.00
May 4	New American Library	113.75
July 5	20th Century Fox	20,000.00
Nov. 29	Appleton	178.20
		25,291.95

The respondent determined that all of the above income from royalties is includable in petitioner's gross income for 1955 and taxable. In the statutory notice of deficiency, he gave the following reason: 'royalty income received from sources within the United States for the period March 28, 1955 to December 31, 1955, is taxable since you engaged in trade or business through a permanent establishment in the United States during part of the year.'

Petitioner is a professional writer of fiction, an eminent author. He writes in French. He is by experience and practice a European novelist. He writes psychological and mystery novels and stories. In his mystery stories, the principal character is Inspector Maigret. All of his literary works, except six, have a European background. His literary works have been published in various countries, including the United States, Canada, and Great Britain, and many have been translated into the English language.

Beginning on July 27, 1950, petitioner rented residential property, called Shadow Rock Farm, in Lakeville, Conn., where he lived with his family until March 19, 1955. * * *

While residing in the United States, petitioner wrote 46 books, novels, and short stories, all of which were written in French and have

French titles. All have European backgrounds and are based on experiences and knowledge which petitioner had acquired in Europe, except six books of novels and stories in which petitioner made use of knowledge acquired in the United States. * * *

In about 1955, petitioner decided to go to Europe. He believed that he could carry on his creative writing better in a European background. He departed from the United States, with his family, on March 19, 1955, and went directly to France, where he remained until June 20, 1956. He then went to Switzerland where he and his family have lived continuously ever since. He has not returned to the United States at any time. * * *

During the period in which petitioner lived at Shadow Rock Farm, he set aside part of the house as his office. He carried on his work as an author and his related business affairs in this office, which he maintained until March 19, 1955. * * *

In his Form 1040 income tax return for the period January 1 to March 19, 1955, petitioner stated that his occupation is 'author,' and he included as part of the return Schedule C, 'Profit (or Loss) From Business Or Profession.' In Schedule C petitioner reported an amount as the net profit from his business after taking several business expense deductions. He included in his business deductions depreciation on his house on the basis of devoting 50 percent of his use thereof to his business; and also on that basis he took a depreciation deduction on furniture and fixtures. The amount of the entire depreciation deduction was computed on the basis of his use of the property, furniture, and fixtures for business purposes during 78 days in 1955, i.e., 31 days in January, 28 days in February, and 19 days in March. Petitioner took business expenses deductions totaling $9,355.46 * * *

Opinion

Royalties from sources within the United States, in the amount of $25,291.95, were paid to petitioner in 1955 after he left the United States on March 19, 1955. Petitioner did not include these royalties in his gross income on his return for 1955. He took the position that they are exempt from the U.S. income tax under the provisions of article 7 of the income tax convention, or treaty, between the United States and France. The respondent made the following determinations: (1) That article 7 of the income tax treaty does not apply because petitioner had a 'permanent establishment' in the United States at some time during 1955. (2) That since the treaty exemption does not apply, the royalties are subject to the U.S. income tax under section 871(c) of the 1954 Code.

The issue for decision is whether the royalties in question, from U.S. sources, are exempt from the U.S. income tax under article 7 of the income tax treaty with France. Section 894 of the Code exempts from the Federal income tax income of any kind, 'to the extent required by any treaty obligation of the United States.' The tax treaty involved is the income tax convention with France which was signed on July 25, 1939, and in due course became effective on January 1, 1945. Article 7 of the convention, in title I, Double Taxation, provides as follows:

Royalties derived from within one of the contracting States by a resident or by a corporation or other entity of the other contracting State as consideration for the right to use copyrights, patents, secret processes and formulae, trade marks and other analogous rights shall be exempt from taxation in the former State, provided such resident, corporation or other entity does not have a permanent establishment there. * * *

(b) Section 514.109 of the regulations of the respondent under article 7 of the tax convention (T.D.5499, supra) provides that royalties are exempt from the Federal income tax provided the individual or entity 'has no permanent establishment within the United States at any time during the taxable year in which such income is so derived.' Petitioner alleged in his petition that his taxable year for the purpose of the U.S. income tax ended on March 19, 1955, 'insofar as treatment of subsequently received royalty income from United States sources under the aforesaid Tax Convention was concerned,' which respondent denied. Petitioner made his return for 1955 on the basis of a short taxable period, January 1 through March 19; he used Form 1040, reporting income as a resident alien during the short period; he took the position that under article 7 of the convention he did not have as a nonresident alien during the balance of 1955 any taxable income from sources within the United States. The pleadings present the question whether petitioner's taxable year was the calendar year 1955, or a short period of less than 12 months. * * *

3.   Treaty Article 7, Permanent Establishment

Respondent determined that petitioner had a 'permanent establishment' in the United States during part of 1955 where he carried on a trade or business. He contends that petitioner maintained an office in his home at Shadow Rock Farm, which constituted a permanent establishment within the meaning of article 7. His contention is limited to the period January 1 to March 19, and to the office at petitioner's home. Respondent's regulation in conjunction with article 7 states that royalties derived from U.S. sources by a nonresident individual, who is a resident of France, are exempt from the U.S. Federal income tax, provided that such individual has no permanent establishment within the United States 'at any time' during the taxable year in which such income is so derived. Sec. 514.109 of the regulations, T.D. 5499, supra. Respondent relies on this construction of 'permanent establishment' in article 7, known as the 'at any time rule.' Article III(A) of the protocol, which is part of the convention, defines the term 'permanent establishment' broadly (see fn. 3), and as including 'workshops,' 'other offices,' and 'other fixed places of business.' Subsection (b) of article III defines 'enterprise' as including 'every form of undertaking whether carried on by an individual, 'corporation, or any other entity. Respondent's position is that petitioner carried on a business in the United States, consisting of his activities as a professional author who wrote stories for the purpose of selling rights in them; that he carried on this business at an office, workshop, and place of business at his home in Connecticut during the period January 1 to March 19, 1955 (and prior thereto); and that he therefore had a permanent establishment in the United States during the taxable year in which the royalties were derived. * * *

'Permanent establishment' is almost a treaty word of art. * * * and nearly all of them (tax treaties) use the term. Furthermore, in each instance the phrase has been qualified by a Treasury regulation conforming it to the 'at any time' rule—the current usage instead of the negative 'at no time'. * * *

Petitioner converted part of his house at Shadow Rock Farm to the use of an office. He reported on his 1955 return that 50 percent of this property was used for his business and took depreciation on that basis; and that furniture and fixtures acquired in 1954 were devoted 100 percent to business use, and he took depreciation on that basis. Respondent has not questioned those deductions and petitioner still adheres to them. * * *

There is nothing in the treaty definition of 'permanent establishment,' insofar as it includes an 'office,' which would serve to exclude from the term 'office' an office at the taxpayer's residence, provided it was devoted to petitioner's business. We are unable to find any merit in petitioner's contention that the office at petitioner's residence cannot be regarded as his 'permanent establishment' in the United States within the treaty definition of that term and its meaning in article 7.

The treaty definition of 'permanent establishment' is a fairly broad and inclusive one in which there is the catchall term 'and other fixed place of business.' The term 'business' has a broad meaning, which has been defined as including 'that which occupies the time, attention, and labor of men for the purpose of livelihood or profit.' Flint v. Stone Tracy Co., 220 U.S. 107, 171. It is also true that whether an occupation constitutes a trade or business must be decided on the facts in each case, Frederick A. Purdy, 12 T.C. 888, and the intent of the taxpayer has a material bearing on the issue, although it is not conclusive, Morton v. Commissioner, 174 F.2d 302, certiorari denied 338 U.S. 828. * * *

The existence of the tax treaty can be good news to *Industrial*. The main benefit is one of simplicity in determining the tax implications of business transactions conducted in the U.S. *Industrial* can do business in the U.S., earn business profits and not pay U.S. tax so long as it does not have a permanent business establishment in the United States. These simple rules replace the tortuous Code rules of sourcing and categorizing the income being generated to determine the tax implications of business transactions under the Code.

Chapter 3

THE OUTBOUND FOREIGN
DIRECT INVESTMENT

SECTION 3.1   THE OUTBOUND FOREIGN DI-
RECT INVESTMENT: PROTECTION UNDER
INTERNATIONAL AGREEMENTS

A.   INTRODUCTION

The outbound FDI, where the host is a developing country, is one of the most active areas in international business transactions. For our purposes, the outbound foreign direct investment is where a U.S. person will be investing or doing business abroad. Since the end of the cold war, countries that were socialist or communist (and even some that continue to be communist) have been receptive to the American concept of free trade and open borders. Recently, developing countries have come to recognize the positive side of foreign direct investment. It is now seen as a means of furthering the country's development strategy.

Foreign direct investment represents capital that can bring development into the country, generate tax revenue, foreign exchange, and provide jobs for the local people. In addition, the typical foreign investment involves the transfer of technology and know-how, both of which are needed in developing countries. Many developing countries are now eager to show the international investment community their openness toward foreign direct investment. The reception is reflected by international agreements that indicate the willingness of these non-free market economies to free market economies. The massive capital flow into these economies is reflective of this new reality.

Many parts of the world–Eastern Europe, Asia and Latin America are engaged in a system of privatizing previously state owned enterprises. If the current liberalization can yield sustainable development, it will last a long time. One of the great opportunities for foreign investors in the Western Hemisphere is the privatization that occurring in Latin America. The countries are welcoming sorely needed foreign capital

154

through a massive privatization of state owned enterprises. The lack of low cost capital, the inefficiency of government run enterprises, and the scarcity of newer technology have fueled the privatization efforts.

The impact of privatization and the liberalization of domestic foreign investment rules are presently being felt in Mexico and other Latin American countries. This certainly will provide great opportunities for private companies, investment bankers, lawyers, and accountants. Latin American privatization efforts have concentrated in those industries where there are natural monopolies—telecommunications, airlines, power, railroads, broadcasting, banking, and steel.

Privatization is occurring at a different pace among the Latin American countries. Some have embraced investment liberalization and privatization with an evangelistic fervor, while other countries like Brazil are slower in privatizing because of weaknesses in its economy. The attorney can bring value to the client's representation by evaluating the investment climate of the host country prior to establishing the foreign investment. The current investment environment in the Americas is positive. The United States has also generally maintained an open policy towards inbound foreign direct investment.

Latin America is embracing free trade as evidenced by Mexico's current attitude. The failure of the import substitution policy with its protectionist tendencies, the plunge in worldwide oil prices and the corresponding economic crisis in 1982 led to a fundamental orientation of Mexican economic policy. The foreign investment rules were liberalized and massive privatization is occurring, as state owned organizations are being sold to privately owned groups. Mexico has the largest economy in Latin America and is one of its strongest leaders. The Mexican decision to spurn import substitution and protectionism in favor of free trade and open borders has been simultaneously embraced by all of the countries in the Western Hemisphere except Cuba.

There has been a decisive change of attitude in Latin America from a region of statist economies to one based on free trade and open borders. International agreements and changes in domestic legislation are removing trade and investment barriers and protecting intellectual property rights of foreigners throughout Latin America. A substantial limitation, however, is the frailty of the economies in the region.

Latin America in general and Mexico in particular have not always maintained a consistent policy on the role that foreign direct investment should play in the economic development of the country. Valid concerns are voiced on the political willingness of the Latin American countries in staying the course on free trade and open borders. Governmental trade development goals are to regulate inbound foreign investment so that foreign interests will not adversely affect the host country. This is essentially a political decision. As described in the Chua article, Latin America has had a love-hate relationship with foreign capital.

THE PRIVATIZATION NATIONALIZATION CYCLE: THE LINK BETWEEN MARKETS AND ETHNICITY IN DEVELOPING COUNTRIES

Amy L. Chua*

95 COLUM. L. REV. 223 (1995).

Privatization has been the source of growing global exhilaration. By the early 1990s, "at least eighty-three countries were conducting some significant form of privatization," prompting commentators to describe the world-wide movement as "profound" and "unprecedented"—an "economic revolution." Policymakers throughout the developing world have embraced privatization as the means to efficiency and productivity, lower prices, economic development and modernization, democracy, equality, justice, maximization of social welfare, and the elimination of social evils.

According to former Argentine economics minister, Rogelio Frigerio, the influx of private capital, particularly foreign capital, "will allow us to increase production, the sole goal of any economic system. Greater production means more work and better salaries, full employment, an improved standard of living, that is to say, a solution to the social problem, both for the urban population and for the rural population." Minister Frigerio's claims are notable because they describe not the privatization initiatives of the 1990s but rather those of the 1950s. This earlier "solution to the social problem" was followed by a return to statist economic policies in the 1960s, a renewed commitment to free enterprise, a swing back to nationalization in the 1970s, and only then by the latest round of Argentinean privatizations.

Similarly, in 1935 President Lazaro Cardenas of Mexico predicted that nationalization would bring "justice for the worker" and the "conversion of Mexico from a poor country to a rich and prosperous nation." But Cardenas's nationalizations of the 1930s were followed by a privatization campaign in the 1940s and 1950s, then by re-nationalization, and now by the current Mexican privatization program that has received so much attention.

In the midst of a global privatization movement, and against the backdrop of the collapse of the former Soviet Union, the temptation is to regard the dismantling of the corporatist state as the culmination of a world-historical learning process. Privatization, according to the former prime minister of Jamaica, is " 'irreversible ... no power on earth can change it.' " Or in the words of a World Bank official: "The present interest in privatization is no fad.... Lessons have been learned.... and today's strategies reflect these lessons."

Today's privatizations by no means represent the first effort to pursue free-market economic policies in Latin America ... On the

* "This article originally appeared at 95 Colum. L.Rev. 223 (1995) Reprinted by permission."

contrary, with few exceptions, the countries … have been cycling back and forth between privatization and nationalization for as long as they have been independent.

The colonial peoples of Latin America achieved independence from Spain and Portugal in a series of revolutions during the first half of the nineteenth century. Following a period of political turbulence that included efforts at monarchical rule, most of the modern nation-states of Central and South America took their present shape by about 1880. While political and economic conditions varied from country to country, in every case the newly emergent national governments embraced the institutions of late nineteenth-century economic liberalism: private property regimes generally accompanied by laissez-faire policies on wealth distribution and the vigorous promotion of capital investment.

Again with considerable variation in the form and pace of change, these regimes were typically followed by a new burst of revolutionary activity that gave rise to the first Latin American nationalization programs. These programs themselves surrendered to a new phase of privatization and free enterprise, which was in turn succeeded by another series of nationalization programs. In many Latin American countries, the current round of privatizations is the fifth phase of a privatization-nationalization cycle.

Unlike the friendly relationship between the U.S. and Canada, the U.S./ Latin American relationship has been filled with mutual contempt, suspicion and dislike. Mexico, like Canada, fears the cultural domination of the U.S., but probably even more importantly fears economic domination by the U.S. through the foreign investor. Despite the large Mexican–American population living in the United States, dealings with Mexico have often been strained and have even included armed conflict between the two countries. Mexico, identifying more with its neighbors to the south, further embraced the import substitution and protectionist policies of other Latin American countries. These activities further alienated the U.S. and chilled any trade and investment related discussions that permeated the U.S./ Canada relationship.

Questions regarding the political will of Latin American governments to stay the course on free trade and open borders will doubtless create much speculation. Whether the current wave of trade and foreign investment liberalization is but one more oscillation that is taking place in Latin America is an important question in international business planning. There is no way of definitively knowing whether the liberalization efforts will be permanent. However, the world is a very different place than existed in the prior oscillations.

Latin America has tried and failed on import substitution and protectionism. Its flirtation with socialist forms of government has also dissipated. The emergence of democratically elected leaders has now promoted free trade and open borders. The United States weighed in on trade liberalization through the Enterprise for the Americas Initiative. All of these factors reached a high point when Mexico entered into the NAFTA and contemporaneously modified its foreign investment law. The possibility remains high that the free trade and open borders decision reflects a fundamental change in Latin America. One important indicator of this shift is the negotiation of major international agreements on trade an investment.

The United States is a substantial exporter of capital. As such, the U.S. government is keenly interested in assuring that the foreign host country treats its nationals fairly. Indeed, a major element in U.S. trade policy is to ensure that the host country promulgate rules that offer market access for U.S. goods and services, as well as protection for capital and intellectual property owned by its nationals. The thrust of the U.S. negotiations has been through bilateral efforts that result in various bilateral investment treaties with various countries. The U.S. has also entered into the North American Free Trade Agreement, which has a complete chapter devoted to the protection of foreign investment. The GATT/WTO trade negotiations have also resulted in the passage of the *Agreement on Trade–Related Investment Measures*, which focus on the removal of trade restrictive investment measures related to the sale of goods.

As mentioned earlier, international agreements are useful devices in facilitating foreign direct investment. The inherent characteristics of an international agreement—a contract between two countries, legal harmonization, and ease in finding the laws with no translation required are very important facilitating factors. Additionally, the international agreement can offer insight on the host country climate toward foreign direct investment. This is especially true where the host is a developing country. In many developing countries, the climate for inbound foreign direct investment has not been hospitable. Usually, when the host is a developed country, the business owners will find rules similar to those found in the United States.

Recall the hypothetical in chapter 1–Delta's Division III owns several valuable patents used in the manufacturing of concrete additives used in oil well drilling. The additive, known as "Quick Dry," is used in concrete to make it harden rapidly. Making "Quick Dry" is a labor-intensive process. Delta has been losing U.S. market share on account of lower cost European additives of comparable quality. Division III is Delta's core business accounting for seventy-five percent of its annual sales.

Delta is convinced that it must reduce its labor cost in manufacturing the additive or risk losing a substantial portion of its market. Delta's Division III is losing market share on account of the high labor cost to manufacture its product. The alternative of licensing the patent to an unrelated licensor to manufacture the additive is not appealing since it represents such a major part of Delta's overall business. Delta has decided to establish a foreign direct investment in a country where the lower labor rate could make it possible to sell its product with a larger profit.

Delta's board of directors anticipates a total investment of fifty million dollars. The plan will ultimately employ two hundred workers. It has not decided on a host country but is considering Mexico or Argentina as possible locations. The following materials analyze the regulatory environment of host countries. The plethora of business/legal issues that emerge in the making of a FDI in the context of an Equity JV are discussed in Section 4.1, infra.

Developed countries generally regulate inbound foreign investment to prevent foreign interests from adversely affecting its security, citizens, or environment. The specifics vary depending on the development level of the country. In developed countries like the U.S., the focus is in restricting foreign investments in certain sensitive industries such as shipping, aviation, telecommunications and energy, or in any case where the national security can be compromised are restricted. Even in non-sensitive industries, the U.S. has been concerned with gauging the amount of foreign investment taking place. In these cases, although there is no outright restriction, reporting requirements are imposed on foreign investors.

Developing countries while being net capital importers are also interested in preventing foreign interests from adversely affecting their country. Historically, developing countries have viewed the foreign direct investor with a certain amount of suspicion. The typical foreign direct investor is thought to be a large multinational enterprise with substantial economic and political strength. Often the developing country believes that left to their own devices, the foreign investor will make exorbitant profits in the country, underpay its employees, strip the natural resources from the country and leave nothing behind. Indeed, this fear and distrust of foreign investors created the environment for the macroeconomic policy of import substitution, which was a dismal failure.

The following excerpt from the World Bank describes what features a domestic legal system should possess in order for it to be deemed friendly towards foreign direct investment. The stated elements are frequently addressed in international investment agreements.

International Economic Law
June 12,1990
Document 111–Hh

WORLD BANK: REPORT TO THE DEVELOPMENT COMMITTEE AND GUIDELINES ON THE TREATMENT OF FOREIGN DIRECT INVESTMENT

Guidelines on the Treatment of Foreign
Direct Investment
The Development Committee

ADMISSION

1. Each State will encourage nationals of other States to invest capital, technology and managerial skill in its territory and, to that end, is expected to admit such investments in accordance with the following provisions.

2. In furtherance of the foregoing principle, each State will: (a) facilitate the admission and establishment of investments by nationals of other States, and (b) avoid making unduly cumbersome or complicated procedural regulations for, or imposing unnecessary conditions on, the admission of such investments.

3. Each State maintains the right to make regulations to govern the admission of private foreign investments. In the formulation and application of such regulations, States will note that experience suggests that certain performance requirements introduced as conditions of admission are often counterproductive and that open admission, possibly subject to a restricted list *of* investments (which are either prohibited or require screening and licensing), is a more effective approach. * * *

4. Without prejudice to the general approach of free admission recommended in Section 3 above, a State may, as an exception, refuse admission to a proposed investment: (i) which is, in the considered opinion of the State, inconsistent with clearly defined requirements of national security; or (ii) which belongs to sectors reserved by the law of the State to its nationals on account of the State's economic development objectives or the strict exigencies of its national interest.

5. Restrictions applicable to national investment on account of public policy (ordre public), public health and the protection of the environment will equally apply to foreign investment.

6. Each State is encouraged to publish, in the form of a handbook or other medium easily accessible to other States and their investors, adequate and regularly updated information about its legislation, regulations and procedures relevant to foreign investment and other information relating to its investment policies including, inter alia, an indication of any classes of investment which it regards as falling under Sections 4 and 5 of this Guideline.

III

TREATMENT

1. For the promotion of international economic cooperation through the medium of private foreign investment, the establishment, operation, management, control, and exercise of rights in such an investment, as well as such other associated activities necessary therefor or incidental thereto, will be consistent with the following standards which are meant to apply simultaneously to all States without prejudice to the provisions of applicable international instruments, and to firmly established rules of customary international law.

2. Each State will extend to investments established in its territory by nationals of any other State fair and equitable treatment according to the standards recommended in these Guidelines.

3. * * * In all cases, full protection and security will be accorded to the investor's rights regarding ownership, control and substantial benefits over his property, including intellectual property. (b) As concerns such other matters as are not relevant to national investors, treatment under the State's legislation and regulations will not discriminate among foreign investors on grounds of nationality.

4. Nothing in this Guideline will automatically entitle nationals of other States to the more favorable standards of treatment accorded to the nationals of certain States under any customs union or free trade area agreement.

A country can indicate a political willingness to favor FDI by encouraging foreign nationals to engage in the transfer of capital. International agreements are useful to commit a country to a path of creating an environment hospitable to FDI. The World Bank guidelines list some concepts that a state should adopt to show that it is willing to encourage and receive foreign direct investment. The World Bank Guidelines can serve as a type of "Hospitality Index" towards foreign direct investment.

The Western Hemisphere has seen brisk activity among its countries in negotiating specific investment treaties or general trade and economic integration agreements with investment components. These agreements generally follow the World Bank Guidelines. As such, they promote foreign direct investment. The agreements focus on six aspects—scope, admission, treatment after admission, the repatriation or transfer of funds, expropriation, and dispute resolution. It is necessary to review the particular agreement to determine the extent of the protections offered.

In agreements deemed favorable, the scope of the investment should cover both the investment and the investor. The investment is typically defined very broadly and includes tangible real and personal property, contracts, joint ventures, loans and intellectual property rights. The investor includes individual and business entities. In some cases there are requirements that when a business entity is used the owners must be residents of one of the signatory countries. This is an anti-treaty shopping mechanism that prevents third country nationals from using the favorable terms of a particular treaty without being entitled to it.

The World Bank Guidelines excerpted above discuss admission standards. The admission standards generally show a willingness to create a favorable climate for the FDI. This is a substantial departure from prior Latin American policy. See Section 1.2, supra. The domestic laws should not discriminate against the foreign capital transferors. The host country is required to have transparency in its rules and regulations involving foreign investment avoiding cumbersome and complicated procedural regulations.

The admission standards recognize the right a host country has in establishing rules that will govern capital flowing into its borders. As noted earlier, the existence of rules and regulations is not the problem. It is only when the rules are unfair or coercive that the flow of capital can be impeded. A country is allowed to restrict the flow of capital into certain sensitive industries. It can also prevent the entry of the capital for national security concerns or in cases where the public order or health may be jeopardized.

Admission standards number three, four, and five restate the international principle that a country has the right to regulate activities within its borders. This is especially true in cases where the investment can impact national security, sensitive industries, public health, the protection of the environment or other concerns of national interest. In these cases, the existence of rules is not deemed to create an unfriendly environment. If you recall, these are the rules the U.S. maintains on inbound foreign direct invest within its borders. The guidelines also include treatment standards that would have the country promise to treat the foreign investment in a non-discriminatory manner.

The agreements also generally require that both the investment and the investor be afforded the better of national or most favored nation treatment. The national treatment standard is a pledge that the investor from a contracting site will be treated as well as the country's own nationals. The exception is where the investment is in some sensitive industry that is reserved only for citizens. The most favored nation requires that it treat an investor from a contracting party no less favorable than they treat the national of some other country. Here too there are exceptions in those cases where a country may be part of a favorable regional arrangement such as a common market.

The next aspect is to see how the FDI is treated after it has been admitted into the country. The treatment characteristic focuses on guaranteeing that the foreign investor will receive fair and equitable treatment in the establishment, operation, management, control, enjoyment and disposal of the investment. The fair and equitable treatment is usually linked to some standard other than the domestic law of the host country. NAFTA, for example, calls for fair and equitable treatment in accordance with international law standards.

Another factor that ranks high in the Hospitality Index is the elimination of performance requirements. The World Bank Guidelines says of performance requirements—"...States will note that experience suggests that certain performance requirements introduced as conditions of admission are often counterproductive..." Performance requirements impact the enjoyment and use of the FDI and are major impediments to the inbound flow of foreign capital . In order to understand the negative impact of performance requirements, one needs to consider the incentives and risks facing the foreign investor.

The incentive for Delta in contemplating a FDI results mainly from external factors—the lowering of costs. High labor and operating costs is making the manufacture of the 'Quick Dry' unfeasible in the United States. However, because of the importance of the patent to Delta's overall profits, it does not want to license the manufacturing to some unrelated Licensee. In order to pick the best host country, it will focus on three important factors—maintaining control over the FDI, limiting its risk, and profit maximization and distribution.

The admission standards of transparency, non-discriminatory and fair and equitable treatment help assuage the fears of the foreign investor pursuant to the risk and control issues. The removal of performance requirements addresses the profit maximization and distribution factors. In order to understand the relationship between profit maximization and distribution with the elimination of performance requirements, one must identify the 'pockets of profit' available to Delta from the FDI. These profit pockets are described in detail in Section 4.1, infra.

There are six sources of benefit or profit that Delta can derive from the FDI. The first benefit is from dividend distributions (as an owner) from the FDI to Delta. The second is from interest income derived from any loans Delta may make to the FDI. The owner/creditor issue is discussed in Section 4.1, infra. The third profit pocket is from gain on the sale of goods and services to the FDI. The fourth is from rental income on the leasing of tangible personal property. The fifth is from royalty income on the licensing of any intangible property. Finally, the sixth benefit derives from the value that can be realized in the case of a subsequent sale of the FDI itself.

Performance requirements limit the pocket profits. For example, forcing Delta to accept a local partner with a fifty-one percent ownership interest can have a substantial negative implication on profit maximization. Other performance requirements include local content requirements on goods produced in the host country, limitations on the amount of royalties that can be repatriated, and the imposition of currency controls. The existence of performance requirements is the best indicator of an inhospitable investment climate.

Performance requirements limiting the transfer of funds from the FDI is anathema to the foreign investor. Modern agreements generally have no impediments to the transfer of funds from the FDI. The funds can come from the FDI as interest, dividends, loans, royalties, sale of goods and services, and the sale of the FDI. In the hospitable environment, countries allow the repatriation to be in usable currency without delay. The developing countries have essentially pledged not to impose currency controls. The agreements also focus on expropriation and dispute resolution, which is discussed infra.

B. THE OUTBOUND FOREIGN DIRECT INVESTMENT UNDER THE NAFTA

1. *Introduction*

The following is an excerpt of the NAFTA investment provisions. Delta will find that the 'Hospitality Index' provided by the NAFTA is high.

The North American Free Trade Agreement

Chapter 11

INVESTMENT

* * *

Article 1101: Scope and Coverage

1. This chapter applies to measures adopted or maintained by a Party relating to: (a) investors of another Party; (b) investments of investors of another Party in the territory of the Party; and (c) with respect to Articles 1106 and 1114, all investments in the territory of the Party.

2. A Party has the right to perform exclusively the economic activities set out in Annex III and to refuse to permit the establishment of investment in such activities. * * *

Article 1102: National Treatment

1. Each Party shall accord to investors of another Party treatment no less favorable than that it accords, in like circumstances, to its own investors with respect to the establishment, acquisition, expansion, management, conduct, operation, and sale or other disposition of investments.

2. Each Party shall accord to investments of investors of another Party treatment no less favorable than that it accords, in like circumstances, to investments of its own investors with respect to the establishment, acquisition, expansion, management, conduct, operation, and sale or other disposition of investments.

3. The treatment accorded by a Party under paragraphs 1 and 2 means, with respect to a state or province, treatment no less favorable than the most favorable treatment accorded, in like circumstances, by

that state or province to investors, and to investments of investors, of the Party of which it forms a part.

4.   For greater certainty, no Party may: (a) impose on an investor of another Party a requirement that a minimum level of equity in an enterprise in the territory of the Party be held by its nationals, other than nominal qualifying shares for directors or incorporators of corporations; or (b) require an investor of another Party, by reason of its nationality, to sell or otherwise dispose of an investment in the territory of the Party.

Article 1103: Most—Favored–Nation Treatment

1.   Each Party shall accord to investors of another Party treatment no less favorable than that it accords, in like circumstances, to investors of any other Party or of a non-Party with respect to the establishment, acquisition, expansion, management, conduct, operation, and sale or other disposition of investments.

2.   Each Party shall accord to investments of investors of another Party treatment no less favorable than that it accords, in like circumstances, to investments of investors of any other Party or of a non-Party with respect to the establishment, acquisition, expansion, management, conduct, operation, and sale or other disposition of investments.

Article 1104: Standard of Treatment

Each Party shall accord to investors of another Party and to investments of investors of another Party the better of the treatment required by Articles 1102 and 1103.

Article 1105: Minimum Standard of Treatment

1.   Each Party shall accord to investments of investors of another Party treatment in accordance with international, including fair and equitable treatment and full protection and security.

2.   Without prejudice to paragraph 1 and notwithstanding Article 1108(7)(b), each Party shall accord to investors of another Party, and to investments of investors of another Party, non-discriminatory treatment with respect to measures it adopts or maintains relating to losses suffered by investments in its territory owning to armed conflict or civil strife.

3.   Paragraph 2 does not apply to existing measures relating to subsidies or grants that would inconsistent with Article 1102 but for Article 1108(7)(b).

Article 1106: Performance Requirements

1.   No Party may impose or enforce any of the following requirements, or enforce any commitment or undertaking, in connection with the establishment, acquisition, expansion, management, conduct or operation of an investment of an investor of a Party or of a non-Party in territory: (a) to export a given level or percentage of goods or services;

(b) to achieve a given level or percentage of domestic content; (c) to purchase, use or accord a preference to goods produced or services provided in its territory, or to purchase goods or services from persons in its territory; (d) to relate in any way the volume or value of imports to the volume or value of exports or to the amount of foreign exchange inflows associated with such investments; (e) to restrict sales of goods or services in its territory that such investment produces or provides by relating such sales in any way to the volume or value of its exports or foreign exchange earnings; (f) to transfer technology, a production process or other proprietary knowledge to a person in its territory, except when the requirement is imposed or the commitment or undertaking is enforced by a court, administrative tribunal or competition authority to remedy an alleged violation of competition laws or to act in a manner not inconsistent with other provisions of this Agreement; or (g) to act as the exclusive supplier of the goods it produces or services it provides to a specific region or world market.

2.   A measure that requires an investment to use a technology to meet generally applicable health, safety or environmental requirements shall not be construed to be inconsistent with paragraph 1(f). For greater certainty, Articles 1102 and 1103 apply to the measure.

3.   No Party may condition the receipt or continued receipt of an advantage, in connection with an investment in its territory of an investor of a Party or of a non-Party, on compliance with any of the following requirements: (a) to achieve a given level or percentage of domestic content; (b) to purchase, use or accord a preference to goods produced in its territory, or to purchase goods from producers in its territory; (c) to relate in any way the volume or value of imports to the volume or value of exports or to the amount of foreign exchange inflows associated with such investment; or (d) to restrict sales of goods or services in its territory that such investment produces or provides by relating such sales in any way to the volume or value of its exports or foreign earnings.

4.   Nothing in paragraph 3 shall be construed to prevent a Party from conditioning the receipt or continued receipt of an advantage, in connection with an investment in its territory of an investor of a Party or of a non-Party, on compliance with a requirement to locate production, provide a service, train or employ workers, construct or expand particular facilities, or carry out research and development, in its territory.

5.   Paragraphs 1 and 3 do not apply to any requirement other than the requirements set out in those paragraphs.

6.   Provided that such measures are not applied in an arbitrary or unjustifiable manner, or do not constitute a disguised restriction on international trade or investment, nothing paragraph 1(b) or (c) or 3(a) or (b) shall be construed to prevent any Party from adopting or maintaining measures, including environmental measures: (a) necessary to secure compliance with laws and regulations that are not inconsistent

with the provisions of this Agreement; (b) necessary to protect human, animal or plant life or health; or (c) necessary for the conservation of living or non-living exhaustible natural resources.

* * *

Article 1109: Transfers

1.   Each Party shall permit all transfers relating to an investment of an investor of another Party in the territory of the Party to be made freely and without delay. Such transfers include: (a) profits, dividends, interest, capital gains, royalty payments, management fees, technical assistance, and other fees, returns in kind and other amounts derived from the investment; (b) proceeds from the sale of all or any part of the investment or from the partial or complete liquidation of the investment; (c) payments made under a contract entered into by the investor, or its investment, including payments made pursuant to a loan agreement; (d) payments made pursuant to Article 1110; and (e) payments arising under Section B.

2.   Each Party shall permit transfers to be made in a freely usable currency at the market rate of exchange prevailing on the date of transfer with respect to spot transactions in the currency to be transferred.

3.   No Party may require its investors to transfer, or penalize its investors that fail to transfer, the income, earnings, profits or other amounts derived from, or attributable to, investments in the territory of another Party.

4.   Notwithstanding paragraphs 1 and 2, a Party may prevent a transfer through the equitable, non-discriminatory and good faith application of its laws relating to: (a) bankruptcy, insolvency or the protection of the rights of creditors; (b) issuing, trading or dealing in securities; (c) criminal or penal offenses; (d) reports of transfers of currency or other monetary instruments; or (e) ensuring the satisfaction of judgments in adjudicatory proceedings.

5.   Paragraph 3 shall not be construed to prevent a Party from imposing any measure through the equitable, non-discriminatory and good faith application of its laws relating to the matters set out in subparagraphs (a) through (e) of paragraph 4.

6.   Notwithstanding paragraph 1, a Party may restrict transfers of returns in kind in circumstances where it could otherwise restrict such transfers under this Agreement, including as set out in paragraph 4.

* * *

The basic safeguards against discriminatory treatment among the three NAFTA member countries are succinctly stated in NAFTA Articles

1102 and 1103. Article 1102 provides for national treatment. Under national treatment, the states pledge that the foreign investor will receive treatment no less favorable than its own citizens. This like treatment, provided for by 1102, extends to investors and the investment. The like treatment standard also covers the establishment, acquisition, expansion, management, conduct, operation, and sale or other disposition of the investment.

In addition to the national treatment standard, NAFTA Article 1103 gives further protection to the member countries by giving them Most Favored Nation (MFN) status as well. Like Article 1102 the MFN status extends to the investor and investment. Likewise, it covers the establishment, acquisition, expansion, management, conduct, operation, and sale or other disposition of the investment as well. The interaction of the two articles provides the member countries the better of national treatment or MFN status.

NAFTA also addresses the important issue of control over the FDI by not permitting forced joint ventures, except in specific areas. Article 1102 (4) states that the parties agree that "... no Party may ... impose on an investor of another party a requirement that a minimum level of equity in an enterprise in the territory of the Party be held by its nationals, other than nominally qualifying shares for directors or incorporators of corporations ..." The so-called forced joint venture are very hostile to the foreign investor. The NAFTA generally eliminates the forced joint venture requirement. In Mexico, there are still instances, however, where a foreign person cannot wholly own an FDI. These exceptions are mandated by law or by business exigencies. The legal issues of these forced joint ventures are discussed in Section 3.3, infra while the business considerations are addressed in Section 4.1, infra.

The NAFTA also addresses the operational control of the FDI. In Article 1107 (1) the parties agreed that "... No Party may require that an enterprise of that Party that is an investment of an investor of another Party appoint to senior management positions individuals of any particular nationality." Thus, the NAFTA thus permits foreign persons to act as senior management. In the case of the naming the board of directors, while the NAFTA [in Article 1107 (2)] permits a party to require that a majority of the board be of a particular nationality, the power cannot be exercised if it impairs the ability of the investor to exercise control over the FDI.

The NAFTA also helps in the important factor of profit maximization and distribution by focusing on the elimination of performance requirements and the elimination of restrictions on payment transfers. Article 1106 prohibits certain performance requirements "... in connection with the establishment, management, conduct, or operation of an investment of an investor of a Party ..." The prohibited performance requirements include export requirements, local content, forced purchase, or the forced transfer of technology except through court order. The article allows a Party to establish performance requirements to meet the health and safety concerns of its nationals so long as the measures are not applied in an arbitrary or unjustifiable manner.

NAFTA Article 1109 focuses on the distribution of profits from the FDI. The foreign investor expects to receive a profit or benefit from the investment. A profitable venture is not useful to the owner unless the profits can be extracted from the FDI. The article states in pertinent part "...Each party shall permit all transfers relating to an investment of an investor of another Party ... freely and without delay. Such transfers include ... profits, dividends, interest, capital gains, royalty payments, management fees, ... other fees, ... returns in kind and other amounts derived from the investment ... payments made under a contract ... including payments made pursuant to a loan agreement ..."

The transfer article is very broad encompassing all of the different types of profit that can be derived from a FDI. In addition it provides that "... Each Party shall permit transfers to be made in a freely usable currency at the market rate of exchange ..." This provision is particularly important in that the FDI will be generating pesos, a soft currency. This essentially is a pledge that Mexico will not impose currency controls. The imposition of currency controls is anathema to foreign direct investment. The article, however, does allow the parties to place transfer controls in the case of bankruptcy, securities trading, and/or criminal or penal offenses.

2. *Minimizing the Risk of Loss on the FDI: The Expropriation Issue*

There are different types of risks facing the foreign investor, however, each type of risk focuses on the potential of losing the capital or investment transferred. One risk is the general business risk of being in the wrong business at the wrong time. This can range from mistakes in the management or operation of the business to selecting a bad joint venture partner. Planning around these business risks is discussed in Section 4.1, infra. The second risk is from action of the host government—the risk of expropriation. These materials focus on the expropriation issue under the NAFTA.

Expropriation occurs when a government takes away property or deprives the owner of its use and enjoyment. It is similar to an eminent domain action in the United States. The taking of property by a government can range from the outright transfer of title to the property or a series of transactions that confiscate, prevent or unreasonably interfere with the investor's right to enjoy the property. The Restatement Third of Foreign Relations Law § 712 refers to this incremental taking as 'creeping expropriation.' The Restatement distinguishes a taking, which violates international law versus governmental regulation, which does not.

Drawing the line between governmental regulation and a taking is difficult. The governmental action must reach the level of nationalization or be confiscatory. The test is whether the government prevents or unreasonably interferes with an owner's enjoyment of its property.

Control is an important element. If the government detains the officers or employees of the business, supervises the work, or takes any of the proceeds of the company—apart from taxation—the action would be confiscatory. Likewise, governmental interference with management or shareholder activities, interference with the appointment of management or directors, or ousting the investor from full management and control of the investment would constitute an expropriation. Non-discriminatory regulation can also be an expropriation. However, the regulation must rise to a confiscatory level as described above.

An expropriation can also occur when a government repudiates a contract. The repudiation may be a taking when it is due to governmental rather than commercial reasons. Restatement § 712 comment h. is helpful in determining when contract repudiation can be an expropriation. It reads in pertinent part: "...A state's repudiation or failure to perform is not a violation of international law under this section if it is based on a bona fide dispute about the obligation or its performance, if it is due to the state's inability to perform, or if nonperformance is motivated by commercial considerations and the state is prepared to pay damages or to submit to adjudication or arbitration and to abide by the judgment or award." The *Azinian* case, infra is an example of a non-expropriation contract repudiation. Other forms of expropriation can include the denial of access to a domestic market and economic impairment if they rise to the level of an expropriation.

The expropriation of property of foreign nationals, whether outright or creeping, has always been the Sword of Damocles hanging over their head. In countries where an investment agreement addresses the issue, the uncertainty is greatly reduced. In other countries uncertainties abound. The expropriation issue has also been the concern of the U.S. government, since the action can deprive U.S. nationals of property. The U.S. State Department under Secretary of State Warren Christopher established an Office of the Coordinator for Business Affairs to help U.S. nationals resolve trade and investment disputes with other governments.

In addition, the United States has established a quasi public corporation—the Overseas Private Investment Corporation (OPIC) to provide insurance against the risk of expropriation. In the case of expropriation, the OPIC is subrogated to the position of the investor. The OPIC then negotiates with the host government. A similar insurance arrangement can be obtained through the Multilateral Insurance Guarantee Agency (MIGA). The MIGA has been formed under the auspices of the World Bank.

The following is an excerpt of the NAFTA expropriation rule:

The North American Free Trade Agreement

Chapter 11

INVESTMENT

Article 1110: Expropriation and Compensation

1. No Party may directly nationalize or expropriate an investment of an investor of another Party in its territory or take a measure

tantamount to nationalize or expropriation of such an investment ("expropriation"), except: (a) for a public purpose; (b) on a non-discriminatory basis; (c) in accordance with due process of law and Article 1105(1); and (d) on payment of compensation in accordance with paragraphs 2 through 6.

2. Compensation shall be equivalent to the fair market value of the expropriated investment immediately before the expropriation took place ("date of expropriation"), and shall not reflect any change in value occurring because the intended expropriation had become known earlier. Valuation criteria shall include going concern value, asset value including declared tax value of tangible property, and other criteria, as appropriate, to determine fair market value.

3. Compensation shall be paid without delay and be fully realizable.

4. If payment is made in a G7 currency, compensation shall include interest at a commercially reasonable rate for that currency from the date of expropriation until the date of actual payment.

5. If a Party elects to pay in a currency other than a G7 currency, the amount paid on the date of payment, if converted into a G7 currency at the market rate of exchange prevailing on that date, shall be no less than if the amount of compensation owed on the date expropriation had been converted into that G7 currency at the market rate of exchange prevailing on that date, and interest had accrued at a commercially reasonable rate for that G7 currency from the date expropriation until the date of payment.

6. On payment, compensation shall be freely transferable as provided in Article 1109. * * *

NAFTA Article 1110 permits expropriation so long as it meets a three-fold test—it must be for a public purpose, on a non-discriminatory basis, in accordance with due process of law while meeting the minimum standard of treatment accorded investments under international law, and the payment of compensation. The due process of law requirement incorporates the minimum standard of treatment provided in Article 1105(1) that states "... Each Party shall accord to investments of investors of another Party treatment in accordance with international, including fair and equitable treatment and full protection and security." Under NAFTA the failure to provide fair and equitable treatment under international legal principles can also be considered an expropriation.

An impediment to the entry of foreign direct investment into Mexico and other developing countries has been the lack of transparency. There is little published law or regulations that can effectively guide the foreign investor on what procedures, permits, and rules are in place. The requirements are discovered in an *ad hoc* manner from people with whom the investor deals. There is little way to ascertain who needs to be involved in the process. As mentioned in Section 1.2, supra the language, cultural, legal, and political differences exacerbate the problem.

The interaction of the various levels of government can pose some severe problems in the transparency area. The NAFTA negotiators saw this problem and included Article 105 which states in pertinent part— "The Parties shall ensure that all necessary measures are taken in order to give effect to the provisions of this Agreement, by state and provincial governments." The case below deals with this issue.

METALCLAD CORPORATION CLAIMANT AND THE UNITED MEXICAN STATES RESPONDENT, INTERNATIONAL CENTRE FOR SETTLEMENT OF INVESTMENT DISPUTES (ADDITIONAL FACILITY)

August 30, 2000, CASE No. A–RB(AF)/97/1. * * *

1. INTRODUCTION

1. This dispute arises out of the activities of the Claimant, Metalclad Corporation (hereinafter "Metalclad"), in the Mexican Municipality of Guadalcazar (hereinafter "Guadalcazar"), located in the Mexican State of San Luis Potosi (hereinafter "SLP"). Metalclad alleges that Respondent, the United Mexican States (hereinafter "Mexico"), through its local governments of SLP and Guadalcazar, interfered with its development and operation of a hazardous waste landfill. Metalclad claims that this interference is a violation of the Chapter Eleven investment provisions of the North American Free Trade Agreement (hereinafter "NAFTA"). In particular, Metalclad alleges violations of (i) NAFTA, Article 1105, which requires each Party to NAFTA to "accord to investments of investors of another Party treatment in accordance with international law, including fair and equitable treatment and full protection and security": and (ii) NAFTA. Article 1110, which provides that "no Party to NAFTA may directly or indirectly nationalize or expropriate an investment of an investor of another Party in its territory or take a measure tantamount to nationalization or expropriation of such an investment ('expropriation'), except: (a) for a public purpose; (b) on a non-discriminatory basis; (c) in accordance with due process of law and Article 1105(l); and (d) on payment of compensation in accordance with paragraphs 2 through 6". Mexico denies these allegations. * * *

2. Metalclad is an enterprise of the United States of America, incorporated under the laws of Delaware. Eco–Metalclad Corporation (hereinafter "ECO") is an enterprise of the United States of America, incorporated under the laws of Utah. ECO is wholly owned by Metalclad, and owns 100% of the shares in Ecosistemas Nacionales, S.A. de C.V. (hereinafter "ECONSA), a Mexican corporation. In 1993, ECONSA purchased the Mexican company Confinamiento Tecnico de ·Residuos In-

dustriales, S.A. de C.V. (hereinafter "COTERIN") with a view to the acquisition, development and operation of the latter's hazardous waste transfer station and landfill in the valley of La Pedrera, located in Guadalcaz'ar. COTERIN is the owner of record ofth e landfill property as well as the permits and licenses which are at the base of this dispute.

3. COTERIN is the "enterprise" on behalf of which Metalclad has, as an "investor of a Party", submitted a claim to arbitration under NAFTA, Article 1117. * * *

V. FACTS AND ALLEGATIONS

A. *The Facilities at Issue*

28. In 1990 the federal government of Mexico authorized COTE-RIN to construct and operate a transfer station for hazardous waste in La Pedrera, a valley located in Guadalcazar in SLP. The site has an area of 814 hectares and lies 100 kilometers northeast of the capital city of SLP, separated from it by the Sierra Guadalcazar mountain range, 70 kilometers from the city of Guadalcazar. Approximately 800 people live within ten kilometers of the site.

29. On January 23, 1993, the National Ecological Institute (hereinafter "INE"), an independent sub-agency of the federal Secretariat of the Mexican Environment, National Resources and Fishing (hereinafter "SEMARNAP"), granted COTERIN a federal permit to construct a hazardous waste landfill in La Pedrera (hereinafter "the landfill"). * * *

B. *Metalclad's Purchase of the Site*
and its Landfill Permits

30. Three months after the issuance of the federal construction permit, on April 23, 1993, Metalclad entered into a 6–month option agreement to purchase COTERIN together with its permits, in order to build the hazardous waste landfill.

31. Shortly thereafter, on May 11, 1993, the government of SLP granted COTERIN a state land use permit to construct the landfill. The permit was issued subject to the condition that the project adapt to the specifications and technical, requirements indicated by the corresponding authorities, and accompanied by the General Statement that the license did not prejudge the rights or ownership of the applicant and did not authorize works, constructions or the functioning of business or activities. * * *

35. On August 10, 1993, the INE granted COTERIN the federal permit for operation of the landfill. On September 10, 1993, Metalclad exercised its option and purchased COTERIN, the landfill site and the associated permits.

36. Metalclad asserts it would not have exercised its COTERIN purchase option but for the apparent approval and support of the project by federal and state officials.

C. Construction of the Hazardous
Waste Landfill

37. Metalclad asserts that shortly after its purchase of COTERIN, the Governor of SLP embarked on a public campaign to denounce and prevent the operation of the landfill. * * *

D. Metalclad is Prevented from
Operating the Landfill

45. Metalclad completed construction of the landfill in March 1995. On March 10, 1995, Metalclad held an "open house," or "inauguration," of the landfill, which was attended by a number of dignitaries from the United States and from Mexico's federal, state and local governments. * * *

50. On December 5, 1995, thirteen months after Metalclad's application for the municipal construction permit was filed, the application was denied. In doing this, the Municipality recalled its decision to deny a construction permit to COTERIN in October 1991 and January 1992 and noted the "impropriety" of Metalclad's construction of the landfill prior to receiving a municipal construction permit.

51. There is no indication that the Municipality gave any consideration to the construction of the landfill and the efforts at operation during the thirteen months during which the application was pending.

52. Metalclad has pointed out that there was no evidence of inadequacy of performance by Metalclad of any legal obligation, nor any showing that Metalclad violated the terms of any federal or state permit; that there was no evidence that the Municipality gave any consideration to the recently completed environmental reports indicating that the site was in fact suitable for a hazardous waste landfill; that there was no evidence that the site, as constructed, failed to meet any specific construction requirements; that there was no evidence that the Municipality ever required or issued a municipal construction permit for any other construction project in Guadalcazar; and that there was no evidence that there was an established administrative process with respect to municipal construction permits in the Municipality of Guadalcazar.

53. Mexico asserts that Metalclad was aware through due diligence that a municipal permit might be necessary on the basis of the case of COTERIN (1991, 1992), and other past precedents for various projects in SLP.

54. Metalclad was not notified of the Town Council meeting where the permit application was discussed and rejected, nor was Metalclad given any opportunity to participate in that process. Metalclad's request for reconsideration of the denial of the permit was rejected. * * *

62. The landfill remains dormant. Metalclad has not sold or transferred any portion of it. * * *

VI.   Applicable Law

70. A Tribunal established pursuant to NAFTA Chapter Eleven, Section B must decide the issues in dispute in accordance with NAFTA and applicable rules of international law. (NAFTA Article 1131(1)). In addition, NAFTA Article 102(2) provides that the Agreement must be interpreted and applied in the light of its stated objectives and in accordance with applicable rules of international law. These objectives specifically include transparency and the substantial increase in investment opportunities in the territories of the Parties. (NAFTA Article 102(l)(c)). The Vienna Convention on the Law of Treaties, Article 31(l) provides that a treaty is to be interpreted in good faith in accordance with the ordinary meaning to be given to the terms of the treaty in their context and in the light of the treaty's object and purpose. The context for the purpose of the interpretation of a treaty shall comprise, in addition to the text, including its preamble and annexes, any agreement relating to the treaty which was made between all the parties in connection with the conclusion of the treaty. *(1d.,* Article 31(2)(a)). There shall also be taken into account, together with the context, any relevant rules of international law applicable in the relations between the parties. *(1d.,* Article 31(3)). Every treaty in force is binding upon the parties to it and must be performed by them in good faith. *(1d.,* Article 26). A State party to a treaty may not invoke the provisions of its internal law as justification for its failure to perform the treaty. *(ld.,* Article 27).

71. The Parties to NAFTA specifically agreed to "ENSURE a predictable commercial framework for business planning and investment." (NAFTA Preamble, para. 6 (emphasis in original)). NAFTA further requires that "[e]ach Party shall ensure that its laws, regulations, procedures, and administrative rulings of general application respecting any matter covered by this Agreement are promptly published or otherwise made available in such a manner as to enable interested persons and Parties to become acquainted with them." *Id.* Article 1802. 1.

VII.   The Tribunal's Decision

72. Metalclad contends that Mexico, through its local governments of SLP and

Guadalcazar, interfered with and precluded its operation of the landfill. Metalclad alleges that this interference is a violation of Articles 1105 and 1110 of Chapter Eleven of the investment provisions of NAFTA.

A.   *Responsibility for the conduct of state and local governments*

73. A threshold question is whether Mexico is internationally responsible for the acts of SLP and Guadalcazar. The issue was largely disposed of by Mexico in paragraph 233 of its post-hearing submission, which stated that "[Mexico] did not plead that the acts of the Municipal-

ity were not covered by NAFTA. [Mexico] was, and remains, prepared to proceed on the assumption that the normal rule of state responsibility applies; that is, that the Respondent can be internationally responsible for the acts of state organs at all three levels of government." Parties to that Agreement must "ensure that all necessary measures are taken in order to give effect to the provisions of the Agreement, including their observance, except as otherwise provided in this Agreement, by state and provincial governments". *(NAFTA* Article 105) A reference to a state or province includes local governments of that state or province. *(NAFTA* Article 201(2)) The exemptions from the requirements of Articles 1105 and 1110 laid down in Article 1108(*l*) do not extend to states or local governments. This approach accords fully with the established position in customary international law. This has been clearly stated in Article 10 of the draft articles on state responsibility adopted by the International Law Commission of the United Nations in 1975 which, though currently still under consideration, may nonetheless be regarded as an accurate restatement of the present law: "The conduct of an organ of a State, of a territorial government entity or of an entity empowered to exercise elements of the Governmental authority, such organ having acted in that capacity, shall be considered as an act of the State under international law even if, in the particular case, the organ exceeded its competence according to internal law or contravened instructions concerning its activity". *(Yearbook of the International Law Commission, 1975, vol. ii, p.61)*

B. NAFTA Article 1105: Fair and Equitable Treatment

74.   NAFTA Article 1105(1) provides that "each Party shall accord to investments of investors of another Party treatment in accordance with international law, including fair and equitable treatment and full protection and security". For the reasons set out below, the Tribunal finds that Metalclad's investment was not accorded fair and equitable treatment in accordance with international law, and that Mexico has violated NAFTA Article 1105(*l*).

75.   An underlying objective of NAFTA is to promote and increase cross-border investment opportunities and ensure the successful implementation of investment initiatives. (NAFTA Article 102(1))

76.   Prominent in the statement of principles and rules that introduces the Agreement is the reference to "transparency" (NAFTA Article 102(1)). The Tribunal understands this to include the idea that all relevant legal requirements for the purpose of initiating, completing and successfully operating investments made, or intended to be made, under the Agreement should be capable of being readily known to all affected investors of another Party. There should be no room for doubt or uncertainty on such matters. Once the authorities of the central government of any Party (whose international responsibility in such matters has been identified in the preceding section) become aware of any scope for misunderstanding or confusion in this connection, it is their duty to

ensure that the correct position is promptly determined and clearly stated so that investors can proceed with all appropriate expedition in the confident belief that they are acting in accordance with all relevant laws.

77.   Metalclad acquired COTERIN for the sole purpose of developing and operating a hazardous waste landfill in the valley of La Pedrera, in Guadalcazar, SLP.

78.   The Government of Mexico issued federal construction and operating permits for the landfill prior to Metalclad's purchase of COTERIN, and the Government of SLP likewise issued a state operating permit which implied its political support for the landfill project.

79.   A central point in this case has been whether, in addition to the above-mentioned permits, a municipal permit for the construction of a hazardous waste landfill was required.

80.   When Metalclad inquired, prior to its purchase of COTERIN, as to the necessity for municipal permits, federal officials assured it that it had all that was needed to undertake the landfill project. Indeed, following Metalclad's acquisition of COTERIN, the federal government extended the federal construction permit for eighteen months. * * *

85.   Metalclad was led to believe, and did believe, that the federal and state permits allowed for the construction and operation of the landfill. Metalclad argues that in all hazardous waste matters, the Municipality has no authority. However, Mexico argues that constitutionally and lawfully the Municipality has the authority to issue construction permits.

86.   Even if Mexico is correct that a municipal construction permit was required, the evidence also shows that, as to hazardous waste evaluations and assessments, the federal authority's jurisdiction was controlling and the authority of the municipality only extended to appropriate construction considerations. Consequently, the denial of the permit by the Municipality by reference to environmental impact considerations in the case of what was basically a hazardous waste disposal landfill, was improper, as was the municipality's denial of the permit for any reason other than those related to the physical construction or defects in the site.

87.   Relying on the representations of the federal government, Metalclad started constructing the landfill, and did this openly and continuously, and with the full knowledge of the federal, state, and municipal governments, until the municipal "Stop Work Order" on October 26, 1994. The basis of this order was said to have been Metalclad's failure to obtain a municipal construction permit.

88.   In addition, Metalclad asserted that federal officials told it that if it submitted an application for a municipal construction permit, the Municipality would have no legal basis for denying the permit and that it would be issued as a matter of course. The absence of a clear rule as to the requirement or not of a municipal construction permit, as well as the

absence of any established practice or procedure as to the manner of handling applications for a municipal construction permit, amounts to a failure on the part of Mexico to ensure the transparency required by NAFTA. * * *

93.   The Tribunal therefore finds that the construction permit was denied without any consideration of, or specific reference to, construction aspects or flaws of the physical facility. * * *

99.   Mexico failed to ensure a transparent and predictable framework for Metalclad's business planning and investment. The totality of these circumstances demonstrates a lack of orderly process and timely disposition in relation to an investor of a Party acting in the expectation that it would be treated fairly and justly in accordance with the NAFTA.

100.   Moreover, the acts of the State and the Municipality—and therefore the acts of Mexico—fail to comply with or adhere to the requirements of NAFTA, Article 1105(l) that each Party accord to investments of investors of another Party treatment in accordance with international law, including fair and equitable treatment. This is so particularly in light of the governing principle that internal law (such as the Municipality's stated permit requirements) does not justify failure to perform a treaty. *(Vienna Convention on the Law of* Treaties, Arts. 26, 27).

101.   The Tribunal therefore holds that Metalclad was not treated fairly or equitably under the NAFTA and succeeds on its claim under Article 1105.

C.   NAFTA, Article 1110: Expropriation

102.   NAFTA Article 1110 provides that "[n]o party shall directly or indirectly expropriate an investment . . . or take a measure tantamount to . . . expropriation except: (a) for a public purpose; (b) on a non-discriminatory basis; (c) in accordance with due process of law and Article 1105(l); and (d) on payment of compensation . . ."

"A measure" is defined in Article 201(l) as including "any law, regulation, procedure, requirement or practice".

103.   Thus, expropriation under NAFTA includes not only open, deliberate and acknowledged takings of property, such as outright seizure or formal or obligatory transfer of title in favour of the host State, but also covert or incidental interference with the use of property which has the effect of depriving the owner, in whole or in significant part, of the use or reasonably-to-be-expected economic benefit of property even if not necessarily to the obvious benefit of the host State.

104.   By permitting or tolerating the conduct of Guadalcazar in relation to Metalclad which the Tribunal has already hold amounts to unfair and inequitable treatment breaching Article 1105 and by thus participating or acquiescing in the denial to Metalclad of the right to operate the landfill, notwithstanding the fact that the project was fully approved and endorsed by the federal government, Mexico must be held

to have taken a measure tantamount to expropriation in violation of NAFTA Article 1110(*l*).

105.   The Tribunal holds that the exclusive authority for siting and permitting a hazardous waste landfill resides with the Mexican federal government. * * *

107.   These measures, taken together with the representations of the Mexican federal government, on which Metalclad relied, and the absence of a timely, orderly or substantive basis for the denial by the Municipality of the local construction permit, amount to an indirect expropriation. * * *

112.   In conclusion, the Tribunal holds that Mexico has indirectly expropriated Metalclad's investment without providing compensation to Metalclad for the expropriation. Mexico has violated Article 1110 of the NAFTA. * * *

In *Metalclad* the plaintiff alleged that Mexico through the local government in *San Luis Potosi* interfered with its development and operation of a hazardous waste landfill. The plaintiff built the plant but was unable to begin operations because the local government would not issue a required permit. It sued Mexico, alleging a violation of the fair and equitable standard promised under NAFTA Article 1105(1). The Tribunal found for the plaintiff by linking the lack of transparency as a violation under Article 1105(1). Mexico has given notice that it intends to appeal the Tribunal's decision.

Returning to the basic expropriation issue, NAFTA Article 1110(1) follows the U.S. conception of the requirements to have a valid "taking" by a foreign state. The public purpose requirement is rarely contested. A sovereign has much latitude under the act of state doctrine and sovereign immunity making a decision to take for a "public purpose" a rare subject of review.

The Restatement Third of Foreign Relations Law is helpful on the issue of discrimination. "Formulations of the rules on expropriations generally include a prohibition of discrimination, implying that a program of taking that singles out aliens generally, or aliens of a particular nationality, or particular aliens would violate international law ... Discrimination implies unreasonable distinction. Takings that invidiously single out property of persons of a particular nationality would be unreasonable ..."[1] The non-discrimination and public purpose test are rarely used by themselves. The usual complaint in expropriations focuses on the compensation issue.

---

1.   Restatement Third of the Foreign Relations Law of the United States § 712 f.

The principal issues on compensation involve three questions—how much will the foreign investor receive? When will the compensation be paid? What currency will be used for the payment? The position of the U.S. government and foreign investor is predictable—full, fair market value, payable immediately in U.S. dollars. Former Secretary State of State Cordell Hull enunciated the U.S. standard of prompt, adequate, and effective compensation after Mexico expropriated the property in Mexico of U.S. oil companies. Developing countries historically had set the payment at a net amount, after making adjustments it deems proper, payable over a long period of time in the currency of the host government.

The standard espoused by developing countries found support in a United Nations Resolution[2] using the phraseology of "appropriate compensation." The "appropriate" standard was intended to reflect a payment over time, at the fair value of the foreign investment, in currency of the host country. Additionally, the concept of fair value allowed a reduction from the fair market value of the foreign investment for certain adjustments. These adjustments reflected the view that many foreign investments were from colonial powers.

The widely held view by the developing countries was that the nationals of these colonial powers had improperly extracted wealth from the host country. The "adjustments" would compensate the host countries for those historical injustices. These two competing positions had been the basis for much disagreement in the foreign direct investment area. The newer investment agreements abandon the U.N. standard.

The NAFTA Article 1110 standard is very similar to the U.S. position. It provides that compensation to the investor be made on the basis of the fair market value of the expropriated investment immediately before the expropriation. (See the materials in Section 2.1, supra for valuation techniques that are used to establish the fair market value of a business enterprise.) The compensation shall be paid without delay and be fully realizable. The payment can be in a hard or soft currency. However, if payment is made in a soft currency the government will adjust the price to reflect any devaluation from the time of expropriation to the time of actual payment.

C. FOREIGN DIRECT INVESTMENT UNDER THE U.S. BILATERAL INVESTMENT TREATY PROGRAM

In addition to investment sections on broader trade agreements like the TRIM agreement under the GATT and the

---

2. G.A. Res. 1803, U.N. GAOR, 17th   A/5217(1963).
Sess., Supp. No. 17, at 15, U.N. Doc.

investment chapter under the NAFTA, countries have entered into agreements specifically related to foreign investment. The agreements are referred to as bilateral investment treaties. These types of agreements are bilateral on account of the political problems encountered in negotiating multilateral investment treaties. For example, the Multilateral Agreement on Investment under the auspices of the Organizations of Economic Cooperation and Development has been in negotiation since 1995 without producing an agreement.

The bilateral investment treaty, known as a BIT, generally is negotiated between a developed country and a developing one. Its term reflects the political willingness of the host developing country to establish an environment of incentives and safeguards for the foreign investment and investor. The U.S. has signed over thirty BITs in its bilateral investment treaty program. Among them is the U.S. Argentina BIT excerpted below.

TREATY WITH ARGENTINA CONCERNING THE RECIPROCAL ENCOURAGEMENT AND PROTECTION OF INVESTMENT

1991 WL 701302.

* * *

LETTER OF TRANSMITTAL

THE WHITE HOUSE, January 19, 1993.
To the Senate of the United States:

With a view to receiving the advice and consent of the Senate to ratification, I transmit herewith the Treaty Between the United States of America and the Argentine Republic Concerning the Reciprocal Encouragement and Protection of Investment, with Protocol, signed at Washington on November 14, 1991; and an amendment to the Protocol effected by exchange of notes at Buenos Aires on August 24 and November 6, 1992. I transmit also, for the information of the Senate, the report of the Department of State with respect to this treaty.

This is the first bilateral investment treaty with a Latin American country to be transmitted to the Senate since the announcement of my Enterprise for the Americas Initiative in June 1990. The treaty is designed to protect U.S. investment and encourage private sector development in Argentina and to support the economic reforms taking place there. The treaty's standstill and rollback of Argentina's trade-distorting performance requirements are precedent-setting steps in opening markets for U.S. exports. In this regard, as well as in its approach to dispute settlement, the treaty will serve as a model for our negotiations with other South American countries.

The treaty is fully consistent with U.S. policy toward international investment. A specific tenet, reflected in this treaty, is that U.S. investment abroad and foreign investment in the United States should receive fair, equitable, and nondiscriminatory treatment. Under this treaty, the Parties also agree to international law standards for expropriation and expropriation compensation; free transfers of funds associated with investments; and the option of the investor to resolve disputes with the host government through international arbitration. * * *

The bilateral investment treaty (BIT) with Argentina represents an important milestone in the BIT program. It is the first BIT concluded with a Latin American country since the announcement of your Enterprise for the Americas Initiative in June 1990. Argentina, like many Latin American countries, has long subscribed to the Calvo Doctrine, which requires that aliens submit disputes arising in a country to that country's local courts. The conclusion of this treaty, which contains an absolute right to international arbitration of investment disputes, removes U.S. investors from the restrictions of the Calvo Doctrine and should help pave the way for similar agreements with other Latin American states.

By providing important protections to investors and creating a more stable and predictable legal framework for investment, the BIT helps to encourage U.S. investment in the economies of its treaty partners. It is U.S. policy to advise potential treaty partners that conclusion of a BIT with the United States is an important and favorable factor for U.S. investors, but does not in and of itself result in immediate increases in private U.S. investment flows.

Argentina has signed BITs with several European countries, including France, as well as with Canada and Chile. The U.S. treaty, however, is more comprehensive than these other BITs.

The Office of the United States Trade Representative and the Department of State jointly lead BIT negotiations, with assistance from the Departments of Commerce and Treasury. The United States has signed nineteen other BITs–with Armenia, Bangladesh, Bulgaria, Cameroon, the Congo, the Czech and Slovak Federal Republic, Egypt, Grenada, Haiti, Kazakhstan, Morocco, Panama, Romania, the Russian Federation, Senegal, Sri Lanka, Tunisia, Turkey, and Zaire–and a business and economic relations treaty with Poland, which contains the BIT elements. * * *

The Argentina treaty satisfies the main BIT objectives, which are:

Investment of nationals and companies of one Party in the territory of the other Party (investments) receive the better of the treatment accorded to domestic investments in like circumstances (national treatment), or the treatment accorded to third country investments in like circumstances (most-favored-nation (MFN) treatment), both on establishment and thereafter, subject to certain specified exceptions;

Investments are guaranteed freedom from performance requirements, such as obligations to use local products or to export goods; Companies, which are investments may hire top managers of their choice, regardless of nationality;

Expropriation can occur only in accordance with international law standards: in a non-discriminatory manner; for a public purpose; and upon payment of prompt, adequate, and effective compensation;

Investment-related funds are guaranteed unrestricted transfer in a freely usable currency; and

Nationals and companies of either Party and their investments, have access to binding international arbitration in investment disputes with the host government, without first resorting to domestic courts.

As does the model BIT, the Argentina treaty allows sectoral exceptions to national and MFN treatment, as set forth in protocol to the treaty. The U.S. exceptions are designed to protect governmental regulatory interests and to accommodate the derogations from national treatment and, in some cases, MFN treatment in existing state or federal law.

Sectors and matters which the U.S. excepts from national treatment are air transportation; ocean and coastal shipping; banking; insurance; energy and power production; custom house brokers; ownership and operation of broadcast or common carrier radio and television stations; ownership of real property; ownership of shares in the Communications Satellite Corporation; the provision of common carrier telephone and telegraph services; the provision of submarine cable services; and use of land and natural resources. The United States also reserves the right to make or maintain limited exceptions to national treatment with respect to certain programs involving government grants, loans, and insurance.

U.S. exceptions from both national and MFN treatment, which are based on reciprocity are mining on the public domain; maritime services and maritime-related services; and primary dealership in United States government securities.

The Argentine exceptions to national treatment are real estate in the Border Areas; air transportation; shipbuilding; nuclear energy centers; uranium mining; insurance; and fishing. "Mining" was included in Argentina's list of national treatment exceptions at the time the treaty was signed but was deleted by an amendment effected by exchange of notes August 24 and November 6, 1992. This will ensure that treaty protections will be extended to an additional sector of significant commercial interest to U.S. investors. In no sectors of the Argentine economy are there restrictions on MFN treatment to be accorded to U.S. investments.

Regarding the obligation not to impose performance requirements, the Argentina treaty contains a protocol provision, which recognizes that Argentina currently maintains performance requirements in the automotive industry. These performance requirements may not be intensified, and Argentina undertakes to exert its best efforts to eliminate them within the shortest possible period, and will ensure their elimination no later than eight years from the entry into force of the treaty. Pending such elimination, Argentina undertakes that these performance requirements shall not be applied in a manner that places existing investments at a competitive disadvantage to any new entrants in this industry.

Achieving such a roll-back of existing performance requirements is a landmark accomplishment and should serve as a model for agreements with other countries which maintain analogous requirements. * * *

The BIT with Argentina provides that an investment dispute between a Party and a national or company of the other Party, including a dispute involving an investment authorization or the interpretation of an investment agreement, may be submitted to international arbitration six months after the dispute arose. Exhaustion of local remedies is not required. The treaty identifies several different procedures for arbitration, at the investor's option: the International Centre for the Settlement of Investment Disputes ("ICSID"), upon Argentina's adherence to the ICSID Convention; the ICSID Additional Facility, if ICSID is not available; or ad hoc arbitration under the Arbitration Rules of the United Nations Commission on International Trade Law (UNCITRAL).

The other U.S. Government agencies, which negotiated the treaty, concur in my recommendation that it be transmitted to the Senate at an early date. * * *

ARTICLE I

1. For the purposes of this Treaty, (a) "investment" means every kind of investment in the territory of one Party owned or controlled directly or indirectly by nationals or companies of the other Party, such as equity, debt, and service and investment contracts; and includes without limitation: (i) tangible and intangible property, including rights, such as mortgages, liens and pledges; (ii) a company or shares of stock or other interests in a company or interests in the assets thereof; (iii) a claim to money or a claim to performance having economic value and directly related to an investment; (iv) intellectual property * * *

2.   Each Party reserves the right to deny to any company of the other Party the advantages of this Treaty if (a) nationals of any third country, or nationals of such Party, control such company and the company has no substantial business activities in the territory of the other Party, or (b) the company is controlled by nationals of a third country with which the denying Party does not maintain normal economic relations. * * *

ARTICLE II

1.   Each Party shall permit and treat investment, and activities associated therewith, on a basis no less favorable than that accorded in like situations to investment or associated activities of its own nationals or companies, or of nationals or companies of any third country, whichever is the more favorable, subject to the right of each Party to make or maintain exceptions falling within one of the sectors or matters listed in the Protocol to this Treaty. * * *

2.   (a) Investment shall at all times be accorded fair and equitable treatment, shall enjoy full protection and security and shall in no case be accorded treatment less than that required by international law.

(b) Neither Party shall in any way impair by arbitrary or discriminatory measures the management, operation, maintenance, use, enjoyment, acquisition, expansion, or disposal of investments. For the purposes of dispute resolution under Articles VII and VIII, a measure may be arbitrary or discriminatory notwithstanding the opportunity to review such measure in the courts or administrative tribunals of a Party.

(c) Each Party shall observe any obligation it may have entered into with regard to investments.

3.   Subject to the laws relating to the entry and sojourn of aliens, nationals of either Party shall be permitted to enter and to remain in the territory of the other Party for the purpose of establishing, developing, administering or advising on the operation of an investment to which they, or a company of the first Party that employs them, have committed or are in the process of committing a substantial amount of capital or other resources.

4.   Companies which are legally constituted under the applicable laws or regulations of one Party, and which are investments, shall be permitted to engage top managerial personnel of their choice, regardless of nationality.

5.   Neither Party shall impose performance requirements as a condition of establishment, expansion or maintenance of investments, which require or enforce commitments to export goods produced, or which specify that goods or services must be purchased locally, or which impose any other similar requirements.

6.   Each Party shall provide effective means of asserting claims and enforcing rights with respect to investments, investment agreements, and investment authorizations.

7. Each Party shall make public all laws, regulations, administrative practices and procedures, and adjudicatory decisions that pertain to or affect investments.

8. The treatment accorded by the United States of America to investments and associated activities of nationals and companies of the Argentine Republic under the provisions of this Article shall in any State, Territory or possession of the United States of America be no less favorable than the treatment accorded therein to investments and associated activities of nationals of the United States of America resident in, and companies legally constituted under the laws and regulations of, other States, Territories or possessions of the United States of America.

9. The most favored nation provisions of this Article shall not apply to advantages accorded by either Party to nationals or companies of any third country by virtue of that Party's binding obligations that derive from full membership in a regional customs union or free trade area, whether such an arrangement is designated as a customs union, free trade area, common market or otherwise.

ARTICLE III

This Treaty shall not preclude either Party from prescribing laws and regulations in connection with the admission of investments made in its territory by nationals or companies of the other Party or with the conduct of associated activities, provided, however, that such laws and regulations shall not impair the substance of any of the rights set forth in this Treaty.

ARTICLE IV

1. Investments shall not be expropriated or nationalized either directly or indirectly through measures tantamount to expropriation or nationalization ("expropriation") except for a public purpose; in a non-discriminatory manner; upon payment of prompt, adequate and effective compensation; and in accordance with due process of law and the general principles of treatment provided for in Article II(2). Compensation shall be equivalent to the fair market value of the expropriated investment immediately before the expropriatory action was taken or became known, whichever is earlier; be paid without delay; include interest at a commercially reasonable rate from the date of expropriation; be fully realizable; and be freely transferable at the prevailing market rate of exchange on the date of expropriation.

2. A national or company of either Party that asserts that all or part of its investment has been expropriated shall have a right to prompt review by the appropriate judicial or administrative authorities of the other Party to determine whether any such expropriation has occurred and, if so, whether such expropriation, and any compensation therefor, conforms to the provisions of this Treaty and the principles of international law.

3. Nationals or companies of either Party whose investments suffer losses in the territory of the other Party owing to war or other armed

conflict, revolution, state of national emergency, insurrection, civil disturbance or other similar events shall be accorded treatment by such other Party no less favorable than that accorded to its own nationals or companies or to nationals or companies of any third country, whichever is the more favorable treatment, as regards any measures it adopts in relation to such losses.

ARTICLE V

1. Each Party shall permit all transfers related to an investment to be made freely and without delay into and out of its territory. Such transfers include: (a) returns; (b) compensation pursuant to Article IV; (c) payments arising out of an investment dispute; (d) payments made under a contract, including amortization of principal and accrued interest payments made pursuant to a loan agreement directly related to an investment; (e) proceeds from the sale or liquidation of all or any part of an investment; and (f) additional contributions to capital for the maintenance or development of an investment.

2. Except as provided in Article IV paragraph 1, transfers shall be made in a freely usable currency at the prevailing market rate of exchange on the date of transfer with respect to spot transactions in the currency to be transferred. The free transfer shall take place in accordance with the procedures established by each Party; such procedures shall not impair the rights set forth in this Treaty. * * *

ARTICLE VII

1. For purposes of this Article, an investment dispute is a dispute between a Party and a national or company of the other Party arising out of or relating to (a) an investment agreement between that Party and such national or company; (b) an investment authorization granted by that Party's foreign investment authority (if any such authorization exists) to such national or company; or (c) an alleged breach of any right conferred or created by this Treaty with respect to an investment.

2. In the event of an investment dispute, the parties to the dispute should initially seek a resolution through consultation and negotiation. If the dispute cannot be settled amicably, the national or company concerned may choose to submit the dispute for resolution: (a)to the courts or administrative tribunals of the Party that is a party to the dispute; or (b)in accordance with any applicable, previously agreed dispute-settlement procedures; or (c) in accordance with the terms of paragraph 3.

3. (a) Provided that the national or company concerned has not submitted the dispute for resolution under paragraph 2(a) or (b) and that six months have elapsed from the date on which the dispute arose, the national or company concerned may choose to consent in writing to the submission of the dispute for settlement by binding arbitration: (i) to the International Centre for the Settlement of Investment Disputes ("Centre") established by the Convention on the Settlement of Investment Disputes between States and Nationals of other States, done at Washington, March 18, 1965 ("ICSID Convention"), provided that the

Party is a party to such Convention; or (ii) to the Additional Facility of the Centre, if the Centre is not available; or (iii) in accordance with the Arbitration Rules of the United Nations Commission on International Trade Law (UNICTRAL); or (iv) to any other arbitration institution, or in accordance with any other arbitration rules, as may be mutually agreed between the parties to the dispute.(b) Once the national or company concerned has so consented, either party to the dispute may initiate arbitration in accordance with the choice so specified in the consent.

4.   Each Party hereby consents to the submission of any investment dispute for settlement by binding arbitration in accordance with the choice specified in the written consent of the national or company under paragraph 3. * * *

The Argentine BIT addresses the major investment issues—scope of the investment, admissions standards, treatment, transfer and funds, expropriation and dispute settlement. The treaty provides a very broad definition of investment that includes equity, debt, service and invest-ment contracts, and various types of intellectual property. There is also a prohibition on nationals of other countries trying to "piggy back" their way into this investment treaty. The U.S. is sensitive to the issue of treaty shopping. The central idea behind the bilateral investment treaty array is to aid developing countries. The U.S. does not want a national of a developed country to establish a subsidiary in Argentina, in this case, and then be able to avail itself of the U.S./ Argentina investment treaty.

The treaty generally provides that the parties will afford their nationals the better of either national or most favored nation treatment. In addition, the parties agree to accord foreign investment fair and equitable treatment no less favorable than allowed under international law. This is similar to the NAFTA standard. Under this test, the foreign person may receive better treatment than a national of the particular country. This is a major concession for Argentina and many developing countries. Additionally, neither party may use arbitrary or discriminato-ry measures in the acquisition, management, use, or disposition of the foreign investment.

There are several major concessions to the United States in these treaties. One important concession is the promise by the parties to not impose performance requirements. The U.S. does not impose these types of requirements so the only country that is acquiescing is the developing country. The prohibition against performance requirements includes not only the acquisition of the foreign investment but also includes the maintenance or expansion of the foreign investment. As can be seen from the terms, the BIT investment regime is very similar to the NAFTA investment chapter.

In the expropriation issue, the U.S./Argentina BIT prohibits the taking of property either directly or indirectly through measures tantamount to a taking unless certain standards are met. The measures 'tantamount to a taking' are also referred to as creeping expropriation and broadly include those measures that a government enacts that have the effect of preventing the use and enjoyment of the FDI by the foreign owner. The standards through which a taking would be permissible include the requirement that it be carried out in accordance with international legal standards. This includes the requirement that the taking be non-discriminatory, for a public purpose and for which prompt, adequate, and effective compensation is paid.

The BIT also provides for the use of international arbitration for the settlement of investment disputes without first having to exhaust local remedies. This is a major departure for Argentina. The idea that a foreigner would not have to resort to Argentine courts to resolve a dispute but rather is permitted to go before an international arbitral tribunal strikes at the heart of the Calvo Doctrine. The fact that the preeminent Argentine Jurist Carlos Calvo formulated the 'Calvo Doctrine' in the first place makes the Argentine approval all the more remarkable. The following section describes the dispute settlement mechanisms under the NAFTA and BIT regime.

SECTION 3.2   THE DISPUTE SETTLEMENT PROCEDURES UNDER NAFTA[3]

There has been a disagreement of long standing between developed and developing countries concerning the role that international law and international tribunals should play in the resolution of foreign direct investment disputes. The historical position by developing countries was that the foreign investor needed to look to domestic courts to settle any investment dispute. This concept has been named the "Calvo Doctrine" after the famed Argentine Jurist Carlos Calvo who framed the concept.

Under the Calvo doctrine the host country asserts exclusive jurisdiction over its territory. Therefore, any claim by a foreign person against the host country must be adjudicated in the courts of the host country. The Calvo doctrine found its way in many foreign investment laws in domestic legal systems through the "Calvo Clause." The typical Calvo clause provides that if the foreigner invokes the protection of its government, the investment is forfeited to the host country. One of the weak links in the foreign direct investment area is the distrust by the foreign investors of the domestic courts of developing countries.

A major concession by developing countries in modern bilateral investment treaties and investment chapters in broader trade agreements is the abandonment of the Calvo Clause. The NAFTA Investment

---

3. I am indebted to my colleague Jack Coe for his knowledge of international arbitration and his willingness to share his thoughts. Any insights in these materials are due in large part to his observations. Any mistakes are, of course, mine.

Chapter and BITS generally mark a substantial departure from the Calvo Doctrine by providing for the settlement of investment by resorting to international tribunals. Specifically, they provides for the submission of the dispute to the International Centre for the Settlement of Investment Disputes (ICSID) or any other arbitration institution that may be agreed upon by the parties. The ICSID was established by the *Convention on the Settlement of Investment Disputes Between States and Nationals of Other States*. The ICSID operates under the auspices of the World Bank.

Alternative dispute resolution has grown rapidly in the United States. The resolution of disputes through mediation and arbitration covers virtually all of the areas of human interaction. The favored dispute settlement procedure in bilateral investment treaties and investment chapters of broader trade agreements has been arbitration. Because of the inclusion of the arbitration option in international agreements, international law provides the rules rather than the domestic legal system. This feature is quite attractive. However, the benefit is tempered by the fact that most international agreements do not have supra-national authority. The domestic systems still play an important role.

International arbitration provides a neutral forum with flexible and private proceedings. The tribunal members are experts in their field and the arbitration result can be enforced through several important treaties. The neutrality applies to both geography and legal rules. International arbitration rules incorporate concepts from both common and civil law systems. In addition, arbitration awards can be appealed on procedural grounds—not substantive ones. Also, the enforcement of arbitration awards is generally more effective than the enforcement of foreign judgments. The following materials describe the dispute resolution procedures under the NAFTA.

RESOLUTION OF INVESTMENT DISPUTES UNDER THE NORTH AMERICAN FREE TRADE AGREEMENT

David A. Gantz
10 Ariz. J. Int'l & Comp. L. 335 (1993).

* * *

Of the many remarkable achievements of the governments of Mexico, the United States and Canada in concluding the North American Free Trade Agreement ("NAFTA"), few are as significant as the framework that has been created for the resolution of investment disputes. This framework, Chapter 11 plus portions of Chapters 14 and 20 of the NAFTA, is unprecedented in any multilateral agreement, and may well serve as a model for similar arrangements in other contexts. These provisions are expected to facilitate investment in all three countries, particularly in Mexico, by investors of the other parties, thereby "ensuring a predictable commercial framework for business planning and investment."

This discussion first reviews the historical antecedents of the NAFTA investment dispute provisions. In essence, the NAFTA represents (A) a resolution of the long-standing disagreement between the U.S. and Mexico over the applicability of international law and international dispute resolution to foreign investment issues; (B) the logical (if not inevitable) evolution of the U.S. bilateral investment treaty; (C) a potentially effective use of the International Center for the Settlement of Investment Disputes through NAFTA incorporation within the scope of the "Additional Facility Rules"; and (D) a significant expansion of the international dispute resolution mechanisms available under the United States–Canada Free Trade Agreement.

Secondly, the article describes and analyzes the legal framework of the dispute mechanism as provided in the NAFTA, with particular attention to the procedural elements of NAFTA and the extent to which these provisions differ from (and improve upon) earlier bilateral or multilateral efforts. Finally, the article speculates on the likely impact of NAFTA on intra-regional investment and on future agreements concerning the protection of foreign investment and resolution of investment disputes.

II.   ANTECEDENTS OF THE NAFTA INVESTMENT DISPUTE MECHANISMS

A.   *Historical Background*

There is surely great irony in the fact that the most comprehensive framework for the settlement of investment disputes ever embodied in a multilateral agreement is incorporated in an agreement in which Mexico and the United States are the leading parties. Certainly, the development of international law relating to state responsibility for economic injuries to aliens, a necessary precondition to international settlement of related disputes, has been greatly affected by bilateral disputes between the United States and Mexico.

Mexican law and jurisprudence has long incorporated the "Calvo Clause," which stipulates that foreign persons operating in Mexico should be considered in all respects as Mexicans, thus limiting the resolution of disputes to local courts adjudicating under domestic law provisions and prohibiting any intervention by the home government. In effect, the Calvo Clause standard, at least in theory, is one of non-discriminatory national treatment. Predictably, one of the earliest invocations of the United States' opposing view that a taking of alien property anywhere in the world requires the payment of "prompt, adequate and effective compensation" is found in an exchange of diplomatic notes in 1938 between U.S. Secretary of State Cordell Hull and the Minister of Foreign Relations of Mexico. * * *

C. *International Center for the Settlement of Investment Disputes*

Consistent with other international efforts to improve the treatment of foreign investments, in 1965 the United States and a group of other nations concluded the Convention on the Settlement of Investment Disputes Between States and Nationals of Other States. As of January 1, 1993, more than 92 countries had become parties to the Convention, including the United States but not Canada and Mexico. Chile, Ecuador, El Salvador, Honduras and Paraguay are the only Latin American parties to date. Others have abstained, presumably because of Calvo Clause concerns. However, most of the English-speaking Caribbean nations, including Barbados, Grenada, Guyana, Jamaica, St. Lucia and Trinidad and Tobago, are parties.

The Convention created a World Bank affiliated institution, the International Center for the Settlement of Investment Disputes ("IC-SID"), located in Washington, D.C. The principal function of ICSID is to act as a secretariat for arbitrations brought under the terms and procedures of the Convention. ICSID is significant not only because as a World Bank affiliate its mechanisms and procedures are perhaps more acceptable among the developing nations than other arbitral mechanisms, but also because it offers the opportunity of international arbitration even to non-member states through its "Additional Facility Rules." These rules make provision for use of the ICSID facilities by non-members who accept ICSID through ad hoc measures or other agreements, such as the NAFTA in the case of Mexico and Canada, discussed in part II(B) below. More than 25 arbitral proceedings have been referred to ICSID since its inception. * * *

III.   SETTLEMENT OF INVESTMENT DISPUTES UNDER THE NAFTA

A. *Chapter 11–Standards for Foreign Investment*

Like the U.S. bilateral investment treaties, Chapter 11 of the NAFTA provides detailed standards for treatment of foreign investment (Section A), and arbitration of disputes relating to those standards (Section B). Chapter 11 applies to "investors" and "investments" of another party. These terms are defined in such a way as to cover natural and juridical persons of one party, and their "investments" (direct or indirectly owned or controlled interests) in the territory of another party. Thus, the ownership interest of a U.S. citizen or U.S. corporation in Mexico or Canada, is covered by Chapter 11.

Significantly, these terms also include third party-owned enterprises that are organized under the laws of a NAFTA party and are carrying out business activities there, when those enterprises invest in another NAFTA party. For example, a Mexican corporation owned by Japanese interests and conducting business in Mexico would be considered a Mexican investor with regard to its investment activities in the United States and Canada, and is, thus, entitled to the protections of Chapter 11.

An exception to this otherwise broad definition exists for investments of a NAFTA party that are owned in turn by investors of a third country, where that NAFTA country receiving the investment either does not recognize the government of that investor, or prohibits financial transactions with that country's nationals or government. This language would, for example, permit the United States to deny benefits, pursuant to the U.S. Foreign Assets Control Regulations, to a company in the United States owned by a Mexican company that in turn is owned or controlled by Cuban, Libyan or North Korean interests.

Section A of Chapter 11 provides investors of the other party with three types of treatment: (1) national treatment; (2) most favored nation treatment; and (3) treatment meeting minimum standards of international law in the event that local treatment (particularly in the event of expropriation) does not meet such standards. In effect, an investor may choose between (1) and (2), depending on which is more favorable in particular circumstances.

Section A further incorporates prohibitions against performance requirements, such as requiring the export of a minimum percentage of production or achieving a specific level of local content. It also affords the freedom to select senior management without regard to nationality, subject to certain exceptions regarding numerical majorities on the board of directors, as well as freedom to transfer or repatriate profits or investment proceeds in freely convertible currency.

Many exceptions and reservations, particularly regarding national treatment, have been entered by the three nations, either permanently or during a phase-out period as reflected in the NAFTA annexes. For example, Mexico may indefinitely preserve its prohibition on foreigners owning property in a 100 km wide strip along the national borders, or within 50 km from its coasts. However, the current Mexican restrictions on foreign ownership of mining operations must be eliminated within five years after NAFTA's entry into force.

Direct or indirect expropriation of investor property is prohibited, except when it is undertaken for a public purpose, on a non-discriminatory basis and in accordance with due process and minimum standards of international law. In all cases of expropriation, compensation equivalent to fair market value based on the value prior to the date of the expropriation must be paid. This compensation must be paid "without delay" and be "fully realizable" in convertible currency, with interest accruing from the date of expropriation to the date of payment.

The Section A standards are general standards for investment. Should inconsistent provisions be found in other chapters, those standards would apply to the matters covered by those other chapters.

B. Chapter 11–Framework for Settlement of Disputes

Section B of Chapter 11 provides a multi-tiered mechanism for resolution of investment disputes between foreign investors and the host country or host country state enterprises. However, Chapter 11 has no applicability to disputes between foreign investors and nationals of the host country, although such disputes may be subject to commercial arbitration.

1. Conciliation and Negotiation

Before there is any resort to arbitration, "disputing parties" are encouraged to seek a solution to their dispute through consultation or negotiation. The requirement of 90 days notice to the other party prior to the filing of a claim for arbitration is apparently designed to encourage such consultation or negotiation.

2. Arbitral Jurisdiction

Once such notice is provided, an investor may demand binding arbitration for a variety of claims on his own behalf or on behalf of an enterprise that he controls, directly or indirectly. These include (1) a claim that the government of another NAFTA party has breached an obligation under Section A of Chapter 11; (2) a claim that a state enterprise of another NAFTA party has acted in a manner inconsistent with the party's obligations under Chapter 11 (investment) or Chapter 14 (financial services) in the exercise of its regulatory, administrative or other governmental authority; or (3) a claim that a state monopoly has acted in a manner inconsistent with a party's obligations under Chapter 11 where the entity "exercises any regulatory, administrative or other governmental authority that the Party has delegated to it...." * * *

Disputes under Chapter 11 are subject to a three year statute of limitations. Actions not brought within three years from the "date on which the investor first acquired, or should have acquired, knowledge of the alleged breach" are barred. If "creeping" expropriation is alleged, i.e., where government actions over time are challenged as being equivalent to a taking, disagreement may arise over the date of the breach of Chapter 11, and, therefore, the time at which the statute of limitations begins to run.

When submitting a claim to arbitration, an investor must consent in writing to arbitration, on his own behalf and on behalf of any enterprise owned or controlled by him that is a party to the arbitration. Further, he must waive the right to initiate or continue administrative or judicial actions in the courts of the affected government, except in proceedings for injunctive, declaratory or other extraordinary relief. The three governments that are parties to the agreement have included as part of the agreement a "blanket" prior written consent to arbitration. Under the "blanket" prior consent rule, in the event an investor demands arbitration under Chapter 11, no further consent by his government is required. Moreover, this "blanket" prior consent also applies to the consent requirements of the ICSID Convention, including consent to the jurisdiction of the Center under the Convention or the Additional Facility Rules, the New York Convention on the Recognition and Enforcement of Foreign Arbitral Awards, and the Inter-American Convention on International Commercial Arbitration. This reference to the ICSID Convention and the Additional Facility Rules is crucial. Because Canada and Mexico are not parties to the Convention, it is this prior consent to arbitration under the auspices of the ICSID Additional Facilities Rules that makes the arbitral provisions binding on the governments of Mexico and Canada.

3. Procedural Rules

Section B provides the procedural rules to be used in the absence of agreement by the parties. These include the number and appointment of arbitrators (normally three), the consolidation of multiple claims involving common issues of law or fact, notice, participation and documentary requirements, the place of arbitration and the use of experts. None of these provisions is particularly unusual, but by specifying explicit rules to be used in the absence of agreement between the arbitrating parties, a possible source of delay in the proceedings is avoided.

In most instances the Secretary General of ICSID serves as the appointing authority, when the parties fail to agree on the choice of arbitrators. Chapter 11 contemplates arbitration under the ICSID Convention or the ICSID Additional Facility Rules using the widely accepted UNCITRAL arbitration rules, as modified by Chapter 11. The governing law is "this Agreement and applicable rules of international law."

4. Limitations and Exclusions

It is recognized that, in some instances, a Chapter 11 dispute may relate to the interpretation of one or more of the parties' reservations under Annexes I-IV of the NAFTA. The arbitral tribunal does not have jurisdiction over such issues. Instead, such questions are to be referred to the Free Trade Commission created under Chapter 20, which must provide its interpretation in writing to the arbitral tribunal within 60 days. That interpretation is binding on the Tribunal.

In addition, certain types of governmental decisions are excluded from arbitration. These include the decision to exclude an investment based on national security grounds, and the decision by Canada under its Investment Canada Act or by Mexico's National Commission on Foreign Investment not to approve an investment. Since the national security exclusion is reviewable under Chapter 20 procedures, a decision by the United States under its Exxon Florio procedures to review foreign acquisitions that have national security implications would presumably be subject to Chapter 20 procedures.

Other exceptions reflect the continuing influence of the Mexican "Calvo Clause" despite its extreme narrowing under the NAFTA. For example, under the NAFTA an investor in Mexico may not submit a claim for breach of obligations by the Mexican government or state enterprises both to arbitration and to the national courts or administrative agencies. Similarly, once a Mexican enterprise owned or controlled by a foreign investor has submitted a claim to the national courts or administrative agencies asserting a breach of rights covered by the NAFTA investment provisions, the same matter may not subsequently be referred to arbitration under Chapter 11. These limitations, particularly the latter one, will require foreign-owned Mexican enterprises to carefully weigh the pros and cons of initially referring a matter to the Mexican internal legal process. The submission of what appears at the time to be a minor matter to the Mexican courts could preclude later arbitration of the same issue, should it be demonstrated that the claim against the government in fact comes within the NAFTA's protections. * * *

Investment disputes between a contracting state and private investor will always involve some assertion that the contracting state is unlawfully expropriating or taking the FDI. The outright taking is an expropriation. The passage of rules that has the effect of preventing the use and enjoyment of the FDI can also constitute a gradual taking or a 'creeping' expropriation. The NAFTA and BITs permit a taking so long as the taking is for a public purpose, non-discriminatory, in accordance with due process of law, and on the payment of compensation.

The outright taking is of course fairly straightforward. The creeping expropriation is harder to identify. The private investor will seek to prove a creeping expropriation has occurred through the action taken by the host government. The NAFTA in Article 1110 (1) describes as a "...measure tantamount to nationalization or expropriation..." In *Azinian* the private investor alleged an expropriation had occurred when Mexico improperly repudiated a contractual obligation. The Azinian case is the first NAFTA Chapter 11 case and is excerpted below.

ROBERT AZINIAN, ET AL. v. THE UNITED MEXICAN STATES
CASE No. ARB(AF)/97/2 (1999).

* * *

AWARD

* * *

4. In early 1992, the Mayor of Naucalpan and other members of its Ayuntamiento (City Council) visited Los Angeles at the invitation of the Claimants to observe the operations of Global Waste Industries, Inc., a company said by the latter to be controlled by them.

5. On 7 October 1992, Mir Azinian, writing under the letterhead of Global Waste Industries Inc. (hereinafter "Global Waste") as its "President," sent a letter to the Mayor of Naucalpan containing a summary of the way "we expect to implement . . . the integral solution proposed for the solid waste problem" of the city. The following representations were made: (1) "The company will replace all the current collection equipment for advanced technology in the area of solid wastes"— specifically including watertight vehicles and metal bins. (2) "The necessary investment to implement an efficient and hygienic solid waste collection, transportation and processing system is approximately US$20,000,000," of which 50% 11 will be directed to the acquisition of collection equipment. (3) "GLOBAL WASTE INDUSTRIES, INC. is a company specialized in the collection and reduction of solid wastes. With more than 40 years of experience, GLOBAL WASTE provides collection services to residences, businesses and industry in the Los Angeles area."

6. In the course of a session of the Ayuntamiento on 4 November 1992, the "Integrated Solution Project" was presented. It was described as involving a consortium including Sunlaw Energy Inc., a U.S. corporation experienced in the conversion of bio-mass to energy, and an investment of US$20 million.

* * *

25. Naucalpan is an important and heavily industrialized suburb of Mexico City. In 1993, when the Concession Contract was signed, it had a population of nearly two million, and 21,800 commercial or industrial establishments. Residential and business waste management was, and remains, an important function of the municipal authorities. Somewhat more than 900

tonnes per day of residential waste were collected, and somewhat less than 900 tonnes per day of commercial and industrial waste. (The latter generates higher revenues for the provider of collection and disposal services.) When DESONA entered the scene, collection, treatment, and disposal left much to be desired. The municipality's equipment was inadequate and obsolete. * * *

28.   Today, as a result of the cancellation by the City of Naucalpan of DESONA's Concession Contract, the Claimants, as shareholders in DESONA, are seeking recovery of the loss of the "value of the concession as an on-going enterprise." The highest of their alternative methods of evaluation (see Section V) results in a figure of some US$19.2 million. The Claimants allege that the actions of the Ayuntamiento of Naucalpan resulted in a violation of NAFTA, attributable to the Government of Mexico.

29.   There are some immediately apparent difficulties with the claim. It must be said that this was not an inherently plausible group of investors. They had presented themselves as principals in Global Waste, with approximately 40 years' experience in the industry. In fact Global Waste had been incorporated in Los Angeles in March 1991, but put into bankruptcy in May 1992—14 months later. Global Waste owned no vehicles, and in the year preceding its bankruptcy had had revenues of only US$30,000. The only Claimant who could be said to have experience in the industry was Mr. Davitian, whose family had been in the business of waste disposal in the Los Angeles area. * * * Even in the case of Mr. Davitian personally, since he was precisely *40* years old in *1993,* a claim of *40* years' experience was preposterous.

30.   As for the other Claimants: Mr. Azinian had no relevant experience, had a long record of unsuccessful commercial litigation, and had been declared personally bankrupt in *1991.* Mr. Goldenstein had a background in a family property business in Argentina and in restaurant management in the U.S., and claims expertise in the financing of major motion picture projects as a result of his studies in Los Angeles. * * *

31.   None of this background was disclosed to the Naucalpan authorities. The Naucalpan authorities thus entrusted a public service to foreign individuals whom they were falsely led to believe were part of an experienced concern possessed of financial and technological resources adequate for the job.

* * *

RELIEF SOUGHT

75.   The Claimants contend that "the City's wrongful repudiation of the Concession Contract violates Articles 1110

("Expropriation and Compensation") and 1105 ("Minimum Standard of Treatment") of NAFTA" (Reply of 19 January 1999, Sec. III, p. 17), and accordingly seek the following relief, as articulated in their Prayer for Relief dated 23 June 1999:

A.   With respect to the enterprise, as follows:

1.   The value of the concession as an ongoing enterprise on March 21, 1994, the date of the taking based upon the values obtained: a. By applying the Discounted Cash Flow QCF) method in the amount of US$11,600,000 (PCV); In the alternative, b. By applying the Similar Transaction Method yielding an amount of US$19,203,000 (PCV); In the alternative, c. Based upon the offer made by Sanifill to purchase the concession in an amount of US$18,000,000; In the alternative, Based upon the lower range value from the fair market value analysis of the concession conducted by Richard Carvell in an amount of US$15,500,000;

* * *

VI.   Validity of the Claim Under NAFTA

A.   The general framework of investor access to international arbitration under NAFTA

77.   For the purposes of the present discussion, the Claimants are assumed to be "investor[s] of a Party" having made an "investment" as those two terms are defined in Article 1139 of NAFTA. * * *

78.   The Ayuntamiento as a body determined that it had valid grounds to annul and rescind the Concession Contract, and so declared. DESONA then failed to convince three levels of Mexican courts that the Ayuntamiento's decision was invalid. Given this fact, is there a basis for the present Arbitral Tribunal to declare that the Mexican courts were wrong to uphold the Ayuntamiento's decision and that the Government of Mexico must indemnify the Claimants?

79.   As this is the first dispute brought by an investor under NAFTA to be resolved by an award on the merits, it is appropriate to consider first principles.

80. NAFTA is a treaty among three sovereign States, which deals with a vast range of matters relating to the liberalization of trade. Part Five deals with "Investment, Services and Related Matters." Chapter Eleven thereunder deals specifically with "Investment."

81. Section A of Chapter Eleven establishes a number of substantive obligations with respect to investments. Section B concerns jurisdiction and procedure; it defines the method by which an investor claiming a violation of the obligations established in Section A may seek redress.

82. Arbitral jurisdiction under Section B is limited not only as to the persons who may invoke it (they must be nationals of a State signatory to NAFTA), but also as to subject matter: claims may not be submitted to investor-state arbitration under Chapter Eleven unless they are founded upon the violation of an obligation established in Section A,

83. To put it another way, a foreign investor entitled in principle to protection under NAFTA may enter into contractual relations with a public authority, and may suffer a breach by that authority, and *still not be in a position to state a claim under NAFTA.* It is a fact of life everywhere that individuals may be disappointed in their dealings with public authorities, and disappointed yet again when national courts reject their complaints. It may safely be assumed that many *Mexican* parties can be found who had business dealings with governmental entities, which were not to their satisfaction; Mexico is unlikely to be different from other countries in this respect. NAFTA was not intended to provide foreign investors with blanket protection from this kind of disappointment, and nothing in its terms so provides

84. It therefore would not be sufficient for the Claimants to convince the present Arbitral Tribunal that the actions or motivations of the Naucalpan Ayuntamiento are to be disapproved, or that the reasons given by the Mexican courts in their three judgements are unpersuasive. Such considerations are unavailing unless the Claimants can point to a violation of an obligation established in Section A of Chapter Eleven attributable to the Government of Mexico.

B. Grounds invoked by the Claimants

85. The Claimants have alleged violations of the following two provisions of NAFTA: Article 1110 (1) "No party may directly or indirectly nationalize or expropriate an investment of an investor of another Party in its territory or take a measure tantamount to nationalization or expropriation of such investment ("expropriation") except: (a) for a public purpose; (b) on a non-discriminatory basis; (c) in accordance with due process of law and Article 1105 (1); and on payment of compensation in accordance with paragraphs 2 through 6."

Article 1105(*l*) "Each Party shall accord to investments of investors of another Party treatment in accordance with international law, including fair and equitable treatment and full protection and security."

86. Although the parties to the Concession Contract accepted the jurisdiction of the Mexican courts, the Claimants correctly point out that they did not exclude recourse to other courts or arbitral tribunals—such as this one—having jurisdiction on another foundation. Nor is the fact that the Claimants

took the initiative before the Mexican courts fatal to the jurisdiction of the present Arbitral Tribunal. The Claimants have
cited a number of cases where international arbitral tribunals
did not consider themselves bound by decisions of national
courts. Professor Dodge, in his oral argument, stressed the
following sentence from the well-known ICSID case of *Amco v.
Indonesia:* "An international tribunal is not bound to follow the
result of a national court." As the Claimants argue persuasively,
it would be unfortunate if potential claimants under NAFTA
were dissuaded from seeking relief under domestic law from
national courts, because such actions might have the salutary
effect of resolving the dispute without resorting to investor-
state arbitration under NAFTA. Nor finally has the Respondent
argued that it cannot be held responsible for the actions of a
local governmental authority like the Ayuntamiento of Naucalpan.

87.   The problem is that the Claimants' fundamental complaint is that they are the victims of a breach of the Concession
Contract. NAFTA does not, however, allow investors to seek
international arbitration for mere contractual breaches. Indeed,
NAFTA cannot possibly be read to create such a regime, which
would have elevated a multitude of ordinary transactions with
public authorities into potential international disputes. *The
Claimants simply could not prevail merely by persuading the
Arbitral Tribunal that the Ayuntamiento of Naucalpan breached
the Concession Contract.*

88.   Understanding this proposition perfectly well, Professor Dodge insisted that the claims are not simply for breach of
contract, but involve 11 the direct expropriation of DESONA's
contractual rights' and "the indirect expropriation of DESONA
itself." (English Transcript, 24.6.99, p. 23, 1. 9–11.)

89.   Professor Dodge then argued that a breach of contract
constitutes an expropriation "if it is confiscatory, 11 or, quoting
Professor Brownlie, *Principles of Public International Law,* 5th
edition at 550, if "the state exercises its executive or legislative
authority to destroy the contractual rights as an asset." Specifically, he invoked a "wealth of authority treating the repudiation
of concession agreements as an expropriation of contractual
rights."

90.   Labeling is, however, no substitute for analysis. The
words "confiscatory," "destroy contractual rights as an asset,"
or "repudiation" may serve as a way to describe breaches which
are to be treated as extraordinary, and therefore as acts of
expropriation, but they certainly do not indicate on what basis
the critical distinction between expropriation and an ordinary
breach of contract is to be made. The egregiousness of any

breach is in the eye of the beholder—and that is not satisfactory for present purposes.

91.   It is therefore necessary to examine whether the annulment of the Concession Contract may be considered to be an act of expropriation violating NAFTA Article I 110. If not, the claim must fail. The question cannot be more central. * * *

C.   The contention that the annulment was an act of expropriation

93.   The Respondent argues that the Concession Contract came to an end on two independently justified grounds: invalidity and rescission.

94.   The second is the more complex. It postulates that the Ayuntamiento was entitled to rescind the Concession Contract due to DESONA's failure of performance. If the Ayuntamiento was not so entitled, its termination of the Concession Contract was itself a breach. Most of the evidence and debate in these proceedings have focused on this issue: was DESONA in substantial non-compliance with the Concession Contract? The subject is complicated by the fact that DESONA was apparently not given the benefit of the 30–day cure period defined in Article 31 of the Concession Contract.

95.   The logical starting point is to examine the asserted original invalidity of the Concession Contract. If this assertion was founded, there is no need to make findings with respect to performance; nor can there be a question of curing original invalidity.

96.   From this perspective, the problem may be put quite simply. The Ayuntarniento believed it had grounds for holding the Concession Contract to be invalid under Mexican law governing public service concessions. At DESONA's initiative, these grounds were tested by three levels of Mexican courts, and in each case were found to be extant. How can it be said that Mexico breached NAFTA when the Ayuntamiento of Naucalpan purported to declare the invalidity of a Concession Contract, which by its terms was subject to Mexican law, and to the jurisdiction of the Mexican courts, and the courts of Mexico then agreed with the Ayuntamiento's determination? Further, the Claimants have neither contended nor proved that the Mexican legal standards for the annulment of concessions violate Mexico's Chapter Eleven obligations; nor that the Mexican law governing such annulments is expropriatory.

97.   With the question thus framed, it becomes evident that for the Claimants to prevail it is not enough that the Arbitral Tribunal disagree with the determination of the Ayuntamiento. A governmental authority surely cannot be faulted for acting in a manner validated by its courts *unless the courts*

themselves are disavowed at the international level. As the Mexican courts found that the Ayuntamiento's decision to nullify the Concession Contract was consistent with the Mexican law governing the validity of public service concessions, the question is whether the Mexican court decisions themselves breached Mexico's obligations under Chapter Eleven.

98. True enough, an international tribunal called upon to rule on a Government's compliance with an international treaty is not paralysed by the fact that the national courts have approved the relevant conduct of public officials. * * * As a former President of the International Court of Justice Put it: "The principles of the separation and independence of the judiciary in municipal law and of respect for the finality of judicial decisions have exerted an important influence on the form in which the general principle of State responsibility has been applied to acts or omissions of judicial organs.

These basic tenets of judicial organization explain the reluctance to be found in some arbitral awards of the last century to admit the extension to the judiciary of the rule that a State is responsible for the acts of all its organs.

However, in the present century, State responsibility for acts of judicial organs came to be recognized. Although independent of the Government, the judiciary is not independent of the State: *the judgment given by a judicial authority emanates from an organ of the State in just the same way as a la w promulgated by the legislature or a decision taken by the executive.*

The responsibility of the State for acts of judicial authorities may result from three different types of judicial decision. The first is a decision of a municipal court *clearly incompatible with a rule of international law.* The second is what it known traditionally as a *'denial of justice.'* The third occurs when, in certain exceptional and well-defined circumstances, a State is responsible for a judicial decision contrary to municipal law. "Eduardo Jimenez de Arechaga," International Law in the Past Third of a Century, 9' 159–1 Recueil des cours (General Course in Public International law, The Hague, 1978). (Emphasis added.)

99. The possibility of holding a State internationally liable for judicial decisions does not, however, entitle a claimant to seek international review of the national court decisions as though the international jurisdiction seized has plenary appellate jurisdiction. This is not true generally, and it is not true for NAFTA. *What must be shown is that the court decision itself constitutes a violation of the treaty.* Even if the Claimants were to convince this Arbitral Tribunal that the Mexican courts were wrong with respect to the invalidity of the Concession Contract, this would not per se be conclusive as to a violation of NAFTA.

More is required; the Claimants must show either a denial of justice, or a pretence of form to achieve an internationally unlawful end.

100. But the Claimants have raised no complaints against the Mexican courts; they do not allege a denial of justice. Without exception, they have directed their many complaints against the Ayuntamiento of Naucalpan. The Arbitral Tribunal finds that this circumstance is fatal to the claim, and makes it unnecessary to consider issues relating to performance of the Concession Contract. *For if there is no complaint against a determination by a competent court that a contract governed by Mexican law was invalid under Mexican law, there is by definition no contract to be expropriated.*

101. The Arbitral Tribunal does not, however, wish to create the impression that the Claimants fail on account of an improperly pleaded case. The Arbitral Tribunal thus deems it appropriate, *ex abundante cautela,* to demonstrate that the Claimants were well advised not to seek to have the Mexican court decisions characterised as violations of NAFTA.

102. A denial of justice could be pleaded if the relevant courts refuse to entertain a suit, if they subject it to undue delay, or if they administer justice in a seriously inadequate way. There is no evidence, or even argument, that any such defects can be ascribed to the Mexican proceedings in this case.

103. There is a fourth type of denial of justice, namely the clear and malicious misapplication of the law. This type of wrong, doubtless, overlaps with the notion of "pretence of form" to mask a violation of international law. In the present case, not only has no such wrong-doing been pleaded, but the Arbitral Tribunal wishes to record that it views the evidence as sufficient to dispel any shadow over the *bona fides* of the Mexican judgments. Their findings cannot possibly be said to have been arbitrary, let alone malicious.

104. To reach this conclusion it is sufficient to recall the significant evidence of misrepresentation brought before this Arbitral Tribunal. For this purpose, one need to do no more than to examine the twelfth of the *27* irregularities, upheld by the Mexican courts as a cause of nullity: that the Ayuntamiento was misled as to DESONA's capacity to perform the concession.

105. If the Claimants cannot convince the Arbitral Tribunal that the evidence for this finding was so insubstantial, or so bereft of a basis in law, that the judgments were in effect arbitrary or malicious, they simply cannot prevail. The Claimants have not even attempted to rebut the Respondent's evidence on the relevant standards for annulment of concessions under Mexican law. They did not challenge the Respondent's evidence that under Mexican law a public service concession

issued by municipal authorities based on error or misrepresentation is invalid. As for factual evidence, they have vigorously combated the inferences made by the Ayuntamiento and the Mexican courts, but they have not denied that evidence exists that the Ayunamiento was misled as to DESONA's capacity to perform the concession. * * *

120. To resume: the Claimants have not even attempted to demonstrate that the Mexican court decisions constituted a fundamental departure from established principles of Mexican law. The Respondent's evidence as to the relevant legal standards for annulment of public service contracts stands unrebutted. Nor do the Claimants contend that these legal standards breach NAFTA Article 1110. The Arbitral Tribunal finds nothing in the application of these standards with respect to the issue of invalidity that appears arbitrary or unsustainable in light of the evidentiary record. To the contrary, the evidence positively supports the conclusions of the Mexican courts. * * *

VIII. Decision

128. For the reasons stated above, and rejecting all contentions to the contrary, the Arbitral Tribunal hereby decides in favour of the Respondent. * * *

Section A of NAFTA Chapter 11 establishes a number of substantive obligations of the contracting states relative to foreign investment. See the materials in Section 3.1, supra for a discussion of these issues. Section B of the investment chapter contains the jurisdiction and procedure rules for the settlement of an investment dispute under the NAFTA. An investor must be able to properly claim a violation of Section A to invoke the NAFTA settlement procedures. Section B sets out the method and procedures by which an investor can seek redress. In *Azinian*, the plaintiffs were alleging that the breach of the contract by the city of Naucalpan was the Section A violation.

The exhaustion of local remedies is a rule of long standing under international law. The rule makes sense from the standpoint that disputants should first seek redress from the domestic legal system where the investment is located. This rule fit well with the *Calvo* doctrine. The problem, of course, was that foreign investors felt that recourse to domestic tribunals was useless. The NAFTA neither abandons nor embraces the exhaustion of local remedies rule. The NAFTA Article requires the investor to waive their right to seek redress before any domestic court or administrative tribunal if they are seeking arbitration under NAFTA for a NAFTA dispute. Article 1121 makes an exception for those cases seeking injunctive or other extraordinary relief.

Some unsettled questions in the exhaustion of local remedies arises out of Mexico's Annex 1120.1 which states in pertinent part—". . . an investor of another party may not allege that Mexico has breached an obligation ... under Section A ... in an arbitration under this Section and in proceedings before a Mexican court or administrative tribunal ..." What if the domestic court purports to apply NAFTA, and concludes, for example, that no breach has occurred? In addition, the U.S. NAFTA implementation act appears to preclude U.S. investors from seeking redress to a NAFTA breach in an U.S. court. Clyde Pearce and Professor Jack Coe in their article[4] examine the relationship between municipal action and the NAFTA rules and provide some thoughtful insights.

Azinian also dealt with the issue of the effect a NAFTA tribunal should accord a domestic court adjudication. In point #98, the tribunal found that "An international tribunal called upon to rule on a government's compliance with an international treaty is not paralyzed by the fact that the national courts have approved the relevant conduct of the public officials." The responsibility of the State for acts of judicial authorities may result from three types of judicial decisions—a decision clearly incompatible with a rule of international law or where there has been a denial of justice. A denial of justice can occur where a court refuses to entertain a suit, if the suit is subjected to undue delay, when there is a clear and malicious misapplication of the law, or if justice is administered in a seriously inadequate way. The claimant must show that the evidence supporting the findings of the domestic court was so insubstantial or so bereft of a basis in law that the judgments were in effect arbitrary or malicious. What must be shown is that the court decision violates NAFTA.

Once the decision to submit a dispute to arbitration is made Section B of the NAFTA provides an orderly systematic process. The beginning point is determining the governing law. Article 1131 (1) provides that investment disputes under this chapter will be resolved in accordance with the applicable rules under international law. This provision essentially abrogates the *Calvo* Doctrine. The investor can seek redress under the UNCITRAL[5] rules or under the ICSID[6]. The ICSID provides for adjudication under the ICSID Convention when the investors and host country are contracting parties under the ICSID Convention. In those cases where the host country is not a party to the ICSID Convention (like Mexico and Canada), the parties must use the arbitration mechanism provided under ICSID's Additional Facility system. The ICSID rules are comprehensive and independent of national legal systems. The ICSID arbitration is administered through the ICSID Institution. Arbi-

4. Clyde Pearce and Jack Coe Jr., Arbitration Under NAFTA Chapter 11—Some Pragmatic Reflections Upon the First Case Filed Against Mexico, 23 Hastings International Law Review 311 (2000).

5. UNCITRAL is an acronym for the United Nations Commission on Internation-

al Trade Law. The UNCITRAL arbitration rules can be found in 24 I.L.M. 1302 (1985)

6. ICSID is an acronym for the International Centre For The Settlement of Investment Disputes established under the auspices of the World Bank and formed pursuant to the Convention.

tration can also be effected on an *ad hoc* basis under the UNCITRAL rules.

The arbitration process begins with a breach under Section A of chapter 11. This is the first trap for the unwary—be careful in seeking local remedies that may preclude action on Section B of chapter 11. In addition, NAFTA article 1118 suggests that the parties first resort to consultation or negotiation to settle the dispute. A six-month 'cooling off' period is imposed by Article 1120. In addition, NAFTA Articles 1116(2) and 1117(2) establishes a three year statute of limitations on any claims. Additionally, a ninety-day pre-filing notice requirement is imposed on the investor under Article 1119. The pre-filing notice requirement must include the name of the investor, the provisions allegedly breached, the issues and factual basis for the claim, the relief sought, and approximate amount of damages claimed. These articles in combination provide an orderly process for the settlement of investment disputes.

For Mexico, the NAFTA Investment chapter represents a substantial departure from its historical attitude towards foreign direct investment. It is not alone. Many developing countries are abandoning restrictive foreign investment regimes. This is a tacit recognition that the developing country's macroeconomic policies have resulted in a dearth of foreign investment.

SECTION 3.3   THE OUTBOUND FOREIGN DIRECT INVESTMENT UNDER THE MEXICAN LEGAL SYSTEM

A.   INTRODUCTION

The Mexican protectionist import substitution policy manifested itself in the Mexican domestic legal system through a highly restrictive foreign investment law.[7] The law was designed to prevent the entry of foreign direct investment. By the mid 1980's the failure of protectionism had become apparent. The Mexican government's political will was changing, creating a hospitable climate for foreign investment. The NAFTA exemplified Mexico's political willingness to open its borders to foreign direct investment.

NAFTA also caused the enactment of sweeping foreign investment legislation in Mexico. The Foreign Investment Law (FIL) enacted in 1993[8] and amended in 1996 is excerpted below. The law haltingly opened Mexico to foreign direct investment. In spite of the willingness to proceed, there continues to be disappointments on the pace and extent of the free trade and open borders environment. The following article from a veteran, knowledgeable commentator offers valuable insight.

---

7. *Ley Para Promover la Inversión Mexicana Y Regular La Inversión Extranjera, Diario Oficial*, Mar. 9, 1973.

8. *Diario Oficial* [Official Gazette], December 27, 1993 and amended on December 24, 1996·

SEEING NAFTA THROUGH THREE LENSES

Ewell E. Murphy, Jr.

23 Can.—U.S. L.J. 73 (1997).

I. THREE LENSES OF PERCEPTION

Knowledge is a rather destructive thing. Our learning curves are littered with the wreckage of invalidated hypotheses, discredited concepts, and failed illusions. The more we come to understand an object, the more we abandon the perspective from which we first glimpsed it. We are like assiduous astronomers, straining to see stars through a telescope of many lenses, discarding each lens, in turn, to observe more clearly through the next.

And yet, those discarded lenses serve a useful purpose. We have to start somewhere. Each of our abandoned perspectives, in turn, enables us to find another. As Ortega wisely noted, *"Sin pre-juicios no cabe formarse juicios."* Without pre-judgments, judgments cannot be formed. It is discouraging to discard lenses, but with each discarding, we better visualize the object of our concern.

Looking at NAFTA is like that. In our attempts to understand the significance of Mexico's joining the free-trade relationship between Canada and the United States, we lawyers of the United States have used and discarded two different lenses of perception, and now we are peering at NAFTA through a third lens. Let us recall how Mexico appeared in those three perceptions, and let us ponder the lessons those three lenses have taught.

A.   The Lens of Economics

The first lens through which U.S. lawyers endeavored to see Mexico's involvement in NAFTA was economics, the preeminent social science of the Modern Age. Economics describes human activity in numbers. It is "GDP this" and "trade balance that" and per capita quantifications all around. So it was in numbers that the economists forecast NAFTA to us. For those of us who do not comprehend numbers very well, the economists furnished graphs; export lines and import lines, zigzagging in dramatic peaks and valleys. Those graphs were very effective. They persuaded even the U.S. Congress to back NAFTA. So it was full speed ahead for NAFTA. Numerically speaking, everything was looking great.

As we lawyers gazed at NAFTA through the lens of economics, it was reassuring to see who was running Mexico. It was a bunch of economists. In earlier times, if you wanted to be a President or a cabinet member of a Latin American country, being a general or a lawyer was the way to go. No longer. Now economists lead the top echelons, nowhere more than in Mexico. Not just ordinary economists, either, but Ph.D.s from the most ivoried towers of the Ivy League. So we lawyers sat back, content that skilled numerologists were authenticating not only those dramatic graphs, but the numbers they depicted.

Looking through the lens of economics, at first we thought NAFTA's objective was trade. That is what the Congress was debating, mostly, and the very name of NAFTA is the "North American Free Trade Agreement." But once we read beyond the title page, we realized that NAFTA aimed at much more than trade. It aimed at investment, for example. In fact, the most perceptive insight into NAFTA was expressed in two short sentences of The Economist back in 1990, when the NAFTA negotiations had just begun. Those sentences read: "The free-trade agreement . . . is not only, or even primarily, about openness of trade. It has more to do with attracting the foreign investment that Mexico will need."

That was a very shrewd insight. Its significance rests on Mexico's historic phobia of foreign investment. In this century that phobia was notably expressed in the land ownership restrictions of the 1917 Constitution, in the oil expropriation of 1938, and in President Avila Camacho's 1944 decree limiting foreign ownership in specified industrial sectors. It culminated in President Echeverria's protectionist Foreign Investment Law of 1973. Theologized by the Calvo Doctrine, that phobia kept Mexico from promising, even for such foreign investment as it deigned to receive, the investment protection commitments of the Convention on the Settlement of Investment Disputes (ICSID), the Convention creating the Multilateral Investment Guarantee Agency, or a Bilateral Investment Treaty with the United States.

Given that phobic tradition, Mexico's undertakings in the foreign investment provisions of the NAFTA Agreement are remarkable. Besides fixing sectoral boundaries to state monopoly and to limitations on foreign ownership, for investment from other NAFTA nations those undertakings grant access to remaining sectors of the Mexican economy and promise standards of protection that more than match the ICSID Convention and a Bilateral Investment Treaty. In the realm of practicality, it is difficult to imagine a more dramatic about-turn from the protectionism of the Echeverrian years.

B.   The Lens of Law

Evaluating NAFTA's opening of Mexico to foreign investment led U.S. lawyers to examine the legal system foreign investment would encounter in Mexico, if it entered. That acquainted us with the imposing infrastructure for domestic and foreign enterprise the Salinas Administration created: a Foreign Investment Law, a Mining Law, commercial arbitration legislation, intellectual property laws, and an Economic Competition Law, all brand-new, enhanced with statutory authorizations for private investment in port services and the generation and sale of electric power and topped off, for U.S. investors, with Mexico's first general income tax treaty with the United States. Additionally the Salinas Administration continued the privatization of Mexican banks the de la Madrid Administration had started. As we were studying that infrastructure the Zedillo Administration embellished it with a new administrative mechanism for privatizations and with additional openings in such significant state monopoly sectors as railroad services, telecommunications, airport services, and the transportation, storage, and distribution of natural gas. We were quite impressed.

We were so impressed, in fact that we began to experiment with a second lens with which to look at NAFTA, the lens of law. Admittedly, we lawyers found that lens to be more user-friendly. As the lens of economics describes human activity in numbers, the lens of law describes human activity in words, and we lawyers have always supposed ourselves to be adept at words. But, aside from its user-friendliness, we honestly concluded that the lens of law was more revealing of the NAFTA that we were trying to see, and that when it came to measuring relationships among the NAFTA nations, numbers were less informative than the words of national law that made those numbers flow.

Then, as we scanned Mexico's foreign investment infrastructure through the legal lens, we were taught a startling lesson about the word "investment" itself. When portfolio investment fled President Zedillo's bungled devaluation of 1994, we learned that there are investments and then there are investments, and some are more skittish than others. To our consternation, some economists seemed as startled as we. That settled it. By the time the U.S. Congress balked at a rescue package for the peso, and President Clinton dared to devise his own, we had discarded the economic lens completely and we were peering at NAFTA exclusively through our comfortable new lens of law.

The more we peered through that lens of law, however, the less sanguine we were of the NAFTA we perceived. What most concerned us were those industrial sectors that President Zedillo was privatizing. They are not your ordinary, everyday industries. Virtually every one of them requires vigilant regulation at both ends, to ensure reasonable returns to suppliers and fair prices to consumers. To make it more difficult, many of the privatizations involve the unpopular downsizing of heavily unionized former governmental staff. Of those privatizations, the most problematical are politically explosive carve-outs from such public sector icons as Petroleos Mexicanos (Pemex) and la Comision Federal de Electricidad (C.F.E.). Overseeing such privatized industrial sectors would be difficult for any nation. For Mexico, which has little governmental experience in impartial and efficient industrial regulation, it will be a very formidable task indeed.

As we pondered those concerns, the birth-rate of Mexican privatizations abruptly dropped. President Zedillo had successfully accomplished, without inordinate public criticism, significant privatizing amputations from two sectors of the state energy monopoly: the generation and sale of electric power and the transportation, storage, and distribution of natural gas. Then he inserted the presidential scalpel to amputate a third. By executive decree key petrochemicals were reclassified from "primary" to "secondary," in order to legalize sales to private investors, both Mexican and foreign, of majority ownership of groups of Pemex plants where those petrochemicals are made.

That struck a very sensitive national nerve. Workers demonstrated; the National Assembly of the ruling political party, el Partido Revolucionario Institucional (the PRI), passed heated resolutions; committees of the Mexican Congress fumed. Cuauhtemoc Cardenas, the once and future candidate for the Mexican presidency, thundered that the proposed plant sale was "a vital part of the plan to re-structure (Mexico's) mechanisms of production, to subordinate them ... to dominant interests in the government and economy of the United States." For privatization of the production of secondary petrochemicals, the result was a "restructuring" that looked like a retreat.

Meanwhile criticism of NAFTA by other outspoken Mexicans was mounting. "The question," Carlos Fuentes muttered, "is how far Mexico can go in honoring an agreement that fatally favors a strong United States over a weak neighbor." From his knitted ski-mask Subcomandante Marcos put it more bluntly: "With the signing of NAFTA, the government of the United States gave its approval for the assassination of millions of Mexicans."

Faced with that troubling scenario, we U.S. lawyers began to understand what we were taught in high school civics, that the viability of legal rules depends on the cultural will to enforce them. The words of law do not make the numbers of economics flow unless cultural attitudes cause those words of law to be obeyed. Photogenic numbers and upbeat graphs do not happen unless the economy they quantify has order. Trade does not move unless somebody polices the market. Investments do not enter—and portfolio investments do not stay—unless somebody enforces the warranties and supervises the stock exchange. And the viability of that policing and enforcing and supervising depends, ultimately, not on words in a statute book, but on a cultural predisposition to due process and the rule of law. We wondered whether Mexico could meet that test.

That reminded us that, while President Salinas and President Zedillo were putting those impressive new words in the statute book, Mexico appeared to start coming apart at the seams: murdering the archbishop in Guadalajara; assassinating the Presidential candidate in Tijuana, and the chief executive of the PRI in Mexico City; an interminable insurrection in Chiapas; smaller rebellions in Guerrero and other states; killings and kidnappings galore.

C. *The Lens of Culture*

We wondered: Is Mexico culturally compatible with the other NAFTA nations? Are those gringo idioms, "due process" and "the rule of law," translatable into the pragmatic vocabulary of Mexican politics? Is the Rio Grande too culturally insurmountable for NAFTA to cross? For answers to those questions, the lens of law seemed as unforthcoming as the lens of economics. And so, to see NAFTA yet more clearly, we U.S. lawyers regretfully discarded our lens of law and turned to a third lens, the lens of culture.

We discovered that culture is a rather tricky lens to look through. For one thing, culture does not describe human activity in numbers or even in words; it describes human activity in feelings—in inarticulate intuitions about the way people should behave. For another thing, culture is interactive. When you look at NAFTA through the lens of culture, you do not see just the other fellow's culture. You see the cultures of all three NAFTA nations impinging on each other. That impinging is very dynamic. Actions from one side of a national border precipitate reactions—sometimes overreactions—from the other side. In that sense, to a U.S. observer of NAFTA, the lens of culture is like a mirror in which you see your own culture flashing back at you. Looking in that mirror, the U.S. observer soon realizes that the mirror-image of one's own culture is not always beautiful.

Look at the frictions between Canada and the United States, for example. The United States has arraigned Canada before the World Trade Organization, charging that a Canadian tax on advertisements in Canadian editions of U.S. magazines is unlawfully discriminatory. So far, WTO panels have sustained that charge, but the issue cannot be evaluated without appreciating the annoyance of Canadians at the enormous tides of trash and trivia that come sloshing over their southern border every day from the U.S. media. That is parallel to the irritation of Mexicans at the rather blatant non-performance by the United States of its NAFTA obligation to open border states to Mexican trucks. Or consider the accusations brought before NAFTA and the Organization of American States and recently raised by the European Union at the World Trade Organization, that the Helms—Burton Act violates international obligations of the United States. To weigh those complaints, one must understand the anger of Canada, Mexico, and other nations at secondary boycotts imposed by an economically intrusive Uncle Sam. And what is the measure of pompous U.S. "decertification" of Mexican efforts at drug control but the festering, in the United States, of the largest and most vicious drug market in the world?

II. THE LENSES RECONSIDERED

Mirror-images like that make U.S. lawyers downright gloomy—so gloomy that now, to tell the truth, we would like to discard our cultural lens and look at Mexico and NAFTA through a fourth and happier lens. The trouble is, we cannot find a fourth lens that pictures things as clearly as the three lenses we have already used. Perhaps we should try putting those three lenses together, and consider contemporary Mexico as the combined projection of the three separate perspectives the three lenses reveal. * * *

In short, when we lawyers of the United States peer at Mexico's relationship to the NAFTA through a combination of our three lenses, we see the numerical optimism of the lens of economics and the verbal assurance of the lens of law, but also the emotional foreboding of the lens of culture. Of those three images, none, by itself, captures the full picture; perhaps, somehow, all three images are correct; conceivably the three images prefigure a Mexico of strength and stability, but we cannot be sure. We are only astronomers, not prophets. We have only a telescope to peer through, not a crystal ball. And, when we look at contemporary Mexico through our telescope of three lenses, those are the three thought-provoking images that we see. * * *

B. FOREIGN DIRECT INVESTMENT UNDER THE MEXICAN LEGAL SYSTEM

1. *The Foreign Investment Law*

In spite of the open borders environment there are still investment areas that are not allowed. The exceptions flow from deeply held sentiments with respect to Mexican Sovereignty. However, the current domestic legal system does greatly enhance the rights of foreign investors in Mexico.

In 1993, keeping with its NAFTA obligations, Mexico enacted a new foreign investment law. The objective of the Foreign Investment Law (FIL) is to promote competitiveness, and to provide clear rules for foreign investment to channel foreign capital into Mexico. The federal legislation assuaged some of the fears because the favorable rules were now found in a legislated federal statute rather than merely in regulations.

MEXICO'S NEW FOREIGN INVESTMENT ACT

Jorge A. Vargas, Esq.
Mexico Trade & Law Reporter (Feb. 1994).

On December 28, 1993, a new federal statute governing foreign investment in Mexico entered into force. The new Foreign Investment Law (Ley de Inversion Extranjera, FIL), published in the Diario Oficial on December 27, 1993), repealed the 1973 Act to Promote Mexican Investment and Regulate Foreign Investment. Until new regulations are promulgated—a legislative exercise that may take a year or so—the new statute provides that the 1989 Regulations will continue to complement and detail the new law's provisions. (An unofficial translations of the FIL begins on page XX).

The new FIL represents another important step in President Salinas de Gortari's overall modernization policies. The FIL is in close symmetry with the North American Free Trade Agreement (NAFTA) and it continues the promotional attitude in favor of foreign investment that characterized the 1989 Regulations. In marked contrast with the 1973 Law, the new statute promotes foreign investment, rather than regulating it. In the official statement that President Salinas sent to Congress last November accompanying the legislative bill, he explained the reasons why Mexico should have this new statute, he said: "The purpose of this bill for a Foreign Investment Act is to establish a new legal framework which, in full compliance with the Constitution, promotes competitiveness in the country, provides legal certainty to foreign investment in

Mexico and establishes clear rules to channel international capital to productive activities."

The content of the FIL may be divided into three large categories, namely: 1) provisions contrary to the 1973 Law; 2) provisions in consonance with the 1973 Law; and, 3) provisions in symmetry with the 1989 Regulations.

Provisions Contrary to the 1973 Law

Say Goodbye to the 49/51 Rule

The new law liberalizes the access to, and the participation of, foreign investment in Mexico. Probably the clearest departure from the rigid text of the 1973 Law was the abolition of the so-called 49/51 rule. Under the old law, foreign investors were allowed to invest up to a maximum of 49 percent, thus relegating foreign investors to a permanent minority position in any Mexican corporation.

The FIL changes this by allowing foreign investment to participate, as a rule, in up to 100 percent in most business and commercial activities in Mexico, except those subject to a specific regulatory regime pursuant to the new Law and the 1989 Regulations.

Foreign Investment Favored

The FIL adopts a clear promotional attitude in favor of foreign investment. The 1973 Law became well-known outside Mexico for its excessive regulatory legal framework and discriminatory provisions directed against foreign investors.

In conformity with NAFTA, the new Law eliminates the imposition of performance requirements upon foreign investors.

In negotiating investment projects with the Secretariat of Commerce and Industrial Development (SECOFI), the federal agency legally empowered to control foreign investment matters in Mexico, it was common for Mexican authorities to impose performance requirements as a condition to authorizing certain foreign investment projects. Those requirements usually consisted, for example, in the creation of a minimum number of permanent jobs, the imposition of export quotas, the buying of supplies from Mexican producers, the use of certain technology, etc.

Provisions in Consonance With the 1973 Law

Unfortunately, the new FIL continues to follow some of the restrictive policies contained in the old law.

Reserved Activities

The FIL maintains a large number of activities exclusively reserved to the Mexican government. These activities are enumerated in the FIL's Article 5 and they include, for example, 1) petroleum; 2) basic petrochemicals; 3) electricity; 4) nuclear energy; 5) radioactive minerals; 6) satellite communications; 7) telegraph services; 8) radiotelegraphic and 9) postal services; 10) railroads; 11) issuance of paper money and 12) minting of money, and 13) control of ports, airports and heliports. Under

Mexican law, the exercise of an exclusive and absolute control on the part of Mexico's government over these natural resources or economic activities is justified for strategic and historical reasons.

Activities Reserved to Mexicans

Furthermore, the new FIL perpetuates the existence of activities exclusively reserved to Mexicans or to Mexican corporations with an "Exclusion of Foreigners Clause."

These activities, contained in article six of the FIL include: 1) national land transportation for passengers, tourism and freight, "not including messenger and package-delivery services;" 2) retail and gasoline sales and liquified petroleum gas; 3) radio broadcasting services, and other services in radio and television, "other than cable television;" 4) credit unions; 5) development banking institutions; and, 6) rendering of professional and technical services.

Regulated Categories

The new FIL continues to limit foreign investment by preserving four regulated categories of economic activity with a specified maximum foreign investment percentage: a) up to 10 percent; b) up to 25 percent; c) up to 30 percent, and d) up to 49 percent in the capital stock of Mexican corporations.

Cooperatives are included in the first category. In the up-to–25–percent bracket, national air transportation, air taxi transportation, and specialized transport are included. The third, 30–percent category, enlists corporations controlling financial groupings, credit institutions of multiple banking services, stock market offices, and stock market experts.

Finally, the 49–percent level enumerates insurance companies, bonds, money exchange, general deposit warehousing, manufacturing and commercialization of explosives, firearms and cartridges, printing and publication of domestic newspapers, cable television, basic telephone services, freshwater and coastal fishing in Mexico's exclusive economic zone, shipping corporations, etc.

Provisions in Symmetry with
the 1989 Regulations

Unquestionably, the new FIL is a continuation of the open and liberal policies enshrined in the 1989 Regulations, as published in the Diario Oficial on May 16, 1989. In general, it may be asserted that the FIL elevated to the constitutional category of a formal, federal statute, the liberal provisions which were previously contained in the text of simple, administrative regulations.

When the new Regulations to the 1973 Law were enacted by President Salinas in mid–1989, some Mexican jurists openly challenged their constitutionality. It was argued, for instance, that since the Regulations actually liberalized the provisions of the 1973 Law, by means of introducing substantive changes to the rigid text of the Law, these departures could only be characterized as unconstitutional.

Moreover, the favorable conditions created by the 1989 Regulations did not provide foreign investors with appropriate legal certainty since it was argued that the Regulations were enacted by means of a Presidential decree, rather than contained in a more formal legislative enactment, such as a federal statute. Therefore, the legal certainty provided by the Regulations was perceived by foreign investors—especially Japanese—as ephemeral, subject to the promulgation of another presidential decree, which could dramatically alter the rules of the game against the interests of foreign investors.

Automatic Approval

Based upon the 1989 Regulations (which continue to be in force until regulations for the new FIL appear), SECOFI automatically approves any foreign investment project under US$100 million in an economic activity not included in the "Classification of Economic Activities." This Classification appeared as an appendix to the regulations.

In addition, any of these projects must comply with the following six criteria: a) a maximum investment of US$100 million in fixed assets; b) direct external funding provided through subscriptions of capital contributions, external credit or foreign funds intermediated by Mexican financial institutions; c) location of industrial plants outside the country's three major industrial metropolitan areas, i.e. Mexico City, Monterrey and Guadalajara; d) at least a balance between foreign exchange income and outlays during the first three years of operation; e) permanent jobs and continuous training for workers; and, f) adequate technology and observance of applicable environmental legislation.

Real Estate Trusts

Simpler fideicomisos (real estate trusts) are needed for Mexican corporations interested in acquiring immovable assets in the "Restricted Zone." Article 10 of the new FIL permits Mexican corporations, with the insertion of the Calvo Clause, "to acquire the direct ownership of immovable assets located in the Restricted Zone" for non-residential activities; namely, assets destined for industrial, commercial or tourism activities. The acquisition has to be registered with the Secretariat of Foreign Affairs.

The Calvo Clause, a common contractual modality practiced throughout Latin America, basically provides, in the Mexican version, "that foreigners who acquire properties of any kind in the Mexican Republic ... agree to consider themselves as Mexican nationals with regard to these properties and not to invoke the protection of their governments with respect to such properties, under penalty, in case of violation, of forfeiting to the Mexican government the properties thus acquired." (Art. 3 of the 1973 Act).

Under Mexican law, the "Restricted Zone" comprises a strip of 100 kilometers along the borders and 50 kilometers along the coasts, pursuant to Article 27, paragraph I of Mexico's Constitution; the Organic Act of Article 27 of the Constitution, and Article 1, paragraph XIII of the 1989 Regulations. In this zone, only Mexicans by birth or by naturalization, and Mexican corporations, may have the direct ownership over immovable assets.

However, foreign natural persons or foreign legal entities interested in obtaining the beneficiary use of immovable assets located within the Restricted Zone must enter into a fideicomiso contract with an authorized Mexican banking institution, when said assets are to be used for residential purposes (Article 11, paragraph II). For the first time, the new FIL defines the concept of "[Use and development of immovable assets located in the Restricted Zone" (Article 12).

The new FIL extends the duration of these fideicomisos from 30 to 50 years, in cases involving both Mexican corporations with the Calvo Clause, and foreign natural persons or foreign legal entities. Furthermore, the renewal of these trust-contracts is virtually automatic and indefinite by means of consecutive trusts, obtainable when the interested party complies with some basic conditions.

Neutral Investments

The new FIL maintains the notion of neutral investments, created by the 1989 Regulations. The FIL defines neutral investment as "that invested in Mexican corporations or in authorized trusts . . . is not taken into account in calculating the percentage of foreign investment in the capital stock of Mexican corporations" (Article 18). This kind of investment was created to liberalize foreign access to the Mexican stock market.

National Commission of Foreign Investments

The FIL enumerates eleven economic activities which require a favorable resolution of the National Commission of Foreign Investments for foreign investment to participate in a larger percentage than 49 percent. Among others, these activities include port services, shipping companies, administration of air traffic terminals, private education, cellular telephones, construction of oil pipelines, drilling of oil and gas wells, etc. (Article 8).

The FIL enlarges the membership of the National Commission of Foreign Investments, and attempts to limit its ample discretionary powers (Article 23). It also simplifies the inscription procedures with the National Registry of Foreign Investments; an issue which had created delays and confusion among foreign investors in the recent past (Articles 31–36).

Sanctions

The FIL devotes its final articles to the imposition of sanctions, "when actions are carried out in violation of the provisions of the Act" by any person, whether a Mexican national, a Mexican corporation, a foreign national or a foreign legal entity (Articles 37–38). Sanctions range from SECOFI's declaration of nullity of the violative acts to the imposition of fines, which may consist of a minimum of US$4,500 to a maximum of US$22,500, depending upon the violation.

Conclusion

The most distinctive feature of Mexico's new Foreign Investment Law is its clear policy to promote, rather than regulate, foreign investment. Although the new federal statute breaks away from the legal and administrative rigidity imposed by the 1973 Law, it still shares some of the old Law's traditional policies. At the same time, the new FIL advances to a higher legal plateau some of the policies of liberalization and flexibility already contained in the 1989 Regulations. Overall, there is no question that the new FIL represents the most progressive legal framework ever formulated in Mexico to govern foreign investment.

The negotiation of the NAFTA provided valuable protection to foreign investors. The enactment of domestic investment legislation buttresses the conclusion that Mexico is looking at an open border in the long run. The NAFTA provides that the countries can get out with six months notice. This fact is not too comforting for a 'bricks and mortar' investment that epitomizes immobility. The foreign direct investor, unlike the foreign portfolio investor, cannot leave the country on a moment's notice. The existence of investment protection under the domestic system is more comforting.

In spite of the open border environment, Mexico continues to limit foreign investment, although it is more in line with U.S. concepts of restricting entry in sensitive industries. The Mexican restrictions, however, are rooted in deeper sentiments. Article 27 of the Mexican Constitution states "Only Mexicans by birth or naturalization and Mexican companies have the right to acquire ownership of lands, waters and their appurtenances, or to obtain concessions for the exploitation of mines, waters or mineral fuels, in the Mexican Republic. The State may grant the same right to foreigners provided that they agree before the Ministry of Foreign Relations to consider themselves as nationals with respect to said properties and accordingly not to invoke the protection of their Governments in regard to them; under penalty, in case of breaches of the agreement, of losing to the benefit of the Nation the properties they may have acquired thereby" * * *. This is essentially the Calvo Clause and its remnants continue to be felt in the new investment legislation.

The prohibition of foreigners of foreign investment includes petroleum and other hydrocarbons, electricity, nuclear energy, satellite communications, telegraph, mail, railroads, and oversight of ports, airports, and heliports. In addition, foreigners may not invest in national surface transportation of passengers, tourism, and freight, retail trade in gasoline, radio broadcasting and other radio and television services different from cable television. These are essentially the sensitive industry's exception. The FIL also limits the percentage ownership interest that foreign persons can make in certain industries.

The forced domestic joint venture is a feature that is not required by U.S. law. Another distinction is that the FIL impacts the formation of companies. A permit from the Secretariat of Foreign Relations is required for the creation of companies. The exclusion of foreigner's clause or the agreement provided for in Article 27 of the Constitution must be included in the by-laws of companies that are created. In addition, foreign companies that intend to do business in Mexico must register with governmental authorities.

2. *The Regulations to the Foreign Investment Law*

The 1993 FIL greatly liberalized the foreign investment rules. The liberalizing trend continues through regulations issued in 1998. The stated purpose of the regulations is to provide a complete and specific set of explanations to the 1993 FIL. The following article describes the new regulations.

MEXICO: THE REGULATIONS TO THE FIL AND THE FOREIGN INVESTMENTS NATIONAL REGISTRY

Juan Francisco Torres–Landa

33 INT'L LAW 747 (1999).

I. INTRODUCTION

Almost five years since the Foreign Investment Law (FIL) was issued, the Regulations to the FIL and the Foreign Investments National Registry (Regulations) have been published in the Federal Official Gazette of September 8, 1998, and have been in force since October 7, 1998. This instrument repealed the Regulations to the Law to Promote Mexican Investment and to Regulate Foreign Investment that had been in force since 1989.

Going back in time, the FIL currently in effect was published in the Federal Official Gazette on December 27, 1993, amended as per decree on December 24, 1996. Issuance of this statute coincided with the period that the North American Free Trade Agreement (NAFTA) entered into between Canada, the United States, and Mexico came into force. The FIL repealed the former Law to Foster Mexican Investment and to Regulate Foreign Investment that had been in place for almost twenty years, and had incorporated a restrictive legal framework that eventually resulted in an obstacle for the economic development of the country. The former regulations marked the beginning of a new era of opening the country to foreign investment, but in some cases using mechanisms that could be considered in conflict with the provisions of the law then in place.

The FIL achieved the important goal of clearly setting up the path of deregulating foreign investment, and therefore, it consolidated the trade opening policy that Mexico adopted at the end of the past decade.

II. Purpose of the Regulations

In general terms, the Regulations' goal is to generate a complete and specific source of information on the following topics, some of which will be addressed in subsequent sections of this article:

(a) To better define legal concepts governed by the FIL, including, among others, what must be understood as foreign investment participation in the capital stock of local companies; confirmation of activities excluded among those subject to foreign investment participation limitations or restrictions; determination of real properties destined to housing and non-housing activities; and series "T" shares that represent the capital contributed in agricultural, grazing, or forest lands;

(b) To establish in a concise, detailed, and orderly manner the procedures and requirements that must be fulfilled in order to perform any of the activities subject to specific regulation by the FIL that benefits from mechanisms provided for in the instrument that may permit avoidance, under certain conditions, of the remaining restrictions in foreign investment matters, as well as to comply with the obligations provided for in the FIL and the Regulations;

(c) To regulate the authority and the operation of the competent agencies addressing this subject matter, basically the Foreign Investments National Commission (FINC) and the Foreign Investments National Registry (FINR); and

(d) To set forth the general rules concerning periodic notices that must be filed by those persons that are subject to registration with FINR, to wit: (1) Mexican companies with foreign investment participation, including those in which the foreigners participate through a trust agreement or neutral investment; (2) foreign individuals or entities that normally perform commercial acts in Mexico and branch offices of foreign investors established in Mexico; and (3) trust agreements granting rights to foreign investors vis-à-vis shares or equity parts, real estate, and/or neutral investment.

III. Activities That Have Specific Limitations for Foreign Investment Participation

The Regulations confirm that the following activities are not reserved for the state to perform, but may rather be performed by private parties, and in the case of foreign investors, they will be able to participate up to the amount allowed in each case. The Regulations now confirm that: (a) transportation, storage, and distribution of natural gas; and (b) electricity generation for self-supply, co-generation, small production, exportation, and emergency purposes are no longer considered as activities reserved to the state pursuant to FIL § 5. 4 Likewise, the Regulations indicate that the construction, operation, and ownership of pipelines, installations and equipment for the transportation and distribution of natural gas no longer need the FINC to issue a specific ruling enabling investors to hold an equity participation in the respective Mexican companies in excess of forty-nine percent of its capital stock.

On the other hand, the Regulations confirm that the following substances encompass the list of basic petrochemicals that are reserved for the Mexican state exclusively: ethane, propane, butanes, pentanes, hexane, heptane, raw materials for black product, naftas, and methane. Other petrochemicals are subject to the general forty-nine percent foreign investment limitation on this area of activities. Finally, the Regulations confirm that Series "T" shares of companies owning farming, livestock, or forestry land, in which foreign investment is limited to forty-nine percent, exclusively represents the capital stock contributed in the form of land or resources to acquire those properties.

The Regulations refer to the existence of rules in the subject matter of foreign investment that are scattered in legal instruments other than the FIL, and that cannot be left out of sight. Therefore, the Regulations provide greater certainty with respect to the legal framework applicable to activities subject to specific restriction, comprised of natural gas, Electric energy public service and petrochemical. These restrictions define in greater detail the activities that should not be considered restricted or limited to those entities with foreign investment participation.

Additionally, the Regulations now provide that the obligation to obtain a favorable ruling from the FINC when a foreign investor wishes to exceed the forty-nine percent capital stock threshold in a Mexican corporation when its assets exceed the annual FINC limit is only applicable with respect to: (i) the acquisition of shares or equity participation of companies already in existence; and (ii) participation in companies that do not carry out activities subject to foreign investment restrictions or specific limitations by the applicable provisions of the FIL. Regarding this subject, the Regulations indicate with greater clarity the requirements and procedures that must be followed in order to secure the respective permits and for the submission of required notices, whether with the Ministry of Commerce and Industrial Promotion (SECOFI) or the Ministry of Foreign Affairs (SRE).

IV.   COMPLIANCE OF OBLIGATIONS REGARDING THE FINR

With the changes to the method of compliance with the obligations imposed by the FIL and the Regulations, the latter contemplate filing with FINR the "corporate, accounting, financial, employment, production, and other data regarding the activity in each establishment" needed to obtain the yearly renewal of the respective FINR registration certificate. According to the Regulations, these reports must be submitted within the seven months following the closing of each fiscal period according to a calendar of submission dates that varies depending on the first letter of the name of the person or legal entity that must file the report (that is, from A to D, during the month of April; from E to J, during the month of May; from K to P, during the month of June; and from Q to Z, during the month of July of each year).

A new adjustment to the Regulations is the obligation to file "data to determine the value of revenue and expenses" derived from: (1) new contributions or withdrawals that do not affect the capital stock; (2) withholding the last fiscal period earnings or distribution of accumulated retained earnings; or (3) loans outstanding as creditors or debtors (under certain events). Submission of this information to the FINR must be made within the twenty business days following the close of each quarter (that is, from January to March, from April to June, from July to September, and from October to December), and only in the case of revenues or expenses, that on quarterly basis exceed the equivalent of three thousand times the minimum wage in force in the federal district (currently approximately U.S. ($9,000.00).

The information referred to in the previous paragraph is included in the report that must be submitted to secure the yearly renewal of the FINR registration certificate. The purpose of this new obligation is to render updated data to the agency to determine the existence of possible new investments or exits of funds that are not necessarily reflected in the capital stock of companies.

V. Acquisition of Real Estate and Trust Agreements

With respect to the purchase of real estate within the restricted zone by foreign individuals or legal entities or Mexican entities without a foreign investment restriction clause, the Regulations indicate that the legal regime will vary depending on the specific housing or non-housing purposes for which the real estate is to be used. In order to distinguish between those classifications, the Regulation includes a list of specific examples to aid in determining housing or non-housing status.

The legal structure under which foreigners may acquire real estate within the restricted zone is a trust agreement. The Regulations now consolidate the specific requirements needed to set up the structure. It is necessary to clarify that a trust agreement allows Mexican companies with foreign investment participation access to housing real estate within the restricted zone, whereas Mexican companies with foreign investment participation may directly acquire non-housing real estate in the restricted zone16. The permits granted to create the trust agreements, or other acquisition vehicles, do not release the respective investor of other environmental, zoning, construction, and related licensing and permitting issues at federal, state, and municipal levels of government.

VI. Incorporation of Companies

Regarding the incorporation of an SRE company and the corporate name permit that is required, the Regulations indicate that name will be granted as long as the respective name has not been reserved by another company, that is, another party previously requested the same name and has already received the SRE permit.

Nonetheless, the reservation will have a duration of ninety business days from the date when the permit is received, at the end of which the creation of the company must be formalized in an instrument granted before a notary public. Otherwise, the reservation will be deemed to be terminated. On the other hand, once the permit issued by the SRE is granted, a six-month term begins in which notification of the incorporation of the company or the change of the corporate name must occur.

The Regulations also provide procedures for filing notices regarding the modification of the foreign investment exclusion clause, permitting foreign investment (the "Calvo Clause," or the agreement foreseen in article 14 of the Regulations); and related to the liquidation, merger or spin-off of companies. Notice of modification of the foreign investment exclusion clause must include a copy of the public instrument containing the amendment to the by-laws and statement regarding company ownership of real estate in the restricted zone and its uses.

As part of the administrative simplification effort, the notices referred to in this section of the Regulations may be secured through the Ministry of Finance and Public Credit (SHCP), when, according to the applicable tax regulations, notices must be filed with the Tax Payers' Federal Registry. The SHCP must deliver the respective information to the SRE within three months of the date on which it receives the data from the interested party. The fourth paragraph of article 18 is the only provision of the Regulations that did not come into force twenty business days after the publication of the Regulations because it will not come into effect within six months after publication.

An important point regarding this title of the Regulations is that, as opposed to the old Regulations, the new Regulations do not indicate the need to establish a series of shares in the capital stock of Mexican companies. In this area, it is necessary to apply the provisions of the special legal instruments to each subject matter (for example, financial institutions, agrarian matters or telecommunications).

VII. Neutral Investment

According to the FIL, neutral investment is a mechanism that allows the inclusion of foreign investment in areas subject to limitations, and it may be performed through instruments issued by trustee agents, special series of shares, or international financial entities for development. The role that the Regulations include for this mechanism is functional, insofar as they simply set forth the requirements to obtain approvals from the FINC and the rules to observe in each one of the referred mechanisms.

VIII. FINC and FINR

With respect to the legal framework of the FINC, the Regulations' goal is to clarify its authority and to set forth the guidelines under which an agency must act for the issuance of resolutions. Likewise, regarding the FINR, the agency in charge of receiving notices for any registration transaction involving foreign investment participation under any of the events foreseen by the FIL, the Regulations implement the manner in which the FINR is divided, as well as the way it must respond to applications submitted within its organization. The goal is to promote an expedited and simplified operation of that body.

As an administrative simplification innovation, the Regulations indicate that, provided a registration request, notice, or report with the FINR is filed without errors or obvious omissions, and the agency does not require the applicant to correct those errors or omissions within twenty business days following their date of submission, those documents will be deemed properly filed. The copy with the receipt stamp from SECOFI is considered the registration certificate, registration renewal certificate, registration cancellation, or confirmation of notice, depending on the case. The FINR will no longer issue official response letters regarding filings made, except when in the form of a request for additional data.

IX. Conclusion

In general terms, the Regulations result in a legal tool that permits a full and complete understanding of the requirements that must be complied with and the guidelines that must be observed in any procedure regarding foreign investment. The Regulations complete and complement the provisions of the FIL, providing additional detail and specifications of the legal concepts governed by the statute. The Regulations accomplish the general goal of adding greater legal certainty to the rules applicable to foreign investors doing business in Mexico.

The environment for the FDI is very favorable in Mexico. The next step in the process is choosing the entity that will be used for the outbound FDI.

———————

Mexican regulations, like regulations promulgated in the United States are intended to merely explain the statute. They are not supposed to expand or contradict the underlying law. In the U.S., an aggrieved party can seek judicial relief to annul an action taken by the Executive branch in cases where it has overstepped its authority in promulgating regulations. This is a clear example of the checks and balances system.

The Mexican tradition with its operational code[9] and *Presidencialismo*[10] undermines the checks and balances systems. As an example, in 1989, then President Carlos Salinas De Gortari promulgated regulations[11] that greatly liberalized the restrictive foreign investment law.

9. See Gordon, Of Aspirations and Operations: The Governance of Multinational Enterprises by Third World Nations, 16 Inter–American L. Rev. 301 (1984).

10. See *Presidencialismo*, supra at Section 1.1.

11. *Reglamento de la Ley Para Promover la Inversión Mexicana y Regular la*

Mexican legal commentators criticized the regulations as exceeding the then existing law. One bold commentator even suggested that the regulations violated the Mexican Constitution.

The 1989 enactment curiously served as a form of protection to the foreign investor because they liberalized the more restrictive statute. The careful lawyer, however, was always concerned about her client making capital investments having only Administrative Regulations as support. The change of Presidents could easily cause a reversal of the liberalization rules—a fact that was supported by history. The 1998 regulations are different because they interpret a statute that has itself liberalized the investment regime.

SECTION 3.4   THE CHOICE OF ENTITY: AN ANALYSIS UNDER THE MEXICAN LEGAL SYSTEM

A. INTRODUCTION

Once the regulatory environment has been assessed, one must select the form of business organization to use for the FDI. Similar to the U.S. system, there are a variety of Mexican entities from which to choose. Although dissimilar in formation procedures, the Mexican *Sociedad Anónima (SA)* and the *Sociedad Anónima de Capital Variable (SA de CV)* are roughly equivalent to the General Business Corporation. The term *Sociedad Anónima* translated literally means 'anonymous society.'

The central idea behind the anonymity concept is that the general public does not know who owns the corporation. Recall that in the U.S. procedure, the sale of shares is made at the organizational meeting which is not public information. Thus, the U.S. corporation is also an ''anonymous society.'

The distinction between the *SA* and *SA de CV* relates to the capital structure. The literal translation of *SA de CV* is 'anonymous society with variable capital. The *SA* must issue all of its authorized shares upon formation. The *SA de CV* has the authority to vary its capital during the life of the corporation. The U.S. Corporation can either be a *SA* or *SA de CV* depending on the action taken at the organizational meeting. See Section 2.2, supra.

Other entities that mirror their U.S. counterpart include the *Sucursal* which is comparable to a branch. The *Sociedad de Riesgo Limitado*, (SdeRL) is roughly equivalent to the Limited Liability Company. The *Sociedad en Nombre Colectivo* (SNC) and *Sociedad en Comandita Simple* (SCP) are roughly equivalent to the general partnership and limited partnership, respectively. The basic legal attributes of the Mexican entities are similar to their U.S. counterparts. It is in the formation of the entity that great differences exist, especially in the role played by the *Notario Público* and *Corredor Commercial/ Público*. The role of the

Inversión Extranjera, Diario Oficial, May,   19,1989.

Notario and *Corredor* is discussed infra. See also the note on the Mexican legal system in Section 1.1, supra.

Similar to our analysis of the U.S. forms of business, no one form is superior over another. The 'best' form is the one that best fits the clients needs. The three important factors must be considered—profit maximization and distribution, limiting the risk, and establishing control over the FDI. Foreign counsel is invaluable in helping the U.S. lawyer and client make an intelligent decision.

B. FORMING THE ENTITY

1. *The Applicable Law*

The rules governing mercantile entities are found in the Federal Commercial Code (*Codigo Comercial*) and specifically under a section of that Code known as the *Ley General de Sociedades Mercantiles* (The General Law of Mercantile Entities, hereafter, the General Law). The General Law provides the rules for the formation, governance, and liquidation of over six business organizations, included within these six forms is the corporation. Additional restrictions on the use of any particular entity or equity limitations are found in Articles 15 and 16 of the Foreign Investment Law. See Section 3.2 B 1, supra.

It is important to remember that merely because an entity is available under the General Law does not mean it can be used by foreigners or that one foreign person can wholly own it. The U.S. restricts foreign ownership in specific industries but leaves the form of business organization generally available to all. In contrast, Mexico imposes industry restrictions and also restricts the use of some business organizations by foreigners. The restrictions, if any, would be found in the Foreign Investment Law. The Mexican General Law is federal law and provides the rules for various types of mercantile entities. In the U.S. system the rules are found in State laws—the Corporation Code, Limited Liability Company Act, Limited Partnership Act, and the General Partnership Act.

2. *Forming the Corporation*

The first step in the incorporation process is for the corporate organizers to obtain a permit to form a corporation from the *Secretaria de Relaciones Exteriores* (The Secretary of Foreign Relations). The certificate obtained from this governmental authority is presented to a *Notario* or *Corredor Público*, so that the *Acta Constitutiva* (roughly equivalent to the Articles of Incorporation of a U.S. corporation) can be prepared. The *Notario* and *Corredor* are the only persons authorized to prepare the *Acta Constitutiva*.

There are substantial differences between the articles of incorporation of a corporation formed under the State law of any U.S. State and Mexico. The Mexican Corporation is constituted rather than incorporated. The formation document is said to be an *Acta Constitutiva* which roughly means an act of constitution. The practical difference is in the size of the document. In the U.S., Articles of Incorporation will frequently be only one page long. In Mexico, and other civil law countries the *Acta Constitutiva* could be fifteen to twenty pages long, containing much of what would be included in the Articles of Incorporation, Organizational Meeting, and by-laws of a common law corporation

Pursuant to the General Law the Articles must contain the name and address of the incorporators, The name of the corporation followed by *Sociedad Anonima de Capital Variable* or *SA de CV,* the address and purpose of the corporation. In a common law corporation a general-purpose clause is legally sufficient. The Mexican system usually will include specific areas of involvement.

The Mexican Articles also must, in accordance with the requirements of Article 31 of the FIL, include the Calvo Clause. The provision obligates the present or future foreign shareholders to formally obligate themselves with the Secretary of Foreign Relations to consider themselves as Mexicans in relation to their investment (either directly or indirectly) in the SA de CV. The investment in the SA de CV includes share ownership, with respect to the goods, rights, and concessions the SA de CV may have, and on contractual undertakings the SA de CV may have with the Mexican government. The foreign persons further obligate themselves to not invoke the protection of their respective governments. Failure to adhere to these obligations will result in the forfeiture of their investment.

3.   *The Role of the Civil Law Notary*

MEXICAN LAW: A TREATISE FOR LEGAL PRACTITIONERS AND INTERNATIONAL INVESTORS

Jorge A. Vargas

West Group 1998.

§ 1.22 The Mexican Public Notary

To a U.S. legal practitioner who is unfamiliar with Mexico and its legal system, the notion of a public notary likely conveys the idea of a minor official who performs unimportant tasks. Nothing can be more erroneous. In Mexico, and in other civil law countries, such as Canada, France or Spain, the public notary (Notario Público) is the most respected member of the legal profession.

A public notary is a professional whose official functions are not only important but indispensable for that country's legal system to work in a proper and efficient manner. They are popularly known as "the attorneys' attorney." They are legal specialists, tax experts, superb drafters of documents and the most authoritative legal counselors a Mexican legal practitioner and his/her clients can have. Public notaries are so successful professionally that most, if not all of them, are counted among the wealthiest professionals in that country today.

Most important legal acts cannot take place in Mexico without the professional and official involvement of a public notary. For example: powers of attorney, real estate transactions, including the drafting of the corresponding title and its official inscription at the Public Registry of Property and Commerce (Registro Público de la Propiedad y del Comercio); the establishment of a Mexican corporation and the drafting of its act of incorporation; domestic and international contracts; the sale of movable assets above $1,000 dollars; formal wills, etc.

Public notaries perform two distinct functions. Above all, they are empowered by statute to execute legal documents exercising their "public faith" power (Fé pública). This means that any assertion advanced by this public official stating that a specific act had been executed by him/her as public notary, is given absolute credence and full legal validity by any Mexican court and by any public authority in Mexico. Accordingly, a notary can assert that a given legal act (Acto jurídico), such as a contract or a will, was executed before him/her, or that a specific occurrence or happening (Hecho jurídico), for example, a fire or a flood, a personal statement or declaration, a visit to a place, an inspection to a corporation, the occurrence of an environmental violation, an injury, or a winner in a lottery or a contest, took place before his/her very eyes as public official on a given date, place and hour.

A formal document issued by a public notary in which such assertions are stated would be accepted as full proof by any Mexican court or by any authority, without any other support, because a public notary, as indicated earlier, is empowered by statute with Fé pública. Furthermore, authorities would not accept, validate or record certain acts or contracts (Actos jurídicos) unless drafted, protocolized and formally executed in a public notary's document known as a "public deed" (Escritura pública). A "notarial minute" (Acta notarial) is another formal document executed by public notaries in which they assert the taking place of factual occurrences.

Secondly, a public notary also functions as a public official whose selection, appointment and professional services are governed and authorized y the Federal District, or by the state where the notary resides. In this capacity of "quasi public official," the public notary, while in the process of executing and issuing any "public deed," is under the obligation to ascertain that the parties involved in a legal transaction are in full compliance with the law and with certain specific statutes, such as the payment of federal or state taxes or, when foreigners are involved in a transaction, ascertain that they possess the correct type of valid visa. When this is not the case, the notary must denounce violations to the competent Mexican authorities, whether federal or state tax authorities on fiscal matters, for example, or to the Secretariat of the Interior (Secretaría de Gobernación, which loosely corresponds to the U.S. Immigration and Naturalization Service) on immigration questions.

Public notaries are governed by notarial statutes enacted by each of the 31 states in the Republic of Mexico and by Federal Congress regarding the Federal District (Mexico City). These statutes regulate the functions, notarial documents, appointments and removals, obligations, State inspections, sanctions and legal liability of these public officials. The body of these rules forms what is known in Mexico as Notarial Law (Derecho Notarial).

Public notaries are appointed by the Governor of the state in question, after passing a demanding and lengthy notarial exam. Each state legislature establishes by statute a fixed number of notaries allowed to function in that state and the requirements to become public notary. Public notaries are appointed for life through the granting of a patent (Patente de notario). Patents are revoked when the notary violates the notarial statute. Unlike other legal practitioners in Mexico, public notaries must belong to the respective College of Notaries (Colegio de Notarios) of a given state of the Federal District. These professionals notarial associations monitor and supervise the proper rendering of notarial services, study legal matters submitted to them by the state government, offer opinions as consultants and recommend the imposition of sanctions to notaries by the government of the state.

Pursuant to the corresponding statute, public notaries are required to have two official books, the "Protocol" (Protocolo) and the "Appendix," without which they cannot function. The protocol is a book in which the notary must transcribe any contracts, deeds (Escrituras públicas) or minutes (Actas) that were subject to his/her authorization. The appendix is formed by the original documents, whether public or private, which the notary utilized for the drafting of the documents in question. Keeping a proper and updated protocol is of the essence. Protocols are subject to a number of formalistic requirements regarding their size, pagination, manner in which written texts should appear in it, the numbering of each document, authorization by a government official, etc., all of which are regulated in detail by the notarial statute. Both the notarial functions, and its working books, are subject to inspections by an official from the state government. Once the notarial books(Libros notariales) are used up, the notary must send each book to the State Notarial Archive (Archivo de Notarías del Estado).

The National Association of Mexican Notaries) Asociación Nacional del Notariado Mexicano), located in Mexico City, embraces most of the public notaries in Mexico, with its membership consisting of some 5,000 notaries. The oldest notarial document at the General Notarial Archive in Mexico City (Archivo General de Notarías de la Cudad de México) is a contract written by Juan Fernández del Castillo in 1525.

Public notaries have a long and distinguished tradition in Mexico. The notarial minutes written by Rodrigo de Escobedo, who accompanied Christopher Columbus in his historical voyage of 1492, were followed by Hernan Cortés, who also utilized the services of a notary to document his discoveries and military conquests in the lands he named the New Spain. Diego de Godoy, on July 10, 1519 wrote the notarial minute of conquest and establishment of the Villa Rica de la Vera Cruz, and the appointment of its government (Ayuntamiento) by Cortés,4 in the palce where the city of Veracruz stands today. It would not be an exaggeration to assert that Spain's maritime discoveries and its territorial expansion in the XV and XVI were built upon the legal expertise of notaries.

C. A SURVEY OF OTHER MAJOR ISSUES

1. *Control Over the Corporation*

In the Mexican system, the supreme corporate authority rests in the shareholders. The shareholders have the power to manage and administer the corporation pursuant to the general shareholder meetings. A supermajority of shareholders is needed for certain fundamental changes to the corporate structure. The shareholders act through regular meetings *Asembleas Generales de Accionistas* or through a special meeting *Asemblea General Extraordinaria* depending on the subject matter.

The Board of Directors (*Consejo de Administración*) or Sole Administrator (*Administrador Único*) whatever the particular case may be, are appointed by the *Accionistas* (shareholders). The *Consejo* or *Administrador* are charged with the responsibility of managing and administering the corporation. Neither the *Administrador* nor members of the *Consejo* (the law requires at least two) need be shareholders. The *Consejo* names the President and Secretary of the board.

The General law also provides for a position that has no statutory analogue in the U.S. system—the *Comisario* (Auditor). A *Comisario* is a person selected by the shareholders. The position is roughly equivalent to an auditor. The duties and obligations of this auditor are found either in the *Acta de Incorporación* or the *Ley General*. Other persons with day-to-day governance responsibilities include the *Director General* (Director General) and the *Gerente General* (General Manager). The Director General and General Manager are named either by the shareholders, the *Administrador*, or the *Consejo*. The U.S. counterpart would be the officers of the corporation.

2. *The Authority to Act on Behalf of a Corporation*

A corporation's status as a 'person' is a legal fiction. In any case where the corporation is to engage in a business transaction some natural person must sign. For example, assume that Delta, Inc., pursuant to its decision to make a foreign direct investment in Mexico, decides to form Delta, SA de CV. The Delta board of directors passed a resolution giving Delta's President, Dennis Wilson, the authority to form the Mexican subsidiary. How can Wilson demonstrate to the *Notario* or *Corredor* that he has the authority to act on behalf of Delta, Inc? This has always been a difficult issue in Mexico and other Latin American Counties. The following article addresses the problem:

Uniform North American Powers of Attorney, Anna Torriente, The National Law Center for Inter–American Free Trade [NLCIFT] * * *

The granting of a power of attorney in a common law jurisdiction such as the United States or British Canada which will enable an agent to conduct business in a civil law jurisdiction such as Mexico has historically been problematic due to basic differences between the common law and law traditions. * * *

In general terms, both the common law and civil law systems define a power of attorney as a verbal agreement or a written instrument authorizing another to act as the grantor's agent or attorney in carrying out one transaction or a series of transactions. A power of attorney may general or special in nature. A general power of attorney gives the agent broader power to exercise his or her discretion in acting on the principal's behalf in performing certain categories of acts. * * *

In contrast, a special power of attorney permits the agent to carry out only those specific acts authorized in the written instrument.

Powers of attorney granted and enforced in the United States need not follow any specific format. As long as the material elements of the agency are contained in the document, the agency will be deemed valid and the agent's acts will, as a general rule, bind the principal.

In contrast, the granting and enforcing of a power of attorney in a civil law country such as Mexico has traditionally been a highly formal process. Parties are not free to execute a power of attorney in whatever format they desire; the specific requirements of the applicable law must be followed. * * *

The creation of these powers entails compliance with various procedural requirements. Some powers must be expressed in the form of a public deed (escritura pública), in general terms, a power granted before a public notary. Other powers may be expressed in a private (non-notarial, consular or judicial) writing. Certain types of powers created and enforced in Mexico must also contain language specified in the applicable state civil code, statutory enactment or administrative act.

Mexican law requires powers of attorney to be legalized and authenticated in accordance with specific procedures. Finally, if the grantor of the power is a foreign legal entity (persona moral), rather than a foreign individual, the power granted by the corporation must demonstrate compliance with the laws of the state of incorporation of the corporation. * * *

Power of Attorney to Incorporate a Joint Stock Company

Finally, the special power of attorney to incorporate a joint stock company permits the agent to appear before a public notary and make all determinations necessary for the preparation of the Articles of Incorporation and Bylaws of the corporation, * * * such as fixing the corporate domicile, the purpose of the corporation, etc. The agent may sign the Articles and Bylaws and is also authorized to invest part of the corporate capital in shares and to place restrictions upon the free circulation of corporate shares, in accordance with the provisions of the Mexican Law of Corporations (Ley General de Sociedades Mercantiles). * * *

Under Mexican law, a corporation, partnership, or other legal entity may not grant a power of attorney without complying with certain additional formalities designed to show that the legal entity in fact had the power to confer the agency. * * *

Under Mexican law, a corporation wishing to grant a power of attorney for its agent to transact business in Mexico must comply with highly detailed formalities. The first step for a corporation granting a power of attorney is to show that it has legal existence and legal personality. These elements must be demonstrated in the power of attorney document. This means that the document must show that the corporation is duly organized under the laws of its state of incorporation and has legal standing and capacity to do business. The elements of legal existence and personality may be shown * * * By attaching a copy of the Articles of Incorporation and Bylaws, and amendments, if any, of the company. The attachments must be copies certified by the Secretary of State and should be accompanied by a Spanish translation of the documents. The purpose and powers of the corporation as contained in the Articles of Incorporation and By-laws may not be in conflict with the activity to be performed by the agent under the power of attorney.

The Secretary of State in some states may simply issue a document called a Certificate of Existence, which could also be used to show the corporation's legal existence and personality. Said certificate, where it is attached, must be accompanied by a Spanish translation. Through such a document, the Secretary of State will certify that the company has been incorporated under the laws of the corresponding state, that a certificate of incorporation has been issued on a determined date and that no Articles of Dissolution or Certificate of Withdrawal have been filed.

Once the legal existence and personality of the company have been shown, the power of attorney document must set forth a "casual link" identifying the individual granting the power of attorney on behalf of the company and establishing that said individual has the authority to grant the power to the person who will ultimately represent the company in the business transactions contemplated. The power of attorney document may demonstrate this casual link in a number of ways, showing that the authority of the person granting the power to the agent derives from the bylaws of the company which identify the appointees or agents of the company, or from the minutes of a shareholders' or Board of Directors' meeting appointing said individual and authorizing the granting of the power. * * *

The crucial principle * * * is the establishment of a chain of causation in the power of attorney document, tracing the authority of the first grantor of the power of attorney to the agent who will ultimately represent the company in the particular series of transactions. The chain of delegation of power from one agent-grantor to another must follow the limitations and the scope of the original power and its subsequent amendments, given that no one may grant a broader power to another than what he or she has the authority to delegate. Further, the grantor's authority to delegate the power or name a substitute must be expressly stated in the attached documents establishing the chain of causation.

By way of example, suppose that company A wishes to conduct business in Mexico and has decided to enter into a joint venture with a Mexican company, company B. Company A wishes to grant a power of attorney to its agent to negotiate and execute the joint venture in Mexico. The following hypothetical diagram demonstrates how Company A could show a chain of causation for purposes of creating a valid power of attorney. Company A would attach to the power the following documents and their translation into Spanish:

A COPY OF THE ARTICLE OF INCORPORATION AND BYLAWS OF THE COMPANY

Such a copy should establish the business purpose of the company and the scope of its activities, which would presumably include the power to execute joint venture contracts. The copy of the Articles and Bylaws would also need to show the name, duration, domicile and authorized capital of the company granting the power. For purposes of our example, the Articles and Bylaws should also show that the company is authorized to enter into a joint venture.

MINUTES OF SHAREHOLDERS' MEETING

The minutes should show the shareholders' appointment of the members of the Board of Directors, including the President of the Board of Directors. These should establish that the shareholders, as the ultimate authority of the company, granted the power to the Board of Directors to negotiate and sign a joint venture contract with company B and to appoint an agent to do so.

MINUTES OF THE BOARD OF DIRECTORS' MEETING

These minutes should show that the Board appointed the President of the Board as its agent to negotiate and sign the joint venture contract with company B on behalf of the company and gave the President the power to delegate that power to a third party.

POWER OF ATTORNEY DOCUMENT

This document should show that the President of the Board of Directors has delegated the power of representation to the company's

Mexican attorney, authorizing him or her to negotiate and sign the joint venture contract with company B.

As the preceding diagram demonstrates, the formalities which must be observed by a corporation in granting a power of attorney to its agent may become more and more complex as additional intermediaries get involved or changes occur in the corporate structure on in the structure of its administrative bodies, such as the Board of Directors. * * *

Once the Form is Completed, What's Next?

Once the document is complete, with above-referenced attachments and translations, as appropriate, the signatures of the grantor and grantee must be authenticated. Previously, this step entailed both parties appearing in person at the closest Mexican consular office and signing the document in front of the consul, who had authority to authenticate the signatures. Of course, this requirement could be problematic when there was no Mexican consulate in the area where the power of attorney was to be granted.

Fortunately, on August 14, 1995, Mexico became a signatory to the October 5, 1961 Hague Convention abolishing the requirement of legalization of foreign public documents. Pursuant to this convention, the signature requirements for a public document such as power of attorney are relaxed. The parties need only complete an apostille form and send the completed form along with the power of attorney to the Central Authority in the country where the power has been prepared. * * *

The Documentation procedure for the formation of a Mexican corporation is cumbersome. The formation of an U.S. corporation in many U.S. States does not even require a common law Notarial Certificate. This is one of many areas where the legal systems are different.

SECTION 3.5 ILLEGAL PAYMENTS TO CORRUPT FOREIGN OFFICIALS

There is a great deal of diversity among the countries of the world—political diversity, economic diversity, legal diversity, and cultural diversity. One major area where there is a problem among cultural diversity is in the area of payments to foreign officials. Governmental salaries in many developing countries are notoriously low. In this environment, the making of payments known as *'mordidas'* to lower echelon foreign officials are almost institutionalized. It is generally accepted that one will be expected to pay officials to get things done. The issue is one more of economics than of morality.

The payments to corrupt foreign officials has taken a more important profile on account of the privatizations and open borders that are taking place. Opportunities to purchase formerly state owned enterprises or opportunities to contract through government procurement laws has elevated the transaction from that of a one hundred dollar payment to a low-level Customs official to a million dollar payment to a high ranking official to snare a contract. The United States took the first step in making a crime out of certain payments to foreign officials.

The Foreign Corrupt Practices Act (FCPA) was enacted in the United States during the Carter Administration. The Act covers publicly held companies as well as other domestic concerns.

THE EXTRATERRITORIAL REACH OF THE U.S. GOVERNMENT'S CAMPAIGN AGAINST INTERNATIONAL BRIBERY

H. Lowell Brown

22 Hastings Int'l & Comp. L. Rev. 407 (1999).

I.   Overview of the Foreign Corrupt Practices Act

The FCPA, originally enacted in 1977, had its genesis in the disclosure by the Watergate Special Prosecutor and SEC of overseas "slush funds" used by U.S. companies to make illegal political contributions to the Nixon re-election campaign and others, and to pay bribes to foreign government officials. Thus, Congress intended the FCPA to address the problem of overseas bribery. The Act approaches this issue in two distinct, though related, ways.

First, the FCPA prohibits the payment or offer of payment either directly, indirectly or through a third party, of money or "anything of value," to an official of a foreign government or political party, with corrupt intent, to obtain or retain business.

Not all payments are prohibited, however. Instead, payments, sometimes referred to as "facilitating payments" or "grease payments," which are intended only "to expedite or secure the performance of a routine governmental action by a foreign official, political party, or party officer," are exempt. Similarly, payments that are legal under the written laws of the foreign country and payments related to the promotion of products or related to the performance of contracts are likewise exempt from the overseas payment prohibitions of the Act.

In addition to these anti-bribery provisions, the FCPA established accounting and controls requirements for companies registered with the SEC pursuant to the Securities Exchange Act of 1934. Establishment of these requirements represented a significant expansion of the SEC's regulatory authority and marked the first time the federal government established standards for the internal management of public companies.
* * *

Enforcement of the FCPA is shared by the SEC and the U.S. Department of Justice. The SEC retained jurisdiction under the Securities Exchange Act of 1934 over issuers; the FCPA gave the Department of Justice jurisdiction to bring civil actions to enjoin violations of the FCPA by "domestic concerns" other than issuers. The Department of

Justice also retained jurisdiction to prosecute violations of the Act criminally.

The penalties for violating the FCPA are substantial. Individuals convicted of violating the anti-bribery provisions may be sentenced for a period of up to five years imprisonment and fined $100,000. A civil penalty of a maximum $10,000 also may be imposed. Additionally, the act prohibits the payment by a corporation of any fine assessed against an individual. A corporation may be fined up to $2,000,000.

Knowing violation of the accounting and controls provisions may also constitute a crime. An individual who committed a knowing violation may be imprisoned for up to ten years and fined up to $1,000,000. Under the same circumstances, a corporation may be fined up to $2,500,000. * * *

In addition to "issuers," the FCPA also applies to "any domestic concern, other than an issuer." Within this class of persons and entities are the following: (A) any individual who is a citizen, national, or resident of the United States; and (B) any corporation, partnership, association, joint-stock company, business trust, unincorporated organization, or sole proprietorship which has its principal place of business in the United States, or which is organized under the laws of a state of the United States, or a territory, possession, or commonwealth of the United States.

In fashioning this definition of "domestic concern," Congress was attentive to the international law implications arising from the assertion of prescriptive jurisdiction beyond readily definable bounds of nationality and territoriality. Congress was well aware of the role played by foreign agents and consultants as intermediaries in corrupt payments to foreign officials. Likewise, Congress had substantial evidence of the use of foreign subsidiaries as repositories for off-book "slush funds" and as conduits for corrupt payments.

To address the problem of foreign subsidiaries, the House bill included within the definition of "domestic concern" an entity: (1) which is owned or controlled by individuals who are citizens or nationals of the United States; (2) which has its principal place of business in the United States; or (3) which is organized under the laws of a state of the United States or any territory, possession or commonwealth of the United States. As the House Committee on Interstate and Foreign Commerce explained:

By so defining domestic concern, the Committee intends to reach not only all U.S. companies other than those subject to SEC jurisdiction, but also foreign subsidiaries of any U.S. corporation. The Committee found it appropriate to extend the coverage of the bill to non-U.S. based subsidiaries because of the extensive use of such entities as a conduit for questionable or improper foreign payments authorized by their domestic parent.

The Senate's definition of "domestic concern" was not so expansive. In conference, the House receded to the Senate definition "with an amendment to make clear that any company having a principal place of business in the United States would be subject to the bill."

The conferees adopted the Senate's more restrictive approach because of their concern for the possible conflict with international law principles if Congress exercised prescriptive jurisdiction over foreign subsidiaries. The conferees emphasized, however, that the U.S. entity, either issuer or domestic concern, would remain liable if it engaged in violative conduct indirectly through a third party. As the conference stated:

In receding to the Senate, the conferees recognized the inherent jurisdictional, enforcement and diplomatic difficulties raised by the inclusion of foreign subsidiaries of U.S. companies in the direct prohibitions of the bill. However, the conferees intend to make it clear that any issuer or domestic concern, which engages in bribery of foreign officials indirectly through any other person or entity, would itself be liable under the bill. The conferees recognized that such jurisdictional, enforcement, and diplomatic difficulties may not be present in the case of individuals who are U.S. citizens, nationals or residents.

Because different jurisdictional considerations apply to U.S. citizens, nationals and residents than apply to foreign nationals or residents, the conferees restricted the liability of persons involved in the affairs of a foreign subsidiary, other than those persons specified in the definitions of "issuer" and "domestic concern," to U.S. citizens, nationals or residents. Foreign nationals or residents who are otherwise subject to U.S. jurisdiction would remain liable for violations of the FCPA in the same way as an issuer or domestic concern. However, this jurisdictional basis over foreign nationals and residents is not a model of clarity. * * *

In enacting the Foreign Corrupt Practices Act, Congress exercised prescriptive jurisdiction to the fullest extent consistent with due process under the Commerce Clause. Congress was deeply concerned by the role that foreign nationals played and the matter in which foreign entities were used in the incidents of foreign bribery that gave rise to the FCPA. Nevertheless, Congress took care not to exercise its prescriptive jurisdiction in a way that conflicted with accepted principles of international law or would otherwise offend the sovereignty of other nations. * * *

Nevertheless, while confirming the FCPA's extraterritorial reach, Congress made clear its wish that the problem of international bribery be addressed globally, on a multilateral basis, and not simply by the unilateral prohibition against bribery by U.S. firms alone. Indeed, the need for an international solution to official corruption has been a recurring theme since the earliest Congressional hearings on questionable payments in 1976. Since that time, U.S. government agencies have undertaken a variety of initiatives aimed at securing international agreement to outlaw bribery. Most recently, these efforts produced official actions by the Organization of American States ("OAS") and the Organization for Economic Co-operation and Development ("OECD"), which, if implemented, could substantively address international bribery and level the playing field of international commerce.

III.   INTERNATIONAL ANTI-CORRUPTION INITIATIVES

Public corruption is rightly viewed as "an international problem that requires an international solution." International corruption not only adversely affects the political, economic and moral fiber of the "receiving country," it also significantly harms vital U.S. interests. The expansion of cross-border trading and the concomitant premium on "hard" currencies increased the incentives for both demanding and making corrupt payments.

Virtually all countries, and certainly all industrialized countries, prohibit the payment of bribes domestically. Nevertheless, the United States is the only country to criminalize the payment of bribes to foreign officials. Similar assertions of extraterritorial jurisdiction engendered hostility among the community of nations, and the FCPA in particular has been susceptible to the charge of moral imperialism.

When the FCPA was first considered, Congress was aware that international initiatives, rather than simple unilateral action, would be necessary to address the problem of international corruption. It was recognized that absent international agreement and cooperation in eliminating official corruption, U.S. companies would be left standing alone. Congress made its view on this subject explicit in the 1988 amendments to the FCPA. However, even before the passage of the FCPA in 1977, intermittent efforts were made to address official corruption multilaterally. These efforts continued over the following two decades and within the past several years resulted in potentially significant breakthroughs by the OAS and the OECD. * * *

C.   Recent Developments

1.   The Organization of American States: The Inter–American Convention Against Corruption

On December 11, 1994, the leaders of the governments of the Western Hemisphere met in Miami, Florida for the "Summit of the Americas." Finding that "[e]ffective democracy requires a comprehensive attack on corruption as a factor of social disintegration and distortion of the economic system that undermines the legitimacy of political institutions," the summit adopted a plan of action. * * *

The anti-corruption measures in the Summit's plan of action served as the basis for the Inter–American Convention Against Corruption, which opened for signature in Caracas, Venezuela on March 29, 1996. The Convention, which at the time was described as "one of the most important developments ever in the international ethics area," called for action at the national and multi-national levels, as well as cooperation among nations to address the problem of corruption. * * *

The Convention is intended to apply to the following: a public official's solicitation or acceptance of a corrupt payment; the offer or payment of money or benefit to a public official in exchange for an act or omission in the performance of a public function; an act or omission by a public official for the purpose of illegally obtaining a benefit either for the official or a third party; the fraudulent use or concealment of property obtained through corruption; and the participation as a principal or a third party ("instigator, accomplice or accessory after the fact") in the commission, attempted commission or conspiracy to commit an act of corruption. The Convention made clear that the enumerated acts were not exclusive and that two or more parties could agree the Convention would apply to other acts of corruption as well. The Convention also provided that States that had not already done so should establish an offense of "illicit enrichment" defined as "a significant increase in the assets of a government official that he cannot reasonably explain in relation to his lawful earning during the performance of his functions."
* * *

Finally, States were to criminalize "transnational bribery." Under that provision, signatories were to enact laws prohibiting and punishing the offering or making of a corrupt payment to a government official of another State "in connection with any economic or commercial transaction in exchange for any act or omission in the performance of that official's public functions." * * *

Thus far, twenty-five nations, including the United States, have signed the Convention; however, only sixteen nations have ratified it. In transmitting it to the Senate for advice and consent to ratification, the President hailed the Convention as "the first multilateral Convention of its kind in the world to be adopted." Others share the President's appraisal. The President also advised the Senate that ratification would not require implementing legislation. Although the OAS Convention represents a significant accomplishment in galvanizing multinational action against corruption, its long-term effectiveness remains to be seen.

2.   The Organization for Economic Cooperation and Development: The 1996 Recommendation on the Tax Deductibility of Bribes to Foreign Officials and the 1997 Convention on Bribery in International Business Transactions

In 1996 and 1997, the OECD realized two major accomplishments in the effort to eliminate bribery as an accepted means of international business. These two initiatives, the 1996 Recommendation on the Tax Deductibility of Bribes Paid to Foreign Officials and the 1997 Convention on Combating Bribery of Foreign Public Officials, were the culmination of over seven years of study and negotiation by the United States and fellow members of the OECD.

The 1996 Recommendation on the Tax Deductibility of Bribes Paid to Foreign * * *

Thereafter, acting on a proposal from the OECD Committee on Fiscal Affairs ("CFA"), on April 11, 1996, the OECD Council adopted a further recommendation addressing the tax deductibility of bribes to foreign officials. The Council recommended "that those Member countries which do not disallow the deductibility of bribes to foreign public officials re-examine such treatment with the intention of denying this deductibility." The Council noted in this connection that "[s]uch action may be facilitated by the trend to treat bribes to foreign public officials as illegal." * * *

b. The 1997 Convention on Combating Bribery of Foreign Public Officials in International Business Transactions * * *

The parties to the Convention recognized that bribery of public officials was a widespread problem that all countries shared responsibility for and required a multilateral response. The Convention solemnized the principal reforms set forth in the earlier recommendation regarding criminalization of foreign bribery, establishment of accounting and controls requirements, clarification of jurisdiction and the rendering of mutual legal assistance in matters of foreign bribery, including extradition. * * *

UNITED STATES v. LIEBO

United States Court of Appeals, Eighth Circuit (1991).
923 F.2d 1308.

* * *

JOHN R. GIBSON, Circuit Judge.

Richard H. Liebo appeals from his convictions for violating the bribery provisions of the Foreign Corrupt Practices Act, 15 U.S.C. ss 78dd–1(a)(1), (3); 78dd–2(a)(1), (3); 78dd–2(b)(1)(B) and 78ff(c)(2) (1988), and making a false statement to a government agency. 18 U.S.C. s 1001 (1988). The jury acquitted Liebo on seventeen other counts. Liebo argues that his convictions should be reversed because of insufficient evidence and because the district court erred in instructing the jury. * * * We conclude that sufficient evidence existed to sustain the convictions and that the court properly instructed the jury * * *

The background leading to Liebo's conviction has all the earmarks of a modern fable. Between January 1983 and June 1987, Liebo was vice-president in charge of the Aerospace division of NAPCO International, Inc., located in Hopkins, Minnesota. NAPCO's primary business consisted of selling military equipment and supplies throughout the world.

In early 1983, the Niger government contracted with a West German company, Dornier Reparaturwerft, to service two Lockheed C–130 cargo planes. After the Niger Ministry of Defense ran into financial troubles, Dornier sought an American parts supplier in order to qualify the Ministry of Defense for financing through the United States Foreign Military Sales program. The Foreign Military Sales program is supervised by the Defense Security Assistance Agency, an agency of the

United States Department of Defense. Under the program, loans are provided to foreign governments for the purchase of military equipment and supplies from American contractors.

In June 1983, representatives from Dornier met with officials of NAPCO and agreed that NAPCO would become the prime contractor on the C–130 maintenance contracts. Under this arrangement, NAPCO would supply parts to Niger and Dornier, and Dornier would perform the required maintenance at its facilities in Munich.

Once NAPCO and Dornier agreed to these terms, Liebo and Axel Kurth, a Dornier sales representative, flew to Niger to get the President of Niger's approval of the contract. They flew to Niger and met with Captain Ali Tiemogo. Tiemogo was the chief of maintenance for the Niger Air Force. Tiemogo testified that during the trip, Liebo and Kurth told him that they would make "some gestures" to him if he helped get the contract approved. When asked whether this promise played a role in deciding to recommend approval of the contract, Tiemogo stated, "I can't say 'no', I cannot say 'yes', at that time," but "it encouraged me." Following Tiemogo's recommendation that the contract be approved, the President signed the contract.

Tahirou Barke, Tiemogo's cousin and close friend, was the first consular for the Niger Embassy in Washington, D.C. Barke testified that he met Liebo in Washington sometime in 1983 or 1984. Barke stated that Liebo told him that he wanted to make a "gesture" to Captain Tiemogo and asked Barke to set up a bank account in the United States. With Barke's assistance, Liebo opened a bank account in Minnesota in the name of "E. Dave," a variation of the name of Barke's then girl friend, Shirley Elaine Dave. Barke testified that NAPCO deposited about $30,000 in the account and that he used the money to pay bills and purchase personal items and that he gave a portion of the money to Captain Tiemogo.

Barke also testified that in August 1985 he returned to Niger to be married. After the wedding, he and his wife honeymooned in Paris, Stockholm and London. He testified that before leaving for Niger, he informed Liebo of his honeymoon plans, and Liebo offered to pay for his airline tickets as a gift. Liebo made the flight arrangements for Barke's return to Niger and for his honeymoon trip. Liebo paid for the tickets, which cost $2,028, by charging them to NAPCO's Diner's Club account. Barke testified that he considered the tickets a "gift" from Liebo personally.

We need not develop the record further other than to provide details of NAPCO's dealings with Niger and the Foreign Military Sales program. NAPCO received two other contracts from Niger. The second contract in the amount of $1,000,000 for the supply of spare parts and maintenance was signed on August 20, 1984. The third contract in the amount of $1,550,000 was signed on August 2, 1985.

Over a two and a half year period beginning in May 1984, NAPCO made payments totalling $130,000 to three "commission agents." The practice of using agents and paying them commissions on international contracts was acknowledged as proper, legal, and an accepted business practice in third world countries. NAPCO issued commission checks to three "agents," identified as Amadou Mailele, Tiemogo's brother-in-law, Fatouma Boube, Tiemogo's sister-in-law, and E. Dave, Barke's girl friend. At Tiemogo's request, both Mailele and Boube set up bank accounts in Paris. Neither Mailele, Boube, nor E. Dave, however, received the commission checks or acted as NAPCO's agent. Instead, evidence established that these individuals were merely intermediaries through whom NAPCO made payments to Tiemogo and Barke. Evidence at trial established that NAPCO's corporate president, Henri Jacob, or another superior of Liebo's approved these "commission payments." There was no evidence introduced at trial, however, that anyone approved the payment for the honeymoon trip.

To obtain Foreign Military Sales financing, NAPCO was required to submit a "Contractor's Certification and Agreement with Defense Security Assistance Agency." In the Contractor's certification submitted in connection with the third Niger contract, Liebo certified that "no rebates, gifts or gratuities have been given contrary to United States law to officers, officials, or employees" of the Niger government. Liebo certified that NAPCO's commission agent under the contract was Amadou Mailele and that he would be paid $47,662. Liebo also certified that no commissions or contingent fees would be paid to any agent to solicit or obtain the contract other than as identified in the certificate.

Following a three week trial, the jury acquitted Liebo on all charges except the count concerning NAPCO's purchase of Barke's honeymoon airline tickets and the related false statement count. This appeal followed. * * *

Liebo first argues that his conviction on Count VII for violating the bribery provisions of the Foreign Corrupt practices Act by giving Barke airline tickets for his honeymoon should be reversed because insufficient evidence existed to establish two elements of the offense. First, Liebo contends that there was insufficient evidence to show that the airline tickets were "given to obtain or retain business." Second, he argues that there was no evidence to show that his gift of honeymoon tickets was done "corruptly." * * *

There is sufficient evidence that the airplane tickets were given to obtain or retain business. Tiemogo testified that the President of Niger would not approve the contracts without his recommendation. He also testified that Liebo promised to "make gestures" to him before the first contract was approved, and that Liebo promised to continue to "make gestures" if the second and third contracts were approved. There was testimony that Barke helped Liebo establish a bank account with a fictitious name, that Barke used money from that account, and that Barke sent some of the money from that account to Tiemogo. Barke testified that he understood Liebo deposited money in the account as "gestures" to Tiemogo for some "of the business that they do have together." * * *

Moreover, sufficient independent evidence exists that the tickets were given to obtain or retain business. Evidence established that Tiemogo and Barke were cousins and best friends. The relationship between Barke and Tiemogo could have allowed a reasonable jury to infer that Liebo made the gift to Barke intending to buy Tiemogo's help in getting the contracts approved. Indeed, Tiemogo recommended approval of the third contract and the President of Niger approved that contract just a few weeks after Liebo gave the tickets to Barke. Accordingly, a reasonable jury could conclude that the gift was given "to obtain or retain business."

Liebo also contends that the evidence at trial failed to show that Liebo acted "corruptly" by buying Barke the airline tickets. In support of this argument, Liebo points to Barke's testimony that he considered the tickets a "gift" from Liebo personally. Liebo asserts that "corruptly" means that the offer, payment or gift "must be intended to induce the recipient to misuse his official position...." Sen.Rep. No. 114, 95th Cong., 1st Sess. 1, reprinted in 1977 U.S.Code Cong. & Admin.News 4098, 4108. Because Barke considered the tickets to be a personal gift from Liebo, Liebo reasons that no evidence showed that the tickets wrongfully influenced Barke's actions.

We are satisfied that sufficient evidence existed from which a reasonable jury could find that the airline tickets were given "corruptly." For example, Liebo gave the airline tickets to Barke shortly before the third contract was approved. In addition, there was undisputed evidence concerning the close relationship between Tiemogo and Barke and Tiemogo's important role in the contract approval process. There was also testimony that Liebo classified the airline ticket for accounting purposes as a "commission payment." This evidence could allow a reasonable jury to infer that Liebo gave the tickets to Barke intending to influence the Niger government's contract approval process. We conclude, therefore, that a reasonable jury could find that Liebo's gift to Barke was given "corruptly." Accordingly, sufficient evidence existed to support Liebo's conviction. * * *

Next, Liebo contends that his conviction should be reversed because the court erred by refusing to give his requested jury instructions distinguishing a "gift or gratuity" from a bribe. * * *

Here, the court instructed the jury that the term "corruptly" meant that "the offer, promise to pay, payment or authorization of payment, must be intended to induce the recipient to misuse his official position or to influence someone else to do so," and that "an act is 'corruptly' done if done voluntarily [a]nd intentionally, and with a bad purpose of accomplishing either an unlawful end or result, or a lawful end or result by some unlawful method or means." Tr. at 166–67. Contrary to Liebo's argument, the instructions as a whole adequately instructed the jury that a gift or gratuity does not violate the Act unless it is given "corruptly." Wagner, 884 F.2d at 1096. See also United States v. Montgomery, 819 F.2d 847, 851–52 (8th Cir.1987). Accordingly, the court did not abuse its discretion by refusing to give the requested instruction. * * *

UNITED STATES v. McLEAN
United States Court of Appeals, Fifth Circuit (1984).
738 F.2d 655.

* * *

W. EUGENE DAVIS, Circuit Judge:

We are presented for the first time with the question of whether the Foreign Corrupt Practices Act (FCPA) permits the prosecution of an employee for a substantive offense under the Act if his employer has not and cannot be convicted of similarly violating the FCPA. We conclude that the Act prohibits such a prosecution and affirm the district court.

I.

During the late 1970's Petroleos Mexicanos (Pemex), the national petroleum company of Mexico, purchased large quantities of turbine compressor equipment to capture and pump to processing plants a high volume of natural gas. The Solar division of International Harvester Company (Harvester) was the dominant worldwide supplier of such equipment. George S. McLean was its vice-president and Luis A. Uriarte was its Latin American regional manager; both were Harvester employees. Crawford Enterprises, Inc., (CEI) was a broker and lessor of gas compression systems which frequently purchased equipment from Harvester for resale or lease. Harvester, as prime contractor, had supplied Pemex with equipment in the mid-Seventies; during the period of accelerated development in the late 1970's, however, Harvester acted as a subcontractor for CEI, which had contracted with Pemex to build complete compression plants.

In early 1979, the United States initiated grand jury investigations into allegations that American businessmen had bribed Mexican officials in violation of the FCPA. On October 22, 1982, a forty-nine count indictment was returned in federal district court charging CEI and nine individuals, including McLean and Uriarte, with one conspiracy count to use interstate or foreign instrumentalities for the purpose of bribing Pemex officials in violation of 18 U.S.C. s 371 (1966), forty-seven substantive counts in violation of the FCPA, 15 U.S.C. ss 78dd–2(a)(1) and (3), s 78dd–2(b) (1981), and one obstruction of justice count in violation of 18 U.S.C. s 1503 (1966).[1] McLean and Uriarte were named

---

1. 15 U.S.C. s 78dd–2 provides, in relevant part: (a) It shall be unlawful for any domestic concern, other than an issuer which is subject to section 78dd–1 of this title, or any officer, director, employee, or agent of such domestic concern or any stockholder thereof acting on behalf of such domestic concern, to make use of the mails or any means or instrumentality of interstate commerce corruptly in furtherance of an offer, payment, promise to pay, or authorization of the payment of any money, or offer, gift, promise to give, or authorization of the giving of anything of value to—

in the single conspiracy count and in forty-three substantive counts of aiding and abetting CEI in violating FCPA and 18 U.S.C. s 2 (1969). Although McLean and Uriarte's employer, Harvester, was not charged in the forty-nine count indictment, the government concedes that all acts of McLean and Uriarte were committed within the scope of their employment with Harvester.

(1) any foreign official for purposes of—(A) influencing any act or decision of such foreign official capacity, including a decision to fail to perform his official functions; or (B) inducing such foreign official to use his influence with a foreign government or instrumentality thereof to affect or influence any act or decision of such government or instrumentality, in order to assist such domestic concern in obtaining or retaining business for or with, or directing business to, any person; (3) any person, while knowing or having reason to know that all or a portion of such money or thing of value will be offered, given, or promised, directly or indirectly, to any foreign official, to any foreign political party or official thereof, or to any candidate for foreign political office, for purposes of— (A) influencing any act or decision of such foreign official, political party, party official, or candidate in his or its official capacity, including a decision to fail to perform his or its official functions; or (B) inducing such foreign official, political party, party official, or candidate to use his or its influence with a foreign government or instrumentality thereof to affect or influence any act or decision of such government or instrumentality, in order to assist such domestic concern in obtaining or retaining business for or with, or directing business to, any person.

The indictment charges the defendants with participating in a plan to bribe Pemex officials in order to sell turbine compression equipment to Pemex.

On November 17, 1982, Harvester entered a guilty plea to a one count bill of information charging conspiracy to violate the FCPA. In the plea agreement with Harvester, the government agreed to bring no further charges against Harvester arising out of its sales to CEI and Pemex. McLean was named but not charged as a co-conspirator with Harvester in that proceeding. The bill of information filed against Harvester included eleven of the twelve overt acts alleged against Harvester or its employees in the forty-nine count indictment charging McLean and Uriarte with conspiracy to violate the Act.

Both McLean and Uriarte filed motions to dismiss the charges pending against them on grounds that the failure of the government to convict Harvester of a violation under the FCPA barred their prosecution. The district court dismissed the substantive counts, but denied the motion to dismiss the conspiracy charge. The court concluded that the

Eckhardt Amendment, 15 U.S.C. s 78ff[2], permits the conviction of an employee under the FCPA only if the employer (termed an issuer or domestic concern under the Act) was convicted of violating the FCPA. The district court concluded that since Harvester's plea of guilty to conspiracy was not a substantive FCPA violation, McLean and Uriarte could not be prosecuted for the substantive counts.

The government presents three arguments on appeal: (1) the "found to have violated" provision does not require that the employer be convicted of a FCPA violation; this requirement may be satisfied by establishing in the employee's trial that the employer violated the Act; (2) McLean, as an individual domestic concern, may be charged with aiding and abetting CEI and; (3) International Harvester's conviction of conspiracy satisfies the "found to have violated" requirement. * * *

The substantive violations of the Act are established in two sections. Section 78dd–1 makes it unlawful for an issuer (defined as an entity subject to the securities registration requirements of s 78l and 78o of Title 15), its officers, directors, employees or agents, to use the mails or other instrumentality of interstate commerce to bribe foreign officials for various purposes including to obtain business. Section 78dd–2 provides generally the same prohibition for a domestic concern, its officers, directors, shareholders and employees. Domestic concern is broadly defined to include any United States citizen, national or resident; or any corporation (other than an issuer), partnership or other entity subject to United States jurisdiction and control.

Section 78ff(c)(3) provides the penalties applicable to employees of issuers. * * * Section 78dd–2(b)(1)(B)(3) contains a similar provision for the employees and agents of a domestic concern. These two sections with the "found to have violated" prerequisite are collectively referred to as the Eckhardt Amendment, after former Congressman Bob Eckhardt, the leading proponent of the provision. * * *

At the hearing, Congressman Eckhardt, the subcommittee chairman, in discussing H.R. 3815 with Harold M. Williams, Chairman of the Securities and Exchange Commission (SEC) and Harvey L. Pitt, general counsel of the SEC stated: "Indeed, the corporations [sic] interest might even be in conflict with that of the agent. The corporation might desire to have Joe Bloke found to have intentionally engaged in bribery and to have been the sole moving agent, that is, the company never agreed to it and the quicker they can convict Joe Bloke, the better off the company is. It is relieved of responsibility and it has a sacrificial lamb in Rome and everybody forgets about the activity. * * *

---

2. Section 78ff U.S.C. 15 provides in pertinent part: (c)(3) Whenever an issuer is found to have violated section 78dd–1(a) of this title, any employee or agent of such issuer who is a United States citizen, national, or resident or is otherwise subject to the jurisdiction of the United States (other than an officer, director, or stockholder of such issuer), and who willfully carried out the act or practice constituting such violation shall, upon conviction, be fined not more than $10,000, or imprisoned not more than five years or both. [Ed. The Eckhardt Amendment was repealed in 1988. Under present law, the employee can be convicted of an FCPA violation without the employer being convicted of a similar violation.]

Congressman Eckhardt pointed out the dependence of the agent on the corporation for an adequate defense since the corporation, due to its superior resources, would be in a much better position than the employer to defend against accusations of wrongdoing in a foreign country. He articulated concern over legislation that would require the agent alone to bear the burden of refuting allegations of FCPA violations. He was also troubled about giving the uncharged corporate employer incentive to both disavow knowledge of the agent's activity and to let the agent bear all responsibility for the wrongdoing. * * *

This problem was avoided * * * because what would become the Eckhardt Amendment "would require the government ... to prove in the first instance that the issuer had violated the section, because that is the condition precedent to the holding of any agent responsible." He noted that if there was doubt about the employer's violation of the Act, then the employee could not be held liable. * * *

Assume USCO manufactures and sells airplane parts and equipment. USCO sells primarily in the domestic market but is interested in making international sales. John Smith, USCO's president was approached by Tomas Garza a resident of Latina. Tomas said he was a 'special consultant' to the Latina Air Force. His job was to locate aircraft parts suppliers.

Tomas told Smith that sales to the Latina Air Force could total five million dollars per year. Smith, in an effort to win the contract authorized the following payments:

Smith and several other USCO officials visited Latina and spent five thousand dollars in entertaining Latina officials in an effort to acquaint them to USCO and its products. The entertainment was not lavish or extravagant.

Smith had promised to send Latina procurement officers samples of USCO's products. USCO paid $1,000 to a Customs official to speed up the process of importing the samples into Latina. The importation of the goods was allowed under Latina law.

USCO, through Smith, paid Tomas $1,000,000 in cash for his services. Although Tomas did not spend much time on the project the payment was made on account of his high level contacts in the Latin Air Force.

Which of these disbursements, if any, violate the Foreign Corrupt Practices Act?

Chapter 4

THE INTERNATIONAL
JOINT VENTURE

SECTION 4.1 THE INTERNATIONAL
EQUITY JOINT VENTURE

A. INTRODUCTION

The previous chapter dealt with the outbound foreign direct investment. The focus was on regulations that the outbound FDI faces through international and domestic legal systems. This chapter continues with the outbound transaction but exploring it through the eyes of a joint venture. The materials need to be read with the impact of law in mind but adding the complexity of the relationship between partners. The term 'partner' in these materials refers to the parties that are engaging in some international joint business adventure not assuming that they have established a partnership.

Joint ventures can be grouped into two categories—contractual joint ventures and equity joint ventures. Contractual joint ventures do not require a capital transfer or a physical presence in the host country. These can include distributorship arrangements where one company purchases goods or takes them under consignment from a foreign company for sale in the domestic market. They can also be service agreements. These joint ventures typically involve a service provider from a developed country with a particular expertise contracting directly with the host government or with a domestic company that has a contract with the government.

Other contractual joint ventures can be strategic alliances—distinct projects that are designed to have a synergy between the two. For example, Developers with adjacent projects can build them in such a way that combines the strengths of both distinct projects. The classic contractual joint venture is where the owner of intellectual property transfers it to another in the form of a franchise agreement or a licensing agreement. The owner of the IPR (the Licensor) receives royalties under the agreement from the Licensee. The License Agreement is discussed in Section 4.2, infra. The international sale of goods and services is discussed in Section 4.3, infra.

The second category is the international equity joint venture (IEJV). The IEJV is the more complex of the two types because it requires both a transfer of capital and a physical presence in the host country. The IEJV itself can be of two types. One is where two or more parties transfer capital and establish a presence in the foreign country but only one manages the business. This arrangement is common in hotel and resort developments. The investor group owns the investment but the hotel and resort operations are run by one of the JV partners. The other type is where two or more of the investor group co-manage the business operations. In this section the term 'JV Partners' means the owners of the International Equity Joint Venture.

Recall in the hypothetical that Delta's Division III was a good candidate for the outbound FDI. Assume that pursuant to Mexico's foreign investment law, since the investment is in the petrochemical industry, Delta must take on a joint venture partner. Assume further, that Delta has made the acquaintance of Juan Gomez and *Industrial*. (See Section 2.1, supra.) The two companies are considering joining forces in the manufacture and sale of the 'Quick Dry' additive. Remember the general rule in planning for international business transactions is that simpler is better. Delta should reflect on its decision at this point—could it realize the desired business goal through some other (simpler) form of transaction? Could Delta simply sell its 'Quick Dry' in Mexico or license its manufacture to *Industrial*? Would *Industrial* be willing to transfer capital but take a limited management role? The decision needs to be made after a thorough analysis of the facts and circumstances.

1.   The Pros and Cons of the IEJV

In cases where a wholly owned subsidiary is permitted, there are certain advantages to going it alone. The foreign investor controls the FDI and reaps all of the benefits that flow from it. This is now possible in Mexico for a variety of foreign investments. The liberalization (privatization) phenomenon makes this a possibility in many other developing countries as well. The investor, when going alone, does not run the risk of getting a bad partner that could increase the risk and perhaps misuse confidential corporate information. The investment is much simpler without having to reach agreement on the business plan or enter into detailed contractual obligations. However, going alone may not be an option.

In some developing countries, although falling into disfavor in the current investment environment, the host government mandates the use of a joint venture (especially in certain industries) where the foreign corporation is a minority partner. Even if not required, the IEJV could also reap benefits. There may be business and political advantages in linking with up with a solid local partner. As one party stated in a negotiation to the foreign partner—"... you provide the know how, we provide the know who ..." The local JV partner may have a good business reputation in the community, an available pool of workers, management, and facilities to engage more quickly in the business effort.

Other reasons to have a JV Partner includes the access and relationships with local banks for any potential loan needs, as well as having access to good legal and accounting professional who know the domestic market and its cultural peculiarities. It is important to have a good rapport with the governmental authorities and to provide access to governmental procurement otherwise statutorily unavailable to the foreign person. Finally, a good local JV partner can generally provide good counsel to the IEJV, preventing traps for the unwary. It is also a useful way to spread the risk and capital investment among two or more parties.

The IEJV is like a marriage. The partners should know what the other expects from them and what they can expect from the other. Finding a good fit can help in ensuring a successful joint venture. Face to face meetings and local counsel are very helpful in this regard. The parties should not avoid the "hard questions." The partners should feel comfortable in the business objectives of the IEJV. The IEJV's plans and objectives should fit well the partner's goals. In short, the partners should get to know each other and have the same priorities relative to the IEJV business plan.

The partners should set clear, reachable objectives for the joint business enterprise. They should expect to know both the benefits as well as the obligations to the JV. The parties should also be reasonable in their negotiating positions. It is important to note that the concept of a joint venture is of recent vintage in Latin America. Indeed the term joint venture is pronounced in English because there is no Spanish word that exactly fits. It is also important to determine that the potential JV partner has the capability to fulfill its commitments. If the domestic JV partner will be the business interface, make sure that the local partner has a good business reputation in the community.

If the JV partner will participate in the operations, one should be satisfied that there is an available pool of workers and facilities sufficient to engage in the business effort. In addition, the partner must have the financial wherewithal to contribute the capital it is supposed to and/or have access and relationships with local banks for any potential loan needs. It should actually know the domestic market and its cultural peculiarities and have a good rapport with the governmental authorities especially if governmental licenses or procurement is important. It is also important to assure that the local partner is capable of assuming the risk and capital investment it is obligating itself to do.

These and other inquiries about the foreign partner can be made through the people with which they do business. Other sources include the local U.S. embassy, court filings, and current and former employees. There should also be care taken that the partner is suitable from an ethical standpoint. The potential loss of confidential information and control is heightened when dealing with companies that may have a reputation for sharp business practices.

2.   *The Role of the Lawyer*

In regards to reasonable negotiating positions—the role of the attorney must be assessed. The lawyer's focus should be on the benefits expected by the client and the liabilities it is facing. The documents should clearly reflect the client's expectations in this regard. The U.S. lawyer has historically played an important role in structuring and negotiating U.S. joint ventures. American businesspeople bring the lawyers in early in the negotiation process. In contrast, Latin American entrepreneurs rarely use lawyers during negotiations. Lawyers are called in, if at all, after the deal is done.

The U.S. lawyer can help make or break a deal depending on the intransigence or cooperation that may exist. I have seen negotiations break down because of American lawyers inundating negotiations with *what ifs* that have a very low probability of occurring. Or else they take such unreasonable positions that makes negotiations impossible. This is not to say that difficult issues should be ignored for fear that feelings may be hurt. However, one should be reasonable, focusing on problems that have a reasonable probability of occurring.

Other problems arise when the lawyer does not distinguish between legal and business issues. The client is the businessperson and usually has more business experience than the lawyer. The lawyer should assist in the legal questions. The lawyer should help the client assess its right and obligations ensuring that the issues are clearly and accurately stated in the documents that will be signed. The final caveat for the lawyer is to understand that differences in culture, legal systems, and political systems exist. A legal system that is different does not necessarily mean it is inferior.

3.   *Structuring the IEJV*

Delta and *Industrial* have decided to embark on an international equity joint venture to jointly pursue business opportunities in Mexico. Assume that in this case both companies will transfer capital and take an active role in the management of the business operations. The parties have agreed that Delta will own forty-nine percent and *Industrial* fifty one percent of the enterprise. The IEJV can be structured in several ways. Delta could purchase *Industrial* shares or Delta and *Industrial* can form a new entity.

a.   *Delta Purchase of Industrial Shares*

Delta can purchase forty-nine percent of *Industrial* shares. *Industrial* could issue new shares sufficient to give Delta the forty-nine percent interest. The legal and business issues arising from this type of transaction are similar to those discussed in the inbound foreign direct investment. Recall that the share purchase transaction is generally not preferable. The purchase of shares from an existing corporation, while seemingly a simple procedure can open a Pandora's Box of liabilities. For a review of the due diligence questions and other issues that arise in the purchase of shares see Section 2.1, supra.

In this particular case *Industrial* may also be reluctant to allow Delta as a shareholder because Delta would then own part of Ace, Inc. and the other divisions of *Industrial*. It is for this reason that the typical IEJV involves two companies forming a third new entity that will be the FDI. Deciding on the form of organization the third entity should use brings the choice of entity decision back to the forefront. For an analysis of the many issues that arise in the choice of entity decision see Sections 2.2 and 3.4, supra. In this section, we will assume that Delta and *Industrial* will form a new third Mexican Corporation—Delta—*Industrial* (DISA). Delta will own forty nine percent and *Industrial* will own fifty one percent of DISA's issued and outstanding common stock.

b.   *The Formation of DISA*

The formation of DISA should be done pursuant to a well thought out business plan. The parties need to make sure the business plan meets with their respective business interests. They should also assure themselves that each party has the financial wherewithal to do the deal. Delta will contribute the following assets to DISA:

	Cost	Fair Market Value
Cash	500,000	500,000
Inventory	500,000	700,000
Quick Dry Additive Patent	$2,000,000	$ 6,800,000
Equipment [Used in manufacturing the 'Quick Dry' Cement]	1,000,000	2,000,000
Total Assets	$4,000,000	$10,000,000

Industrial will contribute cash of ten million five hundred thousand dollars. The cash will be used by DISA to purchase and refurbish the manufacturing and office facilities that will be used by DISA to operate its business. In addition, the parties have each agreed to lend DISA three million dollars to fund DISA'S working capital needs. The parties are to seek independent financing using their DISA shares as collateral. Delta used a U.S. bank while *Industrial* used a Mexican bank. Delta will provide the technical staff to manage the operations. It will also send mid-level executives, who together with managers from *Industrial*, will operate DISA on a daily basis.

B.   KEY FACTORS IN NEGOTIATING THE IEJV

As mentioned earlier, in order to ensure a good fit between partners, the parties should know what each is bringing to the table and have a clear goal on the benefits and obligations that will be assumed. The proper planning for the International Equity Joint Venture (IEJV) must take into account the three important factors mentioned in earlier materials—profit maximization and distribution, control, and limiting the risk. In the IEJV, these three factors take on a new and added importance.

In the earlier examples, where *Industrial* purchases Ace, Inc. or where Delta establishes a FDI as a wholly owned subsidiary the critical factors pitted the private investor against the government. This is especially true in the outbound FDI. In the IEJV you still have the tension between the private investor and the host government. Additionally, the presence of another co-owner raises the complexity of the business negotiations as well. The following materials address these issues from Delta, the minority JV partner's point of view.

1. *Profit Maximization and Distribution*

a.   *The Types of Profit*

An important issue in the case of an FDI is to identify the different profit 'pockets' that exist in the FDI. In chapter 3, the importance of removing performance requirements was discussed. Performance requirements continue to play a role in profit maximization and distribution but added to that are the problems of being a minority shareholder. There are various types of profit that can be generated from the investment. Profit, also known as income or gain, can be divided into two categories—profit derived on account of being an owner and profit derived through contractual undertakings with the FDI.

Profits derived from owning the FDI can be divided into two categories—dividends which constitutes the distribution of corporate profits and gains derived from the sale of the shares. This type of profit can be affected by the vagaries of business. Typically, in order to have dividends the corporation's operations should reflect an excess of revenue over expenses. In addition, in order to realize a gain on the sale of the stock, the corporation usually will have to have been profitable. The profit derived as an owner is also subject to governmental and private control.

Governmental control can be exercised through performance requirements. In developing countries, dividend payments can also be limited by performance requirements that may exist in the applicable foreign investment law. Limiting or restricting the repatriation of profits through dividend payments is a classic performance requirement. Although performance requirements are falling into disfavor in the current international environment, Delta should review the rules of the host country to ascertain the possible impact that performance requirements may have on dividends, as well as the proceeds from any sale or exchange of the stock.

Delta's ability to receive dividends may also be subject to governmental or private control through applicable corporate law statutes.

These can limit the maximum amount of corporate earnings that can be paid. Additionally, dividend payments require action by the board of directors—a private source of control. Making the board declare a dividend is a function of control. Minority shareholders can be subjected to a freeze out of dividends by majority shareholders—Delta is in a vulnerable position in this regard. For possible solutions, see control materials infra.

Delta can also derive profit from DISA on contractual undertakings. There are several types of profit from contracts including gains derived from the sale of goods and services. For further discussions of this type of transaction, see Section 4.3 and Chapters 5, 6 & 7. Contractual profits can also include income from the rental of real or tangible personal property, royalty income derived from the licensing of an IPR (for further discussions see Section 4.2) and interest income from loans made by the partners to the IEJV.

Profits, gain or income from contract are also subject to potential restrictions. The board of directors must initially approve the contract. However, once the contract is approved the payment is made pursuant to the terms in the contract. Therefore, unlike the case of dividend distribution, neither the corporate law or board intransigence can prevent the paying of profits. Delta, the minority shareholder could get considerable benefit by engaging in contractual relations with DISA. Foreign investment laws, through performance requirements, can also negatively impact the distribution of contractual profits. Performance requirements could limit the interest, rental or royalty amount, and/or require the payment for goods and services be made in host currency.

An important role for the attorney is to glean from the client the types of profit that can be extracted from the FDI. Once the type of profit is established, the attorney should review the laws of the affected countries and determine if the scenario will work. For example, assume USCO wishes to license intellectual property to New SA de CV. Assume further that the market value of the IP calls for a royalty payment of 10%. If the host country sets a limit of three percent on royalties paid to foreigners, USCO would not be able to maximize its profit on the licensing of the IPR. In that case, if the royalty payment is a significant priority to USCO, the investment should not be made.

The appropriate time for the analysis of profit potential is before the IEJV is formally organized. The same holds true for any of the profit categories listed above. It is the lawyer's job, together with local counsel, to take into account the regulatory environment in the structuring of the transaction. Additionally, the lawyer should make sure that all of the legal documents are in place so that the profit maximization and distribution can be realized. The documents comprising the IEJV are discussed infra.

b.   *Whose Profit Is to Be Maximized?*

There are three parties in the IEJV–Delta, 49% shareholder, *Industrial*, 51% shareholder and DISA, the FDI. Whose profit is to be maximized? In the context of a wholly owned subsidiary, the issue while important, would not be contentious. In the case of an IEJV, the issue is important and possibly contentious. This is one of the 'hard questions' that must be addressed by the parties before the deal is consummated.

Increasing revenue or decreasing costs maximizes profit. The JV partners may disagree in deciding whose profits to maximize. For example, assume that the FDI is owned by USCO (10%) and by FORCO (90%). Assume that a substantial part of USCO's business is in selling widgets it manufactures to New SA de CV, the FDI. FORCO's interest is in having the FDI pay the least amount possible for the widgets. By doing this, the costs of New SA de CV are lower increasing its profit of which FORCO takes ninety percent. Conversely, USCO wants to sell the widgets at the highest possible price because it will keep one hundred percent of the resulting profit on the sale of the widgets.

USCO has little interest in maximizing the profit of the FDI since it only owns ten percent. There is therefore, a natural tension between the parties as to whose profit to maximize. The solution is to have a clear idea of what the rights, benefits, and responsibilities the parties expect from their investment. The solution is not found in superior drafting, but rather in hammering out the economic details. An IEJV that does not make economic sense to both parties will not last. In the case above, perhaps an agreement of the pricing strategy that USCO will use for the widgets would solve the problem.

2. Exerting Control Over DISA

Control has an important effect on profit maximization and distribution. To a large extent the company in control determines the profit pockets of the business enterprise. It will determine what contractual obligations the FDI will enter into, when dividends will be paid, and who will work for the corporation as officers and employees. Those in control also determine the overall direction of the business, steering it towards priorities that best fits their needs as shareholders. For example, the FDI can pursue business opportunities in a conservative or aggressive manner, depending on the JV partner's corporate culture, analysis and priority. It can take extraordinary action like mergers and dissolution that will fit the synergy of their business and not necessarily that of the FDI.

a. Control at the Company Level

There are two levels of control—the company and operational level. Company level control can be divided into two categories—governmental and private control. The authority for governmental control stems from the virtually unassailable right of a government to regulate transactions occurring within its borders. In the case of developing countries the host government can exert control through the law governing business entities. For example, Mexico governs corporations through the General Law of Mercantile entities, see materials in Section 3.4, supra. Control can also be exerted through applicable investment laws, see e.g. Mexico's Foreign Investment law in Section 3.3 supra. One of the most important tasks for a lawyer is to help the client assess the regulatory environment of the host and exporting country.

There is also a private control at the company level that is effected through the organizing documents. In the typical IEJV the corporate 'partners' own shares in the FDI. The majority corporate shareholder normally controls the corporation, albeit indirectly. This is the reason for developing host government's insistence that one of its nationals take a fifty-one percent ownership in the FDI relegating the foreigner to a forty-nine percent 49% interest. The foreign investor's control over the FDI is severely impacted *vis a vis* the majority shareholder.

There are, however, strategies that can be used in maintaining control in spite of a minority shareholder position. The sources of corporate governance rules include the corporate statute, charter, and by-laws of the corporation. Local counsel is helpful in this regard. In the U.S., effective control by the minority shareholder can be maintained by using these sources of corporate governance to its benefit. The board of directors manages the corporation; therefore, whoever controls the board manages the corporation. The board is elected and serves at the pleasure of the shareholders.

There are a variety of methods wherein minority shareholders can elect a majority of the board. Some of these include establishing a voting trust agreement where the majority shareholder conveys to the minority shareholder its right to vote pursuant to a voting trust. The feasability of these arrangements should be reviewed with local counsel.

Another method is to establish separate categories of stock with each class of stock having the right to appoint a certain number of board members. Effective control at the company level can also be maintained by requiring that a unanimous or super majority of the board is needed to make any major corporate decision. For example, assume that the FDI has a board of five directors where the minority shareholder elects two and the majority shareholder elects three. The majority shareholder would always be able to push their agenda because it has a majority in the board. A possible strategy is to change the majority vote rule. The minority can establish in the by-laws a sort of veto on major decisions by requiring a unanimous or super-majority on major issues facing the FDI.

Another method of limiting the control of the majority shareholder is to remove certain key decisions from the board, reposing it instead in the shareholder and requiring a super-majority or unanimous decision at the shareholder level. For example, assume that a minority shareholder holds a forty-nine percent position, by requiring a super majority of sixty percent, the majority shareholder would be powerless to act without the vote of the minority shareholder. Examples where a super majority would be needed include terminating the joint venture or making substantial changes to the structure of the FDI.

The key to any strategy of this type is to first determine if the corporate code of the particular jurisdiction permits the plan. After that, it is necessary to ensure that the corporate charter and by-laws also permit it. Local counsel can be very useful in implementing these or other strategies.

b. Control at the Operational Level

Even if control cannot be maintained at the corporate level through the procedures described above, control can be maintained at the operational level through contractual arrangements. By using contracts, operational control can be maintained even in the face of a loss of control at the legal organization level. For example, in the example above where USCO owns a ten-percent interest in the FDI, assume the USCO company has contractual agreements with the FDI. Assume the USCO, through valid and enforceable contracts, sells the widgets the FDI needs to operate, rents the premises it uses, licenses the technology it uses, provides key services to the FDI, and lends the FDI money to operate. While the USCO does not control the FDI at the legal level, because it owns only ten percent of the business, it still maintains substantial control at the operational level through its contractual undertakings.

A FDI is particularly vulnerable to operational control when the domestic majority shareholder does not have the technical capacity to run the business operations. For example, assume that the minority shareholder has entered into a licensing agreement with the FDI in a high-tech business operation being conducted in the host country. Assume further that the chief managerial staff of the FDI is composed of employees of the minority shareholder in its capacity as licensor. If the staff leaves, business operations cease. This could make the majority owner much more amenable to work with the minority. Thus, the minority shareholder exerts control over the FDI not on account of its ownership stake but rather on account of the services it is providing.

3. Protecting Against Risk of Loss

Entrepreneurs frequently look at life through rose colored glasses. A large profit potential may distract them from the downside of a FDI. They tend to focus on either establishing or operating a business when things are going well. They usually do not pay much attention to how the affairs should be run if the business is not successful. Lawyers on the other hand are trained to look for problems. The 'problem' is that sometimes lawyers focus on problems that do not exist or have a low probability of occurring. The businessperson that looks at business through the eyes of a lawyer will never do a deal. However, the businessperson that does not consult with a lawyer is doomed to make costly mistakes.

The solution is in realizing the proper role of each person. The lawyer should help the "deal maker" and certainly not be a "deal breaker". With this in mind, the first step in the process of protecting against risk of loss is to determine the nature of the risks involved. The lawyer can also assist the client in developing strategies to shift the risk to some other party either the other JV partner or a third party like an insurer.

The FDI involves the transfer of capital. Therefore, anything that could negatively impact that capital is a risk. Some risks can be covered by insurance, others by contract and still others by the form of legal organization used in establishing the FDI. Insurable risks include damages in tort for defective products or damage caused by the negligence of employees. Expenses for employees being hurt on the job may also be covered by insurance.

Even the value of the FDI can be insured against the expropriation by a foreign government through insurance programs of the Multilateral Investment Guarantee Agency and the Overseas Private Investment Corporation. The solution in managing insurable risks is simple—obtain insurance. In addition, with proper planning, the cost of insurance could even be included in the price of the product being sold.

However, not all risks are insurable. For example, risk from an inability to meet contractual obligations to suppliers, lenders and other creditors of the business are not easily insured against. Losses incurred as a result of general market reversals likewise cannot be insured against. Another creditor that is not easily insured is against the government for income taxes. It is in this category of risk where the lawyer can be most helpful.

Planning for protection against risk of loss in cases where the business is not successful is an important area for the lawyer. One cultural distinction that should be noted is in the lack of use of lawyers by Latin American business entrepreneurs. Typically lawyers are not brought in on the planning stage of business strategies whereas U.S. business people bring lawyers in early. This can create problems because contentious issues may not be exposed as early as they could.

The risks associated with a joint venture mirror those of the parent/subsidiary FDI. However, in the case of a wholly owned subsidiary the corporate owner risks the loss of its entire investment. In the IEJV, the partners share the risk and can even shift the risks between themselves. This risk shifting is the subject of negotiation and strategy. The lawyer can play an invaluable role in structuring a joint venture in such a way that the major part of the risk falls on the shoulders of the other joint venture partner.

Generally the strategy is to limit the capital invested in the FDI. There are several ways in minimizing the capital at risk in the FDI. The type of assets being transferred dictates the strategy of risk minimization. For example, Delta is transferring equipment. The equipment could be leased to the FDI. If the business is a failure, Delta, with respect to the equipment, is a lessor (creditor) rather than owner. Also, Delta has a valuable patent that will be used by the FDI. Instead of transferring the patent as a capital contribution it could license the patent to the FDI thus establishing a creditor relationship.

Delta is transferring assets to the FDI. The transaction could be structured as a part debt/part capital contribution. This could establish Delta as a creditor and owner. To the extent that Delta is a lender it can have more leverage over DISA than as a minority shareholder. For a discussion of this strategy, see the capitalization and valuation issues in Section 4.1 C, infra. Also, Delta and *Industrial* are each to borrow three million dollars. Delta could urge that a local bank be used and the loan established on a non-recourse basis.

C. CAPITALIZATION AND VALUATION ISSUES

1. *The Capitalization Decision*

The capital of a business entity is the accumulated goods, possessions, and assets it owns for the production of profits and wealth. Business enterprises need capital to begin business operations. There are three sources of capital—money or other property contributed in return for an ownership interest (equity capital), loans (debt capital)—either from the owners (inside debt) or from third parties (outside debt), and from business operations (cash flow). This section deals with the initial capitalization, therefore, will not include the capital derived from business operations—the cash flow.

Debt and equity capital have different legal and economic characteristics that impact the three important issues of control, risk, profit maximization and profit distribution discussed above. There are also many important tax differences. The capitalization decision in the FDI is as important as choosing the appropriate entity. The needs of the client and host government regulations must be analyzed to ascertain the appropriate capitalization method. The materials that follow describe the attributes of debt and equity capitalization

a. *Debt Capital*

In a debt investment, the transferee (debtor) agrees to pay the transferor (creditor) the principal amount of the capital transferred (the loan amount) plus an additional amount constituting interest. The repayment plan is evidenced by a loan document calling for the payment of an amount certain on a given date and at a stated amount of interest. The interest payment is income to the creditor but the principal is considered a recovery of capital and is not taxable. The interest increment is typically a deductible expense to the debtor and the payment on the amount of the principal is not deductible.

The non-convertible or straight debt can either be secured or unsecured. In a secured loan the creditor has the debtor's promise to pay. In case of default, the creditor can also foreclose on the debtor's property securing the loan. In case of default on an unsecured debt, the creditor must look for payment from the general assets of the debtor. In a liquidation scenario, the creditor takes priority over the shareholders in asset distributions. In a non-convertible debt the creditor's profit is the interest charged on the loan. Therefore the creditor's profit is not increased nor is the value in the investment increased by the business success of the debtor. The debtor's potential profit is only helpful in assessing its capacity to repay the loan.

Non convertible debt has a limited income potential—the rate of interest charged. Some lenders would like to have the security of a debt instrument but with the possibility of receiving value in the case of the business success of the debtor. The convertible debt can meet this need. On the risk side, the creditor can limit its risk by securing the loan with the debtor's assets. This is usually helpful at the time the business begins. As the business becomes viable, the creditor can convert the debt into ownership. Thus being able to tap into the profits being generated by the business.

b. Equity Capital

The corporation's equity capital is referred to as stockholder's equity. Stockholder's equity is composed of two parts—contributed capital (above referred to as equity capital) and retained earnings. The amount of retained earnings is the cumulative amount of net income the corporation has realized. Equity capital results when the transferee corporation issues shares of capital stock in return for cash or other property received from the transferor (shareholder). The corporation is not obligated to repay the shareholders for the capital received. There is no guarantee that the investor will reap any benefit from the investment. However, if the business is successful the investor can benefit from the payment of dividends and the increase in fair market value of the capital shares due to the business success of the corporation.

Capital stock can be of a variety of categories. Generally, however, there are two types of stock—common and preferred. Each class of stock possesses different economic and legal attributes. In a common stock investment, the shareholder takes a residual ownership interest in the corporation. The common stock investment shares in the profits of the corporation. The common stockholders are the true 'owners' of the corporation—benefiting from the business success and suffering loss in the case of failure. In a liquidation, common stockholders receive corporate property only after the creditors and preferred stockholders.

Preferred stock, sometimes referred to as senior securities, has debt and equity characteristics. A typical preferred stockholder is promised a certain percentage of its par value payable from the profits of the corporation. The percentage can vary but is frequently between five to ten percent. Unlike debt, however, if there is no profit the preferred stockholders do not receive any distributions. If the business fails, preferred stockholders share in the liquidation proceeds after the creditors but before the common stockholders. In the case of success the preferred stockholder's profit is limited to the percentage share of profits based on their par value.

c. Capitalization and the Three Important Factors

(1) The Effect on Control

The control of the business enterprise rests with the owners; therefore, maximum control of the business enterprise will be realized by obtaining a majority equity interest in the business enterprise. Creditors can, however, exert some control over the business enterprise at the entity and operational level. Creditors exert control through contract. For example, the loan documents could prohibit the corporation from taking any action that might harm the repayment of the loan like dividend payments or the sale of corporate assets. A creditor could also require a seat on the board to protect its interest as a creditor. In either case, the creditor can exert some sort of control over the FDI.

(2) The Effect on Risk

The risk and reward goals of the investor usually drive the choice between a debt or equity investment. If the business opportunity offers low risk and high reward, a common stock investment would be the best. If the project involves the purchase of hard assets but is very risky, a secured debt may be the best investment alternative. The creditor's risk is limited to the amount of the loan. The creditor can protect its investment by securing the loan against an asset of the business enterprise and protect the upside potential by using convertible debt.

An unsecured creditor's interest is superior only to the equity holders. In many cases, an unsecured creditor's interest is not much better than that of an equity holder. In a joint venture, the debt versus equity decision can become a contentious issue. The non-lending partner may have an inferior position *vis a vis* the lending partner. The careful lawyer could structure a deal where their client minimizes its risk by taking an equity and either a straight or convertible debt position.

(3) Profit Maximization and Distribution

The important factor to keep in mind is that profit from debt comes from contract and is limited to the amount of interest stated in the loan documents. The payment is not through a declaration of the board but rather pursuant to the loan agreement. An equity investment's profit comes from distributing all or part of the net income of the corporation. Preferred stock is limited to a percentage of its par value whereas common stock can share in all of the profits of the corporation. The potential profit is maximized by an investment in common stock.

As to profit distribution, the decision to distribute profits from the business enterprise follows control. However, even if control is maintained at the company level, governmental rules of the host country may prevent the removal of profits. Those rules must be evaluated to determine the best capitalization mechanism. For example, assume the host government has currency controls on dividends but not on interest. You should set up a debt investment so that the repatriation of the interest may be possible.

2. *Contribution and Valuation Issues*

a. *The Initial Capitalization and Valuation Decision*

In order for the FDI to commence operations the owners must transfer capital to it. The capital can be composed of cash, tangible personal property, real property, or intangible personal property. There are several issues that emerge from this business necessity: Which partners will contribute what assets? What is the value assigned to the non-cash assets? What exchange rate will be used on dollar denominated assets? How will the FDI reflect the transfer of the assets? What are the income tax implications of these capital transfers? The partners should clearly establish what assets they are initially transferring to the IEJV, when they are going to do it and the method they will use.

In the facts of the hypothetical Delta is to contribute equipment, a patent, and cash while *Industrial* to contribute cash. The cash contribution does not create valuation problem but the other non-cash assets could. How can Delta convince *Industrial* that the equipment and patent estimates of fair market value are accurate? Determining the fair market value of an asset is an imprecise art. There may be a need in resorting to an expert on property valuations to properly make these determinations. The valuation decision could also have an income tax consequence, see Section 4.4, infra.

b. *Additional Capital Contributions*

Delta and *Industrial* should have a detailed business plan to determine what amount of capital will be needed initially for DISA to meet its goals. However, business necessities could make those initial projections inaccurate. The parties should provide for the possible need of additional capital. They should agree on the procedures on any future capital calls. Some of the important questions that need to be addressed include— What conditions will trigger a call for additional capital? How will capital calls be made? Who determines when and how much additional capital will be needed?

Other important questions in regards to additional capital contributions are—What happens if a partner is unwilling or unable to meet a future capital call? Will it cause a termination of the business or merely the partner's interest? Will the non-complying partner be forced to sell its interest? At what price will the partner sell its share? The partner with limited resources should be particularly sensitive to this scenario. The above questions are discussed in the section below.

3. *Other Issues*

a. *Issues Relating to Operations and Accounting*

There are also many issues relating to operations and accounting with which to contend. It is important for the lawyer to effectively communicate with the client so that the client's wishes are addressed. The operations issues frequently relate to quality control, and maintaining confidentiality among the partners, and assigning personnel that are bilingual in order to enhance communications.

Another issue is to designate the partner who is primarily responsible for interacting with the host government. This can include obtaining permits, licenses, or visas for personnel. In the area of accounting the questions arise on the preparation of the financial statements. Who is to hire the accountant? Will the financials be prepared in English? Will they be prepared in accordance with US Generally Accepted Accounting Principles? Will there be a right for the partners to audit the books and records? Who will pay? Who will hire the employees? Who is responsible for obtaining visas for the foreign employees? What does the USCO have to do to contend with the FCPA?

b. Reducing the Agreement to Writing

(1) Introduction

As can be seen from the above, the IEJV relationship has many facets. In addition to the relationship as shareholders, in many cases, the partners will also be doing business with the FDI. Indeed, these ancillary business relationships may be a prime motivating force in establishing the FDI in the first place. The various relationships mandate that there be a writing that establishes the rights and obligations of the parties in the entire business relationship contemplated. Good practice dictates that the partners negotiate, draft, and execute all of the applicable documents before the Joint Venture is consummated. Only through this process can all of the possible problem areas be flushed out.

In addition to the business issues, there are some cultural and legal difficulties that may arise here. The common law businessperson wants as many eventualities listed in the agreement as possible. The civil law entrepreneur may believe that the inclusion of so many contingencies is inspired by a lack of trust, favoring instead a procedure where eventualities are discussed and resolved as they arise. This is a difficult concept to bridge. One thing is sure, if there were no problems a one-page agreement would suffice. However, if there is a problem you wish there were a thousand pages explaining the rights and liabilities of the parties in that case.

(2) A Survey of the Contracts That Constitute the IEJV

(A) The Letter of Intent

The letter of intent should be a brief writing between the partners that establishes the salient business, legal, financial, and economic terms of the relationships. The letter is necessary to avoid lengthy and costly negotiations between parties that are not a good fit. The letter of intent should point towards the negotiation and drafting of the more complete document establishing the relationship—the Joint Venture Agreement.

(B) The Joint Venture Agreement

The joint venture agreement should lay out the complete agreement of the parties in their relationship between the IEJV as owners and the ancillary business relationships that are contemplated. The issues described in the materials above should be negotiated and memorialized in the Joint Venture Agreement and/or collateral documents and agreements. It should also include a detailed business plan where the responsibilities, rights and liabilities of the parties are clearly stated including all of the formation, capitalization, operation, and termination issues.

The joint venture agreement should also attach as exhibits and incorporate by reference the organizing documents of the FDI and the collateral agreements entered into. The collateral agreements should include the corporate charter, by-laws, and any other document issued when the corporate FDI is formed including Subscription Agreements, Buy/Sell Agreements, Non–Compete Agreements, and Confidentiality Agreements. It should also include any agreements entered into by and between the parties for the sale of goods, the sale of services, the rental of tangible property, the licensing of any intangible property, and any loan documents.

D.   TERMINATION OF THE JOINT VENTURE

1.   Introduction

There is a tendency among potential partners to overlook shortcomings or faults in the other when the deal is at its inception. The partners should not be reluctant in addressing or dealing with difficult issues for fear of hurting the other person's feelings. It is true that the business-person or lawyer should use courtesy and common sense in addressing possible points of conflict especially in a cross-cultural setting. In any case, good practice dictates that the partners address the issue of IEJV termination.

There are several questions that should be addressed in the termination of the IEJV–What events can cause a termination of either the FDI or a partner's interest in the FDI? What are the consequences of the terminating event? What procedures or mechanisms can be used to have an orderly transfer of interest or termination of the FDI?

2.   Events That Can Trigger a Termination

Trigger events can be business related—business failure on account of unsustainable losses, bankruptcy, or the failure to meet the business plan for reasons beyond the control of the partners. Another trigger event can be expropriation. One danger in making an FDI in a developing country is in the government taking over the investment. See materials in Section 3.1, supra on materials regarding expropriations. The central idea on expropriations is that the taking government pays for the property taken away. Expropriation can be an outright taking or a gradual process wherein regulatory controls make the FDI untenable.

Another trigger event can be partner related. There can emerge a deterioration of relations between the partners, deadlock on the course of business the FDI is taking or on current or future investments. There can be disputes on profit distribution, competitive relationship, corruption, breach of the joint venture agreement or collateral agreements, or a lack of commitment in pursuing the business plan as originally conceived. There are many cases where JV partners reach a point in which there is an unwillingness or inability to go forward on the IEJV. In these cases the business is a success but a changing of priorities or direction by one of the JV partners may not make business sense to continue.

3. *The Consequences of a Terminating Event*

The consequences of a terminating event can be a cessation of the business of the IEJV and a distribution of the assets to the partners. This will frequently arise when the business is a failure or when there is such a division or animosity between the JV partners that a deadlock is impossible to overcome. This termination results in the liquidation and sale of the assets the proceeds of which are distributed to the JV partners. This terminating event frequently results in losses. The forced sale and distribution of assets does not take into account the synergistic value that a set of assets possesses as an operating unit that is generating a profit. In the usual case, if the FDI is a business success, the termination event will lead to the exit of one of the partners but not a cessation of the business.

4. *The Procedures for the Termination*

a. *The Buy–Sell Agreement*

It is in the best interest of all concerned to have a procedure or mechanism in place that will effect an orderly transfer of interest of the departing JV partner. Once the JV partners agree that the business will continue but that one party will leave, the attention turns to various issues—What is the value of the departing party's interest? See the business valuation materials in Section 2.1 supra. Who will purchase the interest—the remaining partner or the corporation? How and when will the departing party be paid? Who will pay the departing party?

Other important collateral issues are—Will the departing party continue to transact business with the FDI? If so, should fresh contracts be drawn up? Will the departing party compete with the FDI? Should there be a non-compete agreement? Is it enforceable in the foreign jurisdiction? If the departing party has transferred confidential information to the FDI what will happen to the information? Will the party be required to return the information? How do you un-ring a bell? What if the departing party gave guarantees to third parties—what happens? Should there be releases given? These and other questions should be addressed through a Buy/Sell Agreement.

b. *How and When Will the Departing Party Be Paid?*

How a departing party will be paid is a function of the bargain between the parties and the economic realities of the entity that is the

FDI. The departing party will want to be paid in cash immediately. The remaining partner may not want or be able to make the payment. It could counter by offering an unsecured promissory note payable over a long period of time. If payment is made in soft currency how will the exchange rate be set? Who will pay the departing party? These questions should be addressed in the Buy/Sell agreement.

There are two candidates for payment—the remaining partner and the FDI entity. If the remaining partner is to buy, the transaction will be called a cross-purchase agreement. If the FDI entity buys the shares the transaction is a redemption. In a cross-purchase agreement, the JV partner agree to purchase the shares from the selling party. The purchaser must fund the buy out with its own after-tax funds. The FDI entity is not directly involved in the transaction.

In a redemption agreement the FDI entity purchases the shares from the selling party and then cancels the shares. In this transaction, the remaining JV partner is not directly involved in the transaction because the entity is purchasing the shares from the selling partner. The usual procedure is to use a redemption agreement. By doing this, pre-tax dollars can be used to fund the transaction.

SECTION 4.2 THE INTERNATIONAL LICENSING AGREEMENT

A. INTRODUCTION

Recall that in the hypothetical Delta's Division III owns a patent used in the manufacturing of concrete additives used in oil well drilling. The additive, known as "Quick Dry" is used in concrete to make it harden rapidly. The making of "Quick Dry" is a labor-intensive process. Delta has been losing U.S. market share on account of lower cost European additives of comparable quality. Division III is Delta's core business accounting for seventy-five percent of its annual sales. Delta is convinced that it must reduce its labor cost in manufacturing the additive or risk losing a substantial portion of its market.

On the facts above, Delta's Division III is probably not a good candidate for the licensing agreement since the manufacturing process accounts for seventy-five percent of its business. It is more likely that Delta would enter into a foreign direct investment instead. If, however, the 'Quick Dry' additive did not represent such a critical aspect of its business Delta would be a good candidate because it is interested in lowering its operating costs and wants access to new markets. In addition, the transfer may be necessary to·comply with the requirements imposed by the host country. Essentially Delta decides on the transfer technology on account of external factors.

An effective way of realizing Delta's needs is by licensing the technology to an unrelated foreign licensor. For a discussion on what constitutes technology see Section 1.1, supra. Delta would transfer the patent and other related intellectual property under license to the foreign licensee. The foreign licensee pays Delta royalties for the use of the patent. These materials focus on the business and legal issues surrounding the International Licensing Agreement. The following is a sample International Licensing Agreement. The contract will serve as the basis for discussing the important legal, business, and tax issues that emerge in a transfer of technology setting.

INTERNATIONAL LICENSING AGREEMENT

RECITALS

This Agreement effective this _____ day of _____, 2000, by and between Delta, Inc., (hereafter Delta) a corporation duly organized under the laws of the State of California and having its principal place of business at 3030 1st Street, Malibu California and *Industrial del Sureste, SA de CV*, (hereafter Industrial) a corporation duly organized under the laws of the Republic of Mexico and having its principal place of business at 1001 Plaza Industrial, Guadalajara, Mexico,

WITNESSETH

WHEREAS, Delta, Inc., is the owner of certain patents, trademarks, and trade secrets duly protected under the laws of the United States, Mexico, and applicable international law;

WHEREAS, Delta, Inc.(hereafter known as Licensor) is desirous of entering into a License Agreement, with Industrial (hereafter known as Licensee);

IT IS RESOLVED, that for ten thousand U.S. dollars paid by the Licensee to the Licensor and for other good and valuable consideration the receipt and sufficiency of which is hereby acknowledged the parties herein agree to be bound by the terms and conditions found in this International Licensing Agreement.

DEFINITIONS

A. "Patent" shall mean the property under United States Letters Patent no. 12567.

B. "Trademark" shall mean the property under the Certificate of Trademark Registration No. 128976 issued by the United States Patent Office on the 1st day of October, 1999.

C. "Sale" shall be deemed to occur at the time of use, of shipment, delivery or other transfer, or at the time of billing, whichever first occurs.

D. "Net Sales" shall mean Licensee's invoice price to its non-related customers less sales or excise taxes or shipping costs actually directly or indirectly by Licensee and separately itemized on Licensee's invoice, and less actual trade discounts, returns and allowances thereon.

ARTICLE 1
GRANT OF LICENSE

A. Upon the terms, royalty payments and conditions set forth herein and under the Patent and Trademark, Licensor hereby grants to Licensee an exclusive license to manufacture and sell the 'Quick Dry' brand concrete additive (hereafter Additive) so long as the additive is manufactured in accordance with the specifications established by the Licensor.

B. Representatives of Licensor will provide detailed specifications to Licensee which relate to the materials for and the manufacture of the Additive. The Licensor has the unqualified right, at any and all reasonable times, and without prior notice, to inspect the materials and manufacturing processes employed by Licensee in the manufacture of the Additive.

C. Licensee shall mark the Additive with a suitable legend, in a form approved in advance by the Licensor, indicating that the Additive is made under license.

D. Licensee hereby acknowledges that any materials provided or revealed to Licensee pursuant to this Agreement including, but not limited to formulas and other written or oral data communicated to Licensee by Licensor constitutes trade secrets of Licensor revealed in confidence to Licensee and Licensee covenants and agrees to keep and respect such trade secrets hereunder reposed.

ARTICLE 2
OWNERSHIP OF PROPERTY AND IMPROVEMENTS

A. Licensee shall at all times recognize the validity of any and all patents, trademarks, and trade secrets of Licensor and the ownership thereof by Licensor, and shall not at any time put in issue or contest, either directly or indirectly, the validity of such patents, trademarks, and trade secrets. In addition, nothing in this Agreement shall give Licensee an interest in any such patent, trademark, or trade secret; it being agreed and understood that there is extended by this Agreement a permission, uncoupled with an interest, to use any and all patents, trademarks, and trade secrets with the licensing program and products of Licensor, said use to be in such manner and with the result of designating Licensor as the source of and origin of said program and products.

B. Licensee agrees that in the event of any actual or suspected infringement of any patent or trademark or piracy of trade secrets of Licensor, the Licensee shall promptly report the same in writing to the Licensor.

C. Licensee agrees that any improvements in the patent, trademark, trade secrets, or knowhow whether developed by Licensor or Licensee, shall be the exclusive property of the Licensor.

ARTICLE 3

ROYALTY AND PAYMENT

A.   Licensee shall pay to Licensor at the end of the first accounting period in which a Sale occurs a royalty of eight percent 8% of the Net Sales Price of the Additive.

B.   The Accounting period shall be on a semi-annual basis, and the account shall be settled on June 30 and December 31 of each year, and payment shall be made within thirty (30) days following each settlement of account.

C.   Licensee shall pay all royalties due hereunder in U.S. dollars. All royalties for an accounting period computed in other currency shall be converted into United States dollars at the buying rate for such transfer for such currency to United States dollars as quoted by Licensor's bank on the last day of such accounting period or the business day thereafter if such last day shall be a Sunday or a holiday.

D.   Licensee shall furnish with each payment a certified written statement of the dollar value of Licensee's Sales of the Additive subject to royalty herein and upon which payment is based in the preceding accounting period setting forth the essential information concerning such Sales. Such information shall further include the Net Selling Price and all other facts necessary to facilitate verification of Licensee's royalty calculation. In the event there are no royalty payments due in any accounting period during the term of the Agreement, Licensee shall so state within thirty (30) days following each such accounting period.

E.   Licensee agrees that it will at all times keep complete, true and correct books of account containing a current record of sales and other data in sufficient detail to enable the royalties payable under this Agreement to be computed and verified. Licensee further agrees to permit Licensor or its duly authorized audit agent to have access to and make copies of said books of account at reasonable intervals during business hours, provided, however, Licensee shall have the right to require such inspection and audit be made by a mutually acceptable independent certified public accountant in which event the costs thereof shall be borne equally by both parties.

F.   Licensee shall be liable for interest on any overdue royalty commencing on the date such royalty becomes due at annual rate of three percent 3% over the prime interest rate quoted by Licensor's bank on the day such royalty becomes due. If such interest rate exceeds the legal rate in the jurisdiction where a claim therefore is being asserted, the interest rate shall be reduced to the maximum rate that is legal in such jurisdiction.

ARTICLE 4

DURATION AND TERMINATION

A.   Unless otherwise terminated as hereinafter set forth, this Agreement shall continue in force and effect for an initial term of three (3) years from the effective date hereof.

B.   In the event of the occurrence of any of the following:

   (1) A party breaches the Agreement and does not cure such breach within forty-five days after notice thereof from the other party specifying such breach;

   (2) Liquidation of a party;

   (3) Insolvency or bankruptcy of a party whether voluntary or involuntary;

   (4) Inability of a party to meet its obligations hereunder;

   (5) Failure of a party to satisfy any judgment against it; or

   (6) Appointment of a trustee or receiver for a party;

   then, and in addition to all other rights and remedies which the other party may have at law or in equity, the other party may, at its option, terminate this Agreement by notice thereof in writing specifying the reason for such termination and a termination date. Such termination shall become effective on the date of termination set forth in the notice of termination, but in no event earlier than forty-five (45) days from the date of mailing thereof.

C.   The waiver of any default under this Agreement shall not constitute a waiver of the right to terminate this Agreement for any subsequent default.

D.   Termination of this Agreement for any cause whatsoever shall in no manner interfere with, affect or prevent the collection by Licensor of any and all sums of money due under this Agreement.

E.   Upon termination of this Agreement for any reason, Licensee's payments required under Article 3, but not yet due, shall become immediately due and payable, and Licensee's inventory of products for which payments are not yet required shall be included in Licensee's payment as though Sales of same had taken place prior to the termination of this Agreement.

F.   Upon termination of this Agreement, Licensee agrees to deliver to Licensor any and all documents, drawings, data or communication relating to the patent, trademark, and trade secrets licensed herein. It also agrees to not exploit, sell or use any knowledge gained under this License Agreement or in its relationship with Licensor.

G.   Any cancellation or termination of this Agreement shall not relieve Licensee of any obligation or liability accrued under any part of this Agreement including but not limited to those obligations found in Article 1, Article 2, Article 3, Article 4F, and Article5A.

ARTICLE 5

MISCELLANEOUS PROVISIONS

A. All notices, requests, demands and other communications under this Agreement or in connection therewith shall be given to or be made upon the respective parties as follows:

To Licensee:

Mr. Juan Gomez

President
Industrial del Sureste SA de CV
1001 Plaza Industrial
Guadalajara, Mexico 45020
To Licensor:

Mr. John Smith
President
Delta, Inc.
3030 1st Street
Malibu, California 90265

B. All notices, requests, demands and other communications given or made in accordance with the provisions of this Agreement shall be in writing, and shall be deemed to have been given when deposited postage prepaid, addressed as specified in the preceding paragraph.

C. This Agreement shall be binding upon and inure to the benefit of Licensor, its legal representatives, successors, and assigns.

D. This agreement shall be binding upon and inure to the benefit of Licensee, but shall not be transferable or assignable without the prior written consent of Licensor, which consent shall not be unreasonable withheld.

E. This Agreement shall be deemed to be a contract made under the laws of the State of California, regardless of where it is signed, and for all purposes shall be interpreted in its entirety in accordance with the laws of said State. In the event this Agreement is translated into any language other than the English language for any purpose, the parties agree that the English language version shall be the governing version.

F. This Agreement embodies all of the understandings and obligations between the parties with respect to the subject matter hereof. No amendment or modification of this Agreement shall be binding upon the parties unless made in writing and signed on behalf of each of the parties by their respective duly authorized officers.

G. Nothing contained in this Agreement shall be construed as conferring by implication, estoppel or otherwise upon Licensee, any license under any trade secrets, or know-how of Licensor and no such license or other rights shall arise from this Agreement or from any acts, statements or dealings resulting in the execution of this Agreement.

H. No representation or warranty has been or is made by Licensor that products made under the Patent or parts thereof may be manufactured, used or sold free of patent rights of others, it being understood that Licensor shall not be liable for any loss, damage or expense arising from any claim of patent infringement upon the manufacture, use or sale thereof.

I. Any disagreements arising under the provisions of this Agreement will be decided by arbitration in accordance with the Rules of the American Arbitration Association, each party to appoint an arbitrator, and the two thus selected to designate a third. If either of the parties fails to appoint an arbitrator within sixty (60) days after receipt of notice of the appointment by the other of its arbitrator, or if the arbitrators fail to appoint a third, then the American Arbitration association will have the power, on the request of either party, to make the appointments which have not been made as contemplated above. The arbitration will be held as promptly as possible at such time and place as the arbitrators may determine. The decision of a majority of the arbitrators will be final and binding upon the parties hereto, and the expense of the arbitration will be shared equally between the parties. Judgment upon the award may be entered in any court having jurisdiction, or application may be made to such court for a judicial acceptance of the award and an order of enforcement, as the case maybe.

J. Licensee agrees that in any proceeding in arbitration, suit or civil action outside the United States, including a proceeding or legal action for royalties recited as payable under the terms of this Agreement it will not, while licensed hereunder, either directly or indirectly contest Licensor's title to or the validity of any issued patent or trademark licensed hereunder.

K. This Agreement shall not constitute or be considered a partnership, joint venture, or agency between the parties hereto and neither of the parties hereto nor any of their employees or agents shall have the power or authority to bind or obligate the other party except as provided by the terms and provisions of this Agreement.

L. In the event Licensor shall, subsequent to the date of this Agreement, voluntarily enter into any license of the same scope as that contained in the Article 1 Grant herein with any other Licensee and at lower rates of royalty than the rates specified therefor in this Agreement taking into account all consideration given by such other licensee, then Licensor shall notify Licensee of such other license and, upon written request by Licensee given not more than sixty (60) days after such notice is given, the rates of royalty specified in this Agreement shall be reduced to conform to the rates specified in such other license, but only for the duration and to the extent to which such lower rates continue under such other license and upon the condition that Licensee shall accept and be bound by the same terms and conditions as all those which are a part of such other license.

In Witness Whereof, the parties have caused their respective officers hereunto duly authorized to execute this Agreement effective the date first written above.

Licensee

Industrial del Sureste SA de CV

By: _____
    Juan Gomez
    President

Licensor:

Delta, Inc.

By: _____
    John Smith
    President

B. ANALYSIS OF BUSINESS AND LEGAL ISSUES

1. *Relationship Between the Licensor and Licensee*

The International Licensing Agreement (ILA) is more complex than a sale of goods transaction. In a sale of goods transaction the seller is interested in getting paid and the buyer is interested in receiving the goods that were bargained for. Interaction between the two is minimal. The sale transaction can be handled fairly easily through the documentary transaction discussed in Chapter 5, infra.

In a Licensing Agreement, however, the parties engage in a relationship that calls for more inter-action and a higher level of trust between them than in a sales transaction. Each party to the license agreement will be called upon to perform certain acts in the completion of the contract. The parties should perform some degree of due diligence on the other party to ensure that it will be able to perform the actions required of it. See the due diligence procedures in Section 2.1 and 4.1 supra.

It is essential, therefore, that each party reaches the conclusion that the other has the financial wherewithal to satisfy its obligations. Also, it is important to see that the parties can be relied upon to maintain confidential information. In short, are the parties ethically and financially capable of living up to their obligations in the agreement. Spending the time to do this investigation initially can be the beginning point of a fruitful licensing arrangement. Furthermore, care should be taken to not contract a business that may be known for sharp business practices.

The legal relationship between the parties is contractual. In the ILA the owner of the intellectual property—patents, trademarks, or trade secrets—(the Licensor) grants permission to a party (the Licensee) to use the intellectual property. In return for the grant of usage, the Licensee will pay the Licensor an amount of money called a "royalty." The Licensor then receives royalty income from the Licensee. The Licensee will make a profit by using the intellectual property to make and sell the goods. To the Licensor, the royalty amount represents the value of the IPR. To the Licensee the royalty is the cost of doing business.

Delta needs to be concerned with the potential loss of ownership of the IPR through piracy or counterfeiting. Also Delta could lose the value of the IPR by not being able to charge or collect its royalties under the agreement. *Industrial* also faces risks. It may incur substantial start up costs only to find the technology that it is licensing is outdated. It could also incur the costs and risks of opening the market for Delta only to be frozen out at the end of the license term. These and other important issues are discussed below.

2. *Protecting the Ownership of the IPR Under International Law*

Protecting the ownership of intellectual property can be effected through U.S. domestic law, Mexican domestic law, and international agreements. The community of developed nations has, for a long period of time sought agreement in the protection of intellectual property rights. Developing countries have not been as favorably disposed to protect the rights of foreign owners particularly in the area of pharmaceuticals. However, in light of the globalization of markets and the free and open borders attitude that is taking place, even developing countries have entered into international agreements and enacted domestic legislation to strengthen IPR laws.

Historically, international agreements have not been very effective in protecting the intellectual property rights of foreigners. Effective protection of IPR's has been found more in domestic legal systems. However, many developing countries have not enforced their domestic IPR laws when a foreign person is the owner. Indeed, many developing countries have not even had a complete system of IPR laws. It is in this environment where international agreements have been helpful. An analysis of the benefits under several treaties is illustrative of the limitations of international agreements.

The International Convention for the Protection of Industrial Property (Paris Treaty)[1] is a self-executing treaty that forms part of U.S. federal Law. The Paris Treaty provides for national treatment of foreign owners of patents and trademarks that are citizens of member countries. The promise of national treatment merely provides for non-discriminatory treatment of the foreign person. The treaty does not create rights for the protection of the patent or trademark. In a similar vein, the Berne Convention for the

1. 21 U.S.T. 1583 53 Stat. 1748.

Protection of Literary & Artistic Works (the Berne Convention) is a non-self-executing treaty which provides for minimum standards and national treatment to owners of copyrights.

The Paris Treaty also establishes a patent priority registration system. If the IPR owner files a patent in one member country it has up to one year to register in other member countries and still keep their priority. In a related treatment, the Patent Cooperation Treaty (PCT) allows for joint filings in selected countries. Any member country (currently about forty) can register in selected countries and the filing is valid for all member countries. The selected countries include the United States, Japan, Sweden, Russia, as well as the European Patent Office in The Hague and Munich.

Note that the treaties described above merely proceed from protection offered at the domestic level. Newer agreements affecting intellectual property rights under the GATT and NAFTA offer more protection to the foreign IPR owner. In addition to providing substantive rules in protecting IPRs they also contain dispute resolution mechanisms. These two agreements have also spurred domestic IPR legislation in countries like Mexico. The provisions of those agreements are discussed below.

a. The TRIPS Agreement

Agreement on Trade Related Aspects of Intellectual Property Rights

Desiring to reduce distortions and impediments to international trade, and taking into account the need to promote effective and adequate protection of intellectual property rights, and to ensure that measures and procedures to enforce intellectual property rights do not themselves become barriers to legitimate trade;

Recognizing, to this end, the need for new rules and disciplines concerning: (a) the applicability of the basic principles of the GATT 1994 and of relevant international intellectual property agreements or conventions; (b) the provision of adequate standards and principles concerning the availability, scope and use of trade-related intellectual property rights; (c) the provision of effective and appropriate means for the enforcement of trade-related intellectual property rights, taking into account differences in national legal systems; (d) the provision of effective and expeditious procedures for the multilateral prevention and settlement of disputes between governments; and (e) transitional arrangements aiming at the fullest participation in the results of negotiations;

Recognizing the need for a multilateral framework of principles, rules and disciplines dealing with international trade in counterfeit goods;

Recognizing that intellectual property rights are private rights;

Recognizing the underlying public policy objectives of national systems for the protection of intellectual property, including developmental and technological objectives;

Recognizing also the special needs of the least-developed country Members in respect of maximum flexibility in the domestic implementation of laws and regulations in order to enable them to create a sound and viable technological base;

Emphasizing the importance of reducing tensions by reaching strengthened commitments to resolve disputes on trade-related intellectual property issues through multilateral procedures;

Desiring to establish a mutually supportive relationship between the MTO and the World Intellectual Property Organization (WIPO) as well as other relevant international organizations; Hereby agree as follows:

PART 1

GENERAL PROVISIONS AND BASIC PRINCIPLES

Article 1

Nature and Scope of Obligations

1.   Members shall give effect to the provisions of this Agreement. Members may, but shall not be obliged to, implement in their domestic law more extensive protection than is required by this Agreement, provided that such protection does not contravene the provisions of this Agreement. Members shall be free to determine the appropriate method of implementing the provisions of this Agreement within their own legal system and practice. * * *

Article 2

Intellectual Property Conventions

1.   In respect of Parts II, III and IV of this Agreement, Members shall comply with Articles 1–12 and 19 of the Paris Convention (1967).

2.   Nothing in Parts I to IV of this Agreement shall derogate from existing obligations that Members may have to each other under the Paris Convention, the Berne Convention, the Rome Convention and the Treaty on Intellectual Property in Respect of Integrated Circuits.

Article 3

National Treatment

1.   Each Member shall accord to the nationals of other Members treatment no less favourable than that it accords to its own nationals with regard to the protection of intellectual property * * *

Article 4

Most-Favored Nation Treatment

With regard to the protection of intellectual property, any advantage, favour, privilege or immunity granted by a Member to the nationals of any other country shall be accorded immediately and unconditionally to the nationals of all other Members. * * *

PART III

ENFORCEMENT OF INTELLECTUAL PROPERTY RIGHTS

SECTION 1: GENERAL OBLIGATIONS

Article 41

1.   Members shall ensure that enforcement procedures as specified in this Part are available under their law so as to permit effective action against any act of infringement of intellectual property rights covered by this Agreement, including expeditious remedies to prevent infringements and remedies which constitute a deterrent to further infringements. These procedures shall be applied in such a manner as to avoid the creation of barriers to legitimate trade and to provide for safeguards against their abuse.

2.   Procedures concerning the enforcement of intellectual property rights shall be fair and equitable. They shall not be unnecessarily complicated or costly, or entail unreasonable time-limits or unwarranted delays.

3.   Decisions on the merits of a case shall preferable be in writing and reasoned. They shall be made available at least to the parties to the proceeding without undue delay. Decisions on the merits of a case shall be based only on evidence in respect of which parties were offered the opportunity to be heard.

4.   Parties to a proceeding shall have an opportunity for review by a judicial authority of final administrative decisions * * *

5.   It is understood that this Part does not create any obligation to put in place a judicial system for the enforcement of intellectual property rights distinct from that for the enforcement of laws in general * * *

SECTION 5: CRIMINAL PROCEDURES

Article 61

Members shall provide for criminal procedures and penalties to be applied at least in cases of willful trademark counterfeiting or copyright piracy on a commercial scale. * * * Members may provide for criminal procedures and penalties to be applied in other cases of infringement of intellectual property rights, in particular where they are committed willfully and on a commercial scale. * * *

PART V

DISPUTE PREVENTION AND SETTLEMENT

Article 63

Transparency

1.   Laws and regulations, and final judicial decisions and administrative rulings of general application, made effective by a Member

pertaining to the subject matter of this Agreement (the availability, scope, acquisition, enforcement and prevention of the abuse of intellectual property rights) shall be published, or where such publication is not practicable made publicly available, in a national language, in such a manner as to enable governments and right holders to become acquainted with them. * * *

2. Each Member shall be prepared to supply, in response to a written request from another Member, information of the sort referred to in paragraph 1. A Member, having reason to believe that a specific judicial decision or administrative ruling or bilateral agreement in the area of intellectual property rights affects its rights under this Agreement, may also request in writing to be given access to or be informed in sufficient detail of such specific judicial decisions or administrative rulings or bilateral agreements. * * *

Article 64

Dispute Settlement

1. The provisions of Articles XXII and XXIII of GATT 1994 as elaborated and applied by the Dispute Settlement Understanding shall apply to consultations and the settlement of disputes under this Agreement * * *

The TRIPS agreement is a major positive step in protecting intellectual property of foreigners. The preamble to the TRIPS essentially adopts the position of developed countries–IPRs are private rights. The signatory countries agree that ineffective or inadequate protections of IPRs are barriers to legitimate trade and that a set of international rules is needed that will provide "... adequate standards and principles concerning the availability, scope and use of trade-related intellectual property rights ..." It also states that there is a need for IPR enforcement mechanisms at the international level and cites a need for an international set of rules for the prevention and settlement of investment disputes.

Essentially the TRIPS adopts the position of developed countries while recognizing that there is a place for public policy objectives in the national systems to develop a domestic technological base and that the needs of the poorest of the poor will be taken into account. Why did developing countries go along with the TRIPS? The TRIPS addresses many of the important IPR issues.

The TRIPS deals with ownership and treatment issues–Articles 1 & 2 obligate the members to give effect to the provisions of the TRIPS. This means that domestic legal systems must be changed to at least comply with the requirements of the agreement and that the provisions of major international agreements like the Paris and Berne Conventions must be adhered to. Articles 3 & 4 require member states to give nationals of other member states the better of national or most favored nation treatment.

The TRIPs also concerns the enforcement and prevention and resolution of disputes. Article 41 mandates that member states ensure that effective enforcement procedures are available under the domestic legal system. Article 61 even requires member states to modify their domestic laws to make the willful violations of certain IPR laws a criminal act. Article 63 focuses on dispute prevention by calling for transparency in governmental decision-making. Finally, Article 64 incorporates IPR rights in the highly developed GATT dispute resolution procedures.

   b.   Protection Under NAFTA

Chapter Seventeen
Intellectual Property

Article 1701: Nature and Scope of Obligations

   1.   Each Party shall provide in its territory to the nationals of another Party adequate and effective protection and enforcement of intellectual property rights, while ensuring that measures to enforce intellectual property rights do not themselves become barriers to legitimate trade.

   2.   To provide adequate and effective protection and enforcement of intellectual property rights, each Party shall, at a minimum, give effect to this Chapter and to the substantive provisions of: (a) the Geneva Convention for the Protection of Producers of Phonograms Against Unauthorized Duplication of their Phonograms, 1971 (Geneva Convention); (b) the Berne Convention for the Protection of Literary and Artistic Works, 1971 (Berne Convention); (c) the Paris Convention for the Protection of Industrial Property, 1967 (Paris Convention); and (d) the International Convention for the Protection of New Varieties of Plants, 1978 (UPOV Convention), or the International Convention for the Protection of New Varieties of Plants, 1991 (UPOV Convention). If a Party has not acceded to the specified text of any such Conventions on or before the date entry into force of this Agreement, it shall make every effort to accede. * * *

Article 1703: National Treatment

   Each Party shall accord to nationals of another Party treatment no less favorable than that it accords to its own nationals with regard to the protection and enforcement of all intellectual property rights. * * *

Article 1714: Enforcement of Intellectual Property Rights: General Provisions

   1.   Each Party shall ensure that enforcement procedures, as specified in this Article * * * are available under its domestic law so

as to permit effective action to be taken against any act of infringement of intellectual property rights covered by this Chapter, including expeditious remedies to prevent infringements and remedies to deter further infringements. Such enforcement procedures shall be applied so as to avoid the creation of barriers to legitimate trade and to provide for safeguards against abuse of the procedures.

2. Each Party shall ensure that its procedures for the enforcement of intellectual property rights are fair and equitable, are not unnecessarily complicated or costly, and do not entail unreasonable time-limits or unwarranted delays.

3. Each Party shall provide that decisions on the merits of a case in judicial and administrative enforcement proceedings shall: (a) preferably be in writing and preferably state the reasons on which the decisions are based; (b) be made available at least to the parties in a proceeding without undue delay; and (c) be based only on evidence in respect of which such parties were offered the opportunity to be heard.

Article 1717: Criminal Procedures and Penalties

1. Each Party shall provide criminal procedures and penalties to be applied at least in cases of willful trademark counterfeiting or copyright piracy on a commercial scale. Each Party shall provide that penalties available include imprisonment or monetary fines, or both, sufficient to provide a deterrent, consistent with the level of penalties applied for crimes of a corresponding gravity.

2. Each Party shall provide that, in appropriate cases, its judicial authorities may order the seizure, forfeiture and destruction in infringing goods and of any materials and implements the predominant use of which has been in the commission of the offense.

3. A Party may provide criminal procedures and penalties to be applied in cases of infringement of intellectual property rights, other than those in paragraph 1, where they are committed willfully and on a commercial scale

Article 1718: Enforcement of Intellectual Property Rights at the Border

1. Each Party shall, in conformity with this Article, adopt procedures to enable a right holder, who has valid grounds for suspecting that the importation of counterfeit trademark goods or pirated copyright good may take place, to lodge an application in writing with its competent authorities, whether administrative or judicial, for the suspension by the customs administration of the release of such good into free circulation. No Party shall be obligated to apply such procedures to goods in transit. A Party may permit such an application to be made in respect of

goods that involve other infringements of intellectual property rights, provided that the requirements of this Article are met. A Party may also provide for corresponding procedures concerning the suspension by the customs administration of the release of infringing goods destined for exportation from its territory.

The GATT and NAFTA IPR rules are very similar. They both embrace the developed country's point of view regarding the protection of intellectual property rights. The NAFTA also served as the impetus for Mexico to enact sweeping domestic IPR legislation. The main source of protecting the IPR ownership is through domestic legislation.

3. *Protection of IPR Ownership Under Domestic Legal Systems*

a. *The Mexican Legal System*

OVERVIEW OF RECENT CHANGES IN MEXICAN INDUSTRIAL PROPERTY LAW AND THE ENFORCEMENT OF RIGHTS BY THE RELEVANT GOVERNMENT AUTHORITIES

Bill F. Kryzda, Shaun F. Downey

CAN. U.S. L.J. (1995).

I.   RECENT HISTORY OF MEXICAN INDUSTRIAL PROPERTY LAW

A.   *Organic Powers from the Mexican Constitution of 1917*

The Mexican Constitution of 1917 grants the federal government the power to grant rights to inventors, pursuant to Articles 28 and 89 (Section XV), and the power to regulate commerce, pursuant to Article 73 (Section X). These powers are vested in the Mexican Congress.

B.   *The Protectionist Period*

1.   *Developments in the 1970s and 1980s*

During the statism period of the 1970s and 1980s Mexico's industrial property laws were extremely protectionist. The Law of Inventions and Marks of 1976 ("La Ley de Invenciones y Marcas") and the Law for Recordation of Technology Transfer and the Exploitation of Patents and Marks of 1972 ("La Ley Sobre el Registro de la Transferencia de Tecnologia y el Uso y Explotacion de Patentes y Marcas") provided almost no protection to foreign rights holders. Needless to say, these laws did not promote the transfer of technology or foreign investment.

2.   *The Placement of Mexico on the U.S.T.R.'s Priority Watch List*

This lack of protection for industrial property rights inside Mexico did not go unnoticed in the United States. In 1989 the U.S. Trade Representative placed Mexico on the "priority watch list" provided by "Special 301" in order to retaliate against inadequate protection and enforcement of industrial property rights. The United States subsequently removed Mexico from the list after it began to improve protections afforded to industrial property as part of the government's overall plan to open the Mexican economy to international competition and the world trading system.

C. Recent Movement Towards Economic Liberalization

Mexico made a giant step forward in the protection of Industrial Property upon implementing the Law for the Promotion and Development of Industrial Property (hereinafter referred to as "Industrial Property Law") ("Ley de Fomento y Proteccion de la Propiedad Industrial"), which took effect on June 27, 1991. The Law abrogated the protectionist Law of Inventions and Marks of 1976 and the Law for Control and Recordation of Technology Transfer and the Exploitation of Patents and Marks of 1982 and prepared Mexico for the commitments that would later be required upon the execution of the North American Free Trade Agreement (NAFTA).

II. Recent Changes in Mexican Industrial Property Laws in 1994

A. General Comments

Mexico further amended the Industrial Property Law with amendments designed to satisfy the commitments made as a result of the signing of NAFTA and to correct deficiencies in the 1991 Industrial Property Law. The amendments, to be discussed below, further strengthened the protection of industrial property rights in Mexico and created an independent entity dedicated to the enforcement of industrial property rights, the Mexican Institute of Industrial Property ("Instituto Mexicano de la Propiedad Industrial"), referred to by members of the profession as the "IMPI."

B. Patents, Utility Models, and Industrial Designs

1. Changes Related to Patents

Amended Article 16 of the Industrial Property Law defines patentability in an all-inclusive manner reversing the previous restrictive listing of what was patentable similar to the Foreign Investment Law where previously such law stated a general rule that Mexican investment of one-fifth percent was required. Now the new law states the reverse, i.e. all investments can be one hundred percent foreign except for a few listed exceptions. Consequently only the following items shall not be patentable including essentially biological processes for production, reproduction and propagation of plants and animals; biological and genetic material as found in nature; vegetable and animal varieties of all classes and species of vegetables, and the human body and the living organisms contained therein. This definition satisfies the requirements of NAFTA Article 1709 related to patents and exclusions from patentability. * * *

C. Trademarks, Commercial Slogans, and Commercial Names

1. Trademarks

The major NAFTA requirements related to trademarks focus on the application of certain provisions of the Paris Convention for the Protection of Industrial Property of 1967 focusing on the determination of the notoriety of a given trademark. The amended Mexican Industrial Property now provides, at Article 90, Section XV, pursuant to NAFTA and the Paris Convention for the Protection of Industrial Property, that in the determination of the notoriety of a trademark account shall be taken of the knowledge of the trademark in the relevant sector of the public. The same Article does not require that the reputation of the trademark extend beyond the sector of the public that normally deals with the relevant goods or services.

Other NAFTA requirements for trademarks focus on use as a prerequisite to registration and the system for trademark registration. NAFTA provides at Article 1708(3) that a signatory may make registrability dependent upon use, but that such actual use may not be a condition for filing an application for registration. In line with these provisions, the amended Industrial Property Law does not make use a prerequisite for registration. However, in line with NAFTA Article 1708, Mexico reserves the right to cancel the registration of a trademark if such has not been used for a period of three consecutive years after registration.

NAFTA also provides at Article 1708(4) general requirements for trademark registration systems requiring, among other things, that the applicant be given notice of the reasons for the refusal to register a trademark and a reasonable opportunity to respond to the notice. Thus, the Industrial Property Law now states, pursuant to Articles 122 and 122, that applicants shall be informed in writing of the failures of the application and shall have two months to correct errors and omissions and to submit arguments in support of the application. Upon the payment of the corresponding fees for the application, prospective applications shall have an additional two months to respond to the rejection.

2. Commercial Slogans

NAFTA does not contain detailed provisions concerning commercial slogans. However, the amendments to the Industrial Property Law provide expanded protection. Article 100 now states that a commercial slogan shall be phrases or sentences of places of businesses or companies related to commerce, industry, or the providing of services intended to be used to advertise such products or services to the public.

3. Commercial/Trade Names

NAFTA also does not directly discuss commercial/trade names. Mexican law provides that commercial/trade names shall be protected without registration. The user of a commercial/trade name may request its publication in the official IMPI publication the Gazette ("La Gaceta"), and such publication shall establish the presumption of good faith usage.

III. TRADE SECRETS AND CONFIDENTIALITY

A. NAFTA Requirements Related to Trade Secrets

NAFTA Article 1711 specifies that all signatories must implement laws to protect trade secrets. These laws must provide legal means for any person to prevent trade secrets from being disclosed to, acquired by, or used by others without the consent of the person lawfully in control of the information in a manner contrary to honest commercial practices. Trade secrets must meet the following requirements to be protected under NAFTA:

(1) The information must be secret in the sense that it is not, as a body or in the precise configuration and assembly of components, generally known among or readily accessible to persons that normally deal with the kind of information in question,

(2) The information has actual or potential commercial value because it is secret, and

(3) The person lawfully in control of the information has taken reasonable steps under the circumstances to keep it secret.

Moreover, NAFTA does not permit any signatory to limit the duration of protection for trade secrets provided that the above listed requirements are satisfied.

B. Current Mexican Protection of Trade Secrets

Based on these NAFTA requirements, Mexico substantially amended the trade secrets provisions of its Industrial Property Law. The current law, at Article 82, defines a trade secret as any information capable of industrial application maintained in confidence which may be useful to obtain or maintain a competitive advantage in the performance of economic activities as long as the owner has taken steps to protect the confidential nature of the information. An industrial secret must be related to the nature, characteristics, or purposes of a product, to methods or production processes, to means or forms of distribution of products, or to the providing of services.

The law further provides that information in the public domain shall not be considered an industrial secret, or any information that would be obvious to an expert or any information which must be disclosed pursuant to law or court order. However, confidential information shall not be considered part of the public domain if such information is disclosed to any authority for the purpose of obtaining permits, registrations, authorization, etc.

The owner of an industrial secret may transfer or license the same to a third party, and such third party is prohibited from transferring the information without the consent of the owner. Any person who, due to employment, charge, position, or in the practice of a profession or in a business relationship, has access to confidential information may not reveal the same without justified cause or without the authorization of the owner or the licensee.

In addition, any person or corporation hiring an employee who renders or has previously rendered services to a competitor to provide services as an advisor, consultant, or professional for the purposes of obtaining industrial secrets of the former employee shall be liable for the payment of damages.

IV.   ENFORCEMENT OF INDUSTRIAL PROPERTY RIGHTS IN MEXICO

A.   NAFTA Requirements Related to the Protection of Industrial Property

Chapter 17 of NAFTA contains various articles related to the enforcement of industrial property rights. The articles focus on general rights to be afforded to the parties, specific procedural and remedial aspects of civil and administrative procedure, the imposition of provisional measures, and criminal penalties and procedures. The numerous requirements contained in these provisions required Mexico to substantially amend its then-existing legal provisions related to the protection and enforcement of industrial property rights.

B.   Current Protection in Mexico of Industrial Property

1.   Patent Infringement

Patent infringement is defined as the manufacturing of patented products, the use of patented methods or processes, the reproduction of industrial models or designs without the consent of the owner or the respective licensee, and the offer for sale of a patented product or industrial model or design without the consent of the patentee provided the seller has knowledge that the product was manufactured without the necessary consent or license.

A patent infringement action cannot be commenced while a patent application is still pending, but once the patent is granted, liability against the infringer shall run from the date of filing.

The modified Industrial Property Law provides that infringing products may be seized pursuant to an order issued by the IMPI. The party bringing the seizure action must post a bond to guarantee the payment of damages to the defendant if the action filed is not successful.

The infringer is also civilly liable for damages and loss of income to the patent owner. The law provides that, at a minimum, the infringer should pay the owner damages equivalent to no less than forty percent of the retail price of the infringing products sold. If the infringer continues to sell pirated products after an administrative declaration of infringement, criminal liability may result.

In order to obtain an infringement declaration, the patent owner must file a petition with the IMPI along with all evidence necessary to prove infringement. The IMPI will then decide from a technical viewpoint whether or not infringement has taken place. Either party may appeal this decision, first at the district court level and later to the Court of Appeals.

2. *Trademark Infringement*

Trademark infringement is defined as the use, without authorization, of a trade or service mark for the same or for similar products or services and includes the use of an identical or confusingly similar mark, the sale of offer for sale of products bearing a registered trademark with knowledge that the products were manufactured without authorization from the trademark owner, and the offer for sale of products from which the original trademark has been changed, altered, or deleted.

Mexican law does not protect unregistered trademarks, but does consider that the first user of a trademark in Mexico or abroad has greater rights. Moreover, the owner of a "well-known" mark is protected under Mexican law pursuant to the above discussed modifications based on the Paris Convention and may request the removal from the trademark registry of any trademark which may be conflicting. The definition of a "well-known" mark was changed in the recent amendments. Now it is not necessary to prove that the mark was "well-known" to the general public, only that it was known to the relevant sector of the public using the product or service with which the mark is identified. The burden of proof to establish both such facts falls on the owner. No administrative action may be taken against possible infringers while a registration application is pending, but once a registration is granted, protection rights are protected retroactively to the date of filing.

If a third party has registered a trademark, such party would not have any liability derived from the use of such mark, even if the same mark is the property of another person or corporation, until the registration is removed from the registry.

Similar to the procedure provided for products that violate copyrights, infringing products may be seized pursuant to an order issued by the IMPI. The party bringing the seizure action generally must post a bond to guarantee the payment of damages to the defendant if infringement is not proven.

Infringement is considered to be an administrative infraction and is punishable with fines of up to 20,000 times the daily minimum wage, approximately $50,000.00 (U.S.) for the initial infringement and of up to 500 times the daily minimum wage, approximately $1,250.00 (U.S.) for each day that the infringement continues. In addition, the authorities have the right to close factories producing infringing products and stores selling the same.

The infringer is also liable to the owner for damages and loss of income. The law provides that the owner shall be entitled to no less than forty percent of the retail price of the infringing products. The IMPI may also order the seizure and destruction of infringing goods provided proof exists that such goods infringe trademark rights.

3. Other Protections Provided

The amended Industrial Property Law, at Article 213, also provides protection against a variety of other infringement actions. A few of the more prominent examples listed as administrative infractions are the manufacture or processing of products covered by a utility model or industrial design without the consent of the owner or respective licensee, the use of a registered commercial slogan or one confusingly similar without consent in order to advertise goods, services, or commercial establishments equal or similar to those for which the slogan is used and the use of a commercial/trade name or one confusingly similar without consent to cover an industrial, commercial, or service establishment in the same or similar line of business. The law provides that infringers of these provisions shall be subject to the same fines and liability described above for trademark infringement.

4. Possible Criminal Sanctions

In line with NAFTA, the modified Industrial Property Law contains possible criminal sanctions to be used against infringers. The following actions, among others, are considered crimes: the continuation of infringement after a final resolution regarding such has been issued, the counterfeit of marks in a fraudulent manner on a commercial scale, and the disclosure or utilization of an industrial secret after receiving notice of the confidentiality of the information.

Infringers found guilty of violating these provisions may be sentenced to prison for terms ranging from two to six years. In addition, criminal offenders are fined. The fine ranges from 100 to 10,000 times the daily minimum wage, approximately $260.00 (U.S.) to $26,000.00 (U.S.). * * *

The Mexican Industrial Property law described in the above article was a substantial departure from prior Mexican law. The U.S. had criticized Mexico in earlier years for lax protection of intellectual property owned by foreigners. It was categorized as a country that permitted counterfeiting and piracy of IPRs. The negotiation of NAFTA also brought about this new legislation covering IPRs. The law is provides substantial protection to foreign IPR owners. However, there is continuing doubt on the enforcement of the rights granted under the law.

b. The U.S. Legal System

The United States is a substantial exporter of intellectual property. It has an impressive array of federal and state rules that effectively protect the ownership of IPRs within the U.S. border. Federal law offers protection for patents 35 U.S.C.A. § 101 *et. seq.*, Copyrights 17 U.S.C.A.

101 *et. seq.*, and Trademarks 15 U.S.C.A. § 1127. In addition, State laws offer protections for trademarks, trade names, and trade secrets. Intellectual property falling into the category of knowhow is generally protected through contract or tort law. The vast amount of intellectual property protection is most effective for violations of intellectual property rights occurring within the U.S.

However, the protection of IPRs in the United States, while formidable, is not as helpful in an international context because of the problems associated with the extra-territorial application of U.S. law. The problem of piracy and counterfeiting occurring outside the U.S. border has also been of great concern. The U.S. effort has been two-fold—keep infringing property from entering into the U.S. and by advocating the strengthening of intellectual property rights of host countries especially when they are a developing country.

In the case of the importation of infringing goods, the United States legal system provides for a private cause of action for infringing on patents and trademarks. The remedies include the recovery of money damages and injunctive relief. The problem with these remedies is that a foreign counterfeiter or pirate is not easily found. Therefore, receiving an award for money damages is not very useful. Furthermore, obtaining an injunction on one company at one location would not prevent them from merely changing names and or location. To assist the U.S. IPR owner federal statutory law provides relief with a focus on the offending products.

Under the Unfair Practices in Import Trade, 19 U.S.C. § 1337 (_____), the International Trade Commission has the authority to order the seizure and exclusion of articles from entering into the U.S. when those articles infringe on valid U.S. patents, trademarks, or copy rights. Thus the IPR owner can prevent the entry of the product into the U.S. The United States Customs Service handles the actual seizure and exclusion of the goods. U.S. trading partners have criticized this statutory rule. They allege that the statute discriminates against foreign produced goods. The European Community filed a complaint against the U.S. As a result, a GATT panel criticized the U.S. statutory formulation. Notwithstanding the criticism, the statute continues in effect. The federal statutory laws used in preventing the entry of offending goods from entering the country are discussed in Chapter 7, infra.

The other major effort in eradicating counterfeiting and piracy is to convince the offending countries to stop allowing this activity within its borders. Indeed the linchpin of U.S. trade policy has been to give trade benefits in return for a certain type of behavior by the foreign country. One such legislation is the so-called *Section 301* proceedings which is codified in 19 USC § 2411 and excerpted below which highlights the carrot and stick approach used by the U.S.

UNITED STATES CODE ANNOTATED
TITLE 19. CUSTOMS DUTIES

Section 2411

§ 2411.   Actions by United States Trade Representative

(a) Mandatory action

(1) If the United States Trade Representative determines under * * * (A) the rights of the United States under any trade agreement are being denied; or (B) an act, policy, or practice of a foreign country-(I) violates, or is inconsistent with, the provisions of, or otherwise denies benefits to the United States under, any trade agreement, or (ii) is unjustifiable and burdens or restricts United States commerce; the Trade Representative shall take action authorized in subsection (c) of this section subject to the specific direction, if any, of the President regarding any such action, and shall take all other appropriate and feasible action within the power of the President that the President may direct the Trade Representative to take under this subsection, to enforce such rights or to obtain the elimination of such act, policy, or practice. Actions may be taken that are within the power of the President with respect to trade in any goods or services, or with respect to any other area of pertinent relations with the foreign country. * * *

(2) The Trade Representative is not required to take action under paragraph (1) in any case in which * * * the Trade Representative finds that—(I) the foreign country is taking satisfactory measures to grant the rights of the United States under a trade agreement, (ii) the foreign country has—(I) agreed to eliminate or phase out the act, policy, or practice, or (II) agreed to an imminent solution to the burden or restriction on united States commerce that is satisfactory to the Trade Representative * * *

(b) Discretionary action

If the Trade Representative determines under section 2414(a)(1) of this title that—(1) an act, policy, or practice of a foreign country is unreasonable or discriminatory and burdens or restricts United States commerce, and (2) action by the United States is appropriate, the Trade Representative shall take all appropriate and feasible action authorized under subsection (c) of this section, subject to the specific direction, if any, of the President regarding any such action, and all other appropriate and feasible action within the power of the President that the President may direct the Trade Representative to take under this subsection, to obtain the elimination of that act, policy, or practice. Actions may be taken that are within the power of the President with respect to trade in any goods or services, or with respect to any other area of pertinent relations with the foreign country.

(c) Scope of authority

(1) For purposes of carrying out the provisions of subsection (a) or (b) of this section, the Trade Representative is authorized to—(A) suspend, withdraw, or prevent the application of, benefits of trade agreement concessions to carry out a trade agreement with the foreign country referred to in such subsection; (B) impose duties or other import restrictions on the goods of, and, notwithstanding any other provision of law, fees or restrictions on the services of, such foreign country for such time as the Trade Representative determines appropriate * * *

(d) Definitions and special rules

For purposes of this chapter * * * Acts, policies, and practices that are unreasonable include, but are not limited to, any act, policy, or practice, * * * which * * * denies * * * provision of adequate and effective protection of intellectual property rights * * *

The statute gives authority to the U.S. Trade Representative (USTR), subject to the specific direction of the President, to suspend or withdraw treaty benefits to offending countries and/or to impose duties or other import restrictions on products proceeding from offending countries. The section also permits the USTR to enter into binding agreements with the foreign country to eliminate the offending action. Although general in scope, *Section 301* is often used to compel foreign countries, especially developing countries, to establish a legal framework for the protection of intellectual property.

The USTR action is either mandated or discretionary depending on the egregiousness of the violation. The USTR action is mandated in those cases where the act, policy, or practice of the foreign country violates a trade agreement entered into with the United States. Mandatory action is also required when the action is unjustifiable and burdens or restricts United States commerce. Under the statute, the term 'unjustifiable' essentially means the violation of a trade agreement. Therefore, the mandatory action is required when there is a violation of an existing trade agreement.

In cases where the action by the foreign country is unreasonable or discriminatory and burdens or restricts United States commerce, the USTR may at her discretion, take the action indicated above. The statute[2] gives a long list of actions that can be unreasonable or discriminatory. The list ranges from the protection of workers and includes the failure to provide adequate protection to IPR owners and the denial of national or most favored nation treatment to U.S. nationals.

The prospects for Delta's not losing its intellectual property to counterfeiting or piracy has never been stronger in Mexico. Delta can

2.   19 U.S.C. 2411(d)(3) & (5)(1999).

avail itself of the protections under the TRIPS Agreement, the NAFTA, Mexican Domestic law, and if applicable U.S. law. Note that in the introductory sections of the International Licensing Agreement, Delta states that it owns certain patents, trademarks, and trade secrets under the laws of the United States, Mexico, and applicable international law. This is the first step—protect the IPR in all of the legal systems involved. This offers the maximum protection.

4. *Protecting the Value of the Intellectual Property Right*

The royalties charged by the licensor is the measure of the value of the IPR. Therefore, anything that can reduce the royalty received will impact the value. The principal mechanism for protecting the value of the IPR is through the International Licensing Agreement. The following provides an analysis of the specific articles.

a. *Article 1—The Grant of License*

This is essentially a business decision. The Licensee should be capable of manufacturing and selling the product made under license. The Licensee should have the operational and financial wherewithal to reach the entire domestic market. If it were unable to do so, the Net Sales figure would not be as high as it could. Since royalties are charged on Net Sales, the royalty or value of the IPR is lessened. The Licensor should ensure that the Licensee is capable of effectively reaching the domestic market. The Agreement could also contain a clause that a breach will occur if the Licensee does not reach a stated percentage of the market in a given period of time.

b. *Article 2—Ownership of Property and Improvements*

This article binds the Licensee to acknowledge that Licensor is the owner of the IPR. Obligating the Licensee under contract to respect the Licensor's ownership of the IPR does not minimize the importance of seeking ownership protection under international and domestic legal protection. It is simply additional protection. The concept of asserting ownership through contract is fairly non-controversial. It is also accepted that improvements made by Licensor should belong to the Licensor.

A more controversial aspect of intellectual property deals with the improvements made to the IPR by the Licensee. Note in Article 2 C. the agreement reads "Licensee agrees that any improvements in the patent, trademark, trade secrets, or know how whether developed by Licensor or Licensee, shall be the exclusive property of the Licensor." This is known as a "grant back" provision and is controversial.

Licensees and the governments of developing countries have looked at grant back provisions very unfavorably. Their idea is that improvements should belong to the person that developed them. This can cause the IPR owner problems. The issue is one of negotiation between the Licensor and Licensee. Overcoming the reluctance of the host country government is more problematic. This is especially true when the host country rules require that the license agreement be registered. In those cases grant back provisions could be the basis for denying the registration of the agreement. The recent modifications in Mexico's industrial property laws removed the registration requirement.

c. Article 3—Royalty and Payment

In an international licensing scenario there are several players—the Licensor, the government of the Licensor, the Licensee, and the government of the Licensee. The Licensor typically is from a developed country. The Licensee oftentimes comes from a developing country. The government of the Licensor is concerned with its national security interests, the IPR protection of its nationals, and collecting the appropriate tax on the royalty transaction. The Licensor, Licensee, and developing host government are concerned with the royalty rate and payment conditions.

The Licensor wants to set the highest royalty paid in U.S. dollars. The license agreement states in pertinent part: Article 3A. & C. "Licensee shall pay to Licensor ... a royalty of eight percent (8%) ... in U.S. dollars." The Licensee and host government would rather pay the lowest royalty in host country currency. As in the grant back provision issue the government may win if the agreement must be registered. Generally the older and simpler the technology, the more the downward pressure on the royalty figure. If the technology is new and can have a high labor effect the Licensor will be in a stronger bargaining position to maintain a high royalty rate.

An issue that is related to the setting of the royalty is the payment. The Licensor wants to get paid in hard currency—U.S. dollars. If payment is made in soft currency it must still be converted into hard currency. The conversion into hard currency can create a loss especially if the soft currency is in a period of devaluation. The payment in hard currency may not be possible if the host country has set currency controls. Again the negotiation with the host revolves around the technology in question and the government's willingness to allow the payment in U.S. dollars.

d. Article 4—Duration and Termination

Typically the Licensor wants a relatively short term. If the business arrangement is a success the Licensor can renegotiate a higher royalty rate sooner or if the market is large and lucrative enough the Licensor may want to establish a foreign direct investment and manufacture its own product and thus cut out the Licensee's profit. In the case where the Licensee is not a god fit, a shorter term allows for the removal of the Licensee sooner. The Licensee and host country government will usually negotiate for a longer term for the very reasons the Licensor wants a shorter term. The duration issue is one of negotiation.

The agreement should also deal with post termination events. Article 4 F states in pertinent part "Upon termination of this Agreement, Licensee agrees to deliver to Licensor any and all documents, drawings, data or communication relating to the patent, trademark, and trade secrets licensed herein. It also agrees to not exploit, sell or use any knowledge gained under this License Agreement or in its relationship with Licensor." The real solution here is in finding the appropriate Licensee in the first place.

SECTION 4.3   THE INTERNATIONAL SALE OF GOODS AND SERVICES

A.   THE INTERNATIONAL SALE OF GOODS

1.   *Contract Formation*

The international sale of goods and services is usually simpler than the foreign direct investment and transfer of technology. However, the international sale of goods and services is generally more complex than a purely domestic sale transaction. The physical transfer of products across national borders involves two governments and three sets of rules—the domestic system of the exporting country, the domestic system of the importing country and applicable international law. In the purely domestic sale only one set of rules are involved.

Recall in the hypothetical Delta's Division I. Delta's oldest division—Division I–manufactures and sells "Blow Out Preventers" (BOP). The BOP is a safety device essential in offshore drilling activities. It is a high-tech device covered by an U.S. patent. It has a very good reputation for reliability and ease of operation. In spite of its high cost it is the most popular brand worldwide. Delta is currently operating below capacity in Division I because of decreased domestic demand. Several potential purchasers in Mexico, Venezuela, Vietnam, and the Peoples Republic of China have approached Delta.

The buyers in Mexico and Venezuela are private companies while those in Vietnam and China are governmental entities. The BOP is of such high demand in these countries that there are no import restrictions. Delta is interested in making these sales. The threshold question is whether the sale can be made. The facts state that the countries have removed the import restrictions. However, the U.S. may have export restrictions that can prevent the sale. These rules are discussed in Chapter 7, infra.

The next hurdle is the business risk. Delta is concerned with getting paid on the sale while the buyer simply wants to receive the product under the conditions and at the bargained price. Delta could minimize its risk by consummating the sales transaction in the U.S. Depending on its bargaining power, the foreign buyer may be compelled to come to Delta's place of business and assume the responsibility to take the product home. Conversely, competition and the realities of the marketplace may oblige Delta to consummate the sales transaction in the buyer's home country. The business community has addressed this risk by developing the documentary transaction financed with a letter of credit. This procedure is discussed in Chapter 5, infra.

These Materials deal with the beginning point for Delta—negotiating the contract for the international sale of goods (CISG). The best approach is for the parties to meet face to face together with their lawyers. At this meeting all of the issues, including the difficult ones, are negotiated and the agreement memorialized in writing. Delta and the buyer need to have a firm grasp on the business issues that need to be identified, negotiated, and resolved. The lawyer's job is to ensure that the client's choices are expressed and her interests protected in the contract.

Contract negotiations are difficult in domestic transactions. They are even more difficult in international transactions. The obstacles in completing international transactions—language, culture, differences in currency, distance between parties, and diverse legal and political systems—all work to intensify the problems associated with contract negotiations and formation. The parties should keep in mind that the contract is the underlying agreement that gives rise to the rights and benefits of the parties in the international business transaction. It should accurately, clearly, and completely describe the rights and obligations of the parties.

The parties should reach agreement on price, quantity, delivery terms, insurance, costs, and other business/economic aspects of the transaction. These issues include but are not limited to payment, delivery, and the transfer of risk of loss. Questions like—what constitutes acceptance or rejection? What warranties are being given? What is the relationship between the parties? What party is responsible for obtaining the export and import permits? Who is to hire the Carrier? Who is to purchase insurance? What law will govern the contract? These questions and those of similar import need to be addressed in the CISG.

The lawyer's role is in reducing to writing the wishes of her client. Sometimes lawyers confuse their roles. Business uncertainties are seen as drafting challenges, problem areas that need to be resolved in her client's favor through deft word selection. To be sure, skillful and clear drafting of the agreement is essential. However, the lawyer is trained to look at life in terms of problems. The lawyer, in a quest for reducing risk and liability to the client, oftentimes imagines worst case scenarios that have very little real probability of occurring. The seasoned executive will use the lawyer's advice as a mechanism to realize the business goals, rather than as a replacement for their business judgment. The effective lawyer helps put the client's thoughts into words in the agreement. This is not to say the lawyer should be a robot who merely reduces the client's thoughts to words.

A thoughtful analysis reveals different areas where the lawyer and the client can make a good team. One prime area is in assisting the client in making a choice of law decision. All properly drafted contracts should have a choice of law provision. The lawyer can provide an invaluable service to the client by analyzing the choice of law question without assuming that the client's home jurisdiction will always be the best. It is said that in a multitude of counselors there is wisdom. In this context, the lawyer would be wise to seek the advice of foreign local counsel to evaluate the client's rights when applying foreign law.

Each party has a natural tendency to choose their own country for jurisdiction and venue. This may not always be the best for the client. U.S. contracting parties and their lawyers frequently take a very hard negotiating position towards using U.S. law and courts for jurisdiction and venue, even if the contract has no operational nexus to the U.S. The position is borne out of distrust for foreign legal systems. This is particularly true in the Western Hemisphere towards Latin American countries. However, this position may create difficulties.

There is much resentment by Latin American business interests and their legal advisors towards U.S. attorneys on this issue. Latin Americans are as distrustful of the U.S. system of courts and justice as their U.S. counterparts are of Latin America's. But beyond these somewhat irrational fears, the choice of law and venue should be a reasoned one, taking into account the realities of the business relationship. The lawyer can make or break a deal in this situation. Thus, intractable positions on the choice of law issue can taint other important points in the negotiation. The result can be no deal and lost profits.

In making the choice of law decision, it may be useful to have an idea on contract formation in civil law countries and Mexico in particular. The materials that follow give a thumbnail sketch of contracting principles found in Mexico. They focus on contract formalities and the role of the civil law notary highlighting the differences between the civil and common law systems.

CONTRACTING IN MEXICO: A LEGAL AND PRACTICAL GUIDE TO NEGOTIATING AND DRAFTING

Rona R. Mears

24 St. Mary's L.J. 737, 740–754 (1993).

C.   Basic Principles of Contracting in Mexico

Certain fundamental principles of commercial contracting in Mexico apply to all types of commercial contracts, regardless of the subject matter of the contract. The following discussion surveys several fundamental elements of contracting in Mexico.

1.   *Freedom of Contracting*

The Commercial Code explicitly recognizes the freedom of two parties to negotiate and reach an agreement and to decide independently their unique set of obligations and privileges under the negotiated arrangement. * * *

This fundamental principle validates the private contract that arises between the parties, and this principle provides the basic matrix for contractual obligations in Mexico, as it does in the United States and in most jurisdictions throughout the world. * * *

2. *Existence and Elements of a Contract* * * *

The two elements required for the existence of a contract under the Civil Code are the following: (1) consent or the act of agreement by the parties regarding the contract; and (2) an object for the contract that may be either the act that the obligor must perform, or must not perform, or the thing to be given by the obligor under the contract terms. Without these two elements, the contract does not exist, or, more precisely, has never been created.

3. *Validity and the Form of a Contract*

In principle, commercial contracts may be either oral or written, provided that the elements required for formation of the contract are present. Two exceptions exist, however, to this basic rule: (1) the Commercial Code (or in certain instances, other Mexican laws) may require some types of contracts to be in writing or memorialized in some particular form; and (2) laws of certain foreign countries may require that contracts entered into in that country be in writing or in some particular form. In both such situations, the form required is essential under Mexican law; without the necessary form, the contracts are void.

* * *

D. PROCEDURAL FORMALITIES AND APPLICABLE LAW

Notwithstanding the general rule that contracts do not require a particular form to be deemed valid, numerous types of contracts must be in writing and must follow specified procedural formalities. The importance of identifying the type of contract under consideration, and determining whether writing and other formalities are required, cannot be overemphasized. Each contract should be reviewed on an individual basis to make this assessment. This review should occur early in the planning and negotiation process with the help of Mexican legal counsel.

1. *Writing*

* * *

The most frequently encountered procedural formality is the requirement that a contract be in written form. As mentioned above, the general principles and statutory provisions regarding commercial contracts in Mexico do not require a writing for a contract to be valid, but there are some contracts that must be in writing.

* * *

The law applicable to determine the form and procedural formalities of certain contracts might be located in any one of several sources: the Commercial Code, the Civil Code, the various Civil Codes of the states, or the subject-specific statutes that govern the type of contract or transaction to which the agreement relates.

* * *

Regardless of the statutory requirements, it is always advisable that parties put their agreement in writing in order to clarify their obligations and to provide evidence at a later time of the terms of their agreement.

2. *Registry*

Certain contracts must be recorded in a public registry. The purpose of such recordation is to make the contract enforceable against third parties and to make available to the public an accessible compilation of facts, actions, agreements, and other legal matters related to a company's operations. Contracts may be valid and effective between the contracting parties, but these contracts will not be effective as to third parties [unless] properly recorded.

* * *

3. *Public Deeds*

Some contracts must be in the form of public deeds. The public deed is a highly formalized document with signatory and notarization requirements that must be followed exactly. To ensure that proper procedures are followed, it is essential to distinguish those contracts that must be public deeds from those that must simply be in writing.

The term "public deed" refers to two documents: (1) the original document as it is fully written in the Notary Public's book of legal acts—called a Protocol—which contains legal acts that have been granted or verified before the Notary Public, and (2) the original document or contract that is operative between the parties, in addition to a brief precis of the agreement recorded in the Notary Public's book. The Notary Public must follow strict requirements in recording documents in the Protocol, in maintaining the Protocol, and in retiring the Protocol to the Public Registry once it is complete.

The grant of a public deed before the Notary Public includes numerous formalities: signatures on each page by both the parties and the Notary Public; the seal of the Notary Public; the statement of detailed identification information about the parties, including date and place of birth, marital status, occupation, and the usual requirements of name and domicile. In addition, agents must prove their authority to represent parties, and the parties must translate foreign language documents into Spanish. A translator must be present when there are parties who do not speak Spanish. The types of contracts that must be in the form of public deeds include corporate formation documents, purchases and sales of real estate, contracts that transfer or create rights in real estate such as mortgages, ship and aircraft purchase/sale contracts, and general powers of attorney or more specific powers of attorney relating to matters that must be finalized by public deed.

* * *

6. Foreign Contract Formalities and Legalization

Contracts created in foreign countries may require certain formalities to be valid if the law of that foreign jurisdiction requires that the contract be in writing, take a certain form, or be validated by certain formalities. In such cases, even though the form or formality may not be required in Mexico, such form must be followed as required in the foreign country, or it will not be valid under Mexican law. As a result, for United States contracts to be effective in Mexico, they must comply with any United States legal requirements regarding form or validity, as well as any requirements under Mexican law.

Private parties who enter into a contract outside Mexico do not generally need to provide any further authentication for the contract to be valid in Mexico, unless it is a type of contract that either must be recorded in a Public Registry or must be registered or approved because of the particular subject matter of the contract. If recordation in a Public Registry is required, then, like comparable Mexican contracts, the parties' signatures must be notarized. The notarization must then be legalized.

Legalization, sometimes called "consularization," is a process of signature authentication required in many countries of the world, including Mexico. In the case of a private contract that must be recorded at a Mexican Public Registry, legalization may include several steps: (1) the signature of the Notary Public who certified the parties' signatures must be authenticated as valid by the local county clerk where the Notary Public is located; (2) the signature of the county clerk must be authenticated by the Secretary of State; (3) the signature of the Secretary of State must be validated by the Mexican Consul, in the United States, that has jurisdiction over the area in which the Notary is located; and (4) authentication by the Ministry of Foreign Relations in Mexico may also be required.

As complex as this process already seems, it is further complicated by the fact that various Mexican consulates throughout the United States are not consistent in requiring all the steps listed above. Some consulates require only one or two of the intermediary authentications, whereas other consulates require all of the authentications. Legalization at the Mexico Embassy in Washington, D.C. requires the additional step of certification of the United States Secretary of State. Detailed instructions should be obtained in the applicable Mexican consulate stating exactly which steps are required for legalization.

Legalization may also be required for authentication of documents issued by foreign authorities. An example of such a document is a corporate certificate of good standing issued by a Secretary of State. This document is often needed as a corollary document to a contractual arrangement. In matters such as the establishment of a branch in Mexico of a United States corporation, numerous organizational documents must be legalized, resulting in an often time-consuming and tedious process. Because of the strict formalities that Mexico requires for a power of attorney, powers of attorney drafted and executed outside Mexico, but granted to be effective within Mexico, must be drafted, signed, notarized, and legalized with particular care, especially if the powers are to be used in a lawsuit in a Mexican court.

* * *

The *Mears* article provides a good overview of contracting principles under the Mexican legal system. The rest of Latin America, while not a mirror image of Mexico, generally follows the same rules since they trace their roots to the civil law system. Despite the differences, common law and civil law countries have many similarities regarding substantive contract issues such as offer, acceptance, legality of subject matter, and legal capacity of contracting parties.

The differences arise more from the procedures involved in entering into an enforceable contract especially in the role of the civil law notary. See Sections 1.1 and 3.4, supra for a discussion of this quasi public official and his counterpart the *Corredor Público* or Commercial Broker. Another important practical difference between the civil and common law beyond the role of the notary is in contract drafting.

The common law, focusing on precedent and case law, makes it important to cover as many eventualities as possible in the contract. Common law lawyers focus on the *"What Ifs"* of commercial relations. In civil law jurisdictions, the parties are more willing to allow the Code to deal with unforeseen events. This difference manifests itself in the size of the contract. It is not uncommon to find a complex common law contract to be in excess of fifty pages where a comparable civil law contract may be a two or three page document. One system is not necessarily better than the other, a general rule is that in the civil law system there is greater flexibility, in the common law greater certainty when the unforeseen event is included in the contract.

Another important distinction between civil and common law contracting is the requisite formalities associated with contract formation. The Code may specify how the contract is to be executed (e.g. signing every page, not only the last page). If one does not follow the Code requirements the contract is not valid. These contract formation rules also may include the intervention of a civil law notary. This can becomes problematic in the case of contracts entered into in a common law jurisdiction where a U.S. notary has signed. If the contract has to be registered in a civil law country with civil law notarial involvement, the common law notary will not suffice.

2. *The Choice of Law Clause*

Understanding the nuances of contract formation in civil law countries and its differences with common law contract principles is very important in negotiating and drafting enforceable contracts. Now the lawyer can start to make an informed decision on what jurisdiction should govern the contract. As mentioned above, a face to face meeting between the parties which results in one document with all of the salient provisions in the contract including a choice of law provision made is the optimum method to obtain an agreement.

In this perfect world, the contracting parties and their counsel meet in one place to iron out all of the substantive business issues including the choice of law issue. Unfortunately, business pressures and large distances separating the parties rarely allow the luxury of face to face meetings between the parties themselves, let alone bringing all of their lawyers. Therefore, a choice of law clause may not be inserted. The contract formation issues with no choice of law clause become even more complex.

Absent a choice of law clause, the domestic choice of law rules must be analyzed to determine what legal system will apply. For example, assume you have a California seller and Mexican buyer. The writings between the parties does not contain a choice of law provision. What law is used to determine the existence of a contract? A California court could decide that California law applies and that venue is proper in California. It could also decide that Mexican law applies but that venue lies in California or that Mexican law applies and that venue is proper in Mexico.

On the other hand, the Mexican court could decide that California law applies and that proper venue is in California. It could rule that Mexican law applies but venue lies in California or that Mexican law applies and that venue is proper in Mexico. As can be seen from the various alternatives illustrated by the example, determining what applicable law has many moving parts that may or may not come together. Couple this with language and cultural differences and the resulting array of alternatives become a Gordian knot.

The array of scenarios on determining the applicable legal system to a contract without a choice of law clause has resulted in international efforts at harmonizing the choice of law rules. The European Community long ago realized that harmonizing choice of law rules giving private parties flexible rules to make choices of law could lead to the free flow of goods, services, and capital leading toward economic integration. The Americas have lagged far behind the flexible, progressive European rules. Recently, however, there has been some good progress made in establishing a framework for international choice of law rules. As in the foreign investment area, changes have been possible by the major shift in attitude of the Latin American countries.

CONTRACT CHOICE OF LAW IN THE AMERICAS

Friedrich K. Juenger

45 Am. J. Comp. L. 195 (1997).

I.   Historical Evolution: A Brief Comparative Overview

In the Americas, the question of what law applies to contracts that cross national frontiers may charitably be described as unsettled. Compared to the Treatment of the subject in European private international law, on this Continent the doctrinal, legislative and judicial responses to the problem were, until fairly recently, seriously underdeveloped.

* * *

C.   Europe

* * * Europe has long recognized progressive choice-of-law approaches that accord private parties the freedom to select the law they wish and, if the parties fail to make a choice, use flexible instead of rigid connecting factors. * * *

Once Western European nations united under the umbrella of what is now called the European Union, they felt a need for conflict of laws conventions, which were thought to promote regional integration. Having experienced a resounding success with codifying rules of international civil procedure in the Brussels Convention on Jurisdiction and the Enforcement of Judgments in Civil and Commercial Matters, these countries also began to tackle choice of law. Since the private international law rules on contracts of the European Union's member states were fairly similar, it appeared logical to start with this subject, which also commended itself because of its commercial importance. These efforts produced the 1980 Rome Convention on the Law Applicable to Contractual Obligations.

* * *

III. THE MEXICO CITY CONVENTION

A. *A New Inter–American Approach to Contract Choice of Law*

As noted earlier, on this Continent approaches to the problems posed to international trade and commerce by the diversity of national laws progressed at a slower pace than in Europe. However, in the Western Hemisphere as well awareness of the fact that legal rules must take into account the realities of a modern world market has prompted a reassessment of private international law tenets. Hence, there were good reasons for putting contract choice of law on the agenda of the Fifth Inter–American Specialized Conference on Private International Law, which dealt with the topic, was chaired by Dr. Parra-Aranguren from Venezuela. The Committee's deliberations focused on a draft prepared by the Inter–American Juridical Committee, which had been revised at a meeting of experts under the auspices of the National Center for International Trade in Tucson, Arizona.

B. *Party Autonomy*

The Inter–American Juridical Committee's draft was largely based on the Rome Convention, a critical analysis of whose virtues and defects helped Committee No. 1 formulate its own set of inter-American choice-of-law rules. Following the European example, the Mexico City Convention made party autonomy the lodestar of inter-American contract choice of law. This fundamental decision—one hopes—will end, once and for all, the sterile academic discussion of whether and how this principle can be reconciled with the classical multilateral choice-of-law system (it cannot). Like its European counterpart, the Mexico City Convention generously endorses the parties' freedom of choice. Article 7(1) allows them to select a neutral law, one that has no contacts whatsoever with their contract. It also condones contractual depecage and permits the parties to change their initial choice (or non-choice) of the applicable law by a subsequent agreement.

Departing from the European model, the Mexico City Convention does not enumerate specific categories of protective laws that cannot be stipulated away by means of a choice-of-law clause. Instead of setting forth narrowly circumscribed choice-of-law privileges for various categories of weaker parties, as the Rome Convention does, article 11 of the Mexico City Convention relies on a general clause that is broad enough to safeguard the protection of consumers and employees, as well as other parties, against over-reaching by the enterprises with which they deal. Allowing the decisionmaker to invoke forum as well as foreign "rules of immediate application" (or, as the Convention calls them, "rules of public policy"), which take precedence over the stipulated law, sufficiently protects these weaker parties against abuses of superior bargaining power.

In marked contrast to the Rome Convention, the Mexico City Convention allows the contracting parties to choose a non-national law, such as the lex mercatoria or its codified version, the UNIDROIT Principles of International Commercial Contracts. Such freedom of choice is better attuned to modern commercial realities than the Rome Convention's strangely retrogressive insistence on limiting the parties' selection to positive laws. Why should individuals or enterprises who choose to arbitrate their differences by allowed to enjoy the benefit of selecting a body of rules, drafted by a distinguished group of experts, which are specifically designed to meet the needs of international transactions, whereas parties who choose to litigate are relegated to national laws? It is certainly difficult to understand what interests (other than those of a doctrinal nature) would be served by impeding the parties from denationalizing their agreement in this fashion.

C. Law Governing in the Absence of a Contractual Choice

The Mexico City Convention's provisions on the law governing in the absence of an effective choice by the parties also differ from those of its European counterpart. Both conventions rely on a "grouping-of-contacts" test that invokes the law having "the closes connection" with the contract. But, once again, the Mexico City Convention has a definite teleological bent. First of all, following a tradition dating back to Dumoulin's notion of a pactum tacitum, article 9(2) of the Mexico City Convention expressly allows the decisionmaker to look at subjective as well as objective factors. Thus, this provision grants the judge or arbitrator a wider leeway of discretion than the Rome Convention does, especially in the event that the parties were unrepresented (or poorly represented) by counsel and failed to make the selection they ought to have made. It also favors the law that best effectuates the contracting parties' objectives. And since they could hardly have intended to enter into an invalid contract, this provision amounts to a rule of validation.

Secondly, the drafters deliberately rejected the notion of further objectifying the choice of the applicable law by means of a "characteristic performance" test. During the deliberations in Mexico City it became clear that this Gordon knot-cutter does not represent sound policy. In many instances it is doubtful which particular performance is the characteristic one, as is true, e.g., in the case of barter transactions, contracts with publishers and distributorship agreements. Moreover, in complex situations (as, for instance, corporate acquisitions or turnkey projects) the simplistic "solution" of exalting one performance over another as the "most characteristic" does not work.

Worse yet, this key concept of the Rome Convention confers a capricious choice-of-law privilege by invoking the home-state law of those who enjoy particular expertise because they habitually supply goods and services in international transactions.

Yet, the Mexico City Convention does not rely exclusively on the "closest connection" test. Rather article 9(1) second sentence, permits the decisionmaker, in determining with which jurisdiction a contract is most closely connected, to take into amount "general principles of international commercial law recognized by international organizations." This formula can of course be faulted for jumbling together wholly incompatible notions-the traditional "seat-of-the-relationship" ideal and the new law merchant. The incongruous admixture of discordant elements reflects a compromise that became necessary upon the rejection of the American delegation's proposal to apply the UNIDROIT Principles in the absence of a valid designation of the applicable law. Article 9 has it now stands signals to the decisionmaker the need to select that law which best accords with substantial justice and the exigencies of international commerce. Sophisticated courts and arbitrators can be expected to prefer principles elaborated by a prestigious international group of experts to idiosyncratic national rules. The parties certainly have no reason to complain if their failure to agree on the law they wish to govern invokes a law of superior quality.

* * *

The Inter–American Convention came into force at the international level on March 17, 1994, when it was approved by the contracting states. Harmonizing choice of law issues alleviates the confusion and uncertainty in contract formation. The Inter–American Convention represents a consensus of the nineteen countries that attended the Mexico City conference. The U.S., Canada, and seventeen Latin American countries represent both the civil and common law systems.

The Convention contains significant concessions by Latin American countries. For example, Article 7 specifically allows the parties to choose the applicable law. The right to choose applicable law in private contracts, known as party autonomy, was not allowed in many Latin American jurisdictions. Article 7 of the Inter–American Convention clearly and succinctly permits party autonomy. Article 9 deals with choice of law when the parties have not made a choice of law by providing that the law of the State with which it has the closest ties shall govern the contract. Paragraph 2 of Article 9 provides that the Court will take into account all objective and subjective elements of the contract to make this determination. It shall also take into account the general principles of international commercial law recognized by international organizations. This was another major concession for many Latin American countries. Up to that time, developing countries had been loath to preempt their domestic law in favor of rules promulgated by international organizations.

Remember that the Inter–American Convention will only point to the legal system that applies. If the international rules establish that U.S. applies then you look to the rules found under U.S. law. In the scenario described above—a California seller and Mexican buyer—What if the international rules establishes that Mexico is the appropriate jurisdiction? The materials on the Mexican legal system highlight the differences in the procedural aspects of contract formation. It also addresses the differences in formality and length of contracts in the common and civil law systems. There are also quite a number of differences in the substantive law of contract formation.

3. *International Substantive Contract Formation Rules*

a. The United Nations Convention on Contracts for the International Sale of Goods

While streamlining and harmonizing the rules in determining the choice of law is useful, it does not affect the problem of applying foreign substantive law, especially if the foreign law is radically different from the home jurisdiction. Countries have long recognized a need for harmonizing substantive contract law. There have been efforts by countries to draft harmonized model laws at the domestic level. This type of harmonization attempts to make domestic laws the same. This is akin to the Uniform Commercial Code and Model Business Corporation Act efforts in the U.S. This system, however, is understandably slow since it requires action by each individual country.

On an international basis, legal harmonization is most effective through international agreements. One area where there have been important strides in harmonizing substantive contract law is in the contract for the international sale of goods. The *United Nations Commission on International Transaction Law (UNCITRAL)* for many years labored to produce an international convention that would harmonize substantive legal rules on the formation of contracts for the international sale of goods. The *UNCITRAL* was successful in its efforts.

In 1988, the *United Nations Convention on Contracts for the International Sale of Goods* (hereafter, the UNCISG) came into force. The UNCISG is an effort to provide substantive international law on contract formation issues, bridging the gap between civil law and common law jurisdictions. In the Western Hemisphere the U.S., Argentina, Canada, Chile, Ecuador, Mexico, and Venezuela are signatory countries. These are some selected articles of the convention and the UCC § 2–207.

THE U.N. CONVENTION ON CONTRACTS
FOR THE INTERNATIONAL SALE OF GOODS

Article 1

(1) This Convention applies to contracts of sale of goods between parties whose places of business are in different States:

(a) When the States are Contracting States; or

(b) When the rules of private international law lead to the application of the law of a Contracting State.

(2) The fact that the parties have their places of business in different States is to be disregarded whenever this fact does not appear either from the contract or from any dealings between, or from information disclosed by, the parties at any time before or at the conclusion of the contract.

(3) Neither the nationality of the parties nor the civil or commercial character of the parties or of the contract is to be taken into consideration in determining the application of this Convention.

* * *

Article 3

(1) Contracts for the supply of goods to be manufactured or produced are to be considered sales unless the party who orders the goods undertakes to supply a substantial part of the materials necessary for such manufacture or production.

(2) This Convention does not apply to contracts in which the preponderant part of the obligations of the party who furnishes the goods consists in the supply of labour or other services.

* * *

Article 6

The parties may exclude the application of this Convention or, subject to article 12, derogate from or vary the effect of any of its provisions.

* * *

Article 8

(1) For the purposes of this Convention statements made by and other conduct of a party are to be interpreted according to his intent where the other party knew or could not have been aware what that intent was.

(2) If the preceding paragraph is not applicable, statements made by and other conduct of a party are to be interpreted according to the understanding that a reasonable person of the same kind as the other party would have had in the same circumstances.

(3) In determining the intent of a party or the understanding a reasonable person would have had, due consideration is to be given to all relevant circumstances of the case including the negotiations, any practices which the parties have established between themselves, usages and any subsequent conduct of the parties.

Article 18

(1) A statement made by or other conduct of the offeree indicating assent to an offer is an acceptance. Silence or inactivity does not in itself amount to acceptance.

(2) An acceptance of an offer becomes effective at the moment the indication of assent reaches the offeror. An acceptance is not effective if the indication of assent does not reach the offeror within the time he has fixed or, if no time is fixed, within a reasonable time, due account being taken of the circumstances of the transaction, including the rapidity of the means of communication employed by the offeror. An oral offer must be accepted immediately unless the circumstances indicate otherwise.

(3) However, if, by virtue of the offer or as a result of practices which the parties have established between themselves or of usage, the offeree may indicate assent by performing an act, such as one relating to the dispatch of the goods or payment of the price, without notice to the offeror, the acceptance is effective at the moment the act is performed, provided that the act is performed within the period of time laid down in the preceding paragraph.

Article 19

(1) A reply to an offer which purports to be an acceptance but contains additions, limitations or other modifications is a rejection of the offer and constitutes a counter-offer.

(2) However, a reply to an offer which purports to be an acceptance but contains additional or different terms which do not materially alter the terms of the offer constitutes an acceptance, unless the offeror, without undue delay, objects orally to the discrepancy or dispatches a notice to that effect. If he does not so object, the terms of the contract are the terms of the offer with the modifications contained in the acceptance.

(3) Additional or different terms relating, among other things, to the price, payment, quality and quantity of the goods, place and time of delivery, extent of one party's liability to the other or the settlement of disputes are considered to alter the terms of the offer materially.

* * *

UNIFORM LAWS ANNOTATED

UNIFORM COMMERCIAL CODE
ARTICLE 2. SALES

§ 2–207.   Additional Terms in Acceptance or Confirmation.

(1) A definite and seasonable expression of acceptance or a written confirmation which is sent within a reasonable time operates as an acceptance even though it states terms additional to or different from those offered or agreed upon, unless acceptance is expressly made conditional on assent to the additional or different terms.

(2) The additional terms are to be construed as proposals for addition to the contract. Between merchants such terms become part of the contract unless:

(a) the offer expressly limits acceptance to the terms of the offer;

(b) they materially alter it; or

(c) notification of objection to them has already been given or is given within a reasonable time after notice of them is received.

(3) Conduct by both parties which recognizes the existence of a contract is sufficient to establish a contract for sale although the writings of the parties do not otherwise establish a contract. In such case the terms of the particular contract consist of those terms on which the writings of the parties agree, together with any supplementary terms incorporated under any other provisions of this Act.

* * *

CONTRACT FORMATION UNDER THE UNITED NATIONS CONVENTION ON CONTRACTS FOR THE INTERNATIONAL SALE OF GOODS AND THE UNIFORM COMMERCIAL CODE: PITFALLS FOR THE UNWARY

Burt A. Leete

6 Temp. Int'l & Comp. L.J. 19 (1992).

* * *

Trading partners in the international community have sought some degree of uniformity in international business transactions for many years. This is particularly true with regard to contracts for the sale of goods.

* * *

The CISG has made some significant changes in the law regarding contract formation and it is likely that in the next several years it will play an increasingly significant role in the drafting of contracts for the international sale of goods. There are several reasons for its developing role beyond the fact that a large number of countries are considering or have already adopted the CISG. For example, if the parties do not make a choice of law as part of the contract, the CISG will apply.

Although one's first impulse might be to exclude the application of the CISG and operate under the familiar domestic law of the United States, the demands of one of the contracting parties may preclude this option. In the event of a dispute as to the appropriate choice of law for the contract, the CISG is a useful alternative for resolving the problem. As people become more familiar and comfortable with the CISG, it will be used more frequently. However, the choice to use it should not be made without serious thought.

* * *

The CISG only applies to contracts for the sale of goods between parties that have both ratified the Convention and whose places of business are in different countries. However, it is possible that the parties may designate the law of a particular country in their contract as the applicable law and thus avoid the application of the CISG.

* * *

There are some significant differences between the approaches taken to acceptance by the CISG, the U.C.C., and the common law. The CISG states that "[a] statement made by or other conduct of the offeree indicating assent to an offer is an acceptance. Silence or inactivity does not in itself amount to acceptance." This flexible approach to the method of acceptance is similar to that taken by the U.C.C. However, important differences exist in the approach taken by the CISG, the U.C.C., and the common law with regard to when an acceptance is considered effective where the acceptance is either mailed or made by performance.

The CISG rejects the common law rule that when mailing is the authorized method of acceptance and the offeror has not stated otherwise, an acceptance is considered effective when mailed. The CISG states instead that an acceptance is not effective until it reaches the offeror. While the effect of the common law rule is to place the risk of a lost acceptance on the offeror, the effect of the CISG approach is to adopt the approach taken by many civil law countries and place the risk on the offeree. Thus, the CISG is consistent in adopting a receipt theory as opposed to a dispatch theory for all the communications concerned with contract formation.

* * *

The CISG also treats acceptance by performance in a manner somewhat different from what the common law lawyer might expect. Both the CISG and the U.C.C. provide that an offer may be accepted by performance. The CISG provides that acceptance by performance may be made without notice to the offeror and that the acceptance is effective when the act is performed.

* * *

Note that this constitutes an exception to the receipt theory of acceptance otherwise adopted by the CISG. Clearly, where performance is authorized as a mode of acceptance either by the offer, by prior practices, or by trade usage, the offer is accepted once performance is begun as in the case of "dispatch of the goods." Hence, while an offeree bears the risk of loss of a communicated acceptance, this is not the case where the mode of acceptance is by performance, such as shipment of the goods.

* * *

Few subjects have received as much attention on the subject of contracts for the sale of goods as the so called "battle of forms" problem. More specifically, the trouble stems from the situation where the purported "acceptance" by the offeree contains new or different terms than were in the offer. The subject is complex and justifies much discussion because of the different approaches taken by common law, Section 2–207 of the U.C.C., and the legal systems of other countries.

* * *

The approach historically taken by the common law is the well known mirror image rule, which requires the acceptance to be in the exact terms as the offer. If it is not, a counter-offer results which is construed as an offer. In order for a contract to result, the mirror image rule requires the parties to continue to make counter-offers until there is total agreement.

* * *

Under the more rigid classical approach, the contract that results most likely will have the terms contained in the "last shot" fired by the party in an exchange of forms. If the offeror (buyer) orders with a form containing his terms and the offeree (seller) invoices on a form with differing terms, under the common law no contract results. No contract will result under this classical approach as long as each party replies to the other with a different form.

* * *

In Section 2–207, the drafters of the U.C.C. attempted to relax the rigidity of the common law by allowing for the formation of contracts where the acceptance deviates in some way from the offer and even where the parties may not be in total agreement as to all the terms. Section 2–207 seems to take a "deal is on" approach to the contract formation process. Thus, a contract can result even where the acceptance does not replicate the exact terms of the offer and contains different or additional terms. The additional terms become part of the contract for merchants unless one of three situations occur: the offer limits acceptance to the terms of the offer; the terms materially alter the offer; or the offeror timely notifies the offeree of objection to the additional terms. Because materiality is not specifically defined by the U.C.C., the courts have some flexibility in interpreting the additional terms. Unlike the mirror image approach, the likely result under the U.C.C. is that a contract will be formed even when the forms exchanged do not "match up."

The U.C.C. also provides for the situation in which a contract results from performance even though a contract did not result from the exchange of documents between the parties. For example, the order form and invoice of the parties may contain terms that are not compatible because each materially alters the other party's terms in such a way that it precludes the formation of a contract under U.C.C. § 2–207(2). However, the buyer may accept some part of the performance tendered by the seller while the documents are being exchanged, suggesting that a contract exists. * * *

The effect of this approach is to hold parties to a contract when it is clear from their conduct that a contract was intended. The contract is not escapable merely because there is no agreement or identical terms. As a result of Section 2–207(2) of the U.C.C., the final contract may contain terms which do not reflect the intent of both or either of the parties. The justification for such an outcome is that both parties indicated by their conduct that a contract was desirable.

* * *

[T]he legislative history of the CISG clearly indicates that a flexible philosophy to contract formation, such as that contained in Section 2–207 of the U.C.C., was rejected by the drafters. While the final draft of Article 19 of the CISG seems to be a compromise between the two philosophies, in reality it is not. Although Article 19(2) allows for material terms which do not "alter the terms of the offer," Article 19(3) defines materiality so broadly that it is hard to imagine a case where an additional or different term would not materially alter the offer. The non-exclusive list of material terms includes matters relating to the settlement of disputes and liability of the parties as well as the price, quantity, and terms of delivery. Thus, the CISG seems clearly to take an approach closer to the traditional mirror image rule than the "deal is on" philosophy of the U.C.C. With regard to the battle of forms issue, it seems clear that the party sending the last form will be the one whose terms prevail.

* * *

Finally, one more potential trap for the contract drafter occurs when both the offeror and offeree specify in their forms that the law of the contract is the law of their own jurisdiction. Article 1 of the CISG provides that it applies to parties from different States "(a) when the States are Contracting States; or (b) when the rules of private international law lead to the application of the law of a Contracting State." Thus, if the parties have designated the law of a contracting state as the law of the contract, then the CISG is applicable even though the parties do not specifically mention the CISG. Notwithstanding this provision, the CISG is not mandatory and the parties may exclude its application or "derogate from or vary the effect of any of its provisions." If these two provisions are read in conjunction with one another, it would seem that simply selecting the law of a contracting State as the law of the contract would not exclude the CISG. The drafter would have to be more specific and state in his or her choice of law provision that the CISG is not to apply. Therefore, standard forms, sent by businesses located in two contracting states that simply select the law of their own states as the law of the contract and do not specifically exclude the CISG, would arguably not be conflicting. Rather, they would be electing the CISG due to the application of Article 1.

* * *

The UNCISG under the U.S. legal system is a self-executing treaty. As the article above mentions, it modifies both common law and *UCC* provisions regarding issues known as the 'mailbox' and mirror image rule. The UNCISG similarly impacts modifies both common law and *UCC* regarding the statute of frauds (Article 11), the remedy of specific performance [Article 46(1)] and (Article 28), the perfect tender rule (Article 49(1)(a) and Article 25), and Damages. For an excellent discussion on these issues see William S. Dodge, *Teaching the CISG in Contracts*, Journal of Legal Education, Volume 50, Number 1 (March 2000).

Another area where the UNCISG affects the *UCC* is in the parol evidence rule. While there is not much case law on the UNCISG, a recent decision analyzed this distinction in the CISG.

MCC-MARBLE CERAMIC CENTER, INC. v. CERAMICA NUOVA D'AGOSTINO, S.P.A.

United States Court of Appeals, Eleventh Circuit, 1998.
144 F.3d 1384.

* * *

BIRCH, Circuit Judge:

This case requires us to determine whether a court must consider parol evidence in a contract dispute governed by the United Nations Convention on Contracts for the International Sale ofGoods ("CISG"). The district court granted summary judgment on behalf of the defendant appellee, relying on certain terms and provisions that appeared on the reverse of a pre-printed form contract for the sale of ceramic tiles. The plaintiff-appellant sought to rely on a number of affidavits that tended to show both that the parties had arrived at an oral contract before memorializing their agreement in writing and that they subjectively intended not to apply the terms on the reverse of the contract to their agreements. The magistrate judge held that the affidavits did not raise an issue of material fact and recommended that the district court grant summary judgment based on the terms of the contract. The district court agreed with the magistrate judge's reasoning and entered summary judgment in the defendant-appellee's favor. We REVERSE.

* * *

BACKGROUND

The plaintiff-appellant, MCC–Marble Ceramic, Inc. ("MCC"), is a Florida corporation engaged in the retail sale of tiles, and the defendant-appellee, Ceramica Nuova d'Agostino S.p.A.("D'Agostino") is an Italian corporation engaged in the manufacture of ceramic tiles. In October

1990, MCC's president, Juan Carlos Mozon, met representatives of D'Agostino at a trade fair in Bologna, Italy and negotiated an agreement to purchase ceramic tiles from D'Agostino based on samples he examined at the trade fair. Monzon, who spoke no Italian, communicated with Gianni Silingardi, then D'Agostino's commercial director, through a translator, Gianfranco Copelli, who was himself an agent of D'Agostino. The parties apparently arrived at an oral agreement on the crucial terms of price, quality, quantity, delivery and payment. The parties then recorded these terms on one of D'Agostino's standard, pre-printed order forms and Monzon signed the contract on MCC's behalf. According to MCC, the parties also entered into a requirements contract in February 1991, subject to which D'Agostino agreed to supply MCC with high grade ceramic tile at specific discounts as long as MCC purchased sufficient quantities of tile. MCC completed a number of additional order forms requesting tile deliveries pursuant to that agreement.

MCC brought suit against D'Agostino claiming a breach of the February 1991 requirements contract when D'Agostino failed to satisfy orders in April, May, and August of 1991. In addition to other defenses, D'Agostino responded that it was under no obligation to fill MCC's orders because MCC had defaulted on payment for previous shipments. In support of its position, D'Agostino relied on the pre-printed terms of the contracts that MCC had executed. The executed forms were printed in Italian and contained terms and conditions on both the front and reverse. According to an English translation of the October 1990 contract, the front of the order form contained the following language directly beneath Monzon's signature:

[T]he buyer hereby states that he is aware of the sales conditions stated on the reverse and that he expressly approves of them with special reference to those numbered 1–2–3–4–5–6–7–8. R2–126, Exh. 3 p 5 ("Maselli Aff."). Clause 6(b), printed on the back of the form states: [D]efault or delay in payment within the time agreed upon gives D'Agostino the right to ... suspend or cancel the contract itself and to cancel possible other pending contracts and the buyer does not have the right to indemnification or damages. * * *

D'Agostino also brought a number of counterclaims against MCC, seeking damages for MCC's alleged nonpayment for deliveries of tile that D'Agostino had made between February 28, 1991 and July 4, 1991. MCC responded that the tile it had received was of a lower quality than contracted for, and that, pursuant to the CISG, MCC was entitled to reduce payment in proportion to the defects.[4] D'Agostino, however, noted that clause 4 on the reverse of the contract states, in pertinent part:

Possible complaints for defects of the merchandise must be made in writing by means of a certified letter within and not later than 10 days after receipt of the merchandise.... Maselli Aff. p 6. Although there is

---

4. Article 50 of the CISG permits a buyer to reduce payment for nonconforming goods in proportion to the nonconformity under certain conditions. See CISG, art. 50.

evidence to support MCC's claims that it complained about the quality of the deliveries it received, MCC never submitted any written complaints.

MCC did not dispute these underlying facts before the district court, but argued that the parties never intended the terms and conditions printed on the reverse of the order form to apply to their agreements. As evidence for this assertion, MCC submitted Monzon's affidavit, which claims that MCC had no subjective intent to be bound by those terms and that D'Agostino was aware of this intent. MCC also filed affidavits from Silingardi and Copelli, D'Agostino's representatives at the trade fair, which support Monzon's claim that the parties subjectively intended not to be bound by the terms on the reverse of the order form. The magistrate judge held that the affidavits, even if true, did not raise an issue of material fact regarding the interpretation or applicability of the terms of the written contracts and the district court accepted his recommendation to award summary judgment in D'Agostino's favor. MCC then filed this timely appeal.

DISCUSSION

* * *

The parties to this case agree that the CISG governs their dispute because the United States, where MCC has its place of business, and Italy, where D'Agostino has its place of business, are both States Party to the Convention. * * * See CISG, art. 1. * * * Article 8 of the CISG governs the interpretation of international contracts for the sale of goods and forms the basis of MCC's appeal from the district court's grant of summary judgment in D'Agostino's favor. * * * MCC argues that the magistrate judge and the district court improperly ignored evidence that MCC submitted regarding the parties' subjective intent when they memorialized the terms of their agreement on D'Agostino's pre-printed form contract, and that the magistrate judge erred by applying the parol evidence rule in derogation of the CISG.

I. Subjective Intent Under the CISG

Contrary to what is familiar practice in United States courts, the CISG appears to permit a substantial inquiry into the parties' subjective intent, even if the parties did not engage in any objectively ascertainable means of registering this intent.[8] Article 8(1) of the CISG instructs courts to interpret the "statements ... and other conduct of a party ... according to his intent" as long as the other party "knew or could not have been unaware" of that intent. The plain language of the Convention, therefore, requires an inquiry into a party's subjective intent as long as the other party to the contract was aware of that intent.

---

8. In the United States, the legislatures, courts, and the legal academy have voiced a preference for relying on objective manifestations of the parties' intentions. For example, Article Two of the Uniform Commercial Code, which most states have enacted in some form or another to govern contracts for the sale of goods, is replete with references to standards of commercial reasonableness. * * *

In this case, MCC has submitted three affidavits that discuss the purported subjective intent of the parties to the initial agreement concluded between MCC and D'Agostino in October 1990. All three affidavits discuss the preliminary negotiations and report that the parties arrived at an oral agreement for D'Agostino to supply quantities of a specific grade of ceramic tile to MCC at an agreed upon price. The affidavits state that the "oral agreement established the essential terms of quality, quantity, description of goods, delivery, price and payment." * * * The affidavits also note that the parties memorialized the terms of their oral agreement on a standard D'Agostino order form, but all three affiants contend that the parties subjectively intended not to be bound by the terms on the reverse of that form despite a provision directly below the signature line that expressly and specifically incorporated those terms. * * *

The terms on the reverse of the contract give D'Agostino the right to suspend or cancel all contracts in the event of a buyer's non-payment and require a buyer to make a written report of all defects within ten days. As the magistrate judge's report and recommendation makes clear, if these terms applied to the agreements between MCC and D'Agostino, summary judgment would be appropriate because MCC failed to make any written complaints about the quality of tile it received and D'Agostino has established MCC's non-payment of a number of invoices amounting to $108,389.40 and 102,053,846.00 Italian lira.

Article 8(1) of the CISG requires a court to consider this evidence of the parties' subjective intent. Contrary to the magistrate judge's report, which the district court endorsed and adopted, article 8(1) does not focus on interpreting the parties' statements alone. Although we agree with the magistrate judge's conclusion that no "interpretation" of the contract's terms could support MCC's position, * * * article 8(1) also requires a court to consider subjective intent while interpreting the conduct of the parties. The CISG's language, therefore, requires courts to consider evidence of a party's subjective intent when signing a contract if the other party to the contract was aware of that intent at the time. This is precisely the type of evidence that MCC has provided through the Silingardi, Copelli, and Monzon affidavits, which discuss not only Monzon's intent as MCC's representative but also discuss the intent of D'Agostino's representatives and their knowledge that Monzon did not intend to agree to the terms on the reverse of the form contract. This acknowledgment that D'Agostino's representatives were aware of Monzon's subjective intent puts this case squarely within article 8(1) of the CISG, and therefore requires the court to consider MCC's evidence as it interprets the parties' conduct.[11]

---

11. Without this crucial acknowledgment, we would interpret the contract and the parties' actions according to article 8(2), which directs courts to rely on objective evidence of the parties' intent. On the facts of this case it seems readily apparent that MCC's affidavits provide no evidence that Monzon's actions would have made his alleged subjective intent not to be bound by the terms of the contract known to "the understanding that a reasonable person . . .

II. *Parol Evidence and the CISG*

Given our determination that the magistrate judge and the district court should have considered MCC's affidavits regarding the parties' subjective intentions, we must address a question of first impression in this circuit: whether the parol evidence rule, which bars evidence of an earlier oral contract that contradicts or varies the terms of a subsequent or contemporaneous written contract,[12] plays any role in cases involving the CISG. We begin by observing that the parol evidence rule, contrary to its title, is a substantive rule of law, not a rule of evidence. * * * The rule does not purport to exclude a particular type of evidence as an "untrustworthy or undesirable" way of proving a fact, but prevents a litigant from attempting to show "the fact itself—the fact that the terms of the agreement are other than those in the writing." Id. As such, a federal district court cannot simply apply the parol evidence rule as a procedural matter—as it might if excluding a particular type of evidence under the Federal Rules of Evidence, which apply in federal court regardless of the source of the substantive rule of decision. * * *

The CISG itself contains no express statement on the role of parol evidence. * * * It is clear, however, that the drafters of the CISG were comfortable with the concept of permitting parties to rely on oral contracts because they eschewed any statutes of fraud provision and expressly provided for the enforcement of oral contracts. Compare CISG, art. 11 (a contract of sale need not be concluded or evidenced in writing) with U.C.C. s 2–201 (precluding the enforcement of oral contracts for the sale of goods involving more than $500). Moreover, article 8(3) of the CISG expressly directs courts to give "due consideration ... to all relevant circumstances of the case including the negotiations ..." to determine the intent of the parties. Given article 8(1)'s directive to use the intent of the parties to interpret their statements and conduct, article 8(3) is a clear instruction to admit and consider parol evidence regarding the negotiations to the extent they reveal the parties' subjective intent.

Despite the CISG's broad scope, surprisingly few cases have applied the Convention in the United States,[14] see Delchi Carrier SpA v. Rotorex Corp., 71 F.3d 1024, 1027–28 (2d Cir.1995) (observing that "there is virtually no case law under the Convention"), and only two reported

---

would have had in the same circumstances." CISG, art 8(2).

12. The Uniform Commercial Code includes a version of the parol evidence rule applicable to contracts for the sale of goods in most states: Terms with respect to which the confirmatory memoranda of the parties agree or which are otherwise set forth in a writing intended by the parties as a final expression of their agreement with respect to such terms as are included therein may not be contradicted by evidence of any prior agreement or of a contemporaneous oral agreement but may be explained or supplemented (a) by course of dealing or usage of trade ... or by course of performance ... ; and (b) by evidence of consistent additional terms unless the court finds the writing to have been intended also as a complete and exclusive statement of the terms of the agreement. U.C.C. s 2–202. * * *

14. Moreover, the parties have not cited us to any persuasive authority from the courts of other States Party to the CISG. Our own research uncovered a promising source for such decisions at http:// www. cisg.law.pace.edu>, but produced no cases that address the issue of parol evidence.

decisions touch upon the parol evidence rule, both in dicta. One court has concluded, much as we have above, that the parol evidence rule is not viable in CISG cases in light of article 8 of the Convention. In Filanto, a district court addressed the differences between the UCC and the CISG on the issues of offer and acceptance and the battle of the forms. See 789 F.Supp. at 1238. After engaging in a thorough analysis of how the CISG applied to the dispute before it, the district court tangentially observed that article 8(3) "essentially rejects . . . the parol evidence rule." Id. at 1238 n. 7. Another court, however, appears to have arrived at a contrary conclusion. In Beijing Metals & Minerals Import/Export Corp. v. American Bus. Ctr., Inc., 993 F.2d 1178 (5th Cir.1993), a defendant sought to avoid summary judgment on a contract claim by relying on evidence of contemporaneously negotiated oral terms that the parties had not included in their written agreement. The plaintiff, a Chinese corporation, relied on Texas law in its complaint while the defendant, apparently a Texas corporation,[15] asserted that the CISG governed the dispute. Id. at 1183 n. 9. Without resolving the choice of law question,[16] the Fifth Circuit cited Filanto for the proposition that there have been very few reported cases applying the CISG in the United States, and stated that the parol evidence rule would apply regardless of whether Texas law or the CISG governed the dispute. Beijing Metals, 993 F.2d at 1183 n. 9. The opinion does not acknowledge Filanto's more applicable dictum that the parol evidence rule does not apply to CISG cases nor does it conduct any analysis of the Convention to support its conclusion. In fact, the Fifth Circuit did not undertake to interpret the CISG in a manner that would arrive at a result consistent with the parol evidence rule but instead explained that it would apply the rule as developed at Texas common law. See id. at 1183 n. 10. As persuasive authority for this court, the Beijing Metals opinion is not particularly persuasive on this point.

Our reading of article 8(3) as a rejection of the parol evidence rule, however, is in accordance with the great weight of academic commentary on the issue. As one scholar has explained: [T]he language of Article 8(3) that "due consideration is to be given to all relevant circumstances of the case" seems adequate to override any domestic rule that would bar a tribunal from considering the relevance of other agreements. . . . Article 8(3) relieves tribunals from domestic rules that might bar them from "considering" any evidence between the parties that is relevant. This

---

15. The Beijing Metals opinion does not state the place of the defendant's incorporation, but the defendant must have been a United States corporation because the court noted that the case was a "diversity action." Beijing Metals, 993 F.2d at 1183 n. 9. Cf. 28 U.S.C. s 1332 (providing no statutory grant for suits between aliens unless a citizen of a State is present); 15 James W. Moore, Moore's Federal Practice s 102.77 (3d ed.1998) (observing that diversity jurisdiction is not present in suits between two foreign citizens).

16. The Fifth Circuit unwittingly may have solved the problem in the very next footnote, where it observed that the agreement between the parties, which attempted to settle a dispute regarding an earlier sales contract, was not itself a contract for the sale of goods and therefore fell outside the Uniform Commercial Code. Beijing Metals, 993 F.2d at 1183 n. 10. See CISG, art. 1(1) ("This Convention applies to contracts of sale of goods. . . .") (emphasis added).

added flexibility for interpretation is consistent with a growing body of opinion that the "parol evidence rule" has been an embarrassment for the administration of modern transactions. * * * Indeed, only one commentator has made any serious attempt to reconcile the parol evidence rule with the CISG. * * * The answer to both these arguments, however, is the same: although jurisdictions in the United States have found the parol evidence rule helpful to promote good faith and uniformity in contract, as well as an appropriate answer to the question of how much consideration to give parol evidence, a wide number of other States Party to the CISG have rejected the rule in their domestic jurisdictions. One of the primary factors motivating the negotiation and adoption of the CISG was to provide parties to international contracts for the sale of goods with some degree of certainty as to the principles of law that would govern potential disputes and remove the previous doubt regarding which party's legal system might otherwise apply. See Letter of Transmittal from Ronald Reagan, President of the United States, to the United States Senate, reprinted at 15 U.S.C. app. 70, 71 (1997). Courts applying the CISG cannot, therefore, upset the parties' reliance on the Convention by substituting familiar principles of domestic law when the Convention requires a different result. We may only achieve the directives of good faith and uniformity in contracts under the CISG by interpreting and applying the plain language of article 8(3) as written and obeying its directive to consider this type of parol evidence.

This is not to say that parties to an international contract for the sale of goods cannot depend on written contracts or that parol evidence regarding subjective contractual intent need always prevent a party relying on a written agreement from securing summary judgment. To the contrary, most cases will not present a situation (as exists in this case) in which both parties to the contract acknowledge a subjective intent not to be bound by the terms of a pre-printed writing. In most cases, therefore, article 8(2) of the CISG will apply, and objective evidence will provide the basis for the court's decision. * * * Consequently, a party to a contract governed by the CISG will not be able to avoid the terms of a contract and force a jury trial simply by submitting an affidavit which states that he or she did not have the subjective intent to be bound by the contract's terms. Cf. Klopfenstein v. Pargeter, 597 F.2d 150, 152 (9th Cir.1979) (affirming summary judgment despite the appellant's submission of his own affidavit regarding his subjective intent: "Undisclosed, subjective intentions are immaterial in [a] commercial transaction, especially when contradicted by objective conduct. Thus, the affidavit has no legal effect even if its averments are accepted as wholly truthful."). * * *

Considering MCC's affidavits in this case, however, we conclude that the magistrate judge and the district court improperly granted summary judgment in favor of D'Agostino. Although the affidavits are, as D'Agostino observes, relatively conclusory and unsupported by facts that would objectively establish MCC's intent not to be bound by the conditions on the reverse of the form, article 8(1) requires a court to consider evidence of a party's subjective intent when the other party was aware of it, and the Silingardi and Copelli affidavits provide that evidence. This is not to say that the affidavits are conclusive proof of what the parties intended. A reasonable finder of fact, for example, could disregard testimony that purportedly sophisticated international merchants signed a contract without intending to be bound as simply too incredible to believe and hold MCC to the conditions printed on the reverse of the contract.[20] Nevertheless, the affidavits raise an issue of material fact regarding the parties' intent to incorporate the provisions on the reverse of the form contract. If the finder of fact determines that the parties did not intend to rely on those provisions, then the more general provisions of the CISG will govern the outcome of the dispute. * * *

Conclusion

MCC asks us to reverse the district court's grant of summary judgment in favor of D'Agostino. The district court's decision rests on pre-printed contractual terms and conditions incorporated on the reverse of a standard order form that MCC's president signed on the company's behalf. Nevertheless, we conclude that the CISG, which governs international contracts for the sale of goods, precludes summary judgment in this case because MCC has raised an issue of material fact concerning the parties' subjective intent to be bound by the terms on the reverse of the pre-printed contract. The CISG also precludes the application of the parol evidence rule, which would otherwise bar the consideration of evidence concerning a prior or contemporaneously negotiated oral agreement. Accordingly, we REVERSE the district court's grant of summary judgment and REMAND this case for further proceedings consistent with this opinion.

---

b. The Role of the INCOTERMS

In a contract for the international sale of goods, many issues need to be addressed including the quantity, price, description of the goods, delivery terms, payment conditions, passage of title, and passage of risk of loss to name just a few. An international, uniform set of commercial terms has emerged which serves as a shorthand communication between the parties on some of the important issues listed above.

The International Chamber of Commerce recognizing the need for standardizing commercial terms has developed a work titled *GUIDE TO INCOTERMS* defining standard commercial terms used in contracts for the international sale of goods. The *Incoterms* enjoy very wide usage in the international sale of goods. The following materials reproduce the two most widely used *Incoterms*—The *FOB* and *CIF* terms.

20. D'Agostino attempts to explain and undermine the affidavit of its representatives during the transaction, by calling Silingardi a "disgruntled" former employee. Appellee's Br. at 11, 39. Silingardi's alleged feelings towards his former employer may indeed be relevant to undermine the credibility of his assertions, but that is a matter for the finder of fact, not for this court on summary judgment.

GUIDE TO INCOTERMS 1990
International Chamber of Commerce

Free on Board (Place of Shipment)

A THE SELLER MUST

A 1 Provision of goods in conformity with the contract

Provide the goods and the commercial invoice, or its equivalent electronic message, in conformity with the contract of sale and any other evidence of conformity which may be required by the contract.

A 2 Licences, authorisations and formalities

Obtain at his own risk and expense any export license or other official authorisation and carry out all customs formalities necessary for the exportation of the goods.

A 3 Contract of carriage and insurance

a) Contract of carriage

   No obligation

b) Contract of insurance

   No obligation

A 4 Delivery

Deliver the goods on board the vessel named by the buyer at the named port of shipment on the date or within the period stipulated and in the manner customary at the port.

A 5 Transfer of risks

Subject to the provisions of B.5., bear all risks of loss or damage to the goods until such time as they have passed the ship's rail at the named port of shipment.

A 6 Division of costs

Subject to the provisions of B.6.

pay all costs relating to the goods until such time as they have passed the ship's rail at the named port of shipment; pay the costs of customs formalities necessary for exportation as well as all the duties, taxes and other official charges payable upon exportation.

A 7 Notice to the buyer

Give the buyer sufficient notice that the goods have been delivered on board.

B THE BUYER MUST

B 1 Payment of the price

Pay the price as provided in the contract of sale

B 2   Licences, authorisations, and formalities

Obtain at his own risk and expense any import licence or other official authorisation and carry out all customs formalities for the importation of the goods and, where necessary, for their transit through another country.

B 3   Contract of carriage

Contract at his own expense for the carriage of the goods from the named port of shipment.

B 5   Transfer of risks

Bear all risks of loss or damage to the goods from the time they have passed the ship's rail at the named port of shipment.

COST, INSURANCE AND FREIGHT (... named port of destination)

A   THE SELLER MUST

A 1   Provision of goods in conformity with the contract

Provide the goods and the commercial invoice, or its equivalent electronic message, in conformity with the contract of sale and any other evidence of conformity which may be required by the contract.

A 2   Licences, authorisations and formalities

Obtain at his own risk and expense any export licence or other official authorisation and carry out all customs formalities necessary for the exportation of the goods.

A 3   Contract of carriage and insurance

a) Contract of carriage

Contract on usual terms at his own expense for the carriage of the goods to the named port of destination by the usual route in a seagoing vessel (or inland waterway vessel as appropriate) of the type normally used for the transport of goods of the contract description.

b) Contract of insurance

Obtain at his own expense cargo insurance as agreed in the contract, that the buyer, or any other person having an insurable interest in the goods, shall be entitled to claim directly from the insurer and provide the buyer with the insurance policy or other evidence of insurance cover.

A 4   Delivery

Deliver the goods on board the vessel at the port of shipment on the date or within the period stipulated.

A 5   Transfer of Risks

Subject to the provisions of B.5., bear all risks of loss of or damage to the goods until such time as they have passed the ship's rail at the port of shipment.

A 6   Division of costs

Subject to the provisions of B.6.,

pay all costs relating to the goods until they have been delivered in accordance with A.4. as well as the freight and all other costs resulting from A.3.a), including costs of loading the goods on board and any charges for unloading at the port of discharge which may be levied by regular shipping lines when contracting for carriage;

pay the costs of customs formalities necessary for exportation as well as all duties, taxes and other official charges payable upon exportation.

A 8   Proof of delivery, transport document or equivalent electronic message

Unless otherwise agreed, at his own expense provide the buyer without delay with the usual transport document for the agreed port of destination.

This document (for example, a negotiable bill of lading ...) must cover the contract goods, be dated within the period agreed for shipment, enable the buyer to claim the goods from the carrier at destination ...

B   THE BUYER MUST

B 1   Payment of the price

Pay the price as provided in the contract of sale.

B 2   Licences, authorisations and formalities

Obtain at his own risk and expense any import licence or other official authorisation and carry out all customs formalities for the importation of the goods and, where necessary, for their transit through another country.

B 3   Contract of Carriage

No obligation

B 4   Taking delivery

Accept delivery of the goods when they have been delivered in accordance with A.4. and receive them from the carrier at the named port of destination.

B 5   Transfer of risks

Bear all risks of loss of or damage to the goods from the time they have passed the ship's rail at the port of shipment.

It is important to remember that *Incoterms* are widely accepted in business transactions as commercial harmonizing terms. They are, however, not law. In order for them to apply, the Sales Contract must incorporate them by reference. If the contract were silent on the use of *Incoterms*, then the relevant domestic system would apply. In cases where *Incoterms* are not incorporated by reference the choice of law and conflict of law analysis would have to be used to determine which legal system would apply. U.S. local law providing guidance on the meaning of commercial terms as well is found in the *U.C.C.* However, the intent of the parties controls over the *Incoterms* and over the gap filling provisions of the *U.C.C.*

B. THE INTERNATIONAL SALE OF SERVICES AND GOVERNMENT PROCUREMENT

1. *The Sale of Services*

Delta's Division II is the geology and engineering group. This division provides technical expertise on the locating of oil reserves and in the drilling of exploratory wells. It also develops plans and strategies to use in the development of oil wells in zones where there are proven reserves. Delta believes there may be a substantial market for these services in light of the market globalization and privatization efforts currently taking place worldwide. The Division has expertise in on-shore as well as off-shore activities.

Its principal business concern is in establishing the access to foreign markets for its engineering services. Providing market access for the international sale of goods has been the subject of cooperation between countries for a long time. Indeed, the great success of the General Agreement on Tariff and Trade (GATT) has been in the removal of trade barriers among the member countries. The rules facilitating the flow of services across national borders are of recent vintage.

Developed countries, chief among them the United States, have promoted the idea of international rules regarding services. The U.S. is the largest service exporter in the world. The service industry is a major component of the U.S. economy. The U.S. economy is transforming from an economy heavy in manufacturing to a service economy. The importance of the service sector has understandably caused the U.S. government to place its enhancement, especially those related to technology, at the forefront of its trade policy objectives. One major U.S. objective has been the opening of foreign markets to U.S. service providers.

Developing countries are service importers. As such, there has not been much interest among them to include rules regarding the free flow of services among countries. Up until the culmination of the Uruguay round the plea for international service rules fell on deaf ears among member developing countries of the GATT. The rules are changing. Among the many achievements of the Uruguay Round was the negotiation of a major multilateral agreement regarding services—The General Agreement on Trade in Services (GATS).

The GATS is a non-self executing treaty that became part of the U.S. domestic legislation through the Uruguay Round Agreement Act which was enacted on April 15, 1994. The purpose of the GATS is to reduce or eliminate governmental measures that prevent services from being freely provided across national borders or that discriminate against locally established service firms. The GATS addresses the removal of barriers to the service industry—market access, non-discriminatory treatment, transparency, and the free flow of payments and transfers. It also provides for dispute settlement procedures in case of conflict.

The standard of treatment that the GATS provides for service providers is the best of either national treatment or most favored nation. This means that member countries must treat services and service suppliers in a manner that is no less favorable than the manner in which they treat services and service suppliers from any other member country. The access of service markets does not apply to measures affecting natural persons seeking access to the employment of a member state. Immigration is still a matter of domestic law. For a summary of the U.S. immigration rules see Section 2.1B, supra.

The NAFTA also addresses the issue of services. NAFTA chapter 12 covers services in a broad context while chapter 14 focuses on financial services. NAFTA chapter 13 addresses telecommunications services. Like the GATS, the NAFTA service chapters do not provide for the immigration of people merely the movement of service providers. NAFTA does address the temporary entry of business-persons in chapter 16. However, chapter 16 still defers to domestic immigration legislation as the main source of rules. See Section 2.1 B, supra for a discussion of these issues. Generally the NAFTA service chapters call for the better of national or most favored nation treatment, transparency, and other rules that facilitate the cross border rendering of services and non-discrimination.

2. *Government Procurement*

Delta's concern in its engineering division is in having market access. However, in many cases the client will be a governmental agency. This brings into play the issue of government procurement rules. Under the GATT, the *Agreement On Government Procurement* provides for national treatment, non-discrimination and transparency in the rule making. The NAFTA's government procurement chapter also calls for non-discrimination and national treatment. The following article describes the NAFTA government procurement chapter.

THE GOVERNMENT PROCUREMENT
CHAPTER OF NAFTA

Carlos Muggenberg R.V.

1 U.S.-Mex. L.J. 295, (1993). * * *

I. INTRODUCTION

The NAFTA provisions dealing with Government Procurement strongly reflect GATT's influence. There are, however, three major differences between the GATT Government Procurement Code and NAFTA's Chapter Ten.

NAFTA covers all government procurement contracts for services while, up to now, GATT does not. The matter of services continues to be a major GATT issue. Only services related to procured goods become subject matter of the relevant GATT code, and only as long as the value thereof does not exceed the value of the goods.

The second difference is that NAFTA goes into much greater detail than GATT in almost every topic. In order to make the parties' obligations clear and accurate, NAFTA even sounds repetitive at times. * * *

II. POINT OF VIEW ANALYSIS

* * * [T]his paper has only two major targets in mind: first, to describe briefly the NAFTA Government Procurement subject matter, and second, to see to what extent the balanced, non-discriminatory, predictable, and transparent government procurement objectives were achieved.

III. NAFTA GOVERNMENT PROCUREMENT PROVISIONS

The NAFTA Chapter Ten article headings are used for the following discussion.

A. Scope, Coverage, and Valuation

Federal government entities and federal government enterprises are both obligated to follow the NAFTA Government Procurement provisions. These entities and enterprises are listed in Annex I to Chapter 10 in a schedule for each party. Exceptions in the areas of transportation, public utilities, research and development, and others are also included in the Annexes. State or other political subdivision government entities are not obligated to follow these provisions; however, the three parties are committed to take the necessary measures in order eventually to make them subject to said provisions.

Goods and services valued at $50,000 and above, and construction contracts of $6,500,000 and above, contracted with Government Entities are subject to NAFTA Chapter 11 rules. Such minimums are increased to $250,000 and $8,000,000, respectively in the case of Government Enterprises. Values will be indexed to the United States inflation rate every two years.

Procurement includes not only the purchases of goods and services, but also lease or rental agreements (with or without purchase options), and excludes government financial and fiscal services. Separation of contracts in order to reduce their value is prohibited and rules to compute the value of renewable contracts are contemplated. Also, rules to compute the value of indefinite lease or rental contracts are established.

Modifications to "Coverage" may be made as long as the other parties are notified and appropriate compensatory adjustments are made. Parties will have recourse to dispute settlement under NAFTA's

Chapter 20. Government reorganizations and divestitures which are considered to be illegitimate by one of the parties can be questioned under the terms of Chapter 10.

B. National Treatment

Only the Rules of Origin established in Chapter 3 of NAFTA may be used to differentiate among parties' suppliers. Therefore, the degree of foreign affiliation or ownership may not be used to discriminate in the award of contracts, unless the supplier is owned or controlled by citizens of a non-party country or does not have a reasonable level of business activity in the territory within which it is originally allowed to do business.

C. Article 1007: Technical Specifications

Performance criteria and international standards, rather than design or descriptive characteristics, will be used in describing procurements. References to industrial property rights shall not be made, unless there is no other way to describe the procurement; but use of the words "or equivalent" should be made in any event. No advice may be obtained in preparing technical specifications from any party involved directly or indirectly in the procurement and which could result in a conflict of interest.

D. Article 1009: Qualification of Suppliers

Conditions for participation in bids must be adequately publicized in advance and be limited to those that are of the essence. Suppliers' business activity in the relevant party territory shall not prevail over global business activity when judging suppliers' capacity. Enough time to qualify must be given to all potential suppliers, even when not listed as such. Changes in or elimination of supplier lists must be published, as well as rejections for lack of acceptable qualifications. Qualification procedures must be uniform or the need for making an exception duly evidenced.

E. Article 1010: Invitation to Participate

Minimum information requirements, such as the nature and quantity of goods or services desired, including future needs, time frames in which options may be exercised, and estimated publication time for recurring agreements, where applicable, must be contained in all invitations to participate. A statement regarding whether bidding is to be open or selective in nature, the date for starting delivery, the address for filing the application and tender, as well as where additional information may be obtained, the submission language, required information and documentation from suppliers, and terms of payment must be published as part of the invitation.

Published notices regarding planned procurement do not eliminate the obligation of having subsequently to publish formal invitations to the suppliers. In the case of selective tendering procedures, annual classified publications of the list must be made together with requirements for qualification and methods to verify such requirements. Validity periods and renewal formalities must also be disclosed.

F. Article 1012: Time Limits for Tendering and Delivery

Time limits should not be used to make foreign supplier qualification more difficult. In principle, the period to receive tenders should never be less than forty days. This period may be reduced to twenty-four days in subsequent publications regarding recurring contracts or to ten days in the event of an emergency.

G. Article 1013: Tender Documentation

In addition to the requirements mentioned in connection with suppliers' qualifications, tender documentation must include the names of those persons authorized to be present at the opening of tenders and the criteria used in awarding contracts.

H. Article 1014: Negotiation Discipline

Negotiation of a procurement is allowed in order to identify the strengths and weaknesses of tenders, as long as the criteria established in the notices and modifications are provided to all suppliers.

I. Article 1015: Submission, Receipt, Opening, and Awarding

Submission is to be made in writing, directly or by mail. If other communication media is acceptable, it must include all required information and must be confirmed by letter. Information initially provided prevails, however, over letter confirmation. Telephone communication is not allowed and electronic transmission requires a confirmation by a letter or signed copy. Correction of unilateral errors is allowed as long as it does not result in discriminatory practices.

Abnormal prices may be questioned. The "public interest" may be used to deny a contract. Prior business activities in the relevant territory may not be argued as the sole reason for awarding a contract. No later *299 than seventy-two days following the award of a contract, notice thereof must be published and must include: a list of the goods and services awarded, the entity awarding, the date of the award, the winning supplier, the highest and lowest tenders, and the procedure used in making the award, unless disclosure might prejudice legitimate commerce, fair competition, or law enforcement.

J. Article 1016: Limited Tendering

Limited tendering is allowed in the absence of sufficient tenders, where collusion has been discovered in connection with one or more tenders, or where there is a lack of conformity with essential requirements. Limited tenders are also permitted to assure the protection of patents, copyrights, or proprietary or confidential information where there exists one sole supplier, in the event of extreme urgency, or in connection with additional deliveries by original suppliers when doing otherwise would compel the purchase of equipment or services not meeting acceptable standards. Limited tenders are also permitted in cases where a prototype has been developed upon request. Similarly, an exception can be made for purchases on the commodity market or where exceptionally advantageous prices are available in the short term for non-routine purchases or in the case of a winner in an architectural contest, if awarded in accordance with NAFTA's Chapter 10.

A report on each such contract awarded shall be prepared and shall remain at the disposal of authorities of the relevant party.

K.   Article 1017: Bid Challenge

Parties must allow any aspect of a bid to be challenged, and a minimum period of ten working days from publication may be authorized for such purpose. A challenge must be resolved fairly and in a timely manner. The reviewing authority must have no substantial interest in the outcome of the challenge, must expeditiously investigate the challenge, and may delay the awarding of the contract pending resolution of the challenge, except in urgent cases or when the public interest is affected. Recommendations made by the reviewing authorities should be given effect by the relevant government entity, but challenge procedures must be made available to interested parties.

L.   Article 1018: Exceptions Applicable to All Parties

Information dealing with essential security interests, the procurement of arms and ammunition or war materials, need not be disclosed, nor measures dealing with public morals, life, health, or protection of intellectual property rights. Exceptions for goods or services produced by handicapped persons, philanthropic institutions, or prison labor may not be interpreted as infringing NAFTA Chapter 10.

M.   Articles 1019 and 1020: Provision of Information and Technical Cooperation

Parties must publish the legal procedures and practices applicable to Government Procurement. In addition, statistics listing the government *300 entities involved, goods and services contracted with the value thereof, and derogations to rules must be published. Exceptions may be allowed where fair competition or commercial interests could be prejudiced.

Cooperation between government and suppliers, personnel training, and the dissemination of information on procurement systems and market opportunities is contemplated in the Agreement, as well as information having to do with small business opportunities.

N.   Annexes

The Annexes to NAFTA's Chapter 10, in addition to listing the government entities and enterprises covered by the procurement regulation, deal mainly with the agreed upon temporary or permanent exceptions to the Government Procurement rules. Such exceptions are made by means of "set asides" and "offsets." "Set asides" are exceptions made by each party regarding the procurement of certain kinds of products or services by specified government entities or where sourced from specified suppliers. An example of United States and Canadian "set asides" are goods and services produced by small and minority businesses. "Offsets" are made when a percentage of certain government contracts is excluded from the rules established by NAFTA's Chapter 11. Mexico, for example, permits government entities to impose a local content requirement that up to forty percent of labor intensive, turnkey projects be contracted locally.

IV. CONCLUSION

NAFTA's Chapter 10 provides the basis upon which the parties can establish a balanced, non-discriminatory, predictable, and transparent legal framework within their own countries. However, the use of non-defined terms such as "foreign affiliation," "substantial business activities," "promptly," "public interest," "proprietary information," "timely manner," and "essential security interest" may result in future inconsistencies between implementing legislation enacted by the parties. * * *

The combination of the General Agreement on Trade in Services and the Agreement on Government Procurement as well as the inclusions of those subjects in the NAFTA have created a favorable environment for Delta. The market access and non-discrimination provisions together with the pledge of increasing transparency on governmental procurement could mean a substantial increase in cross-border services.

SECTION 4.4   THE U.S. FEDERAL INCOME TAX ON THE INTERNATIONAL JOINT VENTURE

A.   THE INTERNATIONAL EQUITY JOINT VENTURE (IEJV)

1.   *Capitalizing the IEJV*

Once the business decision has been made to engage in the IEJV the tax implications on its formation and operation needs to be reviewed. This should be done before the agreement is signed. The first step in the process is to determine the applicable rules. There are three sets of rules that are potentially applicable—the U.S. Internal Revenue Code (Code), the U.S./Mexico tax treaty, and the *Reglamento de la Ley del Impuesto Sobre la Renta* (the Mexican Internal Revenue Code[MIRC]). Delta, as an U.S. citizen is subject to U.S. tax on worldwide income. Also, courtesy of the U.S./Mexico tax treaty 'savings clause' (see Section 2.3, supra), for U.S. tax purposes, Delta is governed by the U.S. Code. Delta may also be subject to the MIRC. However, to the extent that the U.S./Mexico tax treaty governs a particular transaction, it and not the MIRC applies. This is a big benefit to Delta.

Industrial and DISA are both potentially subject to the same set of rules Delta confronts. However, as Mexican corporations, under Article 4 of the U.S./Mexico tax treaty, they qualify as Mexican Residents. As such, they can avail themselves of the U.S./Mexico tax treaty as well. To the extent that it applies, the treaty replaces the Code. Under U.S. law *Industrial* and DISA will be subject to tax if they have business profits (Article 7) attributable to an U.S. permanent establishment (Article 5). See Section 2.3, supra. Under the facts of the hypothetical *Industrial* and DISA will not likely be subject to U.S. tax.

In determining the tax implications facing Delta, the first step is to determine the existence of a taxable event. Under U.S. law, the capitalization of a corporation can be a taxable event. Recall the facts in the hypothetical: Delta will contribute the following assets:

	Cost	Fair Market Value
Cash	500,000	500,000
Inventory	500,000	700,000
Quick Dry Additive Patent	$2,000,000	$ 6,800,000
Equipment [Used in manufacturing the 'Quick Dry' Cement]	1,000,000	2,000,000
Total Assets	$4,000,000	$10,000,000

Industrial will contribute cash of ten million five hundred thousand dollars. In addition, Delta and *Industrial* will each borrow three million dollars from their respective banks to fund DISA's working capital needs. Delta and *Industrial* will use their shares of DISA stock as collateral on the loan together with their respective guarantees.

The Code provides an extensive set of rules governing the capitalization of entities. Tax treaties do not address formation issues. The Code rules for determining the tax effect of an inbound transaction are technical and complex. The outbound rules are even more so. In order to understand fully the Code outbound rules, one must first become acquainted with the inbound rules. Consider the hypothetical involving Delta, *Industrial*, and DISA. **Assume that DISA is a *Texas* corporation.** Assume further the parties formed DISA as described in the hypothetical. Delta will own 49% of the issued and outstanding shares while *Industrial* will own 51%. Under this hypothetical, *Industrial* continues to be a Mexican corporation.

The inbound corporate capitalization—the transfer of assets in return for corporate stock—is a taxable event. *I.R.C § 1001(a) (1986)* uses a formula to determine the gain on the transaction—"... gain from the sale ... of property shall be the excess of the amount realized ...

over the adjusted basis . . ." This sale or exchange treatment can effect the transferors (Delta and *Industrial*) and the transferee, DISA. The 1001 general rule can be devastating to the parties. Fortunately, there are several major exceptions to this harsh general rule.

Consider DISA's tax implications under the general rule. The six million dollars in loans by Delta and *Industrial* is not a taxable event to DISA. The sale of DISA shares to Delta and *Industrial* is subject to the 1001 general rule. The § 1001 amount realized is the ten million dollars in cash and property received from Delta plus the ten million five hundred thousand dollars received from *Industrial* totaling twenty million five hundred thousand dollars. The stock that DISA is selling has a zero basis since it did not cost anything. Therefore, DISA has a potential taxable gain of twenty million five hundred thousand dollars on the capitalization transaction.

Congress recognized that this tax trap could have a substantial chilling effect on corporate formations. As a result, Congress enacted *IRC § 1032 (1986)* that provides in pertinent part: " . . . No gain or loss shall be recognized to a corporation on the receipt of money or other property in exchange for stock . . . of such corporation . . ." Thus, with the help of this taxpayer friendly provision, DISA will not have a taxable event on the sale of its stock. The transferors also have a potential tax effect on their purchase of DISA shares.

Industrial is purchasing DISA shares for cash. Under the § 1001 general rule, the amount realized is ten million five hundred thousand dollars represented by the fair market value of the DISA stock received. The adjusted basis of the property given up—the cash—is also ten million five hundred thousand dollars, therefore, *Industrial's* gain is zero. So far, so good! The cash purchase of stock is a tax neutral event. Notice that the tax implications to *Industrial* are determined by reference to the Code because tax treaties do not cover capitalization issues.

Delta also faces the § 1001 general rule. The amount realized is ten million dollars represented by the fair market value of the DISA stock received. However, the adjusted basis of the property given up (the cash, inventory, patent, and equipment) is only four million dollars. The resulting § 1001 gain is six million dollars. This is another substantial trap for the unwary. If Delta were in the thirty percent tax bracket it's income liability would be one million eight hundred thousand dollars just by capitalizing the corporation! Congress has stepped in on these cases to ameliorate the harshness of the § 1001 rule by enacting *IRC § 351(1986)*.

IRC § 351 states in pertinent part " . . . No gain or loss shall be recognized if property is transferred to a corporation by one or more persons solely in exchange for stock in such corporation and immediately after the exchange such person or persons are in control . . . of the corporation." Control for these purposes is defined as " . . . ownership of stock possessing at least 80 percent of the total combined voting power of all classes of stock entitled to vote and at least 80 percent of the total number of shares of all other classes of stock of the corporation." *IRC § 368(c)(1986)*. The test is met because DISA and *Industrial*, the persons transferring the property, own one hundred percent of the corporation immediately after the exchange. The § 351 rule permits Delta a tax-free corporate capitalization of an inbound transaction.

Now consider the original hypothetical involving Delta, *Industrial*, and DISA where DISA is a Mexican corporation. What are the tax implications in that case? In a domestic setting, although the process was full of twists and turns, Delta was not subject to tax on account of Code § 351. For Delta, the outbound capitalization transaction poses some very negative tax implications from the inbound transaction described above. *Industrial* and DISA, however, under this version of the hypothetical are foreign corporations. As such, they escape the rapacious U.S. income tax rules.

The reasons for the stark difference in the tax effect of an inbound and outbound capitalization transaction traces from the U.S. jurisdiction to tax international transactions. In the inbound transaction, the new entity is located in the U.S. It is subject to U.S. taxation either under worldwide income or territorial principles. The § 351 rule is merely a deferral, not an exemption. If, however, Delta could use section 351(a) to transfer appreciated assets to a foreign corporation a different result would emerge. Delta would not pay a tax on the transfer. DISA could then sell the appreciated assets outside of the United States and escape taxation as well.

To prevent this potential loss of tax revenue the Code essentially sets up a toll charge on outbound transfers by U.S. persons through *I.R.C. § 367 (1986)*. The analysis begins with *I.R.C. § 367(a) (1986)* which provides: "... If, in connection with any exchange described in section ... 351 ... a United States person transfers property to a foreign corporation, such foreign corporation shall not for purposes of determining the extent to which gain shall be recognized on such transfer, be considered to be a corporation." The transfer contemplated by Delta and *Industrial* falls within § 351 and since Delta is an U.S. person and is transferring property to a foreign corporation—DISA, (the foreign corporation) will not be treated as a corporation.

If DISA is not treated as a corporation, the non-recognition rule of § 351 does not apply and Delta is again subject to the § 1001 rule having a gain of four million dollars on the transaction. Therefore, a general rule emerges—a U.S. corporation is subject to the U.S. federal income tax upon the transfer of appreciated assets to a foreign corporation if the transfer is made in return for stock in that corporation. This is a high cost for Delta to pay for using a foreign corporation as the foreign direct investment entity. The unfairness is heightened by the fact that the corporation traditionally is the favored form of business organization.

The unfavorable § 367 rule conflicts with the general U.S. trade policy favoring the exportation of U.S. goods, services, and capital. This harsh tax rule could dissuade U.S. companies from establishing foreign operations. Congress, being mindful of this conflict, enacted a limited exception to the § 367 rule. In traditional fashion however, the exception is limited and is itself subject to various important exceptions. The tax beneficial exception is found in *I.R.C.* § *367(a)(3)(A) (1986)* and applies when the foreign corporation uses the transferred property in the active conduct of a trade or business outside the U.S.

The active conduct of a trade or business exception does not apply in all cases. *I.R.C.* § *367(a)(3)(B)(1986)* causes a transaction that would otherwise qualify for the exception, to revert back to the harsh general rule when certain 'tainted assets' are transferred to the foreign corporation. Delta is transferring cash, inventory, equipment used in the manufacture of the product, and a patent. The inventory and patent are tainted assets under § *367(a)(3)(B)(i)* and *(iv)*. The transfer of cash does not create a taxable event because it is not appreciated property. The equipment, although it is appreciated property, will likely not trigger gain (ignoring the effect of depreciation) on account of the active conduct of a trade or business exception.

The inventory transfer will trigger a gain of two hundred thousand dollars (fair market value of $700,000 and a cost of $500,000). It is a tainted asset and falls outside the § 367(a)(3)(A) rule. Delta should consider not transferring the inventory to DISA on account of the negative tax effect. It could instead replace the inventory with additional cash. This is a prime example of why the parties should determine the tax implications of their actions before obligating themselves. If Delta and *Industrial* had already signed the agreement Delta would either have to ask to amend the agreement or pay the tax consequences of the decision.

The patent is also tainted property and is governed by the forced sales provisions of *IRC* § *367(D)(1986)*. The § 367(d) rule is particularly diabolical for several reasons. First, the transfer is considered a sale even though it is in fact an exchange of a patent for capital stock. Second, the patent's assigned value needs to be commensurate with the income attributable to the intangible. The commensurate with the income standard is not easily determined. See the transfer pricing materials infra. Even an arms-length value established between two unrelated parties (Delta and *Industrial*) of six million eight hundred thousand dollars would not necessarily meet the commensurate with the income standard.

Finally, the income generated by the forced sale is considered as being U.S. source. This has the effect of precluding U.S. tax credits for any Mexican income taxes paid by Delta. The best solution for Delta is to license the patent and avoid the draconian § 367(d) forced sale rule. Otherwise, Delta would have to report a gain of four million eight hundred thousand dollars on the transfer (fair market value $6,800,000 and a cost of $2,000,000). However, the royalty rate set in the licensing of the patent is also subject to the transfer pricing rules described infra with the 'commensurate with income' standard as well. See the transfer pricing materials infra.

2. *Operating the IEJV*

While discussing the full U.S. tax implications of DISA's operations on Delta, *Industrial*, and DISA are beyond the scope of this book, certain broad general rules may be helpful in steering clear of traps for the unwary. This is especially true in decisions relative to business formation and capitalization. We first look to Delta's obligations. Assume Delta owns forty nine percent and *Industrial* owns fifty-one percent of DISA. Assume further that Delta has negotiated three contracts with DISA.

The first is a loan agreement evidencing the loan mentioned in the facts of the hypothetical. Delta is to receive interest income under this agreement. Delta has also negotiated a contract for the sale of goods and services to DISA. It expects to realize a gain from the sale of inventory property as well as services income. It has also signed an International Licensing Agreement (ILA) covering a patent and other intellectual property it transferred to DISA. DISA is to pay Delta royalties under this agreement. Delta decided on the ILA after realizing the negative tax effect of transferring intellectual property in return for stock. The tax effect of the income or gains derived from the contractual undertakings described above are discussed in Section 2.3, supra and 3.4B, infra. Delta could also have income as an owner of DISA on profits generated by DISA. The tax effect of these earnings is discussed here.

Assume DISA has profits for the year of ten million U.S. dollars. Under these facts, DISA and *Industrial*, as Mexican Residents, are not subject to U.S. tax on account of the U.S. Mexico tax treaty. DISA and *Industrial* are subject to tax under the MIRC. In addition, Delta is subject to Mexican tax under the U.S./Mexico tax treaty. See Section 2.3, supra. Furthermore, Delta, as an U.S. person, is subject to U.S. tax on DISA's Mexican earnings. The timing of Delta's tax liability is a function of the type of entity chosen.

For example, if DISA were a Mexican conduit entity like a Limited Liability Company, Delta would have to report four million nine hundred thousand dollars of income in the current year. ($10,000,000 of DISA income x 49%—Delta's ownership interest in DISA.) The income must be reported in the U.S. even if DISA has not paid any cash or property over to Delta. If DISA were a corporation it would not have to report any of DISA's income unless and until there is a dividend payment from DISA to Delta. This deferral of income attribute inherent to the corporate form is one of its major beneficial tax attributes. There are several exceptions to this deferral general rule.

In an international context the principal anti-deferral mechanism is embodied in the Controlled Foreign Corporation (CFC) rules. The CFC rules were enacted in the early nineteen sixties to operate in those cases where an U.S. person is deemed to be using a foreign corporation for an improper tax benefit. The deferral of corporate earnings does not apply in cases where the earnings are generated by a CFC that has subpart F income or invests its earnings (even non-Subpart F earnings) in U.S. property. The effect of the loss of deferral is to convert the foreign corporation into a conduit entity. In our case, if DISA and Delta run afoul of the CFC rules, Delta would have to report income of four million nine hundred thousand dollars even though DISA has not distributed any of its profits to the shareholders as a dividend.

The CFC regime is very complex. These materials are intended to only provide a thumbnail sketch of the rules. *IRC § 957(a)(1986)* defines a controlled foreign corporation as "... any foreign corporation if more than fifty percent of * * * the total combined voting power of all classes of stock of such corporation entitled to vote of * * * the total value of the stock of such corporation, is owned * * * or is considered as owned * * * by United States shareholders on any day during the taxable year of such foreign corporation." The term 'United States shareholder' is defined in *IRC § 951(b)(1986)*—"... means ... a United States person ... who owns ... or is considered as owning ... 10 percent or more of the total combined voting power of all classes of stock entitled to vote of such foreign corporation." The owned or considered as owned is defined in *IRC § 958(1986)*. The code section covers direct, indirect, and constructive ownership of the stock.

DISA may be a CFC. Delta is an U.S. shareholder that directly owns forty nine percent of DISA's shares. It does not own any DISA shares indirectly. However, § 958 also includes any shares that are constructively owned. Recall the materials in Section 4.1, supra where the various ways that Delta could use to maintain control were explored. If Delta is too successful in asserting control and the fact that it is so close to the '... more than fifty percent ...' test stated above, could push Delta as Constructively owning a controlling interest in DISA. If Delta is deemed to have a controlling interest, DISA will be a CFC with the concomitant negative tax effect.

If DISA is a CFC the next step is in determining whether it has any subpart F income. DISA does not become a conduit entity only on account of being a CFC it must also have this type of tainted income. Subpart F Income is defined in *IRC §§ 952 & 954 (1986)*. The Code views income that is easily movable as potential subpart F income. The fact that DISA is engaged in the active conduct of a trade or business militates against this type of tainted income. However, under certain circumstances the loan and transfer of technology agreement[5] and sale of goods[6] and services[7] agreement entered into with Delta could possibly generate subpart F income. The deferral is also lost when earnings are deemed invested in U.S. property as defined in *IRC §§ 952 & 954 (1986)*. The deferral is lost even if the earnings do not result from subpart F income. In the hypothetical the U.S. loan of three million dollars guaranteed by Delta's shares of DISA stock can be construed as an investment in U.S. property under *Treas. Reg. § 1.956–2(c)(2)(1988)*.

---

5. IRC § 954(a)(1) & (c)(1986).   **7.** IRC § 954(a)(3) & (e)(1986).
6. IRC § 954(a)(2) & (d)(1986).

B. TRANSFER PRICING

1. *Introduction*

Recall the materials in Section 2.3, supra where the general U.S. tax rules were discussed. The critical question was in determining the status of the person. A U.S. person under the Code pays tax on worldwide income, likewise a U.S. resident under a tax treaty, for purposes of U.S. taxation, must look to the Code rules for guidance and pays tax on worldwide income as well. Conversely, a non-U.S. person as defined in the Code or non-U.S. Resident as defined in an applicable tax treaty pays tax on U.S. source income only. Taxpayers have used different strategies in an effort to reduce income tax liability. The Internal Revenue Service (IRS) is always on the alert to thwart these efforts. It is a 'cat and mouse' game.

The non-U.S. person could possibly avoid U.S. tax by using the source rules to keep income offshore and by not having a U.S. office. However, in some cases the business exigencies require the creation of U.S. source income. For example, assume a foreign corporation manufactures goods that are sold to U.S. consumers. The sale transaction to the U.S. consumer must take place in the United States. Because the sale takes place in the U.S., the foreign corporation will have U.S. source income subject to U.S. taxation. To eliminate or reduce the tax the foreign corporation could manipulate the sales price.

For example, assume a foreign corporation will sell automobiles at twenty thousand dollars having a cost of ten thousand dollars. The goal is to reduce the potential income of ten thousand dollars. The foreign corporation could form a U.S. subsidiary. The foreign corporation would then sell the automobiles to the U.S. subsidiary for twenty thousand dollars. The transaction is structured so that the sale between parent and subsidiary is consummated outside of the United States. The foreign parent has non-U.S. source income of ten thousand dollars and is thus not subject to U.S. taxation. The U.S. subsidiary will then sell the automobile to the ultimate consumer in the United States for twenty thousand dollars. The U.S. subsidiary has the U.S. source income but the income amount is zero—the sales price of twenty thousand dollars minus the cost to the subsidiary of twenty thousand dollars.

U.S. persons also can use similar transfer-pricing strategies to minimize its income tax liability. Assume a domestic corporation (USCO) manufactures widgets at a cost of ten thousand dollars. It intends to sell them in the country of Europa. Europa has a tax system similar to the U.S. In order to minimize the income tax liability in the U.S. and Europa the USCO forms two foreign subsidiaries—Offshore Ltd., usually located in a tax haven jurisdiction and Europa SA, an Europa corporation.

USCO sells the widget to Offshore at cost—ten thousand dollars. USCO has no gain because the sale price is equal to its cost basis. Offshore then resells the widget to Europa, SA, for twenty thousand dollars. Offshore has the gain of ten thousand dollars—sales price of twenty thousand dollars with a cost of ten thousand dollars. Offshore pays no U.S. tax on the gain because it is a foreign corporation with no U.S. source income. It pays no tax in the tax haven country because there is no tax imposed. Europa, SA pays twenty thousand dollars for the widget then resells it in Europa for twenty thousand dollars reporting no gain in that country.

Congress does not like these types of artificial pricing strategies. In response it gave the IRS a formidable statutory weapon to prevent this type of abuse. Section 482 is the principal code formulation that is designed to prevent transfer-pricing abuse. The entire § 482 text consists of two sentences. The first sentence gives the Commissioner great power to redistribute income or tax credits between related parties. The second sentence adds additional requirements in transfers involving intangible property. The § 482 adjustment is only available to the IRS— not the taxpayer. In the hypothetical situations above the the transactions are entered into between related parties and are subject to § 482 scrutiny.

Section 482 is a blunt weapon. Perhaps that is why the IRS has issued over one hundred pages of regulations attempting to explain the two-sentence statute. Case law is not much help either. The cases are long (some are more than one hundred fifty pages) and fact intensive. They are not very useful for planning purposes. A large percentage of transfer-pricing cases are settled before they reach trial. This statistic perhaps reveals that neither party has a great deal of trust in the available regulations and case law. One helpful procedure is the Advance Pricing Agreement (APA)[8]. An APA can take some of the guesswork out of the transfer-price issue. When the APA rules are followed the IRS will agree to accept the transfer-price as established under the APA.

The basic thrust of § 482 in the sale of tangible property is to put a related transaction in parity with an unrelated transaction. The touchstone is arms-length value. It is believed that the price established by two unrelated parties acting in arms-length will be the true indicator of the fair market vale of the transaction under consideration. Finding a comparable arms-length transaction can be very difficult. In the case involving a transfer of intangible property the process is even more difficult.

Section 482 was amended in 1986 adding the burden that a transfer price in the case of an intangible must be commensurate with the income attributable to the intangible property. This provision dubbed the 'super royalty' provision adds still another level of complexity to the transfer pricing decision. In our hypothetical Delta will be selling goods and services to DISA, a related company. It will also be licensing technology to DISA. These transactions fall within the reach of Section 482. The transfer pricing decision is one of the most important and contentious issues in the tax law. The materials begin with the coverage with the licensing agreement.

8. Revenue Procedure 91–22, 1991–1 C.B. 526

2. *The International Transfer of Technology*

In the hypothetical, Delta has assigned, and the parties have agreed, that the patent and related IPRs being transferred have a value of six million eight hundred thousand dollars. Assume that Delta's marketing and engineering department established the value. The accounting and legal department concurred. Assume also that a royalty rate of twelve percent, in the opinion of the people mentioned above, represents the fair market value of the royalties. Will the IRS honor the rate reached between the parties? The answer is maybe—and that is the problem. The guidelines for Delta are the APA procedures, Treas. Reg. § 1.482—4(1994) and case law.

PROMOTING THE TRANSFER OF U.S. TECHNOLOGY ACROSS NATIONAL BORDERS: THE ENEMY WITHIN

Antonio Mendoza

20 N.C.J. Int'l l. & Com. Reg. 97 (1994).

* * *

I. THE CONFLICT IN U.S. POLICY

A. *Introduction*

The United States is a net technology exporter. Promoting technology exportation is profitable not only for U.S. companies, but for the U.S. economy as well. However, American companies and U.S. policy makers place importance on protecting transferred technology. Congress acts mainly through domestic law in its efforts to protect the transferred technology.

The main goal of American companies is to preserve the financial value of the technology through license and franchise agreements. The U.S. government, wishing to protect the technology, takes aggressive action against counterfeiting, piracy, and other real or perceived unfair business practices of foreign companies or their governments.

The U.S. government, however, has competing interests in regulating technology transfer. It desires to: (1) promote the transfer of technology and protect its financial value; (2) inhibit, for national security purposes, the transfer of certain technology; and (3) prevent the erosion of the U.S. tax revenue base.

Congress reacts to these competing interests by enacting legislation. National security legislation is designed to inhibit the transfer of technology in certain cases; tax legislation is not designed to do so, but in fact, may inhibit the transfer of technology.

B. *The Hypothetical Case of High–Tech, Inc.*

In our hypothetical, High–Tech is a new innovative high technology company, highly successful in developing patents and manufacturing products in the United States. It has been granted a patent on a widget that is designed for nonmilitary applications but which can be converted to military use. Research and development costs for the invention amounted to $100,000. High–Tech believes that widget sales will be very good in Latina, a developing country. * * *

IV. FEDERAL TAX LEGISLATION: WHAT IS THE TAX COST TO HIGH-TECH?

A. *The Tax Avoidance Strategy*

Certainty of a transaction's tax cost is a critical factor in any business decision. High–Tech could incur the expense of the Latina subsidiary and lose the potential profits to the tax man. The problem faced by High–Tech is that it partially fits the profile, albeit inadvertently, of the taxpayer in the classic tax avoidance strategy.

The strategy works as follows. A U.S. company develops a high profit patent. The research and development costs, deductible in the United States, reduce U.S. taxable income. Just before the product which is subject to the patent is marketed, which generates sales income, the U.S. company sells or otherwise transfers the patent to a related foreign affiliate at or below cost. If organized in a tax haven country, the affiliate pays no tax in either the tax haven or the United States.

B. *Federal Legislation to Discourage the Tax Avoidance Strategy*

Through the years, Congress has enacted a formidable array of statutes amending the federal income tax system to discourage the tax avoidance strategy. The question is whether current tax law is a proper response to improper taxpayer strategies, or merely a myopic approach resulting from a preoccupation with revenue. A summary of the rules targeting transfers * * * of appreciated technology property follows. * * *

3. *The Post–1986 Reallocation Provision of I.R.C. s 482: The "Super Royalty"*

a. The Enactment of the Legislation

The technique of transferring intangibles to a related foreign corporation in a low or no tax jurisdiction has prompted concern in Congress with taxpayer behavior. Accordingly, technology transfers, or licenses, to foreign corporations, or possessions corporations, are now subject to a new standard of income allocation.

Dubbed the "Super Royalty," its purpose is to allocate income from intangibles among the members of the multinational group in a manner that reflects the relative economic activities of each. Although admirable in intent, the new standard is very imprecise. It also reflects questionable policy as it erodes the arm's-length standard that the United States has long espoused on an international level. * * *

b. The Attempts to Explain the Statute: Searching for Suitable Explanations

Essentially, the 1986 amendment exacerbates the valuation problem that have long plagued intercompany transactions. Recall that High–

Tech formed Latina, S.A., as its wholly owned subsidiary. It then licensed the widget patent for $200,000 using industry averages to establish the price, reporting a gain on the sale. Will the Internal Revenue Service (IRS) agree with High–Tech on the amount of the gain? The answer is maybe, and thus, turns High–Tech's tax planning into a crap shoot.

Congress recognized that important issues were left unanswered by the language in the amendment. It called upon the IRS to conduct a comprehensive study of the intercompany pricing issue and to modify the rules accordingly. Two years after the Congressional mandate, the IRS issued its much criticized "white paper" explaining the amendment. In January 1992, four years after the issuance of the "white paper," proposed regulations were issued that largely abandoned many of the "white paper" positions. The proposed regulations were themselves repealed after much criticism. In January 1993, temporary regulations were issued. Truly, IRS efforts attempting to explain I.R.C. section 482 have been imprecise and un-illuminating. Final regulations (which were effective as of July 8, 1994), while lengthy and detailed, do not provide much certainty to business planners.

c. The Quest for Certainty Under the Regulations: Searching in Vain

The regulations provide several methods to value intangibles: (1) the comparable uncontrolled transaction method; (2) the comparable profits method; and (3) any other method to reach true arm's-length value. The regulations' intangible property valuation methods resemble those provided in the regulations for tangible property. If experience is any guide, however, the "other method" of valuation will be the IRS's preferred method.

The use of the "other method" provision creates additional problems for High-Tech. The temporary regulations place important limitations on the use of the "other method," by imposing burdensome documentation requirements on the taxpayer, the adherence of which will not necessarily prevent penalties.

V. Conclusion

A. *The Effect of the Amendment and the Regulations*

1. *The Uncertainty Impacting High–Tech*

With the passage of a one-sentence amendment, i.e., I.R.C. section 482, Congress has seemingly imposed a perfect hindsight rule with no safe harbors for U.S. companies. The result is sure to be increased litigation under section 482. High–Tech, and taxpayers similarly situated, will be at a decided disadvantage, and subjected to a whipsaw effect on the earnings of their controlled foreign corporations. * * *

HOSPITAL CORPORATION OF AMERICA v. C.I.R.

United States Tax Court, 1983.
81 T.C. 520.

* * *

HCA was in the hospital management business in the United States. It operated hospitals owned by it or its domestic subsidiary corporations and operated other hospitals under management contracts entered into with the owners thereof. In 1973, HCA decided to pursue an opportunity to contract with the Royal Cabinet of the Kingdom of Saudi Arabia to manage the King Faisal Specialist Hospital in Riyadh, Saudi Arabia. HCA formed a Cayman Islands corporation to negotiate and perform this management contract. HCA performed services for and made available to its Cayman Islands subsidiary its hospital management system, expertise, and experience. * * *

Petitioner decided to form two corporations in the Cayman Islands, a parent and a subsidiary corporation. There were several reasons for incorporating in the Cayman Islands: the country was an English-speaking jurisdiction with familiar corporate codes; it had a stable government; it was readily accessible to the United States; and it imposed no corporate income taxes, if certain conditions were met. The use of a separate corporation to handle the KFSH management contract was generally consistent with petitioner's usual policy of using separate corporations for its HCA-owned hospitals for purposes of identifying the profit picture, assigning responsibility, and limiting liabilities. However, the management contracts with non-HCA-owned hospitals had been handled by HSP, Inc., and the record does not indicate that separate corporations had been set up to handle each management contract in the United States. Tax consequences under both United States and Cayman Islands laws were considered in deciding to incorporate there.

Petitioner hired W.S. Walker and Co., of Georgetown, Grand Cayman, a Cayman Islands law firm, to arrange the incorporation of the two corporations. Robert G. McCullough, a member of the law firm representing petitioner in Nashville, was also involved. The new corporations were named Hospital Corporation International, Ltd. (HCI One) and Hospital Corporation of the Middle East, Ltd. (LTD). HCI One was to be the umbrella corporation for all of petitioner's foreign operations. LTD was to be in charge of negotiating, executing, and performing any contract to manage the King Faisal Hospital. HCI One was a first tier wholly-owned subsidiary of petitioner and LTD was a wholly-owned subsidiary of HCI One and therefore a second tier subsidiary of petitioner.

The Cayman Islands corporations were formed and registered on May 28 and May 29, 1973. Each corporation had capital stock of $1,000 paid in cash. The two corporations were formed and registered as exempt companies under The Companies Law, section 179, which required that the objects of the company be carried out mainly outside the Cayman Islands. The memoranda of association for both corporations specifically provided that neither corporation will "trade in the Cayman Islands with any persons, firm or corporation except in furtherance of the business of the Company carried on outside the Islands...." No income tax was imposed by The Companies Law of the Cayman Islands under which HCI One and LTD were formed. * * *

From the beginning of the KFSH project, tax consequences were considered. Dini had recommended that an offshore company be set up because of "its obvious tax advantages." A memorandum dated October 15, 1973, titled the International Taxation of Foreign Operations was prepared for petitioner by Gary T. Baker, a member of the tax staff of Ernst & Ernst in Nashville. This memorandum concluded that both HCI One and LTD were controlled foreign corporations as defined by section 957(a). * * *

Baker's legal opinion also predicted that it was more likely that respondent would attempt to reallocate income under section 482 than to raise a Subpart F issue. In this regard, Baker advised giving constant attention so that all dealings among petitioner, HCI One, and LTD be at arm's length and warned that the "failure to judiciously comply with that requirement would surely prove to be the greatest potential tax trap facing the international operations." * * *

Ultimate Findings of Fact

1. Hospital Corporation of America, Ltd., is not a sham corporation and is to be recognized for Federal income tax purposes; * * *

3. Seventy five (75) percent of the 1973 net income of Hospital Corporation of America, Ltd., is allocable to petitioner under section 482.

Opinion

* * *

Sham Corporation

Respondent's primary position is that LTD is a "sham" corporation that should not be recognized for Federal income tax purposes. Respondent asserts that LTD was "a mere skeleton; a sham corporation that existed in form only for the purpose of obtaining the tax benefits available to a foreign corporation." Respondent argues that the fees earned from the KFSH management contract were produced by petitioner's professional skill, expertise, know-how, reputation, goodwill, experience, business organization, and procedures and are therefore taxable wholly to petitioner under section 61. Respondent maintains that "the formation of LTD is no more than an old-fashioned anticipatory assignment of income in the guise of a modern-day gimmick known as an offshore tax haven." He asserts that the question is the same as that raised in Lucas v. Earl, 281 U.S. 111 (1930), one of substance versus form, and that in substance the income from the KFSH management contract was earned by petitioner, not LTD.

LTD was properly organized in accordance with the Cayman Islands Companies Law, a fact that respondent does not dispute. It does not follow, however, that LTD will necessarily be recognized for Federal tax purposes. * * * Respondent asks us to disregard LTD's existence for tax purposes.

Generally, the corporate entity will be respected except in "exceptional situations where it otherwise would present an obstacle to the due protection or enforcement of public or private rights." * * * The test of whether a corporation will be recognized as a taxable entity was stated by the Supreme Court in Moline Properties, Inc. v. Commissioner, 319 U.S. 436, 438–439 (1943), as follows:

The doctrine of corporate entity fills a useful purpose in business life. Whether the purpose be to gain an advantage under the law of the state of incorporation or to avoid or to comply with the demands of creditors or to serve the creator's personal or undisclosed convenience, so long as that purpose is the equivalent of business activity or is followed by the carrying on of business by the corporation, the corporation remains a separate taxable entity. (Footnotes omitted.)

These alternative requirements of business purpose or business activity have been restated in a long line of cases in this and other courts. As to the latter requirement, the quantum of business activity may be rather minimal. * * *

Petitioner has the burden of proving that LTD meets either of these requirements. * * * Based on the record in this case, we are persuaded that LTD satisfied both of these tests, and we hold that it is to be recognized as a separate corporate entity for Federal tax purposes.

Our inquiry in that regard is essentially factual. Each case turns on its individual facts and circumstances. * * *

IV. Section 482 Allocation

Respondent's final argument is that all of LTD's taxable income for 1973 in the amount of $1,787,030 should be allocated to petitioner pursuant to section 482. Section 482 authorizes respondent to distribute, apportion, or allocate gross income, deductions, credits, or allowances between or among organizations owned or controlled by the same interests, if he determines that such is necessary in order to prevent the evasion of taxes or clearly to reflect the income of the organizations. As a logical shortcut to allocating gross income and deductions, respondent in certain instances may also allocate net income. * * * We think respondent properly may do so in this instance.

One of the reasons for the enactment of section 482 and its predecessors was to prevent the evasion of taxes by shifting income from a domestic business to a foreign corporation controlled by the same interests. * * * The regulations state that "The purpose of section 482 is to place a controlled taxpayer on a tax parity with an uncontrolled taxpayer, by determining, according to the standard of an uncontrolled taxpayer, the true taxable income from the property and business of a controlled taxpayer." * * *

Section 482 thus permits respondent to examine dealings between controlled corporations and make allocations so as to place these dealings on the same basis for tax purposes as if they had taken place between independent and uncontrolled taxpayers. Achiro v. Commissioner, 77 T.C. 881, 896–897 (1981). On the other hand, if the dealings between controlled organizations are fair and equivalent in result to arm's length bargaining, no allocation is authorized. Hamburgers York Road, Inc. v. Commissioner, supra, 41 T.C. at 835; Ballentine Motor Co. v. Commissioner, supra, 39 T.C. at 357. The standard to be applied in every case is that of an uncontrolled taxpayer dealing at arm's length with another uncontrolled taxpayer. Section 1.482–1(b)(1), Income Tax Regs.

The regulations also provide that "Transactions between one controlled taxpayer and another will be subjected to special scrutiny to ascertain whether the common control is being used to reduce, avoid, or escape taxes." Section 1.482–1(c), Income Tax Regs.

Petitioner and LTD were controlled by the same interests. Section 1.482–1(a)(3), Income Tax Regs., provides that the control may be direct or indirect, whether legally enforceable and however exercisable or exercised. Petitioner had control over LTD since LTD was a second tier subsidiary of petitioner. Moreover, the same individuals who were officers and directors of LTD were also officers and directors of petitioner. The conclusion is inescapable that the requisite control was present.

Section 482, however, does not permit allocation merely because the common interests have the power to shift income. A reallocation under section 482 must be based on actual shifting of income. * * * We must therefore examine whether there has been a shifting of income between LTD and petitioner.

Respondent enjoys broad discretion in his application of section 482. * * * Our review of his determination is limited. * * * Respondent's determination must be sustained unless we find an abuse of discretion— that his determination is unreasonable, arbitrary, or capricious. * * * Whether respondent has abused his discretion is a question of fact. * * * We must examine all of the facts and circumstances to determine whether respondent has abused his discretion.

Respondent, both in his deficiency notice and on brief after the trial in this Court, allocated all of LTD's taxable income to petitioner. By allocating 100 percent of LTD's taxable income to petitioner, respondent has attempted in still another fashion to resurrect his argument that LTD is a "sham' corporation that should not be recognized for tax purposes. Respondent's argument under all of the theories that he has presented is that petitioner could as well have done the things that LTD did and therefore could have received all earnings from the King Faisal Hospital management contract. Since petitioner could have had these earnings, respondent would make it so by exercising his authority under section 482. We answer the argument as we did in Seminole Flavor Co. v. Commissioner, 4 T.C. 1215, 1235 (1945) and Koppers Co. v. Commissioner, 2 T.C. 152, 158 (1943): Petitioner did not do this. Petitioner organized a separate corporation to contract with the Royal Cabinet of the Kingdom of Saudi Arabia to manage the King Faisal Hospital. We have held that LTD is a valid corporate entity that is to be recognized for tax purposes. In these circumstances, section 482 does not authorize an allocation that would in effect disregard the separate corporate existence of LTD. * * * Moreover, section 1.482–1(b)(3), Income Tax Regs., states that section 482 is not intended to effect an allocation as would produce a result equivalent to a computation of consolidated taxable income. See also Seminole Flavor Co. v. Commissioner, supra, 4 T.C. at 1232. We therefore hold that to the extent respondent attempted to shift all of LTD's taxable income to petitioner under section 482, his determination is arbitrary and capricious. * * *

Even though we have rejected respondent's 100 percent allocation of taxable income from LTD to petitioner, the evidence indicates overwhelmingly that an allocation is necessary and proper in this case. * * * Unfortunately, there is little quantitative evidence in this record upon which we can determine what a reasonable allocation of profits would be. Neither party has been particularly helpful to the Court in this regard. However, we must do the best we can with what we have. * * *

The regulations provide as a general rule that where one member of a group of controlled entities performs services for the benefit of another member without charge or at a charge which is not at arm's length, appropriate allocations may be made to reflect an arm's length charge for the services. Section 1.482–2(b), Income Tax Regs. The regulations also provide that where intangibles are made available in any manner by one member of a group of controlled entities to another member of the group for other than arm's length consideration, an allocation can be made to reflect arm's length consideration for the use of the intangibles. Section 1.482–2(d), Income Tax Regs.

Neither petitioner nor respondent has made any attempt to define specific services rendered by petitioner to LTD, to define LTD's use of intangibles belonging to petitioner, or to establish arm's length charges for either. Petitioner argues that the only services that could arguably be said to have been performed by petitioner for LTD during 1973 were in the negotiations of the management contract and in the guarantee. Petitioner further argues that LTD reimbursed petitioner for all of the travel expenses of petitioner's personnel who went to London, Geneva, and Riyadh in 1973, and also reimbursed petitioner for the finder's fee that was paid to Joe Dini. Petitioner also argues that any services which it did perform were merely supervisory services of a parent with respect to a subsidiary that are not subject to allocation under section 482. * * *

The evidence, however, indicates that in 1973 petitioner performed substantial services for LTD within the meaning of section 1.482–2(b), Income Tax Regs., and that it made available to LTD the use of its intangibles within the meaning of section 1.482–2(d)(3), Income Tax Regs. Petitioner played an active role in the contract negotiations. In formulating the contract proposal, some of petitioner's personnel, particularly hospital administrators and accountants, worked under the direction of Todd. * * * Petitioner also made available to LTD the use of intangibles. Section 1.482–2(d)(3), Income Tax Regs., defines intangibles as follows:(3) Definition of intangible property. (i) Solely for the purposes of this section, intangible property shall consist of the items described in subdivision (ii) of this subparagraph, provided that such items have substantial value independent of the services of individual persons. (ii) The items referred to in subdivision (i) of this subparagraph are as follows: (a) Patents, inventions, formulas, processes, designs, patterns, and other similar items; (b) Copyrights, literary, musical, or artistic compositions, and other similar items; (c) Trademarks, trade names, brand names, and other similar items; (d) Franchises, licenses, contracts, and other similar items; (e) Methods, programs, systems, procedures, campaigns, surveys, studies, forecasts, estimates, customer lists, technical data, and other similar items.

In contracting with LTD for the management of the King Faisal Hospital, the Royal Cabinet of the Kingdom of Saudi Arabia definitely looked to petitioner's experience and expertise. At the outset in the contract negotiations, petitioner was told to emphasize in its proposals HCA's experience and expertise. Later, LTD's name was changed from Hospital Corporation of the Middle East, Ltd. to Hospital Corporation of America, Ltd. because the Saudi Arabian officials wanted an "American flavor." The management contract itself is replete with references to and discussions of HCA's experience and expertise in the management of 51 hospitals in the United States. Also the KFSH management contract expressly required that petitioner guarantee LTD's performance of the contract.

* * *

We think that LTD used these intangibles and therefore an allocation is proper. Section 1.482–2(d), Income Tax Regs.

While petitioner has attempted to persuade us that it has no "system" that LTD could use, that attempt has not been successful. Indications of petitioner's system have permeated the entire record in this case. Petitioner's 1973 annual report gives a good indication of what petitioner saw as its management system. The "combination of medical-financial-administrative orientation and skills at all levels of the management structure provides the ideal combination for the effective management of hospitals. It is unique within the health care industry and is one of the company's most important competitive advantages."

* * *

We conclude that petitioner made its system available to LTD in both the negotiations for and the performance of the management contract for the King Faisal Hospital. There is no indication that LTD paid petitioner for the use of the system. Therefore an allocation is proper. Section 1.482–2(d), Income Tax Regs. * * * Using our best judgment on the lengthy but inconclusive record before us, we have concluded and found as a fact that 75 percent of the § taxable income of LTD in 1973 was attributable to petitioner. * * *

U.S. governmental policy in the international transfer of technology area appears to be somewhat in conflict. On the one hand, governmental trade policy favors the outbound flow of technology by negotiating trade agreements that reduce performance requirements and promotes the protection of the ownership of intellectual property. However, tax legislation hinders the transfer by subjecting the pricing decision to a vague standard requiring the transfer price to be "... commensurate with the income attributable to the intangible." The clause adds to the already amorphous § 482 concepts.

The unique nature of an IPR has always made the finding of an arms-length price very difficult. The *Hospital Corporation of America* (HCA) is indicative of many § 482 cases—lengthy and fact intensive. The case reveals the difficulty courts encountered in applying § 482 concepts even before the 1986 amendments. The fact that in many cases taxpayers use tax haven countries as part of their pricing strategy has complicated the issues as well. The IRS in many § 482 scenarios attempts to buttress its position by using a sham argument. The courts also typically do not allow it.

Taxpayers are allowed to order their affairs in such a way as to minimize their tax liability. In one case, Judge Learned Hand wrote what has become the tax lawyer's mantra—"... Any one may so arrange his affairs that his taxes shall be as low as possible; he is not bound to choose that pattern which will best pay the Treasury; there is not even a patriotic duty to increase one's taxes."[9]. The sham argument will prevail when the taxpayer attempts to elevate form over substance.

In HCA the IRS argued also for a one hundred percent re-allocation either as a sham or § 482 adjustment. The court essentially replaced its guess—a seventy five percent reallocation for that of the IRS. The 1986 amendment adding the requirement that the transfer price of an intangible must be commensurate with the income attributable to it greatly complicated the process. The so-called 'super royalty' provisions impose on the technology transferor the obligation to determine the value of the IPR before it is used and without being able to fully rely on industry standards. Adding to the misery, *IRC § 6662(1986)* provides for a penalty of up to forty percent on any gross valuation misstatements.[10] What would the HCA adjustment likely be under the 'commensurate with the income' standard?

---

9. Helvering v. Gregory, 69 F.2d 809 (2d Cir.1934).

10. I.R.C. § 6662(a) & (h)(1986).

The above analysis relates to the amount of income in question as adjusted by § 482. Delta's royalty income is subject to tax by both the United States and Mexico. Since the IPR is being used in Mexico, the Code rules would generally make the royalty income foreign source[11]. This is important because of the potential foreign tax credit available for the payment of any Mexican income tax. Delta will also be subject to Mexican income tax under the U.S./Mexico tax treaty. See Section 2.3, supra.

3. *The International Sale of Services*

Delta's Division II is in the business of providing engineering services to its client. Under the contract with DISA it will have to travel to Mexico to perform the services. For U.S. tax purposes, Delta will pay U.S. tax on income generated by the services by its engineers in Mexico. The income will be foreign source.[12] Delta will not be subject to Mexican tax under the under the U.S./Mexico treaty. See section 2.3, supra. The amount of service income to be included as income is affected by the § 482 rules as well.

UNITED STATES STEEL CORP. v. C.I.R.

United States Court of Appeals, Second Circuit, 1980.
617 F.2d 942.

* * *

LUMBARD, Circuit Judge:

This consolidated appeal from two decisions of the Tax Court, Quealy, J., arises out of the development by United States Steel Corporation ("Steel") of newly discovered Venezuelan iron mines in the 1950's, and the financial arrangements resulting from the creation of two Steel subsidiaries to mine and transport ore. Two distinct questions of tax law are presented: first, what kind of evidence is sufficient for a taxpayer to challenge successfully the Commissioner's determination that payments between a parent and a subsidiary are not "arm's length" and thus are subject to reallocation under s 482 of the Internal Revenue Code * * *

We find that the Tax Court, in the first case, T.C. Memo. 1977–140, did not give sufficient weight to the taxpayer's evidence supporting its contention that charges between the taxpayer and its subsidiary were arm's length, and for that reason we reverse the judgment of the Tax Court sustaining, with modifications, the Commissioner's reallocation of income * * *

I.

THE REALLOCATION ISSUE

Taxpayer, United States Steel Corporation, is a major vertically integrated producer of steel. In addition to steel-making plants, it owns

---

11. I.R.C. §§ 861(a)(4) & 862(a)(4)(1986).

12. I.R.C. § 862(a)(3)(1986).

iron ore mines in the United States and elsewhere. In 1947, Steel discovered a vast new source of iron ore in Cerro Bolivar, a remote part of northeastern Venezuela on the Orinoco River. The transport of Orinoco ore to the Atlantic required the dredging of an extensive channel. Steel proceeded to develop these mines at a cost of approximately two hundred million dollars. In 1949, Steel formed Orinoco Mining Company ("Orinoco"), a wholly-owned Delaware subsidiary, to own and exploit the Cerro Bolivar mines.

Orinoco began selling ore from its mines in 1953. Initially, the ore purchased by Steel from Orinoco was transported to the United States in chartered vessels owned by two independent companies, Universe Tankships, Inc., ("Universe") and Joshua Hendy Corp. ("Hendy"). But in December 1953, Steel incorporated another wholly-owned subsidiary, Navios, Inc., ("Navios") in Liberia. Navios, with its principal place of business in Nassau, in the Bahamas, was a carrier which did not own any vessels. From July 1954 on, Navios, instead of Steel, chartered vessels from Universe, Hendy, and other owners, and Steel paid Navios for the transport of ore from Venezuela to the United States. Navios was an active company, having in the period 1954–60 between 53 and 81 fulltime employees.

Although Steel was by far the largest customer of Navios, Navios sold its transport services to other domestic steel producers (collectively "the independents") and to foreign steel companies. The prices charged by Navios to other domestic ore importers during the relevant period were the same prices charged to Steel, though the rates charged to companies importing ore to countries other than the United States were different.

Like Navios, Orinoco did not sell exclusively to Steel, although its parent was by far its largest customer. Orinoco sold to the independents and to foreign steel companies at the same prices it charged Steel.

Orinoco sold ore bound for the United States FOB Puerto Ordaz, Venezuela in an attempt to arrive at a fair market price in order to minimize conflict with the Venezuelan taxing authorities, who had the power to revalue, for taxation purposes, the price at which Orinoco sold its ore if they considered that price too low. United States prices of iron ore were set, during the period in question, by an annual auction of ore from the Mesabi range of Minnesota, which established the so-called "Lower Lake Erie" price. Through its subsidiary Oliver Mining Co., Steel sold significant amounts of Mesabi ore.

Orinoco was subject to a Venezuelan tax of up to 50% on income, and to a United States tax of 48% on any residue not offset by foreign tax credits. Steel was subject to a United States tax of 48% of net income. Navios was subject to a 2.5% excise tax in Venezuela and no tax in the United States. Dividends paid by Navios to Steel, of course, would be taxed at a rate of 48%.

Navios was a highly successful venture: Steel found itself in 1960 with a wholly-owned subsidiary possessing nearly $80 million in cash and cash equivalents. Navios paid no dividends to Steel during the period involved in this case. In effect, then, Navios became an offshore tax shelter. But, as the Tax Court found, Steel's decision to create Navios is not in itself a justification for the Commissioner's reallocation of income, since Navios served a major business purpose unrelated to tax-shifting: allowing Steel to reap the cost savings of using a non-United States-flag fleet.

In the tax years 1957 through 1960, Navios earned approximately $391 million in gross revenues, all on the transport of iron ore from Venezuela to various points in the eastern continental United States and in Europe. Of this total, revenues from Steel amounted to $286 million, or 73% of the total; and from independent domestic steel purchasers $21 million, or 5% of the total.

Two steel companies, Bethlehem Steel and Eastern Gas and Fuel Associates, used other means of transportation for ore which they purchased from Orinoco. Bethlehem had mines and exported from Venezuela small quantities of ore from the Orinoco area prior to Steel's development of its mines. Bethlehem had earlier set up a transportation system from minehead to the United States to which it adhered during the period in question. Eastern Fuel and Gas, a much smaller concern, contracted directly with shipowners, including its own shipowning affiliates.

During 1957–60, there was no information publicly available from which a "market price" for the carriage of iron ore by sea could be determined. Unlike the practice in the oil tanker industry, for example, ship charter contract prices for ore carriage were not published.

The Commissioner determined that Navios had overcharged Steel by 25%, and allocated income from Navios to Steel * * * the Commissioner asserted deficiencies against Steel as follows:

Taxable Year	Amount Allocated
1957	11,072,585.00
1958	13,042,107.00
1959	13,624,330.00
1960	14,402,384.00
	$52,141,406.00

The Tax Court reviewed the history of Steel's relations with its subsidiaries Navios and Orinoco and concluded that a s 482 reallocation was justified because Steel had caused Navios to charge rates such that, at all times, the delivered price of Orinoco-origin ore in the United States was equivalent of the Lower Lake Erie price. In the Tax Court's view, this equivalence served several purposes. First, it protected Steel's interest in the revenues of its subsidiary, Oliver Mining Co., by insuring that the Lower Lake Erie price was not undercut by cheaper foreign ore. Second, because Steel could be sure of selling its Orinoco production so long as the delivered United States price did not exceed the Lower Lake Erie price, it enabled Steel to earn "extra" profits. Third, such extra profits, because they were earned through Navios, were not subject to Venezuelan tax and were sheltered from United States tax.

Judge Quealy then reviewed the figures used by the Commissioner in his reallocation. The Commissioner had used an approach that looked to profits and determined that a certain percentage of Navios' profits was in excess of what would fairly reflect income. Judge Quealy, by contrast, used two alternative means of arriving at what Navios' revenues would have been had it charged a "market" price for its services. First, he extrapolated hypothetical rates for 1957–60 from what Universe and Hendy charged in their 1954 contracts with Steel, adding adjustments to account for increased costs, risk and profits. As a check on the accuracy of this historical approach, Judge Quealy also constructed hypothetical rates based on estimates of what Navios' costs had been in the taxable years in question, adjusting these estimates to allow for risk and profit. He then chose the method which, for each taxable year, would result in the lowest reallocation in favor of the government.

The figures arrived at by the Tax Court provide for reallocation of income as follows from Navios to Steel:

Taxable Year	Deficiency
1957	$11,100,174.68
1958	10,272,076.07
1959	9,884,214.27
1960	16,814,959.53
	$48,071,424.55

We are constrained to reverse because, in our view, the Commissioner has failed to make the necessary showings that justify reallocation under the broad language of section 482 * * *

The Treasury Regulations provide a guide for interpreting this section's broad delegation of power to the Secretary, and they are binding on the Commissioner. Treas.Reg. 1.482–1(b) states in part that "(t)he standard to be applied in every (s 482) case is that of an uncontrolled taxpayer dealing at arm's length with another uncontrolled taxpayer." This "arm's length" standard is repeated in Treas.Reg. 1.482–1(c), and this subsection makes it clear that it is meant to be an objective standard that does not depend on the absence or presence of any intent on the part of the taxpayer to distort his income.

Treasury Reg. 1.482–2(b) governs the situation presented by the case at bar, in which a controlled corporation performs a service for a controlling corporation allegedly "at a charge which is not equal to an arm's length charge as defined in subparagraph (3) of this paragraph." Subparagraph (3) defines an arm's length charge for a service which is an integral part of the business of the corporation providing it as "the amount which was charged or would have been charged for the same or similar services in independent transactions with or between unrelated parties under similar circumstances considering all relevant facts."

We think it is clear that if a taxpayer can show that the price he paid or was charged for a service is "the amount which was charged or would have been charged for the same or similar services in independent transactions with or between unrelated parties" it has earned the right, under the Regulations, to be free from a s 482 reallocation despite other evidence tending to show that its activities have resulted in a shifting of tax liability among controlled corporations. Where, as in this case, the taxpayer offers evidence that the same amount was actually charged for the same service in transactions with independent buyers, the question resolves itself into an evaluation of whether or not the circumstances of the sales to independent buyers are "similar" enough to sales to the controlling corporation under the circumstances, "considering all relevant facts." In our view, "considering all the relevant facts," the evidence was sufficient to show similar enough transactions with independent buyers to establish that the price Steel paid Navios was an arm's length price.

The evidence referred to above consists of Steel's uncontested showing that the amounts Steel paid Navios for ore transport were the same rates paid by other independent purchasers of Orinoco ore. The Commissioner argues that the payment of the same rates by Steel and by independent buyers does not alone show, "considering all the relevant facts", that Steel paid an arm's length price.

Judge Quealy found that although purchasers of Orinoco ore were not required to use Navios' transport services, "most purchasers would not be in a position to contract independently for transportation of the ore to the site of their mills." (T.C. Memo. 1977–140 at 62). But, as we have stated above, two steel companies, Bethlehem Steel and Eastern Fuel and Gas, did make such independent arrangements. Bethlehem was a large corporation with financial resources comparable to those of Steel, but Eastern was a relatively small company whose ability to do without Navios is persuasive evidence that Judge Quealy's reliance on the notion that independent steel buyers were somehow forced to use Navios out of economic necessity was misplaced.

The following table sets forth the amount of ore carried for some of the larger independent United States buyers, and the resulting charges made by Navios, during the years in question:

Year	Name of Purchaser	Tonnage	Navios
1957	Shenango Furnace	150,027	$1,403,024
	Jones & Laughlin	55,517	497,341
	Pittsburgh Steel	157,252	1,422,247
	Sharon Steel	268,216	814,215
	Youngstown S. & T.	83,697	65,274,437
1958	Shenango Furnace	247,014	2,483,631
	Jones & Laughlin	—	—
	Pittsburgh Steel	54,445	528,535
	Sharon Steel	114,688	1,173,485
	Youngstown S. & T.	74,967	767,532
	United States Steel	8,116,477	76,042,677
1959	Shenango Furnace	299,480	2,975,927
	Pittsburgh Steel	—	—
	Sharon Steel	215,004	2,141,493
	Youngstown S. & T.	79,630	793,150
	United States Steel	8,716,798	80,278,352
1960	Shenango Furnace	66,377	410,863
	Pittsburgh Steel	—	—
	Sharon Steel	163,968	823,119
	Youngstown S. & T.	—	—

These figures show that the shipments of Orinoco ore to independent American buyers represented a series of transactions substantial in both frequency and volume. Although Steel's shipments were larger, transactions on the order of the carriage of 100,000 tons of ore (for which Navios would have charged approximately $1 million) cannot be dismissed as an arrangement a company would make without some attention to the possibility of securing more favorable terms. Nor can purchasers like Pittsburgh Steel, Sharon Steel, Jones & Laughlin and Youngstown Sheet & Tube be considered commercially unsophisticated or incapable of bearing the costs of seeking lower rates. It is true, as the Commissioner points out, that none of the independent domestic purchasers bought enough in one year to fill one of the very largest ore carriers chartered by Navios, but Navios also chartered smaller vessels, down to 20,000 ton capacity, and thus any argument that the independents were forced, in effect, to pool their transport requirements is untenable.

In sum, the record shows that over four years' time half a dozen large corporations chose to use the services of Navios despite the fact that they were not compelled to do so. In such circumstances, we think the taxpayer has met its burden of showing that the fees it paid (which were identical to those paid by the independents) were arm's length prices. We do not say that, had different or additional facts been developed, the Commissioner could not have countered the taxpayer's showing and sustained the validity of his reallocation. Such a counter-showing would have required evidence that Navios' charges, although freely paid by other, independent buyers, deviated from a market price that the Commissioner could have proved existed for example, if worldwide ore-shipping contracts had been recorded and published during the period in question.

The Commissioner also argues that the fact that Steel paid the same rates as the independents is itself sufficient evidence that Steel was overcharged. The reasoning behind this counter-intuitive argument is that, in essence, Steel's relationship to Navios was that of a long-term charterer while the independents were short-term charterers; and that it is axiomatic that a long-term charterer pays a lower annual rate than a short-term charterer, because a shipowner prefers the freedom from market vicissitudes offered by a long-term charter. We are not persuaded by this line of argument. The shipowner who locks himself into a long-term charter bears the risk that charter rates will go up. Moreover, Steel's relationship to Navios was not that of charterer at all; Navios chartered ships from Universe and Hendy, and Steel purchased Navios's services as a carrier. Thus the Commissioner's analogy is not persuasive.

The Commissioner also points out that some of the Orinoco ore was shipped to Great Britain, but that although the distance from Venezuela to Great Britain is, on the average, 54% greater than the distance to the United States, the rates charged by Navios were not 54% higher than the Venezuela-to-United States rates. We do not view this as persuasive. First, there is nothing in the record to support the premise of the Commissioner's argument that charter rates are or should be an arithmetical multiple of distance traversed, nor is there any expert evidence as to the additional marginal cost of transport to Britain. The British rates are therefore of only speculative relevance to this case. Second, it may be, as the Commissioner suggests, that Navios was constrained to set lower rates for its European customers than for its American customers because the effective ceiling on the price of delivered ore in Europe was set by the price of Swedish ore, while the effective American ceiling was set by the Lower Lake Erie price. If the former was lower than the latter, shipping rates to Europe might have to be reduced. But the fact that sellers of ore, providers of ore transport, and ore buyers were all influenced by the price of a competing product does not mean that a price is not an arm's length price. * * *

The transactions between Navios and Jones & Laughlin, Sharon and Youngstown were "independent" in that Steel had no ownership or control interest in any of these firms and thus was not in a position to influence their decision to deal with Navios. To expand the test of "independence" to require more than this, to require that the transaction be one unaffected by the market power of the taxpayer, would be to inject antitrust concerns into a tax statute. But in s 482, a tax statute, it is appropriate to limit the concept of what is not "independent" to actions influenced by common ownership or control.

We do not think that in order so to hold it must be shown that Navios' prices were the result of a perfectly competitive market. Prices arrived at by independent buyers and sellers in arm's length transactions may vary from such a perfect market price depending on factors extraneous to s 482.

Of course, in some markets, all "arm's length" transactions would occur at truly competitive prices. But the more imperfect the market, the more likely it is that "arm's length" transactions will take place at prices which are not perfect market prices. To use s 482 to require a taxpayer to achieve greater fidelity to abstract notions of a perfect market than is possible for actual non-affiliated buyers and sellers to achieve would be unfair. * * *

Nor does the statute require that all independent transactions be at the price taxpayer charged or paid; therefore, the fact that Orinoco ore bought by Bethlehem Steel was transported to the United States at rates different from what Navios charged Steel and other customers is irrelevant. Since there were independent transactions significant in number and dollar amount and occurring over a long period of time, we need not address the question of how many such "independent transactions" at the taxpayer's price would be needed to insulate taxpayer from s 482 in a situation where a preponderance of the "independent" transactions take place at a price far different from the price paid or charged by taxpayer.

The § 482 adjustment also applies in the case of services. However, the "commensurate with the income" standard does not apply. Therefore, finding an arms-length transaction will satisfy the § 482 rule. In the *U.S. Steel* case, an arms-length price was established when it was shown that U.S. Steel used the same price in a sale to an unrelated purchaser. Treasury Regulation § 1.482–2(b) provides some additional rules for the finding of an arms-length price.

4. *The International Sale of Goods*

E.I. DU PONT DE NEMOURS AND CO. v. UNITED STATES
Court of Claims, 1979.
608 F.2d 445.

* * *

OPINION

DAVIS, Judge:

Taxpayer Du Pont de Nemours, the American chemical concern, created early in 1959 a wholly-owned Swiss marketing and sales subsidiary for foreign sales—Du Pont International S.A. (known to the record and the parties as DISA). Most of the

Du Pont chemical products marketed abroad were first sold by taxpayer to DISA, which then arranged for resale to the ultimate consumer through independent distributors. The profits on these Du Pont sales were divided for income tax purposes between plaintiff and DISA via the mechanism of the prices plaintiff charged DISA. For 1959 and 1960 the Commissioner of Internal Revenue, acting under section 482 of the Internal Revenue Code which gives him authority to reallocate profits among commonly controlled enterprises, found these divisions of profits economically unrealistic as giving DISA too great a share. Accordingly, he reallocated a substantial part of DISA's income to taxpayer, thus increasing the latter's taxes for 1959 and 1960 by considerable sums. The additional taxes were paid and this refund suit was brought in due course. Du Pont assails the Service's reallocation, urging that the prices plaintiff charged DISA were valid under the Treasury regulations implementing section 482. We hold that taxpayer has failed to demonstrate that, under the regulation it invokes and must invoke, it is entitled to any refund of taxes.

I. Design, Objectives and Functioning of DISA

* * *

A.   Du Pont first considered formation of an international sales subsidiary in 1957. A decreasing volume of domestic sales, increasing profits on exports, and the recent formation of the Common Market in Europe convinced taxpayer's president of the need for such a subsidiary. He envisioned an international sales branch capable of marketing Du Pont's most profitable type of products—Du Pont proprietary products, particularly textile fibers and elastomers specially designed for use as raw materials by other manufacturers. Du Pont had utilized two major marketing techniques to sell such customized products. One mechanism consisted of technical sales services: an elaborate set of laboratory services making technical improvements, developing new applications, and solving customer problems for Du Pont products. The other was 'indirect selling,' a method of promoting demand for Du Pont products at every point in the distribution chain. These two techniques were to be developed by DISA, Du Pont's international branch in Europe. DISA was not to displace plaintiff's set of independent European distributors, but rather to augment the distributors' efforts by the two marketing methods and to police the independents adequately.

* * *

B.   Neither in the planning stage nor in actual operation was DISA a sham entity; nor can it be denied that it was intended to, and did, perform substantial commercial functions which taxpayer legitimately saw as needed in its foreign (primarily European) market. Nevertheless, we think it also undeniable that the tax advantages of such a foreign entity were also an important, though not the primary, consideration in DISA's creation and operation. During the planning stages, plaintiff's internal memoranda were replete with references to tax advantages, particularly in planning prices on Du Pont goods to be sold to the new entity. The tax strategy was simple. If Du Pont sold its goods to the new international subsidiary at prices below fair market value, that company, upon resale of the goods, would recognize the greater part of the total profit (i.e., manufacturing and selling profits). Since this foreign subsidiary could be located in a country where its profits would be taxed at a much lower level than the parent Du Pont would be taxed here, the enterprise as a whole would minimize its taxes. * * * The details of this planning are set forth in the findings, and they leave us without doubt that a significant objective of plaintiff was to create a foreign subsidiary which would be able to accumulate large profits with which to finance Du Pont capital improvements in Europe.

Du Pont is divided into a series of semi-autonomous departments which report to the Executive Committee. An early draft of a memorandum on this subject to the Executive Committee from the international Department (then known as the Foreign Relations Department) stated that the Treasury Department (responsible for Du Pont's tax planning) was considering the possibility of a 'transfer of goods to a tax haven subsidiary at prices less than such transfers would be made to other subsidiaries or industrial Departments * * *' A memorandum from the Treasury Department reviewed the possibility of an IRS attack on such pricing and concluded: 'It would seem to be desirable to bill the tax haven subsidiary at less than an 'arm's length' price because: (1) the pricing might not be challenged by the revenue agent; (2) if the pricing is challenged, we might sustain such transfer prices (3) if we cannot sustain the prices used, a transfer price will be negotiated which should not be more than an 'arm's length' price and might well be less; thus we would be no worse off than we would have been had we billed at the higher price.' A subsequent Treasury Department report on 'Use of a Profit Sanctuary Company by the Du Pont Company' advised pricing goods to the 'profit sanctuary' at considerably lower levels than other intercorporate sales, suggesting that such prices could probably be sustained against an IRS challenge. In the spring of 1958, an International Department memorandum stated that the principal advantages of a 'profit sanctuary trading company' (dubbed by its initials as a 'PST company') depended 'largely upon the amount of profits which might be shifted (through selling price) from Du Pont to the 'PST company.'' The report concluded that Du Pont could find 'a selling price sufficiently low as to result in the transfer of a substantial part of the profits on export sales to the 'PST company.'' A corporate task force selected Switzerland as the best location for the foreign trading subsidiary, principally because of Swiss tax incentives. The two industrial departments expected to provide the main source of DISA's sales were not overly enthusiastic about a new layer of company organization. However, both departments agreed to formation of DISA for tax reasons. The Elastomer Department concluded: 'The decisive factor in our support of the organization is the potential tax saving.' The Textile Fibers Department recognized that tax considerations 'will command the establishment of lowest practical transfer prices from the manufacturing subsidiaries to Du Pont Swiss (DISA) * * *' A memorandum to the Executive Committee in late 1958 (shortly before the Committee approved DISA) spoke of the modest mark-up (emphasis in original) of goods sold to the foreign trading subsidiary. A prior draft of the memorandum used the phrase 'the 'artificially' low price.'

C. Consistently with that aim, plaintiff's prices on its intercorporate sales to DISA were deliberately calculated to give the subsidiary the lion's share of the profits. Instead of allowing each individual producing department to value its goods economically and to set a realistic price, Du Pont left pricing on the sales to DISA with the Treasury and Legal Departments. Neither department was competent to set an economic value on goods sold to DISA, and no economic correlation of costs to prices was attempted. Rather, an official of the Treasury Department established a pricing system designed to leave DISA with 75 percent of the total profits. If the goods' cost was greater than DISA's selling price, the department would price the item at its cost less DISA's selling expense. This latter provision was designed to insulate DISA from any loss. On the whole, the pricing system was based solely on Treasury and Legal Department estimates of the greatest amount of profits that would be shifted to DISA without evoking IRS intervention.

The individual industrial departments which manufactured goods sold to DISA had little reason to care about the pricing of such goods. Under a special accounting system DISA was ignored in computing departmental earnings, bonuses, etc. All profits from DISA were attributed to the department manufacturing the respective goods. This internal treatment of DISA's profits conflicted with Du Pont's standard practice of treating each subsidiary as a distinct profit center.

As it turned out, for the taxable years involved here, 1959 and 1960, the actual division of total profits between plaintiff and DISA was closer to a 50—50 split. In 1959 DISA realized

48.3 percent of the total profits, while in 1960 its share climbed to 57.1 percent. This departure from the original plan was the result of the omission of certain intercorporate transfers—a result not contemplated in the initial pricing scheme.

D. In operation, DISA enjoyed certain market advantages which helped it to accumulate large, tax-free profits. For its technical service function, the subsidiary did not develop its own extensive laboratories (with resulting costs and risks), but could rely on its parent's laboratory network in the United States and England. DISA was not required to hunt intensively (or pay as highly) for qualified personnel, since in both 1959 and 1960 it drew extensively on its parent's reservoir of talent. The international company's credit risks were very low, in part because of a favorable trade credit timetable by Du Pont. DISA also selected its customers to avoid credit losses, having a bad debt provision of less than one-tenth of one percent of sales. Unlike other distributor or advertising service agencies, DISA, because of its special relationship to the Du Pont manufacturing departments, had relatively little risk of termination. And as explained supra, Du Pont's pricing formula was intended to insulate DISA from losses on sales.

* * *

In operating DISA, Du Pont also maximized its subsidiary's income by funneling a large volume of sales through DISA which did not call for large expenditures by the latter. Many of the products Du Pont sold through DISA required no special services, or already had ample technical services provided. Du Pont routed sales to Australia and South Africa through DISA although the latter provided no additional services to sales in these non-European countries. DISA made sales of commodity-type products and opportunistic spot sales to competitors temporarily short in a raw material, although neither type of sale required DISA's specialized marketing expertise. Du Pont also routed all European sales of Elastomers through DISA, even though the parent had a well-established English subsidiary which had all the necessary technical services and marketing ability.

E. We have itemized the special status of DISA—as a subsidiary intended and operated to accumulate profits without much regard to the functions it performed or their real worth—not as direct proof, in itself, supporting the Commissioner's reallocation of profits under Section 482, but instead as suggesting the basic reason why plaintiff's sales to DISA were unique and without any direct comparable in the real world. As we shall see in Part II, infra, taxpayer has staked its entire case on proving that the profits made by DISA in 1959 and 1960 were comparable to those made on similar resales by uncontrolled merchandizing agencies. DISA's special status and mode of functioning help to explain why that effort has failed. It is not that there was anything 'illegal' or immoral in Du Pont's plan; it is simply that plan made it very difficult, perhaps impossible, to satisfy the controlling Treasury regulations under Section 482.

The § 482 goal in the sale of tangible property between related parties, like in the transfer of technology and services is in finding a comparable arms-length transaction. Treasury Regulation § 1.482–3 provides guidance for the finding of an arms-length amount in the case of sales between related parties. The methods include the comparable uncontrolled price method, the resale price method, the cost plus method, the comparable profits method, the profit split method, and the unspecified method.

Although the regulations thoroughly explain all of the methods, the IRS mostly uses the unspecified method (also known as the 'other method') to support their argument for adjustment. The *Du Pont* case is a good example of how not to approach a transfer pricing decision. It appears that the legal department whose main emphasis was income tax reduction established the price—the very reason § 482 was enacted to prohibit. An important rule to follow in the case of transfer pricing generally is for the seller to examine their strategy—is the price and conditions of the sale set in such a manner that the sale could be offered to an independent buyer? If the answer were yes, the transaction would probably pass the § 482 requirements.

Chapter 5

FINANCING THE INTERNATIONAL SALE OF GOODS

SECTION 5.1 THE DOCUMENTARY TRANSACTION

A. INTRODUCTION

Some of the preceding materials have focused on the issues that surface in forming the contract for the international sale of goods (hereafter the "Sales Contract"). Among the many issues between a buyer and seller that the Sales Contract should address is the payment obligation. The Sales Contract should state how and when the payment will be required under the contract. Each party faces some risk in agreeing to the payment terms.

The risk to the buyer is to pay for the goods but not to receive the quantity and quality of the goods promised by the seller. If the buyer receives non-conforming goods it would have to sue the seller, probably in the seller's home country with the seller already having the buyer's money—not a very good prospect. Conversely, the risk to the seller is to send the goods abroad and to not get paid. Even if the seller maintains control over the goods, they will be in a foreign country. If the product is not sold to the original buyer, the goods will have to be shipped back or sold abroad, perhaps at an unfavorable price.

The seller can avoid this risk by converting the transaction into a domestic sale. In this scenario, the buyer comes to the seller's place of business, orders the goods, and pays cash on delivery. This puts the onus on the buyer. If the seller has the economic and market position dominance over the buyer, it should compel the seller to buy the goods domestically. The buyer can likewise avoid risk by insisting that the seller bring the goods to the buyer and then, only after inspection, be obligated to pay for the goods.

The shifting of risk creates a dilemma. In order for one party to totally avoid risk the other must bear it all. Under these conditions, the business transaction will likely never occur. Neither party will trust the other, especially if they have had no prior dealings with each other. The key is in formulating a transaction where each party assumes part of the risk.

The documentary transaction financed with a letter of credit, hereafter, the 'Documentary Transaction' is the business solution to the risk segmentation issue. The Documentary Transaction divides the risk between the buyer, seller, and one or more banks. By using banks to assume part of the risk, each party can proceed with the transaction with a manageable share of risk. The Documentary Transaction enjoys wide acceptance in the international business community.

The typical Documentary Transaction includes the Seller, Buyer, Carrier, Buyer's Bank, Seller's Bank, Inspector, Customs Agent/Freight Forwarder, and Insurance Carrier. Each has a role in making the documentary transaction work effectively. The following describes the role of the parties and the contractual undertakings that they enter into.

1. *The Parties, Their Roles and the Contractual Undertakings*

The Seller sells the goods to the Buyer and the Buyer buys the goods from the Seller. The Sales Contract memorializes the agreement between the Buyer and Seller, reciting their respective rights and obligations. A properly drafted Sales Contract should include the quantity, quality, price, description of the goods, delivery conditions, payment conditions, a choice of law provision, and the method of payment. In order to use the Documentary Transaction, the method of payment should utilize a documentary or commercial letter of credit.

The Sales Contract governs the rights and liabilities of the parties in case of a breach. If a breach occurs, the parties can sue under the Sales Contract. The payment provision, however, is subject to additional protection through a letter of credit. In effect a bank guarantees the Buyer's payment obligation. The addition of a third party obligor—a bank—is the most valuable part of the Documentary Transaction. In the documentary transaction a breach in the underlying Sales Contract does not affect the bank's payment obligation under the letter of credit. The independence of the letter of credit form the Sales Contract is the linchpin of the Documentary Transaction.

In a Documentary Transaction, the Buyer causes a bank—the Buyer's Bank—also known as the Issuing Bank, to emit a Documentary Letter of Credit naming the Seller as a third party beneficiary. The Letter of Credit defines the relationship between the Buyer's Bank as issuer and the Seller as beneficiary and controls the payment for the international sale of goods. It informs the Seller of the requirements it must meet to get paid. Typically, payment is conditioned upon Seller's delivery of conforming documents to the Issuing Bank during a prescribed period of time.

The Issuing Bank's obligations are predicated on receiving conforming documents—not on the buyer receiving conforming goods—hence the term Documentary Transaction. As mentioned above, although issued pursuant to the Sales Contract, the rights and obligations flowing from the letter of credit are independent from it. This is known as the Independence Principle and it is strictly adhered to except in those cases where there is fraud in the transaction.

The independence principle can create traps for the unwary. For example, a properly drafted Sales Contract will include the documents that are to be presented for payment. The letter of credit also lists the documents upon which payment is to be made. The Issuing Bank's decision to pay is based on the documents listed in the letter of credit, not those in the Sales Contract. If there is a discrepancy between the two documents, only the items listed on the letter of credit will govern the payment obligations of the banks.

Another potential snare involves the goods themselves. The presenter of conforming documents is entitled to payment under a documentary letter of credit even if the goods do not conform to those bargained for in the Sales Contract. The shipment of non-conforming goods does not relieve the payment obligation under the letter of credit even if it constitutes a breach in the Sales Contract. The only exception is where there is fraud in the transaction. The fraud exception is discussed in Section 5.2, infra.

Recall that the Documentary Transaction is an effort to bridge the gap of distrust between the Buyer and Seller. The Documentary Transaction essentially replaces the credit worthiness of the Buyer with that of a Bank—the Issuing Bank. The problem is that the Seller may be reluctant to ship goods on promises made by the Buyer's Bank. After all, it is probably a foreign bank and if the Seller does not trust the Buyer it will probably not trust the Buyer's Bank either.

To resolve the impasse, the Documentary Transaction allows the Seller to interpose a bank of its choosing—the Seller's Bank into the loop. Since the Seller chooses the bank, it will have more trust in it than in the Buyer's Bank. At the very least, the Seller's Bank will probably be in the same jurisdiction as the Seller and can be sued more easily than the Buyer's Bank. The Seller's Bank is also in a good position to know and trust the Buyer's Bank, especially if they are experienced in handling international transactions.

The Seller's Bank, for a fee commensurate with its responsibilities, can serve in one of two capacities—confirming or advising. In a confirming role, it enters into the credit loop by guaranteeing payment to the Seller upon being presented conforming documents. However, as an advising bank, it merely opines on the sufficiency of the documents but does not guarantee payment. As an advising bank, it assists the Seller in determining that the documents presented to the Buyer's Bank are conforming. The Seller chooses the role it deems appropriate for the Seller's Bank to play.

Another important provision in the Sales Contract relates to the delivery of the goods from the Seller to the Buyer. The party responsible for causing the goods to be transported is known as the Shipper. The Shipper can be either the Buyer or the Seller. In the typical Documentary Transaction the Seller is usually the Shipper. The party who physically transports the goods from the Seller to the Buyer is known as the Carrier. The contractual arrangement between the Shipper and Carrier is usually evidenced by a Bill of Lading.

The Bill of Lading is a contract with several functions that are important in the Documentary Transaction. Not only is it a contract of carriage, but it is also a document of receipt and a document of title. In a Documentary Transaction, when payment is made against documents, it is imperative that possessing the documents represents the ownership of the goods. The ownership is established in the Bill of Lading through its function as a document of title. For a more complete discussion of the Bill of Lading and its functions see Section 6.1, infra.

In a Documentary Transaction, the Seller must present conforming documents to a bank in order to get paid. The Seller creates, assembles, and/or receives the various documents called for in the letter of credit. Since payment is made against documents and not goods, controlling the documents is critical in the smooth completion of the transaction. The Seller often uses the services of a Customs Agent/Freight Forwarder (hereafter Customs Agent) in this regard. The Customs Agent assists in the assembly of the documents and facilitates the handing over of the goods to the Carrier. An experienced Customs Agent knows the documents and is well versed in their flow. She can answer many questions that one would otherwise spend hours researching without coming to a satisfactory answer. The Customs Agent is an important, practical person in the documentary transaction.

The Documentary Transaction works very well for the Seller. The Seller presents documents contemporaneously with the shipment of goods and gets paid. At this point the Seller has the money well before the Buyer gets the goods. What if the documents are conforming but the goods are not? The Seller has already been paid. How can the Buyer be protected? The Buyer should have someone it trusts to inspect the goods as they are delivered to the Carrier. This trusted person or company is known as the Inspector.

The Inspector inspects the goods as they are being delivered to the Carrier. It issues a report—the Inspection Report, certifying that the quantity and quality of the goods is that bargained for between the Buyer and Seller. To effectively protect the Buyer, the Inspection Report should be one of the documents called for in the letter of credit. If the Inspection Report is missing, the documents will be deemed non-conforming and the banks will not be obligated to pay.

2. Tracing the Document and Payment Flow

The central idea in the Documentary Transaction is that payment is made upon the presentation of conforming documents. The relevant 'documents' are those listed in the letter of credit. The documents are typically comprised of a bank draft, commercial invoice, negotiable bill of lading, certificate of insurance, inspection report, packing list, and shippers export declaration. The Sales Contract and the actual letter of credit are not documents in this technical sense of the word.

Great care must be taken to ensure that the documents that are required by the Sales Contract and the letter of credit are the same. If not, unfortunate results could occur. For example, assume the Sales Contract calls for the presentation of documents including the Bill of Lading, Shippers Export Declaration, and Inspector's Report. Assume further that the letter of credit calls only for a Bill of Lading and Shippers Export Declaration. The bank will pay on the presentation of the Bill of Lading and Shippers Export Declaration. The Inspector's Report—the only assurance the Buyer has of receiving conforming goods—is effectively removed as a condition precedent to payment.

The error may create a cause of action for breach of the Sales Contract, but because of the independence principle, the breach will not affect the bank's responsibility for payment. There is no responsibility on the part of the bank to peruse the underlying contract for conformity with the letter of credit. That is the responsibility of the parties and their legal advisors.

Assume the following documents are called for in a letter of credit—bank draft, commercial invoice, negotiable bill of lading, certificate of insurance, inspection report, packing list, and shippers export declaration. How are they assembled? In the typical case, the Inspector inspects the goods and prepares her report at the time the goods that are delivered to the carrier. The insurance company issues the Certificate of Insurance. The Carrier executes and delivers the negotiable Bill of Lading when the goods are physically delivered to it. The Seller and/or Customs Agent receives the various documents described above and prepares the shippers export license or other export license as needed, the bank draft, the commercial invoice, and the packing list.

Once assembled, the Seller takes the documents to the Seller's Bank. If the Seller's Bank is a confirming bank and if the documents are in conformance with the letter of credit, the bank pays the Seller. At this point the Seller's Bank has possession of the documents including a properly endorsed Bill of Lading. The Seller's Bank owns the goods and has the risk of loss. The Seller has been paid and is now out of the loop. The risk is now transferred to the Seller's Bank. If the Seller's Bank is an advising bank, it merely opines on the conformity of the documents as required by the letter of credit but does not pay the Seller. In this case the Seller has not been paid since the Seller's Bank is serving as a collection agent for the Seller.

The Seller's Bank then presents the documents to the Buyer's Bank. If the Buyer's Bank finds them conforming it will pay the Seller's Bank. The Seller's Bank, if it is a confirming bank, will receive and keep the payment. If the Seller's Bank is serving in an advisory role it will remit the funds to Seller. At this point the Seller and Seller's Bank are out of the loop and the Buyer's Bank is in possession of the documents, owns the goods, and has the risk of loss. The Buyer's Bank then takes the documents to the Buyer.

The Buyer receives the documents from the Buyer's Bank and pays the amount due. The Buyer's Bank is now out of the loop. The Buyer has possession of the documents that represent the ownership of the goods. At this point the Buyer has the risk of loss but does not have physical possession of the goods. During the time the documents are winding their way from party to party the Carrier is transporting the goods physically to their destination. Upon arriving at the destination the Carrier is obligated to deliver the goods to the holder of the properly endorsed negotiable Bill of Lading.

The Buyer has the Bill of Lading in its possession. It presents the Bill of Lading to the Carrier. The Carrier then delivers the goods to the Buyer and the transaction is complete. At the conclusion of the transaction, the Buyer has the goods, the Seller has been paid, the banks have been paid, and the Carrier has delivered the goods. Each party has assumed a share of the risk so that the deal may be done.

The flow of documents, payment, and goods described above assumes that every party does what they ought and that no problem areas emerge. Unfortunately there are many moving parts to the documentary transaction and points of contention frequently arise. For example, what obligations are the banks assuming? What law applies? What if the documents presented are not conforming? What if the carrier delivers the goods to the wrong person? What if the goods are lost? What if the buyer goes bankrupt? What if there is fraud in the transaction? The materials in the remainder of this chapter as well as in chapter six address some of the problem areas that may arise in a Documentary Transaction. We begin the review by analyzing the typical letter of credit.

B. THE DOCUMENTARY LETTER OF CREDIT

In a documentary letter of credit, the Issuing Bank replaces the financial strength and integrity of the buyer. The bank's promise to pay, evidenced by the letter of credit, can be either revocable or irrevocable. In a revocable letter of credit, the Issuing Bank can revoke its promise to pay at any time. In an irrevocable letter of credit the Issuing Bank cannot revoke its promise to pay prior to the expiration date of the letter of credit. The bank's promise to pay is of critical importance in a Documentary Transaction. The irrevocable letter of credit should always be used. Furthermore, the expiration date should be set far enough in the future that will allow the Carrier time to bring the goods to the named destination.

The form of the commercial (documentary) letter of credit varies as each bank uses its own format. The letter of credit is usually on the letterhead of the issuing bank and should be an Irrevocable Documentary Letter of Credit. A separate letter of confirmation should be obtained from the Seller's Bank. Domestic law determines the rights and obligations of the parties under a letter of credit. However, Courts have recognized that letters of credit are *sui generes*—specialized contractual undertakings occupying a unique position of importance in the financing of the international sale of goods. As a result, many Courts do not use a strictly domestic approach in deciding cases.

The U.S. domestic system governing letters of credit is found in *UCC Article 5*. It is among the most developed in the world. Even so, U.S. courts have used the *UCC Article 5*, applicable international law, common law contract principles, a set of rules known as the *UCP*, described infra, and owing to their unique prominence in international trade, principles from the *lex mercatoria*. Other jurisdictions take a similar course. For example, the Canadian Supreme Court in *Bank of Nova Scotia v. Angelica–Whitewear Ltd.*, 36 D.L.R. 4th 161 (Can. 1987) analyzed the issue before it by using Canadian common law, Canadian civil law, the *UCP*, and the laws of the United States and England.

The *ICC Uniform Customs and Practice for Documentary Credits (UCP 500)*[1] are an important set of international rules that have achieved wide acceptance in the use of letters of credit. The *UCP* embodies banking practice and trade usage. The *UCP* provides rules in all of the major areas of international letters of credit including the form and types of credits, the liability and responsibilities of the various issuing and confirming banks. The rules provide important explanations on documents and standards for their examination. They also provide guidance on notice requirements, discrepant documents, and expiry dates. These rules are examined in part in the section dealing with the presentation of documents.

Although the *UCP* enjoys wide acceptance in the international banking community, it is not law. In order to ensure the applicability of the rules, the letter of credit must incorporate the UCP by reference. Absent an election to invoke the *UCP*, local choice of law rules applies in determining the applicable law. Additionally, a choice of law in the underlying Sales Contract does not impact the choice of law issue in the letter of credit contract. Incorporating the *UCP* is a staple provision in international letters of credit.

C. PRESENTATION OF CONFORMING DOCUMENTS

The Seller presents the documents to the Seller's Bank or the Buyer's Bank if there is no Seller's Bank. The bank examines the documents and must decide either to pay (honor) the letter of credit or to not pay (dishonor). The bank must honor the presenter's draft or demand for payment when the accompanying documents conform to the requirements in the letter of credit. The critical issue is whether the documents conform to the letter of credit. If they do, the bank must honor the letter of credit even if the underlying goods do not conform to the Sales Contract. The letter of credit and sales contract are independent of each other unless there is fraud in the transaction.

---

1. International Chamber of Commerce,   ICC Publication No. 500 (1993).

Once the seller presents the documents to a bank it becomes decision time for the bank—to honor or dishonor the letter of credit. There are several ways a bank may face liability. It may wrongfully honor the letter of credit by paying the presenter when the documents do not conform. It could wrongfully dishonor by not paying when the documents do conform. The action, through error or inadvertence, can cause the bank to be in breach of the letter of credit contract and possibly lose credibility in the international community for not properly handling a letter of credit obligation.

The bank may also intentionally and unlawfully dishonor a letter of credit. For example, assume the Buyer's Bank is presented with conforming documents, but the Buyer's Bank has learned that the Buyer is going into bankruptcy. The bank has an obligation to pay when presented with conforming documents even if someone downstream—the Buyer may be unable to pay. It could decide to dishonor the letter of credit and face a lawsuit rather than paying and not be able to collect from the Buyer.

Another economic motivation to unlawfully dishonor is if the Buyer is an important bank client and the Buyer gets caught in an unfavorable changing market. For example, assume that after the letter of credit is issued the market price of the goods drop substantially. The Buyer may pressure the bank to not pay when the documents are presented because the goods can be acquired from another seller at a lower price. The Buyer's Bank may acquiesce, especially if the Buyer is an important bank customer. Economic considerations can thus play an improper role in the bank's decision to honor or dishonor a letter of credit.

To assist the parties in relying on the process, the *UCC* and the *UCP* provide standards that banks must follow when examining documents and making decisions to pay or not. Under the *UCP*, banks owe a duty of reasonable care. The reasonable care standard extends only to the documents in the letter of credit, not to the goods. The duty of care and/or of good faith merely describes the obligations banks have in examining documents.

After meeting the standards for examination, the banks are still required to determine if the documents are conforming. This is a more difficult task. The *UCC*, *UCP*, and case law provide guidance to banks in determining the conformity of the documents.

1. *The Standards of Document Compliance*

LETTER OF CREDIT TRANSACTIONS: THE BANKS' POSITION IN DETERMINING DOCUMENTARY COMPLIANCE

Paolo S. Grassi*

7 PACE INT'L L. REV. 81 (1995).

* * *

* "Copyright 1995, Pace International Law Review. Reprinted with permission."

As previously stated, in order to function, the entire mechanism of the letter of credit transaction depends on documents. The beneficiary must present conforming documents if he wants the duty to pay from the side of the issuer to be enacted. The documents must satisfy the conditions of the credit and the bank has a right to inspect them. * * *

However simplistic the documentary transaction may initially appear, in reality, the process is complex. One thing is to agree on the delivery of a certain document, another is to provide it in a way that satisfies the credit conditions. A superficially evaluated decision on the documents to be offered in order to cause the issuer to pay may determine the impossibility for the beneficiary to recover immediate payment, i.e. the failure of the efforts to secure the deal.

That the document must comply with the terms and conditions specified in the letter of credit appears therefore to be an easy yet insufficient statement. The issue that the compliance rules attempt to clarify concerns the process pursuant to which the compliance concept can find a practical meaning, i.e. they are designed to give a practical sense to an abstract principle.

The first and generally accepted method of compliance verification is the strict compliance. Pursuant to this rule, to be acceptable the single document must comply word by word with the description specified in the credit. * * *

Pursuant to this theory, the bank examines the documents in a mechanical way by "superimposing" the delivered document to the letter of credit terms. Under this process, the bank looks at the words as if they did not have any meaning and they were a mere combination of letters. No interpretation is allowed, required, or expected; a document is correct, thus acceptable, only if it bears exactly the same words that are included in the letter of credit, regardless of casual typing mistakes or the misspelling of names. Only a strict "word to word" adherence to the terms of the letter of credit is accepted. * * *

The requirement of strict compliance sets pressures on the parties so that they agree in advance on exactly what kind of documents they expect to receive or they are able to provide. It is a matter of negotiation in which the bank is not involved, and that generally puts the customer in a strong position. The standard of strict compliance gives the maximum protection to the bank and to the customer. The latter needs to be sure that the goods he is going to receive are exactly as expected and paid for, i.e. he pays before being able to see the goods so he needs to have all guarantees that the goods are acceptable. However, the customer also ends up being privileged. On one side, if he is eager to receive the goods, he has the right to cause the bank to accept a non-complying document, thus causing payment even in cases in which there could be a refusal. In contrast, the customer has no obligation to accept any amendment of the letter of credit and he can refuse to authorize the bank to pay against non-complying documents.

The bank benefits from considerable protection because it does not have evaluation responsibilities, thus avoiding any risk connected to a misinterpretation of the documents. The rationale behind the strict compliance rule is that the bank is not involved in the underlying transaction and acts only in its function of credit issuer. It does not know the terms of the agreement between the customer and the beneficiary and is therefore not in a position to judge the contents of the documents. Furthermore, the bank is recognized in its function as a services' provider, operational only in the financial sector and therefore neither familiar with commercial practices nor the language. * * *

There are two standards courts apply in determining document conformity—the strict conformance rule and substantial compliance. The strict conformance rule calls for punctilious conformity, *i.e.* the documents must match the letter of credit letter for letter and word for word. Under strict compliance, " ... There is no room for documents which are almost the same, or which will do just as well ..." *Equitable Trust Co. v. Dawson Partners*, 27 Lloyd's List L.R. 49 (1927). If the documents do not conform exactly and literally, the banks may dishonor the letter of credit. The vast majority of U.S. jurisdictions have adopted the strict compliance rule.

The other standard—substantial compliance—injects concepts of equity into the credit transaction. In *Flagship Cruises, Ltd. v. New England Merchants National Bank,* 569 F.2d 699, 702 (1st Cir.1978), the court found it a good thing to have "some relaxation in a strictissimi juris comparison of letters of credit requirements and documents submitted in compliance therewith.... " Strict compliance eschews equity favoring commercial efficiency. In *Alaska Textile Co. v. Chase Manhattan Bank, N.A.,* 982 F.2d 813, 820 (2d Cir.1992), Judge McLaughlin wrote, "Equity's heralded virtue—that it is administered with regard to fairness, as opposed to the rigid rules of the common law—has but a limited role in a credit engagement that demands certainty and predictability if it is to continue its vital role in facilitating international commerce ..." The standards exemplify competing interests: efficiency and equity.

Strict compliance promotes efficiency by permitting document examiners in a bank to perform clerical functions only by comparing the presented documents with those called for in the letter of credit. Under the strict compliance rule banks are not required to know the commercial impact of a discrepancy in the documents. They need only discern whether the documents are facially in compliance, thus speeding up the process. The thrust of the strict compliance rule is that document examiners should not be placed in the position of having to know the commercial significance of a discrepancy in a document.

The rule does not absolve examiners from determining that a defect is truly insignificant; they should not act as mindless robots. Rather, the examiner should exercise discretion in her capacity as a banker. Examples of de minimis errors include transposed letters in a common word, using a lower case letter instead of a capital letter, or obvious typographical errors. The equity concept, promoted in substantial compliance, attempts to inject an analysis of the economic and commercial importance to the non-conforming document.

Consider the old English case of *J.H. Rayner & Co. v. Hambros Bank, Ltd.*, 2 All E.R. 694 (C.A. 1942). In *Rayner*, an issuing bank at the request of a Belgium buyer issued a letter of credit describing the goods as 'Coromandel groundnuts.' The bill of lading covering the goods described them as 'machine shelled groundnut kernels.' The issuing bank rejected the documents as non-conforming and the court agreed even though experts testified that the two descriptions were used in the trade interchangeably. The true motivation for the bank was that after issuing a letter of credit the Nazis overran Belgium and the bank was afraid of not getting paid. Under the substantial compliance standard, the documents would likely be held as conforming.

The careful planner is mindful of agreeing to a term in the document that could render the letter of credit worthless. For example, in *Key Appliance, Inc. v. First National City Bank*, 46 A.D.2d 622, 359 N.Y.S.2d 886 (1974), the letter of credit required that the buyer countersign the commercial invoice. The buyer's refusal to sign rendered the documents non-conforming. By agreeing that the buyer must countersign the invoice, the seller set the stage for allowing the buyer to prevent the documents from ever conforming.

2. *The Role of Custom And Usage*

MARINE MIDLAND GRACE TRUST COMPANY OF NEW YORK v. BANCO DEL PAIS, S.A.
United States District Court, Southern District of New York, 1966.
261 F.Supp. 884.

McLEAN, District Judge.

* * *

The question thus turns upon whether plaintiff properly refused to honor the drafts. Many of the facts are undisputed. They may be summarized as follows: On August 26, 1965, August 30, 1965, September 3, 1965, and September 7, 1965, plaintiff issued its letters of credit numbered respectively 146531, 146576, 146723 and 59425, in the respective amounts of $26,738, $51,000, $53,382 and $120,000, each in favor of Ricardo Nevares Ocampo, Mexico, D.F. Each letter of credit stated that the credit was transferable by Ocampo. In each letter of credit plaintiff undertook to pay drafts presented under it when accompanied by certain specified documents pertaining to shipments of mercury. Three letters of credit specified that the documents should include 'full set clean on board truckers bills of lading.' The fourth letter of credit, No. 146576 dated August 30, 1965, specified 'Full Set Clean On board ocean bills of lading issued to the order of MARINE MIDLAND GRACE TRUST COMPANY OF NEW YORK, N.Y., marked notify:—J. CLETON & CO. N.V., P.O. BOX 193, ROTTERDAM, HOLLAND.'

* * *

On September 17, 1965, defendant presented to plaintiff drafts drawn under letters of credit Nos. 146531, 146723 and 59425 by Alvaro Ocampo Vales, who eventually was shown to be the assignee of Ricardo Nevares Ocampo, in whose favor the credits had been originally issued. These drafts were accompanied by various documents, including a document purporting to be a truckers bill of lading. On September 20, 1965, plaintiff cabled to defendant as follows: 'YOUR OP156/8 CREDITS 59425 $120,000 146723 $53382 146531 $26738 NOT PAID BECAUSE FORWARDERS RECEIPTS PRESENTED INSTEAD ON BOARD TRUCKERS BILLS OF LADING AS REQUIRED STOP UNDERSTAND INSPECTION CERTIFICATE FRAUDULENT PLEASE INVESTIGATE THROUGH SOCIEDAD GENERAL MEXICANA MEXICO D.F. AS BUYERS CONTACTED THEM AND WERE ADVISED CERTIFICATES NUMBERS NOT THEIRS ALSO SIGNER UNKNOWN INSTRUCT'

To this defendant **replied** by cable dated September 23, 1965 (received by plaintiff on September 24), as follows: 'WE REFER TO YOUR CABLE OF THE 20TH INSTANT; WE ARE SURE YOU WILL HONOR YOUR LETTERS OF CREDIT NUMBERS 59425 FOR DOLLARS 120,000.00 146723 FOR DOLLARS 53,382.00 146531 FOR DOLLARS 26,738.00 BECAUSE THE RESPECTIVE DOCUMENTS WHICH WE FORWARDED TO YOU SATISFY THE REQUIREMENTS INDICATED IN YOUR AFOREMENTIONED LETTERS OF CREDIT WE TRUST YOU WILL IMMEDIATELY CREDIT TO US THE AMOUNT OF SAID LETTERS OF CREDIT ADVISING US BY CABLE.'

In the meantime, on September 20, defendant presented to plaintiff a draft drawn by Vales under the fourth letter of credit No. 146576. This is the one, which required on board ocean bills of lading instead of truckers bills of lading.

On September 22 plaintiff cabled to defendant with respect to this draft as follows: 'YOUR REFERENCE LETTER DATED 15TH DOLLARS FIVEONE–ZEROZEROZERO OUR CREDIT 146576 UNPAID COPIES OF BILLS OF LADING PRESENTED NOT ON BOARD SHOWS FREIGHT PREPAID INVOICES SHOW FOB STEAMER PORT OF DISCHARGE OMITTED SHIPMENT EFFECTED SWEDISH AMERICAN LINE STOP UNDERSTAND INSPECTION CERTIFICATE FRAUDULENT PLEASE INVESTIGATE THROUGH SOCIEDAD GENERALE MEXICANA MEXICO DF AS BUYERS CONTACTED

THEM AND WERE ADVISED CERTIFICATE NUMBERS NOT THEIRS ALSO SIGNER UNKNOWN INSTRUCT'

* * *

In my opinion, the documents did not comply. The truckers bills of lading did not state that the goods were 'on board' the trucks. They bore no such notation signed, initialed or stamped by the carrier. This was an essential requirement of the letter of credit and these requirements must be strictly complied with.

* * *

Defendant's affidavits say that in Mexico it is not customary for truckers bills of lading to specify that the goods are 'on board.' They say that these bills of lading were in the customary Mexican form. I believe that the Mexican custom is immaterial.

* * *

Issuers of letters of credit are not held accountable for commercial and trade usage of terms peculiar to the goods involved in the letter of credit. Nor are they responsible for the practices involved in some other contract springing from the sale transaction, e.g. the bill of lading. They are, however, responsible for knowledge of banking industry practices. The *UCP*, with its detailed rules, is a source of bank practice and usage.

Course of dealing or course of performance is irrelevant when the terms in the letter of credit are unambiguous. In those cases the court must decide as a matter of law what the terms of the credit are. *Ward Petroleum Corp. v. FDIC*, 903 F.2d 1297 (10th Cir.1990). Generally, usage or course of dealing will not alter the express terms in a letter of credit. *First State Bank v. Diamond Plastics Corp.*, 891 P.2d 1262 (1995). However, in *Dixon, Irmaos & Cia v. Chase Nat. Bank of City of New York*, 144 F.2d 759 (2d Cir.1944), the court held that a bank must observe bank custom in spite of the fact that the custom affects a change in the meaning of the letter of credit. The *Dixon* case is controversial. Some commentators believe the decision expects too much of bankers in having to decide whether banking custom gives a new meaning to language in the letter of credit.

3. *Waiver and Estoppel*

The strict compliance doctrine is counterbalanced by the corollary rules of waiver and estoppel. These are supplementary rules imposed on banks to prevent the misuse of the strict compliance rule. Under waiver, the party may intentionally relinquish the right to receive perfectly conforming documents. Waiver is mostly used when the document defect has no commercial significance. In the normal business setting, parties often agree to accept discrepant documents. A waiver requires the showing of intent—course of dealings do not give rise to waiver.

Estoppel in a letter of credit context operates to prevent an issuing bank from asserting any objections to the documents that it did not assert promptly. Time is a very critical element to assert estoppel. The two factors at play with respect to timing and estoppel are the expiration date of the letter of credit and the amount of time the banks are given to examine documents. The following case discusses the letter of credit mechanism and the time limits involved.

ALASKA TEXTILE CO., INC. v. CHASE MANHATTAN BANK, N.A.

United States Court of Appeals, Second Circuit, 1992.
982 F.2d 813.

McLAUGHLIN, Circuit Judge:

* * *

Alaska Textile Co. sued Chase Manhattan Bank in the United States District Court for the Southern District of New York (Metzner, J.) for wrongful dishonor of two letters of credits that Chase had issued in favor of Alaska. Alaska conceded that its documents did not conform to the credits, but argued that Chase should be precluded from relying on the discrepancies because Chase violated the timely notice provisions of UCP Article 16(c) [Now Article 14]. See UCP art. 16(e) (issuer violating art. 16(c) "shall be precluded from claiming that the documents are not in accordance with the terms and conditions of the credit"). The district court granted judgment for Chase, holding that Alaska had waived Chase's compliance with Article 16(c) by submitting documents "on approval basis." Alaska Textile Co. v. Lloyd Williams Fashions, Inc., 777 F.Supp 1139 (S.D.N.Y.1991). We now affirm, not on a waiver theory, but on the "reasonable time" mandated by Article 16(c).

* * *

DISCUSSION

* * *

The UCP provides that "[t]he issuing bank shall have a reasonable time in which to examine the documents and to determine, as above, whether to take up or to refuse the documents." UCP art. 16(c) [Now Article 14]. If the issuer does not act in accordance with this provision, it "shall be precluded from claiming that the documents are not in accordance with the terms and conditions of the credit," UCP art. 16(e), i.e., it must honor the credit.

Alaska asserts that, in construing "reasonable time" under the UCP, courts have generally equated it with the Uniform Commercial Code's ("UCC" or "Code") requirement that the issuer act within three banking days, * * * ("Some courts have bridged the difference between the U.C.C.'s rigid rule and the reasonable time rule of the U.C.P. by finding that three days constituted a reasonable time."); * * * ("What constitutes a reasonable time for taking action depends upon the nature and circumstances of the situation."); Dolan, Documentary Credit Fundamentals, supra, at 137–38 ("U.S. authority suggests that from 3 to 5 days is a reasonable period"); Raymond Jack, Documentary Credits: Article 16 Uniform Customs and Rejection of Documents: The Bankers Trust Case, Butterworth's J. of Int'l Bank. & Fin.L. 484, 486 (Oct. 1991) (three-day period is a guideline, not a rule). We expressly avoided ruling on this contention in Bank of Cochin, 808 F.2d at 213 ("we need not decide whether a three-day time period should be read into the UCP's Article [16(c)] reasonable time requirement"); see also Auto Servicio San Ignacio, S.R.L. v. Compania Anonima Venezolana de Navegacion, 765 F.2d 1306, 1310 (5th Cir.1985) (similarly avoiding the issue), but we now reject it.

Courts that bother to offer a rationale for the proposition that "reasonable time" cannot exceed three days generally adopt the reasoning of the district court in Bank of Cochin: Neither the 1983 UCP nor the 1974 UCP defines what constitutes a "reasonable time" to determine if the documents are defective.... When the UCP is silent or ambiguous, analogous UCC provisions may be utilized if consistent with the UCP. The UCC provides for a period of three banking days for the issuer to honor or reject a documentary draft for payment.... The "reasonable time" three-day period should be the maximum time allowable for the notification ... requirement. Bank of Cochin, 612 F.Supp. at 1542–43 (citations omitted), followed in Banque De L'Union, 787 F.Supp. at 1421; Price & Pierce, supra, at 42.

We need not enmesh ourselves in the controversy regarding the interplay of the UCP and UCC under New York law, however, because we find Article 16(c) to be neither silent nor ambiguous: it explicitly provides that issuers shall have a reasonable time to act on a beneficiary's presentation of documents for payment. That "reasonable time" may be imprecise neither makes it ambiguous nor invites interpolation of a fixed time period. In fact, the International Chamber of Commerce gave "[c]onsiderable thought ... to the possibility of replacing 'reasonable time' [with] a specific period of time," but rejected the suggestion. **

Equating the UCP's "reasonable time" with the UCC's three-day limit for examining documents also ignores the contexts in which these provisions appear. The Code and the Uniform Customs adopt vastly different approaches to demands under letters of credit that are not promptly and finally honored. See Bankers Trust Co. v. State Bank of India, [1991] 2 Lloyd's Rep. 443, 448 (A.C.) (UCC three-day limit "is not exactly analogous [to the UCP], since documents are deemed to be rejected [under the UCC], unless they are accepted within three clear banking days, not the other way round"). * * *

Under UCP Article 16(e), if an issuer does not dishonor a demand for payment within a reasonable time, it is deemed to have honored it, whether or not the documents actually conform to the terms of the credit. Thus, in an action for wrongful dishonor, the beneficiary can invoke this rule of strict preclusion to estop the issuer from relying on the documents' nonconformity—regardless of whether the beneficiary has demonstrated detrimental reliance. * * *

An issuer that does not comply with the Code's rigid three-day limitation, however, is deemed to have dishonored the demand for payment, see U.C.C. § 5–112(1) * * * but "the issuer who dishonors by inaction [under the UCC] may raise nonconformity as a defense in the beneficiary's subsequent action for wrongful dishonor." * * * Only if the beneficiary can satisfy the traditional requirements for estoppel (e.g., detrimental reliance) can it prevail on a wrongful dishonor claim if its documents were nonconforming. * * * Dolan, The Law of Letters of Credit, supra, P 4.06[2][c], at 4–30 ("Uniform Customs appear to fashion a strict estoppel rule, while the common-law cases require the beneficiary to establish the traditional elements of common-law estoppel"). In fact, under the UCC, regardless of the issuer's dilatory behavior, a beneficiary that knowingly presents nonconforming documents may not recover for wrongful dishonor. * * *

Thus, the consequences of an issuer's untimely action on a beneficiary's demand for payment are significantly different under the Code and Uniform Customs.

Finally, those that would incorporate the three-day period of UCC section 5–112(1)(a) into UCP Article 16(c) disregard subdivision (b) of section 5–112(1), which provides that the issuer may "further defer honor if the presenter has expressly or impliedly consented thereto." This provision has the salutary effect of tempering the rigid three-day rule, yet no one has suggested that it too should be incorporated into Article 16(c). Thus, were we to accept the argument that "reasonable time" really means three days, the issuer would be left with an absolute duty to act within three days, without exception, and violation of this duty would bring down on the issuer the penalty of strict preclusion. * * * This "rule" bastardizes both the Code and the Uniform Customs, producing a result that resembles neither. We reject it.

"Reasonable time" is a term of art with well-developed implications in the law. What constitutes a reasonable time necessarily depends upon the nature, purpose, and circumstances of each case. * * * In the letter-of-credit context, "what is a 'reasonable time' is to be determined by examining the behavior of those in the business of examining documents, mostly banks." * * *

In this case, Alaska submitted documents with patent, incurable discrepancies and requested that Chase seek a waiver of the discrepancies from Lloyd. Chase examined one set of documents on the third banking day following presentment, and the other set on the fourth day. It informed Lloyd of the discrepancies and, pursuant to Alaska's request, asked Lloyd whether it would waive the discrepancies and authorize payment. At that point, Chase had done all that it could, and the matter was out of its control.

Four banking days later (eight banking days after presentment), Chase informed Merchants of the discrepancies and asked what it should do with the documents. In context, it is clear that Chase was asking whether Alaska wanted Chase to give formal notice of dishonor and to return the documents. Junior demurred and requested that, until he heard otherwise from Alaska, Chase should continue to hold the documents pending Lloyd's decision whether to authorize payment. Fifteen banking days after presentment, Chase sent a telex giving formal notice of dishonor, restating the discrepancies that justified dishonor, and stating that the documents were held at Alaska's disposal.

We hold that Chase acted reasonably under the circumstances. Until either Lloyd decided whether to waive, or Alaska requested action (one way or the other) on its demand for payment, Chase was proceeding as it had been requested, and the matter was out of its control. * * *

To hold otherwise, and thereby impose liability on Chase for credits that were materially discrepant, would create perverse incentives for issuers. A prudent issuer acting on documents submitted on an approval basis would never risk liability by complying with the beneficiary's request that it inquire of the account party regarding waiver. Unless the issuer could secure an immediate waiver, the most sensible course would be to dishonor the demand for payment—a result that none of the participants generally favors.

The letter of credit is intended to grease the wheels of trade and commerce. As many as half of the demands for payment under letters of credit are discrepant, yet, in the vast majority of cases, the account party waives the discrepancies and authorizes payment. * * * This process is efficient, and the law should encourage it, particularly when the beneficiary has acknowledged that its documents are discrepant and has specifically requested that the issuer consult the account party. * * *

Banks have to show reasonable care in examining the documents, but have no obligation to examine the underlying transaction. *Uniform Customs And Practice Article 13(b)* states that banks have a reasonable amount of time to examine documents, not to exceed seven days. The old *UCC* statute allowed three days. The new formulation—*Uniform Commercial Code 5–108(b)* establishes a seven-day rule.

Once the bank has examined the documents, it must inform the presenting party of any defects. *UCP Article 14(d)(i)* states that the banks must give notice of the defect by telephone or some other expeditious means, without delay, but no later than seven banking days. Once a bank has made a decision to dishonor, the notice of the defect must be given to the presenting party without delay. The *UCP Article 14(d)(i)* rule is an outer limit, not a fixed period of time.

To illustrate the effect of this rule, consider *Datapoint Corp. v. M & I Bank*, 665 F.Supp. 722 (1987). In that case documents were presented the day before the expiry date of the letter of credit. The bank made a decision to reject the documents as non-conforming that same day. The bank mailed the documents and the notice of dishonor to the presenter. The court held that the bank should have called the beneficiary to correct the defect. Therefore, the bank was estopped from asserting the defects in the document as a reason for dishonor.

In the case of multiple defects, the bank must give fair notice to the presenter of all the defects it has discovered. The party presenting the documents should deliver the documents at the earliest possible time to allow an opportunity to correct curable defects. If the presenter does not correct the defects prior to the expiry date of the letter of credit, the bank has no obligation to honor the letter of credit.

The bank typically faces an estoppel situation when it rejects documents for a defect and then raises additional defects when the original defect is cured. The expiry date of the letter of credit can loom very large in the mechanics of document presentation. The bank has no duty to honor a letter of credit on documents presented after the letter of credit expiry date. Therefore, the presenter must insure that the documents are presented in time not to run afoul of the *UCP* and *UCC* time limits.

SECTION 5.2   PROPER DISHONOR FRAUD IN THE TRANSACTION

A.   INTRODUCTION

The Documentary Transaction functions on the processing of documents. The Issuing Bank either honors or dishonors the letter of credit based on an examination of documents. The independence principle provides that the letter of credit is separate and apart from the underlying Sales Contract. The policy behind the independence principle is efficiency in the international sale of goods. Requiring payment against conforming documents regardless of the conformity of the goods is a critical element in the functioning of the documentary transaction.

In spite of the favored status of the documentary transaction, courts have fashioned a limited exception to the independence principle when the documents are facially conforming but are forged or fraudulent, or when there is fraud in the transaction. The independence principle and the related concept of fraud in the transaction has been codified in U.S. law:

Uniform Commercial Code, Article 5, Letters of Credit

§ 5–114.   Issuer's Duty and Privilege to Honor; Right to Reimbursement

(1) An issuer must honor a draft or demand for payment, which complies with the terms of the relevant credit regardless of whether the goods or documents conform to the underlying contract for sale or other contract between the customer and the beneficiary. The issuer is not

excused from honor of such a draft or demand by reason of an additional general term that all documents must be satisfactory to it.

(2) Unless otherwise agreed when documents appear on their face to comply with the terms of a credit but a required document does not in fact conform to the warranties made on negotiation or transfer of a document of title (Section 7–507) or of a certified security (Section 8–108) or is forged or fraudulent or there is fraud in the transaction:

(a) the issuer must honor the draft or demand for payment if honor is demanded by a negotiating bank or other holder of the draft or demand which has taken the draft or demand under the credit and under circumstances which would make it a holder in due course (Section 3–302) and in an appropriate case would make it a person to whom a document of title has been duly negotiated (Section 7–502) or a bona fide purchaser of a certified security (Section 8–302); and

(b) in all other cases as against its customer, an issuer acting in good faith may honor the draft or demand for payment despite notification from the customer of fraud, forgery or other defect not apparent on the face of the documents but a court of appropriate jurisdiction may enjoin such honor.

* * *

Uniform Commercial Code, Revised Article 3 Negotiable Instruments Part 3. Enforcement of Instruments

§ 3–302.   Holder in Due Course

(a) Subject to subsection (c) and Section 3–103(d), "holder in due course" means the holder of an instrument if:

(1) the instrument when issued or negotiated to the holder does not bear such apparent evidence of forgery or adulteration or is not otherwise so irregular or incomplete as to call into question its authenticity; and

(2) the holder took the instrument (I) for value, (ii) in good faith, (iii) without notice that the instrument is overdue or has been dishonored or that there is an uncured default with respect to payment of another instrument issued as part of the same series, (iv) without notice that the instrument contains an unauthorized signature or has been altered, (v) without notice of any claim to the instrument described in Section 3–306, and (vi) without notice that any party has a defense or claim in recoupment described in Section 3–305(a).

The independence principle is reflected in *U.C.C. § 5–114(1)*. Under this Code section the Issuing Bank must honor a demand for payment when it complies with the terms of the letter of credit regardless of the conformity of the goods or the documents to the underlying sales contract. The banks are not required to examine the goods or peruse the Sales Contract to detect any discrepancies. This helps streamline the Documentary Transaction.

However, early on the courts saw that the independence principle may sometimes work an injustice to the Buyer. The rule in *Sztejn*[2] has been codified in the uniform Commercial Code. Under *U.C.C.§ 5–114(2)* the buyer has an opportunity, albeit slight, to breach the independence principle. The statute provides for limited relief when documents appear on their face to comply with the letter of credit but in fact do not conform or where the documents are forged or fraudulent. The independence principle may be breached when there is some fundamental problem either with the documents or the goods. The relief is limited because of *U.C.C. § 5–114(2)(a) & (b)*.

The Issuing Bank is compelled to honor a demand for payment when a negotiating bank or other holder in due course is making the demand. Under *UCC § 3–302* a holder in due course is one who took the documents for value, in good faith, without notice of any defect. Therefore, a confirming bank having holder in due course status presents documents to an Issuing Bank, the Issuing Bank must pay regardless of the existence of fraud in the documents or the goods.

Even when the presenter is not a holder in due course, the Issuing Bank, while acting in good faith, can still elect to pay the presenter even if there is notification of fraud, forgery, or other defect not apparent on the face of the documents. Where then is the relief to the buyer? The relief is found in the last part of the last section of *U.C.C.§ 5–114(2)(b)* where it states that "... a court of appropriate jurisdiction may enjoin such honor ..."

B.   FRAUD RELATING TO THE GOODS

Fraud in the transaction can relate to the underlying goods. The critical question is to determine whether there has been a breach in the underlying Sale Contract or whether there is fraud in the transaction. A mere breach does not constitute an exception to the independence principle. Only a fraud in the transaction can create an exception. How do you determine if there has been a breach or fraud?

Assume the Sales Contract calls for the purchase and sale of "Class A" goods. The seller sends "Class B" goods. The Buyer surely has a cause of action for breach of contract against the Seller. Is the discrepancy sufficient to enjoin the issuing bank from paying on the letter of credit—*i.e.* disregard the independence principle? What if the seller sent junk instead of "Class A" goods? Is the following case helpful in drawing that line?

2. Sztejn v. J. Henry Schroder Banking   (1941).
Corp., 177 Misc. 719, 31 N.Y.S.2d 631

UNITED BANK LTD. v. CAMBRIDGE SPORTING GOODS CORP.

Court of Appeals of New York, 1976.
41 N.Y.2d 254, 392 N.Y.S.2d 265, 360 N.E.2d 943.

GABRIELLI, Justice.

* * *

On this appeal, we must decide whether fraud on the part of a seller-beneficiary of an irrevocable letter of credit may be successfully asserted as a defense against holders of drafts drawn by the seller pursuant to the credit. If we conclude that this defense may be interposed by the buyer who procured the letter of credit, we must also determine whether the courts below improperly imposed upon appellant buyer the burden of proving that respondent banks to whom the drafts were made payable by the seller-beneficiary of the letter of credit, were not holders in due course. The issues presented raise important questions concerning the application of the law of letters of credit and the rules governing proof of holder in due course status set forth in article 3 of the Uniform Commercial Code. * * *

In April, 1971 appellant Cambridge Sporting Goods Corporation (Cambridge) entered into a contract for the manufacture and sale of boxing gloves with Duke Sports (Duke), a Pakistani corporation. Duke committed itself to the manufacture of 27,936 pairs of boxing gloves at a sale price of $42,576.80; and arranged with its Pakistani bankers, United Bank Limited (United) and The Muslim Commercial Bank (Muslim), for the financing of the sale. Cambridge was requested by these banks to cover payment of the purchase price by opening an irrevocable letter of credit with its bank in New York, Manufacturers Hanover Trust Company (Manufacturers). Manufacturers issued an irrevocable letter of credit obligating it, upon the receipt of certain documents indicating shipment of the merchandise pursuant to the contract, to accept and pay, 90 days after acceptance, drafts drawn upon Manufacturers for the purchase price of the gloves.

Following confirmation of the opening of the letter of credit, Duke informed Cambridge that it would be impossible to manufacture and deliver the merchandise within the time period required by the contract, and sought an extension of time for performance until September 15, 1971 and a continuation of the letter of credit, which was due to expire on August 11. Cambridge replied on June 18 that it would not agree to a postponement of the manufacture and delivery of the gloves because of its resale commitments and, hence, it promptly advised Duke that the contract was canceled and the letter of credit should be returned. Cambridge simultaneously notified United of the contract cancellation.

Despite the cancellation of the contract, Cambridge was informed on July 17, 1971 that documents had been received at Manufacturers from United purporting to evidence a shipment of the boxing gloves under the terms of the canceled contract. The documents were accompanied by a draft, dated July 16, 1971, drawn by Duke upon Manufacturers and made payable to United, for the amount of $21,288.40, one half of the contract price of the boxing gloves. A second set of documents was received by Manufacturers from Muslim, also accompanied by a draft, dated August 20, and drawn upon Manufacturers by Duke for the remaining amount of the contract price.

An inspection of the shipments upon their arrival revealed that Duke had shipped old, unpadded, ripped and mildewed gloves rather than the new gloves to be manufactured as agreed upon. Cambridge then commenced an action against Duke in Supreme Court, New York County, joining Manufacturers as a party, and obtained a preliminary injunction prohibiting the latter from paying drafts drawn under the letter of credit; subsequently, in November, 1971 Cambridge levied on the funds subject to the letter of credit and the draft, which were delivered by Manufacturers to the Sheriff in compliance therewith. Duke ultimately defaulted in the action and judgment against it was entered in the amount of the drafts, in March, 1972.

The present proceeding was instituted by the Pakistani banks to vacate the levy made by Cambridge and to obtain payment of the drafts on the letter of credit. The banks asserted that they were holders in due course of the drafts which had been made payable to them by Duke and, thus, were entitled to the proceeds thereof irrespective of any defenses which Cambridge had established against their transferor, Duke, in the prior action which had terminated in a default judgment. The banks' motion for summary judgment on this claim was denied and the request by Cambridge for a jury trial was granted. Cambridge sought to depose the petitioning banks, but its request was denied and, as an alternative, written interrogatories were served on the Pakistani banks to learn the circumstances surrounding the transfer of the drafts to them. At trial, the banks introduced no evidence other than answers to several of the written interrogatories which were received over objection by Cambridge to the effect that the answers were conclusory, self-serving and otherwise inadmissible. Cambridge presented evidence of its dealings with Duke including the cancellation of the contract and uncontested proof of the subsequent shipment of essentially worthless merchandise.

The trial court concluded that the burden of proving that the banks were not holders in due course lay with Cambridge, and directed a verdict in favor of the banks on the ground that Cambridge had not met that burden; the court stated that Cambridge failed to demonstrate that the banks themselves had participated in the seller's acts of fraud, proof of which was concededly present in the record. The Appellate Division affirmed, agreeing that while there was proof tending to establish the defenses against the seller, Cambridge had not shown that the seller's acts were 'connected to the petitioners (banks) in any manner.' * * *

We reverse and hold that it was improper to direct a verdict in favor of the petitioning Pakistani banks. We conclude that the defense of fraud in the transaction was established and in that circumstance the burden shifted to petitioners to prove that they were holders in due course and took the drafts for value, in good faith and without notice of any fraud on the part of Duke (Uniform Commercial Code, § 3–302). Additionally, we think it was improper for the trial court to permit petitioners to introduce into evidence answers to Cambridge's interrogatories to demonstrate their holder in due course status.

This case does not come before us in the typical posture of a lawsuit between the bank issuing the letter of credit and presenters of drafts drawn under the credit seeking payment * * * Because Cambridge obtained an injunction against payment of the drafts and has levied against the proceeds of the drafts, it stands in the same position as the issuer, and, thus, the law of letters of credit governs the liability of Cambridge to the Pakistani banks. Article 5 of the Uniform Commercial Code, dealing with letters of credit, and the Uniform Customs and Practice for Documentary Credits promulgated by the International Chamber of Commerce set forth the duties and obligations of the issuer of a letter of credit. A letter of credit is a commitment on the part of the issuing bank that it will pay a draft presented to it under the terms of the credit, and if it is a documentary draft, upon presentation of the required documents of title * * * Banks issuing letters of credit deal in documents and not in goods and are not responsible for any breach of warranty or nonconformity of the goods involved in the underlying sales contract * * * Subdivision (2) of section 5–114, however indicates certain limited circumstances in which an issuer may properly refuse to honor a draft drawn under a letter of credit or a customer may enjoin an issuer from honoring such a draft. Thus, where 'fraud in the transaction' has been shown and the holder has not taken the draft in circumstances that would make it a holder in due course, the customer may apply to enjoin the issuer from paying drafts drawn under the letter of credit * * * This rule represents a codification of precode case law most eminently articulated in the landmark case of Sztejn v. Schroder Banking Corp., 177 Misc. 719, 31 N.Y.S.2d 631, Shientag, J., where it was held that the shipment of cowhair in place of bristles amounted to more than mere breach of warranty but fraud sufficient to constitute grounds for enjoining payment of drafts to one not a holder in due course * * * Even prior to the Sztejn case, forged or fraudulently procured documents were proper grounds for avoidance of payment of drafts drawn under a letter of credit * * * and cases decided after the enactment of the code have cited Sztejn with approval * * *.

The history of the dispute between the various parties involved in this case reveals that Cambridge had in a prior, separate proceeding successfully enjoined Manufacturers from paying the drafts and has attached the proceeds of the drafts. It should be noted that the question of the availability and the propriety of this relief is not before us on this appeal. The petitioning banks do not dispute the validity of the prior injunction nor do they dispute the delivery of worthless merchandise. Rather, on this appeal they contend that as holders in due course they are entitled to the proceeds of the drafts irrespective of any fraud on the part of Duke * * * Although precisely speaking there was no specific finding of fraud in the transaction by either of the courts below, their determinations were based on that assumption. The evidentiary facts are not disputed and we hold upon the facts as established, that the shipment of old, unpadded, ripped and mildewed gloves rather than the new boxing gloves as ordered by Cambridge, constituted fraud in the transaction within the meaning of subdivision (2) of section 5–114. It should be noted that the drafters of section 5–114, in their attempt to codify the Sztejn case and in utilizing the term 'fraud in the transaction', have eschewed a dogmatic approach and adopted a flexible standard to be applied as the circumstances of a particular situation mandate. It can be difficult to draw a precise line between cases involving breach of warranty (or a difference of opinion as to the quality of goods) and outright fraudulent practice on the part of the seller. To the extent, however, that Cambridge established that Duke was guilty of Fraud in shipping, not merely nonconforming merchandise, but worthless fragments of boxing gloves, this case is similar to Sztejn.

If the petitioning banks are holders in due course they are entitled to recover the proceeds of the drafts but if such status cannot be demonstrated their petition must fail. The parties are in agreement that section 3–307 of the code governs the pleading and proof of holder in due course status and that section provides:

(1) Unless specifically denied in the pleadings each signature on an instrument is admitted. When the effectiveness of a signature is put in issue '(a) the burden of establishing it is on the party claiming under the signature; but '(b) the signature is presumed to be genuine or authorized except where the action is to enforce the obligation of a purported signer who has died or become incompetent before proof is required. (2) When signatures are admitted or established, production of the instrument entitles a holder to recover on it unless the defendant establishes a defense. (3) After it is shown that a defense exists a person claiming the rights of a holder in due course has the burden of establishing that he or some person under whom he claims is in all respects a holder in due course.' Even though section 3–307 is contained in article 3 of the code dealing with negotiable instruments rather than letters of credit, we agree that its provisions should control in the instant case. Section 5–114 (subd. (2), par. (a)) utilizes the holder in due course criteria of section 3–302 of the code to determine whether a presenter may recover on drafts despite fraud in the sale of goods transaction. It is logical, therefore, to apply the pleading and practice rules of section 3–307 in the situation where a presenter of drafts under a letter of credit claims to be a holder in due course. In the context of section 5–114 and the law of letters of credit, however, the 'defense' referred to in section 3–307 should be deemed to include only those defenses available under subdivision (2) of section 5–114, i.e., noncompliance of required documents, forged or fraudulent documents or fraud in the transaction. In the context of a letter of credit transaction and, specifically subdivision (2) of section 5–

114, it is these defenses which operate to shift the burden of proof of holder in due course status upon one asserting such status * * * Thus, a presenter of drafts drawn under a letter of credit must prove that it took the drafts for value, in good faith and without notice of the underlying fraud in the transaction * * *.

Turning to the rules of section 3–307 as they apply to this case, Cambridge failed to deny the effectiveness of the signatures on the draft in its answer and, thus, these are deemed admitted and their effectiveness is not an issue in the case. However, this does not entitle the banks as holders to payment of the drafts since Cambridge has established 'fraud in the transaction'. The courts below erroneously concluded that Cambridge was required to show that the banks had participated in or were themselves guilty of the seller's fraud in order to establish a defense to payment. But, it was not necessary that Cambridge prove that United and Muslim actually participated in the fraud, since merely notice of the fraud would have deprived the Pakistani banks of holder in due course status.

In order to qualify as a holder in due course, a holder must have taken the instrument 'without notice * * * of any defense against * * * it on the part of any person' (Uniform Commercial Code, § 3–302, subd. (1), par. (c)). Pursuant to subdivision (2) of section 5–114 fraud in the transaction is a valid defense to payment of drafts drawn under a letter of credit. Since the defense of fraud in the transaction was shown, the burden shifted to the banks by operation of subdivision (3) of section 3–307 to prove that they were holders in due course and took the drafts without notice of Duke's alleged fraud. As indicated in the Official Comment to that subdivision, when it is shown that a defense exists, one seeking to cut off the defense by claiming the rights of a holder in due course 'has the full burden of proof by a preponderance of the total evidence' on this issue. This burden must be sustained by 'affirmative proof' of the requisites of holder in due course status * * *. It was error for the trial court to direct a verdict in favor of the Pakistani banks because this determination rested upon a misallocation of the burden of proof; and we conclude that the banks have not satisfied the burden of proving that they qualified in all respects as holders in due course, by any affirmative proof. * * * The failure of the banks to meet their burden is fatal to their claim for recovery of the proceeds of the drafts and their petition must therefore be dismissed.

* * *

Accordingly, the order of the Appellate Division should be reversed, with costs, and the petition dismissed.

———————

The independence principle is what makes the documentary transaction run smoothly and efficiently. The banks are not required to examine the underlying Sales Contract or the goods to make payment under the letter of credit. The policy of efficient operation clashes with the policy that wrongdoers should not benefit from their wrongful acts. Courts draw the line in the case where the beneficiary commits fraud in the transaction. The independence principle remains intact in cases of breach. However, in cases of fraud the Buyer has a limited means of redress.

Drawing the line between breach and fraud could be difficult. Sending Class B goods instead of Class A is more in the nature of a breach—like a difference in opinion as to quality. An examination of the facts and circumstances of each case must be made to determine if there is fraud in the transaction. Receiving junk instead of Class A goods would be a fraud in the transaction. Courts have construed fraud narrowly finding it in those cases where there has been a total failure of consideration.

In *Cambridge*, the Buyer contracted to purchase boxing gloves and received junk. The court concluded that this constituted fraud on the part of the Seller. However, Seller's Bank paid the Seller claiming to have not known of the fraud. It is now demanding payment. A holder in due course can demand and receive payment in a documentary transaction.

In *Cambridge*, the lower court found that the Buyer had the burden of proof to show that the Seller's Bank was not a holder in due course. The court reversed that holding. The Buyer must establish a prima facie case of fraud in the transaction. At that point the party seeking the holder in due course must prove that it is entitled it. In this case, the Seller's Bank would have to show that they paid value without knowledge of the defect.

C. FRAUD RELATING TO THE DOCUMENTS

Fraud in the transaction is not limited to the goods. It can also apply to the documents. The case below discusses this issue.

SIDERIUS, INC. v. WALLACE CO., INC.

Texas Court of Civil Appeals, 1979.
583 S.W.2d 852.

* * *

SUMMERS, Justice.

* * *

Originally, Siderius was going to sell 5,000 net tons of foreign steel pipe to Melton for approximately $715.00 per net ton. Melton, in a back-to-back transaction, intended to then sell the same pipe to Wallace. This agreement was conditioned upon Wallace's obtaining a letter of credit for Melton's benefit for approximately $4.1 million. Wallace was unable to obtain the letter of credit, and as a result, the deal fell through. Siderius then approached Wallace and offered to sell the pipe to Wallace directly for $715.00 per net ton, conditioned on Wallace's obtaining a letter of credit for Siderius' benefit.

Based upon Wallace's application, Texas Commerce Bank issued an irrevocable documentary letter of credit for Siderius' benefit on August 1, 1974. The terms of the letter of credit specified that: "GENTLEMEN: WE HEREBY OPEN OUR IRREVOCABLE LETTER OF CREDIT IN YOUR FAVOR FOR THE ACCOUNT OF Wallace Company, Inc. P.O. Box 2597 Houston, Texas 77001 FOR A SUM OR SUMS NOT EXCEEDING IN THE AGGREGATE THE SUM OF Three Million Seven Hundred Fifty-Three Thousand Seven Hundred Fifty and No/100 U.S. Dollars ($3,753,750.00). AVAILABLE BY YOUR DRAFTS ON us AT _____ sight _____ TO BE ACCOMPANIED BY:-Commercial Invoice.-Customs Invoice.-Certificate of Origin.-Packing List (Including Tallies) Dock Delivery Order.-Negotiable Insurance Certificate of Policy covering Marine and War risks including All Risk Warehouse to Warehouse for 110% Of full invoice value.-Full set of On Board Ocean Bills of Lading to the order of Texas Commerce Bank National Association, Notify: W. A. Sammis, Wallace Co., Inc., Box 2597, Houston, Texas 77001, Telephone Number 713–675–2661, showing 'Freight Prepaid.' EVIDENCING SHIPMENT from 1. Italian Port, 2. & 3. Israel Port to Port of Houston, Texas U.S.A., not later than November 30, 1974

* * *

The terms of the letter of credit were amended by letters of amendment five times, each of which stated "ALL OTHER CONDITIONS REMAIN UNCHANGED." The shipping deadlines for all three shipments of steel pipe, as specified originally in the letter of credit, were amended by agreement of the parties. In early November, 1974, Siderius requested an extension of the shipping deadline in regards to the pipe to be manufactured in Italy; Wallace consented. In order to reflect this modification, the letter of credit was amended on November 13, 1974, to allow the bills of lading pertaining to the Italian pipe to be dated no later than January 15, 1975. In addition, the expiration date of the letter of credit was postponed to February 28, 1975. Subsequently, Siderius requested that the shipping deadline for the Israeli pipe also be extended. Wallace agreed, and the letter of credit was amended to change the shipping deadline for these portions of the pipe from November 30, 1974, to December 15, 1974. In late December or early January, a request was once again made by Siderius seeking a further extension for shipment of the Italian pipe. Wallace refused to agree to anymore extensions and the January 15, 1975, deadline remained in force. The two shipments of pipe manufactured in Israel were shipped, delivered in Houston, and Siderius' first and second drafts on the letter of credit in regards to these two shipments were honored by the Bank. The dispute in the instant case pertains to the shipment of the portion of pipe manufactured in Italy.
* * *

The pipe in question was to be shipped from the Italian port of Ravenna on board the M/V Slavonija. On February 20, 1975, Siderius presented to the Bank a bill of lading and other documents along with the third draft for payment in an amount in excess of.$1.8 million. The bill of lading was dated January 15, 1975, and on its face appeared to conform to the terms of the letter of credit. Wallace notified the Bank that it suspected that the bill of lading presented by Siderius in the third draft was fraudulent because the shipping requirements had not been met and informed the Bank that it declined to waive any defects. The Bank dishonored Siderius' first presentation of the third draft on February 24, 1975, as nonconforming because the bill of lading was issued under and subject to a charter party, the insurance certificate was short, and the dock delivery order was improper. In addition, Wallace notified Siderius that it was rejecting the Italian pipe on the grounds that the shipment of such pipe failed to conform to the contract terms. It is undisputed that on January 15, 1975, the Slavonija had not yet arrived in the Italian port of Ravenna and did not reach that port until January 24, 1975. The loading of the pipe on board the Slavonija was not completed until January 29, 1975.

Although the letter of credit expired on February 28, 1975, Siderius returned to the Bank and made a second presentation of the third draft on March 7, 1975. A new dock delivery order and copy of the bill of lading with charter party language removed were submitted to the Bank by Siderius. The insurance certificate remained short and the bill of lading continued to be dated January 15, 1975. Wallace refused to waive any defects, including late presentation, and the Bank dishonored Siderius' second presentation of the third draft. Subsequently, Wallace applied for a temporary injunction in order to enjoin the Bank from honoring Siderius' third draft because it was allegedly accompanied by false and fraudulent documents. On March 24, 1975, the trial court so enjoined the Bank. * * *

Letter of Credit

In the case at hand, we are presented with a documentary letter of credit; the issuer agrees to honor a timely draft accompanied by the documents specified in the letter of credit. The issuer deals only in documents and is not concerned with the merchandise, which is the subject of the underlying contract between the buyer and the seller. If the beneficiary presents documents which precisely and strictly conform to the requirements of the letter of credit, the issuer must honor the draft. * * * The rule of strict conformity is necessary because the issuer, dealing solely in documents, should not be required to examine the performance of the underlying transaction to determine if the terms of the letter of credit have been fulfilled. * * *

An exception to this general rule, requiring an issuer to honor a draft which is conforming on its face, is found in Subdivision (b)(2) of sec. 5–114, supra. Under the limited circumstances established by section 5–114(b)(2), supra, the issuer has the option to honor or dishonor, or the customer may enjoin the issuer from honoring such a draft. * * * This rule has been recognized as a codification of the pre-code case law as articulated in Sztejn v. J. Henry Schroder Banking Corporation, 177 Misc. 719, 31 N.Y.S.2d 631 (N.Y.Sup.Ct.1941) and Old Colony Trust Company v. Lawyers' Title and Trust Company, 297 F. 152 (2d Cir.) cert. denied, 265 U.S. 585, 44 S.Ct. 459, 68 L.Ed. 1192 (1924). It is undisputed that Siderius was not an innocent third party as defined in subsection (b)(1) of section 5–114, supra. * * *

The letter of credit, as amended, required that the draft in connection with the Italian shipment be accompanied by a copy of an "on board" bill of lading dated no later than January 15, 1975. * * * The bill of lading presented by Siderius represented that the pipe was so loaded, even though the ship had not yet arrived in the Italian port and wasn't loaded until two weeks later. * * *

In the instant case, the ship arrived into the port of Ravenna after January 15, 1975. The lack of formal notification by the Bank of any fraud in the bill of lading did not prejudice Siderius or prevent cure on the part of Siderius. No cure was possible; therefore the Bank has not waived its right to assert fraud as a defense under section 5–114(b), supra, to Siderius' action for wrongful dishonor.

In the alternative, Siderius asserts that the alleged fraud was insufficient to justify dishonor of the third draft. We disagree. The issuer of a documentary letter of credit, dealing in documents and not merchandise, must be able to rely on the accuracy and integrity of the documents presented by the beneficiary. * * * In the instant case, the fraud related to the documents themselves and not the pipe which was the subject of underlying contract of sale; therefore the fraud was sufficient, upon notification by the customer, to give the Bank the option to honor or dishonor. * * *

The fraud in the transaction exception also applies to documents. The defect must be fraudulent and not merely erroneous. In *Siderius*, the Bill of Lading was dated January 15, 1975. However, the vessel onto which the pipe was loaded did not arrive in the port until January 24, 1975. Furthermore, the Buyer, Wallace, would not waive the discrepancy. The court found this to a fraud in the documents.

In *Siderius*, the beneficiary knew of the defect. The outcome in those cases where the beneficiary is unaware of the defect has been different in some jurisdictions. In the United States the outcome would be the same—the Buyer can assert frauds in the transaction whether or not the beneficiary knew of the problem. In the United Kingdom and perhaps Canada, there is case law that permits dishonor when the beneficiary was unaware of the problem.

D.   ENJOINING THE PAYMENT ON A LETTER OF CREDIT

UCC 5–114(2), provides that in the case of a non holder in due course, an issuer, acting in good faith, may honor the draft or demand for payment despite notification from the customer of fraud, forgery, or other defect not apparent on the face of the documents. The protection for the innocent non-bank party comes under subsection (b) by providing that the party may seek a court of appropriate jurisdiction to enjoin such honor.

Even after establishing that there is fraud in the transaction injunctive relief is available only when the presenter is not a holder in due course. This opens the door to seek injunctive relief under *UCC Article 5–114(2)*. However, the requirements under the particular state's statute for equitable relief must also be met. The requirements for injunctive relief are onerous.

In order to obtain this extraordinary remedy, the petitioner must show irreparable harm where a remedy at law is not sufficient. The party must show probable success on the merits. Failing this, the petitioner must show serious questions going to the merits and balance of hardships tipping decidedly towards the party seeking the remedy. The following case discusses the test that must be met to allow injunctive relief.

AMERICAN BELL INTERN., INC. v. ISLAMIC REPUBLIC OF IRAN

United States District Court, Southern District of New York, 1979.
474 F.Supp. 420.

MacMAHON, District Judge.

* * *

Plaintiff American Bell International Inc. ("Bell") moves for a preliminary injunction * * * enjoining defendant Manufacturers Hanover Trust Company ("Manufacturers") from making any payment under its Letter of Credit No. SC 170027 to defendants the Islamic Republic of Iran or Bank Iranshahr or their agents, instrumentalities, successors, employees and assigns. We held an evidentiary hearing and heard oral argument on August 3, 1979. The following facts appear from the evidence presented:

The action arises from the recent revolution in Iran and its impact upon contracts made with the ousted Imperial Government of Iran and upon banking arrangements incident to such contracts. Bell, a wholly-owned subsidiary of American Telephone & Telegraph Co. ("AT & T"), made a contract on July 23, 1978 (the "Contract") with the Imperial Government of Iran Ministry of War ("Imperial Government") to provide consulting services and equipment to the Imperial Government as part of a program to improve Iran's international communications system.

The Contract provides a complex mechanism for payment to Bell totaling approximately $280,000,000, including a down payment of $38,800,000. The Imperial Government had the right to demand return of the down payment at any time. The amount so callable, however, was to be reduced by 20% Of the amounts invoiced by Bell to which the Imperial Government did not object. Bell's liability for return of the down payment was reduced by application of this mechanism as the Contract was performed, with the result that approximately $30,200,000 of the down payment now remains callable.

In order to secure the return of the down payment on demand, Bell was required to establish an unconditional and irrevocable Letter of Guaranty, to be issued by Bank Iranshahr in the amount of $38,800,000 in favor of the Imperial Government. The Contract provides that it is to be governed by the laws of Iran and that all disputes arising under it are to be resolved by the Iranian courts.

Bell obtained a Letter of Guaranty from Bank Iranshahr. In turn, as required by Bank Iranshahr, Bell obtained a standby Letter of Credit, No. SC 170027, issued by Manufacturers in favor of Bank Iranshahr in the amount of $38,800,000 to secure reimbursement to Bank Iranshahr should it be required to pay the Imperial Government under its Letter of Guaranty.

The standby Letter of Credit provided for payment by Manufacturers to Bank Iranshahr upon receipt of: "Your (Bank Iranshahr's) dated statement purportedly signed by an officer indicating name and title or your Tested Telex Reading: (A) 'Referring Manufacturers Hanover Trust Co. Credit No. SC170027, the amount of our claim $represents funds due us as we have received a written request from the Imperial Government of Iran Ministry of War to pay them the sum of under our Guarantee No. issued for the account of American Bell International Inc. covering advance payment under Contract No. 138 dated July 23, 1978 and such payment has been made by us'. . . . " In the application for the Letter of Credit, Bell agreed guaranteed by AT & T immediately to reimburse Manufacturers for all amounts paid by Manufacturers to Bank Iranshahr pursuant to the Letter of Credit.

Bell commenced performance of its Contract with the Imperial Government. It provided certain services and equipment to update Iran's communications system and submitted a number of invoices, some of which were paid.

In late 1978 and early 1979, Iran was wreaked with revolutionary turmoil culminating in the overthrow of the Iranian government and its replacement by the Islamic Republic. In the wake of this upheaval, Bell was left with substantial unpaid invoices and claims under the Contract and ceased its performance in January 1979. Bell claims that the Contract was breached by the Imperial Government, as well as repudiated by the Islamic Republic, in that it is owed substantial sums for services rendered under the Contract and its termination provisions.

On February 16, 1979, before a demand had been made by Bank Iranshahr for payment under the Letter of Credit, Bell and AT & T brought an action against Manufacturers in the Supreme Court, New York County, seeking a preliminary injunction prohibiting Manufacturers from honoring any demand for payment under the Letter of Credit. The motion for a preliminary injunction was denied in a thorough opinion by Justice Dontzin on March 26, 1979, and the denial was unanimously affirmed on appeal by the Appellate Division, First Department.

On July 25 and 29, 1979, Manufacturers received demands by Tested Telex from Bank Iranshahr for payment of $30,220,724 under the Letter of Credit, the remaining balance of the down payment. Asserting that the demand did not conform with the Letter of Credit, Manufacturers declined payment and so informed Bank Iranshahr. Informed of this, Bell responded by filing this action and an application by way of order to show cause for a temporary restraining order bringing on this motion for a preliminary injunction. Following argument, we granted a temporary restraining order on July 29 enjoining Manufacturers from making any payment to Bank Iranshahr until forty-eight hours after Manufacturers notified Bell of the receipt of a conforming demand, and this order has been extended pending decision of this motion.

On August 1, 1979, Manufacturers notified Bell that it had received a conforming demand from Bank Iranshahr. At the request of the parties, the court held an evidentiary hearing on August 3 on this motion for a preliminary injunction.

Criteria for Preliminary Injunctions

The current criteria in this circuit for determining whether to grant the extraordinary remedy of a preliminary injunction are set forth in Caulfield v. Board of Education, 583 F.2d 605, 610 (2d Cir.1978): "(T)here must be a showing of possible irreparable injury And either (1) probable success on the merits Or (2) sufficiently serious questions going to the merits to make them a fair ground for litigation And a balance of hardships tipping decidedly toward the party requesting the preliminary relief." We are not persuaded that the plaintiff has met the criteria and therefore deny the motion.

A. *Irreparable Injury*

Plaintiff has failed to show that irreparable injury may possibly ensue if a preliminary injunction is denied. Bell does not even claim, much less show, that it lacks an adequate remedy at law if Manufacturers makes a payment to Bank Iranshahr in violation of the Letter of Credit. It is too clear for argument that a suit for money damages could be based on any such violation, and surely Manufacturers would be able to pay any money judgment against it.

Bell falls back on a contention that it is without any effective remedy unless it can restrain payment. This contention is based on the fact that it agreed to be bound by the laws of Iran and to submit resolution of any disputes under the Contract to the courts of Iran. Bell claims that it now has no meaningful access to those courts.

There is credible evidence that the Islamic Republic is xenophobic and anti-American and that it has no regard for consulting service contracts such as the one here. Although Bell has made no effort to invoke the aid of the Iranian courts, we think the current situation in Iran, as shown by the evidence, warrants the conclusion that an attempt by Bell to resort to those courts would be futile. * * * However, Bell has not demonstrated that it is without adequate remedy in this court against the Iranian defendants under the Sovereign Immunity Act which it invokes in this very case. 28 U.S.C. 1605(a)(2), 1610(b)(2) (Supp. 1979).

Accordingly, we conclude that Bell has failed to demonstrate irreparable injury.

B.   Probable Success on the Merits

Even assuming that plaintiff has shown possible irreparable injury, it has failed to show probable success on the merits. * * *

In order to succeed on the merits, Bell must prove, by a preponderance of the evidence, that either (1) a demand for payment of the Manufacturers Letter of Credit conforming to the terms of that Letter has not yet been made, * * * or (2) a demand, even though in conformity, should not be honored because of fraud in the transaction * * *. It is not probable, in the sense of a greater than 50% Likelihood, that Bell will be able to prove either nonconformity or fraud.

As to nonconformity, the August 1 demand by Bank Iranshahr is identical to the terms of the Manufacturers Letter of Credit in every respect except one: it names as payee the "Government of Iran Ministry of Defense, Successor to the Imperial Government of Iran Ministry of War" rather than the "Imperial Government of Iran Ministry of War." * * * It is, of course, a bedrock principle of letter of credit law that a demand must strictly comply with the letter in order to justify payment. * * * Nevertheless, we deem it less than probable that a court, upon a full trial, would find nonconformity in the instant case.

At the outset, we notice, and the parties agree, that the United States now recognizes the present Government of Iran as the legal successor to the Imperial Government of Iran. That recognition is binding on American Courts. * * * Though we may decide for ourselves the consequences of such recognition upon the litigants in this case, Id., we point out that American courts have traditionally viewed contract rights as vesting not in any particular government but in the state of which that government is an agent. Id.

Accordingly, the Government of Iran is the successor to the Imperial Government under the Letter of Guaranty. As legal successor, the Government of Iran may properly demand payment even though the terms of the Letter of Guaranty only provide for payment to the Government of Iran's predecessor, * * * and a demand for payment under the Letter of Credit reciting that payment has been made by Bank Iranshahr to the new government is sufficient. We are fortified in this conclusion and made confident that a court, upon full trial, would reach the same result by Justice Dontzin's decision in the New York Supreme Court earlier this year that the Government of Iran was the legal successor to the Imperial Government of Iran. * * *

Finally, an opposite answer to the narrow question of conformity would not only elevate form over substance, but would render financial arrangements and undertakings worldwide wholly subject to the vicissitudes of political power. A nonviolent, unanimous transformation of the form of government, or, as this case shows, the mere change of the name of a government agency, would be enough to warrant an issuer's refusal to honor a demand. We cannot suppose such uncertainty and opportunity for chicanery to be the purpose of the requirement of strict conformity.

If conformity is established, as here, the issuer of an irrevocable, unconditional letter of credit, such as Manufacturers normally has an absolute duty to transfer the requisite funds. This duty is wholly independent of the underlying contractual relationship that gives rise to the letter of credit. * * * Nevertheless, both the Uniform Commercial Code of New York, which the parties concede governs here, and the courts state that payment is enjoin able where a germane document is forged or fraudulent or there is "fraud in the transaction." * * * Bell does not contend that any documents are fraudulent by virtue of misstatements or omissions. Instead, it argues there is "fraud in the transaction."

The parties disagree over the scope to be given as a matter of law to the term "transaction." Manufacturers, citing voluminous authorities, argues that the term refers only to the Letter of Credit transaction, not to the underlying commercial transaction or to the totality of dealings among the banks, the Iranian government and Bell. On this view of the law, Bell must fail to establish a probability of success, for it does not claim that the Imperial Government or Bank Iranshahr induced Manufacturers to extend the Letter by lies or half-truths, that the Letter contained any false representations by the Imperial Government or Bank Iranshahr, or that they intended misdeeds with it. Nor does Bell claim that the demand contains any misstatements.

Bell argues, citing equally voluminous authorities that the term "transaction" refers to the totality of circumstances. On this view, Bell has some chance of success on the merits, for a court can consider Bell's allegations that the Government of Iran's behavior in connection with the consulting contract suffices to make its demand on the Letter of Guaranty fraudulent and that the ensuing demand on the Letter of Credit by Bank Iranshahr is tainted with the fraud.

There is some question whether these divergent understandings of the law are wholly incompatible since it would seem impossible to keep the Letter of Credit transaction conceptually distinct. A demand which facially conforms to the Letter of Credit and which contains no misstatements may, nevertheless, be considered fraudulent if made with the goal of mulcting the party who caused the Letter of Credit to be issued. Be that as it may, we need not decide this thorny issue of law. For, even on the construction most favorable to Bell, we find that success on the merits is not probable. Many of the facts alleged, even if proven, would not constitute fraud. As to others, the proof is insufficient to indicate a probability of success on the merits.

Bell, while never delineating with precision the contours of the purported fraud, sets forth five contentions, which, in its view, support the issuance of an injunction. Bell asserts that (1) both the old and new Governments failed to approve invoices for services fully performed; (2) both failed to fund contracted-for independent Letters of Credit in Bell's favor; (3) the new Government has taken steps to renounce altogether its obligations under the Contract; (4) the new Government has made it impossible to assert contract rights in Iranian courts; and (5) the new Government has caused Bank Iranshahr to demand payment on the Manufacturers Letter of Credit, thus asserting rights in a transaction it has otherwise repudiated. Plaintiff's Memorandum (Aug. 2, 1979) at 17–18.

As to contention (4), it is not immediately apparent how denial of Bell's opportunity to assert rights under the Contract makes a demand on an independent letter of credit fraudulent.

Contentions (1), (2), (3) and the latter part of (5) all state essentially the same proposition that the Government of Iran is currently repudiating all its contractual obligations with American companies, including those with Bell. Again, the evidence on this point is uncompelling.

Bell points to (1) an intra governmental order of July 2, 1979 ordering the termination of Iran's contract with Bell, and (2) hearsay discussions between Bell's president and Iranian officials to the effect that Iran would not pay on the Contract until it had determined whether the services under it had benefited the country. Complaint Exhibit E; Kerts Affidavit P 3. Manufacturers, for its part, points to a public statement in the Wall Street Journal of July 16, 1979, under the name of the present Iranian Government, to the effect that Iran intends to honor all legitimate contracts. Defendant's Exhibit C. Taken together, this evidence does not suggest that Iran has finally and irrevocably decided to repudiate the Bell contract. It suggests equally that Iran is still considering the question whether to perform that contract.

Even if we accept the proposition that the evidence does show repudiation, plaintiff is still far from demonstrating the kind of evil intent necessary to support a claim of fraud. Surely, plaintiff cannot contend that every party who breaches or repudiates his contract is for that reason culpable of fraud. The law of contract damages is adequate to repay the economic harm caused by repudiation, and the law presumes that one who repudiates has done so because of a calculation that such damages are cheaper than performance. Absent any showing that Iran would refuse to pay damages upon a contract action here or in Iran, much less a showing that Bell has even attempted to obtain such a remedy, the evidence is ambivalent as to whether the purported repudiation results from non-fraudulent economic calculation or from fraudulent intent to mulct Bell.

Plaintiff contends that the alleged repudiation, viewed in connection with its demand for payment on the Letter of Credit, supplies the basis from which only one inference fraud can be drawn. Again, we remain unpersuaded.

Plaintiff's argument requires us to presume bad faith on the part of the Iranian government. It requires us further to hold that government may not rely on the plain terms of the consulting contract and the Letter of Credit arrangements with Bank Iranshahr and Manufacturers providing for immediate repayment of the down payment upon demand, without regard to cause. On the evidence before us, fraud is no more infer able than an economically rational decision by the government to recoup its down payment, as it is entitled to do under the consulting contract and still dispute its liabilities under that Contract.

While fraud in the transaction is doubtless a possibility, plaintiff has not shown it to be a probability and thus fails to satisfy this branch of the Caulfield test.

C.   Serious Questions and Balance of Hardships

If plaintiff fails to demonstrate probable success, he may still obtain relief by showing, in addition to the possibility of irreparable injury, both (1) sufficiently serious questions going to the merits to make them a fair ground for litigation, and (2) a balance of hardships tipping decidedly toward plaintiff. * * * Both Bell and Manufacturers appear to concede the existence of serious questions, and the complexity and novelty of this matter lead us to find they exist. Nevertheless, we hold that plaintiff is not entitled to relief under this branch of the Caulfield test because the balance of hardships does not tip decidedly toward Bell, if indeed it tips that way at all.

To be sure, Bell faces substantial hardships upon denial of its motion. Should Manufacturers pay the demand, Bell will immediately become liable to Manufacturers for $30.2 million, with no assurance of recouping those funds from Iran for the services performed. While counsel represented in graphic detail the other losses Bell faces at the hands of the current Iranian government, these would flow regardless of whether we ordered the relief sought. The hardship imposed from a denial of relief is limited to the admittedly substantial sum of $30.2 million.

But Manufacturers would face at least as great a loss, and perhaps a greater one, were we to grant relief. Upon Manufacturers' failure to pay, Bank Iranshahr could initiate a suit on the Letter of Credit and attach $30.2 million of Manufacturers' assets in Iran. In addition, it could seek to hold Manufacturers liable for consequential damages beyond that sum resulting from the failure to make timely payment. Finally, there is not guarantee that Bank Iranshahr or the government, in retaliation for Manufacturers' recalcitrance, will not nationalize additional Manufacturers' assets in Iran in amounts which counsel, at oral argument, represented to be far in excess of the amount in controversy here.

Apart from a greater monetary exposure flowing from an adverse decision, Manufacturers faces a loss of credibility in the international banking community that could result from its failure to make good on a letter of credit.

Conclusion

Finally, apart from questions of relative hardship and the specific criteria of the Caulfield test, general considerations of equity counsel us to deny the motion for injunctive relief. Bell, a sophisticated multinational enterprise well advised by competent counsel, entered into these arrangements with its corporate eyes open. It knowingly and voluntarily signed a contract allowing the Iranian government to recoup its down payment on demand, without regard to cause. It caused Manufacturers to enter into an arrangement whereby Manufacturers became obligated to pay Bank Iranshahr the unamortized down payment balance upon receipt of conforming documents, again without regard to cause.

Both of these arrangements redounded tangibly to the benefit of Bell. The Contract with Iran, with its prospect of designing and installing from scratch a nationwide and international communications system, was certain to bring to Bell both monetary profit and prestige and good will in the global communications industry. The agreement to indemnify Manufacturers on its Letter of Credit provided the means by which these benefits could be achieved.

One who reaps the rewards of commercial arrangements must also accept their burdens. One such burden in this case, voluntarily accepted by Bell, was the risk that demand might be made without cause on the funds constituting the down payment. To be sure, the sequence of events that led up to that demand may well have been unforeseeable when the contracts were signed. To this extent, both Bell and Manufacturers have been made the unwitting and innocent victims of tumultuous events beyond their control. But, as between two innocents, the party who undertakes by contract the risk of political uncertainty and governmental caprice must bear the consequences when the risk comes home to roost. * * *

The quest for efficiency and a streamlined process in the use of the documentary letter of credit creates a high hurdle for the Buyer to overcome the payment obligation under a letter of credit. The independence principle, which effectively removes the condition of the goods as a factor, can only be breached in cases where there is fraud in the transaction. Even after the finding of fraud, there is no remedy if the presenter is a holder in due course.

In those cases where the presenter is not a holder in due course the bank can still pay so long as it is acting in good faith. It is at this point where the Buyer has a remedy—seek an injunction. But as can be seen from the case above, receiving injunctive relief is not an easy task.

The *Bell* case involved a standby letter of credit. This type of letter of credit is different from a documentary credit in several significant factors. The documentary credit protects the beneficiary (the Seller) against non-payment under the Sales Contract. In a standby letter of credit the beneficiary is the Buyer. The credit protects the Buyer against the non-performance by the Seller.

The document in a standby letter of credit is a certification by the beneficiary (the Buyer) that the Seller is in default. There is no certification by an independent third party like you would find in a standard surety agreement. In a Documentary Transaction the non-payment condition is the presentation of non-conforming documents. It is the unilateral nature of the default trigger by the beneficiary that has earned the standby letter of credit the name of 'suicide credit.'

Chapter 6

THE INTERNATIONAL CARRIAGE AND DELIVERY OF GOODS

SECTION 6.1 THE CARRIAGE OF GOODS BY SEA ACT

A. GOVERNING LAW

1. *Introduction*

The international carriage and delivery of goods is a complex transaction requiring the crossing of national borders. It also typically involves travel across great distances, using singly or in combination sea, land and air transportation. Each type of transportation system has unique legal characteristics that need to be taken into account in any planning scenario. A substantial amount of goods sold in the Americas is delivered by sea, particularly goods sold in bulk emanating from South America, such as oil, agricultural products, phosphates, and minerals.

Land and air transportation is most concentrated in North America, although a substantial amount of bulk products such as oil is delivered by sea as well. For a discussion of the complex legal issues that arise from the multi-modal carriage of goods across national borders see Thomas J. Schoenbaum, *Admiralty and Maritime Law*, Third Edition, West Group, Hornbook Series. These materials focus on the carriage of goods by sea.

The parties and their responsibility for the carriage of goods should be stated in the Sales Contract. A properly drafted contract should clearly state the delivery conditions and should also state whom the Shipper and Carrier will be. The Shipper contracts with the Carrier who physically transports and delivers the goods to their final destination. The Shipper could be either the Buyer or the Seller. The Shipper can be named directly in the Sales Contract or indirectly if the Sales Contract incorporates the *Incoterms* by reference. For a discussion of *Incoterms* see section 4.3, supra.

For example, assume that the Sales Contract includes the delivery term—*FOB Los Angeles*. Under *Incoterms* the *FOB* term imposes on the Buyer the responsibility of contracting with the Carrier for the carriage and delivery of the goods to their final destination; therefore, the Buyer is the Shipper. Assume the Sales Contract provides for a *CIF Buenos Aires* delivery term instead of *FOB Los Angeles*. The *CIF Incoterm* imposes on the Seller the responsibility of engaging the Carrier for the delivery of the goods to Buenos Aires. In this case, the Seller is the Shipper. In a Documentary Transaction the usual delivery term is *CIF Destination*. As such, the Shipper is usually the Seller.

The contractual relationship between the Shipper and Carrier in the carriage and delivery of goods by sea is governed by the Bill of Lading (BOL). The BOL serves as a contract of carriage between the Shipper and Carrier, a document of title to the goods, and a receipt for their delivery. The following materials focus on determining liability in several problem areas—failing to deliver the goods or delivering damaged goods, delivering mis-described goods or delivering the goods to the wrong person.

As these problem areas are reviewed, keep in mind that Carriers are usually large and sophisticated companies that own or lease ocean going vessels, airplanes, railroads or trucks to deliver the goods. The Shipper and Carrier often do not have equal bargaining power. In addition, there are many instances where the Carrier can escape liability.

The BOL as a contract of carriage is important in determining liability in cases where there is a failure to deliver goods or when damaged goods have been delivered. As a document of receipt the BOL describes the goods and provides evidence that the goods have been received by the carrier and loaded for transportation. This attribute is useful in determining liability where mis-described goods are delivered. Finally, the BOL is a document of title. This can be used to determine liability when the goods are delivered to the wrong person. As a document of title it establishes the ownership of the goods. This characteristic is especially important in the Documentary Transaction.

The rights and liabilities of parties in the carriage of goods are determined by domestic legislation. Determining the rights and liabilities of parties in the carriage of goods has historically been a tension between the cargo and vessel interests. The Shipper (the owner of the goods) is interested in protecting the value of the goods. The Carrier (the vessel owner) is interested in protecting the vessel and limiting its liability for any damage to the cargo.

Domestic legislation had traditionally reflected the national vested interests of the particular country. A country with a substantial maritime fleet enacted domestic laws protecting the Carrier. Broad, exculpatory clauses in the BOL, substantially limiting carrier liability were deemed valid. Conversely, a country with a limited maritime fleet and strong cargo interests enacted legislation imposing absolute liability on foreign carriers. This nationalistic approach in regulating the carriage of goods was seen by many countries as stifling international trade.

In the 1890's, the need for international harmonization of carriage of goods rules was gaining recognition by many countries. In 1893, the U.S. Congress took an international leadership role by enacting the *Harter Act*.[1] The *Harter Act*, attempting to strike a balance between the cargo and vessel interests was well received in the international community. It formed the basis for an international convention known as the *Hague Rules*[2] that established international norms for the carriage of goods and are widely accepted throughout most of the world.

The *Hague Rules* themselves have been amended by the *Hague-Visby*[3] and the *Hamburg Rules*.[4] The effort to harmonize international trade rules, although partially realized in many parts of the world, has lagged behind in the Western Hemisphere. Therefore, a review of each domestic system needs to be made to glean the appropriate rules.

2. *The Choice of Law Clause*

In the U.S., the *Carriage of Goods By Sea Act (COGSA)*[5] is the principal legislation governing the carriage of goods by sea to or from ports of the United States in foreign trade. Enacted in 1936, The COGSA is modeled after the Hague Rules. At the time of its enactment, the *COGSA* represented the best international efforts at harmonizing the law regarding the carriage of goods. The *COGSA*, however, does not reflect the changes made by the *Hague-Visby* or *Hamburg* rules. The *Harter Act*, which formed the basis for the Hague rules, still applies to shipments between American ports and foreign ports, as well as to shipments between American ports. It also governs that period of time between delivery to the carrier but before loading and after unloading but before delivery to the consignee.

The BOL is a contract negotiated by parties that often have disparate bargaining power. In the usual case, the BOL selects the law and forum of the Carrier's choosing. The Shipper can either take it or leave it. A point of contention has been in those cases where a Carrier in the BOL chooses a jurisdiction other than the U.S. to apply. U.S. courts had always held as invalid a BOL clause opting out of COGSA. The Supreme Court recently decided a case on the validity of such a choice of law clause.

**VIMAR SEGUROS Y REASEGUROS,
S.A. v. M/V SKY REEFER**
United States Supreme Court, 1995.
515 U.S. 528, 115 S.Ct. 2322, 132 L.Ed.2d 462.

* * *

1. 46 USC §§ 190–196 (1998).

2. Convention for the Unification of Certain Rules Relating to Bills of Lading.

3. 24 ILM 1573.

4. 17 I.LM 603.

5. 46 USC §§ 1300 et. eq. (1998).

Justice KENNEDY delivered the opinion of the Court. * * *

The contract at issue in this case is a standard form bill of lading to evidence the purchase of a shipload of Moroccan oranges and lemons. The purchaser was Bacchus Associates (Bacchus), a New York partnership that distributes fruit at wholesale throughout the Northeastern United States. Bacchus dealt with Galaxie Negoce, S.A. (Galaxie), a Moroccan fruit supplier. Bacchus contracted with Galaxie to purchase the shipload of fruit and chartered a ship to transport it from Morocco to Massachusetts. The ship was the M/V Sky Reefer, a refrigerated cargo ship owned by M.H. Maritima, S.A., a Panamanian company, and time-chartered to Nichiro Gyogyo Kaisha, Ltd., a Japanese company. Stevedores hired by Galaxie loaded and stowed the cargo. As is customary in these types of transactions, when it received the cargo from Galaxie, Nichiro as carrier issued a form bill of lading to Galaxie as shipper and consignee. Once the ship set sail from Morocco, Galaxie tendered the bill of lading to Bacchus according to the terms of a letter of credit posted in Galaxie's favor.

Among the rights and responsibilities set out in the bill of lading were arbitration and choice-of-law clauses. Clause 3, entitled "Governing Law and Arbitration," provided: "(1) The contract evidenced by or contained in this Bill of Lading shall be governed by the Japanese law." (2) Any dispute arising from this Bill of Lading shall be referred to arbitration in Tokyo by the Tokyo Maritime Arbitration Commission (TOMAC) of The Japan Shipping Exchange, Inc., in accordance with the rules of TOMAC and any amendment thereto, and the award given by the arbitrators shall be final and binding on both parties." * * *

When the vessel's hatches were opened for discharge in Massachusetts, Bacchus discovered that thousands of boxes of oranges had shifted in the cargo holds, resulting in over $1 million damage. Bacchus received $733,442.90 compensation from petitioner Vimar Seguros y Reaseguros (Vimar Seguros), Bacchus' marine cargo insurer that became subrogated pro tanto to Bacchus' rights. Petitioner and Bacchus then brought suit against Maritima in personam and M/V Sky Reefer in rem in the District Court for the District of Massachusetts under the bill of lading. These defendants, respondents here, moved to stay the action and compel arbitration in Tokyo under clause 3 of the bill of lading * * *

The leading case for invalidation of a foreign forum selection clause is the opinion of the Court of Appeals for the Second Circuit in Indussa Corp. v. S.S. Ranborg, 377 F.2d 200 (1967) (en banc). The court there found that COGSA invalidated a clause designating a foreign judicial forum because it "puts 'a high hurdle' in the way of enforcing liability, and thus is an effective means for carriers to secure settlements lower than if cargo [owners] could sue in a convenient forum," * * * The court observed "there could be no assurance that [the foreign court] would apply [COGSA] in the same way as would an American tribunal subject to the uniform control of the Supreme Court," id., at 203–204. Following

Indussa, the Courts of Appeals without exception have invalidated foreign forum selection clauses under s 3(8). * * *

[W]e cannot endorse the reasoning or the conclusion of the Indussa rule itself.

The determinative provision in COGSA, examined with care, does not support the arguments advanced first in Indussa and now by the petitioner. Section 3(8) of COGSA provides as follows: "Any clause, covenant, or agreement in a contract of carriage relieving the carrier or the ship from liability for loss or damage to or in connection with the goods, arising from negligence, fault, or failure in the duties or obligations provided in this section, or lessening such liability otherwise than as provided in this chapter, shall be null and void and of no effect." 46 U.S.C.App. s 1303(8). The liability that may not be lessened is "liability for loss or damage ... arising from negligence, fault, or failure in the duties or obligations provided in this section." The statute thus addresses the lessening of the specific liability imposed by the Act, without addressing the separate question of the means and costs of enforcing that liability. The difference is that between explicit statutory guarantees and the procedure for enforcing them, between applicable liability principles and the forum in which they are to be vindicated.

The liability imposed on carriers under COGSA s 3 is defined by explicit standards of conduct, and it is designed to correct specific abuses by carriers. In the 19th century it was a prevalent practice for common carriers to insert clauses in bills of lading exempting themselves from liability for damage or loss, limiting the period in which plaintiffs had to present their notice of claim or bring suit, and capping any damages awards per package. * * *

Thus, s 3, entitled "Responsibilities and liabilities of carrier and ship," requires that the carrier "exercise due diligence to ... [m]ake the ship seaworthy" and "[p]roperly man, equip, and supply the ship" before and at the beginning of the voyage, s 3(1), "properly and carefully load, handle, stow, carry, keep, care for, and discharge the goods carried," s 3(2), and issue a bill of lading with specified contents, s 3(3). 46 U.S.C.App. s 1303(1), (2), and (3). Section 3(6) allows the cargo owner to provide notice of loss or damage within three days and to bring suit within one year. These are the substantive obligations and particular procedures that s 3(8) prohibits a carrier from altering to its advantage in a bill of lading. Nothing in this section, however, suggests that the statute prevents the parties from agreeing to enforce these obligations in a particular forum. By its terms, it establishes certain duties and obligations, separate and apart from the mechanisms for their enforcement. * * *

If the question whether a provision lessens liability were answered by reference to the costs and inconvenience to the cargo owner, there would be no principled basis for distinguishing national from foreign arbitration clauses. Even if it were reasonable to read s 3(8) to make a distinction based on travel time, airfare, and hotels bills, these factors are not susceptible of a simple and enforceable distinction between domestic and foreign forums. Requiring a Seattle cargo owner to arbitrate in New York likely imposes more costs and burdens than a foreign arbitration clause requiring it to arbitrate in Vancouver. It would be unwieldy and unsupported by the terms or policy of the statute to require courts to proceed case by case to tally the costs and burdens to particular plaintiffs in light of their means, the size of their claims, and the relative burden on the carrier.

Our reading of "lessening such liability" to exclude increases in the transaction costs of litigation also finds support in the goals of the Brussels Convention for the Unification of Certain Rules Relating to Bills of Lading, 51 Stat. 233 (1924) (Hague Rules), on which COGSA is modeled. Sixty-six countries, including the United States and Japan, are now parties to the Convention * * * and it appears that none has interpreted its enactment of s 3(8) of the Hague Rules to prohibit foreign forum selection clauses * * * See Maharani Woollen Mills Co. v. Anchor Line, [1927] 29 Lloyd's List L. Rep. 169 (C.A.) (Scrutton, L.J.) ("[T]he liability of the carrier appears to me to remain exactly the same under the clause. The only difference is a question of procedure–where shall the law be enforced?–and I do not read any clause as to procedure as lessening liability"). And other countries that do not recognize foreign forum selection clauses rely on specific provisions to that effect in their domestic versions of the Hague Rules * * * In light of the fact that COGSA is the culmination of a multilateral effort "to establish uniform ocean bills of lading to govern the rights and liabilities of carriers and shippers inter se in international trade," * * * we decline to interpret our version of the Hague Rules in a manner contrary to every other nation to have addressed this issue. * * *

It would also be out of keeping with the objects of the Convention for the courts of this country to interpret COGSA to disparage the authority or competence of international forums for dispute resolution. Petitioner's skepticism over the ability of foreign arbitrators to apply COGSA or the Hague Rules, and its reliance on this aspect of Indussa, supra, must give way to contemporary principles of international comity and commercial practice. As the Court observed in The Bremen v. Zapata Off–Shore Co., 407 U.S. 1, 92 S.Ct. 1907, 32 L.Ed.2d 513 (1972), when it enforced a foreign forum selection clause, the historical judicial resistance to foreign forum selection clauses "has little place in an era when ... businesses once essentially local now operate in world markets." Id., at 12, 92 S.Ct., at 1914. "The expansion of American business and industry will hardly be encouraged," we explained, "if, notwithstanding solemn contracts, we insist on a parochial concept that all disputes must be resolved under our laws and in our courts." * * *

Petitioner's second argument against enforcement of the Japanese arbitration clause is that there is no guarantee foreign arbitrators will apply COGSA. This objection raises a concern of substance. The central guarantee of s 3(8) is that the terms of a bill of landing may not relieve the carrier of the obligations or diminish the legal duties specified by the

Act. The relevant question, therefore, is whether the substantive law to be applied will reduce the carrier's obligations to the cargo owner below what COGSA guarantees. * * *

Petitioner argues that the arbitrators will follow the Japanese Hague Rules, which, petitioner contends, lessen respondents' liability in at least one significant respect. The Japanese version of the Hague Rules, it is said, provides the carrier with a defense based on the acts or omissions of the stevedores hired by the shipper, Galaxie, see App. 112, Article 3(1), (carrier liable "when he or the persons employed by him" fail to take due care), while COGSA, according to petitioner, makes nondelegable the carrier's obligation to "properly and carefully . . . stow . . . the goods carried," COGSA s 3(2), 46 U.S.C.App. s1303(2); * * * But see COGSA s 4(2)(i), 46 U.S.C. s 1304(2)(i) ("[N]either the carrier nor the ship shall be responsible for loss or damage arising or resulting from . . . [a]ct or omission of the shipper or owner of the goods, his agent or representative"); COGSA s 3(8), 46 U.S.C.App. s 1303(8) (agreement may not relieve or lessen liability "otherwise than as provided in this chapter"); * * *

Whatever the merits of petitioner's comparative reading of COGSA and its Japanese counterpart, its claim is premature. At this interlocutory stage it is not established what law the arbitrators will apply to petitioner's claims or that petitioner will receive diminished protection as a result. The arbitrators may conclude that COGSA applies of its own force or that Japanese law does not apply so that, under another clause of the bill of lading, COGSA controls. Respondents seek only to enforce the arbitration agreement. The district court has retained jurisdiction over the case and "will have the opportunity at the award-enforcement stage to ensure that the legitimate interest in the enforcement of the . . . laws has been addressed." * * * Were there no subsequent opportunity for review and were we persuaded that "the choice-of-forum and choice-of-law clauses operated in tandem as a prospective waiver of a party's right to pursue statutory remedies . . . , we would have little hesitation in condemning the agreement as against public policy." * * * Under the circumstances of this case, however, the First Circuit was correct to reserve judgment on the choice-of-law question, * * * as it must be decided in the first instance by the arbitrator * * *. As the District Court has retained jurisdiction, mere speculation that the foreign arbitrators might apply Japanese law which, depending on the proper construction of COGSA, might reduce respondents' legal obligations, does not in and of itself lessen liability under COGSA s 3(8).

Because we hold that foreign arbitration clauses in bills of lading are not invalid under COGSA in all circumstances, both the FAA and COGSA may be given full effect. The judgment of the Court of Appeals is affirmed, and the case is remanded for further proceedings consistent with this opinion.

It is so ordered.* * *

The *Vimar* case is a sharp departure regarding the applicability of the COGSA. *Indussa*, overruled by *Vimar* had been the rule since 1967. The full effect of the decision has yet to be determined. The sharp dissent frames the issues for the counter point of view.

Justice STEVENS, dissenting.

The Carriage of Goods by Sea Act (COGSA), * * * enacted in 1936 as a supplement to the 1893 Harter Act, * * * regulates the terms of bills of lading issued by ocean carriers transporting cargo to or from ports of the United States. Section 3(8) of COGSA provides: "Any clause, covenant, or agreement in a contract of carriage relieving the carrier or the ship from liability for loss or damage to or in connection with the goods, arising from negligence, fault, or failure in the duties and obligations provided in this section, or lessening such liability otherwise than as provided in this chapter, shall be null and void and of no effect." 46 U.S.C.App. s 1303(8).

Petitioners in this case challenge the enforceability of a foreign arbitration clause, coupled with a choice-of-foreign-law clause, in a bill of lading covering a shipment of oranges from Morocco to Boston, Massachusetts. * * * Under the construction of COGSA that has been uniformly followed by the Court of Appeals and endorsed by scholarly commentary for decades, both of those clauses are unenforceable against the shipper because they "relieve" or "lessen" the liability of the carrier. Nevertheless, relying almost entirely on a recent case involving a domestic forum selection clause that was not even covered by COGSA, Carnival Cruise Lines, Inc. v. Shute, 499 U.S. 585, 111 S.Ct. 1522, 113 L.Ed.2d 622 (1991), the Court today unwisely discards settled law and adopts a novel construction of s 3(8). * * *

In the 19th century it was common practice for ship owners to issue bills of lading that included stipulations exempting themselves from liability for losses occasioned by the negligence of their employees. Because a bill of lading was (and is) a contract of adhesion, which a shipper must accept or else find another means to transport his goods, shippers were in no position to bargain around these no-liability clauses. Although the English courts enforced the stipulations, * * * this Court concluded, even prior to the 1893 enactment of the Harter Act, that they were "contrary to public policy, and consequently void." * * *

The Court's holding that the choice-of-law clause was invalid rested entirely on the Harter Act's prohibition against relieving the carrier from liability. * * * Courts have also consistently found such clauses invalid under COGSA, which embodies an even broader prohibition against clauses "relieving" or "lessening" a carrier's liability.

Thus, our interpretation of maritime law prior to the enactment of the Harter Act * * * and the federal courts' consistent interpretation of COGSA, buttressed by scholarly recognition of the commercial interest in uniformity, demonstrate that the clauses in the Japanese carrier's bill of lading purporting to require arbitration in Tokyo pursuant to Japanese law both would have been held invalid under COGSA prior to today. * * *

The Court assumes that the words "lessening such liability" must be narrowly construed to refer only to the substantive rules that define the carrier's legal obligations. Ante, at 2327. Under this view, contractual provisions that lessen the amount of the consignee's net recovery, or that lessen the likelihood that it will make any recovery at all, are beyond the scope of the statute.

In my opinion, this view is flatly inconsistent with the purpose of COGSA s 3(8). That section responds to the inequality of bargaining power inherent in bills of lading and to carriers' historic tendency to exploit that inequality whenever possible to immunize themselves from liability for their own fault. A bill of lading is a form document prepared by the carrier, who presents it to the shipper on a take-it-or-leave-it basis. * * *

When one reads the statutory language in light of the policies behind COGSA's enactment, it is perfectly clear that a foreign forum selection or arbitration clause "relieves" or "lessens" the carrier's liability. The transaction costs associated with an arbitration in Japan will obviously exceed the potential recovery in a great many cargo disputes. As a practical matter, therefore, in such a case no matter how clear the carrier's formal legal liability may be, it would make no sense for the consignee or its subrogee to enforce that liability. It seems to me that a contractual provision that entirely protects the shipper from being held liable for anything should be construed either to have "lessened" its inability or to have "relieved" it of liability.

Even if the value of the shipper's claim is large enough to justify litigation in Asia, contractual provisions that impose unnecessary and unreasonable costs on the consignee will inevitably lessen its net recovery. If, as under the Court's reasoning, such provisions do not affect the carrier's legal liability, it would appear to be permissible to require the consignee to pay the costs of the arbitration, or perhaps the travel expenses and fees of the expert witnesses, interpreters, and lawyers employed by both parties. Judge Friendly and the many other wise judges who shared his opinion were surely correct in concluding that Congress could not have intended such a perverse reading of the statutory text. * * *

———————

The COGSA was modeled after the *Convention for the Unification of Certain Rules Relating to Bills of Lading* commonly referred to as the

Hague rules. The Court in *Vimar* upheld a foreign arbitration clause in a Bill of Lading, saying of arbitration "... It would * * * be out of keeping with the objects of the Convention [The *Hague* Rules] for the courts of this country to interpret COGSA to disparage the authority or competence of international forums for dispute resolution. Petitioners skepticism over the ability of foreign arbitrators to apply COGSA or the Hague Rules ... must give way to contemporary principles of international comity and commercial practice ..." The court through *Vimar* continues to endorse maritime arbitration clauses.

COGSA section 1303(8) disallows forum selection clauses that would result in the lessening of Carrier liability that would follow under COGSA. The section does not specifically relate to choice of forum or method of resolving the dispute. The court did leave open the possibility that 1303(8) would apply if the foreign arbitrators used a law in its decision that would lessen Carrier liability. The court stated that it was premature to reach a conclusion since the case had not yet been submitted to arbitration.

B.   REMEDIES FOR DELIVERING DAMAGED GOODS

1.   *Establishing Liability for the Damage of Goods*

BANANA SERVICES, INC. v. M/V TASMAN STAR
United States Court of Appeals, Eleventh Circuit, 1995.
68 F.3d 418.

BLACK, Circuit Judge:

Plaintiff–Appellant Banana Services, Inc. (Banana Services) appeals the district court's entry of judgment in favor of Defendants–Appellees Star Reefers, Ltd. (Star Reefers), Navegantes Del Oriente, S.A. (Navegantes), and the M/V TASMAN STAR on Appellant's claim for damages due to the spoilation of a cargo of bananas. This appeal requires us to decide whether a carrier, under the Carriage of Goods by Sea Act (COGSA), 46 U.S.C. app. §§ 1300–1315, must first demonstrate it acted with due diligence to provide a seaworthy vessel for transport before the carrier may invoke the "fire defense" of COGSA and the Fire Statute, 46 U.S.C. app. § 182. We conclude that a carrier does not bear this burden, and therefore affirm the district court's judgment. * * *

Navegantes is the owner and operator of the M/V TASMAN STAR. Prior to the events at issue, Navegantes time-chartered the TASMAN STAR to Star Reefers. In September 1990, Star Reefers contracted with Banana Services to transport a cargo of fruit from South America to Florida aboard the TASMAN STAR. The contract between Banana Services and Star Reefers stated Star Reefers accepted "liability for any cargo carried in accordance with the U.S. Carriage of Goods by Sea Act."

In early June 1991, Banana Services delivered boxes of bananas and plantains to the vessel at Puerto Bolivar, Ecuador, and Turbo, Colombia. At both locations, the cargo was accepted, and the crew of the TASMAN

STAR issued clean bills of lading. On June 9, 1991, the vessel departed from Turbo en route to Port Manatee, Florida. That same day, approximately 20 hours into the voyage, a fire broke out in the engine room of the vessel. Although the crew extinguished the fire approximately an hour after it started, the fire damaged the ship's refrigeration control panels. As a result, the vessel was unable to properly refrigerate its cargo of bananas and plantains. The ship's chief engineer determined he could not temporarily repair the refrigeration panels, so the ship's officers decided to return to Turbo, Colombia.

The TASMAN STAR arrived back in Turbo on June 10 and representatives of Star Reefers and Navegantes met to discuss what options were available to protect the perishable cargo. Banana Services participated in these discussions by telephone. Based upon the advice of engineers and technical managers, the parties determined they could not repair the refrigeration system in time given Turbo's limited repair facilities and the need for particular replacement parts. The parties considered transferring the cargo to another vessel chartered by Star Reefers, but this option involved considerable delays and risked damaging the cargo. Moreover, Banana Services indicated that it would not make a final decision regarding transshipment. Navegantes and Star Reefers eventually decided to proceed to Port Manatee with the cargo aboard the TASMAN STAR. The ship departed Turbo approximately 22 hours after returning to port.

The ship arrived at Port Manatee on June 13, 1991. Surveyors for each party inspected the cargo and unanimously agreed the fruit was unmarketable because the pulp temperature of the fruit exceeded industry standards. Banana Services refused to take delivery of the fruit, and Navegantes bore the costs of disposing of the cargo.

Banana Services brought suit against Navegantes and Star Reefers for more than $1.1 million in damages resulting from the loss of the cargo. After a lengthy bench trial, the district court entered judgment against Banana Services. Banana Services appeals, contending the district court misapplied the governing law of COGSA. * * *

Under COGSA, a shipper seeking recovery from a carrier for damages to its cargo bears the initial burden of proving a prima facie case. * * * The shipper establishes a prima facie case by demonstrating the cargo was loaded in an undamaged condition, and discharged in a damaged condition. * * * A clean bill of lading creates a rebuttable presumption the goods were delivered to the carrier in good condition and thus satisfies this element of the plaintiff's prima facie case. * * * The parties do not contest Banana Services established its prima facie case.

Once a shipper establishes a prima facie case, the burden of proof shifts to the carrier to demonstrate either (1) it exercised due diligence to prevent the cargo damage, or (2) the damage was caused by an "excepted cause" listed in 46 U.S.C. app. § 1304(2). * * * This section provides a carrier is not responsible for cargo damage resulting from a fire unless the damage is "caused by the actual fault or privity of the carrier." 46 U.S.C. app. § 1304(2)(b). In addition to the excepted cause for fire, COGSA also preserves a carrier's defense under the Fire Statute, 46 U.S.C. § 182. See 46 U.S.C. § 1308. The Fire Statute exonerates carriers from liability for fire damage to cargo unless the fire was caused by the "design or neglect" of the owner. 46 U.S.C. § 182. * * *

The district court correctly concluded that the cargo was destroyed by fire because the fire in the TASMAN STAR's refrigeration panels prevented the ship from refrigerating the fruit. As a result, the cargo spoiled during the trip from Turbo to Port Manatee. A fire need not directly ignite the cargo to be the cause of damage under COGSA. * * *

Star Reefers and Navegantes invoke both the Fire Statute and section 1304(2)(b) in defense of Banana Services' claim. Banana Services argues they cannot invoke this defense without first demonstrating they acted with due diligence in providing a seaworthy vessel. The district court disagreed with Banana Services' position and concluded that COGSA does not limit the fire defense in this fashion.

There is conflicting authority as to whether carriers must demonstrate due diligence as a prerequisite to invoking the fire defense of COGSA or the Fire Statute. The Ninth Circuit has reasoned carriers must overcome this initial burden before they may raise the defense and shift the burden of proof back to the shipper. The Second and Fifth Circuits, disagreeing with the Ninth Circuit's reasoning in Sunkist, have concluded COGSA does not condition a carrier's right to invoke the fire defense on proving due diligence.

The holding in Westinghouse is consistent with this Court's precedent. We find the reasoning of the Second and Fifth Circuits persuasive, and hold that COGSA does not require carriers to demonstrate due diligence as a condition precedent to invoking the fire defense of section 1304(2)(b) and the Fire Statute. * * *

To invoke the fire defense, Star Reefers and Navegantes only had to demonstrate the cargo was destroyed by fire. The district court correctly refused to impose upon Star Reefers and Navegantes the burden of demonstrating they acted with due diligence as a condition precedent to invoking the fire defense of COGSA and the Fire Statute. * * *

The Banana Services case describes the shifting presumptions under the COGSA. The Shipper makes out a prima facie case against the Carrier by showing that the Carrier received the goods in good condition and upon reaching their destination they were damaged. The burden then shifts to the Carrier who must prove that the damage to the goods was caused by an event that statutorily relieves the Carrier from liability. If the Carrier is unable to meet its burden, liability for the loss will rest on the Carrier.

The COGSA, Hague, Hague–Visby and Hamburg rules still provide for substantial freedom from liability by the carrier. COGSA section 1304 reads as follows:

"(1) Unseaworthiness—Neither the carrier nor the ship shall be liable for loss or damage arising or resulting from unseaworthiness unless caused by want of due diligence on the part of the carrier to make the ship seaworthy, and to secure that the ship is properly manned, equipped, and supplied, and to make the holds, refrigerating and cool chambers, and all other parts of the ship in which goods are carried fit and safe for their reception, carriage, and preservation in accordance with the provisions of paragraph (1) of section 1303 of this title. Whenever loss or damage has resulted from unseaworthiness, the burden of proving the exercise of due diligence shall be on the carrier or other persons claiming exemption under this section."

"(2) Uncontrollable causes of loss—Neither the carrier nor the ship shall be responsible for loss or damage arising or resulting from–(a) Act, neglect, or default of the master, mariner, pilot, or the servants of the carrier in the navigation or in the management of the ship; (b) Fire, unless caused by the actual fault or privity of the carrier; (c) Perils, dangers, and accidents of the sea or other navigable waters; (d) Act of God; (e) Act of war; (f) Act of public enemies; (g) Arrest or restraint of princes, rulers, or people, or seizure under legal process; (h) Quarantine restrictions; (i) Act or omission of the shipper or owner of the goods, his agent or representative; (j) Strikes or lockouts or stoppage or restraint of labor from whatever cause, whether partial or general: Provided, That nothing herein contained shall be construed to relieve a carrier from responsibility for the carrier's own acts; (k) Riots and civil commotions; (l) Saving or attempting to save life or property at sea; (m) Wastage in bulk or weight or any other loss or damage arising from inherent defect, quality, or vice of the goods; (n) Insufficiency of packing; (o) Insufficiency or inadequacy of marks; (p) Latent defects not discoverable by due diligence; and (q) Any other cause arising without the actual fault and privity of the carrier and without the fault or neglect of the agents or servants of the carrier, but the burden of proof shall be on the person claiming the benefit of this exception to show that neither the actual fault or privity of the carrier nor the fault or neglect of the agents or servants of the carrier contributed to the loss or damage."

"It is much to be regretted That your goods are slightly wetted But our lack of liability is plain, For our latest Bill of Lading, Which is proof against evading Bears exceptions for sea water, rust and rain. Also sweat, contamination, Fire and all depreciation That we've ever seen or heard of on a ship. And our due examination Which we made at destination Shows your cargo much improved by the trip ... It really is a crime That you're wasting all your time, For our Bill of Lading clauses make it plain That from ullage, rust or seepage, Water, sweat or just plain leakage, Act of God, restraint of princes, theft or war, Loss, damage, or detention, Lock out, strike or circumvention, Blockade, interdict or loss twixt ship and shore, Quarantine or heavy weather, Fog and rain or both together, We're protected from all these and many more, And it's very plain to see That our liability As regards your claim is absolutely nil, So try your underwriter, He's a friendly sort of blighter, And is pretty sure to grin and foot the bill."[6]

The excerpt humorously but accurately focuses on the many exceptions to carrier liability that is found in the Hague Rules and the COGSA. One of the most criticized sections of the COGSA is the navigational fault exception under 46 USC § 1304(2) where neither the carrier nor the ship shall be responsible for loss or damage arising or resulting from "[a]ct, neglect, or default of the master, mariner, pilot, or the servants of the carrier in the navigation or in the management of the ship." Under this section, the Carrier can escape liability by proving the negligence of its employees.

As noted by Justice Stevens, history reveals that Carriers and/or Shipowners issued BOLs exempting themselves from as much liability as possible. He further contends that BOLs are contracts of adhesion, a contention that the majority refutes. Whether or not a bill of lading is a contract of adhesion, the Shipper is often in a take-it-or-leave-it position with the Carrier, and the Carrier has many avenues to statutorily relieve itself from liability. Even after a carrier is found liable there are significant limitations to the actual amount of liability the Carrier may suffer. The following materials focus on the statutory limitation on carrier liability.

2. *Limitation on Carrier Liability and the Fair Opportunity Doctrine*

ROYAL INS. CO. v. SEA–LAND SERVICE INC.
United States Court of Appeals, Ninth Circuit, 1995.
50 F.3d 723.

BOOCHEVER, Circuit Judge:

Royal Insurance Company insured a yacht shipped by Vantare International, Inc., from Taiwan to Oakland, California. The yacht was shipped on a vessel owned by Sea–Land Service, Inc. The stevedore unloading the yacht, Container Stevedoring Company, dropped it on the dock in Oakland. The yacht was a total loss. The district court found that Vantare's recovery was limited to $500 under a loss limitation clause in the on-board bill of lading. Royal and Vantare appeal, and we affirm. * * *

---

6. Daniel A. Tadros, COGSA Section 4(5)'s "fair opportunity" requirement: U.S. CircuitCourt conflict and lack of international uniformity; will the United States supreme court ever provide guidance? 17 TUL. MAR. L.J. 17, 17–33 (1992).

Vantare International, Inc. ("Vantare") is in the business of buying yachts overseas and selling them in the United States. Its owner and president, Michael Guth, has sold 20–25 yachts since Vantare began operation in early 1987, many bought from Chung–Hwa Boat Building Company ("Chung–Hwa") in Taiwan.

In November, 1987, Vantare and other yacht importers entered into a service contract with Sea–Land Service, Inc. ("Sea–Land"), an ocean carrier, and other ocean carriers who had joined together as the "Asian North American Eastbound Rate Agreement" ("ANERA") (the "Service Contract"). Under the Service Contract, Vantare was entitled to a special reduced freight rate when it shipped on an ANERA carrier. The Service Contract also specified that the individual carrier's bill of lading would determine the terms and conditions of shipment. The tariff governing the Service Contract provided that the carrier's liability would be determined by the carrier's bill of lading. A shipper who desired a higher level of coverage had to so stipulate by showing the value of the goods on the carrier's bill of lading, and had to pay an extra 5.3% ad valorem shipping charge as well as a rate higher than that specified under the Service Contract.

In 1988, Vantare ordered a 58–foot yacht from Chung–Hwa for shipment to Oakland. Chung–Hwa completed Sea–Land's shipping order, requesting shipment under the Service Contract. The yacht was purchased through the use of a letter of credit which required, among other things, presentation of an on-board bill of lading. The yacht was delivered for carriage on March 21, 1988.

The next day, March 22, 1988, after the yacht was on board, Sea–Land issued the bill of lading to cover the carriage. Item 23 on the face of the one-page bill of lading contains a blank allowing the shipper to enter a declared value and states: "If shipper enters a value, carrier's 'package' limitation of liability does not apply and the ad valorem rate will be charged." Vantare did not fill in the blank to declare a higher value. On the reverse side of the bill of lading, a "Clause Paramount" states:

This bill of lading shall have effect subject to all the provisions of the Carriage of Goods by Sea Act of the United States of America.... The defenses and limitations of said Act shall apply to goods whether carried on or under deck.... Clause 17 provides:

VALUATION. In the event of loss, damage or delay to or in connection with goods exceeding in actual value the equivalent of $500 lawful money of the United States, per package, ... the value of the goods shall be deemed to be $500 per package or unit, unless the nature and higher value of goods have been declared by the shipper herein and extra charge paid as provided in Carrier's tariff.... The word "package" shall include ... cargo shipped on a ... cradle....

The bill of lading also provided in Clause 2 that if other parties, including stevedores, were found liable in tort, "the limitations of liability provided by law and by the terms of this bill of lading shall be available to such other persons."

Vantare insured the yacht under an open cover policy which automatically provided coverage when Vantare's insurance broker submitted a declaration to Royal Insurance Company ("Royal") indicating the date of shipment and the value of the yacht.

On April 6, 1988, Container Stevedoring Company ("Container Stevedoring") dropped the yacht while unloading it from the vessel. The yacht was a total loss. Royal paid Vantare $395,000 under the insurance policy.

Royal and Vantare (hereinafter referred to as Vantare) filed suit in federal district court for recovery of $600,000 in damages. Sea–Land and Container Stevedoring denied liability, and asserted that if liability were found, the terms of the bill of lading limited recovery to $500. The parties filed motions for partial summary judgment. The district court granted Sea–Land's motion, limiting recovery to $500. Sea–Land and Container Stevedoring then consented to judgment in the amount of $500, and Royal and Vantare appeal. * * *

The Carriage of Goods by Sea Act ("COGSA"), 46 U.S.C. app. §§ 1300–1315, regulates the terms of international ocean carriage covered by bills of lading. Section 4(5) of COGSA provides that a carrier's liability is limited to $500 per package: Neither the carrier nor the ship shall in any event be or become liable for any loss or damage to or in connection with the transportation of goods in an amount exceeding $500 per package ... unless the nature and value of such goods have been declared by the shipper before shipment and inserted in the bill of lading. 46 U.S.C. app. § 1304(5).

"The shipper may increase the carrier's liability, however, by declaring on the bill of lading the nature and value of the goods shipped and paying a higher freight rate." Travelers Indem., 26 F.3d at 898.

Sea–Land can avail itself of COGSA's $500 liability limitation only if Vantare had a "fair opportunity" to escape the limitation by paying a higher charge. Id. (citing cases). The carrier has the initial burden of producing prima facie evidence showing that it provided notice to the shipper that it could pay a higher rate and opt for a higher liability. Id. This initial burden is met if the language of Section 4(5) is printed legibly in the bill of lading, either by recitation or in language to the same effect. Id. It is not enough merely to incorporate COGSA by reference. Id.

In 1989, we decided Institute of London Underwriters v. Sea–Land Serv., Inc., 881 F.2d 761 (9th Cir.1989), a remarkably similar dropped-yacht case in which Sea–Land and Container Stevedoring were also defendants, and involving the same bill of lading used in this case. Although COGSA by its own terms does not apply to on-deck shipments such as the yacht in this case, London Underwriters held that the "Clause Paramount" of the bill of lading incorporating COGSA meant that COGSA's terms governed the shipment. * * * We also found that because Item 23 on the face of the bill gave the shipper the opportunity to declare a higher value for the cargo, and Clause 17 on the reverse recited the $500 limitation and the means to avoid it, the bill of lading constituted prima facie evidence that the shipper had the opportunity to avoid the $500 limitation. Id. at 766. London Underwriters also held that the shipping of a yacht in a "cradle" was included in the bill of lading's definition of "package." Id. at 768.

London Underwriters thus establishes that COGSA applies to the shipment of the yacht, and that Sea–Land made a prima facie showing that its bill of lading gave Vantare an opportunity to avoid the $500 limitation under COGSA.

Once Sea–Land established that its bill of lading was prima facie proof of Vantare's opportunity to opt out of the $500 loss limitation, the burden then shifted to Vantare to prove that it was denied such an opportunity. * * *

[W]hile the $500 per package minimum may be unrealistic in today's economy, the remedy must come from Congress. Until that occurs, an experienced shipper should not be permitted to gamble that no damage will occur, pay the customarily lower freight rates for goods of undeclared value, and then, when destruction in fact occurs, cry "I did not know" and seek an exception to its own obligation under 46 U.S. Code, sec. 1304(5).

* * *

COGSA SECTION 4(5)'S "FAIR OPPORTUNITY" REQUIREMENT: U.S. CIRCUIT COURT CONFLICT AND LACK OF INTERNATIONAL UNIFORMITY; WILL THE UNITED STATES SUPREME COURT EVER PROVIDE GUIDANCE?

Daniel A. Tadros*

17 Tul. Mar. L.J. 17, 17–33 (1992).

* * *

The specific COGSA provision at the center of this confusion is section 4(5), which provides in relevant part:

Neither the carrier nor the ship shall in any event be or become liable for any loss or damage to or in connection with the transportation of goods in an amount exceeding $500 per package lawful money of the United States, or in case of goods not shipped in packages, per customary freight unit, or the equivalent of that sum in other currency, unless the nature and value of such goods have been declared by the shipper before shipment and inserted in the bill of lading.

* Specific credit line: "Mr. Tadros is a partner in the Admirilty and International Law Sections of the New Orleans firm Chaffe, McCall, Phillips, Toler & Sarpy, LLP."

Under a plain reading of this section, if a shipper does nothing to increase the cargo liability value, a carrier's liability is limited to $500 per package.

However, over the past ten years, "the federal courts, led by the [United States Court of Appeals for the] Ninth Circuit, have added a judicial gloss to [section] 4(5): [a] carrier who does not offer the shipper a 'fair opportunity' to declare a higher value may not obtain the benefit of the package limitation." Although section 4(5) makes no reference to a "fair opportunity" requirement, other circuits have accepted the proposition promulgated by the Ninth Circuit. * * *

B. THE "FAIR OPPORTUNITY" REQUIREMENT

The "fair opportunity" requirement originally was developed by the United States Court of Appeals for the Second Circuit in 1953. Application of this requirement became standard practice in subsequent years as the COGSA $500 per package limitation became more and more devalued.

However, the stringency of the requirement has varied among the circuits. The United States Court of Appeals for the Ninth Circuit has developed a strict version of the requirement that carriers give shippers a "fair opportunity" to declare a higher value. Specifically, the Ninth Circuit has held that the bill of lading must explicitly recite the language of COGSA section 4(5), so that a shipper will know how to avoid the statutory limitation. The United States Court of Appeals for the Fifth Circuit, on the other hand, categorically rejected the Ninth Circuit's approach, and instead considers a choice of rates in the tariff to be adequate to give the shipper a "fair opportunity" to declare a higher value. The United States Court of Appeals for the Second Circuit requires more than a tariff provision, although it accepts a "clause paramount" in the bill of lading as evidence of such "fair opportunity." The United States Court of Appeals for the Fourth Circuit has considered the requirement to be satisfied in disputes involving shipments under "short form" bills of lading that incorporate by reference the "long form" bills of lading which recite the language of section 4(5). The United States Court of Appeals for the Sixth Circuit appears to have adopted the Fourth Circuit's position on the issue. * * *

B. APPLICATION OF THE "FAIR OPPORTUNITY" REQUIREMENT IN COGSA CASES

1. *The Ninth Circuit's Strict Approach* * * *

The Ninth Circuit declared * * * "A significant restriction on a carrier's right to limit liability to an amount less than the actual loss sustained is that the carrier must give the shipper 'a "fair opportunity" to choose between higher or lower liability by paying a correspondingly greater or lesser charge. . . .' " This language provided the basis for all of the current law on the subject of COGSA's "fair opportunity" requirement.

In Komatsu, Ltd. v. States Steamship Co., the * * * shipper Komatsu, had contracted with the carrier States Steamship Company, to ship a tractor from Kobe, Japan to Seattle, Washington. Before Komatsu could present the bill of lading to States Steamship Company, the tractor had been damaged while being unloaded in Seattle. As a result, the typical section 4(5) scenario unfolded when Komatsu brought an action against the carrier to recover for the damaged tractor. The court began its analysis by stating that "the burden of proving 'fair opportunity' is initially upon the carrier" and that only "[e]xpress recitation in a bill of lading of the language contained in COGSA [section] 4(5) is prima facie evidence that the carrier gave the shipper that opportunity. . . ." If the carrier satisfies its burden, then the burden shifts to the shipper to prove that the opportunity did not in fact exist. * * *

Collectively, the Ninth Circuit cases, according to one commentator, require that the carrier appropriately notify the shipper of the availability of a choice. "An explicit clause in the bill of lading is one means to giving notice to the shipper that it may avoid the package limitation by declaring a higher value and paying an increased freight charge."

2. The More Lenient Standards of the Other Circuits

Most of the other circuits that have addressed this issue have diverged from the Ninth Circuit's strict approach. The United States Courts of Appeals for the Second, Fourth, Fifth, and Eleventh Circuits all have applied the "fair opportunity" requirement less rigorously than has the Ninth Circuit. However, the interpretations by these courts also have varied.

In its most recent analysis of section 4(5) limitation of liability, the Second Circuit held that language on the back of the bill of lading incorporating COGSA's provisions, together with a space for declaring excess value provided on the front, sufficiently notified the shipper of the limitation of liability and of the means of avoiding it. * * *

The Fourth Circuit * * * held that a short form bill of lading which incorporated COGSA by reference and also incorporated all terms and conditions of the corresponding long form bill of lading, including section 4(5) limitation of liability, provided the shipper with a "fair opportunity" to avoid the $500 per package limitation of liability. * * *

The Fifth Circuit stated its position as follows: "If the bill of lading declares that the carrier's liability is limited to $500 per package 'unless the shipper declares a higher value,' that is evidence that the option to declare a higher value existed." Similarly, if a tariff filed with the Federal Maritime Commission contains a detailed choice of rates that vary with declared value, the tariff also constitutes evidence that the shipper could have declared a higher value and paid an alternative rate. * * *

The *Royal Insurance* case highlights the harsh results obtained on the application of the $500 per package liability limitation. The yacht has a value greatly in excess of the maximum Carrier liability under the COGSA. The $500 limitation, established in the 1920s, is wholly inadequate for today's modern commerce. The Hague–Visby and Hamburg rules have increased the amount but would still be inadequate to deal with the differences in *Royal Insurance*. To ameliorate the harshness of the result, U.S. courts allow the COGSA limitation to apply only when the Shipper has been given a fair opportunity to state a higher value for the goods.

The five hundred dollar limitation is not available to the Carrier unless it gives the Shipper adequate notice of the limitation and an opportunity to declare a higher value and pay a higher freight charge. Fair opportunity is not given when the Bill of Lading merely makes reference to the COGSA limit. Nor is it given when the print on the Bill of Lading is so small that it cannot be seen by the naked eye. The notice should be included in a readable clause paramount on the Bill of Lading to give the Shipper adequate notice and fair opportunity. The burden of proof is on the Carrier to show that it complied.

Litigation has also arisen over what constitutes a 'COGSA Package.' In *Royal*, the COGSA package was the yacht. Case law has developed several principles that can act as a guide in determining what constitutes a "COGSA Package." The intent of the parties controls as evidenced by the Bill of Lading. Absent an intent gleaned from the words used in the Bill of Lading, the package can be determined by the cargo preparation to facilitate handling, except for the stuffing of containers that are part of the vessel. A container into which goods are stuffed is usually not a COGSA package.

In order to be a COGSA package it must be sufficiently wrapped, bundled, or tied. *Mitsui & Co. v. American Export Lines, Inc.*, 636 F.2d 807, 822 (2d Cir.1981). The definition can have a substantial effect. For example, in *Seguros Illimani v. M/V Popi P*, 929 F.2d 89 (2d Cir.1991), Second Circuit, tin ingots were tied together in bundles of 15. Each ingot was valued at $462.00; the bundles of 15 were valued at $6,930. Sixty-seven bundles (1,005 tin ingots) were lost, thus the total loss was $464,310 (1,005 x $462.00). Applying the *Mitsui* definition of a COGSA Package the court found 67 COGSA Packages. The shipper had maintained that each tin ingot was a COGSA Package. The court's ruling resulted in carrier liability of $33,500 (67 x $500) instead of $464,310 (1005 x $462.00).

3.   *The Limits on the Limitation*

The BOL is a critical document in the Documentary Transaction. In order to preserve the efficiency of the transaction in international trade the parties dealing with the BOL must be able to rely on the statements made in it. This has led to an estoppel doctrine making a Carrier liable in the BOL, in certain cases, relating to the description of goods and their date of shipment. The following case discusses this issue.

BERISFORD METALS CORP. v. S/S SALVADOR

United States Court of Appeals, Second Circuit, 1985.
779 F.2d 841.

* * *

MANSFIELD, Circuit Judge:

Berisford Metals Corporation (Berisford), plaintiff in this cargo-loss action, appeals from an order and judgment of the Southern District of New York, Gerard L. Goettel, Judge, granting its motion for summary judgment against the ship S/S Salvador and A/S Ivarans Rederi (Ivarans), its owner and operator, for loss of 70 bundles of tin ingots valued at $483,214.90 but applying the limitation of liability provision of § 4(5) of the Carriage of Goods by Sea Act, 46 U.S.C. § 1304(5) (COGSA), to limit the defendants' liability to $500 per bundle, or a total of $35,000. Defendants cross-appeal from the district court's denial of their motion for dismissal of the action. We reverse the judgment to the extent that it limits defendants' liability to $500 per bundle and remand the case with directions to enter judgment in Berisford's favor for the full value of the lost cargo. We affirm the district court's denial of defendants' motion to dismiss the complaint.

The material facts are not in dispute. On June 23, 1983, Berisford contracted to purchase from Paranapanema International Ltd. (Paranapanema), located in Sao Paolo, Brazil, 50 metric tons of grade A tin ingots in bundles at a price of $13,140 per metric ton (a price later changed by the parties of $13,300 per metric ton). The terms were F.O.B. vessel at Santos, Brazil, for shipment to New York in January 1984.

Payment was to be made net cash 45 days after ocean bill of lading date against presentation of a "full set of shipping documents," which, in conjunction with the F.O.B. vessel term, was understood by the parties as requiring a clean on board bill of lading. Pursuant to the contract Paranapanema delivered 100 bundles, each containing 30 tin ingots and steel-strapped onto wooden pallets, to Ivarans' agent at Santos, Agencia de Vapores Grieg, S.A. (Grieg), which maintains a terminal located about 5 kilometers from the dock where cargo would be loaded onto Ivarans' ship. Grieg acknowledged receipt of the bundles on December 29, 1983. Grieg stuffed the 100 bundles into four 20–foot containers at its terminal, as follows:

Container No. NICU 901692 35 bundles

Container No. NICU 703002 35 bundles

Container No. IVLU 904540 9 bundles

Container No. IVLU 902420 21 bundles

The containerization was carried out "at ship's convenience", to which Berisford did not object. Clause 6 of the bill of lading later issued by Ivarans authorized the carrier to stow goods "as received or, at

Carrier's option, by means of containers or similar articles of transport used to consolidate goods."

After stuffing of each container its doors were closed, locked and sealed. On January 3, 1984, the containers were transported by Grieg to a Brazilian government-controlled storage yard located near the loading dock. Upon delivery of the containers to that yard they appeared, from the sound and handling of the trucks used to transport them, to be loaded, not empty. The government storage yard issued receipts indicating weights approximately equaling those listed on the shipping documents. At that point the seals and locks appeared unchanged.

On January 4, 1984, the containers were removed from the yard and loaded by stevedores aboard the vessel. On the same date Grieg, acting on behalf of Ivarans and the Master of the S/S Salvador, issued a clean on board bill of lading stating that the ship had received "100 bundles steel strapped on wooden skids containing 3000 refined tin ingots, 'Mamore' brand, with a minimum purity of 99.9%". The gross weight was stated on the bill to be "50,647" kilos and the net weight as "49,845" kilos. Par. 3 of the conditions on the back side of the bill of lading provided that the provisions of COGSA would apply throughout "the entire time the goods [would be] in the carrier's custody, including the period of carrier's custody before loading on and after discharge from the ship". The bill further stated that unless a higher value had been declared in writing prior to delivery and inserted in the bill, the $500 limit per package specified by COGSA would govern the carrier's liability.

Upon the loading of the four containers aboard the ship, neither Ivarans nor its agent Grieg verified the contents or made a tally of the 100 bundles represented by the bill of lading to be in the containers. After being loaded aboard the ship, the containers were not shifted from their place of stowage until the ship arrived in New York on January 19, 1984, at the Red Hook Terminal in Brooklyn. There the four containers were discharged on January 20, 1984, and placed on the ground outside Pier 11 to await stripping. On January 24, 1984, Universal Maritime Services, Ivarans' stevedore, opened the four containers by using a bolt cutter or pliers to cut the seals and found that two of them supposed to contain 70 bundles were empty. Before being broken the seals of the containers appeared to be intact, with no evidence of tampering; in fact, the seals were pitted and rusted. Neither the floors of the two containers nor the snow-covered ground around them near Pier 11 revealed any evidence of recent removal of any cargo from the containers. Each bundle would have weighed approximately 1100 lbs.

On January 27, 1984, Berisford wrote U.S. Navigation, Ivarans' New York agent, charging Ivarans with responsibility for the loss of the 70 bundles. On February 7th Mr. K.W. Hansen, a marine surveyor retained by U.S. Navigation to investigate the loss, rendered a written report which stated that in his opinion the "70 missing bundles of tin ingots were never loaded in the two containers."

In the meantime the Mellon Bank in New York, representing Paranapanema, the seller and shipper of the tin ingots, presented to Berisford in accordance with the purchase contract a full set of shipping documents with respect to the 100 bundles of tin ingots purchased by Berisford, including three original on board bills of lading issued by the carrier (Ivarans), Paranapanema's invoice, weight and analysis certificates, and a draft in the amount of $662,938.50, payable 45 days after the bill of lading date. Since the papers were in order and complied with the parties' purchase contract Berisford accepted the draft and on February 17, 1984, paid the full amount of the purchase price to the Mellon Bank as collection agent for Paranapanema. In addition, Berisford paid Ivarans' freight charges amounting to $10,101.67.

On August 31, 1984, Berisford commenced the present action, seeking $525,000 damages for the missing cargo. Defendants' answer admitted receipt of the shipment of bundles of tin ingots but denied liability, asserting its rights under COGSA and its bill of lading with respect to the shipment, including COGSA's $500 per package limitation on its liability, and alleging that it acted without any fault or neglect. On February 5, 1985, after the parties had conducted pre-trial discovery, including the taking of depositions, Berisford moved for summary judgment, contending that it had paid the purchase price in reliance on Ivarans' representation in its on board bill of lading that the 70 missing bundles had been loaded aboard its ship, that it was committed by its purchase contract to pay the purchase price upon the seller's presentation of the shipping documents, and that the defendant carrier's issuance of a clean on board bill of lading when in fact the ship had not received the 70 bundles constituted a "quasi-deviation," depriving the carrier of the benefits of the bill of lading, including its per package limitation on liability. Berisford sought damages in the amount of $483,214.90 plus interest.

Ivarans did not seriously question the probability that the loss of the 70 bundles occurred prior to its loading of the containers aboard its ship in Santos. Indeed, the evidence that the two containers had not been opened after loading and prior to their being found empty upon their arrival in New York (while still in Ivarans' custody) was overwhelming. Ivarans offered no evidence to the contrary. Its principal defenses were (1) that it could not be faulted for any pilferage that may have occurred while the goods were in the custody of the Brazilian government-controlled dockside warehouse in Santos since it had no control over that warehouse or the government's longshoremen, (2) that Berisford's loss was not caused by its misdescription of the contents of the containers because Ivarans was not required, under the purchase contract's provision for payment against a "full set of shipping documents," to issue an on board bill of lading, and (3) that in any event defendants' liability was limited to $500 per bundle. In opposing plaintiff's motion the defendants, in an affidavit of their attorney, Chester D. Hooper, asked that the complaint be dismissed or in the alternative that Ivarans' liability be limited to $500 per bundle.

In an oral bench opinion Judge Goettel concluded that an evidentiary hearing was unnecessary since the existing evidence demonstrated that the loss had occurred while the cargo was in the possession of the Brazilian government's stevedores in Santos. He rejected Ivarans' argument that it was not responsible for a loss occurring while the cargo was in the possession of the Brazilian Government. However, he also rejected Berisford's contention that Ivarans' issuance of a false on board bill of lading constituted a "quasi deviation" negating the availability of the COGSA per package limitation on liability. Instead, he held that a carrier is estopped from denying that the goods were loaded only upon a showing that it knew that they had not been loaded. He accordingly granted plaintiff's motion to the extent of awarding it judgment in the sum of $35,000, from which both parties appeal. * * *

The central question raised by this appeal is whether a carrier that issues a clean on board bill of lading erroneously stating that certain goods have been received on board when they have not been so loaded should be precluded from limiting its liability pursuant to an agreement binding the parties to the terms of § 4(5) of COGSA, 46 U.S.C. § 1304(5). For the purpose of resolving this issue a brief review of pertinent admiralty law principles is helpful. * * *

[A] negotiable or order bill of lading is a fundamental and vital pillar of international trade and commerce, indispensable to the conduct and financing of business involving the sale and transportation of goods between parties located at a distance from one another. It constitutes an acknowledgement by a carrier that it has received the described goods for shipment. It is also a contract of carriage. As a document of title it controls the possession of the goods themselves. * * * It has been said that the bill and the goods become one and the same, with the goods being "locked up in the bill." Id. 96. As the court stated in Pollard v. Reardon, 65 F. 848, 852 (1st Cir.1895), "In the developments of commerce and commercial credits the bill of lading has come to represent the property, but with greater facility of negotiation, transfer, and delivery than the property itself ... And it has become so universal and necessary a factor in mercantile credits that the law should make good what the bill of lading thus holds out. There is every reason found in the law of equitable estoppel and in sound public policy for holding, and no injustice is involved in holding, that, if one of two must suffer, it should be he who voluntarily puts out of his hands an assignable bill of lading, rather than he who innocently advances value thereon."

The necessity for maintaining the integrity of and confidence in bills of lading has been recognized by us in a line of cases beginning before and continuing after the 1936 enactment of COGSA. * * *

The carrier's responsibility for issuance of false bills of lading was thoroughly considered by this court in Olivier Straw Goods Corporation v. Osaka Shosen Kaisha, which was the subject of two appeals over a period of four years, 27 F.2d 129 (2d Cir. 1928) (Olivier I), aff'd after remand, 47 F.2d 878 (2d Cir.), (Olivier II), cert. denied, 283 U.S. 856, 51

S.Ct. 648, 75 L.Ed. 1462 (1931). In that case, which was remarkably similar to the present one, the shipper delivered 18 cases of hemp to the carrier at its Yokohama dock for shipment by steamer to New York. The carrier issued and delivered to the shipper a bill of lading representing that the cases had been loaded on the ship Alaska Maru when in fact they had not been loaded because that ship had been diverted elsewhere due to an earthquake. The cases of hemp, which had been placed by the carrier in an unprotected dockside shed, were lost as a result of looting. Relying on the bill of lading and other shipping papers forwarded to it by the shipper, the purchaser's bank accepted and paid the shipper's invoice. The purchaser then sued the carrier for the value of the hemp. In an opinion by Judge Augustus Hand, concurred in by Judges Learned Hand and Swan, the court held the carrier liable for the full value of the goods described in the bill of lading, stating:

"The bill of lading recited that the goods were shipped in apparent good order and condition. That statement was a warranty that they were so shipped, and the libelant, as indorsee of the bill of lading, acquired the direct obligation of the carrier and with it the right to sue. . . .

"The warranty that the goods were on board was broken by the failure to ship them, and that breach . . . deprived the carrier of the right to invoke the clauses limiting liability. In The Sarnia, 278 F. 459 [1921], where the cargo had been improperly stowed on deck, we held that the valuation clauses in the bill of lading did not serve to limit damages. We said, at page 461 of 278 F.: 'The general rule undoubtedly is that, if the shipowner commits a breach of the contract of affreightment which goes to the essence of the contract, he is not entitled after such breach to invoke the provisions of the contract which are in his favor.' * * *

"Certainly a breach like the one here, which arose from a failure to ship the cargo at all, with its consequent loss or destruction on land, was no less fundamental than a deviation in the voyage, or than stowage of cargo on deck contrary to agreement, or than misdelivery of goods. In all such circumstances valuation clauses in the bill of lading have been held inoperative to relieve the shipowner. * * *

In support of their contention that a carrier may be held liable for a misstatement in its bill of lading only if it acted intentionally or fraudulently, defendants direct our attention to decisions holding that when a carrier issues a bill of lading to the effect that it has received goods in apparent good condition it may not be held liable beyond a per package limitation for damaged goods contained in the bill of lading or COGSA unless it had actual knowledge of the damaged condition at the time of loading or the damage was readily apparent at that time. * * * These "conditions" cases are readily distinguishable from those applying Olivier II. The "conditions" cases raise the issue of the extent to which a carrier must inspect the condition of goods made, sold and bought by others. Since the imposition of a duty to make a detailed inspection of the condition of the contents of every package received from others would be excessive, the carrier may be held liable only if it knew or could readily see that the packages were not in good condition. A carrier is not required to open every package received from a shipper and inspect the contents before issuing a bill to the effect that they appear to be in good condition.

When a carrier, on the other hand, makes a representation in a bill of lading with respect to its own conduct it is properly held to a higher standard since it is reasonably expected to be aware of its own actions, including whether or not it has loaded cargo, * * * "the duty to load, stow, and discharge cargo–and the consequences for failing to do so properly–fall upon the ship and her owners." 46 U.S.C. § 1303(2) specifically provides, "The carrier shall properly and carefully load, handle, stow, carry, keep, care for, and discharge the goods carried."

Applying the foregoing principles to the present case, we conclude that the defendants must be held responsible for the full value of the lost cargo at the time of shipment in Santos and cannot invoke the $500 per package limitation of liability provision of § 4(5) of COGSA, 46 U.S.C. § 1304(5).

The carrier here, having received 100 bundles of tin ingots from the shipper in Santos, issued a false F.O.B. bill of lading with respect to its own conduct, warranting that on January 4, 1984, it had loaded 100 bundles on its ship when in fact it had loaded only 30. The bill of lading, whether or not intentionally false, enabled the shipper to collect from Berisford, the buyer, the full purchase price for 100 bundles. If the carrier had disclosed that 70 bundles had not been loaded, Berisford would have been entitled to refuse payment and the loss would have fallen on the seller of the goods as required by the conditions of the sales contract. The carrier's misrepresentation therefore amounted to a fundamental breach going to the very essence of its contract and precluding it from invoking those provisions extending the limitation of liability terms of § 4(5) of COGSA to the period when the goods were on shore.

Defendants cannot escape responsibility on the ground that the four containers into which it claims that it had placed the bundles after receipt from the shipper were locked and sealed at the time when the containers were loaded aboard its ship, the S.S. Salvador. It is undisputed that the defendant received from the shipper the 100 separate bundles and that for its own convenience it placed them in the four containers. It was thereafter responsible for verifying the contents before loading the containers and issuing a clean on board bill of lading. The weight of the missing 70 bundles of tin ingots was approximately 78,885 lbs. Even if opening of the containers posed difficulties, at the very least the carrier owed a duty to verify the weight of the containers at shipside before they were placed aboard its ship and before it stated that they contained 100 bundles of tin ingots weighing the equivalent of 50,647 kilos or 111,656 lbs., which would have been 78,885 lbs. in excess of the weight of the containers actually loaded. * * *

Our holding leaves intact the principle that, once goods are aboard the ship as represented, a carrier may be responsible for misdescription of the apparent condition of the goods loaded by it only upon proof of knowledge or intent. The Carso, supra. We hold simply that when a carrier misrepresents its own conduct in loading goods aboard ship it is responsible for the misrepresentation and may not invoke contract provisions incorporating COGSA's limitations on liability.

The order and judgment of the district court is reversed and the case is remanded to the district court with directions to enter judgment in favor of Berisford in the sum of its full damages, plus that portion of freight and handling charges attributable to the lost bundles, and costs and interest from January 20, 1984.

In *Berisford Metals*, the Seller delivered the goods to the stevedores, not to the Carrier. It is important to recognize, however, that the Seller indirectly delivered the goods to the Carrier because the Stevedore acted on behalf of the Carrier. The court in this case determined that the missing cargo was never shipped, and refused to allow a 1304(5) exception to the Carrier. By issuing a clean Bill of Lading, the Carrier misrepresented its conduct when it claimed to have loaded the full cargo. Because their conduct resulted in the loss of cargo, the Carrier was held responsible for the loss.

The $500 per package limitation does not apply in a fact pattern similar to what arose in the *Berisford Metals* case. If there are misrepresentations on the part of the Carrier about their own conduct, then the $500 limitation does not apply. Furthermore, the $500 package limitation will not apply when the Carrier does not give a fair opportunity to the shipper to state a higher value for the goods.

SECTION 6.2   THE FEDERAL BILL OF LADING ACT

A.   THE BILL OF LADING AS A DOCUMENT OF RECEIPT

Under the Hague Rules and COGSA, the Carrier must, on demand of the Shipper, issue a Bill of Lading (BOL) after receiving the goods. The BOL must state the number of packages or pieces received, the quantity or weight of the goods, and the apparent order and condition of the goods. The Carrier's duty is to preserve the condition of the goods as received and to deliver them as described in the BOL. Recall in the documentary transaction, the Seller, with the assistance of the Customs Agent, hands the goods over to the Carrier and receives the BOL. It is critical that the documents reflect the true quantity and condition of the goods when received by the Carrier.

In order to provide this assurance, the documentary transaction requires that the Carrier issue a 'clean' BOL. A clean BOL is one that

" ... bears no clause or notation which expressly declares a defective condition of the goods and/or the packaging."[7] If the BOL contains such a notation it is said to be 'foul.' A foul BOL is a non-conforming document and the presenter cannot compel payment when it presents such documents.

A misrepresentation on the BOL can relate to the quantity and/or condition of the goods. Quantity mis-descriptions include cases where a BOL is issued and there are either no goods or are fewer goods than stated. Misrepresentations as to condition relate only to the external appearance of the packages, not the quality of the goods inside the package. The Carrier is not a guarantor of the quality of the goods.

Carrier liability arises when it issues a clean BOL and in fact the quantity or condition of the goods deserves a foul BOL. The critical elements needed in establishing Carrier liability are a misrepresentation in the BOL, reliance on the misrepresentation by the owner or consignee of the goods, and the suffering of actual damages. Carrier liability in the case of delivering misdescribed goods has changed over the years from no liability to one of strict liability.

Early cases found that Carriers were not liable for mis-descriptions when it was found that the Carrier's agents (its employees) exceeded their authority by issuing false BOLs, either intentionally or through negligence. Eventually, the courts began to assess liability to Carriers on the actions of their employees based on agency principles. Courts declared that Carriers were estopped from denying the existence of the goods when they clothed their agents with authority to act on their behalf.

The Federal Bill of Lading Act[8] (also known as the Pomerene Act) provides the rules for Carrier liability in this area. Under the Pomerene Act, Carriers are liable to a holder of a bill of lading who relied on the bill's description and suffered damage on account of the non-receipt or misdescription of the goods. The Pomerene Act, however, includes important exculpatory clauses that allow carriers to escape liability. The following cases discuss this issue.

INDUSTRIA NACIONAL DEL PAPEL, CA. v. M/V ALBERT F

United States Court of Appeals, Eleventh Circuit, 1984.
730 F.2d 622.

* * *

HATCHETT, Circuit Judge:

In this action, we must determine whether a vessel may be held liable in rem for non-delivery of its cargo described in a clean on board

---

7. ICC Uniform Customs and Practices for Documentary Credits, Article 32a., International Chamber of Commerce (1993).

8. 49 USCA §§ 81–124 (1998).

bill of lading. We affirm the district court which held the vessel liable in rem because it was estopped from impeaching the bill of lading.

On January 9, 1979, the appellee, Industria Nacional Del Papel (Induspapel), ordered 1,500 metric tons of soft wood kraft pulp from Sanca Steel Corporation (Sanca), costing $569,790. In February, 1979, the cargo was loaded aboard the appellant vessel, the M/V ALBERT F, in southern Florida, and the vessel sailed for the Dominican Republic. On the same date, Induspapel paid Sanca.

The M/V ALBERT F arrived in Port Haina, Dominican Republic, on February 19, 1979, without the cargo specified in the bill of lading. Instead, it outturned 505 bales of wastepaper. Induspapel received practically worthless cargo, and sued the vessel and its claimant owner, Fairwind Container Express (Fairwind) to recover the amount it paid. Claiming to be acting on behalf of Induspapel, Sanca originally arrested the M/V "ALBERT F." Subsequently, the vessel was released upon Fairwind's posting of $344,500 as security, and Induspapel was substituted for Sanca as the proper plaintiff. The district court ruled for Induspapel holding that the vessel was estopped from impeaching the clean bill of lading, and therefore, was liable in rem for the non-delivery of the cargo specified in the bill of lading. The M/V ALBERT F contends the district court erred in holding that it was estopped from impeaching the bill of lading and in finding it liable in rem. Induspapel cross-appeals claiming that the district court erred in reducing Induspapel's prejudgment interest award and in denying it an increase in the amount of security posted by Fairwind.

A. ESTOPPEL

The Pomerene Act, 49 U.S.C.A. § 81–124 * * * applies to all "[b]ills of lading issued by any common carrier for the transportation of goods ... from a place in a State to a place in a foreign country...." 49 U.S.C.A. § 81. The Pomerene Act fails to define "carrier," but the Carriage of Goods By Sea Act (COGSA), 46 U.S.C.A. § 1300–1315 * * * defines "carrier" as, "the owner or the charterer who enters into a contract of carriage with a shipper." 46 U.S.C.A. § 1301 * * * "Since COGSA was enacted against the backdrop of the Pomerene Act," we will utilize COGSA's definition of "carrier" to determine whether the M/V ALBERT F is a "carrier" within the meaning of the Pomerene Act. * * *

The Fifth Circuit has held that a vessel is a "carrier" as defined in section 1301 of COGSA where (a) the ship transported and discharged cargo; (b) the bill of lading was issued for the master; and (c) no contractual relationship existed absolving the ship and its owner from liability for the cargo. * * * These factual circumstances exist in this case, and the M/V ALBERT F is a "carrier" within the meaning of COGSA and the Pomerene Act. Since the vessel was a common carrier transporting cargo from the United States to a foreign country, the Pomerene Act applies to this case. 49 U.S.C.A. § 81.

Section 22 of the Pomerene Act provides that a carrier issuing a bill of lading will be liable "[to] the holder of an order bill, who has given value in good faith, relying upon the description therein of the goods, ... for damages caused by the nonreceipt by the carrier of all or part of the goods upon or prior to the date therein shown, or their failure to correspond to their description thereof in the bill at the time of its issue." 49 U.S.C.A. § 102 * * * This provision codified the estoppel principal which held "carriers liable to consignees and good faith assignees for value for misrepresentations in their bill of lading." * * *

Title 49 U.S.C.A. § 102 holds the carrier liable for goods receipted for by him but not actually received. * * * The M/V ALBERT F received certain goods and issued a bill of lading describing 854 tons of soft wood kraft pulp, but the goods received did not conform to the goods described in the bill of lading. The vessel, therefore, is liable for the non-delivery of the goods pursuant to 49 U.S.C.A. § 102. * * *

The M/V ALBERT F contends, however, that the exculpatory provision of the Pomerene Act, 49 U.S.C.A. § 101 * * * exempts it from liability. The vessel claims that certain words contained in the bill of lading free them from liability. The bill of lading declares that "particulars [are] furnished by shipper;" the bill also states the shipper, consignee and owner of the goods and the holder of this bill of lading agree to be bound by all the stipulations, exceptions, and conditions stated herein whether written, printed, stamped, or incorporated on the front or reverse side hereof, as fully as if they were all signed by such shipper, consignee, owner, or holder.

These statements are insufficient to escape liability under 49 U.S.C.A. § 101. The words "particulars furnished by shipper" fail to relieve the carrier of liability under COGSA, and therefore, they do not exempt the M/V ALBERT F from liability under the Pomerene Act. * * * Since COGSA and the Pomerene Act protect the holder in due course from misleading bills of lading, statements insufficient to avoid liability under COGSA should not be permitted to avoid liability under the Pomerene Act. Moreover, the words "particulars furnished by shipper" fail to indicate that the shipper loaded the cargo, because COGSA presumes the shipper will furnish the particulars placed in the bill of lading by the carrier. 46 U.S.C.A. § 1303(3) * * *

The preprinted paragraph in the bill of lading also fails to satisfy the standard in 49 U.S.C.A. § 101. The paragraph does not indicate that the shipper loaded the cargo, and therefore, such an attempted disclaimer of liability is ineffective. * * *

* * *

The judgment of the district court is affirmed.

AFFIRMED.

The Pomerene Act's exculpatory clause "shippers load, weight, and count" provides the Carrier the possibility of escaping liability if the statement is true. What the clause essentially does is to shift the burden of proof onto the Shipper as to the correctness of the loading of the goods and the statements to that effect contained on the BOL.

MITSUI & CO. v. M/V EASTERN TREASURE

United States District Court, Eastern District of Louisiana, 1979.
466 F.Supp. 391.

* * *

CASSIBRY, District Judge:

This case involves the shipment of steel plates from Japan to New Orleans and on to Cincinnati. On or about July 27, 1974 Mitsui and Co. (Mitsui) shipped the steel from Japan to New Orleans aboard the M/V EASTERN TREASURE, which was owned by defendant Liberian Dove Transports, Inc. (Liberian Dove) and was under charter to defendant Daiichi Chuo Kisen Kaisha (Daiichi). There is no question that 183 pieces of steel were loaded onto the M/V EASTERN TREASURE in Japan, as indicated by the bill of lading issued by Daiichi to Mitsui. Once in New Orleans, the cargo was transshipped onto Barge MV–6769, which was owned by defendant The Valley Line Company (Valley Line), for shipment upriver. When the cargo reached Cincinnati for unloading, however, there were only 181 pieces of steel. At issue here is who is responsible to Mitsui for the lost 2 pieces.

The "Shipper's weight, load and count" clause

In New Orleans, the consignment of steel plates was discharged directly over the side of the M/V EASTERN TREASURE into Barge MV–6769. Valley Line issued a bill of lading reciting that Barge MV–6769 had received 183 pieces of steel. That bill of lading, however, contained a clause stating that the shipper, not the carrier, had loaded the cargo onto the barge and the quantity of the shipment was unknown to Valley Line.

The bill of lading issued by Valley Line is covered by the Harter Act, 46 U.S.C. § 190 Et seq. That statute provides that the bill of lading shall be "prima facie evidence of the receipt of the merchandise therein described." 46 U.S.C. § 193. Under this provision, then, the burden would shift onto Valley Line to show that its barge did not in fact take on 183 pieces of steel.

Valley Line argues that because of the insertion of that clause in its bill of lading, the burden should not so shift. The clause reads: ... the said shipment has been loaded by the shipper and the contents, quality, quantity, and condition of the shipment and the packages, if any, are unknown.

Valley Line claims that this clause is a "Shipper's weight, load, and count" clause, allowed under the Pomerene Act, 49 U.S.C. § 81 Et seq. Valley Line's bill of lading was issued for the transportation of goods between two states, and was therefore covered by that Act. 49 U.S.C. § 81. Section 101 of the Pomerene Act allows carriers to insert in bills of lading the words "Shipper's weight, load, and count" or words of similar purport indicating that the goods were loaded by the shipper, not the carrier. If this statement is true, the bill of lading is Not prima facie evidence of receipt by the carrier of the goods described in the bill of lading. Rather, the shipper must produce other evidence to this effect. Under § 101, . . . a bill of lading containing the recital "shipper's load and count" places the burden of proof of proper and correct loading upon the shipper, and such bill of lading without additional evidence does not fulfill this burden. * * * The clause in Valley Line's bill of lading does fall under § 101 of the Pomerene Act, since its meaning is the same as if it had simply recited "Shipper's weight, load, and count."

Only if the recitation is true will the clause have the evidentiary effect outlined above. There is some question in the instant case as to whether the steel was in fact loaded onto Barge MV–6769 by the "shipper," as that term is used in § 101 and the clause in Valley Line's bill of lading. Mitsui was the party that sent the steel to the United States, thus it would conventionally be called the "shipper" in this transaction. Daiichi contends that Mitsui should be considered the "shipper" for purposes of § 101 and the bill of lading. It points out that T. Smith and Son, Inc. (T. Smith), the stevedore, did the actual loading of the steel onto the Valley Line barge in New Orleans. Thus, argues Daiichi, the steel was never loaded onto the barge by the "shipper" within the meaning of § 101 and the recitation in Valley Line's bill of lading. Daiichi cites Carrier Corp. v. Furness, Withy & Co., 131 F.Supp. 19 (E.D.Pa.1955) in support of its position. That case held that because the stevedore that loaded a barge was not the actual agent of the conventional shipper, the barge was not loaded by the "shipper" for purposes of the Pomerene Act. It seems that the statute does not deserve so technical a reading. It intends to distinguish two fundamentally different situations that where the carrier itself actually does (or hires someone to do) the loading; and that where someone other than the carrier, authorized and paid by the shipping interests, does the loading. The former situation is loading "by a carrier" within the coverage of § 100 of the statute; the latter is loading "by a shipper" under § 101. Under my reading of the Pomerene Act, then, the steel in the instant case was surely loaded by the "shipper."

In the instant case, moreover, T. Smith qualifies as the agent of the conventional shipper, Mitsui, and so even the Carrier Corp., standard is satisfied. In Carrier Corp., the court found that neither the stevedore nor the ship's agent ever had any communication with the shipper or the shipper's agent. Here, Mitsui's agent, M. G. Maher & Co., issued a Delivery/Release Order directing that the steel be transferred by the ship to Valley Line's barge. Once Valley Line received this document, it began to prepare to receive the steel. It stayed in touch with the ship's agent, Fritz Maritime, and as the date for transshipment approached, Valley Line stayed in touch with the stevedore, T. Smith. With regard to the transshipment, there was obviously a chain extending from Mitsui and its agent, to the ship and its agent, and to the stevedore. As Mr. Hote, Fritz Maritime's manager, testified, the cost of retaining the stevedore is built into the ship's contract with the shipper.

Accordingly, for purposes of § 101 of the Pomerene Act, the steel was loaded onto Barge MV–6769 by the "shipper." The clause in Valley Line's bill of lading is thus true insofar as it makes this assertion and states that the quantity of the shipment therefore was unknown to the carrier.

Valley Line argues that since the clause's statement is true, the bill of lading should not be prima facie evidence of Valley Line's receipt of 183 pieces of steel. Daiichi and Liberian Dove argue that the Pomerene Act should not be allowed thus to contradict the Harter Act.

There are no cases squarely on point. The few cases that relate to the problem support the position of Daiichi and Liberian Dove. Mississippi Valley Barge Line Co. v. Inland Waterways Shippers Association, 289 F.2d 374 (8th Cir.1961) concerned the carrier's liability for damage due to faulty loading of a barge by a shipper. The bill of lading contained several exculpatory clauses, and contained a "Shipper's weight, load, and count" provision. The court held that the carrier could not relieve itself of its legal duty to handle and stow the cargo carefully, all these clauses notwithstanding. The issue before the court in the instant case is much narrower, for it concerns merely how the "Shipper's weight, load, and count" clause affects the burden of proof on the factual issue of how much cargo the carrier took on board. That issue was before the court in George F. Pettinos v. American Export Lines, 68 F.Supp. 759 (E.D.Pa. 1946), aff'd 159 F.2d 247 (3d Cir.1947). The case involved the Carriage of Goods by Sea Act (COGSA), which covers shipping between this country and foreign ports. The court held that under COGSA a carrier "may not avoid the prima facies of the bill (of lading) merely by entering weight and quantity as 'Particulars Declared by Shipper.' "68 F.Supp. at 764. However the court never mentioned the Pomerene Act and the possible legitimizing influence it might have on the carrier's "Shipper's weight, load, and count" clause.

COGSA, however, specifically retains the provisions of the Pomerene Act insofar as they affect the legal significance of ocean bills of lading. Section 1303(4) of COGSA provides: . . . a bill of lading shall be prima facie evidence of the receipt by the carrier of the goods as therein described . . . Provided, That nothing in this chapter shall be construed as repealing or limiting the application of any part of sections 81 to 124 of Title 49 (the Pomerene Act).

The effect of § 101 of Title 49 with respect to "Shipper's weight, load, and count" clauses has been discussed above. Thus, COGSA specifically allows an ocean carrier to defeat the prima facie effect of its bill of lading by inserting such a clause into the bill. It seems most incongruous for an inland maritime carrier covered by the Harter Act not to be able to provide itself the same protection. The two carriers would then be under different evidentiary burdens with regard to goods which they receive under substantially the same circumstances.

Congress' actions in this area have deliberately avoided that result. In the Harter Act, Congress explicitly allowed a carrier to indicate in its bill of lading that the shipper weighed the cargo, although that phrase had no effect on the prima facie effect of the bill. 46 U.S.C. § 193. The Pomerene Act was passed after the Harter Act. It declared in § 101 that "Shipper's weight, load, and count" clauses were, indeed, to have special exculpatory effect. Congress knew that the Harter Act explicitly allowed such clauses. If it had meant to except such clauses in Harter Act bills of lading from the operation of § 101, it would have carved out an exception to that section. It did not do so, thus § 101 will extend to Harter Act bills of lading. Indeed, in passing COGSA Congress demonstrated its awareness of the necessity of specific exceptions in subsequent statutes. Section 1303(4) of COGSA establishes the broad prima facie effect of COGSA bills of lading. Congress took specific care to retain the Pomerene Act insofar as it affects this aspect of COGSA bills of lading. It thus recognized that if it had not done so, the terms of the subsequent statute would have controlled. Accordingly, Congress has consistently acted to allow § 101 of the Pomerene Act to modify the legal effect that bills of lading would otherwise have under the Harter Act and COGSA.

Valley Line's bill of lading thus is not prima facie evidence that the barge accepted 183 pieces of steel. However, at the trial Daiichi and Liberian Dove produced other evidence to this effect, namely, the testimony of the checker who recorded the transshipment of steel between the M/V EASTERN TREASURE and Barge MV–6769. Robert Cross actually counted 183 pieces of steel being transferred from the ship to the barge. He made a credible witness. He noted that the thickness of the steel plates at issue here made them particularly easy to count. He noted also that the difference in length between the consignment of steel at issue here and the next consignment made it clear where one cargo ended and another began.

Valley Line attempted to show that the plates could not have left the barge at any time before the plates were unloaded and counted short in Cincinnati, thus Robert Cross' testimony should not be accepted. However, Valley Line could only produce direct evidence to the effect that the barge remained unopened until the fleet of which it became a part began to be towed upriver. It did establish that heavy equipment would be needed to open the barge, but it did not adequately negate the possibility that such equipment was employed somewhere along the Mississippi River after the M/V W. J. BARTA began to tow the fleet upriver and before the fleet reached Cincinnati.

The only evidence concerning that part of Barge MV–6769's journey was the logs of the two tugboats that brought the barge upriver. These logs, however, cannot stand as a definitive statement of everything that happened on the voyage upriver. They do not let me reconstruct the voyage sufficiently to conclude that there was no opportunity for the steel plates to have been lost from the Barge MV–6769. Indeed, the logs indicate that the fleet was stopped occasionally. Once Barge MV–6769 was exchanged between the M/V W. J. BARTA and the M/V VALLEY VOYAGER. Even more important, there is a very real possibility, not at all negated by any other evidence, that there were stops or incidents not reported in these logs. The nature and comprehensiveness of the information that is supposed to be recorded in these logs has not been explained to me. Moreover, I have no basis upon which to evaluate the credibility of the persons who made these reports.

In light of the strong, direct testimony of Robert Cross that all 183 pieces of steel were put in Barge MV–6769, I find that the preponderance of the evidence establishes that the loss here occurred while the steel was in the custody of Valley Line. * * *

This question of proof is obviously a close one. However, I could under no circumstance find that the evidence preponderates in favor of Valley Line. If I did not find it more likely than not that the loss of the steel plates occurred while the shipment was in the custody of Valley Line, I would be forced to declare the evidence inconclusive on this question. This being so, liability would still fall on Valley Line, for the principle that "where goods pass through the hands of successive custodians, in apparent good order, any loss is presumed to have occurred while they were under the control of the last custodian" would come into play. * * *

Daiichi and Liberian Dove urge an alternative basis upon which Valley Line should bear liability for the loss in the instant case. The statute controlling the ocean carriage by Daiichi from Japan to New Orleans is COGSA. Section 1303(6) of that statute provides:

Unless notice of loss or damage and the general nature of such loss or damage be given in writing to the carrier or his agent at the port of discharge before or at the time of the removal of the goods into the custody of the person entitled to delivery thereof under the contract of carriage, such removal shall be prima facie evidence of the delivery by the carrier of the goods as described in the bill of lading. If the loss or damage is not apparent, the notice must be given within three days of the delivery.

The port of discharge of the steel from the ocean carrier was New Orleans. Valley Line was the party entitled to delivery thereof at that stage. Valley Line had been designated, in the Delivery/Release Order of Mitsui's agent, as the party to whom Daiichi should release the steel. Valley Line, however, did not give the ocean carrier, Daiichi, the notice required by s 1303(6). The Requests for Admissions propounded by Liberian Dove, and the lack of proper answer or objection thereto, establish these facts. F.R.Civ.P. 36(a). Section 1303(6) therefore dictates that, between these two parties, removal of the steel by Valley Line is prima facie evidence of delivery by Daiichi of 183 pieces of steel. * * * Valley Line's evidence, according to the analysis above, is insufficient to rebut such a prima facie case.

The "Shipper's weight, load, and count" clause does not destroy the prima facie case created under this provision of COGSA. It is § 1303(4) of COGSA that retains the Pomerene Act. The provision of COGSA establishing a prima facie case due to lack of notice of loss or damage is a separate subsection, § 1303(6).

For the foregoing reasons, there should be judgment in favor of plaintiff Mitsui against defendant Valley Line. The stipulated amount of damages is $2,960.60.

The judgment of the district court is affirmed.

AFFIRMED.

The exculpatory language in the Pomerene Act states that if the BOL includes the phrase "shippers load, weight and count," or words of like import, then the Carrier is relieved of liability. The Carrier is responsible for its own conduct and may not rely on exculpatory language when they are at fault. On the other hand, if the misrepresentation is not of the Carrier's conduct, then the limitation would apply under the COGSA. In that case, the Shipper's conduct is in question. This rule is an attempt to relieve the Carrier because the Carrier should not be required to inspect all the goods that are brought on board.

There are limitations to this exculpatory language. Assume that the BOL says "shipper's load, weight and count," but in fact the Carrier loaded, weighed and counted the goods. In that example the exculpatory language will not be relied on because it is not true. In *Mitsui*, although the Shipper was in Japan and the goods were loaded in New Orleans, the clause was valid because the stevedore acted for the Shipper. If the stevedore had been the Carrier's agent, the clause would not have been true and would not be upheld.

The burden of proof rests with the Shipper to prove that, despite the exculpatory language, the Carrier is liable. The mere usage of the term "shippers load, weight and count," does not satisfy the burden that the Shipper actually did load the described goods. This burden can be rebutted with sufficient evidence as in the preceding case where the two pieces of steel were in fact lost when the Carrier had control of them.

A BOL is considered foul if it states that the goods are in apparently good condition but it directs you to an accompanying statement or documents that contain statements that would make the bill foul. However, Article 17 of the Uniform Customs and Practices states that the "shipper's load, weight and count" does not create a foul BOL. The clause is acceptable language to remove the strict liability from the Carrier while maintaining a clean BOL. It would be anomalous to say on the one hand that you can use exculpatory language to limit liability, but if you use it you are not conforming to the documents.

B. THE BILL OF LADING AS A DOCUMENT OF TITLE

A Carrier is obligated to deliver the goods to their owner and is strictly liable for mis-delivery. The type of BOL determines to whom the goods should be delivered. There are two types of BOLs—straight/non-negotiable BOL or an order/negotiable BOL. In a straight/non-negotiable BOL, the Carrier is obligated to deliver the goods to the person named in the BOL (usually the Buyer). The owner of the goods is the person named in the bill.

In an order/negotiable BOL, the Carrier is obligated to deliver the goods to the person in possession of the properly endorsed BOL. The owner of the goods is the holder of the properly endorsed BOL. The straight/non-negotiable BOL should never be used in a Documentary Transaction. Consider the following scenario—Seller delivers the goods to the Carrier and receives a straight/non-negotiable BOL naming Buyer as the owner. Assume that the Issuing Bank pays against the presented documents.

The Carrier is still obligated to deliver the goods to the Buyer even if the Issuing Bank has paid money and is in possession of the documents, and even if Buyer refuses to pay the Issuing Bank. In order for the documentary transaction to function properly, owning the documents must represent owning the goods as well. It is imperative, therefore, that an order/negotiable BOL be used. By using an order/negotiable BOL, the Carrier is obligated to deliver the goods to the person in possession of the properly endorsed BOL. In our case, the Issuing Bank is the holder of the properly endorsed BOL and would be therefore, the owner of the goods.

The Carrier will be strictly liable for delivering the goods to someone either not named in the straight BOL or to someone who is not the holder of a properly endorsed order BOL. The delivery in the case of a straight BOL is fairly straightforward—deliver the goods to the person named in the BOL. Problem areas arise with the order BOL in determining when the order BOL is properly endorsed.

ADEL PRECISION PRODUCTS CORP. v. GRAND TRUNK WESTERN R. CO.

Supreme Court of Michigan, 1952.
332 Mich. 519, 51 N.W.2d 922.

REID, Justice:

Plaintiff brought suit to recover for value of a shipment consisting of a carload of farm machinery shipped upon an order bill of lading, claimed to have been misdelivered by defendant railroad to Hickman Farm Supplies, Inc. (hereinafter called Hickman) at Lansing, Michigan. Defendant claims a justified delivery, but claims that if it is found that the delivery was not justified, that plaintiff ratified the delivery. The jury rendered a verdict for plaintiff for the value of the shipment. Plaintiff had judgment on the verdict. Defendant appeals. No error is assigned on instructions to the jury and the instructions are not in the record. Defendant, relies, for reversal, upon claimed errors in denial of its motion for a directed verdict made at the conclusion of plaintiff's proofs, also on denial of the same motion renewed at the conclusion of all the proofs, and denial of the later motion for a judgment notwithstanding the verdict.

Plaintiff in July, 1948, sold a carload of farm machinery to Hickman, which machinery was for the most part manufactured by Newkirk Manufacturing Company (hereinafter called Newkirk) at Anaheim, California. The manner of the shipment was directed on the part of plaintiff from plaintiff's home office at Burbank, California. The shipment was by plaintiffs' direction made by Newkirk from Anaheim, California, direct to order of plaintiff in Lansing, Michigan.

The question involved are stated by defendant in its brief as follows:

1.   Was the defendant justified as a matter of law under the Federal bill of lading act in delivering the merchandise to Hickman upon the surrendering [by Hickman] to the defendant of possession of the bill of lading? If this court should affirm the lower court's answer [no] to question 1, then,

2.   Under the undisputed evidence in this case, did the plaintiff ratify the delivery of said shipment to Hickman? Walter Noon, a witness for plaintiff, testified that he was employed by Newkirk in July, 1948 as engineer and draftsman; that the shipping clerk, Mr. McMasters, was ill, and that he, Noon, was performing McMasters' duties, and that he had instructions from plaintiff about making up the shipment in question, which instructions were that he, Noon, was to make out a sight draft order bill of lading with one original and three copies; that he was to mail the original and one copy to plaintiff at Burbank, California; that one copy was to be retained by the railroad, and one copy was to be retained by Newkirk, Noon's employer.

Noon testified that he prepared exhibit No. 7, entitled 'uniform order bill of lading' with three copies thereof, that he took the original, exhibit No. 7, and all three copies to the railroad clerk for the Southern Pacific, the common carrier originally receiving the shipment, for his signature. Noon further testified that by mistake he mailed the original, exhibit No. 7, to Hickman, that at that time there was no endorsement on exhibit No. 7 and particularly that the endorsement appearing on the original, exhibit No. 7, at the time of the trial, 'Adel Prec. Prod. Corp.' in typewriting, was not on the exhibit when he mailed it to Hickman. Noon further testified that among other things, 'consigned to order of Adel Prec. Prod. Corp.' was on exhibit No. 7 when he, Noon, mailed it to Hickman. There is no contradiction of Noon's testimony.

There was no testimony that the endorsement, 'Adel Prec. Prod. Corp.' in typewriting was on the original when the original was received by Hickman. The original bill of lading contained the following, 'Notify

Hickman Farm Supplies Inc. corner Grand River & DeWitt Rd. at Lansing, State of Michigan.'

Alton Graeff, general manager of Hickman, testified that he signed 'Hickman Farm Supp. Inc.,' and his own name underneath that of his company under the typewritten 'Adel Prec. Prod. Corp.' endorsement, before exhibit No. 7 was delivered to defendant.

The answer of defendant admits the delivery of the goods to Hickman.

Francis B. Courtney, handwriting expert and expert on typewritings, testified that the disputed typewritten endorsement in question was made by a Royal typewriter machine, and in that particular is different from the other typewritten matter contained in exhibit No. 7, and also different from specimens of typewritings exhibited to the witness from typewriting machines in the office of Hickman and of the defendant.

Witness Noon testified that there was no Royal typewriting machine in the office of Newkirk in July and August, 1948. It does not clearly appear whether there was any Royal machine in the office of Hickman.

Efforts were made by plaintiff by correspondence to get payment from Hickman for the shipment, but Hickman refused to make payment, unless plaintiff would take off Hickman's hands, certain machinery purchased by Hickman from plaintiff, found unsaleable in Michigan. Plaintiff refused to take back the unsaleable goods, and brought the instant suit against defendant, and did not sue Hickman.

Under its claim that the delivery was justified, defendant cites the provisions of § 8 of the Federal Bill of Lading Act, Title 49 U.S.C.A. § 88, as follows: 'A carrier, in the absence of some lawful excuse, is bound to deliver goods upon a demand made either by the consignee named in the bill for the goods or, if the bill is an order bill, by the holder thereof, if such a demand is accompanied by ___ '(a) An offer in good faith to satisfy the carrier's lawful lien upon the goods; '(b) Possession of the bill of lading and an offer in good faith to surrender, properly indorsed, the bill which was issued for the goods, if the bill is an order bill; and '(c) A readiness and willingness to sign, when the goods are delivered, an acknowledgment that they have been delivered, if such signature is requested by the carrier.'

Also, § 9 of the act, Title 49 U.S.C.A. § 89: 'A carrier is justified, subject to the provisions of sections 90–92 of this title, in delivering goods to one who is ___ '(a) A person lawfully entitled to the possession of the goods, or '(b) The consignee named in a straight bill for the goods, or '(c) A person in possession of an order bill for the goods, by the terms of which the goods are deliverable to his order; or which has been indorsed to him, or in blank by the consignee, or by the mediate or immediate indorsee of the consignee.'

Under the order bill of lading in the instant case, exhibit No. 7, the goods were consigned to the order of plaintiff at Lansing.

There was no proper endorsement on the order bill of lading, according to undisputed testimony, because the typewritten endorsement is clearly shown to have been unauthorized.

Defendant cites Pere Marquette R. Co. v. J. F. French & Company, 254 U.S. 538, at page 545, 41 S.Ct. 195, at page 199, 65 L.Ed. 391, and particularly seems to rely upon the words, 'The real cause of the loss was the wrongful surrender of the bill of lading by the Indianapolis bank to Marshall & Kelsey by means of which the car was taken to Camp Taylor and the shipper deprived of the Louisville market', but defendant overlooks the following words, 'Concluding, therefore, that there was a delivery, that it was made to a person in possession of the bill of lading properly indorsed and that it was made in good faith, the important question remains: Does such a delivery exonerate the carrier upon suit by the shipper when it failed to require surrender of the bill of lading as provided in that instrument?' [254 U.S. at page 545, 41 S.Ct. at page 198]

The Pere Marquette case, supra, is to be differentiated from the instant case because of the dissimilarity of the facts in the Pere Marquette case from the facts in the instant case. In the Pere Marquette case, the bill of lading was properly endorsed, while in the instant case, the bill of lading under the finding by the jury, was not properly endorsed, and the ground on which the court in the Pere Marquette case exonerated the common carrier, was different from the ground which the defendant in the instant case claims as a basis for exoneration.

Exhibit No. 7 is on a blank form, 'uniform order bill of lading,' and contains the statement, 'The surrender of this original order bill of lading properly indorsed shall be required before the delivery of the property.'

The opinion of the trial court upon the motion of defendant for judgment notwithstanding the verdict indicates that there had been submitted to the jury (among other things) the questions of whether there was misdelivery and the question whether the original bill of lading was properly endorsed, both of which questions were evidently resolved by the jury in favor of the plaintiff, as to which questions we find there was a sufficient foundation in the testimony for the verdict. We overrule defendant's contention that in those last recited particulars there was reversible error as a matter of law.

The Federal Bill of Lading Act did not authorize defendant, under the circumstances of this case, to deliver to Hickman the goods in question.

Defendant claims and plaintiff denies that plaintiff ratified the delivery after it was made. Defendant cites an Iowa case of Midland Linseed Co. v. American Liquid Fireproofing Co. et al., 183 Iowa 1046, 166 N.W. 573, in which a railroad company as a common carrier is joined as a defendant. Plaintiff in the Iowa case claimed a misdelivery of goods by the railroad company; in that case the plaintiff had sued the wrongful recipient of the goods. The Iowa supreme court said, 166 N.W. at 574,

575, 'The bill was surrendered to the carrier, although it was done after it had delivered the oil. * * * after the plaintiff discovered that the oil had already been delivered, it retained this partial payment [from the buyer, the wrongful recipient]. It demanded payment of the balance of the purchase price from the buyer, and finally it sued it for that purchase price. Why does not this constitute a ratification in favor of the carrier, or, for that matter, * * * [against] the bank? The suit against both carrier and bank is confessedly for conversion, which implies a claim that no title passed to the buyer. A demand for the purchase price implies there was a purchase, and therefore that the buyer obtained title. * * * We hold the carrier cannot be made liable for conversion of the goods, consisting of giving them to some one who was not entitled to them, where the plaintiff declares that the buyer owes him the purchase price. * * * If the delivery was unauthorized, demand of the purchase price ratifies the unauthorized act.'

In a footnote in 15 A.L.R.2d 813, 814, comment is made on the Iowa case as follows: 'In Midland Linseed Co. v. American Liquid Fireproofing Co., 1918, 183 Iowa 1046, 166 N.W. 573, the general principle was stated that 'if the delivery was unauthorized, demand of the purchase price ratifies the unauthorized act.' However, this broad principle is not supported by the facts of the case. It appears from the facts that the shipper accepted part payment of the price of the goods prior to the wrongful delivery, that he retained this partial payment after he had discovered the wrongful delivery, and demanded, and sued for, payment of the balance of the purchase price.'

The facts in the Midland Linseed Co. case (the Iowa case) are materially dissimilar to the facts in the instant case and an important statement of law in that case is contrary to the weight of authority as stated in 15 A.L.R.2d 813, § 7, which recites, 'It appears from the cases collected herein that a mere attempt by one who has sustained a loss on account of wrongful delivery to collect from the recipient of the goods their price or value is not, as a matter of law, ratification of the delivery.'

We conclude that so far as it goes, this statement in A.L.R. is a fair statement of the weight of authority.

The offer of plaintiff to Hickman to treat the matter of the misdelivered goods as an open account with Hickman, was by the latter entirely rejected, and plaintiff thereupon proceeded to the present suit as we have heretofore seen.

It was proper for the trial court to submit to the jury the question of whether plaintiff has ratified the misdelivery. The jury's determination in favor of plaintiff's claim that it was not plaintiff's intention to ratify the misdelivery, is fairly supported by the testimony, and the trial court was not in error in submitting that question to the jury and accepting its verdict thereon. The submission of that question of the jury is indicated in the court's opinion heretofore referred to.

It is the further claim of defendant that in making the shipment, Newkirk was plaintiff's agent, and that plaintiff should have promptly notified defendant of the mistake of Newkirk's clerk in forwarding the order bill of lading to the buyer, Hickman. On this point, witness Noon testified as follows: 'I later discovered the error, approximately that same afternoon.

'Q. What did you do, if anything, or what was done, if anything, if you know? A. Well, I notified Mr. Newkirk immediately of the error.

'Q. Who is Mr. Newkirk? Is he connected with your company? A. He is the president of the company.

'Q. And do you know whether he took any action or not? A. Yes, sir. He called the railroad. I know that.'

This testimony does not support the proposition that notice was given [to] the original carrier. The witness fails to relate what was said to 'the railroad.'

However, Willard Allen, credit manager of plaintiff, testified as follows: 'Knowing that the bill of lading could not be used without an endorsement on it, I assumed that the bill of lading would come back from our customer for endorsement, so I just let the situation ride along. I didn't do anything to find out who the delivering carrier would be so I could wire that carrier not to deliver it. I didn't immediately notify Hickman Company that an error had been made in sending the bill of lading direct to them. I made no special investigation to see if there had been any arrangements made for an open account at that time with the Hickman Company. I just trusted to the fact that the bill of lading would come back to me and then I would take care of the situation.'

Would a prudent business man in witness Allen's position be obliged to assume that there was any likelihood, or anything but a very remote danger, that the order bill of lading sent unendorsed through error to Hickman, a reputable going concern, would be presented by Hickman to defendant with a forged endorsement?

Whether plaintiff was negligent in not taking steps to prevent defendant being defrauded by a forgery of plaintiff's name as an endorsement on the bill of lading, could be considered as a question for the jury; and the jury seems (as we infer from statements in the opinion of the trial judge on denying the motion for judgment notwithstanding the verdict) to have passed on the question of plaintiff's negligence and decided it in favor of plaintiff. We cannot say that such decision finds no sufficient support in the testimony.

'Delivery of carload of grapes by carrier to consignee without shipper's indorsement upon bill of lading, in direct violation of its terms, amounted to conversion, and rendered carrier liable for value of grapes.' Keystone Grape Co. v. Hustis (receiver of Boston & Maine R. Co.), 232 Mass. 162, 122 N.E. 269, syl. 1.

Judgment for plaintiff affirmed Costs to plaintiff.

* * *

In a forged endorsement, the signature is not authentic, as in the Adel case. When a signature is forged there are goods being transported but are delivered to the wrong person. When the BOL is forged there are no goods. The false BOL purports to cover goods that do not exist. If the entire BOL is forged, the Carrier is not liable if it can show that it was not negligent. An innocent Carrier cannot be compelled to deliver goods that do not exist.

Chapter 7

TRADE REGULATION

SECTION 7.1 COUNTRY CATEGORIZATION & PRODUCT CLASSIFICATION

A. INTRODUCTION

1. *Governmental Policy and Trade Regulation*

The Sales Contract establishes the rights and obligations of the respective parties. Apart from the financing and delivery of the goods attention must be given to the governmental involvement as goods move from one country to another. Recall the Delta hypothetical–Delta's Division I manufactures and sells "Blow Out Preventers" (BOP). The BOP is a high technology safety device essential in offshore drilling activities. Delta has buyers in Mexico and the Peoples Republic of China. It must assess the regulatory environment prior to engaging in the sale.

The country from where the goods are emanating (the exporting country) regulates the exporter and the products being exported. The BOP sale will require an U.S. export license—like all products being exported from the U.S. This can be a cumbersome process depending on the product involved and its ultimate destination. For example, the rules for exporting to Mexico—a NAFTA country—are different than exports into the Peoples Republic of China.

The country of destination (the importing country) imposes rules on the importer and the incoming product. The principal import restriction mechanism is the trade barrier. Trade barriers are imposed for a variety of reasons. Some are protectionist—to protect domestic products or industries, and some are used as a deterrent for unfair trade practices taking place abroad that impact products being imported.

The community of nations has been very active in eliminating trade barriers that can impede the sale of goods across international borders. Multilateral trade agreements like the General Agreement on Tariff and Trade and regional agreements like the North American Free Trade Agreement have targeted the elimination of tariff and non-tariff barriers.

443

The success achieved has been quite remarkable. Indeed, the globalization of markets has provoked interest in formerly non-market economies to join in agreements reducing trade barriers.

In spite of the new regulatory environment it is useful to examine the parties that have a stake in trade regulation and how these differences are played out. On the export side you have the government of the exporting country. Governmental export policy is formulated to advance the interests of the particular government. U.S. export policy is a good illustration[1]

" . . . The Congress makes the following declarations: (1) It is the policy of the United States to minimize uncertainties in export control policy and to encourage trade with all countries with which the United States has diplomatic or trading relations, except those countries with which such trade has been determined by the President to be against the national interest. (2) It is the policy of the United States to use export controls only after full consideration of the impact on the economy of the United States and only to the extent necessary-(A) to restrict the export of goods and technology which would make a significant contribution to the military potential of any other country or combination of countries which would prove detrimental to the national security of the United States; (B) to restrict the export of goods and technology where necessary to further significantly the foreign policy of the United States or to fulfill its declared international obligations; and (C) to restrict the export of goods where necessary to protect the domestic economy from the excessive drain of scarce materials and to reduce the serious inflationary impact of foreign demand.

(3) It is the Policy of the United States (A) to apply any necessary controls to the maximum extent possible in cooperation with all nations, and (B) to encourage observance of a uniform export control policy by all nations with which the United States has defense treaty commitments or common strategic objectives."

The U.S., to further the national goals mentioned in the above excerpt, uses export controls. The exporter—either the Buyer or Seller (depending on the Sales Contract)—has the burden of obtaining an export license that is issued pursuant to the guidelines mentioned above. Penalties for noncompliance range from civil penalties, a revocation of the right to export products (a type of death penalty for the company) and imprisonment.

On the import side, governments generally attempt to balance the interests of the parties while furthering its own import regulation policy. The importing country has the right to regulate transactions taking place within its borders. It regulates imports for a variety of reasons—to

1. See 50 USC App. § 2402.

protect domestic industries from foreign competition, protect its citizens from unsafe foreign products, to further its economic, social, and political goals.

U.S. trade policy takes a carrot and stick approach. The carrot is the possible entry into the huge U.S. domestic market. The stick—mandating that countries behave in a certain way—is embodied either in international agreements or federal statutory law. For example, the Andean Trade Practice Act, discussed below, allows certain products from the countries that are parties to the agreement to enter into the U.S. customs region free of tariff. To qualify the country must be a 'beneficiary country.' To qualify as a beneficiary country it must meet certain economic, social, and political guidelines set by the United States. Failing to qualify as a beneficiary country will remove the tax-free status of their products.

U.S. policy is also aimed at eliminating unfair trade practices taking place abroad. As discussed in Section 4.2 supra, products from countries that are havens for the piracy and counterfeiting of U.S. IPR's may be denied entry into the U.S. and/or face a tariff duty. Likewise a foreign company selling its products in the U.S. at an amount below its fair value faces an antidumping duties. Similarly, a foreign company selling its products in the U.S. while receiving unfair export subsidies from their home country will encounter a countervailing duty. For a discussion of antidumping and countervailing duties see Ralph H. Folsom and Michael W. Gordon, *International Business Transactions*, West Publishing Co., (1995), Hornbook Series.

Developed countries like the U.S. embrace a policy promoting the fair and free flow of goods and services across national borders. They champion lower trade barriers, permitting foreign products into domestic markets. Fair foreign competition is seen as a factor in forcing domestic industries to become more efficient. The dislocations in certain industries due to foreign competition are made up by growth in other industries. The import regulations focus more on limiting the entry of products that may be unsafe or harmful to its citizens or are the result of unfair competition from abroad.

Developing countries generally take a much more restrictive view towards free trade than developed countries. The main concern of developing countries is that free and unfettered free trade will inundate the country with foreign, superior products that destroy local industry and eliminate jobs. The protection of domestic industries and fear of relying on foreign products drives the decisions of the developing country.

In the past, Latin America closed its borders to foreign competition, in an effort to protect the precarious domestic industries. The Latin American import substitution policy, discussed in Chapter 1 supra, subjected foreign products to a high tariff rate to protect the domestic industries. The high tariff rate effectively prevented the flow of foreign goods into the region.

This protectionist macro-economic policy has changed. Indeed, one of the most exciting current events in the Americas is Latin American willingness to abandon the protectionism that it had embraced for so long. After many years of protectionism, Latin American borders are flinging open to U.S. and Canadian products. The great "sucking sound" is not of jobs as predicted by some xenophobic politicians, but of goods going into Latin America.

Latin American borders are opening up to foreign products especially those coming from the United States. The under capitalized domestic industries with their outdated technology are no match for U.S. and Canadian industry. These domestic industries are being adjusted and reshaped to reflect the new trade and economic realities. Only time will tell of the ultimate outcome.

2. *The Trade Barrier*

a. *A Balancing of Interests*

The importer can be either the Buyer or the Seller as determined in the Sales Contract. The *Incoterms* can play a prominent role in determining who the importer is. Assume an U.S. Buyer and Argentine Seller. In a *FOB Buenos Aires* term, the Buyer takes the goods from the Seller in Buenos Aires and contracts with the carrier for shipment of the goods to their ultimate destination. The Buyer is the importer in the U.S. If in the same transaction the relevant term was *CIF Los Angeles,* the Seller would be the importer.

The importer has an important stake in trade regulation. It would prefer no regulation. It wants to bring the product into the country and derive the benefits contracted for in the Sales Contract with as little government intrusion as possible. The interests of the importer and the government are usually in conflict with each other. Important preliminary questions the importer faces are whether the product can be sold in the country—a market access issue—and/or what is the cost of importing the product. The latter is a tariffs issue.

Other parties with a stake in trade regulation are the domestic competitors of the importer. In developed countries, like everywhere else, domestic competitors of imported foreign products do not want competition. They would like for the foreign product to not come into the country at all; or, if the products do come in, to be subjected to a high-tariff duty. Here, the country's government may take a position contrary to its citizen's interest. The government must balance the interests of its domestic consumers from the domestic producers. Under what circumstances do the interests of the domestic producer and domestic consumer diverge? What is the proper role of import regulations in these cases?

Despite the willingness to reduce trade barriers they continue to exist. Finding the balance between free trade and protectionism is difficult and fraught with political risks to the countries. Latin America has struggled with the appropriate policy relative to imports. Even the

U.S. has battled with protectionist cycles as the recent presidential election campaigns can attest.

b. The Trade Barrier

(1) The Non–Tariff Barrier

Import regulations are usually referred to as trade barriers. There are two types of trade barriers—tariff barriers and non-tariff barriers. The tariff barrier (TB) increases the cost of the product entering the country. The non tariff barrier (NTB) while not necessarily increasing the cost of the product, may partially or completely restrict the entry of a product into the domestic market.

The stated objective of NTBs can be quite proper. Frequently, stated objectives include the preventing of unsafe products from entering the country, national security, and the overall furtherance of economic and social policy considerations. The NTB is a proper exercise of governmental regulation so long as it is based on real concerns, not disguised trade restrictions. The problem is that NTBs can be disguised efforts at protectionism.

Take for example the following case—Japan imposed a rule that beef could not be sold in Japan if it contained a certain preservative. The Japanese government claimed the preservative was a health hazard and therefore legitimized their denying its entry on account of health and safety considerations. The effect was to prevent U.S. beef suppliers' access to the Japanese market because without the preservative the product coming from the U.S. would spoil en route. There was some dispute on Japan's factual correctness in its assertion. Was the rule truly based on health and safety concerns or was it a protectionist measure favoring the domestic beef producing industry?

This type of problem is not given to easy resolution. The GATT negotiating rounds have had some success at reducing NTBs although not as much as hoped. The problem in removing NTBs is related to their very nature. NTBs arise out of governmental policy focusing on subjective issues like health, safety, and national security. Determining if governmental action is based on valid health, safety, and national security concerns versus protecting inefficient domestic industries can be very problematic.

The GATT negotiating rounds have produced various agreements dealing with non-tariff barriers—the *Agreement on Import Licensing Procedures*, the *Agreement on the Application of Sanitary and Phyto Sanitary Measures*, and the *Agreement on Technical Barriers to Trade* have been negotiated with the principle of reducing NTBs. Also, one of the main objectives of the North American Free Trade Agreement (NAFTA), is the removal of tariff and non—tariff barriers between Canada, the U.S., and Mexico.

(2) The Tariff Barrier

The tariff barrier (TB) is easier to identify and eliminate than NTBs. The GATT negotiating rounds have had great success in reducing tariff barriers worldwide. As a result of the GATT negotiating rounds, tariff rates among the various signatory countries have dropped substantially. During the pre-depression era, tariff rates averaged in the 95–96% range. The current tariff rates averaging from 3–5% are in great part due to the GATT. In addition, many regional and bilateral agreements completely eliminate the tariff barrier altogether.

The TB does not prohibit the entry of the product outright, but it may effectively prevent the entry of the product by elevating the cost of the product over the existing market price. For example, assume a widget sells in country X at one hundred dollars. An U.S. manufacturer (USCO) wants to sell its widgets in country X. The widget manufactured by USCO and the country's domestically produced widget is comparable in every respect. Assume that country X has an import tariff rate of 100% on that widget.

USCO, assuming it is the importer, would have to pay a tariff of one hundred dollars. The tariff raises USCO's cost by one hundred dollars. It would then have to sell the widget for two hundred dollars in country X to make the same profit on a sale in the U.S. for one hundred dollars. The effect of the tariff barrier is that USCO must either greatly reduce its profit or not enter the market altogether on account of the increased cost.

The tariff duty is computed by multiplying the applicable tariff rate by the dutiable value of the goods. The tariff rate is obtained by determining the category of the country, the classification of the product, and the determination of the true origin of the goods. The dutiable value of the goods is determined by applying certain international and/or domestic valuation rules as well as analyzing the costs associated with the transportation of the goods.

Notice the variables in determining the tariff duty—country categorization, product classification, the true origin of the goods, the value of the goods, and the costs that are included or excluded from dutiable values. Each element above is determined by a set of international and domestic rules. The following materials discuss each factor independently. However, all work in unison in determining the tariff duty.

B. CATEGORIZING THE COUNTRY

1. Introduction

The category of the country has a major impact on the tariff rate of the imported product. Country Categorization rules take into account the social, economic, political, and legal linkages between the exporting and importing countries. It is an escapable fact that countries that enjoy friendly relations will treat each other better than countries that are enemies. In addition, countries in close proximity to each other usually have closer trade ties than countries that are separated by great distances.

Another factor that impacts the categorization of the country is its economic development. Developing countries with their unique problems are viewed differently from developed countries. They are likely to be included in a favorable category simply because they represent the poorest of the poor countries. In relationships between developed countries the obligations are reciprocal, *i.e.*, the favorable category is conditioned on the same favorable treatment by the other country. Developing countries are bestowed unilateral trade preferences from the developed country while not expected to reciprocate the favorable treatment.

Country categorization is determined in large part by the trade agreements they have entered into, the relationship among its neighboring countries, and the economic development level. The GATT/WTO agreement has a substantial effect on country categorization. Member countries are bestowed most favored nation (MFN) treatment. In many cases, neighboring countries and poor countries can achieve better than MFN treatment. These exceptions are allowed by the GATT/WTO. U.S. law provides for these three categories of countries as well.

2. *U.S. Categorization Rules*

The products imported into the U.S. from Category 2 countries are either excluded outright through a NTB or face the highest tariff rates. Category 2 provides for tariff rates in the ninety percent range. The rates are the last vestiges of the Smoot–Hawley Tariff Act—the U.S. depression era protectionist tariff system. This category is reserved for countries that the U.S. sees as pariah countries and with which no trade agreements exist. In the cold war days, the Category 2 countries were the communist bloc countries. Presently, Cuba is the sole occupant in the Western Hemisphere.

Category 1—General, are countries that have MFN status. Despite the name, MFN status does not represent the lowest tariff rate. It is the middle of the tariff rates. Prior to World War II MFN countries derived their status from bilateral treaties with the U.S. Since the forming of the GATT in 1947, it has become the primary means of bestowing MFN status. The only U.S. bilateral treaty currently bestowing MFN status is with China. This is also in the process of change as China seeks membership in the GATT.

The GATT excerpt below provides for the reciprocal, non-discrimination, MFN treatment among signatory countries—the essential promise under the GATT.

The General Agreement on Tariff And Trade

* * *

Article 1

General most Favored Nation Treatment

1. With respect to customs duties and charges of any kind imposed on or in connection with importation or exportation or imposed on the

international transfer or payments for imports or exports, and with respect to the method of levying such duties and charges, and with respect to all rules and formalities in connection with importation an exportation * * * any advantage, favour privilege, or immunity granted by any contracting party to any product originating in or destined for any other country shall be accorded immediately and unconditionally to the like product originating in or destined for the territories of all other contracting parties * * *

Article III

* * *

4. The products of the territory of any contracting party imported into the territory of any other contracting party shall be accorded treatment no less favorable than that accorded to like products of national origin in respect of all laws, regulations and requirements affecting their internal sale, offering for sale, purchase, transportation, distribution or use. * * *

———————

Membership in the GATT entitles the country to receive and to bestow at least MFN treatment. The Western Hemisphere countries that presently are GATT signatories include Canada, the United States, Mexico, Chile, Peru, Argentina, Brazil, Costa Rica, Colombia, Bolivia, El Salvador, Guatemala, Honduras, Venezuela, and Panama. In spite of the name—'Most Favored Nation' the most favorable treatment under U.S. law is reserved for those countries that are categorized as Category One—Special countries.

In the U.S. Category 1—Special status is bestowed to Canada and Mexico as members of the NAFTA and the signatory countries in the *The Generalized System of Preferences (GSP)*, *The Caribbean Basin Initiative (CBI)*, and *The Andean Trade Preference Act(ATPA)*. The GSP, CBI, and ATPA are unilateral trade agreements whereas the NAFTA is reciprocal. The following NAFTA excerpt describes the critical provisions in the sale of goods under NAFTA.

North American Free Trade Agreement
Chapter Three
MARKET ACCESS FOR GOODS

Article 300: Scope and Coverage

This Chapter applies to trade in goods of a Party * * *

Section A—National Treatment
Article 301: National Treatment

1. Each Party shall accord national treatment to the goods of another Party in accordance with Article III of the General Agreement

on Tariffs and Trade (GATT), including its interpretative notes, and to, this end Article III of the GATT and its interpretative notes, or any equivalent provision of a successor agreement to which all Parties are party, are incorporated into and made part of this Agreement.

2. The provisions of paragraph I regarding national treatment shall mean, with respect to a state or province, treatment no less favorable than the most favorable treatment accorded by such state or province to any like, directly competitive or substitutable goods, as the case may be, of the Party of which it forms a part. * * *

Section B—Tariffs

Article 302: Tariff Elimination

1. Except as otherwise provided in this Agreement, no Party may increase any existing customs duty, or adopt any customs duty, on an originating good.

2. Except as otherwise provided in this Agreement, each Party shall progressively eliminate its customs duties on originating goods in accordance with its Schedule to Annex 302.2.

3. On the request, of any Party, the Parties shall consult to consider accelerating the elimination of customs duties set out in their Schedules. An agreement between two or more Parties to accelerate the elimination of a customs duty on a good shall supersede any duty rate or staging category determined pursuant to their Schedules for such good when approved by each such Party in accordance with its applicable legal procedures.

4. Each Party may adopt or maintain import measures to allocate in-quota imports made pursuant to a tariff rate quota set out in Annex 302.2, provided that such measures do not have trade restrictive effects on imports additional to those caused by the imposition of the tariff rate quota.

5. On written request of any Party, a Party applying or intending to apply measures pursuant to paragraph 4 shall consult to review the administration of those measures.

* * *

Section C—Non–Tariff Measures

Article 309: Import and Export Restrictions

1. Except as otherwise provided in this Agreement, no Party may adopt or maintain any prohibition or restriction on the importation of any good of another Party or on the exportation or sale for export of any good destined for the territory of another Party, except in accordance with Article XI of the GATT, including its interpretative notes, and to this, end Article XI of the GATT and its interpretative notes, or any equivalent provision of a successor agreement to which all Parties are party, are incorporated into and made a part of this Agreement.

2. The Parties understand that the GATT rights and obligations incorporated by paragraph 1 prohibit, in any circumstances in which any other form of restriction is prohibited, export price requirements and, except as permitted in enforcement of countervailing and antidumping orders and undertakings, import price requirements.

3. In the event that a Party adopts or maintains a prohibition or restriction on the importation from or exportation to a non-Party of a good, nothing in this Agreement shall be construed to prevent the Party from: (a) limiting or prohibiting the importation from the territory of another Party of such good of that non-Party; or (b) requiring as a condition of export of such good of the Party to the territory of another Party, that the good not be re-exported to the non-Party, directly or indirectly, without being consumed in the territory of the other Party.

4. In the event that a Party adopts or maintains a prohibition or restriction on the importation of a good from a non-Party, the Parties, on request of any Party, shall consult with a view to avoiding undue interference with or distortion of pricing, marketing and distribution arrangements in another Party. * * *

The U.S. historically has not been favorably disposed towards non-reciprocal trading arrangements. It has always been a champion of reciprocal free trade. However, after some pressure from other developed countries (notably from the European Community), and since the beneficiary countries of these unilateral trade preferences are some of the poorest countries in the world, the U.S. agreed to develop various unilateral systems to assist them.

The U.S. permits certain products of certain developing countries to enter into the U.S. customs region at a zero percent tariff rate. These arrangements are unilateral because the U.S. does not require the developing country to reciprocate, *i.e.* the developing country is permitted to continue imposing tariffs on U.S. products entering their country. Many of the products from the countries enjoying this special relationship enter into the U.S. free of tariff.

The Generalized System of Preferences (GSP) is the largest unilateral preference trading system to which the U.S. is a party including over 140 countries and over 4,000 products. The beneficiary countries include most of Latin America. The GSP as initially enacted expired in 1995. However, Congress reinstated it in June, 1996. Other agreements are the CBI and the ATPA.

THE ANDEAN TRADE PREFERENCE ACT

Guy C. Smith

21 DENV. J. INT'L L. & POL'Y 149 (1992).

* * *

On December 4, 1991, President Bush signed into law the Andean Trade Preference Act ("ATPA"), which authorizes the President to grant duty-free treatment for ten years to eligible imports from Peru, Colombia, Bolivia, and Ecuador. The ATPA represents one of the chief elements of

President Bush's efforts to create additional incentives to foster trade in legitimate products in the four Andean countries currently fighting the scourge of drug trafficking. The benefits bestowed under the ATPA are in addition to the duty-free benefits these four countries already receive under the U.S. Generalized System of Preferences ("GSP"). When compared with GSP, duty-free treatment under the ATPA extends to a broader array of articles and creates more certainty with respect to the continued eligibility of articles for duty-free treatment. The ATPA also has symbolic importance in that it is a tangible reflection of the U.S. government's commitment to the Andean region. * * *

Under the ATPA, for a period of ten years commencing on December 4, 1991 and ending December 4, 2001, certain eligible articles from designated Andean countries may receive duty-free treatment when imported into the United States. This preferential tariff regime is essentially identical to the tariff regime established under the CBI, except that the CBI regime has been made permanent.

Under the ATPA, only Bolivia, Ecuador, Peru, and Colombia are eligible to be designated as beneficiary countries. On July 2, 1992, President Bush designated Colombia and Bolivia as beneficiary countries under the ATPA. The designation became effective on July 22, 1992. Neither Ecuador nor Peru has yet been designated as a beneficiary country.

A. Country Eligibility

The ATPA has certain country practice standards, which the President must take into account in his decision to designate a country as a beneficiary country. The President is prohibited under the statute from designating any country as a beneficiary if the country: (1) is a communist country; (2) has expropriated property of a U.S. citizen without providing prompt, adequate and effective compensation, or entering into good faith negotiations to provide prompt, adequate and effective compensation, or submitting the dispute to arbitration under the provisions of the International Convention for the Settlement of Investment Disputes or another mutually agreed upon forum; (3) fails to act in good faith in recognizing arbitral awards in favor of U.S. citizens; (4) affords preferential treatment to the products of a developed country and such preferential treatment is likely to have a significant adverse impact on United States commerce; (5) engages in the broadcast of copyrighted material without the express consent of the United States copyright owner or the country fails to work toward the provision of adequate and effective protection of intellectual property rights; (6) is not a signatory to a treaty or convention regarding extradition of U.S. citizens; and (7) has not or is not taking steps to provide internationally-recognized worker rights to its workers. Under the ATPA, the President can waive certain of these requirements if he determines that waiver is in the economic or national security interests of the United States and reports the reasons for such determination to Congress.

The ATPA also has certain additional factors, which the President must take into account in his decision to designate a country as a beneficiary country. These criteria include: (1) the expression by such country of its desire to be designated; (2) the economic conditions in the country, including the living standards of its inhabitants and other economic factors; (3) the extent to which the country has assured the U.S. it will provide equitable and reasonable market access; (4) the degree to which the country follows the rules of international trade as established under the GATT and other trade agreements; (5) the degree to which the country uses export subsidies or imposes export performance or local content requirements; (6) the degree to which the trade policies of the country are contributing to the revitalization of the region; (7) the degree to which the country is undertaking self-help measures to promote its own economic development; (8) whether the country has taken or is taking steps to afford its workers internationally-recognized worker rights; (9) the extent to which the country provides adequate and effective means for foreign nationals to secure, exercise, and enforce intellectual property rights; (10) the extent to which the country prohibits its nationals from engaging in the broadcast of copyrighted material belonging to U.S. copyright owners; (11) whether the country has met the narcotics cooperation certification criteria contained in the Foreign Assistance Act of 1961; and (12) the extent to which the country is prepared to cooperate with the United States in the administration of the provisions of the ATPA.

Under the ATPA, the President has authority to withdraw or suspend the designation of any country as a beneficiary country, or the application of duty-free treatment to any article from any country, if the President determines that because of changed circumstances the country should no longer be designated as a beneficiary country. Before the President renders such a determination, the ATPA provides that written comments from the public will be accepted and a public hearing will be held regarding the proposed action. The President is also required to submit to Congress, until the expiration of duty-free benefits under the ATPA, triennial reports concerning the operation of the ATPA, including the results of a general review of the ATPA beneficiary countries' adherence to the ATPA's country practice criteria. * * *

Under the ATPA, the President may suspend duty-free treatment on any eligible article if the action is proclaimed as import relief under Title II of the Trade Act of 1974, or for national security reasons under Section 232 of the Trade Expansion of 1962. * * *

The benefits provided to the designated beneficiary countries under the ATPA are relatively narrow in scope, but are not necessarily insignificant. The benefits are considerably broader than the benefits the Andean countries currently receive under GSP. Although a significant percentage of exports from these countries (approximately forty-three percent) already receive GSP or most-favored nation duty-free treatment, under the ATPA an additional $324 million or six percent of total imports from the four countries based on 1990 figures are eligible for duty-free treatment. * * *

Finally, the ATPA has symbolic importance. It is a concrete reflection of the U.S government's commitment to the Andean region, and its willingness to provide incentives to encourage trade in legitimate products between the U.S. and the Andean countries. * * *

———————

The carrot and stick approach to trade relationships is very evident in the unilateral trade preference agreements. The foregoing illustrates the importance of trade agreements in country categorization. The U.S. is typical of other developed countries. It offers MFN treatment to GATT members, preferential treatment to those countries in its region and to those countries, which are the poorest of the poor. It also eliminates trade barriers among its neighbors.

The Latin American countries have historically banded together in an attempt to provide a united front against the U.S. Latin America has always embraced the idea of regional economic integration. Although many of the efforts have ended in failure, the success that has been achieved has been most notable in removing tariff and non-tariff barriers.

C. CLASSIFYING THE PRODUCT

The tariff is computed by multiplying the tariff rate by the dutiable value. Categorizing the country and classifying the product that is entering into the U.S. customs region determines the tariff rate. Country categorization is a macro view of trade policy largely determined by international agreements negotiated by the countries. Product classification is a micro view of trade policy.

The product classification procedures are highly technical. However, they can have a substantial effect on tariff rate. Each type of product (which can number in the tens of thousands) entering into the United States must be classified. Understanding and applying the product classification rules is a major part of the work done by lawyers engaged in a customs practice. The following materials give you an idea of how technical they can be.

A FEW POINTERS ON CUSTOMS LAW

E. Charles Routh, Garvey, Schubert & Barer.

ALL-ABA 13.

* * *

With very few exceptions, all goods imported into the United States must be declared with the U.S. Customs Service and are subject to duties under the Harmonized Tariff Schedule of the United States ("HTSUS"). Duties vary with the type of merchandise, its value, its origin, and a number of other factors. Penalties for violating Customs laws or procedures can be quite substantial.

Despite the very high duties (which may be higher than the corporate tax rate), few importers—or their attorneys—give Customs law questions the same thought spent on tax planning or other issues. This is a mistake. The reality for any importer is that duties and fines imposed for Customs laws violations add an extra layer of cost to the item imported and correspondingly reduce the item's competitive worth in the domestic marketplace. If your client does any significant volume of importing business, you should acquaint yourself with the basics of Customs law.

FUNDAMENTALS

The duty payable at the time of entry is a function of four distinct factors:

The first factor is classification. Classification means how the imported goods are described in HTSUS (the Harmonized Tariff Schedule of the United States). The classification determines the duty rate and whether the product is eligible for a duty preference program;

* * *

CLASSIFICATION

Classification refers to the category the product fits into under the Harmonized Tariff Schedule. The Schedule is published by the U.S. International Trade Commission ("USITC"). See USITC Publication 2937 (8th ed. 1996). It was adopted by Congress as part of the Omnibus Trade and Competitiveness Act of 1988 (see 19 U.S.C. s 3007).

System Structure

The merchandise classification system is like a pyramid, beginning at the Section level, such as vegetable, textiles, vehicles, and so forth, and then proceeding to the Chapter level, with articles such as tin items, aircraft, furniture, and so on. Within each Chapter, Headings are further organized by level of processing or by function or use. Subheadings further define products into various categories.

Reading the Headings

The first six digits of the tariff number, which are through the Heading, are standardized by the World Customs Organization, an international organization located in Brussels. Additional subheadings, from the seventh to the tenth digits, are available to individual countries to further make divisions for duty purposes or for purposes of quotas or statistical tracking.

Interpreting the Classifications

All of these breakdowns are subject to nationally and internationally promulgated rules of interpretation. Indeed, by far the vast majority of rulings issued by Customs deal with classification questions. Rulings are issued pursuant to regulation. See 19 C.F.R. pt. 177. More recent rulings are now available on Lexis or can be purchased from Customs or commercial services on floppy disks or CDROM.

General Rules

Section and Chapter notes are subject to General Rules of Interpretation. The notes are found at the start of the Harmonized Tariff Schedule. See USITC Publication 2937 (8th ed. 1996). These rules are designed to resolve classification issues when the same products are seemingly classified under more than one heading.

What's the "Essential Function"?

The rules provide that the heading to be used is the one providing the most specific description of the imported product or, for combinations of materials or multiple function products, the heading for the material, component, or function, which provides the "essential character" of the product. If nothing else, the heading last in numerical order of the Harmonized System prevails.

Classification Change Affects the Duty Rate

The classification determined by Customs can have a significant effect on the rate of duty applied. For example, for years lavatory modules for use in commercial aircraft were imported by commercial aircraft manufacturers as HTSUS 8803.30.00104 (other parts of airplanes). Customs reclassified the modules as HTSUS 9406.00.8090 (prefabricated buildings). The result was an increase in duty from duty free to a duty of 5.7 per cent. Only after a protest was filed was Customs convinced that the original classification was correct.

Finished or Unassembled?

One area in which classification is particularly significant is the treatment of merchandise as finished or unassembled. Certain items may fall under different tariff rates, may be under a quota, or may be subject to dumping duties, depending on whether the item is a component or completed article.

How To Tell the Difference

Harmonized Tariff Schedule General Rules of Interpretation 2(a) states generally that the tariff description of an article must refer to an article as incomplete or unfinished if the incomplete or unfinished article has the essential character of the complete or finished article.

Computer Industry Example

An example was in the news a few years ago. Certain flat panel electronic computer displays typically used in laptop computers were subject to an antidumping duty of approximately 63 per cent when imported into the United States from Japan. USITC Investigation No. 731–TA–469 (final), 56 Fed. Reg. 12,741 (1991). This level of duty made it almost prohibitive to import these panels. However, if the same panels were imported into Canada and assembled into laptop computers there, they could enter the United States as laptop computers under a different classification and tariff schedule. Under certain circumstances they could enter as Canadian goods and thus be subject to the Free Trade Agreement with Canada, greatly reducing the duty that would be paid. The result was a rush of computer companies setting up laptop assembly plants in Canada or various other countries.

Effect of NAFTA

The goal of NAFTA is to eliminate all customs duties on all goods originating in Canada, Mexico, or the United States over a transition period. Now that NAFTA has become effective, it will have a tremendous impact on all aspects of Customs law and practice. To begin with, it will remove all tariffs between the three countries under various timetables, depending on the sensitivity of the particular import. About half of all Mexican tariffs were eliminated on the effective date of the agreement, with the rest to be eliminated over five or 10 years or, in a very few cases, 15 years. Since Mexican tariffs are about two-and-a-half times the U.S. tariff rates, this will have a major impact on trade between the two countries. Canada's rates have already been reduced by the U.S.-Canada Free Trade Agreement and have been further reduced under NAFTA.

As a result of the Customs Modernization Act, passed as part of NAFTA, there have been an increasing number of classification changes. For example, the 1996 Harmonized Tariff Schedule contains some 30,000 changes from the 1995 version. Virtually every Customs Bulletin contains some proposed classification changes.

—————

Engaging in the international sale of goods inevitably leads to dealing with the customs service of a country by one of the parties. The role of Customs varies in its particulars in each country but is generally the same—protecting the borders of the country by regulating the import and export of products. On regulating imports, the U.S. Customs Service (USCS), is responsible for assessing and collecting tariff duties, enforcing non-tariff barriers, and enforcing laws relating to the breach of patents, trademark and copyright laws, and food and drug laws or other unfair foreign competition.

NIDEC CORP. v. UNITED STATES

United States Court of Appeals, Federal Circuit, 1995.
68 F.3d 1333.

* * *

FRIEDMAN, Senior Circuit Judge.

The question is whether the Customs Service properly classified the appellant Nidec Corporation's (Nidec) imported merchandise as electric motors rather than, as Nidec contends it should have done, as parts of electronic data processing machinery. The Court of International Trade upheld Customs' classification. We affirm.

* * *

Nidec's imports are electric rotary motors that include a precision spindle and other components. They are custom designed to be used to rotate the disks in computer hard disk drives in a particular company's computer. Although Nidec's products are referred to by various names, the Court of International Trade found that "[w]hatever the nomenclature, there are three elements, namely, a shaft centering a precision spindle, a stator, and a rotor, imported either separately or loosely connected." The purpose of the spindle is to ensure that the rotation of the computer disks is extremely precise. Precision in rotation is essential because any inaccuracies in speed, positioning, or stability may result in inaccurate storage or retrieval of information.

The United States Customs Service classified the merchandise as electric motors under heading 8501 of the Harmonized Tariff Schedule of the United States (HTSUS). Nidec timely challenged that determination by filing suit in the Court of International Trade. In its complaint, Nidec asserted that "[t]he imported merchandise consists of computer spindles for rigid disk drives" and should have been classified as "Parts and accessories ... suitable for use solely or principally with [automatic data processing] machines" under subheading 8473.30.40 of the 1989 HTSUS.

After trial, the Court of International Trade upheld Customs' classification. The court noted that Rule 1 of the HTSUS' General Rules of Interpretation "mandates that 'classification shall be determined according to the terms of the headings and any relative section or chapter notes and, provided such headings or notes do not otherwise require, according to the [remaining General Rules].' "The court stated that "if the goods are electric motors, even though designed specifically for use in computers, this Rule 1 and Note 2 above require the classification for which Customs opted." The court noted that Nidec had stipulated that "an 'electric motor' is 'a device for transforming electric energy into mechanical power, and includes rotary motors.' "

The court "concur[red]" with the government's position that the description of electric motors in the Explanatory Notes to heading 8501 "is 'sufficiently broad to encompass motors of many types,' including 'motors which are designed to be used in specific machines' "and that "the spindle can be equated with a pulley, gear, or flexible shaft in that it transmits the mechanical energy created by the rotor and the stator to the merchandise's intended load—the discs." It concluded that the "essence" of the function that the spindle performs "is still that of a motor, not of a spindle, the connector to the discs," and that Nidec's product "cannot be classified under the HTSUS as more than that which drives the hard discs in a computer." * * *

A. The Harmonized Tariff Schedule of the United States supplanted the former Tariff Schedule of the United States in 1989. Omnibus Trade and Competiveness [sic] Act of 1988, Pub.L. No. 100–418, 102 Stat. 1107. Heading 8501 of the HTSUS covers: Electric motors and generators (excluding generating sets).

Chapter 84 of the HTSUS, under which Nidec contends its product should have been classified, provides in pertinent part:

Heading 8473: Parts and accessories . . . suitable for use solely or principally with machines of heading 8469 to 8472:

Subheading 8473.30.40: Parts and accessories of the machines of heading 8471: Not incorporating a cathode ray tube.

Heading 8471 covers "[a]utomatic data processing machines and units thereof; magnetic or optical readers, machines for transcribing data onto data media in coded form and machines for processing such data, not elsewhere specified or included."

Section 8501 is an eo nomine provision, i.e., it describes a commodity by a specific name, usually one common in commerce. Absent limiting language or indicia of contrary legislative intent, such a provision covers all forms of the article. See National Advanced Sys. v. United States, 26 F.3d 1107, 1111 (Fed.Cir.1994). Heading 8501 covers "electric motors" and the applicable Subheading, 8501.10.60, covers "Motors of an output not exceeding 37.5W: Of 18.65 W or more but not exceeding 37.5 W." Nothing in the language or legislative history of HTSUS or this heading limits the scope of the provision.

Indeed, note 2(a) of Section XVI of the HTSUS shows that section 8501 covers all forms of electric motors and that an electric motor is properly classified as such even though it also could be classified as a part of another product. Note 2(a) states that "Parts which are goods included in any of the headings of chapters 84 and 85 [which would include heading 8501] . . . are in all cases to be classified in their respective headings." The Explanatory Notes on this section further state that although "parts which are suitable for use solely or principally with particular machines . . . are classified in the same heading as those machines," this rule does "not apply to parts which in themselves constitute an article covered by a heading of this Section . . . [which] are in all cases classified in their own appropriate heading even if specifically designed to work as part of a specific machine. This applies in particular to . . . [e]lectric motors of heading 8501." Although explanatory notes are not controlling authority, they are "generally indicative of the scope of the [HTSUS]." Lynteq, Inc. v. United States, 976 F.2d 693, 699 (Fed.Cir.1992).

Explanatory Note 85.01 to Heading 8501 further illustrates the breadth of the electric motor provision. It states that: (A) Rotary motors produce mechanical power in the form of rotary motion. They are of many types and sizes according to whether they operate on DC or AC, and according to the use or purpose for which they are designed. The motor housing may be adapted to the circumstances in which the motor will operate.... Many motors may incorporate a fan or other device for keeping the motor cool during running. With the exception of starter motors for internal combustion engines (heading 8511), the heading covers electric motors of all types from low power motors for use in instruments, clocks, time switches, sewing machines, toys, etc., up to large powerful motors for rolling mills, etc. Motors remain classified here even when they are equipped with pulleys, with gears or gear boxes, or with a flexible shaft for operating hand tools. The heading includes "outboard motors", for the propulsion of boats, in the form of a unit comprising an electric motor, shaft, propeller and a rudder.

B. Judicial review of a Customs classification "generally entails a two-step process of (1) ascertaining the proper meaning of specific terms within the tariff provision and (2) determining whether the merchandise at issue comes within the description of such terms as properly construed. The first step is a question of law which we review de novo and the second is a question of fact which we review for clear error." National Advanced Sys., 26 F.3d at 1109 (quoting Marcel Watch Co. v. United States, 11 F.3d 1054, 1056 (Fed.Cir.1993)).

The parties stipulated, the Court of International Trade held, and we agree, that an electric motor is a "device for transforming electric energy into mechanical power, and includes rotary motors."

The issue before us, therefore, is whether Nidec's product comes within this description, and therefore properly was classified as an electric motor. We agree with the Court of International Trade that the classification was correct.

As that court pointed out, despite the critical functions it performs in insuring proper rotation of the disk drive, the spindle's "essence is still that of a motor, not of a spindle, the connector to the discs," and it "cannot be classified under the HTSUS as more than that which drives the hard discs in a computer." As the court stated, "the spindle can be equated with a pulley, gear, or flexible shaft in that it transmits the mechanical energy created by the rotor and the stator to the merchandise's intended load—the discs." The explanatory notes to the HTSUS state that merchandise is classified as a motor even if it includes such elements.

Nidec argues that because the principal function of its product is to provide and maintain precision of rotation and stability through the spindle and because the product includes a fan and circuits, which have functions other than to convert electrical energy into mechanical force, it cannot be classified as an electric motor.

The trial testimony, however, repeatedly indicated that the principal function of the merchandise is to drive the disks. The unit performs this function in a way that meets the definition of an electric motor: the interaction of the stator and rotor converts electrical energy into mechanical energy, causing the shaft and spindle to revolve, which in turn causes the disks to rotate.

Indeed, as the Court of International Trade noted, Nidec's own sales literature describes its product as an electric motor and itself as a manufacturer of such motors. Its sales brochure states: Since its founding in July 1973, Nidec has grown to become a world leader in the design and manufacturing of state-of-the-art precision brushless DC electric motors. . . . Spindle Motors (Brushless DC) Spindle motors are designed and manufactured for all sizes of Winchester disc drives: 14", 9", 8", 5.25", 3.5" and smaller, as well as for all optical disc drives. The details of each specific application are closely reviewed with the customer to arrive at a spindle motor design, which yields the desired performance and lends itself to volume production in our automated facilities.

The basic character of Nidec's product as an electric motor is not changed because it is custom designed and made for a particular computer company or because it includes the precision spindle. The Explanatory Notes state that merchandise classifiable as an electric motor is "in all cases classified" as such "even if specially designed to work as part of a specific machine." Moreover, as discussed above, an eo nomine provision such as this one covers all forms of the article unless Congress indicates to the contrary, Hasbro Indus. v. United States, 879 F.2d 838, 840, 7 Fed.Cir. (T) 110, 112 (1989), and Congress has not here so indicated.

C. Under the prior TSUS, a motor that was "more than a motor" because it contained additional components performing different functions, was not classified as a motor. See, e.g., United States v. Acec Elec. Corp., 474 F.2d 1009 (CCPA 1973) (sewing machine motors equipped with clutches are "more than" motors); Servo–Tek Prods. v. United States, 416 F.2d 1398 (CCPA 1969) (motors equipped with gear boxes are "more than" motors); United States v. A.W. Fenton, 49 CCPA 45, 1962 WL 9340 (1962) (gears). Nidec contends that under those cases its product is "more than a motor" and therefore was improperly classified as a motor.

The extent, if any, to which the "more than a motor" doctrine continues under the HTSUS is undecided and unclear. As noted, under that doctrine the presence of clutches, gear boxes or pulleys was held to make a motor "more than a motor." The explanatory note to heading 8501 under the HTSUS states, however, that "Motors remain classified here even when they are equipped with pulleys, with gears or gear boxes, or with a flexible shaft for operating hand tools." Thus, the broad sweep of heading 8501 suggests a Congressional intent to overturn at least some prior applications of the "more than a motor" doctrine.

Assuming without deciding that the doctrine continues to have some application under the HTSUS, we agree with the Court of International Trade that, "a broad eo nomine provision like that at bar still includes all forms of an article." "[E]ach case [involving the 'more than' doctrine] must in the final analysis be determined on its own facts." E. Green & Son (New York), Inc. v. United States, 450 F.2d 1396, 1398 (CCPA 1971). For the reasons previously given, Nidec's product is not "more than a motor" and was properly classified under heading 8501 as an electric motor.

D.   Finally, Nidec challenges as clearly erroneous three of the Court of International Trade's findings: (1) that the merchandise consists of "three elements, namely, a shaft centering a precision spindle, a stator and a rotor, imported either separately or loosely connected"; (2) that its merchandise "drives the hard discs in a computer"; and (3) that the "spindle's remarkable, precise rotation is engendered by the interaction of the rotor and the stator upon electrification." On review of the evidentiary support for those findings, we conclude that they are not clearly erroneous.

Conclusion

The judgment of the Court of International Trade is

AFFIRMED.

———————

The United States Customs Service deals with a tremendous volume of goods, the policing of which is a very difficult task. Dealing with the USCS can be difficult. The process can be a complicated, lengthy, and costly effort. Indeed, the very process of going through customs can be a NTB. Customs procedures for determining the origin, value of products, customs classification of products, import licensing, technical standards, and sanitary and phytosanitary regulations are the primary means of establishing the NTB. Streamlining the Customs procedure was an objective in the NAFTA negotiations. The result was the Customs Modernization Act (CMA), which streamlined customs procedures in trade between the U.S., Canada and Mexico.

Under the CMA, the importer must find the proper product classification and have supporting documentation to defend its decision. The process of classifying the products can itself become a non-tariff barrier because of the way countries enact legislation to classify products. In an effort to minimize non-tariff barriers developed through product classification rules, countries have long sought the international harmonization of rules. The result of the effort was the Harmonized System.

The Harmonized System is a non self-executing treaty that assists in classifying products. Prior to the Harmonized System coming into effect, there were two competing tariff nomenclature systems. One system was the Brussels Tariff Nomenclature System, which was used by most of the world. The other system was the Tariff System of the U.S (TSUS) used by the United States. The U.S. and the other countries eventually agreed on one system and, essentially, the U.S. accepted the Brussels Tariff Nomenclature System. The U.S. adopted the Harmonized System into its domestic system through the enactment of the Harmonized Tariff System.

The function of the Harmonized Tariff System is to create international law to unify and harmonize countries' classification systems. But NTBs die hard—consider the U.S. Customs Service Directive in *Treasury Decision 89–80*—" ... Uniformity in the interpretation of the international system, the HS, is not a function of Customs. Customs is charged with the administration and interpretation of the HTS, the tariff enacted by Congress. The function of maintaining the uniform application of the HS resides with the HSC per Article 7 of the Convention. It is fundamental that the United States did not give up sovereignty when it acceded to the Convention. There is, as such, no obligation on Contracting Parties for uniform application of the HS ..." What effect does such a position have on harmonizing classification rules?

Note on the Exportation of Goods

As in the case of import restrictions, each country regulates the outbound flow of goods in a manner designed to further its interests and the interests of its citizens. In any regulatory scheme, there is a natural tension between the regulators and the regulated. International trade regulation is no exception. Regulating the importation of goods is largely urged by domestic industries seeking to protect their domestic market share. The government goes along, if at all, at the urging of local businesses or industry groups. In the case of export restrictions, however, the government is the driving force. Industry, for the most part, desires unfettered access to export markets.

The government, looking at the good of the country overall, may restrict exports. The United States export regulation policy has several fundamental principles. The export rules generally attempt to further the national security interests of the U.S. The rules also are designed to further the government's policy goals and the retention of scarce resources within the U.S. Another goal is to limit the spread of weapons of mass destruction. The federal statutory rules evidence this broad concern by providing for the inter-action of diverse federal agencies. The affected agencies include the Drug Enforcement Agency, the Department of Energy, the Department of the Interior, the Nuclear Regulatory Commission, the U.S. Patent Office, and the Department of Commerce (DOC). The DOC has the most extensive of rules affecting exports.

Under U.S. domestic law the Constitution empowers the Congress to regulate exports (Art. 1, § 8, cl.3). Congress delegated the authority to the President in the *Export Administration Act of 1979 (EAA)* 50 U.S.C.A. App. 2401 et seq. The EAA expired in 1994. The President instructed the Department of Commerce, Bureau of Export Administration to develop rules governing the exportation of goods. The Export Administration Regulations

(EAR) *15 C.F.R. Parts 730–774* (1998) provides the rules that exporters should use in the exportation of goods. The EAR have been promulgated under the auspices of the *International Emergency Economic Powers Act (IEEPA)* 50 U.S.C.A. § 1701 et seq because the EAA lapsed in 1994.

The EAR, in 15 C.F.R. Part 774, continues to have the product/destination mix through the Commerce Control List (CCL) and the Export Commodity Control Numbers (EECN) but have put the onus more on exporters. Under the new formulations of the EAR, most products do not need a license. However, the exporter is required to be aware of the end use of the product and/or of the end user. Penalties are severe reaching ten times the value of the exports and prison sentences. In the case of companies, the right to export products can be revoked. See 50 App. U.S.C. § 2140 and 15 C.F.R. Part 764 § 764.3.

SECTION 7.2 THE RULES OF ORIGIN

A. THE GATT RULES OF ORIGIN

Determining the category of a country has an important role in the tariff barrier computation. It can also be important in determining the existence of NTBs since they can also be country specific. Countries seeking lower tariff rates or entry into the target country can manipulate country categorization rules. Consider the following example—The United States, Canada, and Mexico are members of the NAFTA. Mexico has entered into a free trade agreement with the EU. Under the Mexico/EU free trade agreement certain EU goods enter into Mexico free of tariffs.

The EU goods once in Mexico could then be transshipped to the U.S. free of tariff through Mexico since Mexico is a NAFTA country. If the EU country had exported the product directly to the U.S., it would have entered into the country at the higher Category 1—General rate (MFN) status instead of the more favorable Category 1—Special rate. A similar strategy could be used to disguise the origin of goods coming from a Category 2 country as either a Category 1—General or Category 1—Special product.

In order to prevent this type of trade deflection, a set of rules are in place designed to determine the true origin of the goods. In our example, only goods originating in Mexico can take advantage of NAFTA to access the U.S. market free of tariff. In order for the EU goods to enter the U.S. free of tariff they must first become Mexican goods. Thus, the EU goods would have to be affected in such a way as to change their place of origin. Determining the origin of the goods is very important and can sometimes be difficult.

Each trade agreement establishes its own set of rules of origin. Although varying in their particulars, all of them employ a combination of three criteria in ascertaining the true origin of the goods. These criteria include—a change in product classification (referred to as a substantial transformation of the product), the amount of value added in a country, and the degree of technical requirements to produce the product. The following materials look at the rules of origin under the GATT, GSP, and the NAFTA.

SUPERIOR WIRE v. UNITED STATES

United States Court of International Trade, 1987.
669 F.Supp. 472.

RESTANI, Judge:

Plaintiff, an importer of steel wire from Canada, challenges the denial of its protest against the exclusion of a shipment of wire made from wire rod produced in Spain. The United States Customs Service (Customs) excluded the wire because it was not accompanied by certificates that would allow its entry under a voluntary restraint agreement (VRA) with Spain covering wire and wire rod. * * *

Plaintiff has been importing wire made from Spanish hot-rolled wire rod since late 1984. It obtains the finished cold-drawn wire from its related company, Big Point Steel Company, in Ontario, Canada. It is the operations of Big Point, which are the main focus here.

The evidence discloses that plaintiff orders the wire rod from Spain for delivery to Canada. The rod arrives in coils of about 2,700 pounds each. The rod is uncoiled, and cleaned during passage through a mechanical descaling machine, which removes a hard oxide crust by reverse bending. The scale is formed during the rod-making process and must be removed to prevent damage to the wire-drawing equipment. The rod is then coated with a spray-on lubricant/rust preventative. The coils are joined by butt-welding, to facilitate feeding the dies, and because the end product is a 2,000 pound coil. Generally, the butt-welding process may also involve annealing across the joint so that the composition of the wire will be the same throughout.

There was no testimony as to whether annealing took place at Big Point. The operation crucial to resolution of this matter is the process, which turns the wire rod into wire. In order to feed the machine, which contains the dies that cold draw the rod into wire, the rod must be pointed and inserted into the machine. The rod is drawn through one, two and possibly, in a few cases, three dies. The testimony was contradictory as to whether one or two die passes were most commonly needed for the sizes of wire drawn by plaintiff, but plaintiff's witnesses seemed to have more familiarity with the process and the court accepts their testimony that two die passes are normally involved. Testimony also indicated that this process increases the tensile strength by thirty to forty percent as the rod is reduced in cross-sectional area by about thirty percent and is elongated. Other evidence indicated this degree of strength increase may be slightly high, but it is not greatly overstated. The final result is a substantially stronger product, which is also cleaner, smoother, "less springy," less ductile, and cross-sectionally more uniform. Seventy percent of the wire imported by plaintiff is intended for use in making wire mesh for concrete sewer pipe reinforcement, which requires the strength of the finished wire. Twenty percent of the wire imported by plaintiff is sold as wire. The wire has about one dozen applications, such as shelving or decking and baskets used in the automotive industry. Wire rod has few uses except for making wire. Only a very small percentage of rod is used directly in concrete reinforcement.

The wire rod is of low carbon content. It is referred to as industrial quality or mesh quality rod. The rod is purchased by plaintiff for its affiliate from the Spanish producer in six sizes which range from 7/32 of an inch to 7/16 of an inch. The sizes of rod imported produce a range of sizes of wire, but the physical properties of the rod limit the range of sizes of wire which may be effectively or economically produced from a particular size of rod. It is also the chemical content of the rod and the cooling processes used in its manufacture, which determine the properties that the wire will have after drawing.

Production of finished cold drawn wire from raw materials, such as scrap metal, involves several processes. The first step is to produce a steel billet. The particular process described at trial was that utilized by a domestic wire rod producer. There was no testimony indicating that the process used to produce the wire rod at issue was significantly different. The billet is a piece of steel about fifty feet long and five and one-eighth inches on each side, if measured cross-sectionally. Depending on the desired composition of the rod to be produced, a selection of different types of scrap are chosen. The scrap is melted in an electric furnace at 2700 degrees Fahrenheit. The molten metal is refined by adding lime, oxygen, and possibly other additives to remove impurities. After the impurities are removed the steel is poured into a ladle and then into a tundish (a brick lined, steel container with holes). The steel then flows into a caster and the billets are formed. The testimony indicated that the scrap costs about one hundred dollars per ton, and at an efficient plant the making of a billet costs about the same.

The next step is the production of wire rod from billets. The billet is reheated to 2100 degrees F. The rod mill described involves twenty-five separate rolling stages (stands) and two lines of billets can be processed at once. The first seven stands are called the roughing stage. The hot billets are passed through horizontal stands, which gradually remove the corners of the billets to achieve a more cylindrical shape. The next four stands are also horizontal and are called the intermediate stage. The third stage also involves four stands but they are alternately horizontal and vertical. Finally, ten carbide rolls size down the rod into its final form. The process is computerized and moves at high speed so that water cooling is required to keep friction from raising the temperature above 2100 degrees. The rod coils produced are then laid out with certain spacing depending on the rate of cooling needed. Air blowers can increase the cooling, and the use of hoods can decrease it.

The testimony indicated that the rolling mill cost between sixty and one hundred million dollars and a new mill would cost perhaps four times that amount. The testimony also indicated that much smaller operations are not economically feasible. The domestic producer's rolling operation involves one hundred and twenty-five employees and another sixty employees for quality control. The cost of producing one ton of rod from billet was placed at between forty and eighty dollars, depending on efficiency. Testimony at trial indicates that a cold-drawing facility can be established for less than two hundred fifty thousand dollars. Plaintiff's operation seems within that range. A used drawing machine may be purchased for as little as thirty-five thousand dollars. Testimony indicated that three employees are needed to run a cold-drawing machine. Plaintiff operates its Canadian plant around the clock five days per week. Plaintiff's accountant stated that recent figures indicated that the cost of cold-drawing the wire from wire rod was about thirty-six dollars per ton. This figure has not been challenged seriously by defendant, and there was some evidence indicating that the figure is slightly understated if viewed in relation to a more general assessment of cost. In early 1987, the price of wire from Big Point to its affiliate was about two hundred eighty dollars per ton. Plaintiff paid two hundred thirty-five dollars per ton for the Spanish rod during the same period.

There seems to be agreement between the parties that the value added in terms of cost of the drawing process is about fifteen percent. During the relevant period domestic wire rod could be purchased for about three hundred dollars per ton. Also during this period, plaintiff sold wire at a substantially higher price to independent customers than it did internally.

Wire rod cannot be hot-rolled to a sufficiently round state to meet specifications of wire. To those in the steel and wire industries, wire rod and wire are different products. They are also classified differently for tariff purposes. * * *

Plaintiff raises two arguments. It asserts that the wire rod was substantially transformed in Canada into wire so that the product it seeks to import is a product of Canada, not Spain, and therefore is not covered by a VRA. * * *

Defendant argues that the operations performed in Canada were minor and that the court should consider the purpose of the VRA and find that the wire is a product of Spain not Canada. * * *

The basic issue before the court is whether the wire sought to be imported is a product of Spain or of Canada for purposes of enforcing the VRA. The parties agree that the court should make its determination on the basis of whether the wire rod imported from Spain is substantially transformed in Canada. * * *

The court now turns to the fundamental question of whether under generally applicable precedent a substantial transformation of the wire rod from Spain occurs when it becomes wire, so as to make the wire a product of Canada, and thus not subject to VRA restrictions. The basic test cited by the parties was set forth in a drawback case * * * which held that a product would be considered the manufacture or product of the United States if it was transformed into a new and different article "having a distinctive name, character or use." The test has been applied in various situations. Cases giving rise to the most generally cited precedent are those involving country of origin for marking purposes, application of the GSP, and drawback. In addition, the parties have cited two import restriction cases which apply the same basic test. See Ferrostaal, 664 F.Supp. at 537; Cardinal Glove, 4 CIT at 45.

Although all recent cases cite the Anheuser–Busch test, they apply it differently, and modify it somewhat. A name change, for example, is not always considered determinative. * * * Therefore, although it is clear that a name change from "wire rod" to "wire" occurred here, this fact is not necessarily determinative. It may support, however, a finding of substantial transformation, as it did in Ferrostaal. Likewise the change in tariff classification which occurred here * * * is not dispositive, although it also may be supportive. * * *

In recent years the courts have concentrated on change in use or character, finding various subsidiary tests appropriate depending on the situation at hand. An inquiry that is sometimes treated as a type of cross-check or additional factor to be considered in substantial transformation cases is whether significant value is added or costs are incurred by the process at issue. * * * values of between one and eight percent were not found to be significant. 628 F.Supp. at 990. In Uniroyal v. United States, 3 CIT 220, 223–24, 542 F.Supp. 1026, 1029 (1982) aff'd, 702 F.2d 1022 (Fed.Cir.1983) (addition of outer sole did not substantially transform shoe upper under marking laws), no percentage was specified, but the cost of the alleged transformation was deemed insignificant. 542 F.Supp. at 1029–30. In Ferrostaal, on the other hand, a value, attributable to the transformation of at least thirty-six to nearly fifty percent of the value of the heat treated steel, reinforced the court's conclusion that galvanizing and annealing steel constituted a substantial transformation. 664 F.Supp. at 540.

A value added test has appeal in many situations because it brings a common sense approach to a fundamental test that may not be easily applied to some products. The fifteen percent added value figure for the wire standing alone does not pull in either direction, but related concepts, including the amount of labor required to accomplish the change and the capital investment required relative to that required to produce the entire article, are also relevant to a determination of whether the change involves minor processing. Minimal processing is part of the factual background of cases such as Murray, National Juice and Uniroyal, all of which involve findings of no substantial transformation. The differences in capital investment and labor needed in the production of wire rod versus wire are enormous. Comparing only the production of wire from wire rod, versus the production of wire rod from billet, it becomes apparent that the processing performed in Canada is a minor finishing step which may be accomplished easily anywhere with a minimal amount of effort and investment. By itself such analysis may not provide the entire answer as to whether a substantial transformation has taken place, but it should comprise part of the analysis in a case involving the type of products and processes at issue here.

Turning to past precedent, the court observes that cases dealing with substantial transformations are very product specific and are often distinguishable on that basis, rather than by their statutory underpinnings. It is difficult to generalize from cases involving combinations of articles to those that involve processing of a single material. In addition, it is frequently difficult to take concepts applicable to products such as textiles and apply them to combinations of liquids or fabrication of steel articles. To determine whether the goods at hand are substantially transformed for purposes of VRA enforcement, the court should examine cases involving processing of metal objects without combination or assembly operations. Torrington Co. v. United States, 764 F.2d 1563 (1985) is one such case. As indicated, it involved the manufacture of needles in a beneficiary developing country. In the first stage of production of needles, a wire is straightened, cut, beveled, and drawn to form a needle blank. The blank is only useful in the needle-making process. In the next stage, an eye is struck into the needle, a groove is made for thread, and the needle is finished by various processes, including hardening, sharpening, and polishing. The Torrington court found that in order for plaintiff to prevail under the GSP statute, two substantial transformations were necessary; the court found both the first and second stages to be substantial transformations.

The second stage of processing discussed in the Torrington case involved a transformation from producers' to consumers' goods. The Torrington court cited with approval the case of Midwood Indus. v. United States, 64 Cust.Ct. 499, 313 F.Supp. 951 (1970), in which rough forgings of the approximate dimensions of the finished products were found to be substantially transformed after being cut, tapered or trimmed, beveled, bored, and subjected to other finishing processes in order to create pipe flanges and fittings. The producer to consumer goods distinction drawn in Midwood, a marking case, however, was found not determinative as to substantial transformation in shoe construction in another marking case, Uniroyal. Although some of the processes involved here are the same as those involved in the second phase of Torrington, there is no clear change from producers' to consumers' goods. Wire rod is primarily intended for wire production, which, in turn, is primarily intended to be used for making wire mesh for concrete pipe reinforcement.

The processes involved in the first stage of Torrington are closer to the ones involved here. In fact, the Torrington court cited in support of its holding a Treasury Decision involving use of dies to draw plate steel into a cup-shaped rear engine housing. See Torrington, 764 F.2d at 1569 (discussing T.D. 78–400, 12 Cust.B. & Dec. 875 (1978)). Two factors distinguish this aspect of Torrington from the case at hand. First, once the needle blanks were drawn they were fit for only one purpose; the raw material was then destined for one end use. This type of transformation does not occur when wire rod is drawn into wire. The composition of the wire rod determines what uses the wire may have. Although the steel and wire industries may have different names for the products, wire rod and wire may be viewed as different stages of the same product. The difference in stages may be important for tariff purposes but it is not determinative here. In contrast, the Torrington court stated, "the initial wire is a raw material and possesses nothing in its character which indicates either the swages [blanks] or the final product." Torrington at 1568. Here, the wire rod dictates the final form of the finished wire. Second, the court cannot escape the statutory basis of the Torrington opinion. Apart from direct references to the purpose of the GSP already mentioned, the court also noted, " . . . Torrington Portuguesa could do no more than it already does in the production of needles. In these circumstances we think Congress intended the GSP statute to apply." Id. at 1571.

The engine housing decision cited by Torrington also differs from the case at hand. Like the wire to needle blank change, the product was transformed from basic steel into a part with a unique destiny. In addition, the decision noted the involvement of a series of dies. Essentially only two die passes are involved here. The wire emerges stronger and rounder after the passes, but the wire loses a few other advantages, such as greater ductility, in the process. It looks much the same. Its strength characteristic, which is important to its end use, is altered, but the parameters of the strength increase was metallurgically predetermined in the creation of the steel billet and very specifically through the fabrication of the wire rod. Under these circumstances the court does not find a significant change in use or character to have occurred.

The court should also mention here the Ferrostaal case. The hot-dipped galvanizing processes involved there, which involved substantial chemical changes, were different from the cold drawing processes involved here. Although, applying broader analytical concepts, the changes in use and character were not greatly different from those involved here, the value added was significant. It appears that a larger capital investment, as well as possibly significant labor, was required to accomplish the transformation in Ferrostaal. Taken together these differences are sufficient to distinguish Ferrostaal from the case at hand.

Here only the change in name test is clearly met, and such a change has rarely been dispositive. No transformation from producers' to consumers' goods took place; no change from a product suitable for many uses to one with more limited uses took place; no complicated or expensive processing occurred, and only relatively small value was added. Overall, the court views the transformation from wire rod to wire to be minor rather than substantial. Accordingly, the country of origin of the wire must be considered Spain rather than Canada.

Judgment is entered for defendant.

———————

Superior Wire involved wire rod from Spain, imported into Canada as wire rod, and then into the U.S. as wire. There existed a voluntary restraint agreement between Spain and the U.S. that Spain would only import a certain amount of wire rod into the U.S. The GATT rules of origin apply here because, at the time, this entry constituted a transaction between two GATT countries. The GATT uses a combination of substantial transformation, valued added and technical requirements to produce the product.

B. THE GENERALIZED SYSTEM OF PREFERENCES

TORRINGTON CO. v. UNITED STATES

United States Court of Appeals, Third Circuit, 1985.
764 F.2d 1563.

DAVIS, Circuit Judge:

The Government appeals from a decision of the United States Court of International Trade (CIT, Carman, J.), holding that certain industrial sewing-machine needles imported from Portugal by appellee (Torrington) are entitled to enter the United States duty free under the Generalized System of Preferences (GSP). 596 F.Supp. 1083 (1984). Agreeing that the imported articles meet the prerequisite for duty-free entry under the GSP statute (and corresponding Customs regulations), we affirm. * * *

The GSP statute, 19 U.S.C. §§ 2461–2465 (1982), enacted as title V of the Trade Act of 1974, Pub.L. No. 93–618, 88 Stat. 2066, represents the United States' participation in a multinational effort to encourage industrialization in lesser developed countries through international trade.

The Act authorizes the President (subject to certain restrictions) to prepare a list of beneficiary developing countries (BDCs), and to designate products of those countries which are eligible for GSP treatment. 19 U.S.C. § 2462. A designated product imported from a listed country may enter the United States duty free. Id., § 2461. One problem with this general program is that it could be used to allow a noneligible country to conduct minimal finishing operations in a BDC, thereby reaping the benefits of the GSP at the expense of American manufacturers, but without the salutary effect of fostering industrialization in the designated country. Congress therefore provided that products from BDCs must meet certain minimum content requirements in order to qualify for duty-free treatment. To this end, 19 U.S.C. § 2463 provides: (b) The duty free treatment provided under section 2461 of this title with respect to any eligible article shall apply only—* * * (2) If the sum of (A) the cost or value of the materials produced in the beneficiary developing country . . . plus (B) the direct cost of processing operations performed in such beneficiary developing country . . . is not less than 35 percent of the appraised value of such article at the time of its entry in the customs territory of the United States.

Section 2463(b) also authorizes the Secretary of the Treasury to "prescribe such regulations as may be necessary to carry out this subsection."

Under this latter authority, the Customs Service has promulgated regulations interpreting the operative phrase in § 2463(b)(2)(A), supra, "materials produced in the beneficiary developing country." 19 C.F.R. § 10.177(a) (1984) states that the words produced in the beneficiary developing "country" [sic, indicating § 2463(b)(2)(A), supra] refer to constituent materials of which the eligible article is composed which are either: (1) Wholly the growth, product or manufacture of the beneficiary developing country; or (2) Substantially transformed in the beneficiary developing country into a new and different article of commerce.

Thus, if the value of the materials described in § 10.177(a)(1) and (2) plus the direct cost of processing operations performed in the BDC account for 35% of the appraised value of the merchandise, the merchandise is entitled to enter duty-free under 19 U.S.C. §§ 2461 and 2463.

The question in this case is whether industrial sewing-machine needles, which Torrington imported, met these minimum content requirements. In the trial court, the parties stipulated to an agreed statement of facts, which formed the basis of the CIT's decision. These facts establish the following:

The sewing machine needles at issue were exported from Portugal to the United States by Torrington Portuguesa, a manufacturing subsidiary of Torrington. The needles are classifiable under item 672.20 of the Tariff Schedules of the United States (TSUS), "Sewing machines and parts thereof." At the time of the exports, Portugal was designated as a BDC and articles classifiable under item 672.20 were eligible products.

Torrington Portuguesa produced the needles from wire manufactured in a non-BDC and brought into Portugal. On this ground the Customs Service denied duty-free treatment to the needles because they did not incorporate any "materials produced" in Portugal, and the direct cost of producing the needles does not account for 35% of their appraised value. In Customs' view the needles failed to meet the minimum content requirements of 19 U.S.C. § 2463(b). Torrington agrees that if Customs' decision not to include the non-BDC wire in the calculation is correct, then the needles do not satisfy the 35% BDC content requirement. On the other hand, if the other requirements are met, then the 35% BDC content prerequisite is also satisfied.

The parties also stipulated to the process by which Torrington Portuguesa produced the needles from the non-BDC wire. Initially, the wire runs through a swaging machine, which straightens the wire, cuts it to a particular length, bevels one end of the wire segment and draws out the straightened wire to alter its length and circumference at various points. The result is known in the needle industry as a "swaged needle blank," a "needle blank," or merely a "swage." In an exhibit before the trial court, the parties included a linear drawing of a swage. The first quarter of a swage has roughly the same circumference as the wire segment from which it was made; the second quarter narrows from that size down to roughly half that circumference; the other half then extends straight out from the second quarter. At this point, the swage is useful solely in the production of sewing-machine needles with a predetermined blade diameter, though the resulting needle may vary in other respects (e.g., eye placement, eye size, and needle length).

The next process in the production of needles is "striking." Striking involves pressing an eye into the swage, forming a spot to provide clearance for the thread, and bending the swage at a particular point. At this stage, the articles are known as struck blanks. The struck blank enters a mill flash machine which removes excess material around the eye and forms a groove along the length of the needle which carries the thread while the needle is in use. The merchandise is then pointed (i.e., sharpened) and stamped with a logo or other information. Finally, the needles are hardened, tempered, straightened, buffed, polished, cleaned and plated. Upon completion, the needle has a sharp point at the narrow end, a long groove running down three-quarters of its body ending near the point, and an eye somewhere in the groove with an indentation in the groove near the eye.

The parties also jointly detailed Torrington's history of trade in swages. In 1973–74, Torrington Portuguesa twice shipped large amounts of swages to Torrington to correct production imbalances between the two companies. Torrington Portuguesa realized no profit on the exchange, and the transfer was accounted for through appropriate entries in the two companies' inventory and receivables accounts. These are the only transactions in swages in which Torrington (now the only U.S. manufacturer of these needles) has participated.

Based on these facts, the Court of International Trade held the needles to be entitled to duty-free entry under the GSP. As a preliminary matter, the court ruled that, under Customs' regulations, the non-BDC wire must undergo two substantial transformations when it is manufactured into a needle if the value of the wire is to be included in the 35% calculation, and that each of these transformations under 19 C.F.R. § 10.177(a)(2) must result in an "article of commerce." The court stated:

It is not enough to transform substantially the non-BDC constituent materials into the final article, as the material utilized to produce the final article would remain non-BDC material. There must first be a substantial transformation of the non-BDC material into a new and different article of commerce, which becomes "materials produced," and these materials produced in the BDC must then be substantially transformed into a new and different article of commerce. 596 F.Supp. at 1086. The court noted that the Customs Service and Treasury Department have consistently interpreted the regulations to require a dual transformation (i.e., two successive substantial transformations) in order to be eligible for GSP treatment, and that the requirement of a dual transformation advances the GSP's goals by requiring greater work in the BDC and by thwarting manipulation of the GSP (which the content requirements were designed to avoid).

The court then turned to the question of whether the production of needles in Portugal satisfied the dual transformation requirement. The court determined that a substantial transformation occurs if a manufacturing process results in an article of commerce, which has a distinctive name, character, or use. 596 F.Supp. at 1086, (citing Texas Instruments, Inc. v. United States, 681 F.2d 778, 782 (CCPA 1982)). Here, the court held, the swaging process constitutes an initial transformation, and the succeeding processes constitute the second. The swage blanks, the court said, have a distinctive name, a different character from the wire segments from which they are made, and a specific use. Moreover, the swages are "articles of commerce" because, on the two documented occasions set forth in the stipulations, they have been the object of large transactions. Thus, the court concluded that the swaged needle blanks are constituent materials of which the needles are made, and their value (which includes the value of the non-BDC wire) should be included in the 35% value added calculation.

* * *

THE DUAL TRANSFORMATION REQUIREMENT.

The parties disagree whether the GSP statute and regulations mandate a dual transformation between raw material and finished product if the latter is to be granted duty-free entry. Torrington contends that its transformation of the non-BDC wire into sewing machine needles—even if considered only a single transformation—was in itself sufficient. The Government counters that a single transformation is insufficient to change the non-BDC wire into a material "produced in the developing country" which, if used in the BDC, may then be considered in the BDC-content evaluation.

Like the CIT, we think that the statutory language of 19 U.S.C. § 2463(b) leads to the Government's position. Congress authorized the Customs Service to consider the "cost or value of materials produced" in the BDC. The parties agree that the wire clearly was not a BDC product. As wire, therefore, it may not be considered a BDC material. However, if Torrington Portuguesa transformed the wire into an intermediate article of commerce, then the intermediate product would be an article produced in the BDC, and the value of that product (including the contribution of the wire to the value of that intermediate product) would be included.

The legislative history of § 2463 supports this reading. Congress used the content requirement to protect the GSP program from untoward manipulation:

The percentage . . . assure[s] that, to the maximum extent possible, the preferences provide benefits to developing countries without stimulating the development of "pass-through" operations the major benefit of which accrues to enterprises in developed countries. H.Rep. No. 571, supra, at 86–87. In the absence of a dual transformation requirement, developed countries could establish a BDC as a base to complete manufacture of goods, which have already undergone extensive processing. The single substantial transformation would qualify the resulting article for GSP treatment, with the non-BDC country reaping the benefit of duty-free treatment for goods, which it essentially produced. This flouts Congress' expressed intention to confer the benefits of the GSP fully on the BDC and to avoid conferring duty-free status on the products of a "pass-through" operation.

Moreover, Torrington's contentions, if accepted, would tend to render the 35% requirement a nullity. If only a single transformation were necessary, then the "material produced" in the BDC as a result of this transformation would be the imported product itself. Customs would then face the problem of determining how much of the appraised value of the import resulted from materials produced in the BDC, when the only material produced was the import. The result would always be 100% since the product would always be a constituent material of itself. Congress clearly envisaged some way of separating the final product from its constituent materials, and the dual transformation requirement achieves this end.

Our predecessor court's ruling in Texas Instruments, supra, supports this reading of the statute, although the dual transformation requirement was not expressly considered as a separate issue. Texas Instruments concerned cue modules for cameras composed primarily of integrated circuits, a photo-diode, a capacitor and a resistor. The court ruled that these cue modules could enter the United States duty-free under the GSP even though the silicon slices which ultimately went into the integrated circuits and photodiode came originally from the United States. The issue on which the court focused its attention was whether the assembly of the component parts into a cue module could in itself constitute a substantial transformation from one product to another. The court ruled in the affirmative, and clearly indicated that it considered this assembly to be the second substantial transformation, the first having been satisfied when the silicon slices were manufactured into separate, packaged silicon chips. 681 F.2d at 783–84.

* * *

The swages—substantial transformation into a new and different article of commerce.

A. In Texas Instruments, supra, the Court of Customs and Patent Appeals adopted the rule, well-established in other areas of customs jurisprudence, that a substantial transformation occurs when an article emerges from a manufacturing process with a name, character, or use which differs from those of the original material subjected to the process.

681 F.2d at 782; cf. Anheuser–Busch Brewing Assn. v. United States, 207 U.S. 556, 28 S.Ct. 204, 52 L.Ed. 336 (1908). The CIT determined here that this substantial transformation test was satisfied when Torrington Portuguesa manufactured needle swages from the wire.

The parties' stipulations sustain the CIT's conclusion. Two critical manufacturing steps separate three items (wire, swage and needle) each of which is markedly different from the others. The initial wire is a raw material and possesses nothing in its character, which indicates either the swages or the final product. The intermediate articles—the swages— have a definite size and shape, which renders them suitable for further manufacturing into needles with various capabilities. At that phase of the production process the material, which emerges is more refined, possesses attributes more specifically applicable to a given use, and has lost the identifying characteristics of its constituent material. It is a new and different article.

This conclusion finds support in prior cases and administrative decisions, which have considered whether a given manufacturing process entails a substantial transformation from one article to another. Manufacturing processes often differ in detail, but we must consider these differences in light of the GSP's fundamental purpose of promoting industrialization in lesser developed countries. Trivial differences in manufacturing processes or techniques will not affect the overall benefit conferred upon the BDCs from the manufacturing conducted in those countries.

A prime source of information in this area of Customs jurisprudence is T.D. 78–400, 12 Cust.B. & Dec. 875 (1978), in which the Treasury Department considered the effect of certain processes in the manufacture of specific types of electric motors for GSP purposes. In the production of a 600 series d.c. motor the manufacturer produced the rear housing assembly in a BDC from flat steel stock of U.S. origin. The manufacturer drew the steel stock through a series of dies to form the cup-shaped motor part. The Department was of the opinion that "the flat steel stock which is drawn into the cup-shaped rear housing is a substantially transformed constituent material, and the entire cost of its component is includable in the costs of materials in computing the 35– per-cent criterion." Id., 12 Cust.B. & Dec. at 676. The Customs Service therefore included the value of this rear housing—which included the value of "its component" (the steel stock)—in the content evaluation. Throughout T.D. 78–400, it was held that various processes, which involved the stamping, dying or molding of metal from a formless article into a shaped component constituted a substantial transformation.

The process by which Torrington Portuguesa formed the swage needle blanks is very similar. A swage is similar to a die and presses metal into a given shape. This new shape results in a product with a new use, a given name different from its component article, and with special characteristics.

Judicial precedent is comparable. For example, in United States v. Pittsburgh Plate Glass Co., 44 C.C.P.A. (Customs) 110 (1957), the court ruled that certain glass louvers were properly classifiable as "manufactures of glass" rather than as plate glass. The court specifically noted that to be a manufacture, the glass must have a different name, character or use from the original material. Id. at 116. The court concluded:

The imported glass louvers were no longer merely sheet glass. . . . They had a new name . . . or several names by all of which the trade witnesses referred to them. . . . The new characteristics were two webbered, round, smooth edges and a specific size. The new use was as jalousie louvers, at least predominantly. As such they were completely manufactured articles. Id. Comparably, the swages in this case were no longer wire; they had a new name by which they were known in the trade; they had new characteristics, including a new shape and size; they had a specific use in the production of needles. "As such they were completely manufactured articles." Id.

B. The CIT also concluded correctly that the swages were "articles of commerce." The Government attacks this determination principally by arguing that the two incidents in which Torrington Portuguesa transferred swages to Torrington in this country should not count in deciding whether swages are articles of commerce. We note initially that the phrase "article of commerce" is found only in the regulation, not in the GSP statute, and therefore we interpret the "of commerce" requirement of the regulation in light of the statute's purpose to further BDC industrialization. By emphasizing that the article must be "of commerce," the Customs regulation imposes the requirement that the "new and different" product be commercially recognizable as a different article, i.e., that the "new and different" article be readily susceptible of trade, and be an item that persons might well wish to buy and acquire for their own purposes of consumption or production.

Two administrative decisions concerning GSP treatment for imported chemicals are consonant with this view. In T.D. 77–273, 11 Cust.B. & Dec. 551 (1977), the Treasury Department concluded that an intermediate chemical (dichloro) involved in the production of technical atrazine does not satisfy the dual substantial transformation requirement. The agency reached this conclusion because (1) the process used to manufacture the technical atrazine is essentially a continuous process, (2) dichloro is not a chemical that is generally bought and sold, and (3) the dichloro resulting in the first step of the Israeli manufacture of technical atrazine would have to be refined (the impurities removed) in order to make shipping practicable. Id., 11 Cust.B. & Dec. at 553–54. In other words, the dichloro was not the result of a first substantial transformation because it was not an "article of commerce," even though the dichloro differed chemically both from the constituent articles from which it was made and the final article, technical atrazine. In sharp contrast, the Customs Service ruled in C.S.D. 79–311, 13 Cust.B. & Dec. 1463 (1979), that another chemical process did include a "substantially transformed constituent material within the meaning of [19 C.F.R. § 10.177(a)(2)]." Id. The Customs Service reasoned:

The evidence includes examples where the product's characterization, preparation process, and uses are enumerated in chemical reference sources. There is a patent on a process by which this product is prepared. A copy of a letter was produced in which an unrelated party indicated willingness to produce and sell this product at a specific price. Id., 13 Cust.B. & Dec. at 1463–64.

Our conclusion is that an "article of commerce"—for the purposes of the pertinent Customs regulation—is one that is ready to be put into a stream of commerce, but need not have actually been bought-and-sold, or actually traded, in the past. Indeed, by requiring proof of actual arms-length transactions by unrelated parties, the Government implies that a new article (never before produced) can never be an article of commerce entitled to GSP treatment—a result not envisaged by Congress. In this instance, we agree with the CIT that the transfer of over four million swaged needle blanks from Torrington Portuguesa to Torrington is an adequate showing that swaged needle blanks are articles of commerce. There is no reason to believe that those articles could and would not be sold to other manufacturers of needles who wanted to purchase them for further manufacture into the final product. * * *

The needles—substantial transformation into a new and different article.

The Government urges that, even if the production of swages from wire constitutes a substantial transformation, the manufacture of the needles from the swages does not. We are referred to paragraph 13 of the parties' stipulations, in which they note that swages "are dedicated for use solely as sewing machine needles with a predetermined blade diameter.... In the majority of cases, a particular type of swaged needle blank becomes only a single particular type of needle." The Government concludes from this that the swages are actually unfinished needles, and do not undergo a substantial transformation into a new article in order to reach their final form. Torrington, also reading from the stipulations, notes that the swages lack the key characteristics of a needle since they have no points or eyes, and that a given swage can be processed into needles with different properties, e.g., eye size.

The Government relies for its position that swages are merely unfinished needles on cases such as Avins Industrial Products Co. v. United States, 515 F.2d 782, 62 C.C.P.A. 83 (1975) and Lee Enterprises, Inc. v. United States, 84 Cust.Ct. 208 (1980). These decisions concern the proper classification of imports under the rule that an item in the TSUS covers the article mentioned in finished or unfinished form. The courts ruled that a product is an unfinished form of an article if the product has been manufactured to the point where it is dedicated solely to the manufacture of that article. Avins, supra, 515 F.2d at 783. However, the Government's reliance on these cases is not pertinent. The proper tariff classification is not dispositive of whether the manufacturing process necessary to complete an article constitutes a substantial transformation from the original material to the final product. Belcrest Linens, supra, 741 F.2d at 1373. Instead, we look—keeping in mind the GSP's fundamental purpose of fostering industrialization in BDCs—to the actual manufacturing process by which the intermediate article becomes the final product.

In Midwood Industries v. United States, 64 Cust.Ct. 499, 313 F.Supp. 951 (1970), the Customs Court (now the CIT) determined that forgings for flanges could enter the United States without permanent country-of-origin markings because the importer substantially transformed the forgings in the United States into pipe. In one case, the importer cut the edges; tapered, beveled and bored the ends; and removed die lines and other imperfections from the surface of the final article. 313 F.Supp. at 955. The court also heard testimony that, in their imported state, the forgings are useless unless processed into the final flange. Id. at 955–56. The decision in that case was that the importer's efforts resulted in a substantial transformation from the rough forgings into "different articles having a new name, character and use." Id. at 957. The court noted that the "imports were producers' goods, and the flanges are consumers' goods," and held: "While it may be true, as some of the testimony of record indicates, that some of the imported forgings are made as close to the dimensions of the ultimate finished form as possible, they, nevertheless, remain forgings unless and until converted by some manufacturer into consumers' goods." Id.

The production of needles from swages is a similar process. The swages are bored (to form an eye), the ridge is carved, and the needle is pointed, cleaned, hardened, plated, etc. The swage is also the approximate size necessary to create the final needle, but, like the forgings in Midwood, they are producers' goods. The final needles are consumers' goods. The production of needles from swages is clearly a significant manufacturing process, and not a mere "pass-through" operation as the Government apparently contends. Portugal certainly reaps the benefit of this manufacturing process; indeed, short of manufacturing the wire itself, Torrington Portuguesa could do no more than it already does in the production of needles. In these circumstances, we think that Congress intended the GSP statute to apply.

For these reasons, we conclude: (1) that a dual substantial transformation in a BDC is a prerequisite for GSP treatment under the GSP statute and Customs regulations, (2) that the swages which Torrington Portuguesa produced are a separate, intermediate "article of commerce," and (3) that the industrial sewing-machine needles imported by Torrington are entitled to duty-free entry. The decision appealed from is therefore affirmed. AFFIRMED. * * *

The Rules of Origin can have a substantial effect on the amount of the tariff. For example, assume a product emanating from a GSP country fails to meet the origin criteria for the GSP. If the true country of origin is a Category 2 or Category 1–General tariff rate will be increased accordingly. As can be seen from the application of the rules in *Superior Wire* and *Torrington*, the analysis is very fact intensive. An importer has the right to seek a Letter Ruling from the U.S. Customs Service under the authority of 19. C.F.R. § 177.9 (c). This procedure can help to ensure that the Customs Service will agree with the importers declaration of origin.

C. THE NAFTA RULES OF ORIGIN

IMPLEMENTING THE NAFTA RULES OF ORIGIN: ARE THE PARTIES HELPING OR HURTING FREE TRADE?

David A. Gantz

12 Ariz. J. Int'l & Comp. L. 367 (1995).

* * *

[T]he NAFTA preferential rules of origin * * * are designed to assure that only goods actually produced within the region, with a substantial regional materials and/or fabrication content, enjoy the benefits of preferential tariff treatment within North America. These highly complex rules, and the uniform customs regulations which implement them, are emerging as significant non-tariff barriers, obstacles to establishing free trade in the region and, ultimately, the Western Hemisphere.
* * *

The NAFTA preferential rules of origin are among the provisions of the agreement, which are most likely to have a significant impact on both regional and non-regional manufacturing. It is these rules, which comprise more than 190 pages of NAFTA's text, that largely determine which goods benefit from the major feature of NAFTA; to wit, a reduced duty or duty-free intra-regional trade. A product classified as originating in North America enjoys NAFTA's preferential tariff rates. A product which does not qualify as "originating goods" under art. 401, even if produced in North America, remains subject to each country's external or "most favored nation" ("MFN") tariffs. Some products, such as textiles, may be subject to quantitative restrictions (quotas) as well. These MFN tariffs are the same tariffs that would be applicable if the product were produced outside North America. Consider televisions: as noted earlier, color televisions imported from Mexico which meet the NAFTA rules of origin enter the United States duty-free; a five percent U.S. duty applies to all televisions made in the region which do not meet the NAFTA rules, as well as all televisions from countries outside NAFTA, or automobiles: NAFTA-origin automobiles trade duty free, while other automobiles are dutiable at 2.5%.

Why were preferential rules of origin necessary for NAFTA? Concern arose that NAFTA's removal of all intra-regional duties, without the inclusion of stiff rules of origin, would allow Mexico, as the low labor cost member of NAFTA, to serve as an "export platform," where foreign owned multinational corporations could establish final assembly ("screw-driver") facilities which import parts and components from Asia or elsewhere, and then assemble them using low-cost Mexican labor. This scheme would evade the U.S. duties regularly applied to the product when it is imported directly from outside the North American region. Among others, the U.S. textile, footwear, electronics, auto, and auto parts industries expressed concerns about such potential "unfair" competition throughout the NAFTA negotiations. Many such firms, and their supporters in Congress, probably would not have supported NAFTA in the absence of a built in mechanism, which prevent screwdriver facilities from exploiting this possible loophole.

A major result of this policy is the restriction of NAFTA preferences to true manufacturing operations in the region. Concomitantly, this encourages regional manufacturers to utilize regionally-produced materials and components, rather than those imported from outside North America.

* * *

In some instances, the country of origin for a product is obvious, whether applying a general or preferential rule. Products in this category include live animals born and raised in a country; fish caught in a country's rivers or within its exclusive economic zone, or taken from the high seas by a country's vessels; products made entirely from such animals or fish; plant and plant products harvested or gathered in a single country; mineral goods extracted from the territory, soil, subsoil, airspace, territorial waters, sea-bed or from beneath the sea-bed of a country; and manufactured goods where all of the materials and components are produced in the country and "do not contain constituents obtained from any other country and which have not undergone processing in any other country at any state of production."

These are the easy cases. The more difficult, and more common situation occurs when particular parts of a product, often in the form of raw materials or components, are from more than one country. This also occurs when the principal manufacturing operation takes place in a country that is not the source of the principal materials and components. This mixing of component parts, which originate in more than one nation, occurs most often with manufactured products. In such instances, any nation, which produced a component part used to manufacture the final product, or where final assembly or manufacture takes place, may arguably be designated as the country of origin. Clearly, an objective means must be found for making such determinations, particularly when one of the potential countries or origin is a NAFTA Party, as to whose goods are subject to preferential treatment, when the other or others is not. * * *

The NAFTA Rule of Origin defines "Originating Goods," a definition similar to and derived from rules of origin found in the Canada—U.S. Free Trade Agreement ("FTA"). It reads as follows:

Except as otherwise provided in this Chapter, a good shall originate in the territory of a Party where: (a) the good is wholly obtained or produced entirely in the territory of one or more of the Parties ... (b) each of the non-originating materials used in the production of the good undergoes an applicable change in tariff classification set out in Annex 401 as a result of production occurring entirely in the territory of one or more of the Parties, or the good otherwise satisfied the applicable requirements of that Annex where no change in tariff classification is required, and the good satisfies all other applicable requirements of this Chapter; (c) the good is produced entirely in the territory of one or more of the Parties exclusively from originating materials; or (d) except for a good provided for in Chapters 61 through 63 of the Harmonized System [clothing, apparel and certain other textile articles], the good is produced entirely in the territory of one or more of the Parties but one or more of the non-originating materials provided for as parts under the Harmonized System that are used in the production of the good does not undergo a change in tariff classification because (i) the good was imported into the territory of a Party in an unassembled or a disassembled form but was classified as an assembled good ... , or (ii) the heading for the good provides for and specifically describes both the good itself and its parts and is not further subdivided into subheadings, or the subheading for the good provides for and specifically describes both the good itself and its parts, provided that the regional value content of the good, determined in accordance with Article 402, is not less than 60 percent where the transaction value method is used, or is not less than 50 percent where the net cost method is used, and that the good satisfies all other applicable requirements of this Chapter.

This definition delineates the identifiable circumstances under which a good originates in a NAFTA country.

a. A designation of NAFTA origin occurs when a good is wholly obtained or produced in the territory of one or several of the parties (delineated in a, above) or is produced entirely in the territory of one or more of the parties exclusively from materials originating in the region (delineated in c, above). As noted earlier, the first category includes mined minerals, plants and plant products, animals and fish, which are taken from the land, soil, or water of a particular country or from the region. The second incorporates articles manufactured or processed from locally grown or produced resources, e.g., flour milled from North American wheat or copper wire drawn in North America from copper ingots derived from copper mined in North America.

b. Where all materials and components are not obtained in the region, NAFTA normally uses the international (non-preferential) Harmonized Tariff System ("HTS") rule of origin (b, above). Under this "tariff shift" rule, when a change in tariff category occurs, the country where that shift occurs is the country of origin. This most commonly occurs when a manufacturing process results in a product that is assigned a tariff category different from the tariff category of the new materials from outside the region (non-originating "material"). The

NAFTA tariff change rule has been relaxed compared to the FTA, which required that all of the parts and components used in manufacturing a product be imported under a different tariff category than the category in which the final product would be classified. NAFTA benefits from a de minimis exception, in which components comprising up to seven percent of the total transaction value of the product need not experience a shift in its tariff category. This permits the use of minor inputs from a third country without causing the finished product to lose the benefits conferred by NAFTA. However, as indicated below, this de minimis exception complicates the corroboration process for manufacturers, importers and customs authorities alike. Moreover, the production process that results in the tariff change must have occurred entirely in the territory of one or more of the NAFTA parties.

This NAFTA tariff shift rule is not conceptually different from the "substantial transformation" approach. This is so because, under the Harmonized Tariff System, a change in tariff classification usually reflects a manufacturing process that causes the shift in tariff category. However, the tariff shift approach has the advantage of predictability; if the tariff classifications of the imported parts and materials and of the finished products, respectively, are accurately determined, and the tariff classification actually shifts as required, the country of origin becomes the country where the tariff shift occurred. With substantial transformation, as noted earlier, each determination must be made on a case-by-case basis, subjecting the good and its owners to the unpredictability and delays of an administrative process which relies to a degree upon subjective criteria when making a determination.

To be considered as originating in the region, the finished product seeking NAFTA origin status must, as noted above, be produced from materials or components that entered the region under a different tariff classification from the finished product. For example, ceramic products classified under chapter 69, headings 6901–6914, of the HTS (e.g., bathtubs, classified under heading 6910), qualify as having regional origin if all the material inputs entered the region under a different chapter, e.g., Kaolin (a type of clay) under heading 2507.

c.   Products which cannot meet the change in tariff classification criterion may nevertheless qualify for regional origin if the product is classified as an assembled good or the applicable tariff heading (four digit category) provides for both the product and its parts without further subdivision and, for both possibilities, the regional value (defined here as the value attributable to materials or manufacturing operations in any of the NAFTA countries) is not less than sixty percent of the total value, when using the transaction value method, or fifty percent of the total cost, when using the net cost method.

d.   However in certain instances, there is a requirement that a product must be demonstrated to contain a specific percentage of regional value content (e.g., sixty percent or fifty percent) in order to qualify for NAFTA tariff preferences. For example, with footwear (HTS headings 6401–6406), there must be a change of tariff heading plus a showing that there is a "regional value content" of not less than fifty-five percent calculated under the net cost method. Likewise, rail locomotives (HTS headings 8601–8606) must show a change in tariff classification from any other heading or a regional value content of sixty percent where the transaction value method is used or fifty percent where the net cost method is used. Automobiles and their engines must demonstrate a regional value content of 62.5% as of the year 2002.

e. Finally, in still other situations, inclusion of a specific regionally produced component or material in the final product controls the designation of origin. For example, a color television receiver with a screen size of more than fourteen inches originates in the NAFTA region only if the color picture tube originates in North American. For a color television receiver with a screen size of fourteen inches or less, all of the printed circuit boards and the tuner must originate within the region. Of course, where a specific component must be of North American origin that component, in turn, must meet the rule of origin specified for it in Annex 401. * * *

In most circumstances where NAFTA requires a determination of regional value content, the calculations may be accomplished using one of two methods. Regional value content is determined by either the "net cost" method, which aggregates the costs of the various inputs, or the "transaction value" method, which begins with the customs or transaction value of the finished products. Under both methods, the non-regional materials inputs are subtracted out. Since the transaction value method usually results in a higher regional content, different minimum percentages are normally specified. Whenever the use of either is permitted, the exporter may use the most favorable methodology. For example, assume that the net cost (NC) of a widget is 100. The transaction value (TV), which is usually the export price to an unrelated purchaser, is 120 and the value of non-originating materials imported from outside the region (VNM) is sixty. Under the transaction value method, the regional value content (RVC) is fifty percent [since RVC = (TV—VNM)/TV x NC = (120—60)/120 x 100 = 50]. Under the net cost (NC) method, the RVC is forty percent [since RVC = (NC—VNM)/NC x NC = (100—60)/100 x 100 = 40]. Here, as in most instances, the transaction value method produces a larger regional value content.

The "net cost" calculations include most normal manufacturing costs, such as materials, labor and overhead, but exclude some items which would be included in calculating the fully allocated cost of production in most accounting systems. Exclusions include expenditures for sales promotion and marketing, after-sales service costs, royalties paid, shipping and packing costs, and non-allowable interest costs that are included in total costs.

"Transaction value" is "the price of a good actually paid or payable for a good or material" to the producer, adjusted in accordance with the GATT Customs Valuation Code and the WTO Customs Valuation Agreement. The transaction value methodology for determining regional value added is usually simpler for manufacturers, importers and customs officials than calculating net cost. The WTO Customs Valuation Agreement provides a generally accepted means for calculating the transaction value of a product. In the vast majority of cases, it is the export value. With the transaction value method, only the value of the non-originating materials must also be calculated; a production cost analysis with all its complexities is normally not required. * * *

Fifth and finally, special rules for the regional value-added calculations also apply to trade in automotive goods. There, the net cost method must be used. In such calculations, non-regional originating goods must use the customs value as the basis for the calculation in order to prevent distortions which result from transfer prices that do not reflect arms-length purchases. Also, when major components, such as the engine, the transmission, and the fuel pump, are assembled within the region, the parts used in that component are factored directly into the regional value content calculations for the completed automobile. This means that non-originating parts and materials used to produce these major components are not counted toward the regional content requirements.

Auto manufacturers, when calculating regional value, may average their calculations across their fiscal/accounting years. Manufacturers benefit from the flexibility of this rule because it permits them to deal with changes in their sources for major parts and materials that affect the finished product's regional content calculations. The flexibility allowed under this rule also aids manufacturers where they use multiple sources, with some being within North America and others being outside of the NAFTA region, for the same parts and components.

In making regional value content calculations, the Uniform Regulations specify that fungible materials may be assigned a country of origin based on any acceptable inventory management method. Packing materials and containers for sale, as well as spare parts or tools delivered with the goods, are generally exempt from the restrictions requiring all components to undergo a change in tariff classification. However, they may be included in regional value calculations. Containers for shipment are excluded in both instances. * * *

As one example in the NAFTA agreement, automotive parts have a local value content requirement of 62.5 percent. In order for an automobile to be said to be a product of Mexico, 65 percent of the goods value must have been added while in Mexico. These percentages are subject of great negotiation, stemming from the fear that exists of Japan using Mexico as a springboard to send cars up to the U.S. free of tariff.

SECTION 7.3 VALUATION OF GOODS & SPECIAL ARRANGEMENTS

A. VALUATION OF GOODS

The tariff amount is obtained by multiplying the tariff rate by the dutiable value of the goods. The tariff rate is obtained by categorizing the country and classifying the product, see the materials supra. The next step in the process is in determining the dutiable value. Dutiable value begins with establishing the fair market value of the imported goods adjusted by certain costs of sale and of carriage. In determining what constitutes fair market value, the relationship between the Buyer and the Seller must be examined.

Fair market value is the amount at which a willing seller is willing to sell and a willing buyer is willing to buy, neither being under a compulsion to buy or sell, and each knowing all relevant facts. In a transaction between an unrelated buyer and seller, the price bargained for between the parties, an amount usually known as the *transaction price*, is accepted as the fair market value. However, in cases where the Buyer and Seller are related, *e.g.*, where the parent sells to a subsidiary, the transaction price is not as readily accepted as the fair market value.

ORBISPHERE CORP. v. UNITED STATES

United States Court of International Trade, 1989.
726 F.Supp. 1344.

* * *

Opinion

MUSGRAVE, Judge.

The primary issue in this case is whether, in valuing plaintiff's products for purposes of customs duties, the Customs Service properly used as its measure of value the "transaction value" of the imported merchandise, or should instead have used the "deductive value" of the merchandise as requested by the plaintiff here. The Court has jurisdiction under 28 U.S.C. s 1581(a), and finds that plaintiff has presented ample evidence to overcome the presumption of correctness of Customs' valuation. The proper basis for valuation of the merchandise is its "deductive value" as claimed by plaintiff. * * *

Plaintiff Orbisphere Corp. (Orbisphere) sells scientific devices that detect, measure, and analyze oxygen and other gases. These devices are manufactured in Switzerland by Orbisphere Laboratories (Orbisphere Labs), a subsidiary of Orbisphere. Both Orbisphere and Orbisphere Labs are incorporated in Delaware. The operation's administrative offices are in Geneva and most of its executive personnel are based there. Orbisphere maintains four sales offices in the United States—in Emerson, New Jersey; Houston, Texas; Mount Prospect, Illinois; and Huntington Beach, California.

At the time of the transactions at issue, sales orders for the analyzers were solicited from U.S. customers by Orbisphere sales staff working at the four U.S. sales offices. Once received, the orders are forwarded to the New Jersey office, which then forwarded the order to the Orbisphere Labs Geneva office where the ordered item was manufactured. The completed item was then shipped from Geneva to the New Jersey office where the merchandise was unpacked, inspected, adjusted if necessary, repacked in a different container, and then shipped to the U.S. purchaser. Invoices were sent to the purchaser from the New Jersey office which office also received payment from the customer and deposited the payment in the company's U.S. bank account. All revenues from these sales in excess of the salaries and other costs attributable to the U.S. sales offices were ultimately remitted to the Geneva office; the U.S. offices, therefore, were "cost centers", not "profit centers".

The prices of products sold by Orbisphere were determined by the Geneva office, in consultation with staff from the American offices, and were distributed in the form of a price list prepared by the Geneva office covering all items produced by Orbisphere. The local U.S. sales offices had no discretion to vary these prices in concluding sales with their customers. The Geneva office also established the terms and conditions of sale of Orbisphere products, and the U.S. sales offices had no authority to vary these terms and conditions either. * * *

The merchandise at issue in this case comprises several oxygen analyzing apparatuses and their accessories manufactured by Plaintiff at its Geneva facility and imported into the United States in late 1985 and 1986. The Customs Service appraised the items for customs purposes on the basis of "transaction value" pursuant to section 402(a) of the Tariff Act of 1930, as amended by the Trade Agreements Act of 1979 (19 U.S.C. s 1401a (b)). Plaintiff contests this appraisal, and contends here that the items should instead be valued on the basis of "deductive value" under section 402(d) of the above act as amended (19 U.S.C. s 1401a(d)). Defendant argues that the items were properly valued based on "transaction value", and in addition asserts two counterclaims alleging that upward adjustments should be made to the appraisals of several of the items. * * *

In support of the Customs Service's use of transaction value for appraising the merchandise in this case, the defendant argues that the sales of the products were consummated not by the U.S. sales offices, but, rather, by the Geneva office directly with the U.S. purchasers. Consequently, argues the defendant, the merchandise was sold by and from the Geneva office for export to the United States, and was therefore correctly appraised on the basis of transaction value under 19 U.S.C. s 1401a(b).

Section 1401a(a) provides that (1) ... imported merchandise shall be appraised, for purposes of this chapter, on the basis of the following: (A) The transaction value provided for under subsection (b) of this section. (B) The transaction value of identical merchandise.... (C) The transaction value of similar merchandise ... if the value referred to in subparagraph (B) cannot be determined. (D) The deductive value provided for under subsection (d) of this section, if the value referred to in subparagraph (C) cannot be determined.... The parties have framed their dispute in this case as a contest over whether the applicable standard for appraisal is the transaction value of the merchandise under subparagraph (A), or the deductive value under subparagraph (D).

Subsection (b) of this section defines "transaction value" as the price actually paid or payable for the merchandise when sold for exportation to the United States, plus amounts equal to—(A) the packing costs incurred by the buyer with respect to the imported merchandise; (B) any selling commission incurred by the buyer with respect to the imported merchandise; (C) the value, apportioned as appropriate, of any assist; (D) any royalty or license fee related to the merchandise that the buyer is required to pay, directly or indirectly, as a condition of the sale of the imported merchandise for exportation to the United States; and (E) the proceeds of any subsequent resale, disposal, or use of the imported merchandise that accrue, directly or indirectly, to the seller. This subsection provides further that the transaction value shall be augmented by the items in paragraphs (A) through (E) above only to the extent that the amount in such a paragraph: (I) is not otherwise included within the price paid or actually payable; and (ii) is based on sufficient information. If sufficient information is not available with respect to one of these amounts, then the transaction value of the product shall be treated as undeterminable, and the product must be valued under one of the alternative bases provided in section 1401a.

In the context of the present controversy, the most critical language in subsection (b) is that defining "transaction value" as the price paid or payable for the merchandise "when sold for export to the United States". The defendant argues that the sales in this case were concluded by Orbisphere's Geneva office directly with the purchasers in the United States. This is so, the defendant claims, because all of Orbisphere's major business decisions were made from the Geneva office by the company's executive personnel, all of whom were based at that office. The Geneva office set the prices at which Orbisphere's products were offered for sale and the terms and conditions governing the sale contracts. The U.S. sales offices, after receiving an order, transmitted to the Geneva office a telex describing the items ordered and stating, "Please accept the following order(s)". After manufacturing the items, the Geneva office shipped the items to the New Jersey office for delivery to the U.S. customer, and paid whatever costs were incurred by the company in transporting the items from Switzerland to New Jersey. When final payment for the items was received by the New Jersey office, these sums were remitted from Orbisphere's U.S. bank account to the Geneva office, less amounts necessary to meet the operating expenses and overhead costs of the U.S. offices.

Additionally, the defendant argues that the commercial practice of Orbisphere in these transactions was accurately stated in the terms printed on the pre-1984 invoices, namely, that all shipments were F.O.B. Geneva, that the risk of loss of the goods shifted to the buyer at that location and, most importantly, that all orders received by the U.S. sales offices were acceptable only by, and at the sole discretion of, the Geneva office. The defendant contends that the changes made in these terms on Orbisphere's invoices after 1983 were merely changes in form, and that the actual practice of the company in later transactions remained the same as that described in the earlier invoices. The U.S. sales, argues the defendant, were always accepted by, indeed could only be accepted by, the Geneva office, and were thus sales "for export to the United States" within the meaning of section 1401a(b).

The plaintiff flatly contradicts the defendant's primary argument and insists that it was the New Jersey office that accepted the orders placed with Orbisphere by customers in the United States. Plaintiff argues further that the ordered goods were shipped from Switzerland F.O.B. New Jersey, and that Orbisphere bore the cost of insuring, and the risk of loss of, the goods during their trans-Atlantic shipment. On the basis of this argument, the plaintiff contends that the sales of the items at issue here were concluded in the United States, and that they were therefore not sales "for export to the United States" as required to make possible transaction value appraisal under section 1401a(b). The plaintiff argues that instead of transaction value, the "deductive value" of the goods is the proper basis for their valuation under section 1401a(d).

"Deductive value" is defined in this section as: . . . (d)(2)(A) . . . whichever of the following prices (as adjusted under paragraph (3)) is appropriate depending upon when and in what condition the merchandise concerned is sold in the United States: (I) If the merchandise concerned is sold in the condition as imported at or about the date of importation of the merchandise being appraised, the price is the unit price at which the merchandise concerned is sold in the greatest aggregate quantity at or about such date. (ii) If the merchandise concerned is sold in the condition as imported but not sold at or about the date of importation of the merchandise being appraised, the price is the unit price at which the merchandise concerned is sold in the greatest aggregate quantity after the date of importation of the merchandise being appraised but before the close of the 90th day after the date of such importation. (iii) If the merchandise concerned was not sold in the condition as imported and not sold before the close of the 90th day after the date of importation of the merchandise being appraised, the price is the unit price at which the merchandise being appraised, after further processing, is sold in the greatest aggregate quantity before the 190th day after the date of such importation. . . . * * *

Plaintiff's argument is in essence that given this scenario the shipments of the products from the Geneva factory to the New Jersey office were merely movements of the goods "from one warehouse to another" * * * that the actual sales were concluded wholly within the United States. * * *

The resolution of this controversy depends substantially upon where the sales of the merchandise are deemed to have occurred. * * *

In the case United States v. Massce & Co., et al., 21 CCPA 54, CAD 3568, the Court of Customs and Patent Appeals, predecessor to the current Court of Appeals for the Federal Circuit, was presented with facts similar to those in the present case. * * *

On the basis of these facts in Massce, the Court of Customs and Patent Appeals upheld the ruling of the trial court that "[e]very element of a United States contract of sale is established by this method of doing business." Deductively, then, there were no sales "for exportation to the United States"; it was therefore not possible to utilize export (or correspondingly, here, "transaction") value appraisal; and the correct measure of value thus was the United States (here, "deductive") value of the merchandise. Because the present case involves statutes, legal issues, and facts similar to those in Massce, the doctrine of stare decisis would seem to require a similar outcome here. In fact such an outcome seems to be required even a fortiori here: while the incorporation status of the plaintiffs in Massce is not wholly clear from that decision, in the present case both Orbisphere and Orbisphere Labs were American corporations, incorporated in Delaware, at the time of the sales at issue; moreover, while it is also unclear what, if any, terms were included on sales or shipping documents used in the Massce transactions, the invoices used by Orbisphere to document the transactions at issue here, supported by testimony at trial, clearly stated that the orders were acceptable at New Jersey, and that title to and risk of loss of the goods passed to the purchasers at that location. * * *

It is the opinion of the Court after consideration of the parties' briefs and the testimony and other evidence proffered at trial, that the proper basis for valuation of the merchandise involved in this case is the deductive value of the merchandise under 19 U.S.C. s 1401a(d)(2). The plaintiff has offered ample evidence to establish that the sales of Orbisphere products at issue here were concluded within the United States by a United States company, to United States customers. Consequently, these products were not sold for exportation to the United States as required for "export value" appraisal to be applicable, and the merchandise should have been appraised on the basis of its "deductive value".

All of the sales orders from U.S. customers were solicited and/or received by the U.S. sales offices of Orbisphere, a U.S. corporation. None was ever solicited or received directly by the Geneva office; indeed the Geneva office never had direct communications of any kind with U.S. customers. The terms and conditions printed on the sales invoices for all of the products involved here clearly stated that orders were acceptable only by the New Jersey office, that title and risk of loss on all sales passed to the buyer on delivery of the products to the ultimate carrier at the FOB point stated in the invoice, and that this FOB point was Orbisphere's Haworth, New Jersey office. These invoices, moreover, were produced by the New Jersey office when the particular orders were received, and copies were sent to the customers by this same office along with the products. All payments for U.S. sales were sent to the New Jersey office which deposited the amounts in Orbisphere's New York bank account. This scenario constitutes the archetypical United States sales contract.

Defendant contests this conclusion primarily with circumstantial evidence. Whatever were the terms and conditions printed on the back of Orbisphere's invoices at times past, all of its invoices during the time of the present transactions contained the terms and conditions described in the preceding paragraph. The company therefore was legally bound by these terms and conditions in these transactions, and consequently, for purposes of this case the provisions should prevail over any inconsistent provisions contained in other invoices from earlier times not relevant here. For reasons already discussed, moreover, the timing of transmittal of these invoices to purchasers in the United States does not change the Court's conclusion.

The defendant also attacks the veracity during testimony at trial of one of plaintiff's witnesses, citing alleged inconsistencies between the statements made at trial by Mr. William Miller and earlier statements made by him at a deposition, concerning the differences in terms and conditions on the earlier and more recent invoices. Mr. Miller at trial openly acknowledged these discrepancies in the terms and conditions, and offered an explanation therefore which the defendant has not controverted otherwise than by casting doubt on Mr. Miller's truthfulness. From its vantage point closest to the testimony the Court accepts Mr. Miller's explanation.

Finally, and underlying its entire argument, the defendant asserts that it was the Geneva office that in realty retained control over all of Orbisphere's important obligations, including the acceptance of orders from U.S. customers. The Court has stated its objections to specific portions of this argument, such as those concerning the invoices and telexes. In conclusion, the Court notes that both Orbisphere and Orbisphere Labs were at all times involved here American corporations. Orbisphere Labs, the manufacturing arm of the company was an American subsidiary of Orbisphere, also an American company. The Geneva office was simply a foreign office of this company. Mr. John Franklin testified that literally there was no entity known as "Orbisphere Switzerland", nor as "Orbisphere Geneva", nor as "Orbisphere New Jersey". Rather there was Orbisphere, Inc., a United States corporation, which sold products to U.S. customers through its New Jersey office. The defendant does not directly contradict this.

Based on these circumstances, the plaintiff has proved to the satisfaction of the Court that the sales at issue in this case were consummated within the United States, thus rebutting the presumption of the correctness of Customs' valuation, and establishing "deductive value" as the correct basis for valuation of the entries.

Both parties agree that in the event of such a finding, the Court should remand the case to the Customs Service under 28 U.S.C. s 2643(b) (1982) for calculation of duties based on the deductive value of the merchandise. The Court hereby finds for the plaintiff, dismisses plaintiff's counterclaims, and remands this case to the Customs Service for a re-calculation of duties on the basis of deductive value, taking into account all relevant data, and in accordance with this opinion. * * *

In a sale transaction between unrelated parties, the Customs Service accepts the transaction value established in the commercial invoice as the fair market value of the product being sold. However, if the Buyer and Seller are related—like where the parent is buying from a subsidiary, the transaction value will not likely be recognized as being the fair market value. The related status of the parties could make the pricing decision artificial and arbitrary.

In the case of a sale between related parties, an alternate statutory valuation method[2] must be used to determine value. The various methods include the transaction value of identical merchandise, transaction value of similar merchandise, deductive value, and computed value. To support the transaction value price as the fair market value, the related seller must demonstrate a sale to an unrelated buyer at the same price and conditions as the sale to the related buyer. An independent sale of identical merchandise to an unrelated buyer is often hard to find because a parent corporation typically buys the entire production of the subsidiary. The unrelated sale of similar merchandise is also difficult to find.

If there is no sale of similar merchandise, the next alternative is to use the deductive value. In the context of the parent/subsidiary sale mentioned above, the price is deduced from a subsequent sale by the parent of the goods bought from the subsidiary. This also has some problems. One would have to look at the operation of the parent, how it may have improved the product, what quantity of goods did it buy from its subsidiary, what quantity did the parent sell, etc. This creates a very complicated scenario.

The last alternate valuation option is to establish the computed value. The computed valuation method builds from the cost of making the product and the addition of a reasonable profit. The costs include the materials, labor, overhead, and any general expenses incurred in the manufacturing of the product. Also included in the costs is a category of benefits the valuation statute refers to as assists *19 USC 1401a(e)(1)(C)*. An assist is a subsidy of sorts, often from the Buyer for the production or sale of exports to the United States.

For example, assume the parent is to purchase product from the subsidiary. In order to manufacture the widgets, the parent purchases one million dollars worth of equipment in the U.S. and transports it to

2. See 19 USC § 1401a. (1998).

Country X. The equipment is used in the manufacture of the widget that will be imported into the United States as a sale from the subsidiary to the parent. The value of the equipment is an assist . .

A value has to be attached to the equipment being used and that value is dutiable. There must be some rational process to attribute the cost of the equipment to a unit or the revenue code rules are used for depreciation. The importer has the obligation to support the assist being claimed. Other types of assists include loans, services, and technical information.

Anything of value that is used in the manufacture of a product is considered to be dutiable. Other additions to value include any royalty or license fees[3] related to the imported merchandise that the buyer is required to pay as a condition of the sale of the imported merchandise for exportation to the U.S. For a royalty to fit under (b)(1)(D), it must be a manufacturing royalty. That is to say, the seller is paying an inventor some amount of money for the use of the patent or a machine that is patented and used to manufacture the product. Selling royalties are not included in the dutiable value if they relate to the sale of the product in the U.S.

B. SPECIAL ARRANGEMENTS

The tariff barrier can loom large in the importation of goods. If the profit margin is small, the tariff rate could mean the difference between a gain and a loss on the transaction. U.S. law provides some relief from tariffs—free trade zones and the *Maquiladora*.

1. Free Trade Zones

ARMCO STEEL CORP. v. MAURICE H. STANS

United States Court of Appeals, Second Circuit, 1970.
431 F.2d 779.

* * *

WATERMAN, Circuit Judge: * * *

Foreign trade zones are areas located in, adjacent to, or nearby, ports of entry, into which foreign merchandise may be brought duty free and 'stored, sold, exhibited, broken up, repacked, assembled, distributed, sorted, graded, cleaned, mixed with foreign or domestic merchandise, or otherwise manipulated, or be manufactured. * * * Section 3 of the Foreign Trade Zones Act, 19 U.S.C. s 81c. Such merchandise, whether in altered form or not, may then 'be exported, destroyed, or sent into the customs territory of the United States. * * *' Id. If 'sent into the customs territory of the United States' the merchandise 'shall be subject to the laws and regulations of the United States affecting imported merchandise. * * *

The creation of a foreign or free trade zone for the purpose of permitting products manufactured in the zone to be subsequently im-

3. See 19 USC 1401a(b)(1)(D) (1988).

ported into the United States allows an enterprise operating within the zone to take advantage of favorable differentials in the tariff schedules between the rates of duty for foreign materials used in the manufacturing process and the duty rates for the finished articles. For instance, in trade zones located in Toledo and Seattle, Volkswagen panel trucks are converted, using domestic labor and materials, into campers and are then imported. The transformation of the vehicles enables them to qualify as passenger vehicles subject to a 6.5% Duty, rather than as trucks subject to a 25% Duty. * * *

In the instant case, the savings differential is so favorable that the duty rate otherwise payable on imported steel is reduced to zero. The parties represent that the tariff on foreign steel of the type used in this case is 7 1/2%, while 'vessels which are not 'yachts or pleasure boats' * * * are not articles subject to the (tariff schedule) provisions.' * * * Thus, steel may be brought into a trade zone from Japan duty free and utilized along with domestic materials to construct barges. When imported from the zone the barges are non-dutiable vessels. The steel used in the construction of the vessels escapes recognition for duty purposes for it is only the end product exported from the zone, the vessels, that triggers the rate of import duty chargeable. * * *

Armco attacks the validity of the Zones Board's order with a variety of contentions. It contends that the Foreign Trade Zone Act, 19 U.S.C. s 81a et seq., does not authorize the action taken by the Zones Board in this case because Congress did not intend the creation of a foreign trade zone: (1) to be used to avoid customs duties when as a result interested domestic industries are placed at a competitive disadvantage, (2) that cannot be operated by a public or quasi-public corporation with equal treatment under like conditions for all business concerns, (3) the purpose of which is to produce vessels because vessels are not 'articles' within the meaning of the tariff laws and products not defined as 'articles' cannot be manufactured in a trade zone, (4) wherein 'heavy' manufacturing, like ship or barge construction, is intended to be conducted for the Act contemplates that only 'light' manufacturing may take place in a foreign trade zone, and alternatively, as to this last contention, that, in any event, barge construction is not 'manufacturing' within the meaning of Section 3 of the Act.

This multi-charged assault on the New Orleans Foreign Trade Subzone involves arguments of policy, which are better designed for consideration by the Congress than by a federal court. The district judge below, Judge Bonsal, concluded as much in a well-reasoned opinion reported at 303 F.Supp. 262, 272 (S.D.N.Y.1969), when Armco's complaint was dismissed upon the grant of defendant-appellees' motion for summary judgment. We agree with the lower court and affirm the judgment entered below. * * *

The Foreign Trade Zones Act was passed in 1934 in the midst of the depression and has a stated purpose 'to expedite and encourage foreign commerce.' * * * Restrictions in the 1934 Act that no manufacturing or exhibition of merchandise was to be permitted in a trade zone were eliminated by amendment in 1950. 19 U.S.C. s 81c. Appellant argues that the original purpose underlying the Act was to create transshipment zones where goods are destined for re-export, and argues that Congress surely did not intend by the 1950 amendment to that Act to allow the manufacture of merchandise in a trade zone, which would then be importable duty-free into the United States in the manufactured form. We have already discussed the possibility that various manufacturers, through utilization of Foreign Trade Zones, may take advantage of differentials built into the tariff rate structure. If a 'hole' is thereby rent in 'the tariff wall,' Congress intended it, for the Foreign Trade Zones Act clearly contemplates that trade zone users may take advantage of differing rates in tariff schedules and thereby, depending on what form a product might take when imported from the zone into the U.S. customs territory, save on customs duties. The Act gives the Trade Zones Board wide discretion to determine what activity may be pursued by trade zone manufacturers subject only to the legislative standard that a zone serve this country's interests in foreign trade, both export and import. * * *

We also reject appellant's argument that the Act contemplates only 'light' manufacturing, and so barge construction of the type to be carried on in the subzone is not authorized.

In support of its claim Armco points to statements made by various Congressmen during hearings on the proposed 1950 amendment by which 'manufacturing' within the trade zones was authorized, that Congress did not contemplate that 'heavy industry or manufacturing activities' (1948 House Hearings 24), 'huge operations' (id. at 17), or 'extravagant manufacturing plan developments' (id. at 32) would result from the passage of the amendment. Appellant's reference to these statements, however, merely establishes that some legislators believed heavy manufacturing would not be feasible in trade zones and although this belief may be entitled to some weight in construing the Act, it is not reasonable to suppose that Congress would leave the broad term 'manufacturing' undefined and unqualified if it had intended strictly to forbid other than 'light' manufacturing activity within a trade zone. The Act reads, 'Foreign and domestic merchandise of every description * * * may * * * be manufactured (in a zone) except as otherwise provided in this chapter. * * * No-where does the Act limit the magnitude of manufacturing allowed in a zone. Even if we could discern ambiguity in the disputed term, the Board's long standing interpretation, which we find to be a reasonable one, allowing 'heavy' manufacturing to be conducted within trade zones is entitled to great weight. * * *

Free trade zones are an important part of international trade. They serve as a place where goods can be received into a country free of tariff while they await further distribution. Once the goods leave this area, however, the appropriate tariffs must be paid. Although tariffs are not originally levied on the goods, countries with free trade zones benefit by renting out storage space and shipping the goods to their final destinations. Goods coming into these areas are also free from most non-tariff barriers. However, countries do reserve the right to exclude those goods that could be a health or safety hazard for their citizens.

2. *The 'Maquiladora'*

THE UNITED STATES v. OXFORD INDUSTRIES, INC.

United States Court of Customs and Patent Appeals, 1981.
668 F.2d 507.

* * *

MILLER, Judge.

This is an appeal from the judgment of the United States Court of International Trade in Oxford Industries, Inc. v. United States, 1 CIT 230, 517 F.Supp. 694 (1981), which sustained appellee's claim that the imported merchandise was entitled to a duty allowance for long and short sleeved shirt collar band components and long sleeved shirt cuff components under item 807.00, Tariff Schedules of the United States ("TSUS"). We affirm. * * *

The imported merchandise consists of men's long and short-sleeved shirts. The shirt components were produced in the United States and shipped to Mexico for assembly. The present controversy centers on buttonholing operations performed on the cuff and collar band components in Mexico[1] by a wholly owned subsidiary of appellant. The collar band components are a front, a back, and a lining. The components of each cuff are a front, a back, and a lining. After assembling the collar band and cuffs, one buttonhole was added to the collar band and two buttonholes were added to each cuff.[2]

The buttonholing operation was performed in the sewing area of the factory by a machine, which stitched and slit the cloth to form the buttonhole in one continuous operation; no fabric was removed by this process. Testimony established that the "standard allowed hours" factor ("SAH")[3] attributable to sewing five buttonholes (one on the collar band and two on each cuff) was 2.89% of the total SAH of sewing the shirt. The SAH attributable to the buttonholing operation on the collar band was 8% of the SAH attributable to the stitching time required for the collar band. The SAH attributable to the buttonholing operation on the cuffs was 10% of the SAH attributable to the stitching time required for the cuffs.

---

1. Buttonholes for the plackets of the shirts were formed in the United States and are not in issue.

2. The pertinent assembly steps performed in Mexico with respect to the collar band and cuffs for the long sleeved shirts are shown by Exhibit 20 as follows: Similar collar and collar band steps were employed with the short sleeved shirts.

3. This is a standardized cost-labor factor used by the trade in analyzing assembly operations.

The parties entered into the following stipulation during the hearing before the Court of International Trade: For the short sleeve shirts and long sleeve shirts in Exhibits 1–A and 1–B, the cost of adding the buttonholes is approximately equal to the cost of cutting the collar band components. That is part one. Two, for the long sleeve shirts, the cost of the four buttonholes in the two cuffs is slightly more than the cost of cutting six cuff components. (Each cuff consists of three components: a front, back, and lining.) Three, for the short sleeve shirts and long sleeve shirts, the cost of adding the buttonholes to the sewn collar band is approximately 8 per cent of the cost of the collar band component. Four, on the long sleeve shirts, the cost of adding the four buttonholes to the two cuffs is approximately 11 per cent of the cost of the six cuff components.

The Customs Service classified the merchandise under item 380.84, TSUS, and disallowed duty free treatment of the long and short sleeved shirt collar band components and long sleeved shirt cuff components under item 807.00, TSUS, because these components were subjected to the buttonholing operations in Mexico.

The Court of International Trade agreed with appellee that the components in issue were exempt from duty under the provisions of item 807.00, TSUS, and stated that Miles v. United States, 65 CCPA 32, C.A.D. 1202, 567 F.2d 979 (1978), and Mast Industries, Inc. v. United States, 1 CIT 188, 515 F.Supp. 43 (1981), "are dispositive of issues at bar," adding that "What the court said in Mast applies equally to the facts at bar, namely, 'Said operations were not such substantial changes as to constitute further fabrication. No new portion of the (shirts) was made, and the cost of performing these operations, in terms of both labor and expense was a small portion of the total cost of assembly.' "

The government argues that the buttonholing operations were further fabrications required before the components could be considered complete, contrary to item 807.00(a), TSUS, and were not incidental to the assembly process, contrary to item 807.00(c), TSUS. According to the government, 807.00(a) and (c) are separate and distinct requirements and must be separately considered; further, time and cost production comparisons apply only to an 807.00(c) determination. Item 807.00(a) was not satisfied, the government argues, because buttonholing was required to complete the garments prior to sale and, therefore, in order to possess commercial utility, the merchandise must be subjected to further fabrication. * * * Regarding 807.00(c), the government asserts that if a new "function or utility" results from the buttonholing operation which does not facilitate the assembly process, then "it is a fabrication and it cannot be incidental to the assembly process." Further, the government proposes that "if the cost and time analyses of the process in issue, when compared to the value of the component, discloses that it is substantial, e.g., it equals or exceeds the value of the component, then it is no longer 'incidental to the assembly process,' and it becomes a prohibitory advancement in value or improvement in condition." (Footnote omitted.)

Appellee stresses that the government has failed to defer to the language of the statute by arguing for a construction that is inconsistent with the express statutory language. It points out that there is no commercial utility requirement or "function and utility" test under item 807.00, TSUS; further, that here there was no preparatory processing of raw material before beginning the assembly process and, as such, the components were "ready for assembly without further fabrication" as required by 807.00(a). Alternatively, appellee argues that 807.00(a) has been complied with because buttonholing is considered by the trade to be an assembly process. Regarding 807.00(c), appellee argues that the evidence establishes that buttonholing is a minor operation which is incidental to the assembly process and is one of the cheapest, fastest, and most automatic operations concomitant with the assembly process. * * *

In support of its point that the buttonholing operation here was "further fabrication" for purposes of item 807.00(a), the government contends that fabrication "must mean a manufacturing or production operation, other than assembly, which creates something new that must be done before assembly can be completed," citing Zwicker Knitting Mills v. United States, 67 CCPA 37, C.A.D. 1240, 613 F.2d 295 (1980), where the out-of-country finger tipping operation completed the glove components in issue. However, we are persuaded that the buttonholing operation here, unlike the tipping operation in Zwicker, was not necessary to enable the components to enter the assembly process. Indeed, as related above, the components of the collars and cuffs were sewn together before the buttonholing operation.[8]

As to item 807.00(c), we are further persuaded that the buttonholing operation was incidental to assembly of the collar and cuff components. Legislative history demonstrates the Congressional intent to permit duty-free treatment of a component manufactured in the United States if subjected to an operation "of a minor nature" occurring before, during, or after assembly.[9] Here the buttonholing operation, which, with the buttons already in place, completed a closure device of the assembly, occurred after the collars and sleeves (with their buttons) had entered

---

8. In United States v. Mast Industries, Inc., decided on appeal concurrently with this case (slip op. 81–18), it was established that the involved buttonholing was a prerequisite to lining up the buttons to be sewn on the garment. That fact alone, however, was held to be insufficient to render the operation a "further fabrication" under item 807.00(a), TSUS. See also Miles v. United States, supra.

9. H.R.Rep.No.342, 89th Cong., 1st Sess. 49 (1965), states: The amended item 807.00 would specifically permit the U.S. component to be advanced or improved "by operations incidental to the assembly process such as cleaning, lubricating, and painting." It is common practice in assembling mechanical components to perform certain incidental operations, which cannot always be provided for in advance. For example, in fitting the parts of a machine together, it may be necessary to remove rust; to remove grease, paint, or other preservative coatings; to file off or otherwise remove small amounts of excess material; to add lubricants; or to paint or apply other preservative coatings. It may also be necessary to test and adjust the components. Such operations, if of a minor nature incidental to the assembly process, whether done before, during, or after assembly, would be permitted even though they result in an advance in value of the U.S. components in the article assembled abroad. (Emphasis supplied.)

the assembly process, because it was necessary for the buttonholes to be lined up with the buttons to enable the assembled components to provide a proper fit.[10] We regard the buttonholing operation as "of a minor nature" considering both the cost and SAH factors relative to the collar and cuff components.[11]

In view of the foregoing, we hold that, for the purposes of item 807.00, TSUS, the collar band components and cuff components of the involved merchandise were exported in condition ready for assembly without further fabrication and were not advanced in value or improved in condition abroad except by operations incidental to their assembly.

The judgment of the Court of International Trade is affirmed.

The labor rate differential between the United States and Mexico created the *Maquiladora* industry. Under the program, Mexico law permits the entry of U.S. goods free of tariff. The goods are then assembled and returned to the U.S. for sale. The goods could then enter the U.S. customs area and would only be taxed on the value added in Mexico. The value amounted to the labor cost. As can be seen in *Oxford*, only assembly is permitted under U.S. law. If there were more than mere assembly, it would be classified as a product of Mexico and taxed accordingly.

Conversely under Mexican law, the U.S. product assembled under the *Maquiladora* program could not be sold in the Mexican domestic market. This rule was established when Mexico had a protectionist system in place. Since the passage of the NAFTA, Mexico has opened its borders to U.S. goods. Accordingly, under Annex I of the NAFTA, Mexico Schedule IM 34 and IM 35, the prohibition of accessing the Mexican Market is being phased out and is scheduled to be eliminated by the year 2001.

10. We note that the Court of International Trade in Mast Industries, Inc. v. United States, 1 CIT 188, 515 F.Supp. 43 (1981), commented with respect to a similar buttonholing operation that "a judicious regard for proper alignment of the affected areas ... dictated the deferral of (the operation) until assembly ... rather than at some prior time."

11. As to the government's argument that the buttonholing was a "fabrication" because it was necessary to enable the involved merchandise to possess commercial utility and resulted in a new "function or utility," we note that neither item 807.00, TSUS, nor its legislative history suggests such a test for determining whether an operation is a "further fabrication" or "incidental to the assembly process." Cost, of course, is only one factor to be considered when making an 807.00(c) determination. Other relevant factors are delineated in the companion case of United States v. Mast Industries, Inc., supra, note 8.

Index

References are to Pages

*